WITHDRAWN

BARCELONA & MADRID

JESSICA JONES

Contents

DISCOVER

Barcelona & Madrid

Spain's two biggest cities could not be more different, and each provides a unique slice of Spanish life.

Cosmopolitan, glamorous, and architecturally stunning, Barcelona is bestowed with a laid-back ambiance, thanks to its location on the Mediterranean. Its infectious energy, seaside location, and fairytale-like Modernisme design have made it one of the world's top destinations. It abounds with famous sights, not least of which is Gaudí's unfinished Sagrada Familia, a mammoth splendor that must be seen in person to be fully appreciated. Away from the big sights, the city is brimming with more off-the-beaten-track experiences, from a tour through a bomb shelter made by locals during the Spanish Civil War to a day cycling or walking in the Collserola hills. Head to up-and-coming neighborhoods for a taste of local life and don't miss a visit to a cava bar to try Catalonia's most famous tipple.

Madrid, meanwhile, as the seat of Spain's government, is seen by some as more serious—but wander around, and you will be surprised at what you find. The main attraction is the life coursing through the veins of the city itself: the buzz of its tapas bars and outdoor terraces, shops that have been selling the

Clockwise from top left: view from the Museu Nacional d'Art de Catalunya; Madrid balconies; Sagrada Familia details; Retiro Park; Barcelona Cathedral detail; Almudena Cathedral.

same lovingly made products for over a hundred years, and the neighborhoods themselves, each one of which feels like its own little village, where neighbors know each other and meet in their local bars. Madrid is also rich in history and art, home to the "Golden Triangle" of art galleries that house some of the world's great masters, from Goya's "Black Paintings" to Picasso's "Guernica." In the 1970s and 80s, the countercultural movement known as La Movida Madrileña gave the city an indie, rebellious vibe that continues to this day.

While Madrid is Spain's political and business center, Barcelona's rich history is strongly tied to its Catalan identity; locals here are quick to tell you that you are in Catalonia, not Spain. The debate over independence—which has been going on for decades—continues, making Barcelona a fascinating place to discover Catalan history, culture, and traditions as well as the city's independent spirit.

Although there is a rivalry between the two cities—so much so that the ongoing competition between the cities' football teams has a name, "El Clásico"—the good news is that you don't have to pick a favorite. Digging into the world-class art, fascinating food culture, and quirky hidden gems in both of Spain's two biggest cities will give you incredible insight into the country as a whole.

Clockwise from top left: Madrid's Gran Vía; Catamaran Orsom; postcards; churros.

15 TOP
EXPERIENCES

1 Stepping inside the color-soaked interior of the **Sagrada Família** cathedral, Antoni Gaudí's unfinished masterpiece (page 70).

2 Enjoying **Plaza Mayor**, Madrid's historic main square, the local way: grab a *bocadillo de calamares*, snag a bench seat, and watch the world go by (page 208).

3 Crowding into a tiny **tapas bar** for some of Spain's tastiest bites (page 26).

>>>

4 Perusing the rich collection of European art, including Velázquez's *Las Meninas*, at the **Prado Museum** (page 223).

<<<

5 Relaxing on one of Barcelona's pristine white **beaches**, followed by a catch-of-the-day dinner in a *chiringuito* (beach hut) (page 91).

>>>

6 Admiring whimsical **Catalan Modernist architecture** (page 78) in Barcelona. **La Pedrera** (page 72) and the Sagrada Familia are among the most famous examples, while Gaudí's **Casa Vicens** (page 82) just opened to the public in 2017.

<<<

7 Standing in front of *Guernica* and seeing up close Pablo Picasso's haunting depiction of the bombing of the Basque town during the Spanish Civil War (page 229).

8 Sipping vermouth, an old-fashioned tipple that is now the aperitif of the moment. The trend is to enjoy it just before lunch, during **La Hora del Vermut**, a.k.a. "vermouth o'clock" (page 28).

>>>

9 Perusing local **markets** for fresh produce, followed by a *caña* (small beer) at a countertop seat in the market (pages 130 and 246).

<<<

10 Taking a whistle-stop tour through a millennium of Catalan art at the **Museu Nacional d'Art de Catalunya** (page 82).

>>>

11 Staying up late in Madrid. The entire city is known for its legendary **nightlife**, but the indie neighborhood of **Malasaña** really sizzles (page 256).

<<<

12 Visiting **Retiro Park**, Madrid's green lung and a beloved local retreat. Bring a picnic, stroll the manicured gardens, or rent a rowboat on the lake for an iconic Madrid experience (page 233).

13 Watching the sun set over the city of Barcelona—and the Mediterranean beyond—from the **Bunkers del Carmel** (page 89).

14 Appreciating the **street art** in Madrid. Two neighborhoods stand out: multicultural **Lavapiés** and trendy **Malasaña** (page 216). Mural by Alice Pasquini.

15 Cheering for the home team at a **football match.** The cities' teams, FC Barcelona and Real Madrid, have a fierce rivalry—it's your pick who you support (pages 135 and 284)!

Planning Your Time

Where to Go

Barcelona

Barcelona is Spain's **cosmopolitan, glamorous,** and **independent** second city and a real highlight of any trip to Spain. With its own language, culture, and identity, Barcelona feels distinct from Spain, a fact that many locals will emphasize. Sitting on Spain's Mediterranean coastline, the city has it all: **beaches,** one-of-a-kind **Catalan modernist architecture,** art, sports, and gastronomy. From the **Sagrada Familia** and Gaudí's other striking masterpieces to the cathedral of soccer, FC Barcelona's **Camp Nou,** in Barcelona everything is big, bold, and beautiful.

Day Trips from Barcelona

Whether you want to explore the rolling vineyards of the **Penedès** wine region and learn all about the Cava-making process or visit the surreal homage to Salvador Dalí at his famous museum in **Figueres,** there are a great range of places to discover within easy reach of Barcelona. Soak up medieval history in **Girona** and see the otherworldly landscapes of **Montserrat,** or just head to the beach and party the night away in **Sitges.**

Madrid

Spain's capital city is known for its legendary social life; the city's streets will enchant you with their sunny **open-air terraces,** beautiful architecture, and **century-old shops.** Art lovers shouldn't miss the city's **Prado** and **Reina Sofía** museums, while history buffs can delve into centuries of intrigue by visiting the city's

Sagrada Familia

Best Views

MADRID

Best Panoramas

- **Círculo de Bellas Artes:** Sip some cava on this stunning rooftop terrace while taking in the 360-degree views over Madrid.

- **Palacio de Cibeles:** The grand Palacio de Cibeles, now home to Madrid's City Hall, has an observation deck with awe-inspiring views of the city, framed by the mountains of the Sierra de Guadarrama beyond.

- **Almudena Cathedral:** Climb to the top of the cathedral for spectacular views across the city's rooftops.

Hemingway's View

- **Gourmet Experience Corte Inglés:** From the ninth floor of the Corte Inglés department store, visitors can view Madrid's Gran Vía from above. The outdoor terrace has views, too: Ernest Hemingway would stand here when the building was the Hotel Florida and watch Franco's Nationalist troops approaching through Casa de Campo park during the Spanish Civil War.

Park View

- **Teleférico de Madrid:** The 11-minute cable car journey to the heart of the Casa de Campo gives travelers views of the Royal Palace, Almudena Cathedral, River Manzanares, and the huge expanse of park below.

- **Temple of Debod:** One of the only Egyptian temples outside Egypt and in a prime elevated position just west of the city center and is a great location for stunning sunset views.

BARCELONA

Barcelona Cityscapes

- **Bunkers del Carmel:** These former anti-aircraft defenses are now a popular local viewpoint. Make the trek up to the bunkers during the cool late afternoon and watch the sunset.

- **Mount Tibidabo:** Scaling Barcelona's Mount Tibidabo gives visitors unforgettable views over the city and the glistening Mediterranean Sea beyond.

- **Park Güell:** Millions visit Gaudí's masterpiece to see the great architect's buildings and designs. Wonderful views over the city and the sea from the slopes of the park are an unexpected bonus.

- **Palau Nacional:** The terrace outside the Palau Nacional, home to the Museu Nacional d'Art de Catalunya and perched on the hillside of Montjuïc, affords visitors wonderful views back over the city.

- **Parc de Collserola:** Escape downtown Barcelona for the surrounding mountains, where locals walk, cycle, and enjoy the fantastic views over the city towards the sea.

- **Mirador de Colom:** Scale the 60-meter-high (200-foot) monument of Christopher Columbus at the end of Las Ramblas for views over the Barri Gòtic and Barcelona's port.

Architectural Views

- **Cathedral:** Gaze over Gothic Barcelona and take in some of the intricate details of the city's cathedral from its rooftop.

- **La Pedrera:** See Barcelona's rooftops through the prism of Gaudí's fairytale design on the rooftop of one of the architect's most famous buildings.

- **Sagrada Familia:** Scale the unfinished cathedral's towers for a glimpse of Gaudí's genius, hidden from spectators below.

View with a Drink

- **Hotel Almanac:** The rooftop bar of the Hotel Almanac has panoramic views across the city, from Tibidabo and the Sagrada Familia to the Mediterranean Sea.

Arab Walls, Royal Palace, and historic plazas. For a thriving European capital, Madrid retains a small-town feel.

Day Trips From Madrid

From Madrid, visitors are spoiled for choice when it comes to day trips, whether it is history, gastronomy, or action on the agenda. Explore Segovia, with its Roman aqueduct and the fairytale castle that is said to have inspired Walt Disney (not to mention its famous roast suckling pig). In **Toledo**, see how three cultures—Christian, Jewish, and Muslim—coexisted and left a unique legacy on the city. And fill your lungs with fresh mountain air on a hike through the **Sierra de Guadarrama**.

When to Go

Barcelona and Madrid are both great year-round destinations; there is always something going on and all the "big sights" are open year-round.

Summer

Summer, especially **July and August,** is high season for tourists. Barcelona in particular experiences some of the biggest tourist crowds of any city in Europe, and summer is peak time. Meanwhile, many Spaniards take their yearly allowance of holiday in August, leading to an exodus from the cities to the coast and mountains. If you visit at this time, you'll encounter a higher percentage of tourists and a low percentage of locals, and many smaller bars, restaurants, and shops close for the entire month.

In terms of weather, Madrid is hit with an intense, dry heat, and summer temperatures can regularly reach the mid-to-high 30s Celsius (95°+ Fahrenheit). In Barcelona, the temperatures may be cooler (28-32°C/82-90°F), but the city is more humid.

Spring and Fall

The best time to visit both cities is spring and fall, with **May** and **September-October** being particularly lovely months—still warm, but cool enough to do plenty of walking around comfortably. Crowds tend to be less intense than during the summer months, but this is still a popular time to visit.

Winter

Madrid in winter is cold, crisp, and sunny, meaning it is still perfectly common to see people sitting out on terraces enjoying the sunshine, but with a warm coat on. Barcelona, too, while more prone to rain, still has its terraces out during the winter months. Tourism tends to slow in November, January, and February, which makes these months good for travel deals. Christmas markets, lights, and decorations make **December** an exciting—and busy—month to visit both cities. The average low temperature is 4°C (39°F) in Madrid, and 7°C (45°F) in Barcelona.

Before You Go

Passport and Visas

Travelers from the **United States**, **Canada**, **Australia**, and **New Zealand** do not need a visa to enter the country for tourist visits of under 90 days. All that is required is a passport valid for at least three months after your intended departure.

EU citizens and residents need a passport or national identity card to enter Spain; no visa is required.

A visa is required for travelers from **South Africa**.

Advance Reservations

There are some reservations that are worth making before you even get on the plane.

BARCELONA

Tickets for the **Sagrada Familia** and **Parc Güell** can sell out if you wait until the last minute. Football at Barcelona's **Camp Nou** are best booked in advance; tickets tend to be released around two weeks ahead of matches. Check online at www.fcbarcelona.com for upcoming matches.

High-end restaurants, including Michelin-starred ones, should be booked well ahead of time (it's worth looking as far ahead as possible to guarantee availability). Hotspots like **Tickets** are known to book up months in advance.

MADRID

As in Barcelona, it's smart to book tickets for **football matches** in advance.

OTHER DESTINATIONS

Girona's **El Celler de Can Roca** has been hailed as the best restaurant in the world. If you'd like to splurge on this Michelin-starred experience, book ahead—reservations are accepted as far as 11 months in advance!

view of Barcelona Cathedral

Transportation

Barcelona and Madrid both have excellent **public transport** networks, and within each city, a combination of walking and using the metro is the best way to get around.

There are several options for **traveling between Barcelona and Madrid**, including domestic budget airlines, train, or bus, depending on your budget and time available. Flying is the quickest option and is often cheaper than the train, but it is worth bearing in mind that taking the train has a much lower carbon footprint than flying. The bus is the cheapest option and takes around eight hours.

In general, renting a car is not necessary, especially if you are staying within the cities of Madrid or Barcelona—public transport is both easier and cheaper. You might want to consider renting a car if you are planning a few day trips; while most destinations are easily accessible by train and bus, the Valley of the Fallen and El Escorial, outside Madrid, are two locations that are much easier accessed by car (bus tours starting from Madrid are available if you'd prefer to go this way).

What to Take

If traveling during the summer months, make sure to take **cool, loose clothing** as well as sun protection.

Pack a **European plug adapter** to make sure you can charge up your phone and camera. They are usually more expensive at airports, so consider buying one before your trip.

To lessen the risk of pickpocketing, consider a **money belt** that can be worn under your clothing and can carry your cards and cash. A cross-body bag with a zip and a flap closure is better than a backpack, because you can keep your eyes and hands on it at all times. Also consider making copies of your passport and travel documents and sending them to yourself in an email, just in case you lose them or they are stolen.

A **refillable water bottle** is a good alternative to buying plastic bottles throughout your trip. It is important to stay hydrated throughout the long, hot summer months, and carrying a bottle of water around during the day is a good idea.

Most hotels supply basic toiletries, so packing shampoo and conditioner is not always necessary.

Best of Barcelona & Madrid

U.S. travelers will most likely book a round trip and therefore will fly both in and out of Madrid or Barcelona, although flying into one and out of the other is possible. For short-haul travelers from Europe, decent one-way deals on budget airlines mean it can be just as reasonable to fly into one city and leave from the other.

Barcelona

DAY 1

Experience the wide boulevard of **Las Ramblas**, one of Barcelona's most famous sights, then a late-afternoon visit to the light-soaked interior of **La Sagrada Familia** (book tickets online in advance to avoid waiting in line), followed by a stroll past other **Catalan Modernist** masterpieces.

DAY 2

See the **Picasso Museum**, then spend the afternoon and evening exploring **El Raval**, a once-gritty neighborhood that's been given a new lease on life with a buzzing food and nightlife scene and an engaging contemporary art museum.

DAY 3: DAY TRIP TO SITGES

Hop on the local Rodalies train from Passeig de Gràcia for a 30-minute journey to the beautiful seaside town of **Sitges**. This charming town of whitewashed villas has long been the playground of artists and locals seeking a relaxing seaside break, and is also one of Spain's most famous LGBT destinations. Spend a day on the beach or walk the town's pretty promenade, see some Modernista masterpieces in the **Museu Cau Ferrat**, and learn how to make a mouthwatering mojito at **Casa Bacardi**, then visit Spain's first *chiringuito* beach bar, **El Chiringuito**. Take an evening Rodalies train back to Barcelona.

DAY 4

Explore a thousand years of Catalan art at the **Museu Nacional d'Art de Catalunya**, then chill on the **beach** next to Mediterranean waters, popping into a *chiringuito* (beach bar) or paella restaurant when hunger strikes. Catch the **sunset over Barcelona** before a meal at award-winning tapas bar **Tickets** (book well in advance).

Las Ramblas

The Tapas Experience

In Spain, tapas are served both in bars—a frenetic, informal, often stand-up affair, where you elbow your way up to the bar and order from the bartender—and in a more formal restaurant setting, where a waiter serves you at the table. Tapas bars are a good place to begin the evening, especially if you're just looking for a light bite or two, and restaurants are a good option if you are looking for a more leisurely experience.

BARCELONA'S BEST TAPAS

- **Cometa Pla:** This restaurant serves fresh, seasonal Catalan produce with a creative spin, plus an organic wine list. Their smoky take on the classic *patatas bravas* is incredible.

- **La Cova Fumada:** This bar's unassuming appearance belies the fact that it's where the legendary *bomba* (a breaded and fried ball of potato filled with beef) is said to have been invented.

- **Tickets:** This aptly named tapas bar is definitely one of the hottest tickets in town. Don't miss their legendary olives, a surprising take on the humble Spanish favorite.

- **Bar Cañete:** Slurp down fresh oysters and sample some sizzling garlic prawns before diving into beef filet with foie gras and truffle sauce.

- **Bar La Plata:** One of the few old-style tapas joints that remains in the Barri Gòtic, this little bar does just four tapas, but does them all to perfection. It is renowned for its fried anchovies (*boquerones*).

MADRID'S BEST TAPAS

- Madrid's La Latina neighborhood—and **Calle de Cava Baja** in particular—is renowned for its tapas offerings.

- **Juana la Loca:** An elevated take on traditional tapas with truffles, featuring quality ingredients. This bar and restaurant serves what is often touted as the city's best *tortilla de patatas.*

tortilla de patatas

- **Casa Labra:** The crisp, fried battered cod is the reason locals flock to this bar, open since 1860.

- **STOP Madrid:** This traditional tavern is a great spot to stop for a *vermút de grifo* (vermouth on tap) and some of the bar's classic tapas.

- **La Musa Latina:** Cool La Latina restaurant, with an international take on classic tapas like tacos, Japanese chicken dumplings, and the poplar Catalan *bomba*.

- **Cabreira:** This traditional restaurant with a great terrace; just off Plaza Dos de Mayo, specializes in Galician tapas, so think octopus, fish, and padrón peppers—and don't miss their Cabreira potatoes!

- **Taberna Maceira:** Laid-back Galician tapas and *raciones* at low wooden tables and wine served in traditional little ceramic bowls.

With More Time

Both Barcelona and Madrid contain treasures that would take a lifetime to explore. If you have more time, here are some suggestions for how to spend it.

IN BARCELONA

Discover Gaudí's earlier work at **Casa Vicens**, the architect's first commission that remained a family home until 2014. On Sundays you can take a tour of **Refugi 307**, a Spanish Civil War bomb shelter that was hewn into the rock of Montjuïc by residents of the Poble Sec neighborhood. Football fans, check schedules in advance and get tickets to a match at the home of **FC Barcelona, Camp Nou**.

IN MADRID

Take the **Teleférico de Madrid** cable car into the middle of the Casa de Campo, Madrid's largest park, and enjoy a walk to its lake, surrounded by restaurants with pleasant terraces overlooking the water. See **Real Madrid** play at the Santiago Bernabéu or take a tour of the stadium, one of the largest in Europe.

If it's Sunday, head to the **Rastro**, Madrid's biggest street market. Wander off the main drag into the side streets for hidden little shops jam-packed with antiques, records, scary dolls, and other curiosities. Stop at a bar for a drink and a tapa en route.

DAY 5

Wander the cool neighborhoods of **Poble Nou** and **Sant Antoni** and enjoy a leisurely brunch at **Federal** before taking an early-afternoon train from Barcelona Sants station to Madrid. Many hotels' check-in time is around 3pm, so you should arrive in time to spend the late afternoon getting your bearings in the new city. Explore the area local to your hotel and spend your first evening in Madrid in a tapas bar or two.

Madrid

DAY 6

Take in **Plaza Mayor, Palacio Real**, and the **Prado Museum**, which houses a wealth of European masterpieces, taking time for a **vermouth** and a bite at a **local market** in between. In the evening, enjoy drinks at some of Hemingway's old haunts in the literary quarter of **Las Letras**.

DAY 7

See Picasso's **Guernica** in the **Reina Sofía**, then spend some time relaxing with locals in **Retiro Park**. Take in the grand architecture of **Gran Vía** and hit some top tapas bars on **Calle de Cava Baja**, Madrid's famed tapas street.

DAY 8

Explore the indie-cool neighborhood of **Malasaña** in the morning, then take in the current exhibition at **Fundación Telefónica**, a hidden gem that even locals miss. Cycle along **Madrid Río**, the city's rejuvenated riverside park, then end your day back in Malasaña for a dose of Madrid's legendary **nightlife**.

DAY 9: DAY TRIP TO SEGOVIA

The high-speed AVE train will take you from Madrid's Chamartín station to Segovia in under 30 minutes. Head straight for the city's awesome **Roman aqueduct**, an incredible feat of engineering. Settle down for a hearty lunch of **cochinillo** (roast suckling pig), then explore the fairytale **Alcázar palace**, before walking the medieval streets of the city's former **Jewish quarter**. Take a late-afternoon train back to Madrid to be back in the city in time for tapas.

DAY 10

Head to the airport for your flight home. Alternately, catch a train or short flight back to Barcelona if you're flying home from that airport.

La Hora del Vermut (a.k.a. Vermouth O'Clock)

Vermouth, a fortified white wine flavored with botanicals, has always been a popular drink in Spain, but while it was long relegated to a drink beloved by grandmas, it has experienced something of a renaissance in recent years.

The drink, known in many other parts of the world as an ingredient in classic cocktails, even has its very own time of day—vermouth hour, or vermouth o'clock—usually before lunch from around 12:30pm, as traditionally vermouth was meant to stimulate the appetite and aid digestion. Spaniards typically drink sweet, red vermouth (*vermút rojo*) with a tapa—be it olives or potato chips, or something a little more elaborate.

Many of the city's old *tavernas* serve the drink *de grifo*, or on tap, with an olive and an orange slice garnish. Order the vermouth *con sifón* (with soda water) if you want to dilute it.

traditional Spanish appetizer with vermouth

WHERE TO TASTE IN MADRID

- **Mercado San Miguel—La Hora Del Vermut:** This bar in one of the center's most buzzing markets is a good place for a pre-lunch vermouth.

- **Taberna la Concha:** This tapas bar's homemade vermouth cocktail, the Manuela, makes a perfect aperitif before lunch in La Latina.

- **Bodegas Ricla:** This little hole in the wall is run by a mother-and-son duo and is a lovely little stop among the more touristy bars around Plaza Mayor.

- **Casa Camacho:** This no-frills bar continues to hold out among the hipster hangouts of Malasaña and is always packed. Try a Yayo: a vermouth, gin, and soda water concoction that's very popular.

- **Sifón:** A more modern bar in Chueca with stylish decor and a charming outdoor terrace.

WHERE TO TASTE IN BARCELONA

- **Senyor Vermut:** A local, reasonably-priced

bar in the swanky Eixample, this is a great place for a vermouth and tapas (try the patatas bravas).

- **Bodega 1900:** At this elevated take on the classic *vermutería* (vermouth bodegas) by star chefs the Adrià brothers, try vermouth alongside old-fashioned tapas dishes in vintage surroundings.

- **La Confitería:** This former confectioner's shop, with original fittings, is an atmospheric spot for a pre-dinner vermouth while propping up its marble counter.

- **Vermutería La Cava:** Pack into the long, thin bar area of this cool Gràcia bar for an evening vermouth.

- **Bar Bodega Cal Pep:** This traditional Gràcia bodega is a great stop-off for a refreshing vermouth and some tapas.

Barcelona

Barcelona is beautiful, from its backdrop of

mountains and sea to its medieval lanes and Modernista architecture. And while many travelers think they might know the city, one of the most visited in the world, there are always new discoveries around every corner.

In the past two decades, the city has cemented itself as the jewel of the Mediterranean, a city-break favorite and Spain's most cosmopolitan metropolis. Its unique Catalan heritage, from the soaring human towers known as *castells* to the real-life towers and fairytale-like *Modernista* architecture of icons like Antoni Gaudí, is evident wherever you look. Art lovers will lap up Barcelona's offerings, from the exquisite Romanesque church paintings preserved in the Museu

Highlights

Look for ★ to find recommended sights, activities, dining, and lodging.

★ **La Catedral (La Seu Catedral):** Barcelona's cathedral is one of the best examples of Gothic architecture in Spain (page 52).

★ **La Boqueria:** Spain's most famous market is a feast for the senses. Pick up supplies for a picnic or grab a seat at one of the many market restaurants and enjoy some fresh local produce (page 53).

★ **Picasso Museum:** Explore Picasso's pivotal years of training in Barcelona, his early artworks, and collections such as his Blue Period and Las Meninas series (page 61).

★ **Sagrada Familia:** Gaudí's towering masterpiece is the world's longest-running architectural project (page 70).

★ **La Pedrera (Casa Milà):** At the time it was built, Casa Milà was nicknamed *La Pedrera* ("the Quarry") by angry locals, for its similarity to a big pile of stone. Today the building is celebrated for its architecture, especially the towering chimney pots crowning the rooftop (page 72).

★ **Park Güell:** This colorful hillside park with spectacular city views is one of Gaudí's most famous legacies (page 78).

★ **Casa Vicens:** Gaudí's first building, which opened to the public in late 2017, is a fascinating insight into the inspirations and beginnings of the city's great architect (page 82).

★ **Museu Nacional d'Art de Catalunya:** Explore a millennium of artwork produced in Catalonia at this excellent museum, which has one of the best collections of Romanesque art in the world (page 82).

★ **Camp Nou:** The home of one of the world's best football teams, FC Barcelona, is a must-visit for sports fans. Get a feel of what it's like to be a player on a stadium tour, or see a match in one of the biggest football stadiums in the world (page 88).

★ **Bunkers del Carmel:** The Spanish Civil War bunkers are a favorite spot for locals to watch the sun set over the Mediterranean (page 89).

★ **La Barceloneta Beach:** What sets Barcelona apart from many other famous European cities is its beach. The Mediterranean provides a stunning backdrop for beach bars, water sports, and lazy days on the sand (page 91).

Nacional d'Art de Catalunya to the vibrant works of Pablo Picasso and Joan Miró. Few big cities have a beach, and Barcelona's seaside location gives it a certain laid-back attitude. The salty sea breeze seems to have a calming effect on people; it's a constant reminder of the city's rich seafaring past.

Food, from traditional bodegas to the most creative Michelin-starred restaurants, is integral to the city. Browsing the local markets, enjoying a long lunch, or moving from tapas bar to tapas bar are at the heart of the city's gastronomic scene. But in stylish Barcelona new trends abound, too, from craft beer to vegetarian cuisine.

Getting to the heart of Barcelona is all about exploring the city like a local—wandering the narrow, medieval streets of the Gothic Quarter, tucking into a huge pan of *fideuá* over lunch by the sea with family and friends, and soaking up the city's many cultural offerings, from the most famous—such as the Sagrada Familia—to the many neighborhood exhibitions, festivals, and cultural spaces.

HISTORY

While there have been settlements on the site of Barcelona since Neolithic times (5000 BC), it was the Romans who founded the city of Barcino as a military camp under the protection of the Emperor Augustus around 10 BC. Its products, including wine and garum—a pungent fish sauce—were exported throughout the Roman Empire.

The medieval period was the city's golden age in trade, culture, and seafaring. Jaume I (1208-1276) took Mallorca, Menorca, Valencia, and Murica from the Moors, marking the beginning of Barcelona's "Golden Age" as a maritime trading power. In this period, the city was under the Crown of Aragon, which controlled many territories, including Naples, and some as far away as Athens. Money flooded the city, and great projects,

including the construction of much of today's "old town," were completed.

Barcelona experienced a period of decline from the 15th-18th centuries as it lost its foothold as a great maritime power and struggled to maintain independence against the Spanish crown. During the 1714 War of the Spanish Succession, Barcelona backed the wrong side (Archduke Charles of Austria over the Bourbon, Philippe of Anjou) and subsequently saw its self-government abolished.

After hundreds of years of decline, the mid-19th century was an important turning point for Barcelona thanks to the Industrial Revolution. The city's economy boomed once again, and the increase in fortunes was accompanied by a cultural movement that revived the Catalan language and the concept of Catalonia as a nation. The old town, by now bursting at the seams, was connected to surrounding villages by a modern new neighborhood, the Eixample—literally, "the extension." Here, the city's new bourgeoisie commissioned grand homes designed by the great architects of Catalonia's art-nouveau movement, Modernisme, including Antoni Gaudí.

In 1895, the Picasso family moved to Barcelona and the 13-year-old Pablo (who had been born in Málaga) began studying at the Llotja School of Fine Arts. His early genius was clear, and many of his early works can be viewed in Barcelona's Picasso Museum. Although he moved to Paris in 1904, he would return regularly to Barcelona until the outbreak of the Spanish Civil War, painting some of his Blue Period works in the city.

The first decades of the new century were marked by political upheaval, as a Republican government rose to power and workers increasingly mobilized against the ruling classes. This all changed in 1936 with the start of the Spanish Civil War, during which Barcelona was bombarded by Italian and German planes. The post-war years were difficult in Barcelona, where the Catalan language

---

Previous: Plaça Reial; Las Ramblas; Park Güell at blue hour.

and culture were more or less stamped out by Franco.

With Franco's death in 1975 and Spain's return to democracy in 1978, Barcelona began a process of renewal and redevelopment that reached its peak with the 1992 Olympic Games. Still talked about as a watershed moment today, the Barcelona Olympics helped to regenerate the city and put it on the world map as a destination, adding new green areas and demolishing waterfront industry to make way for picturesque beaches.

On October 1, 2017, the regional government held a referendum on independence. The question on the ballot papers was: "Do you want Catalonia to become an independent state in the form of a republic?" Ninety-two percent of voters responded affirmatively, but only 43 percent of Catalans came out to vote; many voters who did not support independence stayed at home. The central government in Madrid declared the referendum illegal according to the Spanish constitution. Today, Catalonia is the most visited region in the world's second most visited country.

Planning and Orientation

PLANNING YOUR TIME

Barcelona is one of Europe's most popular weekend break destinations, and a **long weekend** (Fri-Mon) is a decent amount of time to get the feel for the city and see some of its most famous sights.

Barcelona is a popular destination throughout the year, but it can be at its most beautiful in spring (May) and fall (October), when days are warm but not oppressively so—the ideal temperature for strolling around the city. Summer is a good time to visit to make the most of the city's beaches, though temperatures can rise well above 30°C (in Fahrenheit, from the high 80s to the low 100s) and the humidity can be high. Summer also is peak tourist season, meaning queues, crowds, and chaos—and, actually, fewer locals than normal because those who can escape the city for the mountains or beach will do so.

Winter, especially the run-up to Christmas, can be busy. It's a good time to visit to make the most of the city's cozy corners and its sweet treats like hot chocolate, which might not seem quite as tempting in the heat of the summer. Winter temperatures vary, from lows of around 7°C (45°F) to highs of 15°C (60°F).

Daily Reminders

MONDAY

- Picasso Museum has shorter opening hours (10am-5pm).
- Museum of the History of Barcelona (MUHBA) is closed.
- Fundació Joan Miró is closed.
- Born Center of Culture and Memory / El Born Centre de Cultura i Memòria is closed.
- Archeological Museum of Catalonia is closed.
- Museu Frederic Marès is closed.
- Museu de Cultures del Món is closed.
- Palau Güell is closed.
- Museu Blau is closed.
- Fundació Antoni Tàpies is closed.

TUESDAY

- Barcelona Museum of Contemporary Art (MACBA) is closed.

SATURDAY

- Modernisme Museum of Barcelona is closed.

- Museu Nacional d'Art de Catalunya is free from 3pm.

SUNDAY

- Free entrance on the first Sunday of every month to many of the city's major museums, including the Museu Nacional d'Art de Catalunya and the Picasso Museum.
- Mass at the Sagrada Familia is at 9am.
- Tours of Refugi 307 (Civil War bomb shelter) are available only on Sundays by appointment.
- Free admission to CCCB from 3pm-8pm.
- Free admission to Museu Frederic Marès from 3pm-8pm.
- Free admission to Castell de Montjuïc after 3pm.
- Free admission to MUHBA after 3pm.
- La Boqueria is closed.
- Modernisme Museum of Barcelona is closed.

Advance Bookings and Reservations

Tickets for most museums can be bought online ahead of time. One big advantage is that you can then skip the ticket line at the venue. Some tickets that are definitely advisable to book ahead include:

- Park Güell can be visited with timed tickets only (€7.50, book online at www.parkguell. cat).
- Book tickets for the Sagrada Familia by specific date online (from €15, tickets. sagradafamilia.org).
- Soccer games at Camp Nou are best booked in advance; tickets tend to be released around two weeks ahead of matches. Check online at www.fcbarcelona.com for upcoming matches.
- High-end restaurants, including Michelin-starred restaurants, should be booked well ahead of time (it's worth looking as far

ahead as possible to guarantee availability). Hotspots like Tickets are known to get booked up months in advance.

Sightseeing Passes

The Barcelona Card and its shorter time-period alternative, the Barcelona Card Express, are among the best-value cards for their wide range of freebies and discounts, with public transport included. It is worth bearing in mind, however, that admission to some of the most famous Modernista sights in Barcelona, including the Sagrada Familia and La Pedrera, are not included in the cards.

BARCELONA CARD
www.barcelonacard.com

This card gives users unlimited access to public transport (metro, bus, tram, airport metro, and train) as well as free entry into over 25 sights, including the Caixa Forum, the Museum of the History of Barcelona/MUHBA, the Egyptian Museum, the National Museum of Art of Catalonia, the Design Museum, and the Chocolate Museum. It also provides discounts on other sights, experiences, and entertainment. Validate the card by writing the date and time of the first time you use it in the space provided on the front of the card. There are options that cover three days (€45 for adults, €21 for children aged 4-12), four days (€55 and €27), and five days (€60 and €32).

There is also a 48-hour card available, the **Barcelona Card Express**, which gives users the same benefits over a two-day period (€20 for two days). You can obtain a small discount by purchasing your card on the Barcelona Card website, or buy the card at tourist information points around the city.

ARTTICKET
www.articketbcn.org

This single ticket provides access to six of Barcelona's top museums and cultural

Greater Barcelona

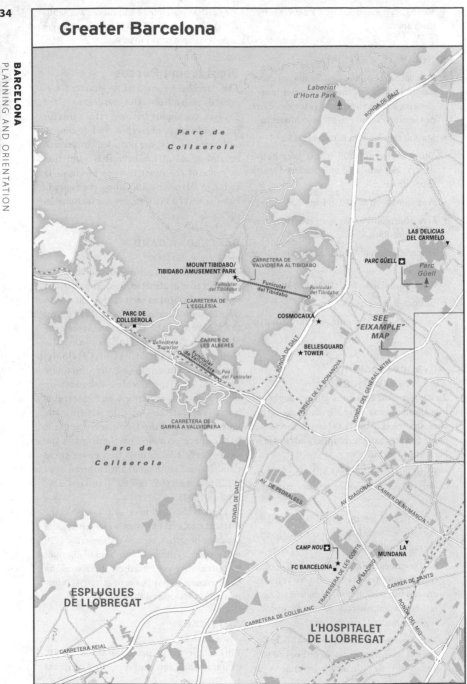

Laberint
d'Horta Park

RONDA DE DALT

Parc de
Collserola

LAS DELICIAS
DEL CARMELO

PARC GÜELL ★   Parc
Güell

MOUNT TIBIDABO/   CARRETERA DE
TIBIDABO AMUSEMENT PARK   VALVIDRERA AL TIBIDABO

Funicular   Funicular   Funicular
del Tibidabo   del Tibidabo   del Tibidabo

CARRETERA DE
L'ESGLÉSIA

PARC DE
COLLSEROLA   COSMOCAIXA ★

Vallvidrera   CARRER DE   SEE
Superior   LES ALBERES   "EIXAMPLE"
Funicular   BELLESGUARD   MAP
de Vallvidrera   ★ TOWER

Peu
del Funicular   RONDA DE DALT

PASSEIG DE LA BONANOVA

CARRETERA DE   RONDA DEL GENERAL MITRE
SARRIÀ A VALLVIDRERA

Parc de
Collserola

AV. DE PEDRALBES

RONDA DE DALT

AV. DIAGONAL   CARRER DE NUMÀNCIA

CAMP NOU ★   LA
MUNDANA

FC BARCELONA ★

TRAVESSERA DE LES CORTS   AV. DE MADRID   CARRER DE SANTS

ESPLUGUES
DE LLOBREGAT

RONDA DEL MIG

CARRETERA DE COLLBLANC   L'HOSPITALET
DE LLOBREGAT

CARRETERA REIAL

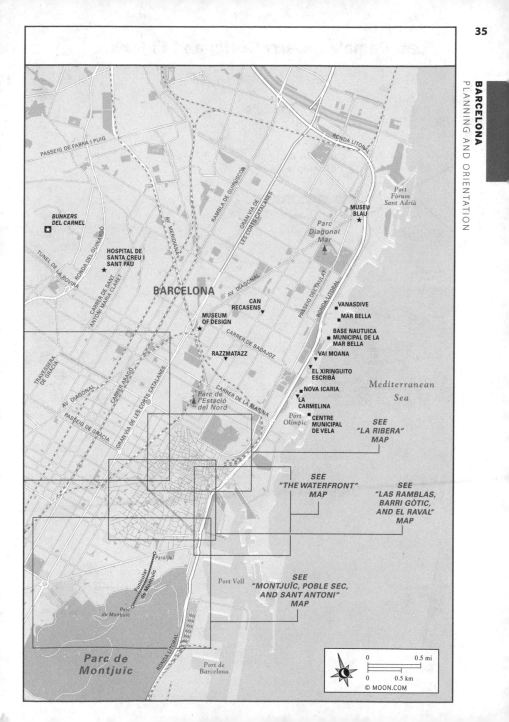

PASSEIG DE FABRA I PUIG

RONDA LITORAL

Port
Fòrum
Sant Adrià

MUSEU
BLAU

BUNKERS
DEL CARMEL

RAMBLA DE GUIPÚSCOA

GRAN VIA DE LES CORTS CATALANES

AV. MERIDIANA

Parc
Diagonal
Mar

TÚNEL DE LA ROVIRA

RONDA DEL GUINARDÓ

HOSPITAL DE
SANTA CREU I
SANT PAU

CARRER DE SANT ANTONI MARIA CLARET

BARCELONA

AV. DIAGONAL

CAN
RECASENS

PASSEIG DEL TAULAT

RONDA LITORAL

VANASDIVE

MAR BELLA

MUSEUM
OF DESIGN

CARRER DE BADAJOZ

BASE NAUTUICA
MUNICIPAL DE LA
MAR BELLA

RAZZMATAZZ

VAI MOANA

EL XIRINGUITO
ESCRIBÀ

TRAVESSERA DE GRACIA

AV. DIAGONAL

CARRER ARAGÓ

CARRER DE LES CORTS CATALANES

CARRER DE LA MARINA

Parc de
l'Estació
del Nord

NOVA ICARIA

LA
CARMELINA

Mediterranean
Sea

PASSEIG DE GRACIA

GRAN VIA DE LES CORTS CATALANES

Port
Olímpic

CENTRE
MUNICIPAL
DE VELA

SEE
"LA RIBERA"
MAP

SEE
"THE WATERFRONT"
MAP

SEE
"LAS RAMBLAS,
BARRI GÒTIC,
AND EL RAVAL"
MAP

Funicular de Montjuïc

Parallel

Port Vell

SEE
"MONTJUÏC, POBLE SEC,
AND SANT ANTONI"
MAP

Parc
de Montjuïc

Parc de
Montjuïc

RONDA LITORAL

Port de
Barcelona

0   0.5 mi

0   0.5 km

© MOON.COM

Las Ramblas, Barri Gòtic, and El Raval

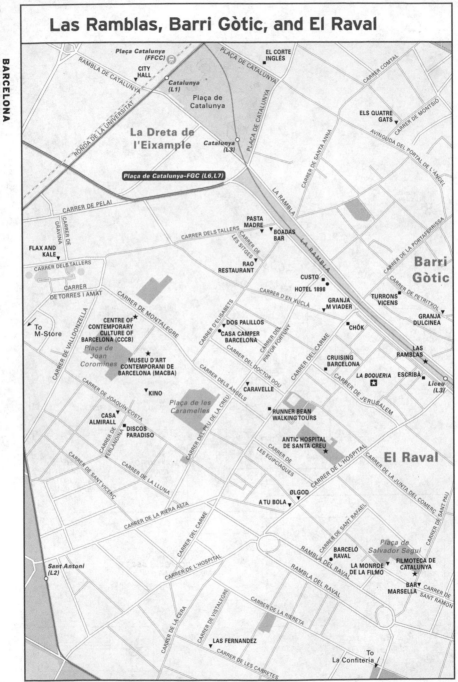

Plaça Catalunya (FFCC)

RAMBLA DE CATALUNYA

CITY HALL

Catalunya (L1)

PLAÇA DE CATALUNYA

EL CORTE INGLÉS

CARRER COMTAL

Plaça de Catalunya

PLAÇA DE CATALUNYA

ELS QUATRE GATS

CARRER DE MONTSIÓ

RONDA DE LA UNIVERSITAT

La Dreta de l'Eixample

Catalunya (L3)

CARRER DE SANTA ANNA

AVINGUDA DEL PORTAL DE L'ANGEL

Plaça de Catalunya-FGC (L6, L7)

LA RAMBLA

CARRER DE PELAI

CARRER DE GRAVINA

CARRER DELS TALLERS

FLAX AND KALE

CARRER DELS TALLERS

PASTA MADRE

BOADAS BAR

CARRER DE LES SITGES

RAO RESTAURANT

LA RAMBLA

Barri Gòtic

CARRER DE LA PORTAFERRISSA

CARRER DE TORRES I AMAT

CARRER DE MONTALEGRE

CUSTO

HOTEL 1898

CARRER D'EN XUCLÁ

GRANJA M VIADER

TURRONS VICENS

CARRER DE PETRITXOL

CENTRE OF CONTEMPORARY CULTURE OF BARCELONA (CCCB)

To M-Store

CARRER DE VALLDONZELLA

Plaça de Joan Coromines

MUSEU D'ART CONTEMPORANI DE BARCELONA (MACBA)

CARRER D'ELISABETS

DOS PALILLOS

CASA CAMPER BARCELONA

CARRER DEL PINTOR FORTUNY

CARRER DEL DOCTOR DOU

CARRER DEL CARME

CHÓK

GRANJA DULCINEA

LAS RAMBLAS

CRUISING BARCELONA

LA BOQUERIA

ESCRIBÀ

Liceu (L3)

KINO

CARRER DE JOAQUIN COSTA

CARRER DELS ÀNGELS

CARAVELLE

Plaça de les Caramelles

CARRER DE JERUSALEM

CASA ALMIRALL

DISCOS PARADISO

CARRER DE FERLANDINA

CARRER DEL PEU DE LA CREU

RUNNER BEAN WALKING TOURS

ANTIC HOSPITAL DE SANTA CREU

CARRER DE LES EGIPCÍAQUES

CARRER DE L'HOSPITAL

El Raval

CARRER DE LA JUNTA DEL COMERÇ

CARRER DE SANT VICENÇ

CARRER DE LA LLUNA

CARRER DE LA RIERA ALTA

CARRER DEL CARME

ÒLGOD

A TU BOLA

CARRER DE SANT RAFAEL

CARRER DE SANT PAU

Sant Antoni (L2)

CARRER DE L'HOSPITAL

RAMBLA DEL RAVAL

BARCELÓ RAVAL

Plaça de Salvador Seguí

LA MONROE DE LA FILMO

FILMOTECA DE CATALUNYA

CARRER DE SANT RAMON

BAR MARSELLA

CARRER DE LA CERA

CARRER DE VISTALEGRE

CARRER DE LA RIERETA

CARRER DE LA RIERETA

LAS FERNANDEZ

CARRER DE LES CARRETES

To La Confiteria

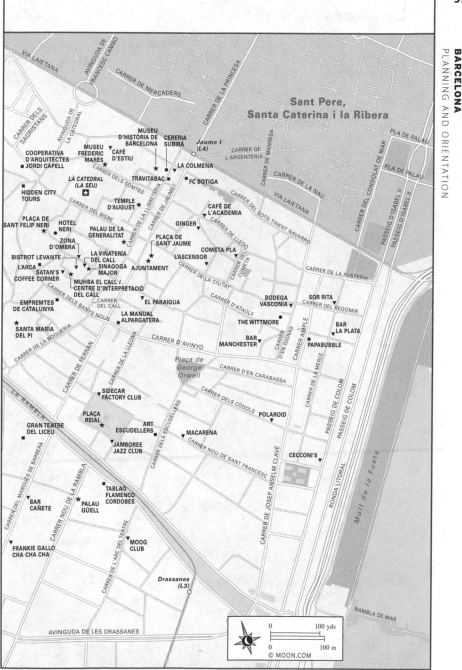

VIA LAIETANA

AVINGUDA DE FRANCESC CAMBÓ

CARRER DE MERCADERS

CARRER DE LA PRINCESA

Sant Pere, Santa Caterina i la Ribera

CARRER DELS SAGRISTANS

AVINGUDA DE LA CATEDRAL

MUSEU D'HISTÒRIA DE BARCELONA

CERERIA SUBIRÀ

Jaume I (L4)

CARRER DE MANRESA

CARRER DE L'ARGENTERIA

CARRER DEL CONSOLAT DE MAR

PLA DE PALAU

COOPERATIVA D'ARQUITECTES JORDI CAPELL

MUSEU FREDERIC MARÉS

CAFÉ D'ESTIU

LA COLMENA

CARRER DE LA NAU

PLA DE PALAU

CARRER DELS COMTES

TRAVITABAC

FC BOTIGA

PASSEIG D'ISABEL II

PASSEIG D'ISABEL II

LA CATEDRAL (LA SEU)

HIDDEN CITY TOURS

TEMPLE D'AUGUST

CARRER DE LA LLIBRETERIA

CARRER DE JAUME I

VIA LAIETANA

CARRER DELS SOTS-TINENT NAVARRO

CAFÉ DE L'ACADEMIA

PLAÇA DE SANT FELIP NERI

HOTEL NERI

CARRER DEL BISBE

GINGER

CARRER DE LLEDÓ

CARRER DE LA FUSTERIA

PALAU DE LA GENERALITAT

PLAÇA DE SANT JAUME

ZONA D'OMBRA

LA VIÑATERÍA DEL CALL

L'ASCENSOR

COMETA PLA

CARRER DEL COMETA

BISTROT LEVANTE

SINAGOGA MAJOR

AJUNTAMENT

L'ARCA

SATAN'S COFFEE CORNER

MUHBA EL CALL / CENTRE D'INTERPRETACIÓ DEL CALL

CARRER DE LA CIUTAT

EMPREMTES DE CATALUNYA

CARRER DELS BANYS NOUS

CARRER DEL CALL

EL PARAIGUA

CARRER D'ATAÜLF

BODEGA VASCONIA

SOR RITA

CARRER DEL REGOMIR

SANTA MARIA DEL PI

LA MANUAL ALPARGATERA

THE WITTMORE

BAR LA PLATA

CARRER DE LA BOQUERIA

CARRER D'AVINYÓ

BAR MANCHESTER

CARRER D'EN GIGNÀS

CARRER AMPLE

PAPABUBBLE

CARRER DE FERRAN

CARRER DE LA LLEONA

Plaça de George Orwell

CARRER D'EN CARABASSA

CARRER DE LA MERCÈ

LA RAMBLA

SIDECAR FACTORY CLUB

CARRER DELS CÒDOLS

POLAROID

PASSEIG DE COLOM

PASSEIG DE COLOM

PLAÇA REIAL

ART ESCUDELLERS

CARRER DELS ESCUDELLERS

MACARENA

GRAN TEATRE DEL LICEU

JAMBOREE JAZZ CLUB

CARRER NOU DE SANT FRANCESC

CECCONI'S

CARRER DE JOSEP ANSELM CLAVÉ

Moll de la Fusta

CARRER DEL MARQUÈS DE BARBERÀ

BAR CAÑETE

PALAU GÜELL

TABLAO FLAMENCO CORDOBES

CARRER NOU DE LA RAMBLA

RONDA LITORAL

FRANKIE GALLO CHA CHA CHA

MOOG CLUB

CARRER DE L'ARC DEL TEATRE

Drassanes (L3)

RAMBLA DE MAR

AVINGUDA DE LES DRASSANES

0   100 yds

0   100 m

© MOON.COM

La Ribera

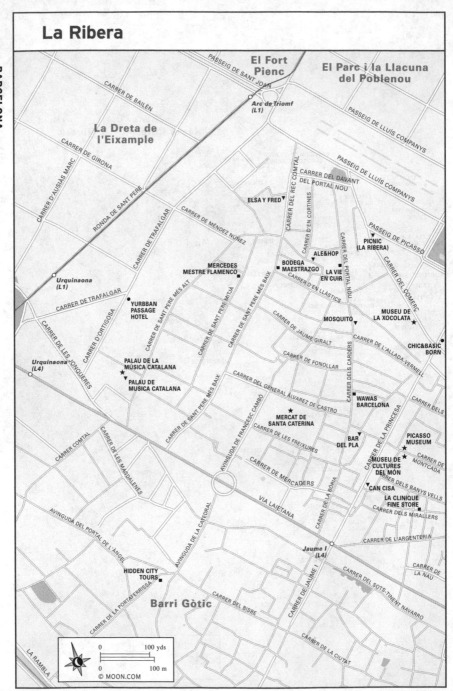

El Fort Pienc

El Parc i la Llacuna del Poblenou

PASSEIG DE SANT JOAN

CARRER DE BAILÉN

Arc de Triomf (L1)

PASSEIG DE LLUÍS COMPANYS

La Dreta de l'Eixample

CARRER DE GIRONA

CARRER D'AUSIAS MARC

RONDA DE SANT PERE

CARRER DEL DAVANT

PASSEIG DE LLUÍS COMPANYS

CARRER DEL REC COMTAL

CARRER DEL DAVANT
DEL PORTAL NOU

CARRER DE MÉNDEZ NÚÑEZ

ELSA Y FRED

CARRER D'EN CORTINES

PASSEIG DE PICASSO

CARRER DE TRAFALGAR

PICNIC
(LA RIBERA)

CARRER D'EN LLÀSTICS

ALE&HOP

CARRER DEL PORTAL NOU

CARRER DEL COMERÇ

Urquinaona
(L1)

CARRER DE TRAFALGAR

MERCEDES
MESTRE FLAMENCO

BODEGA
MAESTRAZGO

LA VIE
EN CUIR

CARRER DE SANT PERE MÉS ALT

CARRER DE SANT PERE MITJÀ

CARRER DE SANT PERE MÉS BAIX

YURBBAN
PASSAGE
HOTEL

MOSQUITO

MUSEU DE
LA XOCOLATA

CARRER DE JAUME GIRALT

CHIC&BASIC
BORN

CARRER DE L'ALLADA-VERMELL

Urquinaona
(L4)

CARRER DE LES JONQUERES

CARRER D'ORTIGOSA

PALAU DE LA
MÚSICA CATALANA

CARRER DE FONOLLAR

CARRER DELS CARDERS

CARRER DELS

PALAU DE
MÚSICA CATALANA

CARRER DEL GENERAL ÁLVAREZ DE CASTRO

WAWAS
BARCELONA

CARRER COMTAL

CARRER DE LES MAGDALENES

CARRER DE SANT PERE MÉS BAIX

AVINGUDA DE FRANCESC CAMBÓ

MERCAT DE
SANTA CATERINA

CARRER DE LES FREIXURES

BAR
DEL PLA

CARRER DE LA PRINCESA

PICASSO
MUSEUM

CARRER DE
MONTCADA

CARRER DE MERCADERS

MUSEU DE
CULTURES
DEL MÓN

CARRER DELS BANYS VELLS

AVINGUDA DEL PORTAL DE L'ÀNGEL

CARRER DE LA BÒRIA

VIA LAIETANA

CAN CISA

LA CLINIQUE
FINE STORE

CARRER DELS MIRALLERS

AVINGUDA DE LA CATEDRAL

CARRER DE L'ARGENTERIA

Jaume I
(L4)

CARRER DE JAUME I

CARRER DE
LA NAU

HIDDEN CITY
TOURS

CARRER DEL SOTS-TINENT NAVARRO

Barri Gòtic

CARRER DEL BISBE

CARRER DE LA PORTAFERRISSA

LA RAMBLA

CARRER DE LA CIUTAT

0   100 yds

0   100 m

© MOON.COM

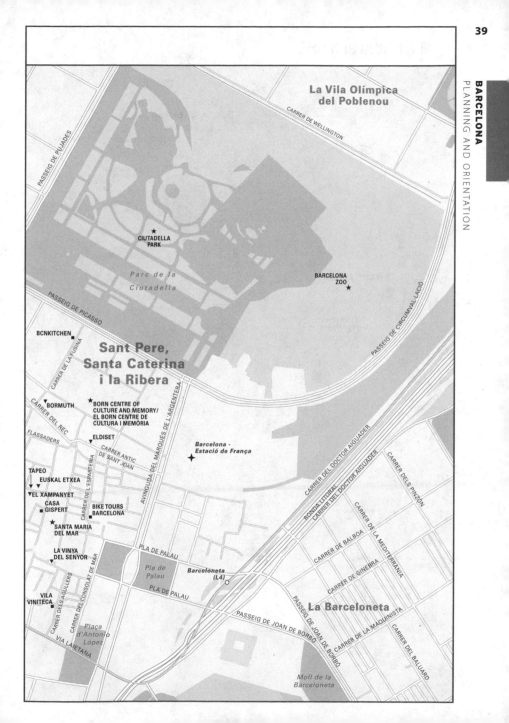

The Waterfront

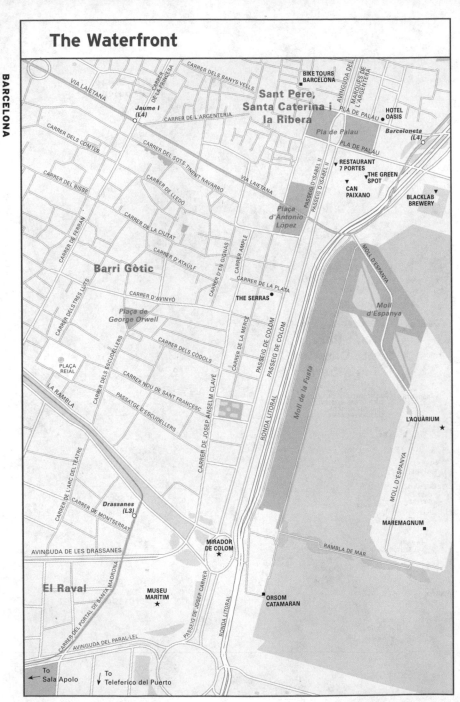

VIA LAIETANA

CARRER DE LA PRINCESA

CARRER DELS BANYS VELLS

BIKE TOURS BARCELONA

AVINGUDA DEL

MARQUÈS DE L'ARGENTERA

Jaume I
(L4)

CARRER DE L'ARGENTERIA

Sant Pere,
Santa Caterina i
la Ribera

PLA DE PALAU

HOTEL
OASIS

CARRER DELS COMTES

Pla de Palau

Barceloneta
(L4)

CARRER DELS SOTS TINENT NAVARRO

PLA DE PALAU

CARRER DEL BISBE

CARRER DE LLEDO

VIA LAIETANA

PASSEIG D'ISABEL II

RESTAURANT
7 PORTES

THE GREEN
SPOT

CAN
PAIXANO

BLACKLAB
BREWERY

CARRER DE LA CIUTAT

Plaça
d'Antonio
López

MOLL D'ESPANYA

CARRER D'ATAÜLF

CARRER DE FERRAN

CARRER D'EN GIGNÀS

CARRER AMPLE

Barri Gòtic

CARRER DE LA PLATA

CARRER DELS TRES LLITS

CARRER D'AVINYÓ

CARRER DE LA MERCÈ

THE SERRAS

Moll
d'Espanya

Plaça de
George Orwell

CARRER DELS ESCUDELLERS

CARRER DELS CÒDOLS

PASSEIG DE COLOM

PASSEIG DE COLOM

PLAÇA
REIAL

CARRER NOU DE SANT FRANCESC

PASSATGE D'ESCUDELLERS

LA RAMBLA

Moll de la Fusta

RONDA LITORAL

L'AQUÀRIUM

CARRER DE JOSEP ANSELM CLAVÉ

MOLL D'ESPANYA

CARRER DE L'ARC DEL TEATRE

Drassanes
(L3)

CARRER DE MONTSERRAT

MAREMAGNUM

MIRADOR
DE COLOM

RAMBLA DE MAR

AVINGUDA DE LES DRASSANES

El Raval

MUSEU
MARÍTIM

CARRER DEL PORTAL DE SANTA MADRONA

PASSEIG DE JOSEP CARNER

ORSOM
CATAMARAN

RONDA LITORAL

AVINGUDA DEL PARAL·LEL

To
← Sala Apolo

To
↓ Teleferico del Puerto

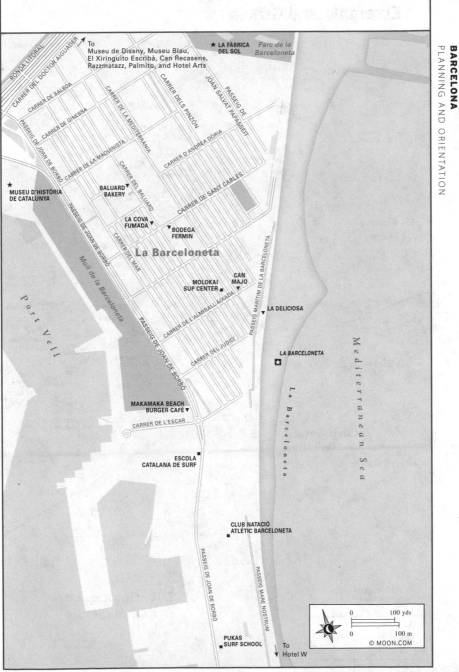

RONDA LITORAL

CARRER DEL DOCTOR AIGUADER

To
Museu de Dissny, Museu Blau,
El Xiringuito Escribà, Can Recasens,
Razzmatazz, Palmito, and Hotel Arts

★ LA FÁBRICA
DEL SOL

Parc de la
Barceloneta

CARRER DE BALBOA

CARRER DE GINEBRA

PASSEIG DE JOAN DE BORBÓ

CARRER DE LA MAQUINISTA

CARRER DE LA MEDITERRANIA

CARRER DELS PINZON

CARRER DE LA MEDITERRANIA

CARRER D'ANDREA DORIA

JOAN SALVAT PAPASSEIT

PASSEIG DE

★ MUSEU D'HISTÒRIA
DE CATALUNYA

BALUARD ▼
BAKERY

CARRER DEL BALUARD

CARRER DE SANT CARLES

PASSEIG DE JOAN DE BORBÓ

LA COVA
FUMADA ▼

▼ BODEGA
FERMIN

Moll de la Barceloneta

CARRER DEL MAR

La Barceloneta

MOLOKAI
SUP CENTER ■

CAN
MAJO
▼

CARRER DE L'ALMIRALL AIXADA

PASSEIG MARITIM DE LA BARCELONETA

▼ LA DELICIOSA

PASSEIG DE JOAN DE BORBÓ

CARRER DEL JUDICI

LA BARCELONETA
✪

P o r t   V e l l

MAKAMAKA BEACH
BURGER CAFÉ ▼

CARRER DE L'ESCAR

ESCOLA ■
CATALANA DE SURF

La B a r c e l o n e t a

M e d i t e r r a n e a n   S e a

CLUB NATACIÓ
ATLÈTIC BARCELONETA
■

PASSEIG DE JOAN DE BORBÓ

PASSEIG MARE NOSTRUM

PUKAS
■ SURF SCHOOL

To
Hotel W

0   100 yds
0   100 m
© MOON.COM

Eixample and Gràcia

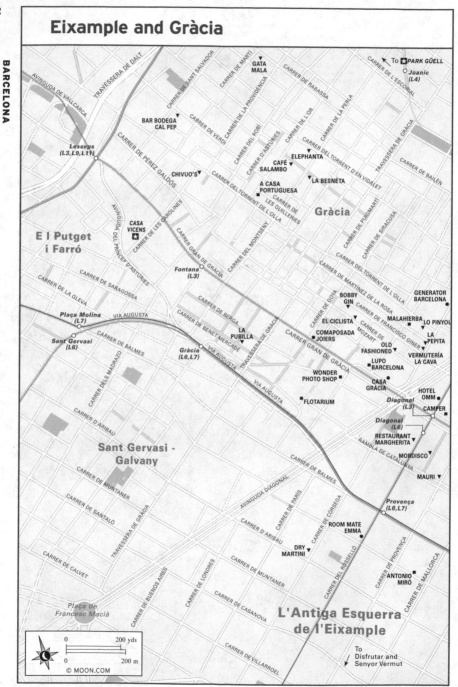

To ✚ PARK GÜELL

○ Joanic
(L4)

AVINGUDA DE VALLCARCA

TRAVESSERA DE DALT

CARRER DE L'ESCORIAL

CARRER DE SANT SALVADOR

CARRER DE MARTI

▼ GATA MALA

CARRER DE RABASSA

CARRER DE LA PROVIDENCIA

BAR BODEGA CAL PEP ▼

CARRER DE VERDI

CARRER DEL ROBI

CARRER D'ASTÚRIES

CARRER DE L'OR

CARRER DE LA PERLA

CARRER DEL TORRENT D'EN VIDALET

TRAVESSERA DE GRACIA

CARRER DE BAILÈN

Lesseps
(L3, L9, L11)

CARRER DE PEREZ GALDOS

CHIVUO'S ▼

CARRER DEL TORRENT DE L'OLLA

ELEPHANTA ■

CAFÉ SALAMBO ▼

A CASA PORTUGUESA ■

LA BESNÉTA ▼

CARRER DE LES GUILLERIES

Gràcia

CARRER DE PUIGMARTI

CARRER DE SIRACUSA

E l Putget
i Farró

AVINGUDA DEL PRINCEP D'ASTÚRIES

CASA VICENS ✚

CARRER DE LES CAROLINES

CARRER GRAN DE GRACIA

CARRER DEL MONTSENY

CARRER DEL TORRENT DE L'OLLA

CARRER DE LA GLEVA

CARRER DE SARAGOSSA

Fontana
(L3)

CARRER DE MARTINEZ DE LA ROSA

GENERATOR BARCELONA ●

Plaça Molina
(L7)

VIA AUGUSTA

CARRER DE BERGA

CARRER DE GOYA

BOBBY GIN ▼

CARRER DE FRANCISCO GINER

MALAHIERBA ■

LO PINYOL

Sant Gervasi
(L6)

CARRER DE BALMES

CARRER DE BENET MERCADE

LA PUBILLA ▼

EL CICLISTA ■

CARRER DE MOZART

COMAPOSADA JOIERS ■

CARRER DE

OLD FASHIONED ▼

LA PEPITA ▼

VERMUTERÍA LA CAVA

Gràcia
(L6, L7)

VIA AUGUSTA

CARRER DELS MADRAZO

TRAVESSERA DE GRACIA

CARRER GRAN DE GRACIA

LUPO BARCELONA ■

WONDER PHOTO SHOP ■

CASA GRÀCIA ●

HOTEL OMM ●

VIA AUGUSTA

FLOTARIUM ■

Diagonal
(L3)

CAMPER ■

Diagonal
(L6)

RESTAURANT MARGHERITA ▼

RAMBLA DE CATALUNYA

MORDISCO ▼

Sant Gervasi -
Galvany

CARRER D'ARIBAU

MAURI ▼

CARRER DE MUNTANER

AVINGUDA DIAGONAL

CARRER DE PARIS

CARRER DE CORSEGA

Provença
(L6, L7)

CARRER DE SANTALO

CARRER DE BALMES

ROOM MATE EMMA ●

TRAVESSERA DE GRACIA

CARRER D'ARIBAU

DRY MARTINI ▼

CARRER DEL ROSSELLO

CARRER DE MUNTANER

CARRER DE PROVENÇA

ANTONIO MIRÓ ■

CARRER DE MALLORCA

CARRER DE CALVET

CARRER DELS BUENOS AIRES

CARRER DE LONDRES

CARRER DE CASANOVA

**L'Antiga Esquerra
de l'Eixample**

Plaça de
Francesc Macià

0   200 yds

0   200 m

© MOON.COM

CARRER DE VILLARROEL

To
Disfrutar and
Senyor Vermut

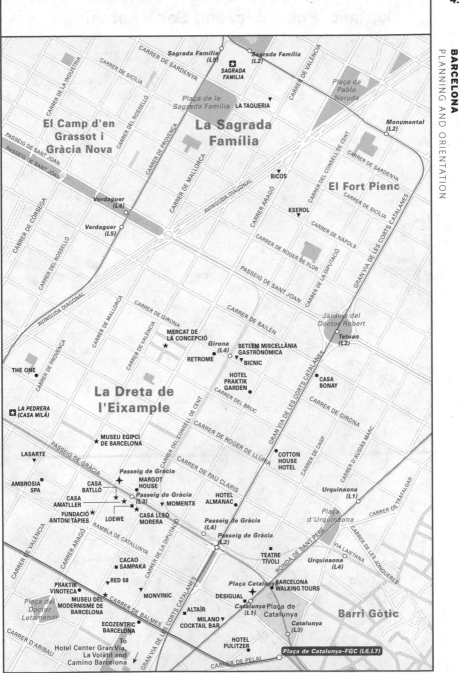

CARRER DE LA INDÚSTRIA
CARRER DE SICÍLIA
CARRER DE SARDENYA
Sagrada Família (L5)
CARRER DE VALÈNCIA
Sagrada Família (L2)
⭐ SAGRADA FAMÍLIA
Plaça de Pablo Neruda
CARRER DEL ROSSELLÓ
CARRER DE PROVENÇA
Plaça de la Sagrada Família
LA TAQUERIA

El Camp d'en Grassot i Gràcia Nova

La Sagrada Família

Monumental (L2)

PASSEIG DE SANT JOAN
PASSEIG DE SANT JOAN

CARRER DE MALLORCA

BICOS

El Fort Pienc

CARRER DEL CONSELL DE CENT
CARRER DE SARDENYA
CARRER DE SICÍLIA

CARRER DE CORSEGA

Verdaguer (L4)

AVINGUDA DIAGONAL

CARRER ARAGÓ

KSEROL

CARRER DE NAPOLS

CARRER DEL ROSSELLÓ

Verdaguer (L5)

CARRER DE ROGER DE FLOR

PASSEIG DE SANT JOAN

CARRER DE LA DIPUTACIÓ

GRAN VIA DE LES CORTS CATALANES

AVINGUDA DIAGONAL

CARRER DE MALLORCA
CARRER DE GIRONA
CARRER DE BAILÉN

Jardins del Doctor Robert

CARRER DE PROVENÇA

CARRER DE VALÈNCIA

MERCAT DE LA CONCEPCIÓ

Girona (L4)
BETLEM MISCEL·LÀNIA GASTRONÒMICA
RETROME
BICNIC

Tetuan (L2)

THE ONE
CARRER DE PROVENÇA

La Dreta de l'Eixample

HOTEL PRAKTIK GARDEN
CARRER DEL BRUC

CASA BONAY

GRAN VIA DE LES CORTS CATALANES

CARRER DE GIRONA

LA PEDRERA (CASA MILÀ)

MUSEU EGIPCI DE BARCELONA

CARRER DEL CONSELL DE CENT

CARRER DE ROGER DE LLÚRIA

COTTON HOUSE HOTEL

CARRER DE CASP

CARRER D'AUSIAS MARC

PASSEIG DE GRÀCIA

LASARTE

CARRER DE PAU CLARIS

Passeig de Gràcia

MARGOT HOUSE

AMBROSIA SPA

CASA BATLLÓ

Passeig de Gràcia (L3)
MOMENTS

HOTEL ALMANAC

Urquinaona (L1)

CARRER DE TRAFALGAR

CASA AMATLLER

FUNDACIÓ ANTONI TÀPIES
LOEWE
CASA LLEÓ MORERA

Passeig de Gràcia (L4)
Passeig de Gràcia (L2)

Plaça d'Urquinaona

CARRER DE SANT PERE

CARRER DE LES JONQUERES

RAMBLA DE CATALUNYA

CARRER DE VALÈNCIA
CARRER ARAGÓ
CARRER DE LA DIPUTACIÓ

CACAO SAMPAKA

RED 58

TEATRE TÍVOLI

RONDA DE SANT PERE

Urquinaona (L4)

VIA LAIETANA

PRAKTIK VINOTECA

MUSEU DEL MODERNISME DE BARCELONA

MONVINIC

Plaça Catalunya
BARCELONA WALKING TOURS

Barri Gòtic

Plaça del Doctor Letamendi

CARRER DE BALMES

ECOZENTRIC BARCELONA

DESIGUAL

ALTAÏR

Catalunya (L1)
Plaça de Catalunya

MILANO COCKTAIL BAR

Catalunya (L3)

CARRER D'ARIBAU

GRAN VIA DE LES CORTS CATALANES

To Hotel Center Gran Via, La Volàtil and Camino Barcelona

HOTEL PULITZER

Plaça de Catalunya-FGC (L6,L7)

CARRER DE PELAI

Montjuïc, Poble Sec, and Sant Antoni

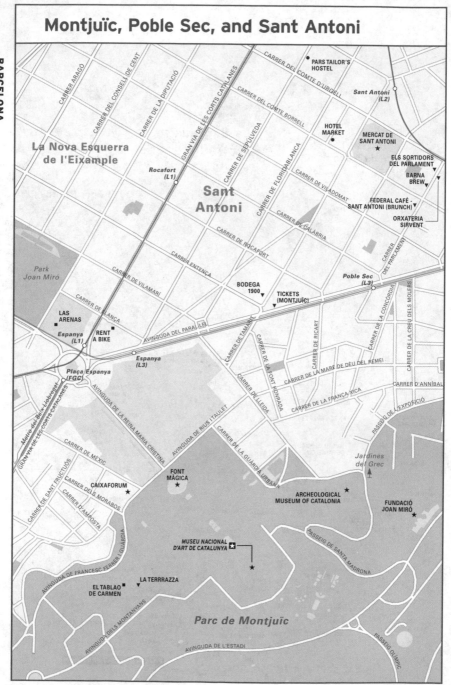

CARRER D'ARAGÓ

CARRER DEL CONSELL DE CENT

CARRER DE LA DIPUTACIÓ

GRAN VIA DE LES CORTS CATALANES

CARRER DEL COMTE D'URGELL

CARRER DEL COMTE BORRELL

CARRER DE SEPÚLVEDA

CARRER DE FLORIDABLANCA

CARRER DE VILADOMAT

CARRER DE CALÀBRIA

CARRER DE ROCAFORT

CARRER ENTENÇA

CARRER DE VILAMARI

CARRER DE LLANÇA

CARRER DE TAMARIT

CARRER DE LA FONT HONRADA

CARRER DE RICART

CARRER DE LA MARE DE DÉU DEL REMEI

CARRER DE LA CONCÒRDIA

CARRER DE LA CREU DELS MOLERS

CARRER DEL PARLAMENT

CARRER DE LLEIDA

CARRER DE LA FRANÇA XICA

CARRER D'ANNÍBAL

PASSEIG DE L'EXPOSICIÓ

La Nova Esquerra de l'Eixample

Sant Antoni

Rocafort (L1)

Sant Antoni (L2)

PARS TAILOR'S HOSTEL

HOTEL MARKET

MERCAT DE SANT ANTONI ★

ELS SORTIDORS DEL PARLAMENT ▼

BARNA BREW ▼

FEDERAL CAFÉ - SANT ANTONI (BRUNCH) ▼

ORXATERIA SIRVENT

BODEGA 1900 ▼

Poble Sec (L3)

TICKETS (MONTJUÏC) ▼

Park Joan Miró

LAS ARENAS ■

Espanya (L1)

RENT A BIKE ■

AVINGUDA DEL PARAL·LEL

Espanya (L3)

Plaça Espanya (FGC)

Metro del Baix Llobregat

GRAN VIA DE LES CORTS CATALANES

AVINGUDA DE LA REINA MARIA CRISTINA

CARRER DE MÈXIC

CARRER DE SANT FRUCTUÓS

CARRER DELS MORABOS

CARRER D'AMPOSTA

AVINGUDA DE FRANCESC FERRER I GUÀRDIA

CAIXAFORUM ★

AVINGUDA DE RIUS I TAULET

CARRER DE LA GUÀRDIA URBANA

FONT MÀGICA ★

Jardines del Grec

ARCHEOLOGICAL MUSEUM OF CATALONIA ★

FUNDACIÓ JOAN MIRÓ ★

PASSEIG DE SANTA MADRONA

MUSEU NACIONAL D'ART DE CATALUNYA ✪

EL TABLAO DE CARMEN ■

LA TERRRAZZA ▼

Parc de Montjuïc

AVINGUDA DELS MONTANYANS

AVINGUDA DE L'ESTADI

PASSEIG OLÍMPIC

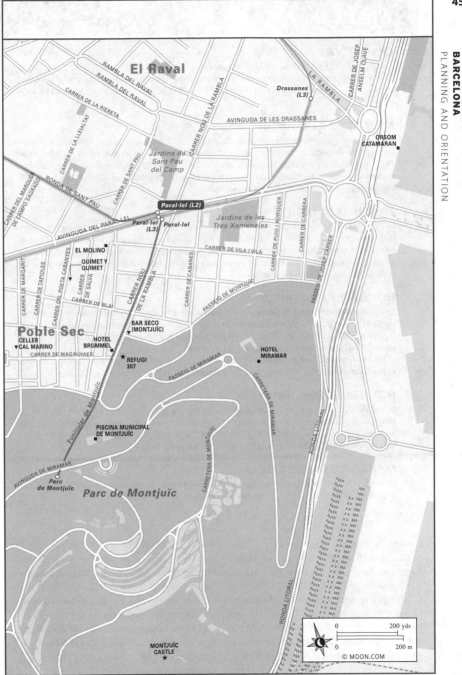

El Raval

RAMBLA DEL RAVAL
RAMBLA DEL RAVAL
CARRER DE LA RIERETA
CARRER DE LA LLEIALTAT

CARRER NOU DE LA RAMBLA

LA RAMBLA

CARRER DE JOSEP ANSELM CLAVÉ

Drassanes
(L3)

AVINGUDA DE LES DRASSANES

ORSOM
CATAMARAN

Jardins de
Sant Pau
del Camp

CARRER DE SANT PAU

CARRER DEL MARQUES DE CAMPO SAGRADO
RONDA DE SANT PAU

AVINGUDA DEL PARAL-LEL

Paral·lel (L2)

Paral·lel
(L3)   Paral·lel

Jardins de les
Tres Xemeneies

CARRER DE PUIG I XORIGUER

CARRER DE CARRERA

CARRER DE CARRERA

PASSEIG DE JOSEP CARNER

EL MOLINO

CARRER DE VILA I VILA

QUIMET Y
QUIMET

CARRER DE MARGARIT
CARRER DE TAPIOLES
CARRER DEL POETA CABANYES
CARRER DE SALVA

CARRER NOU DE LA RAMBLA

CARRER DE CABANES

CARRER DE CABANES

PASSEIG DE MONTJUÏC

CARRER DE BLAI

Poble Sec

BAR SECO
(MONTJUÏC)

CELLER
CAL MARINO   HOTEL
BRUMMEL

CARRER DE MAGALHAES

★ REFUGI
307

HOTEL
MIRAMAR

PASSEIG DE MIRAMAR

CARRETERA DE MIRAMAR

Funicular de Montjuïc

PISCINA MUNICIPAL
DE MONTJUÏC

RONDA LITORAL

AVINGUDA DE MIRAMAR

Parc
de Montjuïc

CARRETERA DE MONTJUÏC

Parc de Montjuïc

RONDA LITORAL

MONTJUÏC
CASTLE
★

0   200 yds
0   200 m

© MOON.COM

What's New?

CASA VICENS

Antoni Gaudí's first housing commission opened to the public in late 2017. This UNESCO World Heritage Site gives visitors a wonderful insight into the inspiration and foundations of the great architect's work. Keep an eye out for themes and motifs that would be used throughout his later designs.

MERCAT DE SANT ANTONI

This wonderful neighborhood market re-opened in May 2018 after nine years and €80 million of slow-going renovations that left locals wondering if it would ever re-open at all. Built between 1879-1882, the market is a neighborhood icon. Fresh food, clothing, and books are all represented on spacious new stalls. Visitors can now see a section of Barcelona's medieval walls on the **-1 level**, which was uncovered during renovations.

MUSEUMS BY NIGHT

In 2018, **Casa Batlló** introduced new nighttime visiting hours. Guests visit Gaudí's famous building after sunset and enjoy live music and a drink in the atmospheric surroundings of one of Barcelona's most iconic buildings. **La Pedrera,** too, offers nighttime hours, during which guests are taken around the building in small groups by a guide and shown projections and light shows, finishing off the visit with a glass of *cava*.

HOTELS AND RESTAURANTS

Traditional Catalan cuisine is getting a creative update, thanks to a host of Michelin-starred restaurants that are pushing the boundaries of the region's traditional dishes. The Adrià brothers' tapas bar **Tickets** is still one of the hottest places in town, while restaurants like **Disfrutar** are showcasing new techniques in a relaxed atmosphere.

Hotel Almanac, which opened its doors at the end of 2017, brings a sleek, sumptuous style to the Eixample district, within easy walking distance of Las Ramblas and the old town.

HOT NEIGHBORHOODS

Sant Antoni, once a leafy quiet area straddling the Eixample and the Poble Sec area of Montjuïc, has a new lease on life thanks to a host of cool new bars, shops, and restaurants and an influx of cool, young creatives. It is now one of Barcelona's hippest districts; a wander down **Carrer del Parlament** is a must for any stylish traveler.

MANAGING TOURIST FLOW

In an effort to control mass tourism, Barcelona has implemented new measures, such as introducing timed visits to Park Güell, Gaudí's famous hillside park.

centers: the Center of Contemporary Culture of Barcelona (CCCB), the Fundació Antoni Tàpes, the Fundació Joan Miró, the National Art Museum of Catalonia, the Museum of Contemporary Art of Barcelona (MACBA), and the Picasso Museum. The ticket costs €30 and is valid for three months from the date of purchase. You can buy the card at participating museums, tourist offices, or online.

ARQUEOTICKET

www.bcnshop.barcelonaturisme.com

One ticket provides access to four historical museums: the Archeological Museum of Catalonia, the Egyptian Museum of Barcelona, the Museum of the History of Barcelona, and the Born Center of Culture and Memory. The ticket costs €14.50 and can be purchased online or at the participating museums.

RUTA DEL MODERNISME

www.rutadelmodernisme.com

This guidebook (available in English, €12) provides a valuable companion to Barcelona's Modernista buildings, as well as a map and discount codes of up to 50 percent for all the Modernista sights in Barcelona including the Sagrada Familia, La Pedrera, Casa Vicens, Casa Batlló, Torre Bellesguard, Hospital de la Santa Creu i Sant Pau, and Casa Amatller.

The guidebook is available from the Modernisme Centre Güell Pavillions (Av. de Pedralbes, 7; Mon-Sun 10am-4pm) and the Institut Municipal del Paisatge Urbà (Av Drassanes, 6, 21st Floor; Mon-Fri 9am-2pm) as well as the Tourist Office on Plaça de Catalunya.

ORIENTATION

Las Ramblas and Barri Gòtic

The Barri Gòtic, the city's Gothic quarter, is a medieval warren of streets hiding beautiful little squares and curiosities at every turn. This is where the **big medieval sites**, like **Barcelona's cathedral** and its former Jewish quarter, are located, while deep below the modern city you can explore the ruins of the Roman city of Barcino.

Las Ramblas, Barcelona's tree-lined boulevard, where generations of locals have promenaded among the flower stalls, is today tourist central, but get there early enough and you can enjoy a peaceful stroll past buildings like the grand Liceu opera house and the **Boqueria market**.

El Raval

West of Las Ramblas was once a seedy, down-at-heel neighborhood, more the domain of prostitutes and drug dealers than tourists. These days El Raval, especially its northern half, has been regenerated and revitalized with a slew of **cultural hubs** like the **Barcelona Museum of Contemporary Art** and the **Filmoteca de Catalunya**. It is also home to some of the city's **oldest bars**, bohemian enclaves that, like the absinthe-peddling

Bar Marsella, have been doing business since the early 19th century.

La Ribera and El Born

Between Via Laietana and Parc de la Ciutadella, just east of the Barri Gòtic, is La Ribera ("The Shore"), an area that flourished during Barcelona's medieval heyday. The street names—*Mirallers* (mirror makers), *Argenters* (silversmiths)—hark back to the craftsmen who once lived there. **Carrer Montcada** was the main thoroughfare, where rich merchants and ship builders constructed huge stone palaces; today five are combined to form the **Picasso Museum**.

The southern part of the neighborhood is named El Born after the 19th-century market that was the center of the area's social and gastronomic life. Nowadays, it is a stylish area of bars, restaurants, and quirky shops.

The Waterfront

Barceloneta, the area of little streets bordering the seafront, was traditionally the fishermen's quarter of the city, full of little hole-in-the-wall bars. The **Port Vell** (Old Port), at the end of Las Ramblas, has been transformed from an industrial area into a smart tourist draw. Old buildings have been preserved (the former shipyards that were at the center of Barcelona's maritime power are now home to the city's Maritime Museum), while a wide boardwalk is lined with **seafront restaurants** and *chiringuitos* (beach huts). **Barceloneta beach** is packed in summer, while further north, the other city beaches (like Nova Icària and Mar Bella) are less crowded and more local.

Eixample

In the 19th century, industrialization and a skyrocketing population meant Barcelona could barely house its own inhabitants. The Eixample ("expansion") was the answer; the brainchild of visionary urban planner Ildefons Cerdà (1815-1876), it was laid out on a grid pattern and joined the city's old town with Gràcia and Sarria, which were then towns outside the city. The new bourgeoisie flooded into the area, commissioning architects to create fantastical new buildings. This is where **Modernisme** flourished, with architects competing to build the most weird and wonderful creations. Today, the Eixample is one of the city's most upmarket areas, home to **designer stores, five-star hotels**, and **Michelin-starred restaurants** as well as some of Gaudí's most famous buildings, including the **Sagrada Familia** and **La Pedrera**.

Gràcia and Park Güell

North of the Eixample, Gràcia was a town outside the city of Barcelona until the late 19th century. There, rich city dwellers built summer homes like **Casa Vicens**, Antoni Gaudí's first building commission. Now, it is a hip neighborhood with a local feel, full of **vintage shops, cool bakeries, bars**, and **restaurants**. In August, the whole neighborhood celebrates the **Festa Major de Gracia** (Gràcia Festival), festooning the streets and

competing to see who can come up with the best decorations. To the north is Park Güell, Gaudí's ambitious failed housing development that is today one of Barcelona's biggest tourist sights.

Montjuïc, Poble Sec, and Sant Antoni

Montjuïc, the hill south of El Raval looking over Barcelona, is home to some of the city's best art museums, such as the **Museu Nacional d'Art de Catalunya** and its millennium of Catalan art, and the **Fundació Joan Miró**, dedicated to the world-famous painter, as well as unusual sights like the theme park that recreates different regions of Spain, **Poble Espanyol**. Its hills are strewn with lush gardens, and a **cable car** brings passengers up from the port. Down the hill, Poble Sec, formerly a working-class area, has a number of great local bars and places to eat, while Sant Antoni, one of Barcelona's most "in" neighborhoods, is craft-beer-and-brunch central.

Itinerary Ideas

DAY 1

Experience the wide boulevard of **Las Ramblas,** one of Barcelona's most famous sights, then plan a late-afternoon visit to the light-soaked interior of **La Sagrada Familia** (book tickets online in advance to avoid waiting in line), followed by a stroll past other **Catalan modernist** masterpieces.

1 Start your day with a visit to **Las Ramblas,** Barcelona's emblematic boulevard. Arrive early to see stallholders setting up and avoid the biggest crowds.

2 Have breakfast of eggs with almost any topping you can imagine at El Quim de la Boqueria in **La Boqueria,** one of the world's most famous food markets, located just off Las Ramblas.

3 Just across Las Ramblas, explore the medieval lanes of the Barri Gòtic, pausing to go inside **La Catedral.** Plaça Sant Felip Neri and Barcelona's former Jewish quarter, El Call, are also nearby and worth a look.

4 A couple of minutes away, see the fascinating remains of the Roman city of Barcino at the **Museu d'Història de Barcelona.**

5 It's a ten-minute walk to **Bar La Plata** for boquerones (fried anchovies), one of just five tapas the bar has been serving since 1945.

6 Take the metro to the **Sagrada Família** and explore Gaudí's unfinished masterpiece—a late-afternoon visit means the golden light will dance through the stained-glass windows for an unforgettable sight inside the basilica.

7 Take the metro back to the Eixample and, as evening falls, stroll down the **Passeig de Gràcia**, lined with Modernista classics like La Pedrera, Casa Batlló, and Casa Amantller.

8 Gràcia is full of restaurants and bars with a cool neighborhood feel. Spend the evening exploring and popping into restaurants like **La Pepita** for tapas.

DAY 2

See the **Picasso Museum,** then spend the afternoon and evening exploring **El Raval,** a formerly gritty neighborhood that's been given a new lease on life with a buzzing food and nightlife scene and an engaging contemporary art museum.

1 Fuel up for the day with a delicious brunch at **Picnic.**

2 After brunch, wander through the streets of La Ribera to the **Picasso Museum**—there will probably be queues, but the rich array of the artist's work inside is worth the wait.

3 The grand **Church of Santa Maria del Mar** is just a two-minute walk away. Built during Catalonia's seafaring heyday in the 14th century, it is an excellent example of Catalan Gothic architecture.

4 Explore the cool shops of La Ribera, stopping for a thirst-quenching craft beer and some veggie tapas at **Ale & Hop,** a ten-minute walk away.

5 Walk (around 15 minutes) over to El Raval. Once a gritty neighborhood, El Raval is now home to hip bars and a multicultural food scene. Explore the rotating modern art exhibits at the **Museu d'Art Contemporari de Barcelona** (MACBA), a colossal white building designed by American architect Richard Meier. Have a drink at KINO (the terrace opposite the museum) and watch the skateboarders outside MACBA do their thing.

6 Explore the nightlife of El Raval, starting with tapas at **Bar Cañete.**

7 Follow up with a bar-hop of century-old drinking dens like **Bar Marsella**, renowned for its absinthe.

BARCELONA LIKE A LOCAL

Explore a thousand years of Catalan art at the **Museu Nacional d'Art de Catalunya,** then chill on the **beach** next to Mediterranean waters, popping into a *chiringuito* (beach bar) or paella restaurant when hunger strikes. Catch the **sunset over Barcelona** before a meal at award-winning tapas bar **Tickets** (book well in advance).

1 Grab a pastry from classic old bakery, **Mauri,** in the Eixample, which has been serving locals freshly made bread, cakes, and desserts since 1929.

2 Take the metro to Espanya and walk up to the Palau Nacional, home to the fantastic **Museu Nacional d'Art de Catalunya**—don't miss the view from its front terrace.

3 Walk past the Olympic Stadium, home to Barcelona's triumphant 1992 summer Olympics, to the **Fundació Joan Miró.**

4 Take the cable car down to the port and enjoy a laid-back lunch at a chiringuito or a paella at one of the restaurants along the seafront, such as **Can Majo.** Pair your lunchtime paella with a glass of crisp white wine, as the locals do.

5 Walk off your lunch along the seafront promenade or spend the afternoon on the beach.

Barcelona Itinerary Ideas

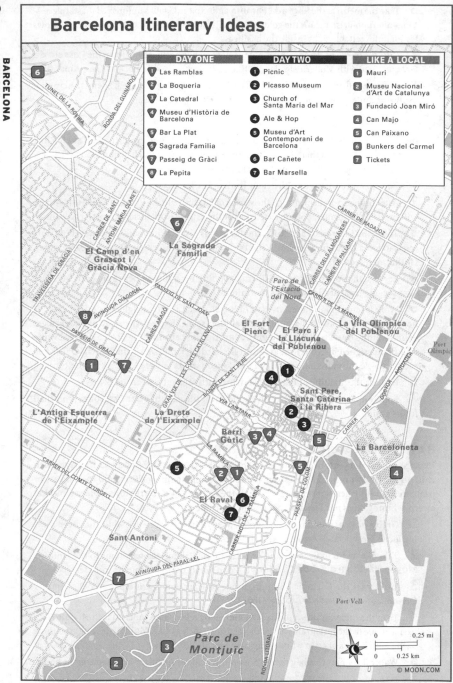

DAY ONE	DAY TWO	LIKE A LOCAL
1 Las Ramblas	**1** Picnic	**1** Mauri
2 La Boqueria	**2** Picasso Museum	**2** Museu Nacional d'Art de Catalunya
3 La Catedral	**3** Church of Santa Maria del Mar	**3** Fundació Joan Miró
4 Museu d'Història de Barcelona	**4** Ale & Hop	**4** Can Majo
5 Bar La Plat	**5** Museu d'Art Contemporani de Barcelona	**5** Can Paixano
6 Sagrada Família	**6** Bar Cañete	**6** Bunkers del Carmel
7 Passeig de Gràci	**7** Bar Marsella	**7** Tickets
8 La Pepita		

© MOON.COM

Hidden Details of the Ramblas

While strolling the Ramblas, be sure to keep an eye out for these details:

- **Miró mosaic:** Look down—Las Ramblas is decorated by some of Spain's most famous artists. Local boy Joan Miró designed a yellow, blue, and red mosaic in 1976 and placed it close to where he was born, on Passatge del Crèdit, at the area of the Ramblas known as Pla de l'Os (where Carrer de l'Hospital meets Plaça Boqueria). It faded over the years as people walked over it, but it was restored to its vivid glory in 2006 to mark its 30th anniversary.

- **Parrots in the trees:** Look up, too! The trees of Las Ramblas are home to a flock of green parrots that were originally pets, but they were released in the 1970s and by now have multiplied into the thousands.

- **Font de Canaletes:** Close to the Plaça de Catalunya, this fountain is named after the medieval northern wall of the city, which was named Canaletes because of the water channels it carried to the old town. It was installed in 1892, and it is said that anyone who drinks from the foundation will return to Barcelona. Since the 1930s, FC Barcelona fans have celebrated their team's triumphs around the fountain.

Either way, don't miss a glass of Cava in **Can Paixano**, a hugely popular local cava bar just off the Waterfront.

6 As evening approaches, take the bus to the **Bunkers del Carmel** to watch the sun set over the city.

7 A magical and theatrical dinner experience at **Tickets** awaits, with a bus ride back into the city center. (Reserve well in advance.)

Sights

LAS RAMBLAS AND BARRI GÒTIC
Las Ramblas

Metro: Catalunya, Liceu, Drassanes

When many people think of Barcelona, they think of Las Ramblas, the city's famous tree-lined boulevard, a place to stroll, shop, and see the sights. It is actually a series of streets in a line: hence the use of the plural, Ramblas. The street, with its two lanes of traffic either side of a wide, pedestrian-friendly central boulevard, is precisely 1.2 kilometers (0.7 miles—about a 20-minute walk) long, stretching from Plaça de Catalunya down to the sea. The street is lined with stalls, from artists selling their visions of Barcelona to newspaper and souvenir kiosks flogging football shirts, fridge magnets, and postcards.

The now-famous street had humble beginnings, as a dried-out stream bed that provided important drainage from the surrounding mountains. Its name is derived from the Arabic *ramla* (sand). In the 15th century, the stream was diverted to allow for an extension of the old town, turning it into a street for the first time. Las Ramblas was built in 1766, following the medieval city walls that bordered the warren-like streets of the old town. At last, locals had a wide avenue where they could stroll, and while it was just seconds from the narrow streets of the Gothic Quarter to the east and El Raval to the west, it was a world away in terms of design. Everyone in the city met here to promenade, and soon key buildings rose up on either side of the Ramblas, such as the city's opera house (the Gran Teatre del Liceu) and the Boqueria food market.

Today, the Ramblas is best visited in the morning, when the flower stalls located close to La Boqueria are setting up, and there is an—albeit fleeting—sense of peace; locals will be on their way to work, and most visitors will have yet to arrive. By 10 or 11am, the street is thronged with tourists seeking out some of the most emblematic sights.

Skip the cafés and restaurants along the street, which tend to be packed with tourists and don't offer good value. Instead, enjoy an early wander and weave off the street into the Bari Gòtic when it's time for breakfast or a mid-morning coffee.

★ La Seu Catedral
(La Catedral)

Pla de la Seu; www.catedralbcn.org; Cathedral: Mon-Sat 8am-7:30pm, Sun 8am-7:30pm, Cloister: Mon-Sat 8:30am-12:30pm, 5:15pm-7pm, Sun 8:30am-1pm, 5:15pm-7pm; €7; Metro: Jaume I

One of the best examples of Gothic architecture in Spain, Barcelona's cathedral is a huge island in the sea of little warrens of the Gothic Quarter. The Catedral de la Santa Creu i Santa Eulàlia, known as La Seu, a Catalan word meaning "the seat" (of the diocese) or "cathedral," stands out in the Barri Gòtic for its richly decorative façade, home to gargoyles and animals. Ironically, this is the one part of the cathedral that was added later (in the late 19th century); the rest of the structure was built between the 1298 and 1448 on the site of an earlier Christian basilica.

The cathedral is open mornings for worship and prayer, with free entry to the cathedral floor and cloister, and afternoons for cultural visits (€7) that include entry to the cathedral floor and cloister, the roof, the choir, the cathedral museum, and the Chapel of Lepanto. Don't miss the hidden oasis in the heart of the building—its 14th-century cloister, home to 13 quacking geese.

Visit during the early morning for a tranquil experience or during the paid afternoon session (roughly 1pm-5pm) when there are fewer visitors and you can access more of the cathedral.

INTERIOR

The vast interior of the cathedral is divided into a central nave surrounded by 28 chapels. In the middle of the nave is the choir, whose stalls feature the coats-of-arms of the knights of the Order of the Golden Fleece, who gathered here during the visit of Emperor Charles V in 1517.

Of the cathedral's chapels, don't miss the **Chapel of the Holy Sacrament** and of the **Holy Christ of Lepanto** (first chapel on the right from the main façade entrance), which holds a crucifix that rode on the front of the galley of Juan of Austria during the Battle of Lepanto in 1571. Legend has it that when a cannonball was careering towards the cross, it leaned out of the way, which gives it its inclined shape.

The **Chapel of Santa Llúcia**, with an entrance at the south-west corner of the cloister, is one of the oldest sections of the cathedral, part of the Romanesque church built prior to the Gothic cathedral. Constructed between 1257 and 1268, it consists of a single nave and two doors, and houses the remains of the 13th-century bishop Arnau of Gurb and the 14th-century canon Francesc of Santa Oloma.

CRYPT

In front of the main altar, a staircase leads down to the cathedral's crypt, home to the remains of one of two of Barcelona's patron saints, **Saint Eulalia**, to whom the cathedral is dedicated. It is said the teenage Eulalia was martyred during the Roman rule over the city. She was subjected to 13 tortures for refusing to give up Christianity, some of which are depicted on the sides of her tomb. Inside the crypt, visitors can see the polychromed marble **sarcophagus** where Saint Eulalia's remains are interred. The sculptor, who is known to have come from Pisa, Italy, engraved key scenes from the young girl's life into the side of the sarcophagus; the story should be read from left to right, from the time Eulalia left her parents' home to her trial, martyrdom, and death.

ROOFTOP

Take the elevator (€3) from the chapel of the Innocent Saints, next to the door of San Ivo (to the left of the choir, inside the cathedral and straight to the back, and to the left when you enter), up to the cathedral's rooftop for spectacular views of the cathedral's spires and the heart of Gothic Barcelona.

CLOISTERS

The Gothic cloister, a rectangular space of four galleries lined in arches and columns, is home to the **Well of the Geese**. 13 white geese live among the tall palm trees of the tropical garden that fills the center of the cloister; the number is kept at 13 because Saint Eulalia was said to have been 13 years old when she was martyred. Look out for the Romanesque door between the cloister and the cathedral, made from white marble, which is said to have come from the Romanesque cathedral that stood on the spot before the current one was built. The cloister's arches are separated by pillars, engraved with scenes from the Old Testament.

★ La Boqueria

Las Ramblas, 91; tel. 93/318-2584; www.boqueria. barcelona; Mon-Sat 8am-8:30pm; Metro: Liceu

Mercat de la Boqueria, commonly referred to as La Boqueria, is one of the world's most famous food markets, a sensory delight where all of Barcelona unites in its love of food. The low rumble of the crowds—the booming voices of stallholders and the chatting visitors—combines with the tempting aroma of fried seafood and the multicolored stands of fruit that are as vivid as any Miró painting.

The current structure dates back to the 19th century, but a market in one form or another has stood on Las Ramblas since at least the 13th century. In 1835 the Carmelite Convent of St. Joseph was destroyed by a fire during the riots on the feast day of Saint James, and once it was demolished, market stalls moved onto the site. The early 20th century brought Modernista touches to the market; the arches that mark the entrance off Las Ramblas were designed by Antoni de Falguera in 1913, and in 1914 the metal roof was added, finally protecting stallholders from the weather.

The market, one of the biggest in Europe, sits midway down Las Ramblas and is hard to miss for the crowds of people congregating at its main entrance. Stalls are a mixture of specialty food vendors (including butchers, cheesemongers, and fruit and vegetable stalls), and small restaurants where you can take a seat at the bar for breakfast or lunch.

Despite its popularity with tourists (there has been talk of banning large tour groups, which tend to display a look-but-don't-buy attitude), it remains a place where locals—and local chefs—come to buy their produce. Do as they do and arrive early, during the first hour after the 8am opening, to buy picnic provisions including Spanish cheeses, jamón Ibérico, fresh fruit, and juicy olives.

Museu d'Història de Barcelona (Museum of the History of Barcelona)

Plaça del Rei; tel. 93/256-2100; www.ajuntament. barcelona.cat/museuhistoria/ca; Tues-Sat 10am-7pm, Sun 10am-8pm; Metro: Jaume I

The Museum of the History of Barcelona (MUHBA), which opened in 1943, gives visitors a fascinating tour of Roman Barcelona, or Barcino as it was called when it was founded by the Emperor Augustus in around 10BC.

The museum is set in the late-15th-century Casa Padellàs on the Plaça del Rei, which was moved brick-by-brick to the site in 1931 when the Via Laietana was being built. During the removal process, archaeologists discovered the well-preserved Roman and medieval streets below the square, buried in centuries of history.

As you enter, pick up your free (and interesting) audio guide and descend into the Roman streets of Barcino. Raised walkways cross over the excavated Roman ruins. See Roman lookout towers, wine factories, tanneries, and laundries, as well as artefacts discovered during the excavations, including jewelry and kitchenware. The *garum* (fish

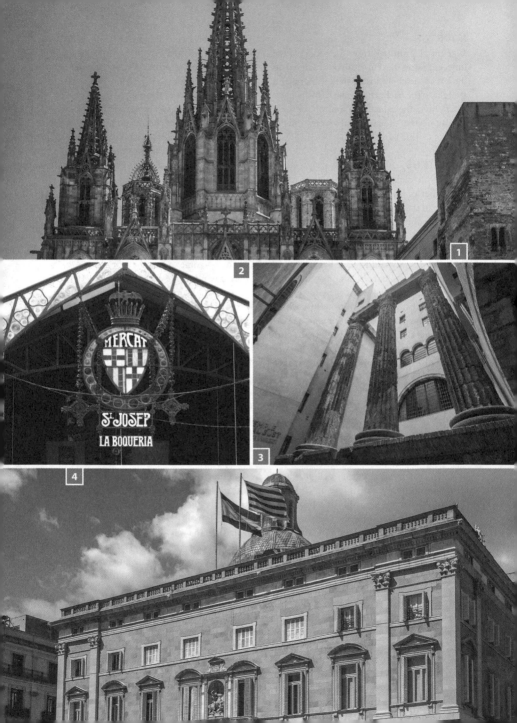

La Boqueria's Best Eats

Lunch is the most popular time to eat there; the market does not open for dinner.

- **El Quim de la Boqueria** (Mon midday-4pm, Tues-Thurs 7am-4pm, Fri-Sat 7am-5pm, www. elquimdelaboqueria.com, €16): This lively place, run by the eponymous Quim, opens early for breakfast (try the two fried eggs with a variety of additional toppings) and is a buzzing lunchtime spot (just finding a seat can prove difficult). Specialities include red tuna with soya and sesame reduction, wild mushrooms in port wine, and Catalan butifarra sausage with beans and garlic sauce. There are plenty of vegetarian options, too. Look out for the bright yellow stall, down the second row on the left from where you walk in off Las Ramblas.

- **Bar Central** (Mon-Sat 8am-8pm, €15): Fish and seafood, cooked fresh to order. Razor clams, king prawns, lobster; pull up a stool and order a seafood feast (seafood platters also available). It is located on the far right-hand side of the market, close to where you enter from Las Ramblas.

sauce) factories and wineries made produce that was exported throughout the empire.

The visit ends in the Palau Reial Major, the residence of the counts of Barcelona and, subsequently, the kings of the crown of Aragon. The Saló del Tinell, or great hall, with its six-arched ceiling, was where Christopher Columbus had an audience with Isabella and Ferdinand (Isabel y Fernando), the Catholic monarchs, on his return from his first trip to the Americas in 1493. Visitors walk into the hall and find themselves back in the 15th century.

You can easily spend two to three hours exploring the museum.

Temple d'August

Carrer del Paradís, 10; tel. 93/256-2122; www. ajuntament.barcelona.cat/museuhistoria/es/muhba-temple-daugust; Tues-Sat 10am-7pm, Sun 10am-8pm, Mon 10am-2pm; admission free; Metro: Jaume I

The unassuming and wonderfully named Carrer del Paradís (Paradise Street), a narrow passage in the Barri Gòtic, takes you into a small medieval courtyard that is home to one of Barcelona's most surprising hidden gems—the remains of the Roman Temple of Augustus. At over 2,000 years old, the remains are around the same age as Barcelona itself.

1: La Seu Cathedral; 2: La Boqueria; 3: Temple d'August; 4: Palau de la Generalitat.

The four gigantic stone columns (made all the more colossal by now lying within this small courtyard, surrounded by buildings) are all that remain of the temple, built in the early 1st century BC as part of the forum in the Roman city of Barcino. The columns are nine meters (30 feet) high and would have once surrounded the entire building. The remains of the temple were discovered in the 19th century and today are part of the Barcelona City History Museum (MUHBA).

Plaça de Sant Jaume

Metro: Jaume I

The Plaça de Sant Jaume has been the political heart of Barcelona since the days when it was home to the Roman forum. Today, it is home to the Palau de la Generalitat (the headquarters of Catalonia's regional government) and the Ajuntament (City Hall) and is the scene of most big demonstrations, protests, and festivals. Locals pack into the square and *castells* (human towers) rise up from the crowds during local festivals.

Palau de la Generalitat

Plaça de Sant Jaume, 4; tel. 93/402-4600; www. presidencia.gencat.cat/ca/ambits_d_actuacio/ historia_generalitat_i_palau/visites; second and fourth weekends of every month; Metro: Jaume I

The headquarters of Catalonia's regional government, the Generalitat, was built between the 15th and mid-17th centuries as a permanent base for the Corts Catalanes, founded in 1283 and often cited as the first parliament in Europe. It is one of the few medieval buildings in Europe that has been home to the government since its inception. Its oldest part is the fifteenth-century exterior on Carrrer del Bisbe, designed by Marc Sefont.

Its long construction period resulted in a mixture of architectural styles, including Gothic, Renaissance, and baroque, behind a neoclassical façade. The much-photographed Bridge of Sighs, connecting the Palau de la Generalitat with the former canons' houses (now the residence of the President of the Generalitat) across the narrow Carrer del Bisbe, might look ancient, but was actually added in 1928.

Opportunities to visit the Palau de la Generalitat are limited to free visits on the second and fourth weekend of each month as well as to open-door days on Dia de Sant Jordi (Saint George's Day—April 23), the Diada Nacional de Catalunya (Catalonia's National Day—September 11), and la Mercè (Barcelona's annual city festival—September 24). Tours take place every hour and last for approximately one hour; online booking ahead of time is essential.

Ajuntament

Plaza Sant Jaume, 1; tel. 93/402-7000; Sundays 10am-1:30pm; Metro: Jaume I

The Ajuntament, also known as the Casa de la Ciudad, is the home of Barcelona's City Hall. The building is a hodgepodge of renovations and additions; the façade looking out onto the Plaça de Sant Jaume was built in the 19th century, while the façade around the corner on the Carrer de la Ciutat includes the building's original Gothic entrance.

There are free visits on Sundays (10am-1:30pm) and open-door days (April 12, April 23, May 30), during which visitors can see the grand marble interiors, including the Great Hall (Saló de Cent) deigned by Pere Llobet in the 14th century. Other highlights are the Saló de Cròniques, with murals by Josep Maria Sert from 1928, and the Gothic staircase off the lobby, which has sculptures by leading Catalan artists.

Plaça de Sant Felip Neri

Metro: Jaume I

This charming little square, which takes its name from the church of Sant Felip Neri, hides a few secrets. Located in the heart of the Barri Gòtic, its beauty belies its bloody and traumatic recent history. During the Spanish Civil

Plaça Reial

War, on January 30, 1938, a Nationalist bomb fell on the square, killing 42 people, many of them children from the square's School of Sant Felip Neri who had sought refuge in the air-raid shelter below the Sant Felip Neri Church (which gives the square its name). It was the second most deadly bombing raid on Barcelona during the war. Francoist authorities started a rumor that the bomb damage was actually caused by machine guns used by Republicans to murder the clergy during the war in an attempt to cover up the bombings. There is a plaque today in honor of the victims, and the pockmarked exterior of the church shows the effect of the bombing. The school is still running today; its pupils play on the square during recess.

Plaça Reial

Metro: Liceu

Just off Las Ramblas, Plaça Reial (Royal Square) is one of Barcelona's most beautiful plazas and a popular hang-out spot for young Barceloneses. Built on the site of the former Capuchin convent of Santa Madrona, the square was designed by architect Francesc Molina in the mid-19th century.

The porticoed square is filled with palm trees, fountains, and, on either side of the central fountain of the Three Graces, two street lamps designed by Antoni Gaudí in 1879, one of his first commissions.

The square was once known for prostitution and drugs, but these days is a popular tourist sight and nightlife spot, with bars and restaurants inside the porticos bringing out terraces in the warm weather.

The square hosts street parties during the La Mercè festival in September and on New Year's Eve.

Santa Maria del Pi

Plaça del Pi, 7; tel. 93/318-4743; www.basilicadelpi. com; €4; Metro: Liceu

Turn a corner from one of the narrow streets of the Barri Gòtic and you are met with this wonderful example of Gothic architecture, the Church of Saint Mary of the Pines. Its Catalan Gothic style includes a single nave and simple decoration, beautifully lit by stained-glass windows. Burned out in 1936 during the Spanish Civil War, the church was restored, complete with a replica of its rose window. At 10 meters (33 feet) wide, the window is one of the biggest in the world.

Guided tours—of the crypt, museum, garden, and bell tower, which has fantastic views over the city—take place on weekdays at midday and 1pm, and every day from July to September at midday, 1pm, 3pm, 4pm, and 5pm (€8.50). They last around 45 minutes and are available in English.

The charming square in front of the church, Plaça del Pi, holds an artisanal food market on the first and third Friday, Saturday, and Sunday of each month. It is so named because of a pine tree that was planted on the square in 1568. That tree was destroyed and later replaced, marking the beginning of the tradition to plant a new tree whenever the existing pine dies. The current tree was planted in 1985.

MUHBA El Call / Centre d'Interpretació del Call

3, Placeta de Manuel Ribé; tel. 93/256-2122; Wed 11am-2pm, Fri 11am-2pm, Sat-Sun 11am-7pm; €2.20; free for children under 16; Metro: Liceu

This small museum, in the heart of what was once the city's Jewish quarter of El Call, recounts the history of Barcelona's medieval Jewish community. The museum, which belongs to the Museum of the History of Barcelona (MUHBA), is set in the former home of a local veil maker. It shows pieces discovered during excavations of the area, including dishes, tombstones with Hebrew inscriptions, and a facsimile of the Sarajevo Haggadah, an illustrated manuscript depicting the Passover Haggadah, produced in Barcelona in the 14th century and thought to have been smuggled out after the expulsion of the Jews in 1492.

Sinagoga Major

Carrer de Marlet, 5; tel. 93/317-0790; www.

El Call—Barcelona's Jewish Quarter

Between the 11th and the 14th centuries, Barcelona was home to a thriving Jewish community centered around the areas of El Call Major and El Call Menor (a smaller Jewish development from the 13th century) in the Gothic quarter. (The word "call" means "little street" or "alley" in Catalan.) In 1079 there were 70 Jewish families, but by the 14th century the number had grown to well over 4,000 people. Most of the Jews in El Call were craftsmen (silk veil weavers, shoemakers, goldsmiths, and book binders).

In the early years, Jews and Christians got on relatively well and in the court of the kings Jews held important positions, such as tax collectors and ambassadors, and even caretakers of the kings' lions (many of which were presented as gifts from overseas).

Things started to sour in the 13th century. James I (Jaume I) forbid Jews from holding public office in 1215, and during the Black Death, rumors that Jews were poisoning the water began to circulate, resulting in violence and the deaths of several Jews. (Eventually, King Peter asked the Pope to make an official statement that the accusations against the Jews were lies.)

Anti-Jewish sentiment had spread throughout Spain by the 14th century and came to a head in Barcelona on August 5, 1391, when angry locals attacked El Call. Around 300 Jews were killed, and others fled or were baptized as Christians to escape persecution. Properties were torched, and it was essentially the end of what had been Barcelona's thriving Jewish quarter.

Today, the small Jewish quarter trail features signs in Spanish, Catalan, and English at points of interest around the area. The starting point is at **MUHBA El Call** (Placeta de Manuel Ribé, 3). El Call Major was bordered by Carrer de Sant Honorat in the east, Carrer de Sant Sever and Baixada de Santa Eulàlia in the north, Carrer d'Avinyó in the west, and Carrer de Call in the south. Carrer de Sant Domènec was the main street of the Call. El Call Menor was located between Carrer de la Boqueria, Carrer de Rauric, Carrer de la Lleona, and Carrer d'Avinyó across an area of five city blocks.

sinagogamayor.com; Mon-Fri 10:30am-6:30pm, Sun 10:30am-3pm; Metro: Liceu

The Main Synagogue is one of the few original Jewish buildings still standing in Barcelona. The building it is housed in was all set to be converted into a bar, until it was discovered in the 1990s that the unassuming space held the oldest of Barcelona's medieval synagogues.

It was the largest and most important of Barcelona's five synagogues, and it is said to be one of Europe's oldest—it served as a religious center from around the fourth century AD until the massacre of the Jews in 1391. The synagogue was the center of the community and the site of study, prayer, and special festivals like Rosh Hashanah and Hanukah.

While it does not have a regular congregation, the small room can be used for special occasions such as Bar Mitzvah. In 2003, a Canadian couple were the first people to be married in the synagogue in over 600 years.

Visitors can see the synagogue by guided tour by a member of Barcelona's Jewish community. The space is divided into two small rooms; the first includes architectural evidence dating back to Roman times and a section of the city's 13th-century walls. The second, the heart of the synagogue, is an intimate room with stone walls—two windows in the south-east wall face towards Jerusalem—and remnants of original Roman city walls.

Museu Frederic Marès

Plaça Sant Iu, 5; tel. 93/256-3500; Tues-Sat 10am-7pm, Sun 11am-8pm; €4.20; Metro: Jaume I

Catalan sculptor Frederic Marès (1893-1991) donated his private sculpture collection to the city of Barcelona in 1946. The collection spans the ancient world to the 19th century and is set in the grand surroundings of part of the old Royal Palace of the Counts of Barcelona, later the headquarters of the Spanish Inquisition in the city.

The basement, ground floor, and first floor of this five-floor museum are dedicated to Marès' vast collection of Medieval

Barri Gòtic Walking Tour

The Barri Gòtic, Barcelona's Gothic Quarter, was constructed during a heady period of commerce, exploration, and riches for the city that peaked during the 14th century. The streets of the Barri Gòtic are narrow and meandering, and suddenly open out onto grand buildings like the cathedral. The sunlight hits the stone at angles, lighting up a statue here or a street shrine there.

As you explore, be sure to look up, and you will notice that every street in the Barri Gòtic has a sign saying entrada (entrance) or salida (exit). The signs, which all feature a picture of a horse and cart, were designed to control the flow of transport through the narrow streets—carts were only allowed to go in one direction. Start your tour at **Liceu metro station.**

street shrine in the Barri Gòtic

- Head into the Barri Gòtic off Las Ramblas and north up Carrer del Cardenal Casañas, which takes you to Plaça del Pi, dominated by the huge **Church of Santa Maria del Pi.** Note the pine tree in the middle of the square—the first was planted in the 16th century and now it is tradition to replace the tree whenever it dies. This one was planted in 1985.

- Leave the square, heading north on Carrer de l'Ave Maria, and walk up the Baixada de Santa Eulàlia, dedicated to one of Barcelona's two patron saints (look out for the **shrine to Santa Eulàlia,** who was martyred by Romans at the age of 13 when she refused to renounce her Christianity). It is located where Baixada de Santa Eulàlia meets Carrer de Sant Sever, and is fixed high on the wall. It features a painting of the saint covered in a little roof, with space in front for flowers or offerings.

- To the right of Baixada de Santa Eulàlia is the former Jewish quarter, **El Call**; a small museum, MUHBA El Call, recounts the life of the Jewish community in Barcelona during its medieval peak, while the Sinagoga Mayor, newly discovered in the 1990s, was the area's largest synagogue.

- To the left of Baixada de Santa Eulàlia, Carrer de Sant Felip Neri takes you onto the beautiful and shady **Plaça de Sant Felip Neri,** which takes its name from the church on the square. Look out for the bombing damage on the side of the church; a bombing during the Spanish Civil War killed 48 people, many of them children, who had been sheltering under the church.

- Leave the square by its northeast exit, down the Carrerde Montjuïc del Bisbe, which takes you to the Carrer del Bisbe, running along the side of the cathedral. Turn left and you will emerge in front of the **cathedral,** one of the great Gothic buildings in Spain. 13 geese live permanently in its cloister, because 13 was the age of Santa Eulàlia—to whom the cathedral is dedicated—when she died.

- Head down the left-hand side of the cathedral, down Carrerde la Tapineria towards the Plaça del Rei, and on the way you can see remnants of Barcelona's Roman walls on Plaça de Ramon Berenguer el Gran. Around Plaça del Rei is the brilliant **Museum of the History of Barcelona,** where you can explore excavated Roman streets and buildings that were discovered under the city.

- From Plaça del Rei, head south down the Carrer de la Pietat, then turn left onto Carrer del Paradis. On the corner, at number 10, duck into an unassuming doorway and see one of the city's incredible hidden treasures, the four gargantuan columns that made up the **Temple of Augustus.** As old as the city itself, the 2000-year-old, nine-meter-high (30-foot) columns would have surrounded the whole building, which was constructed in the early 1st century BC.

sculpture, dominated by a number of poly-chrome wooden crucifixes from the 12th to the 15th century. The collection goes much further back in time with Roman busts. Some of Marès' own sculptures are displayed in the Library-Studio on the second floor.

Marès was an avid collector of just about everything, and the Collector's Cabinet, on the second and third floors of the museum, shows a range of everyday items the sculptor collected both in Spain and on his travels. The unlikely treasures, including over 300 intricately detailed ladies' fans from Spain, carved smoking pipes from Turkey and India, shell vases from the Catalan coast, and one of the city's most important collections of 19th-century photography, give interesting insight into daily life at the time.

Don't miss the building's lovely courtyard garden, which is dotted with *orange* trees. Its summer café, **Cafè d'estiu** (April-Oct; Tues-Sun 10am-10pm; www.cafedestiu.com), is a lovely oasis in the heart of the old town.

EL RAVAL
Museu d'Art Contemporani de Barcelona (MACBA)

Plaça dels Àngels, 1; tel. 93/481-3368; www.macba. cat; Mon 11am-7:30pm, Wed-Fri 11am-7:30pm, Sat 10am-8pm, Sun 10am-3pm; €10; Metro: Universitat

This huge, white, glass-fronted contemporary art museum, opened in 1995, is one of the buildings that has helped regenerate the area of El Raval, a neighborhood formerly known for its seedy street scenes. Designed by Pritzker-winning American architect Richard Meier, the minimalist space is bathed in natural light, while a walkway takes visitors up through the museum's four floors. Outside, the area in front of the museum reverberates with the sound of skateboarders doing tricks.

The museum hosts regular temporary exhibitions on the first and second floors as well as a continuously rotating number of works from its own permanent collection on the ground floor, which includes works from the 1950s to the present day by artists

such as Antoni Tàpies, Joan Miró, and Paul Klee.

The admission ticket is valid for one month and allows multiple entries to all current exhibitions. Guided one-hour tours in English take place on Mondays at 4pm (no advance booking, just ask at reception where the meeting point is). Times are subject to change, so it's worth checking the time of the tour by calling.

Admission is free on Saturdays from 4pm-8pm.

Centre de Cultura Comtemporània de Barcelona (CCCB)

Carrer de Montalegre, 5; tel. 93/306-4100; www. cccb.org; €6 entry to one exhibition, €8 entry to two exhibitions; Metro: Universitat

Just around the corner from MACBA, the Center of Contemporary Culture of Barcelona (CCCB) is a huge arts space housed inside a former workhouse. The refurbished space, with a gigantic exterior glass wall, is a cultural hub that holds regular exhibitions, debates, film screenings, and concerts. Recent exhibitions include "World Press Photo," "Black Light: Secret Traditions in Art Since the 1950s," and "Political Prisoners in Contemporary Spain." Check its website for upcoming events.

There is a bar and bookshop (Mon-Sun 10:30am-8pm) inside the center.

Palau Güell

Carrer Nou de La Rambla, 3-5; tel. 93/472-5775; www.palauguell.cat, Tues-Sun 10am-5:30pm; €12; Metro: Liceu

In a city packed with famous Gaudí treasures, this relatively unassuming—at least from the outside—mansion is one of the architect's hidden gems. Palau Güell was one of Gaudí's first commissions, built between 1886 and 1890. It was commissioned by the Barcelona industrialist Eusebi Güell (who later commissioned the architect to build Parc Güell) as an extension to his family home on Las Ramblas. Opened in 2012 after several years of renovations, it is well worth a visit to see the germ of ideas that would go on to decorate the likes of the Sagrada Familia and La Pedrera.

Despite being an early work, Palau Güell displays several of Gaudí's trademark styles, including Islamic and *Modernista* influences and a use of wrought iron and ceramic mosaics. The huge central hall is topped with a dome with holes to allow the light to pour in; it resembles a sky full of stars. The room's massive organ is played during the day, and the hall is often used for evening recitals. Don't miss the rooftop, with its chimneys decorated in broken ceramic mosaics that bring to mind Gaudí's later work on La Pedrera. An exhibition in the attic recounts the construction and restoration of the building.

Lines aren't nearly as long as those for Gaudí's more famous works; still, you can purchase tickets online ahead of time if you like. An audioguide, included in the ticket price, is a useful companion to the visit. It takes about an hour to tour this large family home.

Antic Hospital de Santa Creu

Carrer de l'Hospital, 56; Metro: Liceu

Antic Hospital de Santa Creu once served as Barcelona's main hospital—and you can only imagine the scenes it witnessed during its more than 500 years in use. It is famously the place where Antoni Gaudí died after being run over by a tram, just a month before the hospital closed in 1929.

The hospital is one of the oldest sights in El Raval. Construction began in 1401, with the aim of uniting six of the city's hospitals into one, up-to-date complex. The Hospital de Santa Creu was renowned as one of Europe's best hospitals during its medieval peak, but as the centuries wore on, its reputation significantly diminished until it was moved to a fancy new *Modernista* site—the Hospital de la Santa Creu de Sant Pau—in 1929.

Today, the building is home to several institutions, including the Biblioteca de Catalunya (Catalan Sate Library, Mon-Fri 9am-8pm, Sat 9am-2pm) on the first floor.

The vast, 70-meter-long library, with vaulted wooden ceilings and exposed brick walls, is where the hospital wards were once located. The Institut d'Estudis Catalans (Institude of Catalan Studies) is located in what was once the 17th-century Casa de Convalescència de Sant Pau. You can visit its internal patio, where there is a statue of Saint Paul. Look for the ceramics decorating the entrance (on the Carrer del Carme).

You can also see the central courtyard of the building and walk around the cloisters; its former chapel holds regular art exhibitions.

Filmoteca de Catalunya

Plaça de Salvador Seguí, 1-9; tel. 93/567-1070; www. filmoteca.cat; €4; Metro: Liceu

Since 2012, Catalonia's main film archive has been located in the heart of the Raval, just one of the additions that has helped to give the formerly run-down area a new lease on life. The huge concrete-and-glass building houses two cinemas, a bookshop, a film library, and regular film-related exhibitions. It runs themed seasons, from Turkish cinema to May 1968, and children's films at weekends; check its website to see the upcoming schedule. Films are €4 and are shown in their original versions with Catalan or Spanish subtitles. Wandering around an exhibition or buying your ticket for an indie film screening, you'll blend right in with the locals at the cinema, far off the tourist trail.

LA RIBERA AND EL BORN
★ Museu Picasso

Carrer Montcada, 15-23; tel. 93/256-3000; www. museupicasso.bcn.cat; Mon 10am-5pm, Tues-Wed 9am-8:30pm, Thurs 9am-9:30pm, Fri-Sun 9am-8:30pm; €12, €7 for people between 18-25 and over 65, free for university students and under 18s; Metro: Jaume I, Arc de Triomf

Dominating five large Gothic palaces on a narrow street in La Ribera, the Picasso Museum is a key reference for the early works and inspirations of one of Spain's most famous painters. Although born in Málaga, Picasso spent a lot of his adolescence and youth in Barcelona; you could say that it was in this city that he learned how to be an artist. The museum opened in 1963, the first dedicated to Picasso to be opened during the artist's lifetime. The museum is worth visiting for its setting alone; the five interconnected palaces have peaceful courtyards, stone staircases, and large galleries that make a wonderful backdrop to the artwork on display.

Don't expect to see too much of Picasso's later, Cubist work. Where this museum really shines is in tracing Picasso's early influences and documenting the beginning of his journey to world-wide acclaim. Across the 4,251 works in the permanent collection, we can trace the early genius of the child and teenage Picasso through his drawings and sketches, through his famous Blue Period and into Cubism.

VISITING THE PICASSO MUSEUM

The Picasso Museum is one of Barcelona's top museums, so expect lines; get there as early as possible to avoid the biggest crowds. Fortunately, you can book tickets, audio guides, and tours online ahead of time. Hour-long tours are available in English on Thursdays at 7pm, Wednesdays at 3pm, and Sundays at 11pm (€6 plus the price of the ticket). A good audio guide (€5) provides background and context to 51 key works, or for visitors in a rush, there is a short version that covers 12 works. Children's audio guides (€5) help little visitors explore using all their senses, making for an enjoyable introduction to Picasso. There are free hours on Thursdays, 6pm-9:30pm, and on the first Sunday of each month, 9am-8:30pm.

PICASSO MUSEUM HIGHLIGHTS

The museum is generally organized along chronological lines. Picasso's earliest work from his training in Barcelona is displayed in rooms 1-3, and the rooms progress in chronological order, including paintings from Paris (rooms 5-7) and the Blue Period (room 8),

and culminating in Picasso's versions of Las Meninas in rooms 12-15.

A highlight of Picasso's early work is **Science and Charity** (1897, room 3)—completed when the artist was just 15 years old. Its social realism is at stark contrast with Picasso's later Cubist works. His own father, José Ruiz Blasco, modeled as the doctor in the painting, while Picasso gave a woman he found on the street with her baby 10 pesetas to model as the sick mother and child.

Paintings produced in Paris around the turn of the 19th century nod to the styles of other painters of the day. **End of the Number** (1901—room 6), depicting a French singer waving at the end of a performance, brings to mind the work of Toulouse-Lautrec, who inspired Picasso during his time in Paris.

The artist said the sadness at the death of his friend Carles Casagemas in 1901 led him to paint in blue, kicking off what is known as his Blue Period. **Woman with Bonnet** (room 8) was painted during this time. It depicts an inmate at Saint-Lazare, a women's prison and venereal-disease hospital in Paris. It reflects Picasso's growing interest in the depiction of the downtrodden in society.

Picasso's later, Cubist style is best represented in the museum by the wonderful collection of his own interpretations of Las Meninas, the 1656 painting by Diego Velázquez that hangs in Madrid's Prado Museum. Picasso became obsessed with the painting in the late 1950s, dedicating himself to reproducing it dozens of times in his own style. His **Las Meninas Series** (rooms 12-14) shows his own take on the famous artwork.

Museu de Cultures del Món
(Museum of World Cultures)

Carrer de Montcada, 12-14; tel. 93/256-2300; www.museuculturesmon.bcn.cat; Tues-Sat 10am-7pm, Sun 10am-8pm; €5; Metro: Arc de Triomf

Just opposite the Picasso Museum, the Museum of World Cultures is a wide-ranging

---

1: Filmoteca de Catalunya; 2: Museu Picasso; 3: Basílica de Santa Maria del Mar.

collection of art and artefacts from outside Europe, housed in two former medieval palaces.

The museum is intriguing to wander around for two reasons: its magnificent palace-mansion setting (a much quieter setting in which to see the medieval mansions along Carrer de Montcada than visiting the nearby Picasso Museum), and its host of fascinating displays, including everything from West and Central African statues and masks to Buddhist and Hindu sculpture and Japanese and Afghan art. Highlights include Moai carved by the Rapa Nui of Easter Island and ancient cave sculptures from the Karawari River in Papua New Guinea. Entry is free on Sundays from 3pm-8pm.

Mercat de Santa Caterina
Av. de Francesc Cambó, 16; tel. 93/319-5740; www. mercatsantacaterina.com; Mon, Wed and Sat 7:30am-3:30pm, Tues, Thurs and Fri 7:30am-8:30pm; Metro: Jaume I

Immediately recognizable for its wavy, multicolored roof, the Santa Caterina market was built in 1845 and was given its colorful roof renovation in 2005. While its exterior looks modern, on the inside things remain very traditional, with greengrocers, fishmongers, and butchers' stalls dominating the space. During the Spanish Civil War, many people from the surrounding areas would come into Barcelona to shop at the market. Today, the charcuterie, olive, and cheese stalls are great places to pick up food for a picnic.

Museu de la Xocolata
Carrer del Comerç, 36; tel. 93/268-7878; www. museuxocolata.cat; Mon-Sat 10am-7pm, Sun 10am-3pm; €6; free for children under 7; Metro: Arc de Triomf

This small museum traces the history and production of chocolate, from its use as a spicy drink by the Mayans to its introduction to Europe by Spanish conquistadors. You will learn that Barcelona had a considerable part to play in bringing the now-beloved treat to Europe. (Suddenly, the city's proliferation of

chocolate shops will make a lot more sense.) A cool feature is that your ticket into the museum is a chocolate bar, which really should be the case in all museums.

It doesn't take long to walk around the one-floor exhibit; 30-45 minutes should do it. It's a good activity for children—there are chocolate sculptures and a shop and café at the end where you can indulge in a hot chocolate. Children's workshops and activities are available on the weekends; check the website for details.

Basílica de Santa Maria del Mar
Plaça de Santa Maria, 1; tel. 93/310-2390; www. santamariadelmarbarcelona.org; Metro: Jaume I

Rising like a giant wave from the narrow streets of La Ribera, the Church of Santa Maria del Mar (Saint Mary of the Sea) is one of Barcelona's finest religious buildings. With towering ceilings and widely spaced columns, its sheer scale is staggering, especially as you emerge from the narrow, winding alleys of the surrounding area.

During the 13th century, the area surrounding the present-day church was at the height of its mercantile and seafaring powers; local craftsmen, ship builders, and wealthy merchants demanded a grand, new church in their neighborhood. The church was designed by Berenguer de Montagut and built between 1329 and 1384—a fast construction at a time when churches of this scale typically took well over a century to build. Merchants donated money toward construction, and rock was hewn from Montjuïc mountain. (Look for the images of the porters of La Ribera, who helped carry the stones for construction, on the church's main doors.) The distance between the church's columns is the greatest of any medieval building in the world—13 meters (43 feet). This adds to the sense of its width and height, giving Santa Maria del Mar seemingly giant proportions in line with the giant ambition of its medieval creators.

Look for the stained-glass windows at the back of the church, which range in completion date from the 15th to the 20th centuries—the newest, completed in 1995, is next to the sacristy and was designed by José Fernández Castrillo to commemorate the 1992 Olympic Games. (On the left-hand side at the back of the church, see if you can spot the FC Barcelona shield in one of the stained-glass windows, added in the 1960s when the club donated money to help restore the windows that were damaged during the Spanish Civil War.) One of the church's most famous pieces is its Rose Window, which was destroyed by an earthquake in 1428 and remade afterwards. Its surprisingly bare interior is due to a fire in 1936 that destroyed many of its more decorative and artistic elements.

Two different tours in English are available daily at 1:15pm, 2pm, 3pm, and 5:15pm. The complete tour (€10, €8 for students and seniors) includes the church, the galleries, and the crypt, and takes around an hour. The 40-minute Towers and Rooftops tour (€8, €6.50 for students and seniors) grants visitors access to the church towers and rooftop (up a narrow spiral staircase), a great spot to gaze out over the city's Gothic rooftops and top sights, such as the Cathedral and the Sagrada Familia. Tours can be booked online or at the ticket office.

Ciutadella Park

Passeig de Picasso, 21; Metro: Ciutadella | Vila Olímpica
This famous park was originally the site of a great citadel, built by Philip V after he took Barcelona during the War of the Spanish Succession. (The citadel, which was intendended to prevent locals from rising up against the central powers in Madrid, was detested by locals and finally demolished in 1869.)

The 70-acre park as we know it today is a popular leisure spot and is a great place to stop if you have children in tow. It was constructed for the 1888 Universal Exhibition. Its new buildings showcased a contemporary style of architecture that would come to define the city in the decades to come—Catalan Modernisme. Architect Josep Fontsère

designed the park, and his young apprentice Antoni Gaudí assisted with the construction of the huge fountain, the Cascada, in front of the park's lake. Note that the water basin in front of the fountain features dragons, a common figure in the architect's later work.

Other examples of Catalan Modernisme include what was the 1888 Exhibition's restaurant and café, Castell dels Tres Dragons, an exposed brick building designed by Lluís Domènech i Montaner, with castle battlements and four towers in its corners. The building is now home to the Zoology Museum of Barcelona. The Arc de Triomf, built as the main access gate to the 1888 Universal Exhibition, crosses over the pedestrianised promenade on the Passeig de Lluís Companys, leading to the park.

Barcelona Zoo

Parc de la Ciutadella; www.zoobarcelona.cat; daily 10am-7pm; €19 adults and €12 children; Metro: Ciutadella | Vila Olímpica
Barcelona's zoo, set within the Ciutadella Park, was founded in 1892. It is a great family-friendly place and home to over 2,000 animals, including the endangered Sumatran tiger and Iberian wolf, as well as rhinoceros, elephants, giraffes, and penguins.

The "Land of Dragons," a newly renovated facility, is home to a Komodo dragon enclosure as well as other species from southeast Asia. Other areas include the gorilla area, the primate gallery, and the aquarama, home to the zoo's sea lions.

Children are well catered for, with a petting zoo, a train that snakes around the complex, and pony rides. The feeding of the penguins takes place 11am-1pm daily. You can also watch how the keepers care for and train the dolphins when the dolphin enclosure opens to the public, 11am-2pm and 3pm-6pm daily.

Palau de la Música Catalana (Palace of Catalan Music)

Calle Palau de la Música, 4; tel. 93/295-7200; www.palaumusica.cat; Metro: Urquinaona
Rising from a narrow street in the Ribera

neighborhood, the Palau de la Música Catalana (Palace of Catalan Music) is one of Barcelona's *Modernista* masterpieces. While most of Barcelona's most famous Modernista buildings are in the Eixample, this is one rare example in the city's old town, built between 1905 and 1908 by Lluís Domènech i Montaner for the Orfeó Català, a choral society founded in 1891.

The building, which was declared a UNESCO World Heritage Site in 1997, is designed around a central metal structure covered in glass, bathing the interior in natural light. The concert auditorium is a stunning space—its central skylight floods the space with light while a huge organ above the stage dominates the eyeline. It is marked with motifs of nature, including flowers, palms, and fruit.

Seeing a concert there is one of the best ways to experience the building, but if you can't get tickets, you can take a 55-minute tour of the building (€20, or €16 when booked online 21 days before your visit).

El Born Centre de Cultura i Memòria
(Born Center of Culture and Memory)
Plaça Comercial, 12; tel. 93/256-6851; www. elbornculturaimemoria.barcelona.cat; Tues-Sun 10am-8pm; €6; Metro: Jaume I

In the early 2000s, builders renovating the Born Market were surprised to unearth well-preserved streets and houses under the market that dated back to the 1700s, complete with homes and shops. They had been destroyed to make way for the city's hated citadel, built by Philip V to help control locals following the War of the Spanish Succession.

The light-drenched interior of the former market, a glass and iron structure built in 1876, now houses the archaeological remains found onsite. There is also an exhibition space with period items that explains the destruction of the area, as well as temporary exhibitions and activities.

There are daily one-hour guided tours in English (€6.60 per person) at 4:30pm; tours

can be booked by calling 93/256-6850 on weekdays or by emailing reserveselbornccm@bcn.cat.

THE WATERFRONT
Teleferico del Puerto
Access points at Av. Miramar (highest point) and Passeig de Joan de Borbó, 88 (lowest point, in port); €11 one way, €16.50 round trip; Metro: Barceloneta

This cable car, which dates back to 1931, takes passengers from the port up to the top of Montjuïc hill, a 1,300-meter (4,265-foot) journey with stunning views over Barcelona. With no seating, passengers (a maximum of 19) stand cramped together; it's not the most comfortable ride, but it is short (around 10 minutes), and kids will love it.

The line passes through the Tower of Jaime I, which during the Spanish Civil War was used as a lookout and a gun station; it was a strategic position of defense for the Port of Barcelona.

Museu del Disseny
(Museum of Design)
Plaça de les Glòries Catalanes, 37; tel. 93/256-6800; www.ajuntament.barcelona.cat/museudeldisseny; Tues-Sun 10am-8pm; €8; Metro: Glòries

Nicknamed "the stapler" (la grapadora) by locals for its hard-edged, chunky shape, Barcelona's Museum of Design is a gray, concrete building whose sharp lines contrast with the smooth curves of the Torre Glòries skyscraper just behind (formerly the Torre Agbar).

The museum, which opened in 2014, brings together collections from other museums (including the Museum of Decorative Arts and the Museum of Textiles) to provide visitors with a snapshot of design in its many different guises. The first floor is home to (mainly Catalan) product design from the 20th and 21st centuries—from the BFK Butterfly chair, designed in 1938, to the latest innovations in eco-design and

---

1: Palau de la Música Catalana; 2: Museu del Disseny.

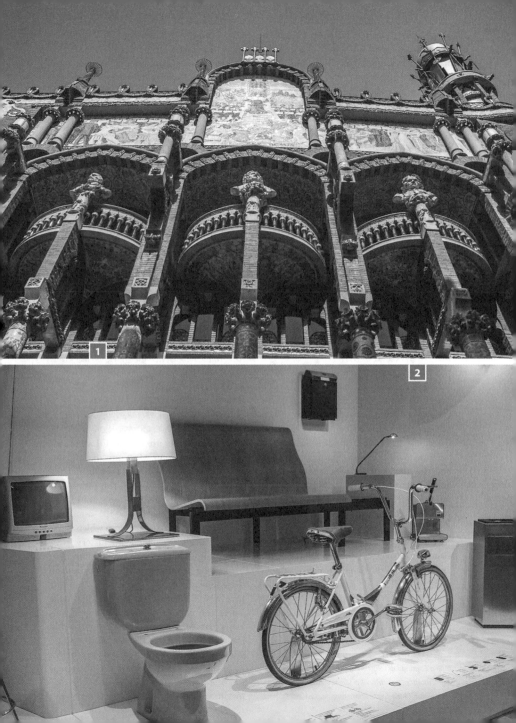

3D printing. The second floor houses the museum's eclectic collection of decorative arts, which includes everything from 16th-century clocks to gigantic 18th-century carriages. The third floor provides an interesting overview of fashion from the 17th century to the present day, from the tiniest corsets to 20th-century dresses by Spanish greats like Cristóbal Balenciaga, whose 1932 little black dress seemed to bring fashion into the modern age. On the fourth floor, you will find the museum's collection of graphic arts.

While the information cards could be more detailed, the museum is an interesting visit for those fascinated by design; another plus is that it is rarely busy, allowing visitors to browse at their own pace. There are temporary exhibitions as well as a café. The museum missed an opportunity by not having a design-themed gift shop, but some products, like tote bags and badges, are available to buy at the reception desk.

Mirador de Colom

Plaça Portal de la pau; daily 8:30am-7:30pm; €6; Metro: Drassanes

Marking the end of Las Ramblas and the beginning of the seafront area of La Barceloneta, the Columbus monument rises tall over Barcelona, the explorer standing on his plinth pointing towards the sea. The monument was built for the 1888 Universal Exhibition to honor Columbus, who sailed into Barcelona in 1483 to tell the Catholic monarchs Isabel and Fernando (Isabella and Ferdinand) of his discovery of America.

A lift hidden inside the monument takes visitors up 60 meters (197 feet) for panoramic views over the city, from the Collserola mountains to the Port Vella, with its Maritime Museum, yachts, and industrial port, while the base of the monument features reliefs depicting the explorer's life and travels.

L'Aquàrium

Moll d'Espanya del Port Vell; tel. 93/221-7474; www. aquariumbcn.com; Mon-Fri 10am-7:30pm, Sat-Sun 10am-8pm (June-Sept, 9pm, July-August, 9:30pm);
€20, children aged 5-10 €15, children aged 3-4 €7; Metro: Barceloneta

One of the most comprehensive aquariums in Europe, L'Aquàrium Barcelona, in the Port Vell, is home to over 11,000 animals and makes for a fun day out for kids. It recreates all the underwater environments found on earth (including coral reefs), but specializes in Mediterranean ecosystems. An 80-meter (262-foot) tunnel takes visitors underneath the gargantuan Oceanarium, home to sharks that swim around you as you walk through the depths.

The *¡Explora!* (Explore!) area is a must-see for children. It houses over 50 interactive games that teach little ones all about the marine world.

Check the aquarium's website for regular activities, including feeding time (penguins are fed at 11:30am daily, other animals vary), diving with sharks (with or without a cage, from €150), and weekend family activities that include sleeping in the shark tunnel—an unforgettable experience for shark-loving kids.

Museu Marítim
(Maritime Museum)

Av. de les Drassanes; tel. 93/342-9920; www.mmb. cat; Mon-Sun 10am-8pm; €10; Metro: Drassanes

There could be no better location for Barcelona's Maritime Museum than the former Royal Shipyards (Drassanes Reials), the center of shipbuilding from the 13th to the 18th century. The huge Gothic buildings, which could hold 30 galleys at the same time, are an atmospheric backdrop in which to explore Catalonia's rich seafaring history.

Highlights include a replica of the 60-meter-long Royal galley, which was built in these shipyards before a battle in 1571. At the time of building, it was the largest galley in the world. It is painted in the red and gold (yellow) colors of Spain, and the rear of the ship is elaborately decorated with paintings and sculptures, many of them religious in theme.

In the courtyard, visitors can see a replica of Ictíneo I, one of the world's first submarines, created by Catalan inventor Narcís

Monturiol in 1859. Monturiol was originally inspired to make the four-meter (13-foot) olive wood construction—a ship that could sail under the water—in order to help coral harvesters work safely. The submarine could dive to a depth of 20 meters (66 feet) and moved using hand-cranked propellers, which meant its speeds were slow.

The ticket price also gets visitors onto the schooner Santa Eulàlia, a 46-meter (151-foot) vessel dating from 1918 that is moored in Barcelona's harbor just opposite the museum. The restoration project, which began in 1997 and was the first of its kind in Spain, refurbished the ship to its original state, and represented an important stage in the city's rediscovery of its important seafaring history. Admission is free on Sundays after 3pm.

Museu d'Història de Catalunya
(Museum of Catalonian History)

Palau de Mar, Plaça de Pau Vila, 3; tel. 93/225-4700; www.mhcat.cat; Tues, Thurs-Sat 10am-7pm, Wed 10am-8pm, Sun 10am-2:30pm; €4.50 for permanent exhibition, €6.50 for permanent and temporary exhibitions combined; Metro: Barceloneta

This comprehensive history of Catalonia is housed in one of the warehouses of Barcelona's Port Vell (Old Port), which have been renovated into a cool shopping, culture, and dining area.

The four-floor space is divided into eight areas representing different historical periods, arranged in chronological order. The historical journey begins with the Greeks founding Empúries, and covers the Romans, Catalonia's Golden Age, the Industrial Revolution, the Civil War, and the 20th century, right up to the present day. Period artefacts—from Roman vases and looms of the Industrial Revolution to modern-day election posters—bring the fascinating history of the region to life, providing essential background on what makes Catalans different and why many feel separate from Spain. Kids especially love the interactive areas of the museum, such as the chance to ride a king's horse. Some information panels are in Spanish and Catalan only.

La Fàbrica del Sol

Pg. Salvat Papasseit, 1; Tues-Sat 10am-2pm, Tues-Fri 4:30pm-8pm; www.ajuntament.barcelona. cat/lafabricadelsol/en; free admission; Metro: Barceloneta

This yellow and red-brick Modernista building was once home to the old gasworks administrative building. Today, it is a reference for sustainable energy, set up by the city council with the aim of publicizing environmental sustainability. For architecture fans, a walk past to see the exterior, with Modernista details such as exposed brick, is worthwhile.

Strolling around the building, you can also see various examples of sustainability, including an interior vertical garden, geothermal heat pump, and solar panels on the roof. Information panels are in Catalan and Spanish only, but there is an introductory film in English, and English notes are available at reception. Don't miss the rooftop, featuring solar panels, a garden, and views over the gasworks' original water tower.

Museu Blau
(Blue Museum)

Plaza Leonardo da Vinci, 4-6; tel. 93/256-6002; www.museuciencies.cat; Oct-Feb, Tues-Fri 10am-6pm, Sat 10am-7pm, Sun 10am-8pm; Mar-Sept, Tues-Sat 10am-7pm, Sun 10am-8pm; €6; Metro: El Maresme | Fòrum

Dedicated to the natural world, the Museu Blau (Blue Museum) is the shiny showpiece of the city's Museum of Natural Sciences. It opened in 2011 in the Forum Building, a distinctive triangular wedge of a building that has more than 9,000 square meters (29,527 square feet) of exhibition space.

The permanent exhibition, "Planet Life," traces the origins of planet Earth using interactive exhibits and specimens across three areas: Biography of the Earth, Earth Today, and Islands of Science. Small children will love the Science Nest, an area dedicated to teaching little ones all about science, while bigger kids will like the interactive screens, videos, and dinosaur skeletons.

The museum has a gift shop and small café.

Timed tickets can be booked online in advance. The museum is not too large and can be explored in around an hour. Situated right on the seafront, it's a good location from which to walk along the promenade afterwards.

EIXAMPLE

Eixample is home to a cluster of *Modernista* architecture. Casa Batlló by Gaudí, Casa Lleó Morera by Domènech i Montaner, Casa Amantller by Josep Puig i Cadafalch, and Casa Mulleras by Enric Sagnier are all located on one block, which is known as the "mansana de la discòrdia" or the **block of discord**, named because of its unusual buildings of wildly different designs, shapes, and themes, all built around the same time by some of the most famous proponents of Catalan *Modernisme*.

TOP EXPERIENCE

★ Sagrada Familia

Carrer de Mallorca, 401; tel. 93/208-0414; www. sagradafamilia.org; Nov-Feb, daily 9am-6pm; Mar, 9am-7pm; Apr-Sept, 9am-8pm; Oct, 9am-7pm; basic ticket €15, audioguided visit €22, guided experience €24, top views €29; Metro: Sagrada Familia

Barcelona's most famous monument is the Basilica and Expiatory Church of the Holy Family, aka the Sagrada Família. The construction of Antoni Gaudí's ambitious design was begun in 1882 and is projected to be completed in 2026, the centenary of Gaudí's death. The longest-running architectural project on earth is a firm fixture of the Barcelona skyline, its soaring spires and yellow cranes a sign of the work still to be done on this famously unfinished church. When he was asked, as he often was, when the church would be finished, Gaudí would reply, "Don't worry, my client is in no hurry. God has all the time in the world."

Gaudí designed the church to be the tallest building in Barcelona, its spires rising so high that they would unite heaven and earth. He aimed to depict the history of Catholicism in the façade of the church, a mammoth task that the architect always knew would take more than one lifetime to complete. The design of Gaudí's masterpiece came to obsess and dominate his later life, to such an extent that he would often sleep in his on-site workshop.

At least an hour is recommended to really appreciate the building. Getting there early is a good idea to beat the biggest crowds.

TICKET OPTIONS

All tickets can be purchased online ahead of time; it's worth it since they can sell out. The audioguide costs €7 extra, but lets visitors explore at their own pace with the help of an audioguided tour that lasts approximately 45 minutes. You can also book a guided experience in English (€24, 50 minutes), with a qualified guide who will take you around as part of a group tour, letting you in on secrets and hidden details in Gaudí's work.

Attending **mass** (Sundays, 9am) is a special experience that allows visitors to experience the church in the way it was intended to be used. There is an international mass open to members of the public in several different languages. There is no charge, but space is limited. Doors open at the Nativity façade (Carrer de la Marina) 8:30am-9am.

HISTORY

The Sagrada Familia was commissioned by bookseller Josep Maria Bocabella, founder of the religious society the Spiritual Association of Devotees of St. Joseph, as a church that would atone for the sins of all the inhabitants of Barcelona.

Architect Franscico de Paula del Villar began work on the project, which he envisioned as a standard Gothic-style church, in 1882. It was when Gaudí took over the project in 1883, after the original architect resigned, that it transformed from a straightforward, classical design into something radically different. Gaudí's new design was for a cathedral-sized church that would sport 18 spires, representing the twelve apostles as well as the Virgin Mary, four Evangelists, and—the pinnacle and largest spire—Jesus Christ himself.

He left detailed models of how the church

should be completed. These were destroyed during the Spanish Civil War, leaving subsequent architects scratching their heads at how to tackle the ambitious scale and detail with no plans. They painstakingly pieced together some of Gaudí's destroyed models and plans; more recently, they have employed the most up-to-date aeronautical engineering software to help them figure out the complex design, which at the time was unlike anything ever conceived.

Pope Benedict consecrated the Sagrada Familia as a basilica in 2010; it was the first mass to take place there in its 128-year history.

While the Sagrada Familia attracts millions of visitors every year and is one of Spain's biggest tourist attractions, it has not been without its critics. George Orwell called it "one of the most hideous buildings in the world." Whether or not today's work reflects Gaudí's vision, and whether the great architect would like what he saw if he were to return to 21st-century Barcelona, is up for debate. Some critics say the church can never truly resemble Gaudí's ideal, whereas others applaud the architects and engineers who have overcome huge obstacles to follow the original design as faithfully as possible.

NATIVITY FAÇADE

The only facade to be completed during Gaudí's lifetime, the Nativity façade—facing eastwards at the front of the cathedral onto Carrer de la Marina—was designed between 1894 and 1930. It is split into three porticos representing Hope, Faith, and Charity. On the Charity portico is the manger, surrounded by the shepherds, the three wise men, and angels. Gaudí used plaster casts of locals to create many of the figures, even casting chickens and stillborn babies in his quest for a lifelike depiction.

It represents the birth of Jesus and is highly decorative, with motifs from nature visible throughout; notice the tortoises and turtles—to represent the land and the sea—at the base of the columns separating the porticos.

INSIDE THE CHURCH

As you step inside, you are immediately struck by the tree-like columns, which bring to mind a forest of stone. The design was intentional; Gaudí felt that it was in a forest that man felt closest to God. Gaudí chose red porphyry stone from Iran for the columns that bear the heaviest load, because it is one of the strongest stones in the world.

The stained-glass windows, in shades of amber and red and green and blue, are more than two stories high. They filter in more light at the top and are darker at the bottom, with illustrations and texts. This helps draw the eye upward toward the heavens and toward the architectural details high up in the church, illuminated by the colored light. The streaming light, filtered by the stained glass, lends the white walls a bejeweled look.

Light also plays off the organ's pipes. Installed in 2010, the organ will eventually be one of several positioned at different points around the church—a solution to the challenge of the church's acoustics. They will be playable separately, or all together from one keyboard.

PASSION FAÇADE AND GLORY FAÇADE

The simple design of the Passion Façade—on the western side facing Carrer de Sardenya, opposite where you entered—is in stark contrast to the busy, intricate detail of the Nativity Façade. It is designed in harsh lines that bring to mind the bones of a skeleton, and depicts the suffering and crucifixion of Jesus. Gaudí wanted this facade to strike fear into the onlooker (which is why he began with the more accessible Nativity Facade).

In 2002, construction began on the Glory Façade, on the south side of the building, which will be the church's largest and will show man's ascension to God. It will also depict purgatory, hell, the seven deadly sins, and the seven heavenly virtues.

TOWERS

Of the 18 planned towers, four have been built over the Nativity facade and four over the Passion facade, representing eight of the apostles. The central spire, representing Jesus, will be topped with a gigantic cross—its height (170 meters or 558 feet) will be one meter lower than Montjuïc hill, as expressly designed by Gaudí, who believed man's creations should never surpass those of God. The completed spires will make the Sagrada Familia the tallest church in the world.

A tower-visit ticket (€29) includes a visit up one of the 65-meter (213-foot) towers, either the Nativity Façade or the Passion Façade. At the top of the towers, visitors can appreciate Gaudí's use of mosaics, color, and quirky detailing. You can ascend the towers via a lift, but you do have to descend the quite claustrophobic staircase; people with mobility, cardiac, or pulmonary issues should not climb the towers.

TOP EXPERIENCE

★ La Pedrera (Casa Milà)

Passeig de Gràcia, 92; tel. 93/214-2584; www. lapedrera.com; daily 9am-8:30pm; €25; Metro: Diagonal

What would be Gaudí's last private home design was commissioned by local lawyer Pere Milà and his wife Roser Segimon, a widow of a wealthy businessman, who put much of her money into the project. At the time, Casa Milà, with its curved stone façade, wrought-iron balconies and doors, and artisanal creative touches in murals, doorknobs, and furniture, was unlike anything seen before. Today it is one of Antoni Gaudí's most famous works, but it angered locals when it was built (between 1906 and 1912) for not adhering to traditional style. The project, whose official name is Casa Milà, was scornfully nicknamed *La Pedrera* ("the Quarry") by angry locals, for its similarity to a big pile of stone.

As well as the *Modernista* design, the building's other innovations included an underground garage (one of the first of its kind

in the world) for Pere Milà, who was one of the city's first car owners. As was common in those days, the Milà family would live in a spacious first-floor apartment and rent out the upper floors. Roser Segimon lived in the first-floor apartment until her death in 1964; during subsequent years, more apartments were made out of the buildings' rooms, and it even housed a bingo hall.

The building originally was going to be much more overtly religious—the Catholic Gaudí had planned statues of the Virgin Mary and excerpts from the Rosary—but after the Tragic Week (July 25-August 2, 1909), during which anarchists attacked convents and other religious buildings, Milà decided against the religious additions.

In 1984, UNESCO declared La Pedrera a World Heritage Site, and the building underwent significant renovations during the same decade.

VISITING LA PEDRERA

The visit does not take in the whole building, so it can be done in around an hour—arriving early is a good idea to beat the biggest crowds. Book tickets online to avoid the (sometimes very long) lines. The self-guided tour takes in the rooftop, attic space, and fourth-floor apartment. An audio guide, included in the price, gives visitors context and information about Gaudí's architectural style.

Arrive early and take the elevator straight to the building's crowning glory: its magnificent rooftop. Like a set from a surreal theater production, the rooftop is populated with gigantic chimney pots that look like guards watching over the building. The views from here across Barcelona are spectacular.

The attic, once home to the building's laundry area, is now home to the Espai Gaudí, with displays on the history and architecture not just of La Pedrera, but also of the entirety of Gaudí's work.

On the fourth floor, visitors can tour the Pedrera Apartment, decorated as it would

1: Sagrada Familia; 2: Casa Batlló; 3: La Pedrera.

have been in the early 20th century. Note the apartments' irregular layout and design to provide each a view from the main façade. Also note the ceilings—some wavy, some bearing inscriptions—intended to mirror the wavy exterior.

Ironically, Roser Segimon was never keen on the over-the-top furnishings and design of her apartment, and when Gaudí died in 1926, she had it completely redecorated in a more understated style.

At the bottom of the building, don't miss the Passeig de Gràcia and Career de Provença courtyards and exhibition rooms, located on the main floor where the Milà family used to live.

A new experience for 2018 is the "Gaudí's Pedrera: The Origins" tour, a nighttime tour during which visitors are led around the building in small groups by a guide; you'll watch a light show and projections, and finish off with a glass of cava in the building's courtyard. Tours take place daily, 9pm-11pm (€34 per person).

Casa Batlló

Passeig de Gràcia, 43; www.casabatllo.es; daily 9am-9pm; from €24.50; Metro: Passeig de Gràcia

Built as an apartment block in 1877 by Emilio Sala Cortés (one of Gaudí's architecture professors), this building was bought in 1903 by Josep Batlló y Casanovas, a textile magnate and prominent Barcelona businessman, who employed Antoni Gaudí to fully renovate the house. Batlló had originally planned to completely demolish the building and start again, but Gaudí persuaded him to keep the structure and let the architect loose creatively, to completely recreate its design. It was fully reformed between 1904 and 1906.

Gaudí changed the exterior and the internal layout of the building, adding characteristic touches such as his broken mosaics, ceramics, and curved designs (there are no straight lines in nature so there should be none in the building, he said).

Locals christened the building the *casa del drac* ("house of the dragon") and the *casa dels ossos* ("house of bones"); the roof's metallic-looking tiles could be a dragon's scaly skin, and the entire roof could be a dragon spread out, taking a nap. Also note the sword-like cross on the roof, leading many to deduce that the roof is a homage to Saint George (the patron saint of Catalonia) and the dragon. Its balconies, which seem edged in bones, gave the building its second, rather macabre nickname.

In 1995, the house was opened to the public; today it welcomes more than one million visitors every year. If you want to just view the façade, go early in the morning to see the first beams of daylight illuminate the building, its tiles almost coming to life as it is bathed in sunlight.

TICKET OPTIONS

Several ticket options, including the Casa Batlló + FastPass (€29.50 online, €33.50 from ticket office), allow visitors to skip the line. You can purchase a regular Casa Battló ticket (€24.50 online, €28.50 from ticket office; children under seven go free). It is worth buying tickets via the official Casa Battló website for a discount.

All ticket options include the SmartGuide, an augmented-reality mobile device, available in 11 languages, that gives guests an immersive experience of the building. The guide transports users back to the original building, showing what it would have looked like when Gaudí had finished his revolutionary design, as well as bringing key elements to life (see a fish swim straight off the wall, for example).

A new ticket for 2018 is the **Magic Nights ticket** (€39), which includes a nighttime visit, live music, and two drinks, allowing guests to enjoy the space in a more relaxed atmosphere. Visits are available daily and start at 8pm.

VISITING CASA BATLLÓ

You can get around the house in under an hour (the smart guide lasts 45 minutes). The visit starts on the main floor, home to the salon that looks out onto the Passeig de Gràcia; note the swirling ceilings and rounded wooden door and window frames (there are no straight lines in this building, giving it a fairytale fantasy feel that could have come straight out of Hansel and Gretel). Take the stairs up to the attic to admire the interior patio, completely tiled in dark and light blue. Up in the attic, where the laundries were once located, the sparse white color contrasts with the vivid shades below. The sharply curved ceiling makes you think that this is what standing inside a whale might feel like. Green, blue, and pink ceramics give it a snakeskin sheen.

Casa Amatller

Passeig de Gràcia, 41; tel. 93/216-0175; www.amatller. org; daily 11am-6pm; €24; Metro: Passeig de Gràcia

Like Casa Batlló and Casa Lleó Morera, Casa Amatller was a refurbishment of an existing residential building. Around that time (1898-1900), prominent architects were refurbishing homes to compete for the urban awards convened by Barcelona City Council. Casa Amatller was the first of the three to be refurbished.

The original building was constructed by Antoni Robert in 1875, and in 1898, chocolatier Antoni Amatller's family commissioned Catalan architect Josep Puig i Cadafalch to refurbish the building as a family home. Josep Puig i Cadafalch worked with some of the city's finest artisans and craftsmen to transform a regular building into a wonderful flight of fancy, with a façade featuring knights, dragons, and other creatures. The architect used Germanic elements in his redesign, completely rebuilding the façade, and added technological advances such as an electric elevator and a rotating platform for Amatller's car.

In the entrance foyer, note the huge stained-glass entry doors by the staircase; upstairs in the first-floor museum, note the period *Modernista* furniture. Made of wood and often elaborately carved, these tables, chairs, and cabinets often furnished the buildings of the great *Modernista* architects.

You can visit the first floor, now a museum

with period furniture and decor, by guided tour (€24 tickets can be booked on the official website) or with a 40-minute visit using a video guide (€19).

Casa Lleó Morera

Passeig de Gràcia, 35; www.casalleomorera.com; Metro: Passeig de Gràcia

Casa Lleó Morera is perhaps the least wacky of the buildings that make up the Illa de la discòrdia. Today, it functions as part of a Loewe store and cannot be visited as a museum.

Casa Lleó Morera was commissioned by Francesca Morera and designed by Lluís Domènech i Montaner in 1902. The building was named after her son. The corner building was the only one on the famous block to be awarded the Barcelona Council's Annual Artistic Building Prize, in 1906. Its gray exterior is marked by curved balconies decorated with carvings of animals and plants, most notably the mulberry—Morera means mulberry in Spanish.

The project was a real team effort and combined master craftsmen from different disciplines, including sculpture, stained glass, woodcarving, and mosaics. Sadly, much of the ground floor—including a pair of female statues by the sculptor Eusebi Arnau—were destroyed during the redesign for the Loewe shop during the 1940s. A caretaker is said to have salvaged the female heads, which had been left on the sidewalk, and later to have sold them to Salvador Dalí, who displayed them at the Theatre-Museu Dalí in Figueres.

Museu del Modernisme de Barcelona
(Museum of Barcelona Modernism)

Carrer de Balmes, 48; tel. 93/272-2896; www.mmbcn. cat; Mon-Fri 10:30am-2pm, 4pm-7pm; €10; children between six and 16 €5, students and over 65s €7; Metro: Passeig de Gràcia

Though Modernisme found its most famous expression in the architecture of Barcelona, the movement was far more wide-reaching, encompassing furniture, sculpture, and art, all of which are on display at the Modernisme

Antoni Gaudí

Antoni Gaudí i Cornet was one of the most creative and imaginative architects of his era, changing the language of architecture with his ambitious projects, including Barcelona's most famous sight: **La Sagrada Familia.**

EARLY LIFE

Antoni Gaudí i Cornet was born on June 25, 1852 in Reus, Catalonia. The son of a coppersmith, the young Gaudí loved mathematics and nature but was a sickly child.

In 1870, he moved to Barcelona to study architecture; he was a mediocre student who only occasionally displayed flashes of the genius to come. When he graduated from the School of Architecture in 1878, the school's director, Elies Rogent, said, "I do not know if we have awarded this degree to a madman or to a genius; only time will tell."

mosaic details at Gaudí's Park Güell

EARLY WORK

One of Gaudí's first jobs was designing two lamp posts for Barcelona's Plaça Reial. In 1883, he was commissioned to create his first residential building, a summer house named Casa Vicens in Gràcia.

The house, which can be visited today, shows several motifs that the architect would use again and again, such as intricate wrought-iron work, a focus on curves and nature, and a new technique called trencadís, which used broken ceramic pieces to make colorful mosaics.

Gaudí's works would be heavily influenced by his passion for nature and his devout Roman Catholic religion (he was nicknamed "God's architect").

PERSONAL LIFE

Gaudí, who in his youth had been finely dressed and sociable, regularly attending the theater and literary gatherings, increasingly withdrew from public life as he got older. He never married; it is said he had one great love—a teacher, Josefa Moreu—but his love was not reciprocated. So Gaudí dedicated himself to his faith and his work.

A celibate vegetarian, Gaudí was an unusual man for the times, with an unusual vision for his architecture.

LATER LIFE

Gaudí was 31 when he started work on the Sagrada Familia. His grandest project, which he knew would never be finished in his lifetime, consumed him to such an extent that he would often sleep in his workshop. He wore threadbare clothes and took little care of his appearance.

When he was walking to mass on June 7, 1926, he was struck by a tram. He was so unkempt that the tram driver and several passersby refused to help him, assuming he was a tramp. He was eventually put in a taxi and taken to Santa Creu Hospital, where he died on June 10, aged 73. Two days later, a huge crowd packed the crypt of his beloved Sagrada Familia, where the great architect was laid to rest.

Museum of Barcelona. This two-floor museum is compact and rarely busy, allowing visitors to browse its items and artworks at their leisure. It is worth a visit if you want more context for Modernisme; here you can explore how it manifested across many other artworks in addition to its famous architectural examples.

The ground floor focuses on furniture, with a section of pieces by Antoni Gaudí, including desks, mirrors, and chairs, all featuring the architect's signature whimsical nature motif. Many of the pieces are from buildings that the architect designed himself, including Casa Batlló and Casa Milà (La Pedrera).

Downstairs, the focus is on paintings, featuring works by the likes of Ramon Casas, Gaspar Camps, and Arcadi Mas i Fondevila. The artwork is one of the most interesting parts of the museum, perhaps in part because Modernisme, so famed for its architecture and furniture, is lesser known for its artistic output. Some paintings feature common Modernista themes of nature and religion, while others seem to channel the Art Nouveau style of painters like Toulouse Lautrec.

The gift shop features Catalan produce, including chocolates and cava.

Museu Egipci de Barcelona

Carrer de València, 284; tel. 93/488-0188; www. museuegipci.com; Jan 7-June 21 and Sept 12-Nov 30, Mon-Fri 10am-2pm, 4pm-8pm, Sat 10am-8pm, Sun 10am-2pm; Dec 1-Jan 5, Mon-Sat 10am-8pm, Sun 10am-2pm; June 22-Sept 11, Mon-Sat 10am-8pm, Sun 10am-2pm; €12; students and those over 65 €8.50; Metro: Diagonal

This private collection of Egyptian artefacts by hotelier Jordi Clos includes over 1,000 pieces displayed across three floors. The museum is divided into different themes (the Pharaoh, jewelry, cosmetics, and funerary beliefs and practices) that give visitors a sense of the daily lives of Egyptians and the make-up of Egyptian society.

The collection includes a leather bed (2920-2649 BC), a granite statue of the pharaoh Rameses III (1194-1163 BC), and beautifully intricate collars that were popular jewelery items. An incredible inscribed gold ring (664-525BC) is one of only a handful of similar surviving pieces in the world.

There is a charming rooftop terrace café and a gift shop.

Fundació Antoni Tàpies

Carrer d'Aragó, 255; tel. 93/487-0315; www. fundaciotapies.org; Tues-Thurs and Sat 10am-7pm, Fri 10am-9pm, Sun 10am-3pm; €7, students and over 65s €5.60; Metro: Passeig de Gràcia

This cultural center and museum is both an impressive Modernista building and the home of the works by 20th-century Catalan artist Antoni Tàpies. Tàpies created the foundation in 1984 to promote contemporary art. It opened its doors in 1990, and today holds the largest collection of the artist's work, which is shown on a rotating basis alongside temporary exhibitions. It's worth seeking out for its exterior, or to visit inside—30-45 minutes is ample time to wander through the exhibitions.

The building was designed 1880-1882 by Catalan Modernist architect Lluís Domènech i Montaner (who also designed the Palau de la Música Catalana and the Hospital de Sant Pau, as well as the nearby Casa Lleó Morera) for the publishing house Editorial Montaner i Simon, and was one of the earliest examples of the new Modernista style that would sweep through the city in the coming years. The building mixes exposed red brick and the wrought iron that typified many Modernista buildings with the work of Tapiés himself, and is crowned with his huge sculpture *Núvol i cadira* (Cloud and Chair, 1990). The sculpture represents a chair (a recurring motif in the artist's work) jutting out of a cloud, and it makes a surreal cherry-on-top of the building. Another key feature of the building is its Islamic influence, both inside and out, as seen in the exposed brickwork and geometrical design.

Tàpies' work is wide-ranging across styles and genres. He was inspired by Miró and flirted with surrealism, but found his niche in an abstract style known as pintura matèrica,

Catalan Modernism

Catalan Modernism (also known as Modernisme) was an architectural, artistic, and literary movement towards the end of the 19th century that sought to find a cultural expression of Catalan identity. Part of a general trend that swept Europe toward the turn of the century, including Art Nouveau in France and Jugendstil in Germany, Catalan Modernism developed its own unique identity.

The First Barcelona World Fair in 1888 set the Modernista wheels in motion by showcasing some of the first Modernista creations, including the **Castle of the Three Dragons** by Lluís Domènech i Montaner, located within today's Ciutadella Park.

In the years that followed, many Modernista buildings were commissioned by industrialists and entrepreneurs in the new neighborhood of the Eixample (built in the late 19th and early 20th centuries), including Gaudí's **Sagrada Familia**, La Pedrera, and Casa Batlló. A block in the neighborhood on Passeig de Gràcia, between Carrer del Consell de Cent and Carrer d'Aragó, was christened the "Illa de la discòrdia," a play on words in Catalan; it means both "block of discord" and an expression that matches the English "bone of contention." Famous buildings on the block comprise works by major architects in the movement, including Antoni Gaudí (**Casa Batlló**), Lluís Domènech i Montaner (**Casa Lleó Morera**, now the Loewe flagship store), and Josep Puig i Cadafalch (**Casa Amatller**). The buildings, though all Modernista, have clashing styles; this is one reason—along with the fierce competition between the architects to design the most impressive building in the area—for the moniker, "block of discord."

Catalan modernism was characterized by its use of the curve over the straight line, intricate detail including motifs of nature, and several artists and cráftsmen working together on a single project. Architects, furniture designers, and sculptors would collaborate to make one vision, which means the style encompassed much more than the architecture for which it is best known.

Other famous Modernista buildings include the **Palau de la Música Catalana** in the Ribera, the **Hospital de Santa Creu i Sant Pau,** and Gaudí's first building commission, Casa Vicens.

which used unusual, not traditionally artistic materials—he added marble and clay to the paint and used string, rags, and paper in his works. He also did large-scale sculptures, and in the '60s and '70s, his works were increasingly politically charged.

The beautiful library on the top floor, which still has the original shelves from the publishers that used to be housed here, has a compressive archive of Tàpies' work.

Mercat de la Concepció

Carrer d'Aragó, 313-317; Mon 8am-3pm, Tues-Fri 8am-8pm, Sat 8am-3pm; Metro: Girona

In the heart of the Eixample, this market is known for its flowers; it's where locals come for a bouquet to brighten up their apartments. It also has stalls selling fresh fruit and vegetables, meat, and fish, as well as olives, cheese, and other items ideal for a picnic. Built in 1888, the market is a lovely place to wander, especially for the green-thumbed traveler.

GRÀCIA AND PARK GÜELL
★ Park Güell

Carrer de Larrard; www.parkguell.cat; October 28-March 24, 8:30am-6:15pm; Mar 25-Apr 29, 8am-8:30pm; Apr 30-Aug 26, 8am-9:30pm; Aug 27-Oct 27, 8am-8:30pm; €7.50 online, €8.50 from ticket office; Metro: Lesseps

Park Güell, with its much-photographed dragon sculpture and mosaic benches overlooking the Mediterranean, is one of the most emblematic Gaudí sights in Barcelona.

The park originated as a high-class housing

Ruta del Modernisme sign

Visitors to Barcelona can follow the city's **Ruta del Modernisme** (the Modernisme Route, www.rutadelmodernisme.com); tiles mark it out on the street, and there is a guidebook (in English, €12), which comes with a map. It is available to buy at the Tourist Information Center on Plaça de Catalunya (number 17). You can also buy it at **Modernisme Centre Güell Pavillions** (Av. de Pedralbes, 7 Mon-Sun 10am-4pm) and **Institut Municipal del Paisatge Urbà** (Av Drassanes, 6, 21st Floor, Mon-Fri 9am-2pm). The guide also includes discount codes of up to 50 percent for key Modernista sights.

estate. Gaudí was commissioned by entrepreneur Eusebi Güell to design the complex, set on Carmel Hill in the north of Gràcia, which would combine the latest technology with a Modernista style. The housing estate was not a commercial success, perhaps due to Gràcia's distance from the center at that time, and only two houses (one inhabited by the Güell family) were built. In 1923 the Güell family gave the land to the city to be used as a public park. It was inspired by the English garden-city movement, hence the use of the English "Park" and not the Catalan "Parc." In 1984, Park Güell became a UNESCO World Heritage Site.

Today, most locals enjoy the park for what it is: a park. There are pathways that snake around, and benches where you can sit and take in the incredible views over Barcelona. It is also a massive tourist attraction, so consider arriving early (you can get into the monumental precinct for free before 8:30am) if you really want to beat the crowds and experience an unforgettable sunrise over the city.

TICKETS AND TOURS

Once free and an open part of the park, the central Monumental Core (which includes the famed mosaic benches) is now part of a separate area that charges admission. Tickets can be bought online for timed entry; definitely take advantage of this, as time slots do sell out, and people who arrive without tickets may have to settle for a slot 2-3 hours later in the day. The tickets allow a visit for 30 minutes after the designated time (e.g., a 3pm ticket allows entry from 3pm until 3:30pm).

Guided tours of the park are also available. The 50-minute tour, in English, gives visitors insight into the history, context, and symbols of the park. The general guided tour is with a group of about 25 people and costs €7, plus the price of the ticket to the Monumental Core. English tours take place daily at 10am, 11am, noon, 3pm, 4pm, 5pm, and 6pm. Private tours (€36/person) are also available; see website for details.

VISITING PARK GÜELL

The park is on a hill, and steep paths and staircases trail up or down, depending on where you enter.

The Monumental Core is at the center of the park. It includes the much-photographed mosaic benches, a vibrant color-clash of ceramics that overlooks the city and the Mediterranean beyond. The benches are on a platform raised by columns. Take some steps down and you will see the famed dragon ("el drac" in Catalan), a mosaic reptile that is one of Barcelona's most photographed sculptures.

Snaking around the Monumental Core are a series of modernista "viaducts," originally designed so that carriages could easily travel from the bottom to the much higher top of the park. Typical of Gaudí, they feature strong nature motifs: the stone columns resemble trees and vines, while the top of the balustrades double as plant pots, topped with real plants.

The **Gaudí House Museum** (93/219-3811, Oct-Mar 10am-6pm; Apr-Sept 9am-8pm; www.casamuseugaudi.org), located to the right of the Monumental Core when entering from Carrer d'Olot, was the home of Antoni Gaudí from 1906 to 1925, and was a showhouse for the planned housing estate of Park Güell. It was designed by Gaudí's friend and assistant, Francesc d'Assís Berenguer i Mestres. In the 1960s, it was opened as the Gaudí House Museum, and today it looks just as it would have when the great architect lived there.

At the lower entrance on Carrer d'Olot, you will find the two entrance houses that resemble a fairytale house made of candy. Here, too,

is the **Casa del Guarda** (Caretaker's House, included in ticket price), home to the exhibition "Güell, Gaudí and Barcelona: Expression of an Urban Ideal," which provides interesting background to the Park Güell project and focuses on the house, the park, and the city.

Away from the concentration of Gaudí buildings at the bottom, the wooded park, with landscaped areas and pathways throughout, is a lovely area for a stroll or a picnic, with the bonus of fantastic views over the city.

Hike to the highest point in the park, the *Turó de les tres creus*, three crosses on a hill of stones marking the spot where Gaudí planned to build a chapel, for fantastic views across the city.

GETTING THERE

There are three entrances into the park. The main entrance, on Carrer d'Olot, is at the bottom of the hillside park, closer to the Monumental Core. Another entrance is at top of the park, at the end of a series of escalators, on the steep Baixada de la Glòria. A third entrance is at Carretera del Carmel, number 23-and-a-third.

From Lesseps metro station (line 3) it is a 20-minute walk to the entrance on Baixada de la Glòria—this leads you into a high point of the park, from which you can wind down to the bottom and leave at the main entrance on Carrer de Larrard.

Bus lines H6, D40, 24, and 92 all get you closer to the park than the metro. From the bus stop on Travessera de Dalt (lines H6 and D40), it is a 10-minute walk to either the Baixada de la Glòria or the Carrer d'Olot entrance.

No public transport gets you right to the park, so for those with mobility issues, a taxi is the best bet. The journey from the Barri Gòtic to Park Güell takes around 15 minutes and should cost approximately €8. There is a taxi rank on Carrer de Marianao if you want to leave by taxi.

1: Park Güell; 2: Casa Vicens interior; 3: Museu Nacional d'Art de Catalunya.

★ Casa Vicens

Carrer de les Carolines, 20; www.casavicens.org;
10am-8pm daily; €16, free for children under 16;
Metro: Fontana

Gaudí might be famed the world over for the Sagrada Familia and La Pedrera, but Casa Vicens is where it all started for the local architect. Casa Vicens was commissioned as a summer residence by businessman Manel Vicens i Montaner in Gràcia, a village that was then separate from Barcelona (it would later be swallowed up by the city) and that was a popular summer retreat for prosperous city dwellers. Built between 1883 and 1885, this was Gaudí's first building commission, and it showcases the early foundations of the architect's style, with features that cropped up again in Gaudí's later work such as the use of tiles and motifs of nature.

The building, with its green, white, and yellow ceramics and cupola crowning the rooftop, stands out against the surrounding plain brick buildings, and you can't help but wonder what people made of it in 1885, this completely new style that heralded the beginning of Modernisme. The use of tiles on the outside of buildings, which we now associate with Gaudí and other Modernista architects, was at the time highly unusual. Little did people realize that this wacky new style would, over the years, become synonymous with Barcelona and draw visitors from across the globe.

The house opened to the public in 2017 after extensive restoration work that began in 2014. Visitors can see the three-floor house, a UNESCO World Heritage site since 2005, as well as its gardens and rooftop.

Inside, highlights include the ground-floor blue and gold smoking room, which had its own team of restorers; it's a wonderful space, meant for relaxation, that features Islamic detailing and papier-mâché wall detailing. Upstairs, you can explore the bedrooms, terrace, and bathrooms; Casa Vicens was a pioneer in using running water in its very own indoor bathrooms, decorated just as ornately as the dining room or smoking room. The attic holds a permanent exhibition on the history of the house, while outside, Gaudí's first accessible rooftop features domes and towers that bring to mind Islamic architecture. An extension, added in 1925 by Joan Baptista Serra de Martínez, has been turned into an exhibition space to show visitors the evolution of Gaudí's work, as well as the evolution of Barcelona itself (don't miss a fascinating eight-minute video on the expansion of the city and the rise of Catalan Modernism).

Wander the house at your own pace; there are guides along the route to answer any questions and provide visitors with background information, or you can opt for a guided-tour ticket (€19).

MONTJUÏC, POBLE SEC, AND SANT ANTONI

★ Museu Nacional d'Art de Catalunya
(National Museum of Art of Catalonia)

Palau Nacional, Parc de Montjuïc; tel. 93/622-0376;
www.museunacional.cat; Oct-Apr, Tues-Sat
10am-6pm, Sun 10am-3pm; May-Sept, Tues-Sat
10am-8pm, Sun 10am-3pm; €12; Metro: Espanya

The grand Palau Nacional, with its domes and jutting towers, is a relatively recent addition to the city, built to show off Catalonia for the 1929 International Exposition. Today it is Catalonia's national art gallery, home to a thousand years of the region's art. It is hard to beat for its sheer breadth of works, from Romanesque altarpieces of the middle ages to Spanish Civil War posters from the 1930s. Famous artists including Salvador Dalí and Joan Miró are also represented.

The building itself is well worth a visit; expansive and light-filled, its grandeur and its domes make it seem much older than it is. Its sheer size means that it rarely feels as busy as the likes of the Picasso Museum. Depending on how much you want to see, a visit could be a half-hour spin around the museum's

Romanesque pieces or a whole morning or afternoon checking out all the different galleries.

One of the museum's highlights is its collection of Romanesque art from the 11th-13th centuries, in the left-hand galleries on the ground floor. Frescoes that were painstakingly removed from churches high in the Pyrenees in northern Catalonia are beautifully presented here; the museum has recreated the shape of some of the churches, so visitors can see how the altarpieces and wall murals might have looked *in situ*. Many of the frescoes remain surprisingly well-preserved because of the isolation of the churches in which they were painted, and today they are considered one of the most important collections of early Medieval art in the world. They are remarkable for their vivid color, which, coupled with their two-dimensional appearance, gives them a modern-art look that is remarkable, given that they are nearly a thousand years old. Also on the ground floor, on the right-hand galleries, is the museum's collection of Gothic, Renaissance, and Baroque art.

On the first floor, there is a wonderful collection of contemporary Catalan art arranged by theme, spanning Modernisme, Noucentisme (an early-20th-century Catalan cultural movement that was largely a reaction against Modernisme), and the Civil War. Highlights include Salvador Dalí's "Portrait of My Father" and a fascinating range of Spanish Civil War posters. Joan Miró's murals dominate the first-floor Dome Room (look up to see an intricate fresco in the dome by painters Manuel Humbert, Josep de Togores, and Francesc Galí).

There are also regular temporary exhibitions. Not all descriptions are in English, so the audio guide (€4) is useful to discover more about the artworks (a combined ticket with audio guide can be purchased online for €14).

There's a terrace out front, with lovely views back down toward Plaça d'Espanya and across the city. Many come just for the views from the terrace (you don't have to pay to access it) without even entering the museum, and it is a good spot to recharge your batteries with a drink and a sit-down before checking out some more of Montjuïc. On the terrace is a small kiosk where you can buy drinks and snacks.

To get here, walk up from the Plaça d'Espanya Metro stop towards the Palau Nacional. There are escalators to the museum at the top of the hill. The €12 entry ticket is valid for two days during the month after the purchasing date.

CaixaForum

Av. de Francesc Ferrer i Guàrdia, 6-8; tel. 93/476-8600; www.caixaforum.es/Barcelona; daily 10am-8pm; €4; Metro: Espanya

The cultural arm of the Catalan CaixaBank is the home of the building society's extensive collection of modern art, some of which is on permanent display here in a former texile factory and warehouse, the Casaramona factory, designed by Modernista architect Josep Puig i Cadafalch. It opened as the first CaixaForum in Spain (there are now branches in Madrid, Valencia, and other cities) in 2002.

From the outside, the building's turrets make it look like a medieval castle. Inside, the bones of the factory have been kept intact, making the building just as interesting for its original architecture as for its often fascinating exhibitions.

As well as its permanent collection, the space holds impressive and eclectic international exhibitions; recent themes include Walt Disney, Andy Warhol, and the musician in antiquity. A 400-seat auditorium is the scene of regular concerts, talks, and film screenings. Visitors can easily spend an hour checking out the latest exhibitions.

A free audio guide giving background to the architecture of the building can be downloaded onto your phone or picked up at reception. Tickets, valid for all current exhibitions, are €4 and can be purchased online or at the ticket office in reception.

Refugi 307

Carrer Nou de La Rambla, 175; tel. 93/256-2100;
www.ajuntament.barcelona.cat/museuhistoria/es/
muhba-refugi-307; by tour only: English tours Sunday
10:30am; €3.50; Metro: Paral·lel

The Spanish Civil War was one of the first conflicts to use aerial bombardment; Italy and Germany helped their Spanish Nationalist allies by bombing the country, and Barcelona was heavily hit. To protect themselves, locals dug their own bomb shelters using picks and shovels. Everyone joined in, especially women and children, as most men were away fighting.

One of the biggest bomb shelters in Barcelona is now open for visits. Refugi 307, one of some 1,400 bomb shelters in the city, was hewn into the rock of the Montjuïc hill by locals of the Poble Sec neighborhood and had room for around 2,000 people.

After the war it fell into disrepair, but today, visitors can walk through 400 meters (1,312 feet) of tunnels (just over two meters tall and between 1.5-2 meters wide) to see the sick bay, the latrines, and the benches where locals sat, sometimes for hours and at times for days, waiting for the bombing to pass and unsure of what would await them when they emerged from underground.

The only way to visit the site is on a tour.

Tours are limited to around 10 people, and by appointment only (book by calling the number above); they are led by knowledgeable guides, mostly historians who have worked for years in the local neighborhood, chronicling the stories of locals during the Spanish Civil War.

The visit, around an hour long, brings the war to life and leaves a lasting impression of the hardship suffered by the people of Barcelona during the conflict.

Fundació Joan Miró

Parc de Montjuïc; tel. 93/443-9470; www.fmirobcn.
org; Nov-Mar, Tues, Wed, Fri 10am-6pm; Apr-Oct,
Tues, Wed, Fri 10am-8pm, year round, Thurs
10am-9pm, Sat 10am-8pm, Sun 10am-3pm; €12,
under age 15 free; Montjuïc Funicular from Metro
Paral·lel

Joan Miró, born in Barcelona in 1893, was one of the 20th century's most famous surrealist painters, known for his use of vivid primary colors and distorted shapes in paintings, ceramics, sculpture, and murals (look for his murals at the Barcelona Airport). This museum, which opened in 1975, was created by the painter himself, and he bestowed it with much of his personal collection. The white, light-filled building was designed by Miró's

Refugi 307 Spanish Civil War bomb shelter

close friend, Josep Lluís Sert, who also designed the painter's Mallorca studio.

The museum is a tour through Miró's career, from his early paintings, depicting his family summer home in Mont-roig, through his huge canvas paintings to his ceramics and bronze sculptures. Set aside an hour for a visit to the museum, which has the dimensions of a large villa. One wing is dedicated to the private Kazumasa Katsuta collection (with more than 32 works loaned to the musum by private collector Kazumasa Katsuta, owner of the world's largest private collection of works by Miró), while its surrounding gardens are peppered with sculptures and make for a peaceful stroll with impressive views down over the city.

The museum is a 10-minute stroll from the Museu Nacional d'Art de Catalunya (MNAC) (check out the Miró murals there before diving into the artist's life and work at the Miró museum). There are free one-hour guided tours in English (tour included in admission price) every Thursday at 1pm and on the first Sunday of every month at 11am (no booking necessary). Although crowds tend to be manageable, arrive early to have more of the museum to yourself.

Museu d'Arqueologia de Catalunya
(Archeological Museum of Catalonia)

Passeig de Santa Madrona, 39-41; tel. 93/423-2149; www.macbarcelona.cat; Tues-Sat 9:30am-7:30pm, Sun 10am-2:30pm; €5.50; Metro: España

The ancient history of what is now Catalonia is on full display at the Archeological Museum of Catalonia, set in the Graphic Arts palace from the 1929 World Exhibition.

Displays take visitors from prehistoric times through Greek and Roman occupation to the medieval period of the Visigoths. Highlights include discoveries from the Greek site of Empúries on the Costa Brava, such as the statue of Asclepius from the 3rd century BC and a 53,200-year-old Neanderthal jaw from Sitges, south of Barcelona. Rooms 14 and 18 are dedicated to Barcino, the Roman name

for Barcelona, and include statues, tombstones, and inscriptions discovered around the city. Interactive displays bring the pieces to life.

The relatively compact museum can be done in 30-45 minutes, longer if you linger at each display.

Castell de Montjuïc
(Montjuïc Castle)

Carretera de Montjuïc, 66; tel. 93/256-4440; www.ajuntament.barcelona.cat/castelldemontjuic; Nov 1-Feb 28, Mon-Sun 10am-6pm; March 1-Oct 31, Mon-Sun 10am-8pm; €5; Metro: Paral·lel

Perched 173 meters (568 feet) above the port on the top of Montjuïc hill, Montjuïc Castle is a military fortress that dates back to 1640. The castle is a symbol of the long history of repression for many Catalans, and it became especially infamous during the Spanish Civil War, when political prisoners were tortured and executed there. Catalan President Lluís Companys was executed in Montjuïc Castle in 1940. Today, this strategic military point is worth the visit for its spectacular views over the Mediterranean and the port area.

The castle you see today dates from the 18th century. It is surrounded by defensive ditches and walls, and its original moat is now a landscaped garden. Inside, a museum traces the history of the castle. There are some fascinating tombstones dating from the 11th century from the old Jewish cemetery on Montjuïc.

The best way to reach the castle is to take the funicular railway (included in metro passes) from Paral·lel up to Parc de Montjuïc, right next door to the station of the **Teleferico de Montjuïc cable car**, which gives passengers spectacular views across the city. The cable car ticket is €12.70 for adults and €9.20 for children.

There is free entry on Sundays after 3pm.

Font Màgica
Plaça de Carles Buïgas, 1; www.barcelona.cat/en/ what-to-do-in-bcn/magic-fountain; April 1-May 31,

Thurs, Fri, Sat 9pm-10pm; June 1-Sept 30, Wed-Sun 9:30pm-10:30pm; Oct 1-Oct 31, Thurs, Fri, Sat 9pm-10pm; Nov 1-Jan 6, Thurs, Fri, Sat 8pm-9pm; Mar 1-Mar 31, Thurs, Fri, Sat 8pm-9pm; Jan 7-Feb 28, closed for annual maintenance; Metro: Espanya

Designed by Carles Buigas for the 1929 International Exposition, the Font Màgica (Magic Fountain) is Barcelona's largest ornamental foundation and one of the city's biggest tourist attractions. Its thrice-weekly one-hour music and light displays start between 8pm and 9:30pm, depending on the time of year. On Thursday, Friday, and Saturday evenings, the fountain's waters are illuminated in different colors as the water dances to music against the backdrop of the grand, floodlit Palau Nacional. Make sure to get there early to get a good spot around the fountains (crowds stand rather than sit, with kids on their parents' shoulders, to take in the show). Definitely more a tourist attraction than a local hangout spot, the Font Màgica is worth seeing if you have the time.

Check online for times, which are subject to change.

Mercat de Sant Antoni

Carrer Comte d'Urgell, 1; tel. 93/423-4287; www. mercatdesantantoni.com; Mon-Sat 8am-8pm; Metro: Sant Antoni

This historic neighborhood market reopened to great fanfare in May 2018 after nearly a decade of extensive renovations. It was built between 1879-1882 by architect Antoni Rovira i Trias; it was the first market outside the old city, and today it has a range of spacious stalls selling all kinds of foods. The renovation has extended each stall, giving stallholders more space to display their stock and visitors more space to browse. It may have had an expensive makeover, but Sant Antoni remains a neighborhood market, with fresh fruit and vegetables, butchers, and fishmongers sitting alongside traditional old bars, where stallholders can have a quick break and punters can enjoy a quick café con leche or caña.

BEYOND THE CENTER
Mount Tibidabo

At 500 meters (1,640 feet) above sea level, Tibidabo—crowned by a vintage amuseument park—is the highest point in the Collserola Ridge, with wonderful views over Barcelona.

If rides aren't your thing, you can still go up to the park area (for free) to enjoy the views and to visit the Temple de Sagrat Cor high on the hill. This neo-Gothic church, built in 1806, is topped with a statue of the sacred heart. It's worth the trip for the funicular ride and the views, especially if you take a picnic. The Panoramic Area of the park is free to enter and has terraces with benches as well as (pricey) cafés and snack bars plus fantastic views over Barcelona.

GETTING THERE

The Funicular del Tibidabo, the best way to get to the top of Tibidabo, is located at Plaça de Dr. Andreu. To get there, take metro line 7 to Avinguda Tibidabo, then take bus number 196 up the hill to the funicular. (Alternately, you can walk from the metro stop to the funicular, which will take around 30 minutes.) The funicular rail ticket costs €7.70, or €4.10 with entry to the amusement park.

Tibibús T2A departs from Plaça Catalunya (stop on the corner of Plaça Catalunya and Rambla Catalunya, in front of Desigual shop) from 10am on days when the park is open. Buses (€3 one way) run every 20 minutes and take around 30 minutes to reach the park.

A taxi from Plaça de Catalunya should take around 30 minutes and cost approximately €14.

Parc d'Atraccions Tibidabo
(Tibidabo Amusement Park)

Plaza del Tibidabo, 3-4; tel. 93/211-7942; www. tibidabo.cat; Mon-Fri 11am-6pm, Sat-Sun 11am-9pm; €28.50, €10.30 for children under 120 centimeters (4 feet) tall; Metro: Av. Tibidabo

Spain's oldest amusement park sits high above Barcelona, perched on the peak of Mount Tibidabo. The park was opened at the

Barcelona Off the Beaten Path

Barcelona is home to some of the world's most iconic sights, but there are plenty of more under-the-radar places that are well worth exploring. They will likely have fewer tourists, so you'll be able to visit in relative peace.

GAUDÍ ARCHITECTURE

- In the Gràcia neighborhood, you can visit Antoni Gaudí's first-ever house commission, **Casa Vicens** (Carrer de les Carolines, 20; daily 10am-8pm; Metro: Fontana), which gives a fascinating insight into the inspiration and early works of the acclaimed architect.

- **Bellesguard Tower** (Carrer de Bellesguard, 20; tel. 93/250-4093; Tues-Sun 10am-3pm; www.bellesguardgaudi.com), which opened in September 2013, is one of the lesser known works of Gaudí. The manor house, in the Sant Gervasi neighborhood, can only be visited on a tour that can be booked online.

SPANISH CIVIL WAR HISTORY

- The anti-aircraft fortifications known as the **Bunkers del Carmel**, built in 1938 during the Spanish Civil War, are today a perfect spot to watch the sun set over the city.

- **Refugi 307**: One of more than 1,400 bomb shelters built by the people of Barcelona during the Spanish Civil War, Refuge 307 was one of the biggest, with room for around 2,000 people. It can be visited as part of a guided tour only; the English tour takes place at 10:30am on Sundays.

PARKS

- **Parc del Laberint** (Passeig dels Castanyers, 1; tel. 66/667-7722; daily 10am-7pm; Metro: Mundet): Barcelona's oldest gardens are home to a magical maze dedicated to the Greek god of love, Eros.

- **Parc de Collserola**: The mountains surrounding Barcelona give visitors the chance to escape the packed city streets in a matter of minutes; you can quickly be in the greenery of the mountains. It's a popular spot for picnics, hiking, and cycling, and it affords visitors incredible views of the city below.

NEIGHBORHOODS

- **Poble Sec:** On the lower hills of Montjuïc, Poble Sec was originally a poor neighborhood, but recently it has been making a name for itself with its food scene and buzzing bars.

- **Sant Antoni:** The leafy, tree-lined streets have become a hipster haunt, with craft beer bars and brunch spots.

beginning of the 20th century by Dr. Salvador Andreu i Grau, who took advantage of the new Tamvia Blau (Blue Tram), inaugurated in 1900 to open up the top of the mountain. (Note: the Tramvia Blau was closed at the time of research for modernization work on its infrastructure.) A funicular railway, which took passengers up the mountain from the last stop of the Tramvia Blau, was a new and exciting mode of transport at the time, and eventually it became an attraction in itself.

The park is popular with both tourists and local families. It's a mixture of century-old rides and modern additions (all 25 rides are included in admission price). Don't miss the Avió airplane ride, a little red "aeroplane" that has been flying passengers out over the edge of the mountain since 1928. The aeroplanes are a replica of the first plane to fly between Barcelona and Madrid in 1927.

The Giradabo big wheel, with its multicolored cabins, opened in 2014 on the highest point of the mountain to give passengers incredible views over Barcelona. The amusement park makes the most of the views with its Sky Walk (open from 11am).

★ Camp Nou

Carrer d'Aristides Maillol, 12; 902189900; www.fcbarcelona.com/tour; Mon-Sat 9:30am-7:30pm, Sun 10am-2:30pm; from €25; Metro: Collblanc

Home to local football legends FC Barcelona since 1957, Camp Nou is the largest stadium in Europe, seating 99,354 fans. A tour of the grounds is a must-do for any sports fan.

The self-guided tour, with an optional audio guide (€5), takes visitors around the stadium's highlights, including visits to the stands, field, dugout, players' tunnel, the away side's changing rooms, and the commentary boxes. The tour provides interesting context to one of the world's greatest football teams, and both soccer-loving kids and adults are sure to be entertained. Standing pitch-side and looking up into the towering stands, you realize quite how huge the stadium is.

There are a few different ticket options. The standard **Camp Nou Tour** (adults €25, children 6-13, 70+ and students €22) and the **Camp Nou Tour Plus** (€35) can be booked online. The Tour Plus ticket includes a multimedia audio guide, complete with tablet and virtual reality glasses; it really brings the stadium to life and is worth it for die-hard football fans.

If you want to pretend you are Barça's latest signing, the **Players' Experience Tour** (€120) gives visitors a personal tour of the stadium with a tour guide, as well as exclusive access to the FC Barcelona changing room, a walk along the pitch, and a visit to the press room to announce your new signing.

All tickets also include entry into the **FC Barcelona Museum**, located inside Camp Nou, which includes an audiovisual trip through the club's 120-year history, a space

dedicated to striker Lionel Messi, and the trophy room.

The club shop is the place to stock up on Barça memorabilia, from football shirts to mugs, scarves, and hats.

The best way to reach Camp Nou is by metro; the stadium is a 10-minute walk from the Collblanc metro stop.

CosmoCaixa

Carrer d'Isaac Newton, 26; tel. 93/212-6050; www.agenda.obrasocial.lacaixa.es; daily 10am-9pm; €4; Metro: Av. Tibidabo

Barcelona's huge science museum, with its hands-on displays and awe-inspiring exhibits, is a must-visit if traveling with children. Run by the social arm of the Caixa bank, the museum aims to promote science in all its forms. The building itself melds Modernista architecture with a 2004 extension that expanded the space, adding a cavernous six levels underground.

The Bosc Inundat (Flooded Forest) is a highlight; 1000 square meters (10,764 square feet) of Amazonian rainforest, featuring animal and plant life typical of the ecosystem, including piranhas, caimans, and giant catfish. The Geological Wall contains seven sections of rock that represent the earth's different geological structures, while the Planetarium takes visitors on a tour of the Universe, with stunning 3D shows (daily).

The metro is the best way to get to the museum, which is a 15-minute walk from the Av. Tibidabo stop.

Bellesguard Tower

Carrer de Bellesguard, 20; tel. 93/250-4093; www.bellesguardgaudi.com; Tues-Sun 10am-3pm; €9; Metro: Avenida Tibidabo

One of Antoni Gaudí's lesser known works, Bellesguard Tower was built between 1900 and 1909 in the well-to-do Sant Gervasi neighborhood of the city, on the slopes of Tibidabo. The site was originally home to the medieval castle of King Martí "The Humane," the last king of the Catalan dynasty of the House of Barcelona, who died in 1410. Gaudí restored the ruins of the medieval palace, which now form part of the grounds.

Gaudí's building blends Art Nouveau and Gothic influences with a use of straight lines that differs significantly from the architect's other work, which is famed for its curves (note the straight parapets and the vertical lines of the tower). The interior adheres more closely to Gaudí's famous Modernista style, with vivid stained-glass windows and wrought-iron detailing.

The building opened to the public at the end of 2013. There are two kinds of tours available. The audio guide visit (available in English, €9 per person) allows visitors to explore the exterior spaces at their own pace and includes a visit inside the building; it begins every 30 minutes and is led by a guide. The weekend hour-long guided tour (in English, starts at 11am, €16 per person) is led by a qualified guide who directs groups around the exterior and the interior of the building, telling fascinating stories about its history.

The best way to get to the sight is by metro; it is a 15-minute walk from the Avenida Tibidabo stop.

TOP EXPERIENCE

★ Bunkers del Carmel
Carrer de Marià Labèrnia; tel. 93/256-2122; open daily

During the Spanish Civil War, the new tactic of carpet bombing, which would show its full force during the Second World War, was tested over Barcelona. The city responded in 1938 by building these anti-aircraft fortifications at the top of the Turó de la Rovira, 262 meters (860 feet) above sea level. Despite the name, there has never been a bunker at the top of the hill; rather, the fortifications held four Vickers 105mm guns. After the war, the shantytown of Los Cañones grew up on the hill—it was only removed in the early 1990s, ahead of the 1992 Olympic Games.

The bunkers belong to the Museum of the History of Barcelona (MUHBA). Access to the outside of the bunkers is free all day, every day of the year.

In 2015 a museum space opened at the bunkers, the **MUHBA Turó de la Rovira** (part of the Museum of the History of Barcelona— Sat 4:30pm-8:30pm, Sun 10:30am-2:30pm, 4:30pm-8:30pm, Wed 4:30pm-8:30pm, free admission) that recounts the history of the fortifications. But it's the 360-degree views of the city that really attract visitors to this site, especially at sunset; watching the sun disappear below the horizon over the sea is a magical experience. While the space is becoming increasingly known by tourists, it is still an informal and local favorite where people come to watch the sun set, eat, strum guitars, and generally enjoy the incredible view of the city below.

The best transport option is by bus (you can take number 24 from Plaça de Catalunya or Passeig de Gràcia to Ctra del Carmel-Mühlberg, around a 40-minute journey; from there it's a 10-minute walk); that option leaves visitors closest to the bunkers. There is a steep, 10-minute walk up to the top and there is no shade once you get there, so if you are visiting during the summer, take appropriate sun protection.

Hospital de Santa Creu i Sant Pau
Carrer de Sant Quintí, 89; tel. 93/291-9000; self-guided visit €17, guided visit €19, audio guide €3, children under 12 free; Metro: Guinardó | Hospital de Sant Pau

This former hospital, built between 1901 and 1930 by Modernista architect Lluís Domènech i Montaner, showcases how Modernista design was not only used in fancy private apartment blocks, but also for much-needed public services.

Hospital de Santa Creu i Sant Pau was built because of the growing concern about health in the city. After studying solutions used in other European cities, Domènech i Montaner designed a set of separate pavilions linked by underground walkways; the pavilions are surrounded by gardens that create large, clear

expanses of space, on a site equivalent to nine blocks of the Eixample. Adhering to the latest thinking in hygiene and sanitation, his pavilions kept infectious patients apart from the general population. In 1930, all services moved here from the Hospital de la Santa Creu in El Raval, which had been the city's main hospital for centuries.

Hospital de Santa Creu i Sant Pau was a functioning hospital until 2009, opened as a museum and cultural center in 2014. It is a UNESCO World Heritage Site, along with the Palau de la Música Catalana.

In the Sant Rafael Pavilion, a high-ceilinged space with aquamarine arches and tiled walls, a 1920s hospital ward has been recreated with 10 beds, vintage heaters, and a day room where patients would have received visitors. An exhibition space shows how the hospital was run in the early years. Don't miss a walk through the underground tunnels that connected the hospital's pavilions; you can imagine what a hive of activity they must have been, with doctors and nurses running from one patient to another.

The self-guided tour (€17) comes with a multimedia audio guide; it gives a 12-stage tour through some of the highlights, recounting the history of the hospital as well as providing photographs and videos to help visitors understand what the site was like in the early 20th century. Guided tours in English are also available (€19) daily from 10:30-11:45. They last approximately an hour and 15 minutes.

Beaches

TOP EXPERIENCE

One of the things that makes Barcelona special and unique is its 4.5 kilometers (2.8 miles) of beaches. In minutes, you can go from the narrow lanes of the Gothic Quarter to the wide, sandy beaches and blue seas of the Mediterranean.

In summer, the water is warm enough for swimming, and beaches are kept safe by lifeguard patrols. In winter, you'll seldom see anyone braving the little waves (apart from some watersports fans trying their hand at surfing or sailing).

Do as the locals do and take a cool bag/box with picnic supplies, such as crusty ham sandwiches, olives, cheese, and chocolate. You can also pick up supplies and cooling ice-lollies from the beach kiosks, or duck into a *chiringuito* (beach hut) when the sun gets too hot. The beaches are very mixed, from older couples in their fold-up chairs reading the paper and groups of students topping up their tans, to young families building sandcastles.

1: Parc d'Atraccions Tibidabo; 2: La Barceloneta with Hotel Arts in background.

Barcelona City Council operates a **beach visitors center** (Passeig Marítim, 25) on the boardwalk opposite the Hospital del Mar. It has information on the beaches, coastal walks, events, beach activities, and games and sports equipment to use on the sand.

★ LA BARCELONETA

Metro: Barceloneta

Barcelona's famous city beach is located next to the Port Vell and the traditional fishing neighborhood of Barceloneta, renowned for its excellent seafood and traditional tapas bars. Lifeguards monitor the busy beach, which has showers, public toilets, sun loungers available to rent (around €10), changing rooms, and kiosks selling drinks and snacks—as well as Wi-Fi so you can upload all those holiday snaps. This is the beach closest to the city, and it's the most crowded.

NOVA ICÀRIA

Metro: Ciutadella | Vila Olímpica

Close to the Port Olímpic and north of La Barceloneta, the gently curving Nova Icària is a more peaceful beach, popular with families

Chiringuito Beach Huts

Chiringuito—or sometimes xiringuito—is a bit of a catch-all term to describe informal bars and restaurants located along the beach. They usually sell drinks, snacks, and tapas dishes and are united by their relaxed vibe. Their laid-back décor—think deck chairs, fairy lights and, often, a beach-shack-like appearance—adds to the chill appeal. They are a great place to head to when the sun gets a bit too hot, or when you need some sustenance after all that swimming. Prices are generally reasonable and there is usually no need to make a reservation—just head in and grab a seat.

VAI MOANA

Av. Litoral; tel. 93/309-1291; www.vaimoanabeachbar.com; Mon-Sun 10am-2am; Metro: Ciutadella / Vila Olímpica

Handily located along the boardwalk between Nova Icària and Mar Bella (on Bogatell, the beach in between), this tropical-themed beach bar is a laid-back spot with deck chairs, parasols, and a cool young crowd day and night, sipping on healthy juices and creative cocktails. It calls itself a "gastronomic chiringuito," which makes it a great place to grab something to eat. It offers breakfasts and sandwiches (think pulled pork and BLTs) to its tapas, burgers, and salads.

LA CARMELINA

Av. Litoral, Nova Icària, 620; tel. 93/611-7070; daily 9am-2am; €15; Metro: Ciutadella / Vila Olímpica

Right on Nova Icària, this lovely beach restaurant is open all day long, catering to beach goers during the day, then later the dinner crowd, who eat at tables topped with candles to a soundtrack of waves lapping on the shore. Its pastel colors, from the awning to the wicker chairs, are modern and stylish, and its menu features crowd-pleasers like tacos, burgers, and paella.

LA DELICIOSA

Paseo Marítimo de Barcelona; tel. 93/309-1291; www.ladeliciosabeachbar.com; daily 9am-midnight; Metro: Barceloneta

This beach bar, right on La Barceloneta, is a favorite with families and young people for its hearty food (burgers, sandwiches, etc.), friendly staff, and fun, relaxed atmosphere. Its décor philosophy is based on recycling, so expect lots of "upcycled" crates, chairs, and seats that give the space a cool, vintage vibe.

and groups of friends. You can reach it by walking north along the boardwalk from La Barceloneta, which takes around 20 minutes. It's bordered by a wide boardwalk and plenty of beach bars and is close to the city's two big skyscrapers, which were built just before the 1992 Olympic Games (if in doubt, head toward the skyscrapers to find the beach). It's a good spot for sports, and it has a beach volleyball court as well as table tennis. The Centre Municipal de Vela offers dinghy-sailing courses (by the hour), kayaking, and windsurfing. Facilities include cloakrooms, showers, public toilets, changing rooms, sun loungers, beach umbrellas, drinks and ice cream kiosks, restaurants, and Wi-Fi.

MAR BELLA

Metro: Poblenou

North of Nova Icària, the wide expanse of Mar Bella, which leads onto Llevant beach, is popular with young people and draws a local crowd (be aware that part of it is a nudist beach). If you want to get active, there is beach volleyball, table tennis, a skate park, and basketball hoops. The Base Nàutica Municipal de la Mar Bella (Av. del Litoral; tel. 93/221-0432; daily 9am-8pm) offers sailing trips and kayak rental; VanasDive (Av. del Litoral, 86-96; tel. 93/221-0548) is a diving center that runs diving courses for beginners and PADI and SSI scuba-diving certifications.

Food

Barcelona is famed for its cuisine, from its traditional tapas bars to its explosively creative high-end restaurants, which have invented a whole new language for Catalan cuisine by using weird and wonderful techniques to distill flavors into their purest forms.

Sitting right on the Mediterranean, the city of course has incredible seafood—the restaurants in Barceloneta, right along the seafront, have long been famed for their excellent fish, brought in from the port just steps away. Paella, too, though really from Valencia down the coast, is a popular dish in Barcelona, best shared among family or friends and enjoyed outdoors with the salty sea aroma in the air. A popular version in Barcelona is *fideuá*, in which thin little noodles are substituted for the rice. Do like the Spaniards and order it at lunch alongside a glass of crisp white wine.

Of all the regional cuisines represented in Barcelona, Basque (Euskal) may be most abundant—and exciting. *Pintxo* bars, the Basque version of tapas bars, serve *pintxos*, Basque tapas that consist of delicious morsels, usually on top of a piece of crusty bread, all laid out along the top of the bar. Customers can see everything on offer and choose whatever takes their fancy.

LAS RAMBLAS AND BARRI GÒTIC
Catalan and Spanish
★ COMETA PLA

Carrer del Cometa, 5; tel. 64/619-7845; www. cometapla.cat; Mon 7:30pm-11pm, Tues-Thurs 1pm-4pm, 7:30pm-11pm, Fri 1:30pm-4pm, 7:30pm-11pm, Sat 1pm-4pm, 7:30pm-11pm; €10; Metro: Jaume I

Highlighting seasonal and organic Catalan produce with an emphasis on vegetables, Cometa Pla is a cozy, cool restaurant on a little side street in the Gothic Quarter. You're immediately hit by the tempting aromas from the open kitchen, where chefs put a creative spin on Catalan produce. The menu consists of small tapas plates with plenty of vegetarian options, while the wine list includes Catalan organic and natural wines—the friendly staff are happy to advise on wine or food options. Don't miss the restaurant's take on *patatas bravas*, a smoky dish of potatoes with paprika and garlic sauces; seasonal dishes like grilled artichokes are also excellent. There's a ground-floor dining room, with wooden tables and low-strung lights, and a mezzanine floor above. Reservations recommended.

CAFÉ DE L'ACADEMIA
Carrer dels Lledó, 1; tel. 93/319-8253; Mon-Fri 1pm-3:30pm, 8pm-11pm; €15; Metro: Jaume I

This atmospheric restaurant, in the heart of the Barri Gòtic, does Catalan cuisine in a smart, elevated fashion. Open only on weekdays, it's a popular spot with locals for its lunchtime *menu del día* (€15); by night, it's a warm and romantic setting, especially in summer when it opens its outdoor terrace. Inside, the stone walls and wooden beams make for a cozy atmosphere in which to enjoy dishes like traditional Catalan escudella stew, fideuà, and fresh cod with tomato and black olives.

LA VIÑATERÍA DEL CALL
Carrer de Sant Domènec del Call, 9; tel. 93/302-6092; daily 7:30pm-1am; €15; Metro: Jaume I

Nestled in the narrow streets of the Jewish quarter, this lovely restaurant harks back to days gone by with its wooden beams, dark wood furniture, and low lighting—a romantic setting for dinner (it gets busy, so reservations are recommended). It specializes in classic dishes, from cheese and meat boards to chorizo in cider, meatballs, and fried padrón peppers.

Tapas

★ BAR LA PLATA

Carrer de la Mercè, 28; tel. 93/315-1009; www.
barlaplata.com; Mon-Sat 9am-3:15pm, 6:15pm-11pm;
€3; Metro: Barceloneta

One of the most authentic old bars in the Gothic quarter, Bar La Plata has been serving the same four dishes to loyal patrons since 1945. Salted anchovies, sausage, and a simple tomato salad are the standard tapas, but it is the fried anchovies (*boquerones*) that are the real star of the show; the bar goes through some 40 kilograms (88 pounds) of anchovies a week. Tables are scarce; this is a place to prop up the bar or spill out onto the street, like the locals.

BODEGA VASCONIA

Carrer d'en Gignàs, 13; tel. 93/488-6882; Tues-Fri
2pm-midnight, Sat-Sun 1pm-midnight; €10; Metro:
Jaume I

Going strong since 1905, this local bar, with its blue and green tiled walls, might be popular with tourists as well as locals, but it hasn't lost its feel of a true local haunt, with friendly staff and good-quality tapas. Try some crunchy fried seafood, a satisfying wedge of *tortilla de patatas*, or some Galician-style octopus (drizzled with oil and a dash of paprika), washed down with a glass of house wine.

International

BISTROT LEVANTE

Placeta de Manuel Ribé, 1; tel. 93/858-2679; www.
bistrotlevante.com; Wed-Fri 5pm-midnight, Sat-Sun
10am-1am; €10; Metro: Jaume I

This Middle Eastern bistro, opened in 2017, is a cool new addition to El Call, Barcelona's old Jewish quarter. The spacious dining room is stylish, with low-hanging lights and plants cascading from the ceilings. Brunch and all-day dining make this an excellent stop whatever the time. Morning meals include Lebanese poached eggs and spicy *shakshuka*. At night, the restaurant does a range of *mezze*, tapas-style small plates ideal for sharing. Many are vegetarian, including roasted sweet

Steering Clear of Tourist Traps

It's only too easy to fall into a tourist trap in Barcelona, so a few key tips should help you avoid the overpriced rubbish and find something more authentic. Firstly, avoid menus with photos—they're almost always an indication that the food is not worth stopping for. Secondly, head off that main drag—i.e., Las Ramblas—where you're likely to find touristy places, and explore the streets just behind, where bars and restaurants will likely have a much more local flavor.

potatoes with charred Brussels sprouts and excellent hummus.

CECCONI'S

Passeig de Colom, 20; tel. 93/220-4640; www.
cecconisbarcelona.com; Mon-Thurs midday-1am,
Fri-Sat midday-2am, Sun 12pm-midnight; €20-€25;
Metro: Drassanes

Cecconi's, the Italian restaurant at Barcelona's Soho House, mixes the modern with the classic; whitewashed, exposed-brick walls and a forest of green plants provide the backdrop to elegant tables with white tablecloths. The open kitchen produces high-quality Italian fare, from handmade pasta to seafood dishes typical of northern Italy. It serves an Aperitivo Italiano on weekdays from 6-8pm and a brunch buffet on Sundays midday-5pm (€40 per person).

Cafés

CAFÈ D'ESTIU

Plaça Sant Iu; tel. 93/310-3014; www.cafedestiu.com;
Apr-Oct, Tues-Sun 10am-10pm; €6; Metro: Jaume I

In the peaceful courtyard of the Museu Frederic Marès, this lovely café has an outdoor terrace that is a hidden oasis of calm in the streets of the tourist-heavy Gothic quarter. It is open April-October and is a lovely place to relax with a coffee while checking out the surrounding medieval architecture. There's

Catalan Specialties

Catalan cuisine is, at its heart, classic Mediterranean cooking, using fresh ingredients, not usually very spicy, cooked in a variety of different ways. Grilling is popular in this part of Spain, whether it is to cook fresh vegetables for the Catalan dish *escalivada*, calçots when the popular vegetable is in season, or delicious fresh seafood, straight from the market.

- **Bomba:** Resembling a big, round croquette, this breaded and fried ball of mashed potato filled with beef mince was invented in Barcelona and is usually served drizzled in spicy brava sauce or aioli.

- **Pa amb Tomaquet:** The staple of any Catalan breakfast is Pa amb Tomaquet, or tomato bread—thin, Catalan coca bread (a thin bread typical of this part of Spain) rubbed with tomato and covered with olive oil and a liberal pinch of salt.

Pa amb tomàquet aka tomato bread

- **Calçots:** This kind of green onion is eaten across Catalonia during calçot season, usually between November and April. During celebrations known as calçotadas, the vegetables are grilled over a hot fire and peeled by hand, before being dipped into *romesco* sauce, made with red peppers, roasted garlic, almonds, and olive oil. Many restaurants serve calçots during the harvest season, so keep an eye out for them on menus.

- **Crema Catalana:** Catalonia's most famous dessert is its take on the classic crème brulee, a rich custard base with a thin, crunchy crust on top.

- **Escalivada:** This smoky grilled vegetable dish is a great Catalan vegetarian option, typically including roasted eggplant, bell peppers, onion, and tomato with olive oil garlic and salt. It is often served as a tapas dish in Barcelona.

- **Butifarra:** This spicy pork sausage is typical of Catalan cuisine and comes in several varieties. *Butifarra negra* (black butifarra) is made with pork and pork blood, while you can also buy uncooked butifarra to grill or barbecue.

- **Escudella:** *Escudella i carn d'olla*, or *escudella* for short, is a traditional Catalan stew made using meatballs spiced with garlic as well as vegetables, butifarra sausage, and other meat. It is traditionally eaten in two parts: first the soup, served with pasta or rice, followed by the meat, served with the vegetables used in the broth.

- **Esqueixada:** This salad, particularly popular in summer, is made with shredded salt cod, onions, tomatoes, olive oil, and vinegar. The salt cod is always shredded by hand to get the correct texture.

- **Fideuá:** This dish, which comes from Valencia but is also popular throughout Catalonia, is a take on the traditional paella but substitutes thin, small noodles for the rice.

- **Suquet de Peix:** This Catalan seafood stew is served with potatoes, garlic, and tomato. Lots of different types of seafood can be used, depending on what has been caught that day.

a small tapas menu and a range of different drinks options.

Breakfast and Brunch
SATAN'S COFFEE CORNER
Carrer de l'Arc de Sant Ramon del Call, 11; tel. 66/622-2599; www.satanscoffee.com; Mon-Sat 8am-6pm, Sun 10am-6pm; €7; Metro: Jaume I

This cool café full of young creatives takes its coffee very seriously. Founded in 2012 as a small storefront in the Raval, the brand has grown through word-of-mouth fame to become one of the city's most well-loved speciality coffee roasters. The coffee is delicious—there is a weekly rotating menu of speciality brews—and its food menu, from Japanese breakfasts to sandwiches, salads, and cakes, is designed to pair perfectly with the coffee on offer.

Bakeries and Dessert
GRANJA DULCINEA
Carrer de Petritxol, 2; tel. 93/302-6824; www.granjadulcinea.com; daily 9am-1pm, 5pm-9pm; €4; Metro: Liceu

Your inner child will burst out when you see the chocolatey treats on offer at Granja Dulcinea, a vintage *granja* (dairy shop) on Carrer de Petritxol, a historic street that for decades has been home to several granjas and their chocolatey wares. Inside, the tiled floor, dark wood furnishings, and pictures of family members hark back to the café's past—it was founded in 1941 and quickly became a favorite of locals for a snack or a thick hot chocolate topped with cream (ask for a *suís*).

★ LA COLMENA
Plaça de l'Àngel, 12; tel. 93/315-1356; www.pastisserialacolmena.com; daily 9am-9pm; €2; Metro: Jaume I

Since 1849, La Colmena has been making passersby stop and marvel at its tempting window displays of meringues, chocolates, and pastries. One of Barcelona's oldest cake shops is a great place to stock up on a few sweet treats, made using centuries-old recipes.

ESCRIBÀ
Las Ramblas, 83; tel. 93/301-6027; daily 9am-9:30pm; Metro: Liceu

The Escribà family has been making delectable chocolates, pastries, and other sweet treats since 1906. Its Las Ramblas branch, with its Modernista façade, is quintessentially "Barcelonés." It's hard to walk past without peering into the windows to see what's on

La Colmena

offer. Inside, you can pick up little handmade pastries, ideal for breakfast or an afternoon snack while exploring the old town.

EL RAVAL
Catalan and Spanish
LAS FERNANDEZ

Carrer de les Carretes, 11; tel. 93/443-2043; www. lasfernandez.com; Tues-Sun 8:30pm-2am; €10; Metro: Sant Antoni

Run by the three Fernandez sisters, this popular local restaurant in El Raval hits you with its bright red color scheme, which makes the locale look like it has stepped right out of a Pedro Almodóvar film. The friendly staff serve dishes made with fresh, local ingredients like "fish of the day," pulled pork, and classics like *patatas bravas* and Catalan meats and cheeses.

RAO RESTAURANT

Carrer de les Sitges, 3; tel. 65/559-7021; www.raobcn. com; Mon-Sat 7pm-11pm; €10; Metro: Plaça de Catalunya

This modern restaurant is a stylish spot. Its long dining room features low and high tables, exposed brick walls, and Scandinavian-inspired low-hanging lights. It's a good spot for couples or groups, as it specializes in small sharing plates from classic *tortilla de patatas* and *bomba* to crunchy fried squid, English-style roast beef, and Galician-style octopus.

Tapas
LA MONROE DE LA FILMO

Plaça de Salvador Seguí, 1-9; tel. 93/441-9461; www.lamonroe.es; Tues-Thurs midday-1am, Fri-Sat midday-2am, Sun midday-1am; €9; Metro: Liceu

This tapas bar, just next door to the Filmoteca (from where it gets its name), has a buzzing outdoor terrace and a cool industrial-themed interior. It's a favorite with locals, and a great place to grab a drink and some tapas before or after a film next door. There are various food options, from tapas like croquettes and prawns to sandwiches, and larger, main courses at night.

★ BAR CAÑETE

Carrer de la Unió, 17; tel. 93/270-3458; www. barcanete.com, Mon-Sat 1pm-midnight; €15; Metro: Liceu

Bar Cañete is an example of how the once seedy Raval has become one of the coolest areas in the city. It mixes vintage touches, like red banquettes, with a bustling open kitchen and long wooden bar, where diners can sit and watch the chefs at work. Food is fresh, with seasonal vegetables and fish from local Catalan markets. Fresh oysters and the local tapa favorite *la bomba*, a beef and potato croquette, are offered alongside wild tuna Tataki with seaweed and aged beef steak with foie and truffle sauce.

KINO

Carrer de Ferlandina, 23; tel. 93/179-8409; www. kinobcn.com; daily 11am-2am; €8; Metro: Universitat

This cool terrace in front of the Barcelona Museum of Contemporary Art (MACBA) is an ideal stop for lunch/snack/coffee/wine while you're visiting the museums. KINO's menu is an all-day affair: breakfast, such as satisfyingly tasty breakfast wraps (including vegetarian options) and bagels, is served until 2pm every day. For lunch and dinner, there are burgers, tapas, salads, sandwiches, and meat and fish options—i.e., something for everyone.

International
DOS PALILLOS

Carrer d'Elisabets, 9; tel. 93/304-0513; www. dospalillos.com; Tues-Wed 7:30pm-11:30pm, Thurs-Sat 1:30pm-3:30pm, 7:30pm-11:30pm; tasting menu from €90; Metro: Liceu

Former El Bulli chef Albert Raurich earned a Michelin star for his take on east-meets-west at Dos Palillos, in the cool Casa Camper hotel. The restaurant specializes in the creative fusion of Japanese, Chinese, and other southeast Asian flavors with Spanish produce, so dishes might include fresh Spanish prawns with Asian spices, covered in seaweed as if caught in a net. The front bar area does Asian tapas (no reservations taken), while deeper inside the restaurant, a square bar surrounding an open kitchen is where the real magic happens. Diners opting for the tasting menus (€90 for the 17-course Dos Palillos Menu, or €110 for the 19-course Dos Palillos Festival menu) get a front row seat as chefs grill, steam, and fry an amazing array of ingredients.

FRANKIE GALLO CHA CHA CHA

Carrer del Marquès de Barberà, 15; tel. 93/159-4250; Mon-Thurs 7pm-1:30am, Fri-Sat 1pm-2am, Sun 1pm-1:30am; €12; Metro: Liceu

Neapolitan-style pizzas made in its wood-fired pizza oven are the mainstay at Frankie Gallo Cha Cha Cha, a hip restaurant with a laid-back atmosphere and long, wooden tables set in an old storehouse in the heart of El Raval. The industrial decor matches the cool, young crowd of mainly locals. The sourdough pizzas feature inventive toppings, including truffle, bacon, and smoked salmon.

PASTA MADRE

Carrer dels Tallers, 3; tel. 93/639-4087; Mon-Sun 9am-2am; €3; Plaça de Catalunya

If your tummy is rumbling when visiting Las Ramblas, this small Italian place does a tasty slice as well as pastas, pizzas, and take-out options that will hold you over while you continue your sightseeing. Slices are around €2.50, while meal deals, which include a drink, go for around €4. It's a great, cheap food option when exploring the old heart of the city.

A TU BOLA

Carrer de l'Hospital, 78; tel. 93/315-3244; www. atubolarest.com; €6; Metro: Liceu

This excellent little place in El Raval does its own spin on gourmet street food, centered around all kinds of meats (and veggies) shaped into balls, all made fresh. Vegetarian options include falafel and sweet potato balls, while there are meat versions such as classic beef, Asian-style chicken, and Mexican-style pork. Diners choose a plate, a pita (three balls) or tapa (one ball), and pack into the small dining area to enjoy the flavorsome eats. It's a great budget option. Cards are only accepted on orders over €20.

Breakfast and Brunch
CARAVELLE

Carrer del Pintor Fortuny, 31; tel. 93/317-9892; www.caravelle.es; Mon-Tues 9:30am-5:30pm, Wed-Fri 9:30am-midnight, Sat 10am-midnight, Sun 10am-5:30pm; €12; Metro: Liceu

Close to the Barcelona Museum of Contemporary Art (MACBA), Caravelle is great for brunch, whatever the day of the week. Home-toasted muesli with passion-fruit yogurt, Moroccan-style baked eggs, and coconut French toast with fresh strawberries and ice cream are just some of the dishes on offer. Caravelle's philosophy is that if something can be done in-house, they'll do it; therefore, they make their own sauces, smoke their own pork, and pickle their own vegetables. Arrive early on weekends because it gets busy for brunch. It's a cool location with a mixture of industrial and period features. Its tacos and craft beer are particularly good if you're passing by later in the day.

FLAX AND KALE

Carrer dels Tallers, 74b; tel. 93/317-5664; www. teresacarles.com/fk; Mon-Fri 9am-11:30pm, Sat-Sun 9:30am-11:30pm; breakfasts from €3; Metro: Universitat

"Eat better, be happier, live longer" is the slogan of this restaurant in El Raval, the first "flexitarian" restaurant in Barcelona, which means 80 percent of the menu is plant based while the other 20 percent is fish based. If that all sounds a bit too pretentious, the restaurant itself is a lovely, light-filled, modern space that does breakfast, lunch, and dinner as well as weekend brunch (Sat-Sun 9:30am-5pm). There are lots of delicious vegan and gluten-free options, from gluten-free maple-glazed doughnuts and avocado toast to grilled smoked tofu wraps. There are kids' options on the lunch and dinner menu, too.

Bakeries and Dessert

GRANJA M VIADER

Carrer d'en Xuclà, 4-6; tel. 93/318-3486; www.
granjaviader.cat; Mon-Sat 9am-1:15pm, 5pm-9:15pm;
€4; Metro: Liceu

Now in the fifth generation of ownership by the same family, this *granja* (a dairy-chocolate shop) was opened in 1870 and today still specialises in dairy products. The Viader family invented **Cacaolat**, the most popular chocolate milk in Barcelona, served in a now-iconic glass bottle with yellow label. The tiled floors, marble-topped tables, and wooden chairs take you right back through the decades to when the shop first opened. It's a popular spot for grandparents and grandchildren enjoying an after school treat. Try a hot chocolate with whipped cream (*suís*) for a taste of chocolatey heaven.

CHÖK

Carrer del Carme, 3; tel. 93/304-2360; www.
chokbarcelona.com; daily 9am-9pm; Metro: Liceu

One thing is for sure about Chök—they really love their chocolate. Anyone with a sweet tooth will be stopped in their tracks by the shop's window displays, full of delectable donuts, chocolates, and cronuts (a croissant-donut hybrid). Try the signature chök, the gourmet donut made to the shop's special recipe with less sugar and fat, making it a lighter—if no less indulgent—bite. Donuts range from €3-€4, and you can can sit in the small café at the back or take away.

LA RIBERA AND EL BORN

Catalan and Spanish

ELDISET

Carrer Antic de Sant Joan, 3; tel. 93/268-1987; www.
eldiset.com; Mon-Fri 7pm-3am, Sat-Sun 1pm-3am;
€8; Metro: Barceloneta

With its cool, Scandinavian-inspired interior with light wood and low-hanging lights, Eldiset is a stylish wine bar and restaurant that does creative toasts and tapas. Friendly staff and a cozy atmosphere make it a romantic spot for couples, or a cozy hangout among friends. Try some local Catalan wines and opt for food from the cold, hot, or classic tapas menus. Options include hummus, spicy sausage and goat cheese, wild asparagus, croquettes, and cheese and ham boards.

Tapas

TAPEO

Carrer de Montcada, 29; tel. 93/310-1607; www.
tapeoborn.cat; daily midday-midnight; €10; Metro:
Arc de Triomf

This charming tapas bar is just down from the Picasso Museum. The long bar area is dotted with high tables and stools, lending it a laid-back vibe. Although in a touristy area, the bar is just as popular with locals, and run by a friendly husband-and-wife team. Traditional Catalan dishes like Fideuà sit alongside more innovative and seasonal tapas, like chicken legs with soy and ginger and beef sweetbreads with wild mushrooms, bone marrow, and figs.

EUSKAL ETXEA

Calle de Jovellanos, 3; tel. 91/531-4593; Mon-Fri
9:30am-midnight, Sat 11am-midnight; €4; Metro:
Barceloneta

This Basque tavern, at the front of the Euskal Etxea Basque community center, does pintxos—Basque tapas—the traditional way, all lined up on the bar top. Simply take a plate and choose what you want; the toothpicks holding your pintxos will be counted at the end to see how many you had. It's a stand-up kind of place and can get very busy, so aim for an early (midday or 7pm-ish) bite to beat the crowds, although they are often part of the atmosphere and the full "pintxo bar" experience.

BAR DEL PLA

Carrer de Montcada, 2; tel. 93/268-3003; www.
bardelpla.cat; Mon-Thurs midday-11pm, Fri-Sat
midday-midnight; €7; Metro: Jaume I

This tapas bar is beloved by locals for its fresh, seasonal tapas that include octopus bombs, squid in ink croquettes, and classics like Catalan sausage, beef cheek, and *callos* (tripe

Tasting Tapas

The concept of tapas is now one that is known all over the world, with tapas restaurants from Tokyo to Toronto—but Spain is where it all originated. The word *tapas* comes from the Spanish word *tapar*, to cover. There are several theories about the origin of tapas. One story goes that, hundreds of years ago, Spanish inns and bars would serve a bite to eat on a piece of bread, which visitors would use to cover their glasses to keep the flies out—hence the name "to cover." This bread "tapa," or lid, was usually topped with some ham, chorizo, or cheese.

tapa

TAPAS BARS AND RESTAURANTS

In a traditional **tapas bar,** no reservations are necessary, and patrons order from and are served at the bar. In a **tapas restaurant,** which could well be a more formal area at the back of a more informal bar, patrons tend to sit down and are served by a waiter or waitress.

A **Basque pintxo bar** is a different experience. Here, *pintxos* (Basque tapas, served on a slice of bread) are all laid out on the bar-top, so diners can see what is on offer and choose what they want. *"Pintxo,"* which literally means "spike," refers to the toothpick that usually holds the *pintxo* in place on the bread.

ORDERING TAPAS

Tapas can be either hot or cold. A single tapa or a single *pintxo* is traditionally a small individual serving for one person. A *ración*, which you might also see on tapas menus, is a larger plate meant for sharing (for example, a ración of squid will be a larger plate to share).

The price of tapas differs, depending on the dish and the tapas bar—traditional bars with basic décor and a local clientele will be much cheaper than the latest trendy opening. As a rule, you can probably expect tapas dishes to be under €10.

While you can get some excellent tapas in Barcelona, the city is not renowned for its freebies. Unlike cities in the south of the country (and even Madrid), Barcelona bars are unlikely to offer punters a free tapa with a drink—if they are on offer, they will often be at an extra cost.

TYPICAL TAPAS

Typical tapas to order in Barcelona include a *bomba* (a meat-filled, round potato croquette drizzled in spicy brava sauce), *patatas bravas* (potatos in the same spicy sauce), *croquetas* (croquettes filled with different ingredients and bechamel sauce) and, of course, seafood like anchovies and *chipirones* (deep-fried baby squid).

stew). The narrow room with vaulted ceilings has a long bar on the left-hand side and high tables and stools to the right; it opens out into a wider dining area at the back.

International
MOSQUITO

Carrer dels Carders, 46; tel. 93/268-7569; www.mosquitotapas.com/mosquito; Tues-Sun 1pm-midnight, Mon 6pm-midnight; €4; Metro: Arc de Triomf

The place for Chinese dumplings in Barcelona, Mosquito has cornered the market in "Asian tapas" at this cool bar/restaurant in La Ribera. Alongside the dumplings on the menu are noodles, soups, and vegetable dishes. It also stocks a good range of craft beers. Its over 20 tapas options are a mix of Asian classics including Vietnamese pho, steamed pork dumplings, and noodles with smoked duck.

Breakfast and Brunch
ELSA Y FRED
Carrer del Rec Comtal, 11; tel. 93/501-6611; www. elsayfred.es; €7; Metro: Arc de Triomf
Sink into a leather armchair and soak in the cozy living room surroundings of this cool café/bar in the Ribera neighborhood. It's a great place for a relaxed breakfast (options include tomato bread and eggs) or a huge weekend brunch. By night, cool locals pack in to sink a few beers and cocktails to the cool jazz and indie-rock soundtrack.

★ PICNIC
Carrer del Comerç, 1; tel. 93/511-6661; www. picnic-restaurant.com; Mon-Fri 10:30am-4pm, Sat-Sun 10:30am-5pm, Wed-Sat 8pm-Midnight; €10; Metro: Arc de Triomf
This bright, modern café is a buzzing brunch spot popular with cool locals of all ages (young families, couples, and groups of friends) and in-the-know travelers. The Chilean-American hybrid does incredible quinoa hash browns (order them as a side and you won't regret it). Pancakes are fluffy and stacked high, covered in strawberries and syrup, while the veggie eggs are served with fried green tomatoes. Ingredients are fresh and the whole place is filled with mouth-wateringly good smells from the open kitchen.

THE WATERFRONT
The waterfront area of Barcelona is one of the best places in the city to try seafood, whether that comes in the form of fried fish in a laid-back local tapas bar or a feast of seafood paella for a big family lunch.

Catalan and Spanish
RESTAURANT 7 PORTES
Passeig d'Isabel II, 14; tel. 93/319-3033; www.7portes. com; daily 1pm-1am; €20; Metro: Barceloneta
Founded in 1836 as a café, 7 Portes was turned into a restaurant in 1929 and soon became a Barcelona classic, attracting artists, writers, and politicians for its take on traditional Catalan cuisine. Named after its seven doors, its history is preserved in its checkerboard floors, wooden-beamed ceilings, tiled walls, and little plaques showing where famous diners once sat. It is famous for its paellas, but also does excellent seafood.

EL XIRINGUITO ESCRIBÀ
Av. del Litoral, 62; tel. 93/221-0729; www. xiringuitoescriba.com; daily 1pm-10:30pm; €22; Metro: Ciutadella | Vila Olímpica
This beachside restaurant is a local favorite for one of Spain's most famous dishes: paella. Eat it at lunchtime, as Spaniards do. There are lots of different varieties to choose from, including seafood, black rice paella, and green vegetable paella. Many are also available as *fideuà*, a take on paella popular in Barcelona that uses thin noodles instead of rice. There are plenty of appetizing starters to tuck into while you wait for the paella, including fried cod, squid, sardines, and prawns. It is located between the beaches of Nova Icària and Mar Bella, a 10-minute stroll north from La Barceloneta.

CAN MAJO
Carrer de l'Almirall Aixada, 23; tel. 93/221-5455; www.canmajo.es; Tues-Sat 1pm-3:30pm, 8pm-11:30pm, Sun 1pm-3:30pm; €20; Metro: Barceloneta
With its outdoor terrace set at the edge of Barceloneta beach, Can Majo has been a popular local spot to dig into some of the city's freshest seafood since it opened in the 1960s. The *caldero de arroz con Bogavante* (a lobster-and-rice dish) is a house speciality, as well as paellas, seafood platters, and fried fish that give diners the change to sample a whole range of fresh local seafood.

Tapas
★ LA COVA FUMADA
Carrer del Baluart, 56; tel. 93/221-4061; Mon-Wed 9am-3:15pm, Thurs-Fri 9am-3:15pm, 6pm-8pm, Sat 9am-1pm; €3; Metro: Barceloneta
Opened in 1944, this legendary family-run tapas bar close to the port is said to be where

the *bomba*, a breaded and fried ball of potato filled with pork or beef that is a staple on Catalan tapas menus, was invented. Little has since changed in the bar, with its old blackboard, marble-topped tables, and no-frills atmosphere. The bar may not be much to look at, but people come here for the food: fresh seafood (prawns, squid, octopus, sardines served with olive oil), fried artichokes, *butifarra* (Catalan sausage), and *bacalao* (salt cod).

PALMITO

Carrer de Ramon Trias Fargas, 2-4; tel. 93/224-0407; www.encompaniadelobos.com/en/palmito; daily midday-3am; €8; Metro: Ciutadella / Vila Olímpica

In front of the Port Olímpic, this laid-back beach bar has tables under palm trees (great shade in the summertime) with views out onto the sea. Drinks include juices, smoothies, and cocktails (€10), while tapas include croquettes, *patatas bravas*, and Galician-style octopus. There is also a range of salads and main courses, including club sandwiches, hamburgers, and chipotle chicken tacos. It attracts a cool, diverse crowd.

CAN RECASENS

Rambla del Poblenou, 102; tel. 93/300-8123; Mon 8:30am-1:30pm, 5pm-11:45pm, Tues-Thurs 8:30am-1:30pm, 5pm-1am, Fri 8:30am-1:30pm, 5pm-3am, Sat 9am-1pm, 9pm-3am, Sun 9pm-1am; €12; Metro: Poblenou

Deli by day, cozy and romantic dinner spot by night, Can Recasens has several interconnected rooms decorated with fairy lights. It is a temple to two beloved Spanish products: ham and cheese. Opt for a cheese board or a plate of *jamón Ibérico* or go really cheesy with a fondue. Rambla del Poblenou is located in the Poble Nou neighborhood, just behind the seafront. Reservations are a must on weekends; it tends to be slightly quieter during the week.

International
MAKAMAKA BEACH BURGER CAFÉ

Passeig de Joan de Borbó, 76; tel. 93/221-3520; www.makamaka.es; Mon-Thurs midday-midnight,

Fri midday-2:30am, Sat 11am-2:30am, Sun 11am-midnight; €8; Metro: Barceloneta

This laid-back beach bar channels 1970s vibes and serves up a crowd-pleasing menu of burgers, beers, cocktails, and smoothies. Try the burgers, including the Hot Mama (a beef burger with smoked Scamorza cheese and homemade spicy cream-cheese sauce) and the vegetarian Mr Nice Guy (a soya burger with avocado, red pepper, mozzarella, and mango sauce). The outdoor terrace with deck chairs is the ideal place to kick back on a sunny day.

THE GREEN SPOT

Carrer de la Reina Cristina, 12; tel. 93/802-5565; www.encompaniadelobos.com/the-green-spot; daily 1pm-midnight; €15; Metro: Barceloneta

This modern restaurant with wooden furnishings is a creative and stylish vegetarian option close to the beach. It bills itself as "veggie for non-veggies," i.e., the food is just so good that even the most committed carnivore will relish it. The extensive menu covers aperitifs (kale chips, mini corn satay, nachos), salads and soups, pasta, rice, pizza, and dishes from around the world, including kimchi and avocado quesadilla, black bean burger with pretzel bread, and tofu and mushroom bao.

Bakeries and Dessert
★ BALUARD BAKERY

Carrer del Baluard, 38; tel. 93/221-1208; www.baluardbarceloneta.com; Mon-Sat 8am-9pm; €2; Metro: Barceloneta

Known for baking some of the best bread in Barcelona, Baluard is beloved by locals for its excellent loaves at affordable prices. Founded by fourth-generation breadmaker Anna Bellsolà, Baluard is a simple bakery that, at its core, is all about excellent bread, baked in wood-fired ovens. A great place to stock up on provisions for a beach picnic, it also sells sweet items like fruit tarts, brioche, and brownies. Try the Barceloneta, a long-fermented loaf sprinkled with Atlantic sea salt.

EIXAMPLE

Of all the central neighborhoods in Barcelona, Eixample is home to some of the most expensive restaurants. It offers relatively affordable options, but dining prices at many of its restaurants tend to be on the more expensive side.

Catalan and Spanish

★ DISFRUTAR

Carrer de Villarroel, 163; tel. 93/348-6896; www. ca.disfrutarbarcelona.com; Mon-Fr 1:30pm-2:30pm, 8pm-9:30pm; €120; Metro: Hospital Clínic

Led by a trio of chefs from legendary Spanish restaurant el Bulli—Mateu Casañas, Oriol Castro, and Eduard Xatruch—this modern Mediterranean restaurant is a creative journey of the senses, and fully deserves its two Michelin stars. There are three tasting menus, ranging from €120-€185. A wine pairing, also available at an extra price, selects around 14 wines with the courses. Highlights include olives that burst in the mouth with a concentrated flavor, a "smoked cider" made at the table using liquid nitrogen, and a spherified corn on the cob that tastes more like corn than anything you've ever tasted. The dining area, with its clean white walls and huge windows and skylights, features an open kitchen and big windows looking out onto a terrace, where diners can have an aperitif. Disfrutar can also adapt its tasting menus for vegetarian or pescatarian diners. Reservations, made far in advance, are essential, and the restaurant will contact you via email two days before your date to confirm your reservation. Make sure you do confirm, or it will be canceled. Staff are friendly, and the atmosphere is refreshingly relaxed for a fine dining experience.

MORDISCO

Passatge de la Concepció, 10; tel. 93/487-9656; www. grupotragaluz.com/en/restaurant/mordisco; €12; Metro: Diagonal

Set in a leafy conservatory on a cute little street just off the Passeig de Gràcia, Mordisco is a favorite of cool locals for its fresh, seasonal produce and creative dishes. A vegetarian-heavy menu is both a novelty and a welcome surprise in Spain, and Mordisco gives dishes a special extra sparkle. The menu is split into appetizers, starters, rice and pasta, and meat and fish dishes, but most are designed to share, so come with a group and try a little of everything. Highlights include the seasonal charcoal grilled artichokes, vegan tacos, and charcoal tuna and babaganoush. The kitchen

Disfrutar

is open all day, so it's also a good option for a bite to eat outside traditional dining hours.

LASARTE

Carrer de Mallorca, 259; tel. 93/445-3242; www.restaurantlasarte.com; Tues-Sat 1:30pm-3:30pm, 8:30pm-11pm; €55, tasting menu €235; Metro: Diagonal

In the heart of the high-end Eixample, the three-Michelin-starred Lasarte is one of Barcelona's top fine-dining experiences. Basque chef Martin Berasategui earned his third Michelin star for this restaurant in 2017. Diners, who sit in a clean, modern dining room with light wood walls and floor, can order a la carte (mains are around €55, including sea bass with mantis shrimp broth and charcoal grilled pigeon with citrus and black olive) or opt for the tasting menu (€235). Dress code includes long trousers and closed shoes, and while there is no doubt this is fine dining, there is no stuffy atmosphere here.

MOMENTS

Passeig de Gràcia, 38-40; tel. 93/151-8781; www.mandarinoriental.com/barcelona/passeig-de-gracia/fine-dining/restaurants/catalan-cuisine/moments; Tues-Sat 1:30pm-3:30pm, 8:30pm-10:30pm; €176 tasting menu; Metro: Passeig de Gràcia

Spanish chef Carme Ruscalleda has already won seven Michelin stars for her restaurants in Spain and Tokyo, and Moments, which she runs alongside her son, Raül Balam, has two. Both an a la carte and tasting menu are on offer, based around seasonal Catalan cuisine. The Ecosystems tasting menu (€176) takes diners through the different ecosystems of the planet, while main courses are around €56. The dining room is elegant, with amber hues and a large window onto the kitchen that gives diners a glimpse of the action.

BICNIC

Carrer de Girona, 68; tel. 69/090-4614; www.bicnic.com; Tues-Sat 1:30pm-3:30pm, 8:30pm-11pm; €19; Metro: Girona

A gastronomic picnic awaits at this cool restaurant, which started life as a food truck. The front "Fast Bar" does some of the food-truck classics and is aimed at more casual diners who want to perch on a stool and enjoy a few tapas or small dishes. (Dishes include marinated squid, croquettes, falafel, and lentils with foie). At the back, the "Slow Restaurant" is a more relaxed area where diners can take their time and enjoy a full meal. The menu has starters designed to share, including a porchetta platter and roasted chicken salad, and main courses including veal cheek and monkfish with green onions.

Tapas

KSEROL

Carrer de Nàpols, 184-186; tel. 93/639-3342; www.kserol.com; Mon 9am-6pm, Tues-Sat 9am-midnight; €10; Metro: Monumental

This great tapas bar, run by a Frenchman, does breakfasts, *menus del día*, and nighttime tapas in a stylish atmosphere, with prices that won't break the bank (a welcome fact in the usually pricey Eixample). The three-course *menu del día*, which changes on a weekly basis, is a bargain at €12.90. Tapas feature Spanish favorites, like croquettes, alongside more international flavors, from French paté to nachos. It's a friendly spot with a neighborhood feel to it.

BICOS

Avenida Diagonal, 287; tel. 93/611-8227; www.bicosrestaurante.com; Tues-Sun 12:30pm-4pm, Tues-Thurs 7pm-11pm, Fri-Sat 7pm-midnight; €12; Metro: Monumental

This stylish restaurant three blocks from the Sagrada Familia specializes in the cuisine of Galicia in northwest Spain, and has a buzzing, local feel of somewhere just off the beaten track. Typical dishes include fresh octopus with bread and olive oil, Galician *empanadas* (a filled pastry), and *raxo*, a Galician dish of peppery pork. There are interesting fusions, too, like the Portuguese-style cod tacos. What all dishes have in common is excellent ingredients, prepared simply and lovingly to get the very best out of them. Wash down your meal with a glass of crisp Albariño, a white wine from Galicia.

BETLEM MISCELLÀNIA GASTRONÒMICA

Carrer de Girona, 70; tel. 93/265-5105; www.betlem. es; Sun-Wed 9am-midnight, Thurs-Sat 9am-1:30am; €10; Metro: Girona

Chef Victor Ferrer makes local ingredients really sing in his range of creative tapas at this lovely bar/restaurant. Its outdoor terrace brings to mind Parisian sidewalks; it's the ideal place to indulge in some people watching. Try the lovingly made tapas, including king crab ravioli with coconut and lime, artichokes, and Spanish omelette with black Catalan sausage and mushrooms.

SENYOR VERMUT

Carrer de Provença, 85; tel. 93/532-8865; Tues-Wed 6pm-11pm, Thurs midday-4pm, 6pm-11pm, Fri-Sat midday-11pm, Sun midday-4pm; €5; Metro: Hospital Clínic

A great spot for a vermouth aperitif and some tapas, this is a reasonably priced option in Eixample, a neighborhood that often veers towards the expensive. With *patatas bravas* under €3 (practically unheard of in Barcelona), homemade croquettes, and a lively atmosphere, it's a great place to start a night in the Eixample.

International
RESTAURANT MARGHERITA

Carrer del Rosselló, 253; tel. 93/611-5667; Mon-Sat 11am-midnight, Sun 11:30am-11:30pm; €15; Metro: Diagonal

The friendly staff and modern, exposed-brick interior make this Italian restaurant in the Eixample a cozy place to grab dinner. The menu includes Neapolitan-style pizzas, homemade pasta, and a selection of daily specials. This restaurant attracts locals and tourists alike, and the romantic atmosphere makes it ideal for a date.

Bakeries and Dessert
★ MAURI

Carrer de Provença, 241; tel. 93/215-1020; www. pasteleriasmauri.com; daily 8am-10pm; Metro: Diagonal

This classic local bakery was founded in 1929 and retains a refined feel. Its counters are filled with beautiful-looking baked goods, both sweet and savory, ideal for breakfast or an afternoon snack. You can order to take out or sit in the café, where your order will be loaded onto a card that you take to the till near the door to pay at the end of your meal. Try an *ensaimada* (€1.25), a sweet pastry originally from Mallorca that's a local favorite, and wash it down with a *café con leche* (coffee with milk). Late mornings attract an older crowd, who catch up on the newspaper with a leisurely coffee.

GRÀCIA AND PARK GÜELL
Catalan and Spanish
CAFÉ SALAMBO

Carrer de Torrijos, 51; tel. 93/218-6966; www. cafesalambo.com; Mon-Thurs midday-1am, Fri-Sat midday-3am, Sun- midday-midnight; €13; Metro: Joanic

The grand, wood-clad café attracts a mixed clientele of young and old, be it for the tasty *menu del día* (€13), afternoon coffee, or a drink to discuss the latest arthouse flick at the nearby cinema. The café's relaxed, friendly vibe makes it a great stop, whatever the time of day. The food menu is a mixture of Spanish classics, like *patatas bravas*, and international flavors like tuna tataki and beef bourguignon.

LA PUBILLA

Plaça de la Llibertat, 23; tel. 93/218-2994; www.lapubilla.cat; Mon 8:30am-5pm, Tues-Fri 8:30am-midnight, Sat 9am-midnight; €16; Metro: Gràcia

This local favorite, with an unassuming exterior, does market-fresh Catalan cuisine accompanied by great wine. Chef Alexis Peñalver celebrates traditional local flavors and elevates grandma-style cooking into something that—while having a bit more panache—still gives diners that comforting feeling of a great, home-cooked meal. Try Catalan classics like *esqueixada* (shredded cod salad) and—when in season—grilled calçots, or try the weekend brunch or weekday *menu del día*.

Tapas
GATA MALA
Carrer de Rabassa, 37; tel. 63/639-3610; Tues-Sat 6:30pm-midnight; €8; Metro: Joanic

This great little tapas bar offers something practically unheard-of in Barcelona . . . a free tapa with every drink ordered. Staff are friendly, and the buzzing atmosphere (it's usually packed) contributes to a great—and cheap—selection of tapas, from little toasts topped with cheese and morcilla (blood sausage/black pudding) to plates of local hams and cheeses.

LA PEPITA
Carrer de Còrsega, 343; tel. 93/238-4893; Sun-Mon 7:30pm-midnight, Tues-Sat 1pm-4:30pm, 7:30pm-midnight; €9; Metro: Diagonal

This popular tapas bar straddles the Eixample and Gràcia neighborhoods. Try the "Pepitas," their version of the pepito pork sandwich, accompanied with some delicious *patatas bravas*. The small space means it's better for couples or smaller groups. The restaurant does not take reservations, so get there early to grab a table. La Pepita has a little sister a couple of doors down, *vermutería* (vermouth bar) **La Cava** (Carrer de Còrsega, 339; 93/348-3909), a packed, long bar that is a great place to start the night with a vermouth.

International
LA TAQUERIA
Passatge de Font, 5; tel. 93/126-1359; www.lataqueria.eu; Tues-Sun 1pm-4:30pm, 8:30pm-11:30pm, Fri-Sat 1pm-4:30pm, 8:30pm-midnight; €7; Metro: Sagrada Familia

A couple of blocks from the Sagrada Familia, this buzzing local Mexican spot does Mexican street-food-style dishes for a reasonable price. Inside is an explosion of color; the bright green and pink walls make a lively backdrop to spicy dishes like tacos and quesadillas.

CHIVUO'S
Carrer del Torrent de l'Olla, 175; tel. 93/218-5134; www.chivuos.com; Mon-Sat 1pm-5pm, 7pm-midnight; €8; Metro: Lesseps

Slow street food and craft beer are the name of the game at this cool Gràcia restaurant (with other branches in Eixample and Raval). It specializes in big, satisfying burgers and sandwiches, including the Chivuo's burger with caramelized onions and bacon, pulled pork with bbq, and Philly cheese steak (all €8). There's also a good selection of craft beers.

Bakeries and Dessert
LA BESNÉTA
Carrer de Torrijos, 37; tel. 93/415-3839; www.labesneta.com; Tues-Sun 10:30am-9pm, Mon 10:30am-5:30pm; Metro: Joanic

It's no surprise that the trendy Gràcia neighborhood is home to Barcelona's first vegan bakery. Inspired by her Argentine great-grandmother, owner Daniela combines Argentinian and Catalan flavors to make a mouth-watering array of vegan baked goods, including cakes, biscuits, pastries, and cookies. The friendly owner and amazing array of sweet treats will leave you wanting to come back for more.

A CASA PORTUGUESA
Carrer de l'Or, 8; tel. 93/021-8803; daily 10:30am-9pm; www.acasaportuguesa.com; Metro: Fontana

This cute shop specializes in Portuguese produce and has a tempting baked-goods section at the front. Their *pasteis de nata* (Portuguese custard tarts) are a must-try; they also offer savory options, like quiche, that make good on-the-go lunches. Portuguese cherry liquor Ginginja is delicious.

MONTJUÏC, POBLE SEC, AND SANT ANTONI
Catalan and Spanish
★ TICKETS

Av. del Paral·lel, 164; tel. 93/292-4252; www. ticketsbar.es; Tues-Fri 7:30pm-10:30pm, Sat 1pm-3pm, 7pm-10:30pm; €14; Metro: Poble Sec

This tapas bar, opened by Albert and Ferran Adrià, formerly of El Bulli, is the hottest ticket in town and one of the world's best restaurants. It is a laid-back and (mercifully) affordable affair that puts the fun back in dining. With its circus-themed dining room and creative takes on Spanish and international cuisine, dinner becomes theater, with diners interpreting each new dish as they would a performance. The food is a mixture of world flavors and Catalan classics, and individual dishes are surprisingly affordable considering the pedigree of the chefs. Simple dish names bely the complexity and creativity of the offerings. Highlights include Tickets' take on the classic El Bulli dish of the spherified olive (€2.50 each), crunchy suckling pig taco with hoisin mayonnaise and pickled cucumber, and crunchy octopus with kimchi mayonnaise and Tickets' cucumber (€17.80). Making reservations online, as far in advance as possible, is a must—the waiting list has been known to run for months.

BODEGA 1900

Carrer de Tamarit, 91; tel. 93/325-2659; www. bodega1900.com; Tues-Sat 1pm-4pm, 7pm-10:30pm; €12; Metro: Poble Sec

Adventurous eaters will love this place, run by the famed Adrià brothers, located just over the road from their more famous restaurant, Tickets. In Bodega 1900, the brothers pay homage to Barcelona's traditional vermuterías (vermouth bodegas), where locals traditionally went for a glass of the popular fortified wine and some small plates. This blast-from-the-past restaurant takes diners through early-20th-century flavors, with salted, preserved, and chargrilled products. Sea urchins and cured cow tongue sit alongside Spanish cheeses and cured hams, squid, and chargrilled leeks. There's a touch of the modern, too; they serve the Adriàs' famous spherified olives, a burst-in-the-mouth surprise. Reservations recommended.

Tapas
★ QUIMET Y QUIMET

Carrer del Poeta Cabanyes, 25; tel. 93/442-3142; Mon-Fri midday-4pm, 7pm-10:30pm; €2.50; Metro: Paral·lel

Lines form outside this standing-room-only bar in Poble Sec before it even opens because of its century-old charm and tasty tapas. It opened as a shop selling homemade wine in 1914, and today it's still in the same family. Behind the bar, shelves are filled with wine and spirit bottles and tins of conserves. It specializes in *montaditos* (€2.50)—bread topped with a huge range of options, like baby squid and onion and foie gras with volcanic salt—made by Quim, the great-grandson of the original owner.

Cafés
BAR SECO

Passeig de Montjuïc, 74; tel. 93/329-6374; www. bar-seco.com, Tues-Sun 9am-5pm; €10; Metro: Paral·lel

In the shadow of Montjuïc hill, this popular neighborhood bar is a cool chill-out spot whether you're looking for a satisfying brunch, a lazy afternoon coffee, or some delicious burgers and craft beers. There's an outdoor terrace and a healthy, seasonal menu of crowd-pleasing dishes and snacks.

Breakfast and Brunch
FEDERAL CAFÉ

Carrer del Parlament, 39; tel. 93/187-3607; www. federalcafe.es/barcelona; Mon-Thurs 8am-11pm, Fri 8am-1am, Sat 9am-1am, Sun 9am-5:30pm; €8; Metro: Poble Sec

This hip breakfast and brunch place in the cool Sant Antoni area was founded by Australians (the country that, aptly, invented the "flat white," a popular accompaniment to breakfast). Get there early for weekend brunch, because it fills up early. There's a huge range of tempting dishes, from the virtuous fruit bowls and avocado toast to the decadent morning bacon burger, French toast, and pancakes.

Bakeries and Dessert
ORXATERIA SIRVENT

Carrer del Parlament de Catalunya, 56; tel. 93/441-2720; www.turronessirvent.com; daily 9am-9pm; Metro: Poble Sec

Since 1920, the Sirvent family has been creating thick, sweet *Orxata* (Horchata), a refreshing drink originally from Valencia, made from tiger nuts and delicious *turrón*, a Spanish kind of nougat. Their little bar, with its stainless-steel counter, stools, and huge pictures of the ice-creams also on offer, is a great stop for a sweet pick-me-up or for dessert; it has been a local children's favorite treat spot for decades.

BEYOND THE CENTER
Tapas
LAS DELICIAS DEL CARMELO

Carrer de Mühlberg, 1; tel. 93/429-2202; www.barrestaurantedelicias.com; Tues-Sun 10am-4pm, Tues-Thurs 7pm-10:30pm, Fri-Sat 8pm-11pm; €8; Metro: El Carmel

This authentic tapas bar and restaurant is a local favorite and serves up heaped plates of *patatas bravas* (potatos with a spicy sauce), fried squid, and Galician-style octopus. It's a great spot for a family lunch, and its location, close to the out-of-the-way Carmel Bunkers, makes it a good stop-off point between Park Güell and the popular lookout point. Plus, you'll need to fuel up before walking up the hill to the bunkers.

LA MUNDANA

Carrer del Vallespir, 93; tel. 93/408-8023; www.lamundana.cat; daily 1pm-3:30pm, 8pm-11:30pm; €12; Metro: Sants-Estació

Part *vermutería*, part modern tapas restaurant, La Mundana fuses Catalan and Mediterranean ingredients and flavors with Japanese and French influences to create inventive tapas dishes that are hard to forget. It offers 14 different types of vermouth paired with specific dishes. Tapas are divided into cold and hot, including Korean ribs, pulled pork ravioli, and "Asian-style" calamari. The interiors are modern and stylish, with funky wallpaper and vintage-style seltzer bottles to top up your vermouth. It's between Sants train station and Camp Nou, making it a handy option for a tasty meal if you're catching a train or an FC Barcelona match.

Bars and Nightlife

Barcelona is a city renowned for its nightlife, and whatever your cup of tea—from a chill evening in a local bar to classy rooftop cocktails—the city has you covered.

Nightlife in Barcelona is inextricably linked with food; going to a local *bodega* (wine shop) for some wine and cheese, hitting a few tapas bars, or trying out a great new opening is the locals' favorite way to spend a night out. Barcelona's bodegas, from decades-old traditional joints that seem to have changed barely at all to a new breed of modern bodegas mixing vintage with hip new trends, get to the heart of what makes Barcelona so enjoyable. They are laid-back, welcoming, and have been at the center of the city's social fabric for decades. Pop in for a rustic spread of meats, cheeses, simple tapas, and, often, wine straight from the barrel.

Barcelona is surrounded by Spain's cava-producing region, and the sparkling wine is one of the most popular aperitifs in the city. The city is also home to some vintage cava bars, where locals pack in for a glass of the (surpringly reasonable) bubbly.

NIGHTLIFE DISTRICTS

Barri Gòtic

Las Ramblas is a buzzing area whatever the time of day (and thronging with people by night); however, it's a very touristy spot, so it's best to weave into the warren-like streets of the Barri Gòtic rather than to stick to Las Ramblas. Here, you'll find stylish cocktail bars, hip grungy bars closer to the seafront, and, around **Plaça Reial**, some great live music venues and clubs.

El Raval

What was once known as the seedy underbelly of Barcelona has done a lot to clean up its act, but some bars that hark back to its bohemian past are still going strong, like the absinthe-soaked Bar Marsella, and Casa Almirall, which opened in 1860 on **Carrer de Joaquín Costa** (now a strip of hip bars patronized by cool, young locals).

El Born

In the south of the neighborhood of La Ribera, El Born is one of Barcelona's most stylish nightlife spots, packed with hip creatives following in the footsteps of artists like Pablo Picasso, whose museum is now located in the area. Its medieval lanes are packed with wine and tapas bars, and there's a cool, laid-back vibe.

Eixample

The wide boulevards of the Eixample are home to some of Barcelona's most exclusive restaurants and bars. It might be high-end, but there are plenty of accessible, interesting places to visit, from acclaimed cocktail bars to underground electronic clubs and rooftop bars with incredible views over the city. The area between Passeig de Gràcia and Diagonal metros, either side of the main **Passeig de Gràcia** street, is home to cocktail bars and some cool hotel rooftops.

Gràcia

What was once a village on the outskirts of the city (before it was gobbled up at the end of the 19th century) retains its small-town feel. This is the place to come for laid-back evenings on the local square, **Plaça de la Vila de Gràcia**, or to check out its huge range of bars, from historic bodegas to chic cocktail bars.

Montjuïc

Below Montjuïc hill, two neighborhoods are really making a name for themselves as Barcelona's trendiest nightlife spots: **Poble Sec** and **Sant Antoni**. In Poble Sec, head to the bar-lined **Carrer de Blai** for drinks and tapas. The tree-lined streets of the formerly quiet Sant Antoni, on the border of the Eixample, are now some of the coolest in the city. Check out **Carrer del Parlament** for craft beers and a relaxed vibe.

BARS

Las Ramblas and Barri Gòtic

L'ASCENSOR

Carrer de Bellafila, 3; tel. 93/318-5347; Sun-Thurs 6pm-2:30am, Fri-Sat 6pm-3am; Metro: Jaume I

Slide the elevator door to enter L'Ascensor (The Elevator), an atmospheric cocktail bar down a little side street in the Barri Gòtic. Patrons are a mixture of ages, everyone seeking a relaxed night and sinking back into the red velvet banquettes. Low lighting gives a romantic air and the extensive cocktail list has something for every taste.

ELS QUATRE GATS

Carrer de Montsió, 3; tel. 93/302-4140; www.4gats. com; daily 9am-midnight; Metro: Jaume I

The hub of Barcelona intellectual and artistic life at the turn of the 20th century, this storied old tavern was a favorite hangout of Pablo Picasso and Catalan artist Ramon Casas, who paid for the interior decor. Casas also painted "Ramon Cases and Pere Romeu on a Tandem," which depicts the painter and one of the café's promoters riding a bike (a copy now hangs above the bar; the original is in the National Art Museum of Catalonia). The café, set in Casa Martí, a Modernista building designed by architect Josep Puig i Cadafalch, opened in 1897 and organized literary discussions (known as *tertulias*) and art exhibitions, including Picasso's first one-man show. Closed due to financial difficulties in 1903, it was restored to its former glory in the 1980s. Today, while somewhat of a tourist haunt, you can still get a sense of the café's history over a coffee or beer in its atmospheric bar, with high ceilings, yellow walls, and some furniture designed by Puig i Cadafalch.

BAR MANCHESTER
Carrer de Milans, 5; tel. 62/773-3081; Mon 6:30pm-midnight, Tues-Wed 6:30pm-2:30pm, Thurs-Fri 6:30pm-3am, Sat-Sun 6:30pm-2:30am; Metro: Jaume I

Bar Manchester, founded by a couple of Chilean friends, pays homage to all the great bands that have come out of the northern English city of Manchester. Young Catalan regulars come here to listen to the likes of The Stone Roses, Joy Division, and The Smiths spinning on the decks. It's even had some of the big names of the period, like Mani from the Stone Roses, pop in for a beer. Its grungy, laid-back atmosphere, with records decorating the walls and low lighting, is ideal for a chilled-out drink.

POLAROID
Carrer dels Còdols, 29; tel. 93/186-6669; www. polaroidbar.es; Sun-Thurs 7:30pm-2:30am, Fri-Sat 7:30pm-3am; Metro: Jaume I

Polaroid bar prizes fun above all else, with good drinks and décor that includes old film posters, video cassettes, and action-figure displays that hark back to the 80s. It also hosts regular film nights, and gives out popcorn with drinks, adding to the vintage movie-theater vibe. Prices are low, and the crowd is a laid-back mixture of locals and visitors.

SOR RITA
Carrer de la Mercè, 27; tel. 93/176-6266; www. sorritabar.es; Sun-Thurs 7:30pm-2:30am, Fri-Sat 7:30pm-3am; Metro: Jaume I

The queen of kitsch, Sor Rita's decor is a leopard print, high-heeled homage to the Spanish

film director Pedro Almodóvar. Stilettos jut out like stalactites from the ceilings, while Barbies in an array of positions make for interesting decorative touches. Try a mojito as you take in the wonderfully over-the-top surroundings.

BOADAS BAR
Carrer dels Tallers, 1; tel. 93/318-9592; www. boadascocktails.com; Mon-Thurs midday-2am, Fri-Sat midday-3am; Metro: Catalunya

Barcelona's oldest cocktail bar, just off the Ramblas, opened its doors in 1933 and counted the likes of Joan Miró and Ernest Hemingway as regulars. These days, it's undoubtedly a tourist favorite, but also has the power to transport you back in time with its dark wood interiors. The small, triangular-shaped bar area can get packed.

GINGER
Carrer de la Palma de Sant Just, 1; tel. 93/024-3152; Tues-Thurs 6:30pm-2:30am, Fri-Sat 6:30pm-3am; Metro: Jaume I

This great cocktail bar in the old town features Art Deco interiors, leather armchairs, and a range of tapas dishes. A favorite of thirty-something-plus locals, it's an elegant stop for a late-night cocktail.

El Raval
BAR MARSELLA
Carrer de Sant Pau, 65; tel. 93/442-7263; Mon 6pm-2am, Tues-Sun 10am-2pm, Tues-Thurs 6pm-2am, Fri-Sat 6pm-2:30am, Sun 6pm-2am; Metro: Liceu

Smoke-stained ceilings and a ramshackle look mark Bar Marsella, a staple of the Raval since it opened in 1820. Ernest Hemingway used to sink an absinthe here, and it still specializes in the drink known as "the green fairy." It's a great spot for a late-night tipple; sample the house speciality, if only to learn the important way of drinking it—the absinthe is served in a glass with a sugar cube. Drip water on the sugar cube until it has dissolved into the absinthe, and voilá. Take it easy, though: it doesn't take much to make the room spin.

CASA ALMIRALL

Carrer de Joaquín Costa, 33; tel. 93/318-9917; www.casaalmirall.com; Mon 5:30pm-1:30am, Tues-Wed 5:30pm-2am, Thurs midday-2:30am, Fri-Sat midday-3am, Sun midday-12:30am; Metro: Universitat

One of Barcelona's oldest bars, Casa Almirall opened in 1860 and was a bohemian hangout in the late 19th century. Today, little has changed in the bar's decor, with marble table tops and wooden floors, combined with vintage tills and the cast-iron muse from the 1888 World's Fair. Try a pre-lunch vermouth or a late-night glass of wine, and drink in the surrounding history. If only those walls could talk.

LA CONFITERÍA

Carrer de Sant Pau, 128; tel. 93/140-5435; www. grupoconfiteria.cat; Mon-Thurs 7pm-3am, Fri 6pm-3:30am, Sat 5pm-3:30am, Sun 5pm-3am; Metro: Poble Sec

This atmospheric bar was a confectioner's shop until the 1980s and has retained many of the original fittings, including the original cabinets, old marble countertop, and colorful tiled floor. Grab a high wooden stool at the bar (if it's not too busy) and enjoy a pre-dinner vermouth. It's also a great late-night spot for a drink.

La Ribera and El Born

BORMUTH

Plaça Comercial, 1; tel. 93/310-2186; Sun-Thurs 12:30pm-1:30am, Fri-Sat 12:30pm-2am; Metro: Arc de Triomf

This cozy bar in Ribera, with wooden floors, high tables, stools, and a split-level dining room, does tapas and beers. It combines a cool, modern vibe with traditional tapas like tortilla and *patatas bravas*. It's popular with a mixed, local crowd and is ideally located, close to the Picasso Museum.

The Waterfront

BODEGA FERMIN

Carrer de Sant Carles, 18; tel. 93/112-4303; Sun-Thurs 11am-midnight, Fri-Sat 11am-1am; Metro: Barceloneta

This Barcelona bodega is a friendly local joint with wooden wine barrels behind the bar. Try a vermouth or one of their long list of craft beers from both Spain and further afield. Wine is good and cheap, and the atmosphere is vintage Barcelona bodega: wooden tables and a hodgepodge of old paraphernalia decorating the walls. There is a good range of tapas, from olives and cheese boards to jamón, to go with your drinks.

Eixample

DRY MARTINI

Carrer d'Aribau, 162-166; tel. 93/217-5072; www. drymartiniorg.com; Mon-Thurs 1pm-2:30am, Fri 1pm-3am, Sat 6:30pm-3am, Sun 6:30pm-2:30am; Metro: Diagonal

Consistently voted one of the best bars in the world, this stylish, wood-clad cocktail bar is all about elegance. Slink back into a leather chair in the warmly lit space, dominated by the laboratory of cocktails—the bar. The white-coated and black-tied waiters are serious about cocktails and bring a scientific precision and an artistic creativity to their creations. They will happily provide suggestions, or you can go for a Dry Martini and channel the serious James Bond vibes.

Gràcia and Park Güell

EL CICLISTA

Carrer de Mozart, 18; tel. 93/368-5302; www. elciclistabar.com; Sun-Thurs 7:30pm-2am, Fri-Sat 7:30pm-3am; Metro: Diagonal

Intimate cocktail bar El Ciclista (The Cyclist) is decorated in all things bicycle-related, from bike-wheel light shades and tables to the ingenious rope-and-pedal door opening. With its extensive menu of cocktails and laid-back vibe, it's a great spot for a late-night drink in Gràcia and a great photo opportunity for cycling fans.

BOBBY GIN

Carrer de Francisco Giner, 47; tel. 93/368-1892; www.bobbygin.com; Sun-Wed 4pm-2am, Thurs 4pm-2:30am, Fri-Sat 4pm-3am; gins from around €11; Metro: Diagonal

This temple to gin in the stylish

neighborhood of Gràcia is a great place for a nighttime tipple. Take a seat at the bar to watch the barmen work; their knowledge of gin, and their finesse at adding different garnishes (depending on the type of spirit), is mesmerizing. The bartenders are friendly and, if you tell them your favorite ingredients, will rustle you up a bespoke gin and tonic. The bar is famous for its GinFolk gins, which have been enhanced with smoking or infusing. As is the norm in Spain, gins are served in huge, fishbowl-like glasses, so if you fancy some food to soak up some of the drink, there's a menu of tasty burgers, croquettes, and other sharing dishes.

VERMUTERÍA LA CAVA

Carrer de Còrsega, 339; tel. 93/348-3909; www.lapepitabcn.com; Mon-Sat midday-midnight; Metro: Diagonal

This long bar, in Gràcia, is a popular place for an early-evening vermouth, and it can get packed (watch your bags!). Grab a stool at the bar and try your hand at adding some *sifón* (soda water) to your vermouth from the high-pressured, colorful soda siphons dotted along the bar top. There are tables in the back, where the walls are exposed brick and graffiti-strewn. Small tapas plates are available for when you're feeling peckish.

ELEPHANTA

Torrent d'en vidalet, 37; tel. 93/237-6906; www.elephanta.cat; Mon-Thurs 6pm-2:30am, Fri-Sat 6pm-3am, Sun 5pm-10pm; Metro: Joanic

This cozy bar with green banquettes and pink stools specializes in cocktails. The smart bar staff are only too happy to make recommendations, or you can try one of the 40 different kinds of gin. If you fancy something non-alcoholic, opt for one of its extensive menu of teas.

OLD FASHIONED

Carrer de Santa Teresa, 1; tel. 93/368-5277; www.cocktailsbarcelona.oldfashionedbcn.com/wp; Tues-Thurs midday-2am, Fri midday-3am, Sat 5pm-3am, Sun-Mon 5pm-2am; Metro: Diagonal

Creative cocktails and friendly bar staff make

Old Fashioned, with its corner bar packed with spirits, a popular haunt in Gràcia. The menu is as long as your arm, but the staff, in their braces-and-tie uniforms, are happy to concoct cocktails based on your personal tastes and favorite flavors.

WINE AND CAVA BARS
Las Ramblas and Barri Gòtic
ZONA D'OMBRA

Carrer de Sant Domènec del Call, 12; tel. 93/500-5802; www.zonadombra.es; Sun-Thurs midday-11pm, Fri-Sat midday-midnight; Metro: Jaume I

This wine-bar-meets-shop is a lovely, cozy spot in the Gothic Quarter to while away a few hours over some wine. The staff are friendly and eager to impart their considerable knowledge of Spanish *vinos*. There are rotating specials and a good range of wines available by the glass, as well as a menu of snacks like olives, cheeses, and toasts. It's a good pre-dinner spot.

La Ribera and El Born
EL XAMPANYET

Carrer de Montcada, 22; tel. 93/319-7003; Tues-Sat midday-3:30pm, 7pm-11pm, Sun midday-3:30pm; Metro: Jaume I

Pack into one of Barcelona's most famous cava bars for a glass of something sparkling, served in a delicate coupe glass and accompanied by some tasty tapas snacks, including mini tortillas on bread, olives, pimientos de padrón, and tomato bread. It can get very busy, so don't be afraid to elbow on in towards the bar. The crowd is a mix of old locals meeting for an aperitif and tourists eager to sample one of Catalonia's most famous drinks.

LA VINYA DEL SENYOR

Plaza Sta Maria, 5; tel. 93/310-3379; Mon-Thurs midday-1am, Fri-Sat midday-2am, Sun midday-midnight; Metro: Jaume I

Close to the church of Santa Maria del Mar, this lovely wine bar, with an outside terrace overlooking the grand medieval church, has a great number of wines from Catalonia and around Spain. In summer, the small outdoor terrace is a picturesque spot to people-watch over a glass of cava.

CAN CISA
Carrer de la Princesa, 14; www.cancisa.cat; tel. 93/319-9881; Mon-Thurs 1pm-4pm, 7pm-1:30am, Fri-Sat 1pm-1:30am; Metro: Jaume I
This hip bar, a favorite with young and stylish locals, specializes in natural wines and has an impressively long wine list. Bar staff are friendly and well-informed, and they will happily give you recommendations for great local wines. The adjoining **Bar Brutal** does excellent tapas with a modern twist, like grilled hearts of romaine and asparagus with romesco sauce and sautéed clams and mussels with tomato, garlic, and basil.

The Waterfront
★ CAN PAIXANO
Carrer de la Reina Cristina, 7; tel. 93/310-0839; www.canpaixano.com; Mon-Sat 9am-10:30pm; Metro: Barceloneta
Also known as **La Xampanyeria**, this incredibly popular little cava bar, founded in 1969, is usually packed with a range of locals and tourists of all ages, here to sample the house sparkling wine. The rustic decor, with sausages hanging from the ceiling, contrasts with the most popular drink—rosé cava served in delicate little coupe glasses. A house rule (Grandma-style) is that if you're drinking, you're eating. Satisfying sandwiches (check the options on the huge boards behind the bar) make a great accompaniment to the wine—barmen will expect you to eat something, so be aware! And don't mind the pushing: there's a lot of it here, but it's all part of the experience.

Eixample
MONVINIC
Carrer de la Diputació, 249; tel. 93/272-6187; www.monvinic.com; Mon 7pm-10:30pm, Tues-Fri 1:30pm-3:30pm, 8pm-10:30pm, Sat 7pm-10:30pm; Metro: Passeig de Gràcia
This sleek and spacious temple of vino is great for wine buffs or those looking to learn a thing or two about Spanish wines. The team of sommeliers are knowledgeable and happy to guide you, depending on the flavors you like. Explore the digital wine list on tablets along the bar, and order wines by the glass or half-glass, a great way to sample lots of different vinos. There is also a menu of sharing plates to accompany the wines. While prices can spiral into the big bucks, a glass of wine starts at just a few euros. Lit by golden hues, it's a modern and romantic setting for some serious wine exploration.

LA VOLÀTIL
Carrer de Muntaner, 6; tel. 93/172-1199; www.lavolatil.com; Tues-Thurs 1pm-11pm, Fri-Sat 1pm-11:30pm, Sun 1pm-11pm; Metro: Universitat
This modern bar in the Eixample puts natural and organic wines front and center—quite literally, in its huge, glass-fronted wine cabinets. Its mossy-green tiled bar and clean white walls bring to mind a modern country kitchen, and the relaxed ambiance is ideal for enjoying a glass or two from the extensive cellar. There are plenty of options available by the glass, as well as a range of good tapas dishes to pair with your drinks.

Gràcia and Park Güell
LO PINYOL
Carrer del Torrent de l'Olla, 7; tel. 93/217-6690; www.lopinyol.com; Tues-Sat midday-4pm, 7pm-midnight, Sun midday-4pm; Metro: Diagonal
Gràcia bodega Lo Pinyol pairs vintage interiors—a beautiful tiled floor, wooden tables, and old wine barrels behind the bar—with friendly service and easy-on-the-wallet prices. It's a great spot for a vermouth and a little tapa (around €3 for both) before lunch, or an early-evening drink before dinner. Handily, the wine list is color-coded by type and flavor to help you choose something that is perfect for you.

Spanish Wine

Wine has been produced in the Iberian Peninsula since the first century AD. Remnants of a Roman wine press were found in Teia, near Alella, 20 minutes from Barcelona. Wine was widely exported during the Roman Empire, so it would have been perfectly common for border soldiers in England and Germania to drink wine that had been produced in Spain.

Spain's wine industry suffered under the dictatorship of Francisco Franco, who banned exports and believed the drink should be used only in church services. He made an exception, however, for a certain US president. When he heard that Dwight Eisenhower was partial to a glass of sparkling wine, he asked cava makers Perelada to produce a special wine for the president's visit to Spain in 1959. The resulting cava, Gran Claustro, is still produced today.

Barceloneses often drink wine with lunch or dinner (a glass usually comes included in a *menu del día*), especially at weekends. Depending on its make and where you are drinking, your wine can cost an average of €3.50/€4 per glass.

WINES

Although more than 400 grape varieties are planted in Spain, more than 80 percent of wine production focuses on 20 grapes. Wines in Spain are often described by grape rather than by area, so **Albariño** wines, which pair well with seafood, come from the Albariño grape, typically used to make white wine in the northwest region of Galicia. **Tempranillo** grapes, some of the most popular in Spain, make full-bodied reds.

In Spain, the Denominación de Origen (DO) appellation system controls the quality of wine—79 wine areas across the country have DO wines; two have the even more prestigious Denominación de Origen Calificada (DOC and DOQ in Catalonia)—La Rioja and Priorat, an area of Catalonia known for its sparking wine, or Cava, made using the classic Champagne method. Each DO has bodies that regulate production, including grape variety and the length of time the wine is aged in barrels.

Handily, most Spanish wine is pre-aged so you can enjoy it straight away. **Crianzas** are aged at least two years, including one year in oak barrels, **Reservas** are aged at least three years, including one year in oak barrels, and **Gran Reservas** are aged for five years, including two years in barrels.

White wines pair well with seafood and fish—typical Catalan dishes, like *esqueixada* (flaked fish salad) and fideuá, will wash down nicely with a bottle of chilled white wine, while heartier meat dishes pair well with a full-bodied Rioja.

BAR BODEGA CAL PEP

Carrer de Verdi, 141; tel. 93/218-5885; Mon-Fri 7am-4pm, 6pm-9:30pm, Sat 8:30am-3pm; Metro: Lesseps

This traditional bodega in the heart of Gràcia is well worth seeking out for a refreshing vermouth and a snack while exploring the neighborhood. There are wine-barrel-turned-tables to stand around at the front, a few low tables farther back, and walls lined in local paraphernalia, like ring buoys from Barceloneta beach, flags, photographs, and sketches—many reflecting the surrounding neighborhood.

Montjuïc
ELS SORTIDORS DEL PARLAMENT

Carrer del Parlament, 53; tel. 93/441-1602; www.elssortidors.com; Mon 5pm-11pm, Wed-Sun noon-11pm; Metro: Sant Antoni

On the trendy Carrer del Parlament, this popular local bodega lined in huge wine barrels offers a great range of both Catalan and international wines. Grab a spot at a barrel-table and choose from the wine list or buy from the shop (corkage fee €4) and pair your wine with some cured meats and cheeses or a few tapas dishes from the food menu.

bottles of Spanish wine

CAVA

Cava is a Spanish sparkling wine made using the same methods as Champagne. Grapes (usually macabeu, xarello, and parellada) are fermented and mixed with sugar and yeast, then bottled, sealed, and kept in cellars for around nine months for a second fermentation.

Like Champagne, cava has different sweetnesses according to how much sugar was used in the fermentation—Brut (less than 20g/liter), Sec (20-30g/liter), Semisec (30-50g/liter), or Dolç ("sweet," including more than 50g/liter). Brut and Sec are most commonly consumed with savory food; sweeter varieties resemble dessert wines.

About 95 percent of all cava is produced in the Penedès region of Catalonia, centered around the village of Sant Sadurní d'Anoia, 60 kilometers (37 miles) west of Barcelona. The biggest brands are Freixenet and Codorníu, both based in the village.

There are several traditional cava bars in Barcelona where you can try local bubbly, such as El Xampanyet and Can Paixano.

CELLER CAL MARINO

Carrer de Margarit, 54; www.calmarino.com; Mon-Thurs 7:30pm-11:30pm, Fri-Sat midday-3pm, 7:30pm-11:30pm, Sun midday-3pm; Metro: Poble Sec

This spacious bodega features wine barrels behind the bar and a good range of tapas dishes to pair with the great range of wines. Prices are reasonable, and beers and vermouth are also on offer for those who fancy something other than wine. The atmosphere is buzzing—lots of locals and regular live music nights add to the lively vibe.

CRAFT BEER
La Ribera and El Born
★ ALE & HOP

Carrer de les Basses de Sant Pere, 10; tel. 93/126-9094; www.aleandhop.com; Mon-Wed 5pm-1:30am, Thurs 5pm-2:30am, Fri 5pm-3am, Sat 1pm-3am, Sun 1pm-1.30am, Metro: Arc de Triomf

This modern bar is a temple to craft beer, with 10 beers on tap and over 70 by the bottle. It has an excellent menu of mainly vegetarian and vegan tapas, made with produce from the owner's farm on the outskirts of the city. Vegan burgers, croquettes, and a vegan "pulled pork" sandwich are highlights. Bar staff are friendly and knowledgeable, and they will recommend you a drink based on your tastes. There's usually a mixed crowd of young locals and curious foreigners.

El Raval
ØLGOD
Carrer de l'Hospital, 74; tel. 93/443-9082; www. olgodbcn.com; daily midday-2am; Metro: Liceu

With a name that means "God of beer," Ølgod is a must-visit for fans of a good craft brew. This Danish craft-beer bar in the bohemian Raval has 30 taps behind the long, concrete bar, with a good selection of Danish and local Catalan brews, as well as beers from other parts of Europe. There's also a "beer cocktail" menu if you fancy something a bit more adventurous. The menu of vegetarian tapas provides some tasty dishes ideal for chomping on alongside the beers. Regular DJ nights keep the atmosphere lively.

The Waterfront
BLACKLAB BREWERY
Palau del Mar, Plaça Pau Vila, 1; tel. 93/221-8360; www.blacklab.es; Mon-Wed 12:30pm-1:30am, Thurs-Fri 12:30pm-2am, Sat-Sun 10:30am-1:30am; Metro: Barceloneta

In front of Port Vell, this large craft beer bar with exposed brick walls and comfy seating is a must-visit for beer aficionados. Part brewhouse, kitchen, and bar, its extensive menu features beers brewed on-site (see the large, stainless steel vats behind the glass wall off the main seating area). Among the most popular house brews are Claudia (an IPA) and the Little Sister, a lighter version with less alcohol. The bar also offers seasonal beers and a tasty menu of Asian and American-influenced dishes, including fries with the utterly addictive secret house sauce.

Montjuïc
BARNA BREW
Carrer del Parlament, 45; tel. 93/706-5229; www. barnabrew.com; Tues-Thurs 5:30pm-11:30pm, Fri 5:30pm-1:30am, Sat midday-1:30am, Sun midday-11:30pm; Metro: Sant Antoni

On the Carrer del Parlament, the epicenter of bars and restaurants in the hip Sant Antoni neighborhood, Barna Brew is a local brewpub that makes its own craft beers and draws a cool local crowd of Barceloneses and expats. Many beers are Belgian-inspired, thanks to the English owners' time spent in Brussels. The award-winning beers, brewed on-site in the bar's very own brewery, include the refreshing Pils Parlament, named after the street on which the bar is located.

CLUBS
Las Ramblas and Barri Gòtic
CITY HALL
Rambla de Catalunya, 2-4; tel. 93/238-0722; www. cityhallbarcelona.com; daily midnight-6am; cover from €10; Metro: Catalunya

Dance the night away in the grand surroundings of the 19th-century Teatro Barcelona at City Hall, a trendy club with a mainly electronic soundtrack. Local DJs spin the discs at this night spot with themed nights. Its outdoor terrace and bar are the ideal place for a post-dance chill.

MACARENA
Carrer Nou de Sant Francesc, 5; tel. 93/301-3064; www.macarenaclub.com; Fri-Sat midnight-6am, Sun-Thurs midnight-5am; €10 cover; Metro: Liceu

This postage-stamp-sized club has an ambience like no other: the DJ booth is in the middle of the dance floor, and some of the best international and local DJs spin electronic and house music. Housed in a former *flamenco tablao*, it is an intimate venue in which to enjoy some of the best electronic music in Barcelona.

El Raval
MOOG CLUB
Carrer de l'Arc del Teatre, 3; tel. 93/319-1789; www. masimas.com/en/moog; daily midnight-6pm; cover from €5; Metro: Drassanes

Moog Club is a crowd pleaser, with an upstairs "mirror room" dedicated to pop and a low-ceilinged downstairs space that plays techno and house music. It attracts techno aficionados and tourists drawn by its location (just off Las Ramblas) and the fact it is open every day of the year. Wednesday is traditionally the day when big international names perform, but there is a good mix of international and local DJs.

Eixample
RED 58

Carrer del Consell de Cent, 280; advance tickets from €5; www.red58club.com; Thurs-Sat midnight-6am, Metro: Passeig de Gràcia

Near the Plaça de Catalunya, this club opened in 2017 and does stripped-back bass and house for a discerning crowd of music lovers. The 250-person capacity makes it an intimate space; it attracts locals keen on good music to see its rotating roster of both international names and up-and-coming local DJs.

Montjuïc
LA TERRRAZZA

Av. de Francesc Ferrer i Guàrdia; tel. 68/796-9825; www.laterrazza.com; Fri-Sat midnight-6am; tickets online from €10; Metro: Espanya

The quaint Poble Espanyol, a recreation of different regions of Spain on Montjuïc hill, is the surprising home to this summer open-air club, where international and local DJs spin house and techno. It's a glamorous crowd, but the dress code is pretty laid-back: jeans and trainers are fine, but sportswear and bikinis are a no-no. Because the bar is far from the metro, a taxi is your best bet (make sure to write down the address—it can be difficult to find). The cab ride takes around 15 minutes and costs approximately €8 from Plaça de Catalunya.

LIVE MUSIC
Las Ramblas and Barri Gòtic
SIDECAR FACTORY CLUB

Plaça Reial, 7; tel. 93/302-1586; www.sidecar.es; Mon-Thurs 7pm-5am, Fri-Sat 7pm-6am; Metro: Liceu

Sidecar, just off the Plaça Reial, has become one of Barcelona's classic music venues over the past 30 years for its alternative, indie, and rock music. The intimate club plays host both to bands and to DJs, and always draws a good crowd of both locals and tourists.

EL PARAIGUA

Carrer del Pas de l'Ensenyança, 2; tel. 93/317-1479; www.elparaigua.com; Sun-Wed midday-midnight, Thurs midday-2am, Fri-Sat midday-3am; Metro: Jaume I

El Paraigua (The Umbrella) has been hosting live music in the Gothic quarter since 1968. Upstairs is a cocktail bar; the basement with exposed brick walls and a cozy atmosphere is where bands play on Friday and Saturday nights at 11:45pm. Music is eclectic, from Spanish guitar and latin to blues. Musicians take to the small stage, and the crowd sips on cocktails while they watch.

Eixample
MILANO COCKTAIL BAR

Ronda Universitat, 35; tel. 93/112-7150; www.camparimilano.com; Tues-Fri midday-3am, Sat midday-2:30am, Sun 6pm-2:30am, Mon 6pm-3am; Metro: Catalunya

The red leather banquettes and smart waiters give this cocktail bar and jazz venue the feel of a vintage jazz club. There are jazz, blues, and swing concerts most nights of the week, and an extensive menu of cocktails and tapas is offered so guests can eat and drink while they listen to the music. Check the website for details on upcoming performances.

Performing Arts

SARDANA DANCES

The Sardana, the traditional circle dance of Catalonia, is celebrated on weekends, when locals gather in front of the cathedral to dance. The dancing usually takes place on Saturdays at 6pm and some Sunday mornings just after 11am.

FLAMENCO

Las Ramblas and Barri Gòtic
TABLAO FLAMENCO CORDOBES

Las Ramblas, 35; tel. 93/317-5711; www. tablaocordobes.es; €45 for show and drink, €80 for a show and dinner; Metro: Liceu

One of Barcelona's most historic *flamenco tablaos* (flamenco venues) has been bringing the best flamenco dancers, singers, and guitarists to the city since it opened its doors on Las Ramblas in 1970: There are three nightly performances of around an hour each, and ticket options include ticket and a drink or ticket and dinner. The venue, with its arched low ceilings and seating close to the stage, lends performances an intimate atmosphere and lets the crowd see the dancers close-up. Performers change week by week, giving shows a fresh and exciting feel. Check online for upcoming shows.

Montjuïc
EL TABLAO DE CARMEN

Av. de Francesc Ferrer i Guàrdia, 13; tel. 93/325-6895; www.tablaodecarmen.com; shows at 6pm and 8:30pm, from €43; Metro: Espanya

Amid the surreal surroundings of Poble Espanyol, the "Spanish village" on Montjuïc hill that recreates architecture, culture, and crafts from regions across Spain, is El Tablao de Carmen. It opened in 1988 as a tribute to Barcelona-born flamenco dancer Carmen Amaya. The venue's whitewashed patio, with plant pots dotting the walls, is modeled after a typical Cordoban patio and is a lovely spot for a pre-show drink. There are two hour-long shows a night (6pm and 8:30pm), and you have the option of having a drink (€43) or a full dinner (€61) while watching the show.

CONCERTS

Las Ramblas and Barri Gòtic
JAMBOREE JAZZ CLUB

Plaça Reial, 17; tel. 93/304-1210; www.masimas.com/ en/jamboree/jazz-club-barcelona; jazz club hours 7:30pm-11:30pm, club from midnight, Metro: Liceu

Its low ceilings and exposed brick give Jamboree the look of a mythical jazz club, a great atmosphere to watch one of its two nightly concerts (8pm and 10pm). Blues, funk, swing, and (most of all) jazz are the name of the game here. Since it opened in 1960, the club has welcomed the most famous names in jazz, such as Chet Baker. At 12:30am, it turns into a nightclub, Jamboree Dance Club, where R&B and hip-hop DJs do their thing. Tickets are around €15 (€13 when booked online). It's a smallish venue, so the atmosphere really sizzles once the musicians get going.

La Ribera and El Born
PALAU DE MUSICA CATALANA

C/ Palau de la Música, 4-6; tel. 93/295-7207; www. palaumusica.cat; Metro: Urquinaona

One of Barcelona's most emblematic concert venues, the Palau de Musica Catalana was commissioned by the Orfeó Català, a Catalan choral society, and built between 1905 and 1908 by one of the city's leading Modernista architects, Lluís Domènech I Montaner. Seeing a concert is one of the best ways to appreciate the wonder of the building, whose design was like nothing ever seen before it opened. It is one of Barcelona's leading venues for choral and classical music, with up to 100 concerts per season. It also hosts flamenco concerts. Check online for upcoming concerts and to purchase tickets—prices vary depending on the performance. The large venue's

Castells

Castells, or human towers, are a popular tradition across Catalonia during local fiestas; they are comprised of men, women, and children known as *castellers.* The towers are constructed first by a scrum of people standing at the bottom to provide support. Then, members of the group form the trunk, with men at the bottom, women in the middle and, typically, children at the top. At their very highest, they can reach up to ten levels, or 30 feet, high. They are always topped by a child, called the *enxaneta,* who has to raise one hand when he or she reaches the top to show the castell has been completed. They are dramatic and heart-stopping to witness—there is no safety net, and if they collapse there is a serious risk of injury—but castellers train hard to make sure they can be as safe and secure as possible.

the Vila de Gràcia castell group

The history of castells dates back to the 18th century, when they were first recorded at Valls in southern Catalonia. They were inspired by Valencian street dances, and they gained popularity throughout the 20th century. Their popularity surged as Catalans rediscovered their traditions following the cultural repression of General Francisco Franco, and the art became more competitive when (with the addition of women in the 1980s) towers could be built higher and higher.

For Catalans who take part, it is an important social activity. Many families train together; different neighborhoods have different castell groups, which train in community centers or even in their own purpose-built training centers.

In 2010, UNESCO named castells a Masterpiece of the Oral and Intangible Heritage of Humanity.

Visitors are most likely to see castells during local celebrations, such as the Festa Major de Gràcia (August) and the Festa de la Mercè (September).

---

seats are divided into stalls and boxes, with a range of prices available starting at around €25.

The Waterfront
RAZZMATAZZ
Carrer dels Almogàvers, 122; tel. 93/320-8200; www. salarazzmatazz.com; Metro: Marina

Set in a big industrial building behind the seafront in the cool Poble Nou neighborhood, Razzmatazz is a concert venue, club, and entertainment space all rolled into one. Its five concert halls have hosted acts such as Coldplay, The Strokes, Kanye West, and Kraftwerk, while they also have regular club nights, from techno and indie rock to hip hop

and reggeton. It's a casual crowd—no dress code necessary.

SALA APOLO
Carrer Nou de la Rambla, 113; tel. 93/441-4001; www. sala-apolo.com; Metro: Drassanes

This cavernous concert hall and nightclub, with a large central room with balconies on either side, has regular club nights with names like Nasty Mondays, Cupcake, and Cannibal Sound System. As a popular concert venue, it also plays host to international acts. Buy tickets online (€15 or €6 for early entry between midnight and 1am) or at the door. The dress code is casual, and the vibe from the mainly younger crowd is indie-cool.

THEATER
Eixample
TEATRE TÍVOLI

Carrer de Casp, 8; tel. 93/215-9570; www.
grupbalana.com/es/teatros/salas/teatre-tivoli; Metro:
Passeig de Gràcia

The second-largest theater in Barcelona (after the Liceu opera house), Teatre Tívoli opened in 1919 and hosted theater, opera, and *zarzuelas* (a Spanish kind of musical theater). Today, it is the place to see some of the best Spanish musicals, ballet, and theater. Check the website for upcoming shows. Ticket prices depend on the show, but they can start at around €20.

Montjuïc
EL MOLINO

Carrer de Vila i Vilà, 99; tel. 93/205-5111; www.
elmolinobcn.com; Metro: Paral·lel

"The Windmill" is a legendary music hall that opened its doors in 1898. It was known as the Petit Moulin Rouge from 1910 until 1939, when the dictatorship of Francisco Franco made it exchange its foreign name for something Spanish. The theater has a range of shows, including cabaret, burlesque, flamenco, music, and theater. Check

its website for upcoming schedules and to buy tickets.

OPERA
GRAN TEATRE DEL LICEU

La Rambla, 51-59; tel. 93/485-9900; www.
liceubarcelona.cat; Metro: Liceu

Barcelona's premier opera house, located right on Las Ramblas, has been the center of the city's intellectual and cultural life since it opened in 1847. Originally a private opera house, it burned down in 1861 and was rebuilt the following year. In 1893, during a performance of William Tell, an anarchist threw a bomb into the crowd, killing 20 people. In 1994, another fire gutted the building when a spark hit a curtain that was part of the set. The original 1847 façade as well as the grand *Saló de Miralls*, or hall of mirrors, were retained when the building reopened in 1999.

With 2,300 seats, the Liceu is one of Europe's largest opera houses. It hosts ballet performances, concerts, and classical recitals as well as opera. Ticket prices start from as little as €10 (for the seats farthest from and highest above the stage). Tickets can be purchased online; check upcoming shows well in advance to get the best deals before tickets sell out.

Festivals and Events

Barcelona has a host of festivals that are popular with locals and visitors alike. The electronic music festival Sonar draws performers and crowds from around the world, with many making the trip to Barcelona specifically for the festival. For locals, the most beloved festivities include Sant Joan (which also draws plenty of foreigners to the city) and neighborhood celebrations such as the Festa Major de Gràcia.

SPRING
DIA DE SANT JORDI

Various locations, Las Ramblas; April 23

Saint George might be better known as the

patron saint of England, but he is also the patron saint of Catalonia and is celebrated on April 23, which happens to be World Book Day. (Spanish literary great Miguel de Cervantes died on the same day.) The two collide in the day's traditions: women give men a book, and men give women a rose. Book and flower stalls are set up across the city, but Las Ramblas is a particular hive of book- and flower-buying activity. The **Government Palace** (Palau de la Generalitat de Catalunya, Plaça de Sant Jaume, 4) is also open for free visits on April 23—an old tradition saw locals visit the chapel of Sant Jordi inside the Government Palace.

EASTER / HOLY WEEK

Various locations

Good Friday processions are common throughout the city, but head to Barcelona Cathedral for a sure-fire sight. Easter Monday is also a public holiday in Barcelona, and it is when children eat the *Mona de Pascua*, a sponge cake traditionally consumed at Easter and typically filled with jam or chocolate. The cakes come in lots of different styles, from spring-themed creations to ones featuring the latest cartoon characters. Expect to see lots of wonderful window displays featuring the cakes in bakeries around the city; you can pick one up for yourself if you fancy.

PRIMAVERA SOUND

Parc del Fòrum (Carrer de la Pau, 12); end of May-beginning of June, www.primaverasound.com

One of Barcelona's most famous music festivals takes place at the end of May in the Parc del Fòrum, a spacious outdoor seaside location. Some of the world's best pop, rock, indie, and alternative acts have played the three-day festival, including The Cure, The Pixies, Public Enemy, Patti Smith, Arcade Fire, and Neil Young. A weekend pass ticket is around €215 and can be booked online via the Primavera Sound website (www.primaverasound.com). Day tickets are also available (around €85). Book early, because tickets sell out quickly.

SUMMER

SANT JOAN

Barceloneta beach; June 23-24

This popular feast day celebrates the beginning of summer with bonfires on the beach and the crackle of fireworks across the city. Catalans call it the "Nit del Foc" (Night of Fire). Many families buy their own fireworks and hold parties on their balconies and terraces. One of the best places for visitors to experience Sant Joan is down on the beach. It is typical to bring picnics to watch the fireworks and listen to the musicians who set up on the beach. Head to the beach early (before 9pm) to get a good spot because it fills up quickly.

BARCELONA PRIDE

Various locations; end of June; www.pridebarcelona.org

Barcelona's Pride festival takes place in late June-early July, with concerts, activities, and cultural events across the city, all celebrating diversity. The main concert stage is on the Avenida de Maria Cristina, between Plaça de Espanya and the Palau Nacional in Montjuïc. The week-long festivities end with a huge pride march through the city, starting at the Jardins de les Tres Xemeneies, close to the seafront, and ending on Avenida de Maria Cristina.

CRUILLA FESTIVAL

Parc del Fòrum; July; www.cruillabarcelona.com; three-day ticket €120, day ticket €75

This summer festival at the sprawling Parc del Fòrum, close to the seafront just north of the central beaches, welcomes acts from around the world to its three stages and is one of the city's most varied music festivals. It is also more under-the-radar than the better-known Sonar and Primavera Sound, making for smaller crowds and a more local vibe. The eclectic lineup is ideal for music lovers who want to see a wide range of acts. Recent performers have included Jack White, Seasick Steve, Damien Marley, and Fatoumata Diawara.

FESTA MAJOR DE GRÀCIA

Gràcia; mid-August

This festival, which takes place in the neighborhood of Gràcia (once a town in its own right before it was gobbled up into an expanding Barcelona), kicks off on August 15 and lasts for a week to ten days. Locals decorate their streets, competing to see who can come up with the most creative designs. There's a whole range of events, such as concerts and parades featuring giant-headed characters; by night a general party atmosphere rules and by day cultural traditions prevail, including *castells* (human towers) and *correfoc* (firerunning), when some locals dress as devils and set off fireworks into the crowd from their spears. The crowd dresses to protect themselves from the sparks, and others—more sensibly—watch from a safe distance.

SÓNAR

Various locations, mid-June, sonar.es, €155 for a three-day ticket

This three-day festival brings some of the best electronic acts in the world to Barcelona with previous performers including New Order, The Chemical Brothers, and M.I.A. It is split into two distinct parts—daytime Sónar, held in the Fira Montjuïc conference center (Avinguda de la Reina Maria Cristina) and nighttime Sónar, held in the Fira Gran Via L'Hospitalet (Av. Joan Carles I), south of the city.

FALL

FESTA DE LA MERCÈ

Various locations; Sept 24; www.lameva.barcelona. cat/merce/en

Barcelona's annual festival is a city-wide event first celebrated in 1871, when the city government organized a fiesta to commemorate the feast day of Our Lady of Mercy ("La Mare Déu de la Mercè" in Catalan). Festivities begin a few days before the main feast day of September 24, with performances and parades across the city showcasing the best of Catalan culture, including *castells* (human towers), processions of *gegants i capgrossos* (giant papier-mâché models), and lots of dancing of the *sardana*, Catalonia's traditional dance.

Hundreds of events, spread across plazas, parks, and streets, are all free—check the festival's website for a full program.

DIADA NACIONAL DE CATALUNYA

Various locations; September 11

Catalonia's national day has been, in recent years, a day of demonstrations for Catalan independence. It—strangely—commemorates the fall of Barcelona during the War of the Spanish Succession on September 11, 1714. Celebrated since the late 19th century, it was banned under the dictatorship of Francisco Franco and observed for the first time in nearly 40 years in 1977. Locals usually celebrate the day with marches and flag-waving. It's interesting to see, but decidedly more political than other local festivals.

WINTER

EPIPHANY

Various locations; Jan 5/6

Spanish children wait in excited anticipation for January 5, when the Three Wise Men arrive from the East to bring them presents. In Spain, it is the *Tres Reyes* (Three Kings) who traditionally bring children presents, not Santa Claus, although today most lucky children receive presents from both.

On January 5, the Three Kings parade on huge floats through the center of Barcelona. The festivities usually kick off at around 4:30pm, when they arrive on a boat in the Port Vell, where they are greeted by the Mayor of Barcelona. The parade proper begins at around 6pm and snakes around the city, the Three Wise Men throwing sweets to the children waiting along the route. It ends at around 9:30pm, close to the Magic Fountain in Montjuïc.

CARNIVAL

Various locations; Feb/March

Carnival takes place before Ash Wednesday, a last hurrah of fun, frolics, and excitement before the 40 days of Lent in the run-up to Easter. The Carnival begins with *Dijous Gras* or Greasy Thursday, when people typically enjoy a last pig-out before they rein in the indulgences during Lent. The weekend sees lots of local carnival parades, including one in the Ribera area of the old town, La Taronjada, that takes place on carnival Sunday and ends with a huge battle of orange balloons and confetti at the end of the route.

The end of the carnival on Ash Wednesday sees the Burial of the Sardine— the traditional conclusion of the carnival festivities in Barcelona. (The origin of this practice is disputed and perhaps lost to history, but people around Spain have long buried a sardine on the eve of or on Ash Wednesday to mark the end of the abundant carnival season.) A funeral cortege followed by a brass band will make its way through the streets, usually to a main square, where the sardine's will is read out and then the effigy of the fish is set on fire. It is common to eat fish on this day.

Shopping

It's not for nothing that Barcelona is known as a great shopping location. With its mixture of decades-old family-run stores, designer names, and exciting modern brands, the city caters to everyone from the casual shopper to the confirmed shopaholic.

Quirky shops are well represented in Barcelona and are a brilliant place to pick up some unique souvenirs. Local designers and artists often sell their designs in smaller, independent stores, which are a joy to browse (many of these quirky shops are centered around cool neighborhoods like El Born, El Raval, and Gràcia). Barcelona is also great city for markets, and from the bric-a-brac of the Encants street market to the gourmet bites of La Boqueria, foodies should definitely make a beeline for the city's *mercados*.

Prices tend to be on par with those at Madrid and other big European cities, and the best bargains are to be found with local brands and independent shops.

SHOPPING DISTRICTS
Passeig de Gràcia
Eixample is where the city's designer stores can be found, especially on and around the Passeig de Gràcia, where the world's most recognizable designer brands (including Chanel, Gucci, Versace, and more) have huge shops in the grand 19th-century buildings. It's a lovely street to walk, even if you're just window shopping, and is also home to some of Barcelona's most famous Modernista architecture.

PLAÇA DE CATALUNYA
The large square at the top of Las Ramblas is home to Spain's major deparment store, El Corté Inglés (if in doubt, you'll probably find anything you need there). The area around the square is also home to many international brands, from makeup giants Sephora to H&M and Uniqlo.

EL RAVAL / GRÀCIA
Both areas are home to a range of more independent, local shops, featuring work by young designers. From record shops to shops specializing in Portuguese gourmet food, half the fun is just wandering around these neighborhoods and seeing where your shopping trip takes you.

LAS RAMBLAS AND BARRI GÒTIC
FC Barcelona Merchandise
FC BOTIGA
Carrer de Jaume I, 18; tel. 93/269-1532; www. fcbarcelona.com/camp-nou/card/fcbotiga; daily 10am-9pm; Metro: Liceu
Sports fans should stop off in the official FC Barcelona store to stock up on merchandise based around the city's world-famous team. While tourist shops and stalls sell football merch, this is the place to get official souvenirs in the famous blue and claret colors. There are thousands of products, from football kits to pencil cases, notebooks, scarves, and footballs. An official adult's shirt is around €85.

Clothing and Accessories
L'ARCA
Carrer dels Banys Nous, 20; tel. 93/302-1598; www. larca.es; Mon 11am-2pm, 4:30pm-8:30pm, Wed-Sat 11am-2pm, 4:30pm-8:30pm; Metro: Liceu
This wonderful treasure trove of a shop

Best Souvenirs

CHOCOLATE

Visit the Museum of Chocolate and you will realize what an important part Barcelona played in introducing the foodstuff to Europe. You might have already realized the city has a special relationship with the sweet just from walking around the streets and noticing how many chocolate shops there are. Pick up a local brand, such as Amatller, to take home.

CAGANER

This unusual figurine, a staple in many Catalan Christmas cribs and nativity scenes, has got to be one of the weirdest Christmas traditions in the world. The *caganer* (literally, the "crapper") is a figurine of a Catalan peasant wearing a traditional red cap, squatting down and defecating on the floor. The figure has been used at least since the 18th century. Today, you can buy *caganers* modeled after royalty, presidents, and prime ministers, and famous footballers, musicians, and actors. Prices are around €15. You can purchase *caganers* at many souvenir shops around the city, including **Travitabac**, as well as the **Corte Inglés** gift department. Kiosks 36 and 41 on La Rambla dels Estudis (the part of La Rambla between the junctions with Carrer del Bonsuccés/Carrer Canuda and the Carrer Canuda) also sell *caganers*. Whether you go for someone you love or loathe is completely up to you!

CERAMICS

You can find ceramics from all around Spain at shops like **Art Escudellers**. Even if you don't have much space in your luggage, mementos such as egg cups, mugs, or small dishes can be used again and again and will always remind you of Spain.

ESPADRILLES

Espadrilles are a summer staple in Spain; these rope-soled shoes have been made at **La Manual Alpargatera** since the 1940s.

FOOTBALL MERCHANDISE

A customised Barcelona FC football shirt could be a special memento from your time in Barcelona and can be picked up at the team's official store, of which there are several around the city, including **FC Botiga** (Carrer de Jaume I; tel. 93/269-1532).

FOOD

Pick up a bottle of cava (such as Freixenet or Codorníu) or vermouth, artisanal olive oil (La Chinata is one brand), or a packet of saffron to help recreate those fantastic paellas at home.

---

specializes in vintage women's clothing and supplies stage and screen (one of Rose's/Kate Winslet's dresses in *Titanic* came from here). One of its specialities is wedding dresses, so if you're on the hunt for something unique and vintage, this could be a special place to search. It's also a great place to pick up accessories (which are, thankfully, more affordable than the ballgowns and wedding dresses), like gloves and brooches.

CUSTO

Las Ramblas, 109; tel. 93/481-3930; www.custo. com; Mon-Fri 10am-9pm, Sat 10am-9:30pm, Sun midday-8pm; Metro: Liceu

This Barcelona brand is known for its eye-catching T-shirts and clothing for men and women, with funky designs and vivid color palettes. It was founded by brothers Custo and David Dalmau in the '80s after a road trip through California. Inspired by the laid-back surfer vibe, the brothers began making

T-shirts (around €60) and today offer a wide range of womenswear and menswear, including accessories like scarves and bags, in their three Barcelona stores.

Shoes
LA MANUAL ALPARGATERA
Carrer d'Avinyó, 7; tel. 93/301-0172; www.
lamanualalpargatera.es; Mon-Fri 9:45am-1:30pm,
4:30pm-8pm, Sat 10am-1:30pm, 4:30pm-8pm;
Metro: Liceu

La Manual started making *espadrilles* in the 1940s, when the traditional Spanish rope-soled shoe, which before then had been the footwear of the working classes, began to gain a fashionable following. The handmade shoes are available for women, men, and children in a huge range of patterns and colors, all stacked onto the floor-to-ceiling wooden shelves of the shop. Take a seat on the original smooth wooden benches to try on the shoes. They're lovely souvenirs from Barcelona or the ideal footwear for a day along the beach.

Food and Wine
PAPABUBBLE
Carrer Ample, 28; tel. 93/268-8625; www.
pappabubble.com; Mon-Fri 10am-2pm, 4pm-8:30pm,
Sat 10am-8pm; Metro: Barceloneta

A kaleidoscope of candy colors awaits you in this temple to all things sweet, a must-visit for children or the child at heart with a sweet tooth. Founded in Barcelona in 2004, Papabubble aimed to recover the art of artisanal candymaking. Watch sweet experts craft multi-colored candies before your eyes, from lollipops and gummy candies to sweet sushi, and pick up a few packets to take home as gifts (or eat on the plane). From its humble beginnings, the brand now has stores as far afield as Tokyo, Sao Páolo, and New York, so take the opportunity to visit the original.

TORRONS VICENS
La Rambla, 111, Kiosk 43; tel. 62/932-8255; www.
vicens.com; Mon-Sat 10am-8:30pm, Sun 11am-8pm;
Metro: Liceu

This family-run business has been creating *turrón (turró* in Catalan), a Spanish nougat made from almonds and especially popular at Christmas, since 1775. It produces over 150 varieties of turrón using both hard and soft nougat, including chocolate, coconut, praline, and cava flavors, and has several stores across the city. Its kiosk, which opens directly onto Las Ramblas, is packed with packets of *turrón* and a convenient location where you can stock up on a traditional Spanish product to take home.

Design and Décor
CERERIA SUBIRÀ
Baixada de la Llibreteria, 7; tel. 93/315-2606; www.
cereriasubira.cat; Mon-Thurs 9:30am-1:30pm, 4pm-8pm,
Fri 9:30am-8pm, Sat 10am-8pm; Metro: Jaume I

Barcelona's oldest shop began selling candles on Carrer Corders in 1761 and moved to its current location—a former luxury clothing store, compete with grand, winding staircase—in the 19th century. Candles, which come in every imaginable color, are still made using traditional methods with the finest beeswax and paraffin.

ART ESCUDELLERS
Carrer dels Escudellers, 23; tel. 93/412-6801; www.
artescudellers.com; 11am-11pm; Metro: Liceu

This spacious store stocks ceramics and pottery made by over 200 artisans based around Spain, including Barcelona. The street it sits on has been linked to potters since the 13th century, and today "escudeller" in Catalan means ceramicist or potter. The shop aims to preserve traditional handicrafts in the face of industrialization, which threatens craftsmen around the country (and the world). From cups and bowls to intricate mosaic figurines in every color imaginable, the shop's many wares make great souvenirs.

EMPREMTES DE CATALUNYA
Banys Nous, 11; tel. 93/342-7520; http://ccam.gencat.
cat/ca/arees_actuacio/artesania/centre_artesania/
botiga_empremtes; Mon-Sat 10am-8pm, Sun
10am-8pm; Metro: Liceu

This spacious, modern handicraft shop, run

by the Generalitat de Catalunya (Catalonia's regional government), brings together products from across the region to highlight Catalonia's rich history, culture, and artistic traditions. Products are wide-ranging and include jewelery, pottery, fans, clothing, books, and much, much more.

TRAVITABAC

Baixada de la Libreteria, 8; tel. 93/315-1555; Mon-Fri 9am-9pm, Sat-Sun 10am-9pm

This tobacconist, in the Barri Gòtic, stocks a range of *caganers* from one of the main producers in Catalonia, www.caganer.com.

Books
COOPERATIVA D'ARQUITECTES JORDI CAPELL

Plaça Nova, 5; tel. 93/224-3932; www.lacapell.com; Mon-Fri 9am-2:30pm, 4pm-7pm, Sat 10am-2pm; Metro: Jaume I

For such an architecturally rich city, a visit to Barcelona's only architecture bookshop is an interesting stop. As well as thousands of books (some in English), the shop, set on two levels—a ground floor and a raised mezzanine walkway—features products designed by architects and designers as well as a stationery shop to stock up your office with stylish pens, pencils, and other essentials. It's a relaxed place to avoid the crowds and soak up some culture.

Department Stores
EL CORTE INGLÉS

Plaça de Catalunya, 14; tel. 93/306-3800; www. elcorteingles.es; Mon-Sat 9:30am-9pm; Metro: Plaça de Catalunya

Spain's biggest and last remaining department store chain, El Corte Inglés, has a huge store on Plaça de Catalunya. The eight-floor store has departments for women's, men's, and children's fashion and accessories, sports, homewear, electronics, books, and DIY. There's a food hall and supermarket in the basement, useful to stock up on essentials. El Corte Inglés Viajes, the department store's in-house travel agent, can book tickets for RENFE

trains if you don't want to/can't manage to book online.

Other Corte Inglés stores in Barcelona are on Avinguda del Portal de l'Àngel, 19 and Avinguda Diagonal, 471.

EL RAVAL
Music
DISCOS PARADISO

Carrer de Ferlandina, 39; tel. 93/329-6440; www. discosparadiso.com; Mon-Fri 11am-9pm, Sat midday-8pm; Metro: Universitat

This sleek record store, with its new and second-hand vinyl, specializes in electronic and house but also stocks some alternative, rock, and other genres. It's a cool space, with white brick walls and minimalist design. Turntables and headphones along the front wall mean you can listen to records before you buy.

LA RIBERA AND EL BORN
Clothing and Accessories
LA VIE EN CUIR

Carrer del Portal Nou, 7; tel. 93/017-4881; Mon-Sat midday-8pm; Metro: Arc de Triomf

A lovely little shop full of leather accessories, all made by local craftsmen with local materials. Products range from supple bags and satchels to shoes, wallets, and belts. Some products are made on-site in the small workshop area, so you can see exactly where your new souvenir was handmade.

MERCEDES MESTRE FLAMENCO

Sant Pere Mitjà, 69; tel. 93/280-9027; www. mercedesmestre.com; Mon-Fri 11am-8pm; Metro: Urquinaona

This flamenco atelier, the only one of its kind in Barcelona, is run by designer Mercedes Mestre, who makes incredible flamenco dresses of all colors, shapes, and elaborate designs for women and girls. From the tassled shawl draped over the balcony to the displays of vibrant accessories, the shop is a feast for the eyes. The ruffled designs are incredible, but if you aren't quite ready to invest a few hundred euros in a dress, you can pick out some accessories like earrings, necklaces, flower crowns, and bags.

Food and Wine
CASA GISPERT
Sombrerers, 23; tel. 93/319-7535; www.casagispert. com; Mon-Fri 9:30am-2pm, 4:30pm-8:30pm, Sat 9:30am-2pm, 5pm-8:30pm; Metro: Jaume I

Since 1851, Casa Gispert has been selling exotic ingredients that arrived in the city from overseas, from dried fruit and nuts to coffee and spices. Visitors won't be able to resist its floor-to-ceiling wooden shelves and little wooden drawers holding hundreds of products. Little has changed inside the intimate shop, except maybe for its embrace of organic produce. The family business has been recognized for the best roasted nuts in Europe. Its nuts achieve a smoky flavor by being roasted next to but never in the fire.

VILA VINITECA
Carrer dels Agullers, 7; tel. 90/232-7777; www. vilaviniteca.es; Mon-Sat 8:30am-8:30pm; Metro: Barceloneta

If you've ever wanted to see a space entirely decorated with wine bottles, this is the place for you. This wine shop, which has been selling wine since 1932, is something of a Barcelona institution and is now run by the third generation of the same family. Every available bit of space in the shop, with its wooden ceiling beams, seems to hold a bottle of wine. One of the most highly regarded wine merchants in Europe, it stocks both Spanish and international wines. Its Barcelona shop and deli are stocked floor to ceiling with wine bottles and is a favorite with local gourmands and wine lovers.

BODEGA MAESTRAZGO
Carrer de Sant Pere Més Baix, 90; tel. 60/231-0265; www.bodegamaestrazgo.com; Mon 5pm-10pm, Tues-Sat 11am-3pm, 5pm-10pm; Metro: Arc de Triomf

This small bodega in El Born has been dispensing advice on the best wines and vermouths since 1952, and its seemingly haphazard collection of wine-stacked shelves is a library waiting to be explored for vino fans. It sometimes hosts wine tastings (see its website for upcoming events). There is a good list of wines by the glass, as well as over 1,000 bottles. Whether you're a wine connoisseur or a beginner keen to explore the world of wine, take a seat at a wine-barrel table in the adjoining wine bar and settle in to sample some vino and enjoy local cheese, hams, and other tapas.

Design and Décor
WAWAS BARCELONA
Carrer dels Carders, 14; tel. 93/319-7992; Mon-Sat 11am-2pm, 5pm-9pm; Metro: Jaume I

Founded by sisters Anna and Silvia Franquesa, this cool souvenir shop, close to the Picasso Museum, started selling alternative postcards of Barcelona and today stocks quirky and artistic products made in the city by local creatives. From postcards designed by local artists to ceramics, guidebooks, artwork, T-shirts, mugs, and chocolate bars branded with "Barcelona," you'll find excellent souvenirs or gifts for friends back home. Ceramics by Spanish brand Cha Cha are ideal for recreating the tapas feel back home.

THE WATERFRONT
SHOPPING CENTERMAREMAGNUM
Moll d'Espanya, 5; tel. 93/225-8100; daily 10am-9pm; Metro: Barceloneta

This shopping center, set in a huge building on Barcelona's Port Vella, is a popular weekend hangout with locals, especially on Sundays when it is one of the only places in the city where shops stay open. It is home to a range of fashion, sports, accessories, and make-up shops as well as to restaurants and cafés, some with lovely views across the old port from terraces on the wooden boardwalk surrounding the shopping center. Barcelona brand **Desigual** (93/225-8116, www.desigual. com), with its funky patterns, is a good place to look for some local designs, while **Enrique Thomas** (93/225-8034, www.enriquetomas. com) specializes in the finest Spanish *jamón de bellota*—a great gourmet souvenir.

Flea Market
MERCAT DEL ENCANTS

*Carrer de los Castillejos, 158; tel. 93/246-3030; www.
encantsbcn.com; Mon, Wed, Fri and Sat 9am-8pm;
Metro: Glòries*

The "Old Charms" flea market, about a mile from the waterfront, is the biggest of its kind in Barcelona and one of the oldest flea markets in Europe. It was given a new lease on life in 2013, when a mirrored roof was added. It makes the huge space seem even larger, reflecting stalls and shoppers back at themselves. The market dates to the 14th century, and today its 500 stalls sell everything from antiques and second-hand clothes to furniture and electronics. There's definitely a garage-sale vibe. Saturdays are especially busy, so go during the week, and early, to avoid the crowds.

EIXAMPLE
Clothing and Accessories
DESIGUAL

*Plaça de Catalunya, 9; tel. 93/343-5940; www.
desigual.com; Mon-Sat 9am-9pm, Metro: Plaça de
Catalunya*

Founded in Ibiza in 1984, Desigual has become one of Spain's most recognizable brands for its bright colors and bold patterned and patchwork clothing for women, men, and children. The store has branches around the city, with its flagship store located on the Plaça de Catalunya. The biggest store, it has women's, men's, and children's clothing and accessories over three floors.

LOEWE

*Passeig de Gràcia, 35; tel. 93/216-0400; www.loewe.
com; Mon-Sat 10am-8:30pm; Metro: Passeig de
Gràcia*

Spanish luxury fashion house Loewe's Barcelona flagship store is located in the grand surroundings of the Casa Lleó Morera and is worth a visit if just to see its building. Founded in 1846, the brand is known for its high-quality leather goods, especially women's and men's bags. Today, Loewe also sells women's and men's apparel as well as accessories and homewear.

ANTONIO MIRÓ

*Carrer d'Enric Granados, 46; tel. 93/113-2697; www.
antoniomiro.es; Mon-Sat 10:30am-8:30pm; Metro:
Diagonal*

Barcelona fashion designer Antonio Miró designs clothes and accessories for men and women. His store also features perfumes, sunglasses, homewear, and stationery. Founded in 1979, the Spanish brand is known for its elegant formalwear, trademark tailoring, and shirts. Its large, flagship store on Enric Granados makes for a relaxing shopping experience, while the store's Espacio Miró often plays host to concerts and events.

LUPO BARCELONA

*Passeig de Gràcia, 124; tel. 93/455-5940; www.
lupobarcelona.com; Mon-Sat 10am-8:30pm; Metro:
Diagonal*

Founded in 1920, Lupo Barcelona is a luxury bag brand that takes some of the city's key artistic and architectural influences (we're looking at you, Gaudí) and puts them into its products. It is the official maker of the Pedrera bags (including a camera bag—€540, bucket bag—€540, and cross-body bag—€480), inspired by Gaudí's nearby buildings. It also has a range of Joan Miró-inspired bags that capture the painter's bright primary colors.

Shoes
CAMPER

*Passeig de Gràcia, 100; tel. 93/467-4148; www.
camper.com; Mon-Sat 10am-9pm; Metro: Diagonal*

The Fluxà family already had a long history of shoemaking when Lorenzo Fluxà founded the brand Camper in 1975—they had been making shoes on the island of Mallorca since 1877. With a rich shoemaking heritage, the company went on to design classic, casual footwear for men, women, and children. Its key design traits are its smart-casual look and its unisex lines, as well as the fact that it is always innovating, bringing out new styles every year. There are stores all over the city, but its Passeig de Gràcia location is particularly spacious and pleasant to browse.

Food and Wine

CACAO SAMPAKA

Carrer del Consell de Cent, 292; tel. 93/272-0833; www.cacaosampaka.com; Mon-Sat 9am-9pm; Metro: Passeig de Gràcia

This gourmet shop is a haven for all things chocolate, and it immediately draws in the eye with its striking black and white façade. Inside, it's like a factory for grown-up chocolate, with multicolored packaging neatly stacked onto sleek shelves and displays. From traditional blocks to surprising combinations, the shop stocks everything a chocoholic could desire. The café in the back is a great place to enjoy a hot chocolate, pastries, cakes, or even chocolate sandwiches.

Books

ALTAÏR

Gran Via de les Corts Catalanes, 616; tel. 93/342-7171; www.altair.es; Mon-Sat 10am-8:30pm; Metro: Passeig de Gràcia

This wonderful bookshop is two floors of travel inspiration. Whet your wanderlust by flicking through travel guides, memoirs, and accounts of exploration across the continents. Although the majority of books are in Spanish or Catalan, English-language books can be found among the Spanish-language versions. There is a good range of maps of Spain and further afield, and a small downstairs café where you can read through your new purchases over a coffee.

MONTJUÏC

Shopping Center

LAS ARENAS

Gran Via de les Corts Catalanes, 373-385; tel. 93/289-0244; www.arenasdebarcelona.com; Mon-Sat 9am-9pm; Metro: Espanya

In a sign of Catalans' disdain for bullfighting, Barcelona turned this former bullring into a shopping mall, and it's worth the visit to see its architecture. It is home to fashion brands like Mango and Desigual as well as to restaurants, a cinema, and a rooftop viewing platform. The lift to the platform costs €1, but escalators inside the shopping center will take you to the rooftop for free. From here, enjoy the excellent views over the Plaça d'Espanya, Montjuïc, and Mount Tibidabo.

Design and Décor

M-STORE

Ronda de Sant Antoni, 39; tel. 93/825-3232; www.moritz.cat; daily 10am-10pm; Metro: Urgell

Part of the Moritz Beer Factory, the M-Store is an industrial-chic space with exposed brick walls and long metal tables holding a range of interesting products, both beer- and non-beer related. Pick up beer mugs, books, and gadgets, as well as Moritz-brewed craft beers and locally designed products such as Papabubble sweets. There's a book and magazine section (international magazines on music, fashion, and art). It's a good spot to pick up a quirky gift or souvenir. Moritz is brewed in Barcelona and is a popular beer in bars and restaurants across Catalonia. It prides itself on being the only beer in the world whose labeling is entirely in Catalan.

GRÀCIA AND PARK GÜELL

Clothing and Accessories

LA CLINIQUE FINE STORE

Carrer dels Mirallers, 7; tel. 68/750-7325; www.lacliniquefinestore.com; Mon-Sat 11:30am-3pm, 4pm-8pm; Metro: Diagonal

This stylish store specializes in vintage eyewear from the 1950s to the 1990s, as well as other vintage pieces that have been beautifully curated in the minimalist shop. Private appointments, either in-store or at your hotel, can be made for a more personal approach. This is no bric-a-brac store; pieces are high-end and unworn and can have prices to match, but if you're after a luxurious and one-of-a-kind treat, this is the place to splurge.

MALAHIERBA

Bonavista, 26; tel. 93/513-5818; www.malahierba.es; Mon-Sat 11am-8:30pm; Metro: Diagonal

This cool local brand, started by two young designers whose headquarters is this Gràcia

Barcelona's Food Markets

Visiting the local market for fresh fruit and vegetables, along with the butchers and fishmongers for meat and fish, is common in Barcelona. Most neighborhood markets are indoors. Many have been going for more than 100 years and are as interesting for their architecture as for their buzzing daily life. They are all also home to some "old man" bars, where you can pull up a stool and watch the world go by over a *café con leche* or a *caña*.

La Boqueria might be the city's most famous market, but with its narrow lanes crowded with tourists, it is far from its most local—and prices tend to be at a premium. If you want to get a real feel for Barcelona, make sure to check out some of its other markets.

MERCAT DE LA BOQUERIA

Spain's most famous market, right on Las Ramblas, draws thousands of tourists every day, but if you arrive early, you can still experience the thrill—like some local chefs—of buying great local produce and browsing at a more leisurely pace (page 53).

MERCAT DE SANTA CATERINA

Located near the Picasso Museum, Mercat de Santa Caterina is immediately recognizable for its wavy, multicolored roof, the result of a refurbishment in 2005. Originally built in 1845, it was the first covered market in the city (page 64).

MERCAT DE LA CONCEPCIÓ

A neighborhood meeting place in Eixample, this market is famed for its flowers but also has a range of fresh produce stalls, as well as stalls selling olives, wine, and vegetarian food (page 78).

MERCAT DE SANT ANTONI

This neighborhood market, on the border of Eixample and Sant Antoni, reopened in May 2018 after a multi-million-euro renovation. Its spacious stalls are packed with fresh produce, and little bars offer a spot for a quick coffee after picking up your picnic supplies (page 86).

shop, features a range of youthful designs and quirky patterns across dresses, tops, skirts, and coats. All products are made right here in Barcelona, and there is also a range of accessories and footwear. The store is light, with wooden floors and a welcoming atmosphere. The brand releases two collections a year and its designs are sold in boutiques as far-flung as Japan and Scotland.

COMAPOSADA JOIERS

Carrer Gran de Gràcia, 42; tel. 93/415-8408; www. barcelonajewels.com; Mon-Sat 10am-2pm, 5pm-8pm; Metro: Diagonal

This family-run business specializes in what it calls "cultural jewelery"—collections inspired by the works of great cultural figures including Picasso, Gaudí, and Dalí. The

collections, unique takes on famous architectural landmarks and artworks, are designed and produced in Barcelona and displayed in this spacious shop in the heart of Eixample. From necklaces inspired by Barcelona's beginnings as the Roman town of Barcino to beautiful brooches, rings, necklaces, and earrings inspired by several different Gaudí works around the city, these jewels make for unique souvenirs.

Design and Décor
WONDER PHOTO SHOP

Carrer Gran de Gràcia, 1; tel. 93/408-8787; www. wonderphotoshop.es; Mon-Sat 10am-9pm; Metro: Diagonal

A fun playground for photo fanatics, the Wonder Photo Shop is the first of its kind to open in Europe and is dedicated to the Fujifilm brand. You can print off photos from your smartphone or create custom photoshoots and photo albums as well as attend regular workshops and events. Lots of cameras and accessories are for sale in this shop that offers a tribute to both digital and analog photography.

Recreation and Activities

PARKS AND HIKING

Ciutadella (along with Park Güell) is the city's most famous park, but there are a host of others as well, including Parc de Collserola, a popular hiking destination that's relatively near the city.

PARK DEL LABERINT

Passeig dels Castanyers, 1; tel. 66/667-7722; daily 10am-7pm; Metro: Mundet

The Parc del Laberint (Labyrinth Park) is home to the oldest gardens in the city, laid out in the late eighteenth century. The showpiece is a maze of cypress hedges, El Laberint, created for the estate's owner, the Marquis de Llupià i Alfarràs, in 1792. It was designed as a riddle to love, and a statue of Eros, the Greek god of love, lies in wait for anyone lucky enough to find the center. The rest of the park, part Neo-classical, part Romantic, features pavilions, fountains, and a pond. It's a magical spot way off the tourist trail, where locals come to stroll and escape the hectic pace of the city.

PARC DE L'ESTACIÓ DEL NORD

Parque de la Estacion del Norte; daily 10am-10:30pm; Metro: Arc de Triomf

Close to Barcelona's Arc de Triomf, this small urban park is a great place for the kids to run around and clamber over the blue mosaic, wave-like structures that emerge from the grass, designed by American artist Beverly Pepper. The park is set on the spot where the Estació del Nord train station stood until 1972.

JARDINES DEL GREC

Pg Santa Madrona, 38; daily 10am-7:30pm; Metro: Paral-lel and cable car

On the slopes of Montjuïc, this park is modeled on ancient Greece, and is even home to a replica of a Greek amphitheater that holds regular concerts throughout the summer as well as a special series of performances as part of the city's Festival del Grec. Originally created as a rose garden for the 1929 International Exposition, the gardens are a charming place to wander, high above the busy city below.

PARC DIAGONAL MAR

Carrer de Llull, 362X; daily 10am-9pm; Metro: Selva de Mar

Kids will adore this park known by locals as the "giant slide park." It's close to the city's Parc del Forum, which hosts concerts and festivals. Located on a disused factory site, the park is divided into seven different areas, all united by one theme—water. It is dotted with lakes and modern sculpture fountains as well as a tubular structure that snakes around the park (it irrigates the gardens with groundwater, part of the park's high sustainability credentials). The park's giant slides are free to use.

PARK JOAN MIRÓ

Carrer d'Aragó, 2; daily 10am-11pm; Metro: Espanya

Just behind the bullring-turned-shopping-center Las Arenas is this park dedicated to Barcelona artist Joan Miró. His 22-meter-tall (72-foot) sculpture *Dona i Ocell* (Woman and Bird) looms high over the green space, once the site of the city's main slaughterhouse.

Barcelona with Children

Barcelona is a great city for children. A feast for the senses, its sights, sounds, smells, and tastes will leave little ones fascinated, engaged, and eager to explore.

TIBIDABO AMUSEMENT PARK

The fun begins with a ride on the funicular up to the highest peak in the Parc de Collserola, Tibidabo, which rises to over 500 meters (1,640 feet) above the city. At the top is an amusement park with a mixture of old-fashioned rides and funfair stalls as well as more modern rides for all ages.

MUSEUMS

Far from the stuffy stereotype, Barcelona's kids' museums are fun, engaging, and interactive. The **Chocolate Museum** is a quick look at the history of chocolate, Barcelona's important role in bringing it to Europe, and—probably best of all for the kids—your admission ticket is an actual chocolate bar. Very Willy Wonka.

CosmoCaixa, the huge science museum, will leave little mouths gaping at the wonders of the universe. It features gigantic dinosaurs and an enormous slice of Amazon rainforest, complete with caimans, piranhas, and other native species.

BARCELONA ZOO

Barcelona's Zoo, set within the Ciutadella Park, has a range of species including rhinoceros, elephants, giraffes, tigers, and penguins, as well as kid-friendly activities in a farmyard zoo and the always-popular pony rides. There are fun play parks, a train that takes visitors around the zoo, and plenty of food options.

L'AQUÀRIUM

Barcelona's aquarium, right on the seafront, is home to over 11,000 animals and attractions, including a tunnel under the shark tanks and animal feeding. Check the aquarium's website for regular

PARC DE COLLSEROLA

Carretera de l'Esglesia, 92; 93/280-3552; Metro: Baixador de Vallvidrera

Barcelona's green lung, the Parc de Collserola is where locals go to escape the hustle and bustle of the city and is a popular spot for walking, cycling, and running. Free to visit, the park offers more than 8,000 hectares (30.8 square miles) of protected pine and oak forests with trails, picnic areas, springs, and lookout points.

A good place to start is the park's **Information Center** (Carretera de l'Església, 92; tel. 93/280-3552; Metro: Baixador de Vallvidrera), where you can pick up maps, find out about hiking trails, and locate facilities such as restrooms. It's an easy, ten-minute walk from the metro station.

The 10-kilometer (6-mile) **Carretera de les Aigües** is a gravel trail popular with cyclists, runners, and walkers; it's one of the most accessible spots in the Serra. To get there, take the Funicular de Vallvidrera (on lines S1 and S2 from Plaça de Catalunya—journey time around 25 minutes), which has a stop right on the trail (stop: Carretera de les Aigües).

CYCLING

In recent years Barcelona's City Hall has made considerable efforts to encourage locals to get around the city by bike. You will notice many cycle paths—today there are more than 180 kilometers (112 miles) of bike lanes around the city; whether pedestrians and cars respect them or not is another matter. Be sure to wear a helmet and, if cycling when dark, reflective material.

Chocolate figures at the Museu de la Xocolata / Chocolate Museum

activities, including feeding time (penguins are fed at 11:30am daily, other animals at various times), diving with sharks (with or without a cage), and weekend family activities.

THE BEACH

Barcelona has the advantage over most cities of being right on the beach, so when the kids get sick of wandering the busy streets, you can spend some time building sandcastles and splashing about in the waves. **La Barceloneta** beach is the closest to the city and the most crowded. Further along is the newer **Nova Icaria Beach**, bordered by a wide boardwalk and plenty of beach bars, and the quieter **Mar Bella**; both are more popular with local families.

Bicycle Rentals

RENT A BIKE

Carrer de Llança, 13; 93/315-6313; www.rentabikebcn. com; daily 9:30am-8pm; Metro: Espanya

Rent a Bike operates this store close to Plaça Espanya, from where cyclists can easily get up onto Montjuïc Hill. City bikes are €5 for two hours and €8 for a day, and mountain bikes are €15 for five hours and €20 for a day rental. It also has a location in the Barri Gòtic (Carrer Regomir, 33, 933193702, daily 9:30am-8pm, Metro: Barceloneta), with easy access to Barcelona's seafront.

CRUISING BARCELONA

Carrer de Jerusalem, 32; 93/011-0311; cruisingbarcelona.com; daily 10am-8pm; Metro: Liceu

Cruise Barcelona offers a range of bikes to rent, from two hours (€6) to a full day (€12). E-bikes and tandems can be rented for €12 for two hours, €18 for five hours, or €22 for a full day. This location is in the Eixample. There's a second branch in Gràcia (Carrer de Santa Tecla, 7, 935187533). Bike tours around the city are also available.

BIKE TOURS BARCELONA

Carrer de L'Esparteria, 3; 93/268-2105; www. biketoursbarcelona.com; daily 10am-7pm; Metro: Barceloneta

Bike Tours Barcelona rents bikes for one hour (€5), two hours (€7), four hours (€10), or a day (€12). Multi-day hires are also available, as are bike tours around the city.

Cycle Routes

Maps of current cycle paths are available from the Plaça de Catalunya tourist information center, or online at www.bcn.cat/bicicleta.

PASSEIG MARÍTIM BOARDWALK

A nice easy route along the seafront, the Passeig Marítim boardwalk is ideal for a leisurely cycle. There are also plenty of stop-off points for an ice cream or a drink along the way. The traffic-free path stretches about 10 kilometers (6 miles) along the seafront from the Carrer de la Drassana (a good place to start) to the Parc del Fòrum.

PLAÇA ESPANYA TO MONTJUÏC CASTLE

The whole area of Montjuïc, with its steep slopes and curved roads, is popular with cyclists. Get those legs pumping with the 7-kilometer (4-mile) ride from Plaça Espanya up to Montjuïc Castle, mainly on quiet roads that can be pretty steep in places (the ride up to the Fundació Joan Miró via Avinguda Francesc Ferrer I Guàrdia and Avinguda de l'Estadi is not too bad because of the gentle zig-zag roads; the steepest ascent is up Passeig Olimpic, Carrer Doctor i Font Quer, and Carrer de Can Valero, which lead to the Passeig del Migdia and the castle). You'll cycle past key sights like the Fundació Joan Miró and the 1992 Olympic park and through a landscape of pines that makes you feel far away from the busy city below. You'll be rewarded with great views from the top and—best of all—a breezy downhill ride on the way back. Get out early to avoid the heat.

CARRETERA DE LES AIGÜES (PARC DE COLLSEROLA)

One of the best places to cycle in Barcelona is the Parc del Collserola, in the hills surrounding the city. You will be treated to spectacular views over Barcelona and the Mediterranean Sea beyond.

There are numerous bike trails in the park for all abilities. The 10-kilometer (6-mile) gravel Carretera de les Aigües ("Road of the Waters," named for the water pipes that once ran along the route) is ideal for cycling and weaves its way across the mountains, giving riders fantastic views of the city. The easiest way to get to the trail is by the Funicular de Vallvidrera (on lines S1 and S2 from Plaça de Catalunya—journey time around 25 minutes), which has a stop right on the trail (stop: Carretera de les Aigües). The funicular permits up to four bikes at once.

SURFING

In summer, the waters off Barcelona are still, but in winter, small waves are common, which make it ideal for beginners (including children) who don't want to tackle anything too intimidating.

PUKAS SURF SCHOOL

Passeig de Joan de Borbó, 93; tel. 93/118-6021; www.pukassurf.com/barcelona; Mon-Fri 10am-7pm, Sat-Sun 9am-7pm; Metro: Barceloneta

This Basque company, which makes surfboards and has surf schools around Spain, is handily located just off the Barceloneta. It offers lessons (from €26/hour for groups, €55 for individuals), rents out boards (€13/hour) and stand-up paddle boards (from €26/hour), and even offers surfboard pilates, if that's your thing.

ESCOLA CATALANA DE SURF

Passeig Joan de Borbó, 78; tel. 93/710-6430; www. escolacatalanadesurf.com; Wed-Sun 10:30am-6pm, Metro: Barceloneta

Since 2003, the Catalan Surf School has been teaching people to surf, and its instructors really know their stuff, giving fun, informative lessons that will plunge you straight into the action. Choose from two-hour lessons to week-long courses at both beginners' and improvement levels. There are children's and adult classes that start at €40 (per person) for a two-hour surf lesson. You can also rent equipment (surfboards from €15 per hour) if you are confident enough to go it alone.

WATERSPORTS

Being right on the beach, Barcelona is also an ideal spot to try out some watersports. Paddle boarding, though a relatively recent trend, is very popular, as are sailing and diving.

MOLOKAI SUP CENTER

Carrer de Meer, 39; tel. 65/408-2099; www. molokaisupcenter.com;Tues-Sat 10am-7pm, Sun 10am-6pm, Metro: Barceloneta

The place to try out stand-up paddleboarding (SUP) in Barcelona, Molokai offers boards to rent as well as classes where you can learn the basics if you've never tried SUP before. A basic two-hour private lesson is €60 for an individual and €80 for a couple. The price is €30 per person for a group (maximum of six people). Board rentals cost €15 for an hour and €25 for two hours.

CENTRE MUNICIPAL DE VELA

Moll de Gregal; tel. 93/225-7940; www. velabarcelona.com; daily 9am-6pm; Metro: Ciutadella | Vila Olímpica

On Barcelona's Nova Icària beach, just west of the Barceloneta, the Centre Municipal de Vela offers dinghy sailing (two-hour lessons from €56), kayaking and windsurfing courses, and kayaks and paddle boards to rent.

BASE NÀUTICA MUNICIPAL DE LA MAR BELLA

Av. del Litoral; tel. 93/221-0432; www.basenautica. org; daily 9am-8pm; Metro: Poblenou

Located on Mar Bella beach and popular with couples and families, Base Nàutica Municipal de la Mar Bella offers a range of courses, including windsurfing (two-hour class from €70), paddle surfing (90-minute class from €40), and catamaran (three-hour class from €70).

VANASDIVE

Av. del Litoral, 86-96; tel. 93/221-0548; www. vanasdive.com; Metro: Poblenou

This diving center, on Mar Bella beach, runs diving courses for beginners and offers PADI and SSI scuba diving certifications. Its Try Scuba Diving course (€45pp), during which divers reach a maximum of 6 meters (20 feet), is ideal for beginners.

FOOTBALL MATCHES

TOP EXPERIENCE

FC Barcelona

Camp Nou stadium, C. d'Aristides Maillol, 12; www. fcbarcelona.com; tickets from €69; Metro: Collblanc

Soccer is more than a sport in Spain; it is a religion. FC (Football Club) Barcelona is one of the country's top teams; it plays on weekends during the season (August-May) at the Camp Nou stadium.

Matches (90 minutes) are lively, with singing in Catalan; the waving of the Catalan flag, the *estalada* (the "starred flag"—commonly waved by supporters of an independent Catalonia), is a common sight. The atmosphere is always upbeat, with singing, horn honking, and general merriment; violent behavior is rare. Fans tend to wear the blue and claret team colors. The atmosphere is family-friendly, and you shouldn't worry about taking older children to a match.

The stadium opens 90 minutes ahead of kick-off on match days—it is worth getting to the stadium nice and early to enjoy the build-up and find your seat in plenty of time. The stadium, open to the elements, can get cold in winter, so take layers for extra warmth. The cheaper seats higher up in the stadium tend to be more filled with tourists and fewer regular attendees. You'll find many of the local fans sitting behind the goals or lower down, closer to the pitch.

Alcoholic drinks are not sold inside the stadium, which only offers alcohol-free beer in the run-up to and during the match, and you are not allowed to bring alcohol into the stadium. Fans are free to bring food and soft drinks—in fact, most local fans do so, with some of the most common snacks being satisfyingly big baguette sandwiches filled with ham and cheese. (There are snack stalls inside the stadium, but there is not a great amount

FC Barcelona

Barcelona's home football team, known as *Barça* to its fans, is much more than just a sports team. Its motto, "Més que un club" (more than a club), points to its status as an important symbol of Catalan culture and tradition.

When the Catalan language and culture were severely repressed under dictator Francisco Franco, one relatively safe way to embrace Catalan identity was to be a supporter of FC Barcelona and to make the weekly pilgrimage to its gigantic stadium, Camp Nou. The club has never shied away from wading into politics—several big names associated with Barça, from former coach Pep Guardiola to defender Gerard Piqué, have expressed their support for independence.

The club was founded in 1899 by a group of English, Swiss, and Catalan footballers and played in mainly amateur competitions until 1910.

In 1928, Barça and several other teams founded *La Liga,* Spain's premier football division. The team holds the distinction (along with Athletic Bilbao and arch-rivals Real Madrid) of never having been relegated from the league.

The team is known for its blue- and red-striped football shirt, which local legend says was chosen because blue and red were the colors of FC Basel, the home team of Swiss Barça founder Joan Gamper. The shirt has been worn by some of the world's greatest players, from legendary Johan Cruyff, who went on to manage the team, to Brazilians Ronaldo and Ronaldinho and today's Lionel Messi.

Barcelona holds dozens of records, including being the team with the most European trophies (16) and the only team to have won the treble of Cup, League, and Champions League—twice. The team has a notorious rivalry with Real Madrid, known as El Clásico.

of choice, so bring a little picnic and you'll fit right in.)

It's best to book tickets in advance; they usually become available on the team's official website (www.fcbarcelona.com/tickets/football/football-tickets) around four weeks before matches. Tickets can also be booked on TicketMaster (www.ticketmaster.es), which sells tickets at the official price. Bear in mind that match days and times are often not confirmed until around two weeks beforehand, so it could be a good idea to wait until they are officially confirmed than risk a change and miss the match.

The best way to get to the stadium is by metro. Get off at Collblanc or Les Corts. The road between, the Travessera de les Corts, is lined with bars where fans can stop for a pre-match beer and get into the game day spirit.

SWIMMING POOLS

Barcelona's beaches are generally clean, and it is safe to swim in the sea off them. The city also has many municipal swimming pools.

CLUB NATACIÓ ATLÈTIC BARCELONETA

Passeig de Joan de Borbó, 79; tel. 93/221-0010; www.cnab.cat; Mon-Fri 6:30am-11pm, Sat 7am-11pm, Sun 8am-8pm; Metro: Barceloneta

This seafront sports center has one indoor pool and two outdoor pools with loungers, just off the beach. Day tickets are around €13.

PISCINA MUNICIPAL DE MONTJUÏC

Avinguda Miramar, 31; tel. 93/423-4041; June 29-Sept 2 (exact dates may vary); 11am-6:30pm; Metro: Montjuïc Funicular from Metro Paral-lel

This pool boasts the best views of any pool in the city. Set high up on the hill of Montjuïc, it has a 25-meter (82-foot) swimming pool and a diving pool, built so that the diving competition during the 1992 Olympic Games would have a spectacular backdrop. It is open only during the summer (July and August). Entrance is €6.65 for adults and €4.60 for children aged 6-14 years old; under-fives go free.

SPAS

AMBROSIA SPA

Passatge de Domingo, 9; tel. 93/186-3342; www.ambrosiaspabcn.com; Mon-Sat midday-9pm; Metro: Diagonal

In the heart of the swanky Eixample, this city spa offers a range of treatments from facials to massages, following the latest wellness trends. The invitingly named Wine Therapy (€125) includes a grapeseed body scrub, a 60-minute body massage, and a glass of wine with chocolates.

FLOTARIUM

Plaça de Narcís Oller, 3; tel. 93/217-3637; www.flotarium.com; Tues-Sat 10am-9pm, Sun 10am-3pm, Mon 3pm-9pm; Metro: Diagonal

This alternative relaxation experience involves floating in your own individual capsule; the zero-gravity atmosphere helps you to relax. The Flotarium contains 600 liters (158 gallons) of water and 300 kilos (661 pounds) of Epsom salts, causing the body to easily float on the water. The 50-minute session (€40 per person) is said to help ease everything from migraines to jet lag.

TOURS

Whatever your interests, there is a tour for you in Barcelona. An increasing number of small tour companies specialize in specific facets of the city, from its gastronomy to its fascinating history.

Bus Tour

BARCELONA TURISTIC BUS

tel. 93/465-5313; www.barcelonabusturistic.cat; Winter: 9am-7pm, summer: 9am-8pm; every 5-25 mins depending on the season; €30 for one day, €40 for two days; 4-12-year olds €16 or €21

The hop-on-hop-off bus takes passengers all around the city on three routes: red (south of the city to the sea front), blue (north of the city), and green (east of the city along the sea front). All the big names, including the Sagrada Familia, Camp Nou, and the Cathedral, are accounted for, and the bus goes further, including outer neighborhoods of Sant Gervasi and Sarrià. There are stops outside places of interest that makes it easy to hop off, see a sight in more detail, then hop back on another bus later on. There is an audio guide pointing out interesting places along the way, as well as free Wi-Fi. The red and blue routes are approximately two hours long, while the green route is around 40 minutes.

Buy tickets online (there's a 10 percent discount for online purchases) or at the city's tourist offices. Stops are clearly marked with the company's logo. The recommended starting point for the red and blue route is the central Plaça de Catalunya, and for the green route, the seaside Port Olímpic.

Boat Tour

ORSOM CATAMARAN

Moll de Drassanes, Portal de la Pau; tel. 93/441-0537; www.barcelona-orsom.com; Metro: Drassanes

One alternative way to see the city is from the Mediterranean Sea. Orsom Catamaran takes passengers out of the port area and around along the seafront during the 90-minute journey affording views of the Sagrada Familia, Mount Tibidabo, and the Torre Agbar.

Options include the **Catamaran Sail & Skyline** (adults €15.50), the **Jazz & Chill Out Sail** (adults €1.50), and the **Sunset Cruise** (adults €19.50). Passengers can get comfortable on the catamaran's nets and enjoy a drink from the bar during one of the cruises on offer.

The launch point is directly opposite the Mirador de Colom (Columbus Monument); you can buy tickets there or reserve them online. Be aware that the catamaran does not sail in bad weather, so call ahead to double check.

Walking Tours

BARCELONA WALKING TOURS

Plaça de Catalunya, 17; 93/285-3832; http://bcnshop.barcelonaturisme.com; daily 8:30am-9pm; Metro: Plaça de Catalunya

Several tours run by the Oficina d'Informació de Turisme de Barcelona provide a useful introduction to the city, with information on history, culture, art, and cuisine. The two-hour **Barri Gòtic tour** (€14.40) covers Barcelona's oldest city, exploring its history from Roman Times to the Middle Ages. Other tours include the two-hour **Gourmet Walking Tour** (€19.80) that takes visitors around some of the city's best markets and gourmet food shops and the two-hour **Modernisme Tour** (€14.40), an introduction to the style and works of architects, including Gaudí. Get 10 percent off all tours by booking online via the Barcelona Tourism website.

RUNNER BEAN WALKING TOURS

Carrer del Carme, 44; tel. 63/610-8776; www.
runnerbeantours.com; daily 9am-6pm; Metro: Liceu
Spanish-Irish couple Gorka and Anne-Marie started Runner Bean tours in 2010, and since then their guides have been showing visitors around the city. Free walking tours (donations are welcomed) include the two-and-a-half-hour **Gothic Quarter tour** (meeting point Plaça Reial, for which the closest metro stop is Liceu) and the **Gaudí tour** (meeting point Plaça Reial). Fixed-price tours include the **Kids & Family walking tour** (€16 per

person—meeting point outside Jaume I metro stop).

Booking ahead is not required, but space is limited, so it's advised either to book online or to arrive 20 minutes before the tour starts to ensure you get a place. Guides hold a lime-green Runner Bean Tours umbrella and are easy to spot.

HIDDEN CITY TOURS

Plaça Nova, 3; tel. 65/558-5156; www.
hiddencitytours.com
Previously homeless people guide visitors around the city, showing them a different side to Barcelona in a tour that is designed to provide work for the city's homeless (or previously homeless) population. Tours mix some local history with the homeless population's experience of the city. One option is the two-hour **Barcelona Classic Walking Tour** (€16), an eye-opening socio-historic tour through the city's Gothic Quarter that's just as likely to point out local soup kitchens as local historic sights. Groups are small, so it's easy to really see the city through someone else's eyes and ask questions. It's a great way to give something back to locals and see a completely different side of Barcelona. All guides speak English.

Orsom Catamaran

CIVIL WAR TOUR

Guides and history buffs Nick Lloyd and Catherine Howley give an engrossing and in-depth tour exploring the Spanish Civil War and how it affected Barcelona. You'll visit central areas, including the Plaça de Catalunya and Barri Gòtic, and learn what happened before and during the war at each site. Props and photographs enhance the experience and bring the stories to life. Those interested in history will be impressed. Groups are limited to a manageable number, and at €30 per person for a five-hour tour, it's an excellent value. Tours depart Monday, Tuesday, Thursday, Friday, and Saturday—contact Nick by email for meeting place, queries, and bookings. Private tours (€290) are also available.

Food Tours

DEVOUR BARCELONA FOOD TOUR

tel. 69/511-1932; www.devourbarcelonafoodtours.com

Devour Spain runs food tours in cities across the country, using local, knowledgeable guides and partnering with neighboring, often family-run businesses to give visitors an authentic taste of Spain. It currently runs eight tours in and around Barcelona. The three-and-a-half-hour **Tapas, Taverns and History Tour** (€99 per person) is a two-in-one tour that covers the history of Barcelona as well as visits to some of its most authentic old taverns. Discover a more local side to Barcelona with the two-and-a-half-hour **Tapas Like a Local: Sant Antoni Neighborhood Tapas Tour** (€69 per person), during which you will encounter the true art of a tapas bar crawl, walking from bar to bar and tucking into excellent tapas at each one.

Bicycle Tours

One of the best ways to dip your toe into cycling in the big city is to do a bike tour.

CRUISING BARCELONA

Carrer de Jerusalem, 32; www.cruisingbarcelona.com

Started by a Dutch couple in 2005, this company runs daily group and private bike tours, as well as offering bike rental. The three-hour **Original Tour** (€24 per person, daily 11am), with an English-speaking guide, takes you through several different districts of the city including the old town, the Modernista buildings of the Eixample, and the seafront. A nice extra is that you can keep the bike for the rest of the day for an extra €4. Cruising Barcelona has a second location at Carrer de Santa Tecla, 7 in Gràcia.

BIKE TOURS BARCELONA

Carrer de L'Espartería, 3; 93/268-2105; www.biketoursbarcelona.com; daily 10am-7pm; Metro: Barceloneta

Since 1995, Bike Tours Barcelona has been working closely with the city council to promote cycling in the city. It offers daily bike tours (€25 per person, 11am in the Plaça de Sant Jaume outside the tourist office—look out for the red-T-shirt-wearing guides). The tour goes through the Gothic quarter and Ciutadella Park, past the Sagrada Familia, and down along the seafront.

CLASSES

Cooking

BCNKITCHEN

Carrer de la Fusina, 15; 93/268-1253; www.bcnkitchen.com; €70 per person; classes run from 10am-7:30pm; Metro: Arc de Triomf

bcnKITCHEN offers a four-hour Market Visit and Spanish Cooking Workshop in English. Each class begins with a visit to a market—either the iconic La Boqueria or the beautiful neighborhood market Santa Caterina—where your chef will help you pick out your ingredients. Then it's back to the kitchen, where you will cook a five-course meal under the guidance of your chef—including *tortilla española* (Spanish potato omelet), gazpacho, paella, and *crema Catalana*, a typical Catalan dessert. You'll then enjoy a meal and a glass of wine. It's a fun experience that will teach you some valuable skills, so you can recreate some Spanish classics back home.

Language

CAMINO BARCELONA

Carrer Comte d'Urgell, 78; tel. 93/467-8585; www. caminobarcelona.com; Metro: Urgell

This language school, certified by Spain's Instituto Cervantes, offers many different language-class options. Teachers are all qualified native speakers, and class sizes are small (maximum 10 people per class). An intense one-week course of 20 lessons for a complete beginner starts at €159. There is optional on-site accommodation or the possibility of being placed with a host family. The school also offers courses such as "Spanish and Salsa," "Spanish and Flamenco," and "Business Spanish."

Accommodations

The center of the city is relatively compact, so basing yourself in Eixample or the Barri Gòtic is a good option for both public transport and walking. If you want to stay closer to the beach, Barceloneta is a good option; it's close to Las Ramblas and has good metro links into the city center.

LAS RAMBLAS AND BARRI GÒTIC

€200-300

★ HOTEL 1898

Las Ramblas, 109; tel. 93/552-9552; www.hotel1898. com; €260; Metro: Catalunya

With a great location right on Las Ramblas, Hotel 1898 was opened in 2005 in the former headquarters of the General Philippines Tobacco Company, built in 1881 by Catalan architect Josep Oriol Mestres. Its early 2000s renovations preserved many of the period interiors. Rooms range from the comfortable classic room to the exquisite Colonial Suite, complete with its very own terrace and swimming pool. The hotel's spa is housed in the former coal bunker, with exposed-brick walls, pool, steam bath, hydromassage, and dry sauna, as well as a fitness room. La Isabela rooftop terrace has a pool, bar, and spectacular views across the city. In summer, guests can enjoy their breakfast on the rooftop terrace.

HOTEL NERI

Carrer de Sant Sever, 5; tel. 93/304-0655; www. hotelneri.com; €250; Metro: Jaume I

This boutique hotel in the old Jewish quarter, just steps from Plaça Felip Neri and the cathedral, is set in two historic palaces, one built in the 12th century, the other the 17th. Its 22 rooms include classic rooms on the first and second floors, deluxe rooms (some with a private terrace), and the Suite Neri, which comes with a separate living area. All rooms feature amenities such as kettles with tea and coffee-making facilities and bluetooth speakers. A rooftop terrace bar has great views over the city, while a terrace on the Felip Neri square is a lovely, relaxing spot.

Over €300

THE WITTMORE

Carrer de Riudarenes, 7; tel. 93/550-0885; www. thewittmore.com; €350; Metro: Jaume I

On a small side street in the Gothic quarter, this intimate 22-room five-star hotel is a luxurious, adults-only accommodation. Photographs are strictly forbidden, giving it an old-world charm devoid of the modern thirst for selfies. It has a British design twist, with sumptuous fabrics, wooden furniture, and design additions like Roberts radios. There are five different room sizes to choose from, from the cute "tiny" to the

Where to Stay If...

You want to be in the heart of Barcelona's Modernista masterpieces
... the Eixample.
You want to explore Barcelona's rich medieval history
... Barri Gòtic.
You want to stay by the beach
... the Waterfront.
You want a small town, off-the-beaten-track feel
... Gràcia.
You want to stay in one of the city's coolest neighborhoods
... Poble Sec and Sant Antoni in Montjuïc.
You're on a budget
... Gràcia.
You value peace and quiet
... Montjuïc.
You're a night owl or party animal
...Barri Gòtic / El Born.

palatial suites. A beautiful rooftop sun deck is the ideal place to relax after a long day of sightseeing. The hotel restaurant, Witty, does breakfast, lunch, and dinner as well as cocktails.

EL RAVAL
€100-200
★ **CASA CAMPER BARCELONA**
Carrer d'Elisabets, 11; tel. 93/342-6280; €180; www. casacamper.com; Metro: Universitat
This hip boutique hotel in the heart of El Raval belongs to the Spanish shoe brand Camper and is also home to the Michelin-starred Dos Palillos restaurant. Its 30 rooms and 10 suites are modern and minimalist, with splashes of color on bright red walls. Instead of the usual mini bar, guests can enjoy the complimentary "tentempié," a buffet of sandwiches, salads, soups, fruits, desserts, snacks, soft drinks, and tea and coffee in the lobby, room, mini lounge, or terrace. The rooftop terrace is ideal for breakfast with a view or an evening drink while the sun sets. There is a gym, and the Dos Billares bar comes complete with pool tables and other games.

BARCELÓ RAVAL
Rambla del Raval, 17-21; tel. 93/320-1490; www. barcelo.com/en-gb/barcelo-hotels/hotels/spain/ barcelona/barcelo-raval; €120; Metro: Liceu
Hip design and reasonable prices make this hotel a great option close to Las Ramblas (on the grittier El Raval side). Rooms—including doubles, triples, and interconnecting rooms ideal for families—feature rain-head showers, LCD TVs, and exquisitely comfortable beds. The 360-degree rooftop terrace, with swimming pool, is a great place to relax at the end of the day.

LA RIBERA AND EL BORN
€100-200
★ **CHIC & BASIC BORN**
Carrer de la Princesa, 50; tel. 93/295-4652; www. chicandbasic.com/hotel-barcelona-born; €120; Metro: Arc de Triomf
Set in a 19th-century apartment block, this minimalist hotel proves that "budget" doesn't have to mean "boring." Rooms are all-white and light-filled, and they range from singles and basic doubles to deluxe doubles with balconies looking out onto

Best Accommodations

★ **Hotel Almanac:** This stylish five-star hotel opened in late 2017. With a prime location (in the Eixample, close to Plaza de Catalunya) and stunning rooftop bar, it's one of the city's coolest new openings.

★ **Praktik Vinoteca:** This wine-themed hotel in the upmarket Eixample features reasonably priced rooms and a welcome glass of wine on arrival.

★ **Pars Tailor's Hostel:** This hostel, run by a mother-daughter team, is designed like a tailor's shop and brings a huge dose of style to the usually soulless hostel sector.

★ **Casa Gràcia:** Casa Gràcia is part of a new wave of hip hostels for the discerning traveler on a budget. Social activities like tapas crawls bring travelers together.

★ **Margot House:** This home away from home (if you lived in the pages of Architectural Digest, that is) is a beautifully designed oasis in the heart of the city.

★ **Hotel 1898:** A luxurious setting with excellent transport right on Las Ramblas, this stylish hotel has its own spa and rooftop pool.

★ **Casa Camper Barcelona:** This 30-room hotel is a hip destination in El Raval for its vivid decor, rooftop terrace, and its own Michelin-starred restaurant.

★ **Chic & Basic Born:** A great budget option in the heart of the cool Born district, this hotel is easy on the wallet but doesn't compromise on comfort or style.

the street. Shower cubicles in the rooms are somewhat of a feature—but this may be better for couples than friends sharing rooms, because of the lack of privacy. The common area is cozy, with big sofas and free tea, coffee, and water.

€200-300
YURBBAN PASSAGE HOTEL

Carrer de Trafalgar, 26; tel. 93/882-8977; www.yurbbanpassage.com; €230; Metro: Urquinaona

This chic boutique hotel and spa in the hip Ribera district is housed in a former textile factory and has retained some of its former industrial-design touches throughout. Rooms are minimalist but comfortable, with mini bars stocked with Catalan products, pillow menus, and satellite TVs. A restaurant manned by a Michelin-starred chef, a luxury spa, and a magnificent roof terrace with sun loungers and pool add to the high-end atmosphere.

THE WATERFRONT
€100-200
HOTEL OASIS

Plà de Palau 17; tel. 93/319-4396; www.hoteloasis.es; €160; Metro: Barceloneta

Hotel Oasis is a comfortable base that prides itself on being excellent value for money. Its handy location, close to both the beach and old town, means the city's major sights are an easy walk away. Rooms are simple and comfortable, with white bedding and wooden accents. A daily breakfast buffet and snack bar will keep you full, and a cute summer outdoor terrace and pool are great for cooling off.

€200-300
THE SERRAS

Passeig de Colom, 9; tel. 93/169-1868; www.hoteltheserrasbarcelona.com; €270; Metro: Barceloneta

This boutique hotel, in the building where

Picasso had his first studio, gives guests the best of both worlds; it is located on the edge of the Gothic Quarter and a short stroll away from Barceloneta beach. The 28 guest rooms and suites are bright and stylish, with either sea views or views onto the Barri Gòtic. Rooms feature coffee machines and designer toiletries, plus a smart phone with complimentary international calls that you can take out into the city to navigate. The rooftop terrace has great views over Barcelona's marina, while Catalan cuisine and cocktails are on offer in its restaurant and bar. Make your reservation well in advance.

Over €300
HOTEL W
Plaça De La Rosa Dels Vents, 1 Final, Passeig de Joan de Borbó; tel. 93/295-2800; www.w-barcelona.com; €400; Metro: Barceloneta
The hotel W, the glass, sail-shaped hotel on the seafront, has its own luxurious town within its sleek walls—from its stunning rooftop bar and infinity pool that looks out over the Mediterranean to a range of restaurants, a spa, and beachside bars with sun loungers—and you may never want to leave once you've checked in. Glass-walled rooms look out onto either the sea or the city; request your preferred vista when booking. Well-located for the beach, the magnificent seafront location means the Hotel W is actually a bit of a walk from Barcelona's old town and center.

HOTEL ARTS
Carrer de la Marina, 19-21; tel. 93/221-1000; www. hotelartsbarcelona.com; €370; Metro: Ciutadella | Vila Olímpica
Hotel Arts is set inside the blue skyscraper on Barcelona's seafront. The upper-floor suites, especially, have spectacular views over the sea, city, or—in some cases—both. The outdoor pool and easy beach access make this a great luxury option. The Club, on the 33rd floor, is available to guests who book club rooms and suites, and it offers a private check-in and a lounge that serves five complimentary gourmet buffets every day. Opened

in 2018, the ground-floor P41 Bar specializes in cocktails based on the 41st parallel (which Barcelona sits on) and is a cool place to wind down. With restaurants, a luxury spa with jaw-dropping views, outdoor pool, and Michelin-starred restaurant, guests are spoiled for choice for entertainment and dining options. Surprisingly, guests in standard rooms pay extra for Wi-Fi.

EIXAMPLE
Under €100
HOTEL CENTER GRAN VÍA
Gran Via Corts Catalanes 573; tel. 93/451-2898; www.centergranvia.com; €90; Metro: Universitat
The 15-room Hotel Center Gran Vía is a good budget option in the typically upmarket Eixample neighborhood. Set out like a typical Spanish *pensión*, or guesthouse, the hotel is located on the first floor of the building, a five-minute walk from Plaça de Catalunya. Rooms are a good size; some feature balconies with a table and chairs. Bathrooms include essential toiletries and a hairdryer. Note that reception is manned only between 9:30am-2pm and 7pm-midnight. If you arrive between 2pm and 7pm, the hotel will send you an entry code and your room number and will leave the key in your room.

HOTEL PRAKTIK GARDEN
Carrer de la Diputació, 325; tel. 93/467-5279; www. hotelpraktikgarden.com; €90; Metro: Girona
The Praktik hotel chain has a handful of hotels in Barcelona and Madrid, and it aims to provide reasonably priced accommodation without compromising on design or style. Praktik Garden gets its name from its leafy garden terrace on the first floor, complete with sun loungers—a cool place to chill out. Rooms are minimalist, clean, and white, with comfortable beds, essential toiletries, and a hairdryer.

ECOZENTRIC BARCELONA
Calle Balmes, 23; tel. 93/412-2118; www.ecozentric. com; €70; Metro: Universitat
Many of Barcelona's hotels are increasingly

environmentally friendly, but EcoZentric Barcelona is a dedicated eco-guesthouse. Eco-friendly features include low-consumption LED TVs and thermostat showers, and a part of every payment goes to tree planting and the reforestation of local woodland. Several doubles, some with a balcony or terrace, are available in the guesthouse, which takes up one floor of a grand building in the Eixample. Rooms are simple and amenities, basic, but for the price and location, EcoZentric Barcelona is a good option if you're on a budget.

€100-200
★ PRAKTIK VINOTECA
Carrer de Balmes, 51; tel. 93/454-5028; www. hotelpraktikvinoteca.com; €140; Metro: Passeig de Gràcia
This wine-themed hotel, part of the stylish budget Praktik hotel chain, is a great inexpensive option that doesn't sacrifice style. It's ideally located a five-minute walk from Plaça de Catalunya and the start of Las Ramblas. Guests are welcomed with a complimentary glass of wine, and wine tastings, from €18 per person, are available with the hotel's own sommelier. Breakfast is a buffet of local produce served in the stylish, wood-clad dining room. Rooms are simple, light, and comfortable, and are decorated with wine-themed touches, such as paintings of vintage wine bottles.

RETROME
Carrer de Girona, 81; tel. 93/174-4037; www.retrome. net/barcelona; €155; Metro: Girona
In the heart of the Eixample, Retrome is a stylish, retro-themed boutique hotel that is easy on the wallet. Rooms include the small retro double, the romantic retro studio with terrace, and the retro duplex studio with patio. Rooms are comfortable, with high-quality beds and little design touches like armchairs, lamps, and colorful wall paintings. Downstairs, the Retrome Café and Lounge has an outdoor terrace on the street.

CASA BONAY
Gran Via de les Corts Catalanes, 700; tel. 93/545-8050; www.casabonay.com; €190; Metro: Girona
A stylish project by a group of Barcelona creatives, the 1869 building that houses Casa Bonay has been completely renovated, both to preserve the historical elements and to inject a huge dose of style—with features like antique tile floors, designer lighting, and bathroom products. Rooms include nice touches like yoga mats and complimentary movie streaming. A public rooftop beach bar is a cool place to grab a drink, while the private rooftop space is for guests only. The Libertine Bar serves breakfast as well as all-day food and drinks.

ROOM MATE EMMA
Carrer del Rosselló, 205; tel. 93/238-5606; room-matehotels.com/es/emma; €145; Metro: Provença
The stylish Room Mate chain of boutique hotels gives each its different hotels a name and personality that describes the kind of person who stays there. Room Mate Emma is "daring, cheerful, and very creative," and has a futuristic, space-age-themed interior. Rooms are modern with splashes of color—bright pink runs throughout the hotel—and range from the comfortable (if compact) standard to deluxe, triples, and suites with terraces, some with plunge pools. A good buffet breakfast will set you up for a day of exploring.

HOTEL PULITZER
Carrer de Bergara, 8; tel. 93/481-6767; www.hotelpulitzer.es; €180; Metro: Catalunya
This boutique hotel close to Plaça de Catalunya is a cool spot with a fun-loving atmosphere. Both locals and guests hang out on its buzzing rooftop bar, which regularly hosts DJ and music nights. Its 91 rooms are elegant, with leather armchairs, dark wood, and designer lighting. Facilities include a restaurant and lobby bar, as well as the option to rent Brompton bikes and order your own personal trainer or yoga instructor.

€200-300
★ MARGOT HOUSE
Paseo de Gracia 46; tel. 93/272-0076; €200; www.
margothouse.es; Metro: Passeig de Gràcia

Named after Wes Anderson heroine Margot Tenenbaum, the nine-room Margot House could have leapt straight off the screen for its quirky decor that's dripping with style. Its small size makes it feel like you are staying in the home of a very stylish friend. Each room is decorated differently, with light wood, designer lamps, and cozy textiles made in Spain, as well as designer toiletries and statement features (like a roll-top bath in the middle of the room). There's a daily breakfast buffet with delicious local produce. It's a calm oasis in the heart of the city.

COTTON HOUSE HOTEL
Gran Via de les Corts Catalanes, 670; tel.
93/450-5045; www.hotelcottonhouse.com; €280;
Metro: Passeig de Gràcia

Set in Barcelona's former Cotton Guild, this five-star hotel has a feel of old-fashioned luxury, from its friendly, smartly-dressed staff to its Art-Deco-inspired decor. Standard double rooms are labeled "cozy," which is possibly a charming way to say "small"—but they are packed with luxurious touches like sumptuously soft sheets, comfortable beds, and a well-stocked mini bar. Some rooms also have a balcony with a table and chairs, a lovely place to wind down after a busy day. There's a gym, a rooftop terrace with a small pool, and a spacious outdoor terrace with bar. A delicious daily breakfast includes a buffet and dishes made to order.

THE ONE
Carrer de Provença, 277; tel. 93/214-2070; www.
hotelstheone.com; €260; Metro: Diagonal

Five-star hotel The One (part of the H10 hotel group, which holds several hotels around the city) straddles the high-end Eixample neighborhood, home to some of Gaudí's most well-known works, and the hip Gràcia, which has much more of a neighborhood feel—and it's a great base from which to explore both. The helpful concierges are happy to answer questions and provide recommendations. Rooms are comfortable, with muted color palettes and stylish, colorful armchairs and artworks. In summer, the rooftop terrace, complete with bar and plunge pool, is a great place to cool off. Other facilities include the Despacio Spa, a 24-hour gym, and the Somni restaurant and cocktail bar.

Over €300
HOTEL OMM
Carrer Rosselló, 265; tel. 93/445-4000; www.
hotelomm.com; €330; Metro: Diagonal

Hotel Omm is a stylish oasis, visited just as much by locals (as a place to hang out in the bar, or for their regular events) as by travelers. It is home to a spa, hair salon, and rooftop terrace with a small pool (open to guests only during the day and to the public on summer evenings, when it plays host to live music). Rooms include doubles, superior doubles, and junior and senior suites (with four-poster beds). Toiletries are bespoke and locally produced; Bose speakers, room service, and mini bars that include a range of local produce are nice touches. Breakfast is a buffet with pastries, breads, and vegetarian options like tortilla and tomato bread, as well as made-to-order dishes.

★ HOTEL ALMANAC
Gran Via de les Corts Catalanes, 621; tel.
93/018-7000; www.almanachotels.com/barcelona;
€360; Metro: Passeig de Gràcia

Opened in December 2017, the stylish Hotel Almanac is a five-star slice of laid-back luxury just a couple of minutes from Plaça de Catalunya. Its 91 rooms (including 30 suites) have luxurious touches, such as bespoke toiletries and tablets that you can take out with you during the day (and that can put you directly in touch with the hotel's concierge). All rooms come with breakfast and a free minibar stocked with snacks and drinks, including the hotel's own craft beer. The stunning roof terrace has a bar and pool, as well as panoramic views over the city. Don't miss the breakfast—a substantial savory and sweet buffet is accompanied by plates to order, including eggs and pancakes. The Liana restaurant, where breakfast is served, has five dedicated pastry chefs, so unsurprisingly the sweet options—including the mouth-watering almond croissant—are excellent.

GRÀCIA AND PARK GÜELL
€100-200
GENERATOR BARCELONA

Carrer de Còrsega, 373; tel. 93/220-0377; www. *generatorhostels.com/destinations/barcelona; €30* *dorms, €180 privates; Metro: Diagonal*

This hip hostel chain's Barcelona outpost is more than just accommodation; it's the place to party the night away or to enjoy a laid-back beer in its bar. Located in the hip Gràcia neighborhood, its own village within the city, there are dorm and private room options, including twin and triple rooms. The penthouse with terrace sleeps up to four people. Generator's bar, with its 300 hanging ceiling lanterns, serves breakfast, lunch, and dinner.

★ CASA GRÀCIA

Passeig de Gràcia, 116 Bis; tel. 93/174-0528; www. *casagraciabcn.com; dorms €40, doubles €150;* *Metro: Diagonal*

Set in a stylish Modernista townhouse, the large Casa Gràcia is part of a new wave of hostels that ditches cramped, uncomfortable accommodation for something much more stylish. Dorms (mixed and female-only) and single, double, three-, four-, five-, and six-person private rooms have high ceilings and cool, minimalist décor (and are ideal for groups). Common spaces are comfy and cool; there's a communal kitchen for guests to use, as well as La Paisana restaurant, which serves tapas and Catalan-inspired cuisine. Regular activities include yoga classes, tapas tours, and music nights.

MONTJUÏC
Under €100
★ PARS TAILOR'S HOSTEL

Carrer de Sepúlveda, 146; tel. 93/250-5684; www. *parshostels.com; dorms €40; Metro: Urgell*

This design hotel is inspired by a 1930 tailor's shop, and there are design nods to its past throughout, from vintage sewing machines to lush fabric wall hangings. The hotel was founded and designed by a mother-and-daughter team, who sourced furnishings from Barcelona flea markets. Rooms are themed around different fabrics (cashmere, kimono, polka dot) and include six-, eight-, and 12-bed mixed dorms and 12-bed female dorms. There's a fully equipped kitchen for guests to use, and regular social activities such as free tours and paella nights.

€100-200
HOTEL BRUMMEL

Nou de la Rambla, 174; tel. 93/125-8622; www. *hotelbrummell.com; €175; Metro: Paral·lel*

Located in the cool Poble Sec neighborhood, Hotel Brummel is a hip hotel with a laid-back feel. It's slightly off the beaten track, meaning you get a neighborhood feel just a five-minute walk from the nearest metro station (from there, it's a 10-minute metro ride into the heart of the city). The stylish rooftop, complete with swimming pool, gives a real sense of calm, as does the urban garden courtyard. Guests can enjoy breakfast and brunch on the leafy patio. The 20 rooms, which include the poolside classic and penthouse, are modern and comfortable.

HOTEL MARKET

Carrer del Comte Borrell, 68; tel. 93/325-1205; www. *hotelmarketbarcelona.com; €130; Metro: Sant Antoni*

Located in the heart of the hip Sant Antoni, Hotel Market is a stylish boutique hotel at a reasonable price. Rooms, including singles, doubles, and suites, have wooden floors and stylish interiors, with black accents on headboards and frames. There's a downstairs restaurant that does classic Catalan food and offers free mineral water at reception.

Over €300

HOTEL MIRAMAR

Plaça de Carlos Ibáñez, 3; tel. 93/281-1600; www.
hotelmiramarbarcelona.com; €350; Metro: Espanya
This pink-hued, five-star luxury hotel sits majestically on the hillside of Montjuïc with spectacular views out over the sea. Its location high up on the hill means it is far from public transport—a taxi (which would take around 15 minutes and would cost around €10 from the city center) would be the best way to get there. A secluded location gives guests a peaceful ambiance; the terrace is a fantastic place from which to drink in the views with a glass of cava. Rooms, which have designer toiletries and TVs with international channels, include deluxe, premium, and two different suite options.

Information and Services

TOURIST INFORMATION CENTERS

Barcelona's main **Tourist Information Center** (Plaça de Catalunya, 17; daily 8:30am-9pm) provides maps, guides, a hotel booking service, tour and ticket sales, and a gift shop.

Other tourist information centers include: Plaça de Sant Jaume (Ciutat, 2 [Barcelona City Hall]; Mon-Fri 8:30am-8:30pm, Sat 9am-7pm, Sun 9am-2pm), Sants Station (Plaça dels Països Catalans; daily 8am-8:30pm), Airport Terminals 1 and 2 (daily 8:30am-8:30pm), Cathedral (Plaça Nova, 5; Mon-Sat 9am-7pm, Sun 9am-3pm), Columbus Monument (Plaça Portal de la Pau; daily 8:30am-8:30pm; also includes a Wine Tourism and Wine Information Point).

Information booths, located close to the city's main sights, also provide tourist and cultural information. Some key locations include Plaça de Catalunya, Plaça Espanya, Sagrada Familia, and World Trade Center.

HEALTH AND SAFETY

Robberies

Unfortunately, Barcelona has a reputation for its notorious pickpockets; keeping your bag and valuables with you at all times is absolutely essential. Do not put bags on the floor; it is best to keep the strap over you when sitting down to eat. Make sure bags are secure, with a zip and another fastening if possible. Pay particular attention while on public transport or in busy areas such as markets, Las Ramblas, and busy, stand-up bars.

Immediately report any robbery to the local police. The Guàrdia Urbana station (Las Ramblas, 43; tel. 93/256-2430) has English-speaking staff. You will need to fill out a police report (*denuncia*) for insurance. If your passport has been stolen, you can request an emergency passport at your country's consulate.

ID is technically required to be carried, but a photocopy of your passport will usually suffice.

Emergency Numbers

The main emergency telephone number in Spain is 112, used to contact the police, fire brigade, and ambulance service. In Barcelona, calls are taken in Catalan, Spanish, English, and French. There is a help center for tourists who have been a victim of crime or have had an accident; it is open 24 hours a day (Las Ramblas, 43; tel. 93/256-2430).

Hospitals

If you need a hospital, head to one of the following: **Hospital de la Santa Creu i Sant Pau** (Sant Quintí, 87; tel. 93/291-9000) in northern Barcelona; **Hospital Clínic** (Carrer de Villarroel, 170; tel. 93/227-5400) in Eixample; **Hospital Dos de Maig** (Carrer del Dos de Maig, 301; tel. 93/507-2700) near Sagrada Familia; or **Hospital del Mar**

(Passeig Marítim, 25-29; tel. 93/248-3000) near the seafront/Barceloneta.

Pharmacies

Look out for the illuminated green cross of pharmacies, which are generally open 9am-2pm, then 4pm-8pm. There are an increasing number of 24-hour pharmacies, especially in the city center. A list of 24-hour pharmacies can be found in the window of every pharmacy.

Farmàcia Clapes (Rambla, 98; tel. 93/301-2843; Metro: Liceu) is a centrally located 24-hour pharmacy right on Las Ramblas.

COMMUNICATIONS
Wi-Fi

Barcelona city council operates a free Wi-Fi (pronounced "wee-fee" in Spanish) network, including hotspots around the city (www.ajuntament.barcelona.cat/barcelonawifi/en). Many cafés, restaurants, and bars also offer free Wi-Fi for patrons.

Newspapers

Spain's biggest daily newspaper is *El País*, on the center-left (there is a Barcelona edition). Conservative Catalan paper *La Vanguardia* has a decent arts and culture section on Fridays. *Avui* is the main nationalist paper and is printed in Catalan.

Getting There

AIR
Barcelona-El Prat Airport

Most flights arrive at **Barcelona-El Prat Airport** (BCN; www.aena.es), 12 kilometers (7.5 miles) southwest of the city center. The airport has two terminals, the newer Terminal 1 and the older Terminal 2.

AIRPORT TRANSPORTATION

There are several ways to get into the city center from the airport, but the train is the fastest. **Metro:** It takes 32 minutes from terminals T1 and T2 of the airport to the Zona Universitària metro station on line L9Sud (orange line). Trains leave every seven minutes 5am-midnight, and a single ticket costs €4.50.

From Zona Universitària, you can change onto metro line L3 (green), which goes to central stations including Catalunya, Liceu, and Passeig de Gràcia (the journey takes around 20 minutes).
Bus: Aerobús (tel. 90/210-0104; www.aerobusbcn.com) runs buses (line A1) from terminal T1 to Plaça Catalunya (35 minutes, single €5.90, return €10.20). The buses leave every five minutes from 5:30am-1:05am. Tickets are valid within 15 days of purchase.

Aerobús's A2 line runs from terminal T2 to Plaça Catalunya (30 minutes). Buses leave every 10 minutes from 5:30am-1am. Buy tickets on the bus or on the Aerobús website (valid for one year from purchase).
Train: The train from terminal T2 to the central Passeig de Gràcia station takes 27 minutes on line R2. Trains leave every 30 minutes from 5:21am-11:38pm. A one-way ticket is €4.10. (If you arrive at terminal T1, you can take a free shuttle bus to T2 that takes 10 minutes).
Taxi: A taxi from either terminal into the city takes around 30 minutes and costs around €25.

Girona-Costa Brava Airport

Some budget airlines arrive at **Girona-Costa Brava Airport** (GRO, www.girona-airport.net), 90 kilometers (56 miles) north of Barcelona.

The **Sagalés Airport Line** bus (tel. 90/213-0014; www.sagalesairportline.com) takes passengers from the airport directly to Barcelona Nord bus station (€16 one way, €25 return); the journey takes around 75 minutes, and buses run from 8:45am to around midnight daily. Barcelona Nord station is less than a minute's walk from Arc de Triomf metro station (Line 1, red line); it can take you into the center in a couple of minutes (it is one stop to Plaça de Catalunya).

Reus Airport

Some budget airlines arrive at **Reus airport** (REU, www.reus-airport.com), 110 kilometers (68 miles) south of Barcelona.

From Reus airport, the **Hispano Igualadina bus** (tel. 90/229-2900; www.igualadina.com) goes to Barcelona Sants train station (which has a metro station, Sants Estació, connected to line 3 and line 5). Bus tickets are €16 one way, and the journey time is 90 minutes. Buses are coordinated with flight times and you can check the timetable on their website.

TRAIN

Spain's national rail operator is **RENFE** (tel. 90/224-0202; www.renfe.es).

Rail links with most cities in Spain and Europe arrive at **Barcelona-Sants Station.** There is a metro station inside the train station, called Sants Estació. Line 3 runs direct to Liceu on Las Ramblas, and Catalunya on Plaça de Catalunya.

Some coastal trains from the north arrive at **Plaça de Catalunya**, and some trains from other areas of Catalonia arrive at **Passeig de Gràcia.** Both stations are connected to Barcelona's metro system. Some intercity trains may arrive at **Estació de França**, close to Barceloneta metro station.

BUS

The main intercity bus station is the **Estació del Nord** (tel. 90/226-0606; www.barcelonanord.cat). Travelers arriving here can hop on the metro at Arc de Triomf (Line 1), directly opposite the station, which is just two stops from Catalunya, on the central Plaça de Catalunya.

Some international bus services depart from the bus terminal behind Barcelona-Sants Station.

CAR

It is 625 kilometers (388 miles) from Madrid to Barcelona, and the drive can take around six hours. Leave Madrid on the **A-2** and take the **AP-2/E-90** in the direction of Zaragoza; continue along the **E-90/Autopista del Nordeste**, then continue along the **AP-7/E-15/E90**. Keep going along the **AP-2/E-90**, then take the **B-23** and you will arrive in Barcelona along the Avinguda Diagonal. Expect tolls of around €35.

Driving into Barcelona is straightforward, but parking is both expensive and difficult to find. A car is not needed if you are sticking to the city and its surrounding areas.

CRUISE SHIP

Barcelona is Europe's leading cruise harbor, with annual passenger arrivals of two and a half million. Cruise ships dock in Barcelona's Port, which is home to seven cruise terminals. The three terminals at the World Trade Center are 400 meters (1,312 feet) from metro and buses (Metro: Drassanes). Terminals A, B, C, and D, known as the Adossat Quay terminals, are serviced by the T3 PORTBUS shuttle (single ticket €3, return ticket €4, can only be purchased on the bus), which takes cruise passengers to Plaça de Colón, at the foot of the Ramblas.

Getting Around

The best way to get around Barcelona is on foot, and for longer distances, the metro is hard to beat—it is fast, reliable, and covers the entire city and its outskirts.

PUBLIC TRANSIT

Single **tickets** (€2.20) can be purchased on all public transport (metro, bus, and tram), but if you're spending a few days in the city, consider buying a *tarjeta*, a discount ticket that can be used multiple times and can be bought at metro, train, and tram stations (but not on buses). The **T-10** (€10.20) is valid for 10 separate journeys and can be shared between passengers. You may be asked to choose which zone you want your pass to cover when buying from a machine, and if so, just go for Zone 1, which includes the entire city of Barcelona, along with the airport.

The **Hola BCN card** (www.tmb.cat/en/barcelona/fares-metro-bus/barcelona-travel-card-hola-bcn) offers unlimited journeys on metro, bus, and the rest of Barcelona's public transport network for two (48 hours, €15), three (72 hours, €22), four (96 hours, €28.50), or five (120 hours, €35) consecutive days. The card also includes journeys from Barcelona airport into the city center. Buy online for a 10-percent discount. The clock starts ticking on your pass once you have validated it on your first journey. Unvalidated cards expire on February 28 of the year following purchase.

Metro

Barcelona's metro is split between two different companies, **Transports Metropolitans de Barcelona** (TMB, www.tmb.cat) and **Ferrocarrils de la Generalitat de Catalunya** (FGC, www.fgc.cat), which share the running of its eight color-coded lines. Metro stations are marked by a red, diamond shape with an "M" in the middle. The metro runs Mon-Thurs 5am-midnight, Fri 5am-2am, Sat continuous service all night, and Sun until midnight.

You can pick up metro maps at metro stations or consult it online (www.tmb.cat/en/barcelona-transport/map/metro). Be aware that changing between lines at some stations can involve a long walk to the next platform, even though it is part of the same station.

You can buy single tickets and travel passes from machines—with English-language options—inside the metro with either cash or credit card.

Bus

The metro will usually be an easier transport option in Barcelona, but there are circumstances when the bus is better. One destination better reached by bus is the Bunkers del Carmel. Buses also tend to be more wheelchair-friendly, with a designated space for wheelchair users (not every metro station has an elevator). Passengers can buy tickets on board the bus; multi-journey tickets (that cover all public transport) can be purchased at ticket machines in metro stations.

The **Nitbus** (night bus, www.ambmobilitat.cat/principales/busquedanitbus.aspx) traverses 17 routes, most of which go through Plaça de Catalunya, where it is possible to transfer between routes. This is the bus that runs at night through the city.

Access more detailed information about bus routes and times at **Bus Barcelona** (www.tmb.cat/ca/barcelona/autobusos/linies).

Tram

Barcelona's tram network (www.tram.cat) mainly covers the city's suburbs, so you will perhaps be unlikely to use it. It is particularly useful, however, when wanting to travel from the Glòries area (home to the Mercat del Encants and the Museum of Design) to the Waterfront or Ciutadella Park—take line T4 from the Glòries stop to the Ciutadella/Vila Olímpica stop.

Tram travel is also included in the Hola BCN card.

TAXI

Barcelona's taxis are black with yellow panels on the side doors. An illuminated green light on the roof means they are free. There are taxi ranks close to central points, for example at Plaça de Catalunya and Passeig de Gràcia, and you can usually easily flag one down in the street. If leaving from your hotel, the front desk will be happy to call or hail you a cab.

There is a minimum fare of €2.15, and after that it's €1.13 per kilometer (slightly more on weekends and evenings). There are surcharges for airport and train station pickups, as well as for storing luggage in the trunk. Most taxis take credit card payment.

Taxi companies include **Radio Taxi** (tel. 93/303-3033; www.radiotaxi033.com). **Taxi Amic** (tel. 93/420-8088, www.taxi-amic-adaptat.com) specializes in travelers with reduced mobility. Booking at least a day in advance is recommended.

CAR

For city breaks in Barcelona, a car is unnecessary. If you are planning on driving around the wider Catalonia region, you can rent a car. Major car rental companies, including **Hertz** (tel. 90/240-2405, www.hertz.com), **Europcar** (tel. 90/210-5030, www.europcar.com), and **Avis** (tel. 90/218-0854, www.avis.com), have branches at the Barcelona airport and Barcelona-Sants train station. While car parks do vary in price, expect to pay around €20-€25 per day.

BICYCLE

Barcelona has more than 100 kilometers (62 miles) of cycle lanes and a city bike system, the **Bicing** (www.bicing.com). Bicing stands full of red bikes dot the city, but they are aimed more at locals making short journeys than at tourists (you have to register, then receive a welcome pack containing your bike card, which is sent to your address 10 days after you register; once you receive your card, you must then register it online—all in all, it's too much effort for a tourist who might be in the city for a short period of time).

A more tourist-friendly and easier option is renting bikes by the hour or day. There are dozens of bike-rental companies in Barcelona. Some of the nicest areas to cycle include the seafront at La Barceloneta and, for fans of mountain biking, the Parc de Collserola.

Barcelona Day Trips

From a historic Catalan pilgrimage site nestled in the rocky mountains of Montserrat to the medieval old town of Girona to a seaside Roman amphitheater in Tarragona, there are fascinating places to explore within easy reach of Barcelona. Art lovers can take their appreciation further at Salvador Dalí's funhouse of a museum in Figueres, while beach bums can relax in the beautiful seaside town of Sitges, or taste cava at the wineries where the sparkling beverage is produced.

PLANNING YOUR TIME

All of the destinations in this chapter are easily doable as a day trip from Barcelona using public transport or by car. For the most part,

Highlights

Look for ★ to find recommended sights, activities, dining, and lodging.

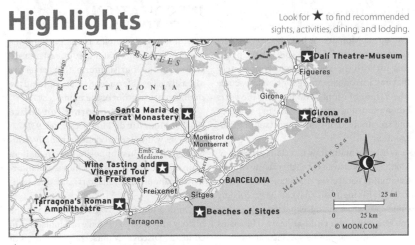

PYRENEES

CATALONIA

R. Gallego

★ Dalí Theatre-Museum
Figueres

Girona

★ Santa Maria de Monserrat Monastery

★ Girona Cathedral

Monistrol de Montserrat

Emb. de Mediano

★ Wine Tasting and Vineyard Tour at Freixenet

Freixenet

Sitges

BARCELONA

Mediterranean Sea

★ Tarragona's Roman Amphitheatre

★ Beaches of Sitges

Tarragona

0   25 mi
0   25 km

© MOON.COM

★ **Santa Maria de Montserrat Monastery:** Spain's second most important pilgrimage site after Santiago de Compostela is an important Catalan symbol and home to a much-praised relic of its patron saint (page 155).

★ **Girona Cathedral:** The grand medieval marvel stands majestically over Girona's old town (page 161).

★ **Dalí Theatre-Museum:** The quirky creativity of Spanish surrealist Salvador Dalí comes out in force at the museum he designed in his hometown of Figueres (page 167).

★ **Beaches of Sitges:** Channel laid-back Spanish sophistication at this popular summer playground, gay-friendly destination, and beautiful seaside town all rolled into one (page 172).

★ **Tarragona's Roman Amphitheatre:** Tarragona's fascinating Roman heritage is encapsulated in its most impressive Roman remain: this seaside amphitheatre with a backdrop of the Mediterranean (page 176).

★ **Wine tasting and vineyard tour at Freixenet:** Explore Catalonia's main Cava-producing Penedès region with a wine tasting and visits to the rolling vineyards of one of the world's biggest Cava brands (page 181).

all are also easily navigated on foot once you arrive.

Sitges, the glamorous seaside town famed for its gay scene and nightlife, is also a popular weekend or overnight destination, where locals go to escape the city and enjoy the more laid-back pace of life—if only for a day or two.

Figueres' main draw is the museum dedicated to the work of Salvador Dalí, which can be easily visited in a morning or afternoon, while **Girona**, with its narrow medieval lanes, pretty riverside homes, and one of the most famous restaurants in the world, could be worth an overnight stay if time permits. Only 15 minutes apart by high-speed train, Figueres and Girona can be easily combined into a packed day trip or a more leisurely overnight trip.

Montserrat is ideal as a day trip, whether to make a pilgrimage to the monastery or to hike some of the surrounding trails. The **Penedès wine region** is a lovely day out and displays a very different side of Catalonia to the metropolis of Barcelona. It can also be visited as an extension of a trip to Sitges.

Montserrat

Montserrat is a jagged mountain range 50 kilometers (31 miles) northwest of Barcelona. The name Montserrat literally means "serrated mountain," for its spiky, bare peaks that jut into the air. Home to a monastery that has a strong meaning for Catalan people (the Virgin of Montserrat has over the years become a strong symbol of Catalan patriotism and spirituality), it is an important pilgrimage site.

While the main draw is certainly the abbey, Montserrat is also an excellent place to explore Catalonia's nature; the mountain range is dotted with hiking trails that can be reached by cable car, an exciting experience whether you're a child or a child-at-heart. The vistas from Montserrat can be spectacular and visitors can even see as far as Mallorca, in the Balearic Islands, on a clear day.

Montserrat is one of the most popular day trips from Barcelona, and the abbey can get crowded with visitors, especially on weekends and on April 27, the feast day of Our Lady of Montserrat. If you really want to beat the crowds, stay the night before and arrive early in the morning—the abbey opens at 7:30am.

INFORMATION AND TOURS

The monastery complex is compact and the monastery, Montserrat museum, restaurants, cafés, and the tourist information center are all easily accessible on foot, located around the main square in front of the monastery.

The **Montserrat Information Office** (08199, Monestir de Montserrat; tel. 93/877-7701; www.montserratvisita.com; daily 9am-8pm,), located just opposite the Cremallera train station, has maps, brochures, and information about the monastery and surrounding area.

Guided tours are available, which put the history and artistic heritage of Montserrat in context. "Discover Montserrat: 1,000 years of spirituality, history and art" is a two-hour, 30-minute tour (€15, free for under 14s); available in English, it takes visitors around the monastery and into the museum, explaining the history and artistic heritage of Montserrat. Several other daily tours start at the **Montserrat Information Office**.

Tourist information kiosks at the monastery provide maps and information.

Previous: Girona; Sitges; Dalí Theatre-Museum.

Day Trips from Barcelona

	Why Go?	Travel Time from Barcelona
Montserrat	Montserrat abbey; mountainous hiking routes	1 hour by train and cable car; 1 hour 20 minutes by car
Girona	Medieval old town, magnificent cathedral, ancient Jewish quarter, one of the best restaurants in the world	40 minutes by high-speed train; 1 hour 40 minutes by car
Figueres	Salvador Dalí museum, Catalan cuisine	1 hour by high-speed train; 2 hours by car
Sitges	Beaches, Modernista architecture, party scene, gay-friendly	40 minutes by train; 1 hour by bus; 1 hour by car
Tarragona	Roman architecture	35 minutes by high-speed train; 1.5 hours by bus; 1 hour 20 minutes by car
Penedès wine region	Touring vineyards and cellars; tasting cava and wine at the source	45 minutes by train; 1 hour by car

SIGHTS
★ Santa Maria de Montserrat Monastery

08119, Montserrat; tel. 93/877-7777; www. abadiamontserrat.net; daily 7:30am-8pm; access to La Moreneta 8am-10:30am, midday-6:30pm; choir performance weekdays at 1pm, Sun midday and 6:45pm; admission free

Clinging to the rocky hillside of the Montserrat range, the monastery of Santa Maria de Montserrat is one of Catalonia's major tourist and religious sites. It is also still a functioning Benedictine monastery, home to around 70 monks.

The monastery was founded in 1025 on the site of an earlier hermitage and was destroyed by Napoleon's troops in the early 19th century, after which much of it was rebuilt. Parts of the old building remain, such as its 15th-century cloisters. The grand, 19th-century façade that depicts Saint George and Saint Benedict looks out onto the Plaça de Santa Maria, a grand square surrounded on other sides by restaurants, souvenir shops, and other buildings.

The basilica, the only one of the religious buildings open to the public, is a sprawling space that can take anything from 20 minutes to well over an hour to explore, depending on how much time you want to spend taking in the architecture and whether you attend a choir performance or mass. The basilica can be busy, especially on weekends, so aim to arrive early for the most tranquil and reflective experience.

Montserrat is famous for Our Lady of Montserrat, aka **La Moreneta** (the Black Virgin), a Romanesque polychrome carving of the Virgin and Child from the 12th century. In the 1100s pilgrims started climbing Montserrat to venerate the Virgin, who became the patron saint of Catalonia in 1881 (she shares the accolade with Saint George). The Virgin can be found at the back of the chapel, surrounded by a golden altar. Her feast day, when thousands make their way to Montserrat to kiss or touch the statue, is on April 27. (Her other nickname is "the April Rose.") Visitors can see La Moreneta daily from 8am-10:30am, midday-6:30pm.

Barcelona Day Trips

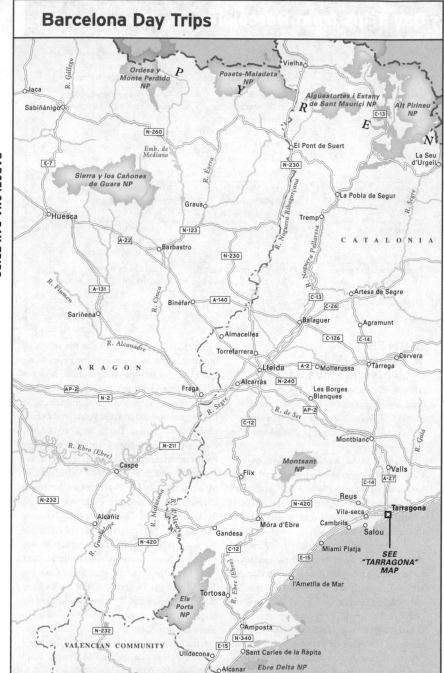

Jaca

Sabiñánigo

R. Gállego

Ordesa y Monte Perdido NP

P

Posets-Maladeta NP

Y

Vielha

Aigüestortes i Estany de Sant Maurici NP

R

C-13

Alt Pirineu NP

E

N

N-260

Emb. de Mediano

E-7

Sierra y los Cañones de Guara NP

R. Ésera

El Pont de Suert

N-230

La Seu d'Urgell

Huesca

Graus

La Pobla de Segur

R. Segre

A-22

N-123

Barbastro

N-230

Tremp

R. Noguera Ribagorzana

R. Noguera Pallaresa

C A T A L O N I A

R. Flumen

A-131

Sariñena

R. Cinca

Binéfar

A-140

C-13

C-26

Artesa de Segre

Agramunt

R. Alcanadre

Almacelles

Balaguer

C-126

C-14

A R A G O N

Torrefarrera

Lleida

A-2

Mollerussa

Tàrrega

Cervera

AP-2

N-2

Fraga

Alcarràs

N-240

R. Segre

Les Borges Blanques

AP-2

R. de Set

C-12

Montblanc

R. Gaià

R. Ebro (Ebre)

N-211

Montsant NP

Caspé

Flix

Valls

C-14

A-27

N-232

N-420

Reus

Tarragona

Alcañiz

R. Matarraña

R. d'Algars

Móra d'Ebre

Vila-seca

Cambrils

Salou

Gandesa

N-420

C-12

R. Ebre (Ebre)

Miami Platja

E-15

SEE "TARRAGONA" MAP

R. Guadalope

Els Ports NP

Tortosa

l'Ametlla de Mar

N-232

VALENCIAN COMMUNITY

N-340

Amposta

E-15

Ulldecona

Sant Carles de la Ràpita

Alcanar

Ebre Delta NP

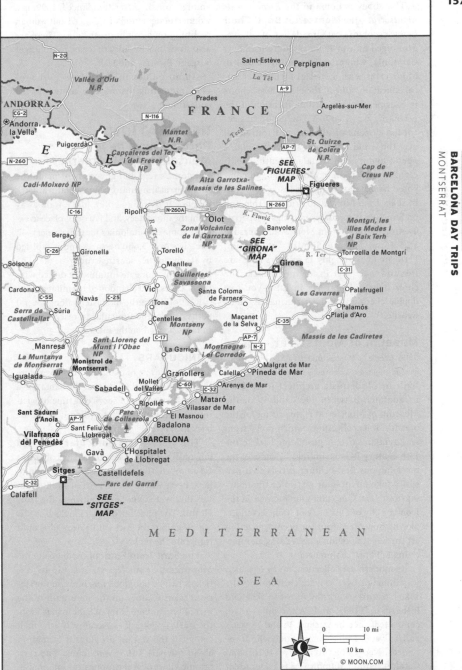

The abbey is home to the *Escolania de Montserrat*—the **Montserrat Boys' Choir** (www.escolania.cat), made up of 50 students aged nine to 14 years old from all over Catalonia, who attend boarding school in Montserrat with a special focus on musical education. One of the oldest boys' choirs in Europe, the first written mention of the Escolania was in 1307. The group has recorded dozens of albums and toured all over the world. The choir sings *el Virolai*, a poetic hymn about Catalan identity, dedicated to the Virgin of Montserrat and composed by Catalan composer Josep Rodoreda in 1880, from Monday to Friday at 1pm and on Sundays at midday, and sings Vespers—evening prayers—from Monday to Thursday at 6:45pm and on Sundays at 6:45pm. Performances, roughly 15 minutes long, are free and take place inside the basilica. The choir does not perform in July—you can double-check upcoming performances on its website.

Museum of Montserrat

08199 Abadía de Montserrat; tel. 93/877-7745; www.museudemontserrat.com; daily 9am-5:45pm; €7

Built by Modernista architect Josep Puig i Cadafalch between 1928 and 1933, the Museum of Montserrat is surprising for the breadth of its collections, which range from an Egyptian sarcophagus dating back to the 13th century BC to paintings by some of the most famous 21st-century artists that can easily take up an hour or two of time during your visit. One exhibition focuses on the Iconography of Our Lady of Montserrat, exploring how the Virgin has been depicted in art through the centuries, shedding an interesting light on La Moreneta.

Its modern art collection, much of which was donated by a private collector in the 1980s, features works by Picasso ("The Old Fisherman," 1895, and "Altar Boy," 1896, completed when he was just 14 and 15 years old), Salvador Dalí ("Composition with three figures, Neo-Cubist Academy," 1926), and Catalan painter Ramon Casas ("Decadent young woman. After the dance," 1899, is a wonderful depiction of a danced-out woman reclining on a bright green sofa). There are also drawings by Edgar Degas, John Singer Sargent, Picasso, and Dalí.

Audio guides in English (€2.20) provide interesting history and context to the collections.

RECREATION
Parc Natural de la Muntanya de Montserrat

Catalonia's regional government made the Montserrat mountain range a Natural Park in 1987. It is free to enter, just a walk away from the monastery, and is a great place to explore some of Catalonia's natural scenery—it stretches over 3,600 hectares and is typified by its dramatic, soaring, rocky peaks. The rugged limestone mountains are dotted with trails, caves, and abandoned hermitages. You can set off from the monastery along several paths or take the funicular to reach the hermitages nestled on the hillside.

FUNICULARS

You can take one of two funiculars to explore the mountainside. (Note that the Santa Cova Funicular was out of service at time of writing, and it was uncertain when it would be back in service.)

The **Santa Cova Funicular** takes you downhill to the 17th-century chapel of **Santa Cova** (open all day, admission free), said to have been where the Virgin of Montserrat was discovered and also known as the Holy Grotto. The pink-hued chapel looks like it is clinging onto the rocky hillside, and is built right into the rock.

The **Sant Joan Funicular** (opposite the Montserrat Cremallera station; €13 return; tickets can be bought at machines in the station) takes visitors up the mountain to the incredible vantage point of Sant Joan station, the starting point for several walks. A small center in the station provides information about the park's flora and fauna. The panoramic views over the monastery, mountain, and (it seems) the whole of Catalonia are well worth the price of the funicular (don't forget your camera!). The funicular runs every 20 minutes from 10am until 4:30pm in winter and 6:30pm in summer, and the ride lasts 5-7 minutes.

HIKING

Several well-signposted mountain tracks zigzag up from the monastery. Pick up maps and get more information at the **Montserrat Information Office**, opposite the Cremallera de Montserrat railway station (08199, Monestir de Montserrat; tel. 93/877-7701; www.montserratvisita.com; daily 9am-8pm). The whole mountain is dotted with little hermitages that were abandoned during the 19th century when the French invaded. Today, they provide eerie signposts along the route.

From the top of the Sant Joan Funicular, you can walk the 20 minutes to the **Sant Joan Hermitage**, a small stone chapel perched on the rocks, with a stunning backdrop of the valley below. (You cannot actually enter the hermitage.)

There is also the hour-long hike from the Sant Joan Funicular (the top station) to the **Sant Jeroni Hermitage**, another abandoned chapel that was rebuilt in the 19th century. It is the furthest hermitage from the monastery, and up here hikers should look out for wildlife like eagles and hawks. It's another 10 minutes up a flight of concrete steps to reach the summit of Sant Jeroni. The 1,236-meter-high (4,055-foot) peak is the highest point in the Montserrat massif and is where all the views so far combine into one incredible panoramic vista, looking over the other-worldly Montserrat peaks and the Llobregat valley below, as well as over the twinkling Mediterranean Sea and—on a clear day—even as far as the island of Mallorca.

It's also possible to walk the 40-minute downhill trail from the monastery (be aware that it is very steep on the way back uphill), known as the **Way of the Rosary**, to the 17th-century chapel of **Santa Cova** (open all day, admission free). It is flanked by statues depicting events in the lives of Jesus and Mary. You will be treated with fantastic views over the mountains and the steep drops to the valley below.

ROCK CLIMBING

Unsurprisingly, the rocky mountain is also excellent for rock climbing. Introductory rock-climbing sessions (half-day; €170 for two, €180 for three or four people; all equipment included) can be booked via the Visit Montserrat website (www.montserratvisita.com/en/ideas-for-your-visit/nature/1465). The rock climbing is led by expert guides and is available in English.

FOOD

Much of the food on offer around the abbey is cafeteria-style, standard fare. There is a picnic area with picnic benches for those who want to bring their own supplies. Essentials can be purchased at a small supermarket, **Supermercado Queviures** (Montserrat Monastery main square; Mon-Fri 9am-5:30pm, Sat-Sun 9am-6:30pm). There is usually also a small market of local producers set up opposite the Mirador dels Apostols building (daily 10am-5pm) selling local cheeses, baked goods, honey, and other foodstuffs.

RESTAURANT ABAT CISNEROS

Plaza del Monasterio; tel. 93/877-7701;
12:30pm-3:30pm, 8pm-9:45pm; from €28 for a
fixed-price lunch

Located inside the Hotel Abat Cisneros, just next to the monastery, this restaurant is a more formal option than the cafeteria-style dining that is abundant at Montserrat. The atmospheric dining room, once 16th-century stables, has a stone-arched ceiling, while the stone walls make you feel like you are dining deep inside the mountain itself. The restaurant serves Catalan classics and a range of traditional fish and meat dishes. There is a set lunch menu for €27.50 per person. It is worth booking in advance to guarantee a table.

BO2 RESTAURANT & BOTIGA

Carrer Sant Joan, 32; tel. 93/828-4313; www.
bo2restaurant.dabmedia.cat; Mon, Tues, Thurs
and Sun 1pm-4pm, Fri and Sat 1pm-4pm,
8:30pm-10:30pm, €15-€20

Located in the little town of Monistrol de Montserrat, connected to the monastery by the Cremallera de Montserrat railway, this lovely restaurant is a great option for lunch away from the crowds. Its menu comprises tapas and Catalan dishes, using fresh local ingredients. If you visit Montserrat on a morning, the restaurant makes a good lunch stop on the way home (it's a 10-minute walk from Monistrol de Montserrat train station).

ACCOMMODATIONS

APARTAMENTOS MONTSERRAT ABAT MARCET

Plaça de L'abat Oliba; tel. 93/877-7701; www.
montserratvisita.com; €85

The Apartamentos Montserrat Abat Marcet were built in the 1960s and provide accommodation right next to Montserrat's abbey. The 120-plus apartments are hard to beat for sheer proximity to the abbey and are clean and functional, if a little bare (the bargain option has a slightly dorm-room or hostel feel). Kitchen amenities include a fridge, oven, and hob (a ring on top of a stove). Options include studios and one- or two-bedroom apartments, all with TVs.

HOTEL ABAT CISNEROS

Plaza del Monasterio; tel. 93/877-7701; www.
montserratvisita.com; doubles from €120

Hotel Abat Cisneros, operated by the same company as Apartamentos Montserrat Abat Marcet, is another option for visitors who would prefer hotel accommodation to apartments. Located right next to the monastery, the hotel affords guests incredible views over the mountain and valley. The 82 comfy rooms include singles, twins, doubles, adjoining rooms, and rooms with views over the mountains. Demand can be high, so try to book as far ahead as possible.

GETTING THERE

The easiest way to get to Montserrat without a car is by train and then cable car or mountain railway (the cable car is a fun option for children and is the quickest way to the monastery, taking just five minutes). While it might seem complicated due to the number of trains/cable cars/mountain railways/funiculars on or leading to Montserrat, the actual journey is quite straightforward, especially because there are likely to be many other visitors doing the exact same one as you.

Train and Cable Car

From Barcelona's Espanya station (on Plaça d'Espanya), take the FGC train, line R5, direction Manresa. Trains leave every hour, and the journey to Montserrat Aeri, where you can connect to a cable car, takes around 55 minutes. The first train leaves at 7:36am and there are trains every hour until 5:36pm. A single adult ticket is €12.15 one-way and €22 return. (You can buy tickets from machines inside the station.)

The **Aeri de Montserrat** (www.aeridemontserrat.com) cable car has been taking day-trippers and pilgrims up to Montserrat since 1930. The ride lasts five minutes and is a fun way to reach the monastery. Prices: adult round trip €11, child (between 4-13) round trip €5.50. Tickets can be booked online in advance but must be redeemed within six months of booking. Schedule: March 1-Oct 31 daily 9:40am-7pm; Nov 1-Feb 28, weekdays 10:10am-5:45pm, weekends and public holidays 9:40am-6:15pm. Departures are frequent, sometimes every five minutes, depending on number of passengers.

Mountain Railway

Start your journey as above, by taking the FGC train, line R5 direction Manresa, from Espanya metro station in Barcelona. Trains leave every hour from 7:36am, with the last train at 8:36pm. Get off at the Monistrol de Montserrat station (journey time around one hour). The **Cremallera de Montserrat** (www.cremallerademontserrat.cat), the

Montserrat Mountain Railway, departs from the Monistrol de Montserrat station (the stop after Montserrat Aeri) and takes 20 minutes (tickets €6.30 one-way and €10.60 return; first train 8:48am, last train at 6:48pm; trains depart every 20 minutes).

Travelers can buy combined tickets online and from the Plaça de Catalunya tourist information office in Barcelona. The ticket, which covers the entire round-trip via metro and train, is €35.30.

Bus

Autocars Julià (www.autocaresjulia.es)

buses depart from Barcelona Sants station at 9:15am daily, returning 5pm (Oct-May) and 6pm daily (June-Sept). A one-way ticket is €5.10. The trip takes around 1.5 hours.

Car

Leave Barcelona by Avinguda Diagonal and take the B-23 dual carriageway northwest and the A-2 Barcelona-Lleida motorway northwest (Manresa exit). Take the C-55 north to Monistrol de Montserrat and the BP-1121 south to Montserrat. The journey takes around one hour, 20 minutes. Parking at the Monastery is €6.50 per day.

Girona

The old city of Girona (pop. 100,000), 85 kilometers (53 miles) northeast of Barcelona, is a criss-cross of intriguing alleyways, cobbled streets, and mesmeric medieval architecture. Home to what has been named on several occasions the best restaurant in the world, the city is also a worthwhile pilgrimage for fine-dining foodies.

Over the years Girona has had a thriving Jewish Quarter, Moorish occupiers, and a range of different Spanish rulers, giving it a captivating mixture of historic, artistic, and architectural influences. The compact nature of the old town makes it easy to explore on foot within a day. The new and old towns are separated by the river Onyar, whose footbridges are a perfect vantage point to snap a few pictures of the reflection of the colorful riverside homes that line its banks. A new kind of television tourism has also been flourishing in the city since it was used as a filming location for the fantasy TV series *Game of Thrones*.

SIGHTS

Girona's compact **Old Town** (Barri Vell) is on the east side of the river and is roughly located between the Torre Gironella and the old city walls (Carrer de la Muralla) on one side and

the River Onyar on the other. It is home to the city's oldest sights, such as the cathedral and the Arab baths. The streets are cobbled, narrow, and in places very steep, with little alleyways snaking off wider main streets. They are lined in stone buildings. The area is also known as the Força Vella because it lies within the triangular-shaped fortress built by the Romans in the first century BC.

★ Girona Cathedral

Plaça de la Catedral; tel. 97/242-7189; www. catedraldegirona.org; July-August 10am-7:30pm, Nov-March 10am-5:30pm, rest of year 10am-6:30pm; €7, €5 for pensioners and students
Dominating the heart of Girona's medieval old town is the cathedral, officially the Cathedral of Saint Mary of Girona. It is a mixture of architectural styles due to its prolonged build—it was constructed between the 11th and 18th centuries.

Visitors approach the cathedral up a grand set of 17th-century steps. What is immediately arresting about the cathedral is its lack of aisles and the width of its nave—at 22 meters (72 feet), it is one of the widest in the world, second only to St. Peter's Basilica in Rome. It was started in the 11th century in a Romanesque style, which by the 13th

Girona

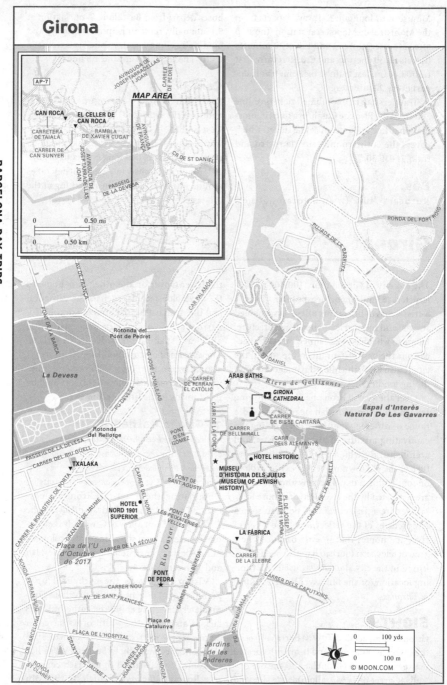

MAP AREA

AP-7

AVINGUDA DE JOSEF TARRADELLAS I JOAN

CARRER DE PEDRET

CAN ROCA
EL CELLER DE CAN ROCA

CARRETERA DE TAIALÀ

RAMBLA DE XAVIER CUGAT

CARRER DE CAN SUNYER

AVINGUDA DE JOSEP TARRADELLAS I JOAN

AVINGUDA DE FRANÇA

CR DE ST DANIEL

PASSEIG DE LA DEVESA

0   0.50 mi

0   0.50 km

RONDA DEL FORT ROIG

PUJADA DE LA BARRUFA

A DE FRANÇA

PONT DE LA BARCA

CAP PALAMÓS

Rotonda del Pont de Pedret

CAP ST. DANIEL

PG JOSE CANALEJAS

La Devesa

CARRER DE FERRAN EL CATÒLIC

ARAB BATHS
Riera de Galligants

GIRONA CATHEDRAL

Espai d'Interès Natural De Les Gavarres

PG DEVESA

CARRER DE BISBE CARTAÑÀ

CARRER DE LA FORÇA

CARRER BELLMIRALL

CARR DELS ALEMANYS

Rotonda del Rellotge

PONT D'EN GOMEZ

PASSEIG DE LA DEVESA

CARRER DEL RIU GÜELL

TXALAKA

HOTEL HISTORIC

MUSEU D'HISTORIA DELS JUEUS (MUSEUM OF JEWISH HISTORY)

CARRER DE BONASTRUC DE PORTA

CARRER DEL NORD

PONT DE SANT AGUSTÍ

PL DE JOSEP FERRATER I MORA

CARRER DE LA MURALLA

GRAN VIA DE JAUME I

HOTEL NORD 1901 SUPERIOR

LES PEIXATERIES VELLES

PONT DE

LA FÀBRICA

CARRER DE LA LLEBRE

Plaça de l'U d'Octubre de 2017

CARRER DE LA SÈQUIA

Riu Onyar

CARRER DE L'ALBEREDA

PG SOTA MURALLA

CARRER DELS CAPUTXINS

RONDA FERRAN PUIG

CARRER NOU

PONT DE PEDRA

AV. DE SANT FRANCESC

CARRER DE LES PEDRERES

CR BARCELONA

PLAÇA DE L'HOSPITAL

GRANVIA DE JAUME I

Plaça de Catalunya

CARRER DE JOAN MARAGALL

PG MENDOZA

Jardins de les Pedreres

RONDA ST CLARET

0   100 yds

0   100 m

© MOON.COM

century had changed into a more Gothic form. Remnants of the original Romanesque architecture remain in the cathedral's cloisters and bell tower.

A €7 entry ticket—including audio guide—allows entry into the nave, treasury, and cloister, as well as the Basilica of Sant Feliu, which was Girona's first cathedral until the 10th century.

A highlight of the cathedral's treasures is the **Tapestry of Creation**, an 11th-century Romanesque tapestry considered one of the finest surviving specimens of this kind of work.

Arab Baths

Carrer Ferran el Catòlic; tel. 97/219-0969; www. banysarabs.org; Mar-Oct, Mon-Sat 10am-7pm, Sun 10am-2pm; Nov-Feb, Mon-Sun 10am-2pm; €2

At the foot of the cathedral's sweeping stone staircase are some of the best-preserved ancient baths in all of Spain. The baths were first constructed in 1194, in a Roman style with Arab influences—hence the name. Not actually Arab baths, they were built a few centuries after the Moors left Girona.

The three interconnected rooms, with pools of different water temperatures, served as public baths until the 14th century, when they stopped being used as baths. Later, they were incorporated into a nearby convent; the nuns used what were once the pools as a laundry room. The baths were restored in the 20th century to their original design.

Although not in use as baths today, visitors can walk through the different rooms of the baths, entering through the apodyterium (the "undressing room"). At the center of the central bathing area, a cupula surrounded by stone columns lets light pour in and gives a sense of the grandeur in which medieval locals bathed.

Jewish Quarter

Girona's former Jewish Quarter, El Call, is located within the Old Town around the Carrer de la Força, and has retained its medieval character with narrow, winding lanes studded with balconies, shop fronts, and archways, leading onto secret little patios. It is one of the best-preserved Jewish quarters in Europe.

Museu d'Història dels Jueus (Museum of Jewish History)

Carrer de la Força, 8; tel. 97/221-6761; www.girona. cat/call/eng/museu.php; July-August, Mon-Sat 10am-8pm, Sun 10am-2pm; Sept-June, Tues-Sat 10am-6pm, Mon and Sun 10am-2pm; €4

Explore the history of Jewish life in both Girona and the wider region of Catalonia at this fascinating museum, which charts Jewish history through 11 galleries including "Origins," "Synagogue," "Family," and "Converted Society and Inquisition." The first Jewish families settled in Girona in the 9th century and the museum uses archaeological finds and illustrations to tell their story. The audio guide is €2 and the museum is free for children under the age of 14. There is free entry for everyone on the first Sunday of every month.

Pont de Pedra

Joining Plaça del Vi with Carrer Nou

This footbridge, built in 1856 using Girona stone, is one of the best viewpoints of the vibrantly colored houses along the banks of the river. It joins Plaça del Vi, on the eastern Old Town side, with Carrer Nou in the Mercadal neighborhood on the western side of the river. The next bridge along the river, Pont de les Peixateries Velles, made of red steel, was built by Gustav Eiffel and his company in 1877.

FOOD
★ EL CELLER DE CAN ROCA

Carrer de Can Sunyer, 48; tel. 97/222-2157; www. cellercanroca.com; Tue, 12:30pm-2pm, Wed-Sat, 12:30pm-2pm and 8pm-9:30pm; set menu €180/€205

El Celler de Can Roca, opened in 1986 by brothers Joan, Josep, and Jordi Roca, has been named best restaurant in the world several times over. For dedicated foodies, the three-Michelin-starred restaurant is itself worth a trip to Girona, with its avant-garde take on Catalan cuisine and its expansive wine list.

Fideuà

Paella is one of Spain's most famous dishes, but you might notice a rival to the traditional rice dish when visiting the Catalan coast. *Fideuà* is a version of paella made with thin pasta noodles instead of rice; *fideuà* comes from the Catalan word *fideuada*, which means "a large amount of noodles."

The dish is said to have first been prepared on a ship in the early 20th century; the captain was said to like rice so much that he would often not leave enough paella for the other sailors. The cook decided to substitute rice for noodles, but it became a big hit, spreading through the town of Gandia and, soon, farther afield.

Like paella, *fideuà* is cooked in a wide, shallow pan and includes a variety of seafood, meat, and vegetables. It is, also like paella, a popular dish up and down the coast, including in Catalonia. It is commonly eaten for lunch.

The restaurant is housed in a modern, light-filled space, with floor-to-ceiling glass windows that open out onto its small courtyards, planted with trees. The atmosphere is relaxed but expectant—everyone knows they are here for something special. The dishes—from amuse-bouches like liquid truffle bonbons, and main courses (including the restaurant's special take on Iberian suckling pig), to a tobacco leaf and chocolate dessert—are a constant surprise and delight. It's not just the food that is creative but the methods of plating and serving; some dishes come balanced on little trees or inside a miniature doll's house, giving the whole experience an elevated sense of theater.

Booking in advance is a must—reservations can be made online up to 11 months in advance, and you can add your name to a waiting list if the dates you want are not available. The restaurant is quite far out of the town center, so taking a taxi is a good idea (10 minute ride, around €7).

TXALAKA

Carrer Bonastruc de Porta, 4; tel. 97/222-5975; daily 1pm-4pm, 7.30pm-11.30pm

This is a great place to sample typical Basque tapas or *pintxos* (bread topped with different ingredients, from prawns to tortilla Txalaka); it's a traditional Basque tavern with dark wood walls and a buzzing atmosphere, serving its fares the traditional way, laid out on the bar top. Simply take a plate and load it up with what strikes your fancy. Sample an array of seafood, as well as pintxos topped with *jamón Ibérico* and lots of tasty local cheeses.

LA FÁBRICA

Carrer de la Llebre, 3; tel. 97/229-6622; www. lafabricagirona.com; daily 9am-3pm

This cool café does healthy sandwiches and great coffee, making it the ideal breakfast or lunch stop while exploring the old town. Opened by a Canadian couple—one of whom is a former professional cyclist—the café has a rustic charm, with stone walls and cyclist memorabilia, as well as a small outdoor terrace. The couple also own the nearby **Espresso Mafia** coffee shop (Carrer de la Cort Reial, 5; tel. 63/307-8075; Mon-Thurs 9am-7pm, Fri-Sat 9am-8pm, Sun 10am-5pm).

CAN ROCA

Ctra. de Taialà, 42; tel. 97/220-5119; Mon-Fri, 1pm-4pm, 9pm-10.30pm, €11

A world away from the molecular gastronomy of El Celler de Can Roca, this restaurant serves the hearty, homemade food of the Roca brothers' childhoods and is—perhaps surprisingly—where they started out (it is still run today by the Rocas' parents, now in their eighties). The €11 weekday lunch menu (available from around 1pm) is a great deal; this is

1: Girona Jewish Quarter; **2:** Dalí Theatre-Museum; **3:** Girona Cathedral.

the place to come for traditional Catalan cuisine, from escudella stew to fideuà, in a rustic, cozy atmosphere.

ACCOMMODATIONS

There is a city tax in Girona of €0.99 per person per night that will be added to your hotel bill.

HOTEL HISTORIC

Carrer Bellmirall, 4A; tel. 97/222-3583; www. hotelhistoric.com; €115

Just steps away from the cathedral, this atmospheric, family-run hotel is located in a period building with historic features, from wooden beams to original stone walls, around every corner. Its eight rooms feature doubles, twins, and two different suites, one with its own private terrace. This is a great base from which to explore Girona's old town.

HOTEL NORD 1901 SUPERIOR

Carrer Nord, 7-9; tel. 97/241-1522; www.nord1901. com; €100

Across the river from the Old Town, this family-run four-star hotel with outdoor pool and sun loungers is a relaxing location within easy walking distance to Girona's main sights. Double and twin rooms feature air conditioning and TVs, while the hotel also has one- and two-bedroom apartments (from €110) located in nearby buildings—ideal for larger groups or families. A buffet breakfast is served in the garden in summer.

INFORMATION AND SERVICES

Girona Tourist Office (Rambla de la Llibertat, 1; tel. 97/201-0001; www.girona.cat; Apr-Oct, Mon-Fri 9am-8pm, Sat 9am-2pm, 4pm-8pm, Sun 9am-2pm; Nov-Mar, Mon-Fri 9am-7pm, Sat 9am-2pm, 3pm-7pm, Sun 9am-2pm) has maps, brochures, books, and info about the city and its attractions.

The **Gironamuseus card** (www. gironamuseus.cat) is a discount card for six museums in the city (Museum of Archeology of Catalonia, Art Museum, History Museum of Girona, Museum of Jewish History, Museum of Cinema, and Casa Masó). With the card, visitors will pay the full price at the first museum and then 50 percent at all the others. The card is free and can be picked up from the Tourist Office.

GETTING THERE

Trains (faster and often cheaper than buses) are your best bet for getting from Barcelona to Girona.

Train

The high-speed AVE train, run by Spain's national train operator RENFE (www. renfe.com), has hourly routes between both Barcelona Sants and Passeig de Gràcia stations and Girona that take around 40 minutes and cost around €26 return (first departure 7am, last departure 9:40pm). There are also slower, regional trains, which take around an hour and a half and are slightly cheaper—but for a day trip the AVE is the best bet. Trains arrive at Girona's main train station, in the new town, across the river from the old town—a short, 10-minute walk away. Alternately, you can take a taxi from the station (approximately €6).

Bus

Buses leave from Barcelona's Estació Nord (www.barcelonanord.cat) and take just under two hours. Buses leave around every 90 minutes. The first departure is at around 7:40am, and the last bus from Girona to Barcelona is at 7:30pm. Prices are around €29 return.

Car

Go up the AP-7 north of Barcelona, which takes around one hour and 40 minutes. It can be tricky to find parking spaces close to the old town. There is a free car park next to the train station, and a larger free car park next to the Mercadona supermarket on Avinguda de Franca, a 15-minute walk north of the center.

GETTING AROUND

Once in Girona, most tourists will stick to the old town and the more modern shops of the new town, just across the river. Both areas are very walkable, so the need to use public transport is minimal. **Gitaxi** (tel. 97/222-2323; www.gitaxi.cat) runs taxis throughout the city and also does airport transfers.

Figueres

Figueres (pop. 46,000), a small town in the north of Catalonia, 140 kilometers (87 miles) north of Barcelona, was a pretty, if unknown, town before the surrealist artist Salvador Dalí (who was born here) put it on the tourist map with the Dalí Theatre-Museum. Dalí designed the museum, which holds many of his creations and is a journey into the bizarre and the brilliant. The museum is by far the biggest draw for day trippers, but Figueres itself is home to a lovely tree-lined main boulevard as well as plenty of good tapas bars and shops, making it an attractive place to linger.

SIGHTS

★ DALÍ THEATRE-MUSEUM

Plaça Gala i Salvador Dalí, 5; tel. 97/267-7500; www.
salvador-dali.org/en/museums/dali-theatre-museum-
in-figueres; Tues-Sun: Jan 1-Feb 28 10:30am-6pm,
Mar 1-Mar 31 9:30am-6pm, Apr 1-Sept 30
9am-8pm, Oct 1-Oct 31 9:30am-6pm, Nov 1-Dec 31
10:30am-6pm; €14, students €10

Opened in 1974, the sprawling Dalí Theatre-Museum is a homage to surrealism and the work of Spanish artist Salvador Dalí. It is housed in what was originally the original Municipal Theatre, where Dalí held his very first exhibition, in 1919, when he was 15 years old.

Dalí transformed the former theater into a wacky feast for the imagination, personally designing the architectural elements and large-scale installations inside the museum. He was originally asked to donate one work to the town, but instead said he would make an entire museum: "Where, if not in my own town, should the most extravagant and solid of my work endure, where if not here?" Dalí said.

Visitors are immediately struck by its exterior: a huge glass dome and red towers topped with egg shapes and golden human figures that look like they are about to dive off the edge. Inside, the museum takes visitors through the work of Dalí in a roughly chronological order, from his beginnings through his surrealist peak and his interest in mysticism and science. The museum's collection includes paintings, drawings, sculptures, installations, holograms, and photography—of which over 1,500 items are on display. Key works include "Self-Portrait with l'Humanité" (1923), "Portrait of Gala with Two Lamb Chops Balanced on Her Shoulder" (1933), and "Leda Atomica" (1949). There are works by other Catalan artists on display, as well as art collected by Dalí over the years by the likes of El Greco, Marcel Duchamp, and Marià Fortuny.

Dalí also created several works especially for the museum, such as the "Mae West Room," a sculptural montage of the famous actress—including a disjointed bright red lips sofa, a blonde wig, two pictures of eyes, and a nose—that, when viewed through a mirror, come together into one, surreal face. Another famous installation is the "Rainy Taxi," a Cadillac with mannequins inside. Put a euro in the slot and watch it start raining inside the taxi.

Your ticket also allows admission into Dalí-Joies, housed in an annex building of the museum. It contains a series of jewels designed by Dalí, as well as his original drawings of the jewel designs.

It is best to visit on a weekday and get there early to avoid the biggest crowds of tourists. Tickets can be reserved online in advance.

The museum also opens at night, from

Figueres

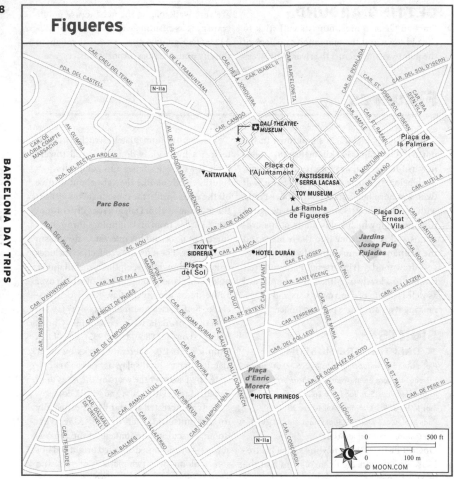

© MOON.COM

10pm to 1am July 28 to September 1, giving visitors a unique experience of the space.

TOY MUSEUM

Carrer de Sant Pere, 1; tel. 97/250-4585; www. mjc.cat; Oct-May, Tues-Fri 10am-6:30pm, Sat 10:30am-7:30pm, Sun 10:30am-2:30pm; June, July, Sept, Mon-Fri 10:30am-7pm, Sat 10:30am-8pm, Sun 10:30am-2:30pm; Aug, Mon-Sat 10:30am-8pm, Sun 10:30am-2:30pm; €7, children aged 6-16 and over 65s €5.60

This three-story museum charts the history of European toys, from ancient games through 20th-century classics. A comprehensive collection of toys spanning the end of the 19th century to the modern day include porcelain dolls, German mechanical toys, magic lanterns, and a gigantic Meccano Eiffel Tower from 1929. Some toys have been donated by famous Catalans, so you can see Salvador Dalí's childhood teddy bear and a whistle figurine belonging to Joan Miró.

The second floor houses an analogue model railway, built by train-lover Andreu Costa Pedro, who took eight years to complete the intricate display.

FOOD

TXOT'S SIDRERIA

Av. Salvador Dalí, 114; tel. 97/267-8523; www. sidreriatxots.com; daily midday-midnight

This traditional Basque pintxo bar serves pintxos the traditional way: lined up on top of the bar for customers to pick themselves. The Basque cider is poured from on high to add bubbles, providing a touch of theater to proceedings. As well as Basque classics, there are local Catalan flavors like *escalivada* (smoked vegetables) on toasted bread and a menu especially for children. The tapas bar is at the front while a more formal, sit-down restaurant is found towards the back.

ANTAVIANA

Carrer de Llers, 5-7; tel. 97/251-0377; www. estaurantantaviana.cat; Tues-Sun 1pm-3:30pm, Tues-Sat 8pm-10:30pm

Located close to the Dalí museum, Antaviana offers elevated tapas, such as anchovies with tomato bread, ham croquettes, and squid from Cap de Creus on the nearby coast, and a good-value lunchtime fixed-price menu (€18.50 for three courses). The classic dishes are presented with a flourish of style. Decor is rustic-meets-contemporary, with exposed brick walls and wooden tables, each overlooked by its own standing lamp.

PASTISSERÍA SERRA LACASA

Plaça Ajuntament, 6; tel. 97/250-0581; Mon-Fri, 9am-2pm, 5pm-9pm, Sun 9am-3pm

This lovely bakery, in the heart of Figueres just off La Rambla, is over a century old and is a great place to try some local specialities. *Flaones*, a typical Figueres pastry filled with a custard cream, makes the perfect sweet snack. You can also pick up chocolates, other typical pastries, and sweets like boxes of *turrón*, a Spanish nougat popular at Christmastime.

ACCOMMODATIONS

HOTEL DURÁN

Carrer Lasauca, 5; 97/250-1250; www.hotelduran.com; €65

Run by the Durán family since 1910, this central hotel was a favorite of Salvador Dalí himself whenever he returned to his home town. Its 65 rooms are comfortable and easy on the wallet, while its restaurant specializes in fresh local ingredients and delicious Catalan cuisine—there is a degustation menu for €49 and main courses range from €20-€25. A good-value, three-course lunch menu (€22) is available on weekdays.

HOTEL PIRINEOS

Avinguda de Salvador Dalí i Domènech, 68; tel. 97/250-0312; www.pirineoshotelfigueres.com; €70

The four-star Hotel Pirineos, a less-than-10-minute walk from the Dalí Theatre-Museum, offers neat and modern accommodation across its double and triple rooms. Décor is neutral, with white walls and warm, biscuit colors throughout. Rooms have all the standard amenities like air conditioning, flat-screen TVs, and hairdryers, and some have balconies with views over the city. A lounge-bar area is a good spot for a nightcap and a good buffet breakfast is served every morning.

GETTING THERE

The best and fastest travel option between Barcelona and Figueres is the high-speed AVE train.

Figueres is only 15 minutes from Girona by high-speed train, so could easily be combined with a day trip or overnight stay in Girona.

Train

FROM BARCELONA

RENFE's high-speed AVE trains run from Barcelona Sants station to Figueres-Vilafant station, 1.5 kilometers (1 mile) from the center of Figueres. Trains take 55 minutes and prices start at €11 one-way. (The first train leaves at approximately 7am, and the last train back from Figueres at 8:45pm. There are roughly 25 trains a day leaving every half-hour or so.) There's a taxi stand and a bus stop outside the station; the 5-10-minute taxi ride will cost around €5.

Slower RENFE trains and the local commuter train (called the Rodalies, which runs on the R11 line) run from Barcelona Sants to Figueres station (a different station from Figueres-Vilafant) around every hour. The journey takes between one hour 40 minutes and two hours, with the first train of the day usually at around 6am and the last train from Figueres at around 8:30pm. Buy tickets from machines inside the station. From Figueres train station it is a 10-minute walk into the center of town, so there is not much need for a taxi. If you have heavy luggage or want to rest your legs, there is a taxi rank outside the station (10-minute journey of around €6).

FROM GIRONA

The high-speed AVE runs from Girona to Figueres Vilafant (15 minutes, from €6.90 one way), with the first train at 7:45am and the last train back from Figueres at 8:45pm.

Car

From Barcelona, get on the AP-7 motorway north, which takes around one hour and 50 minutes. From Girona, it is a 40-minute drive north to Figueres along the AP-7 motorway.

There is a fee-paying carpark behind the Dalí Theatre-Museum and below the Rambla de Figueres. Free street parking is pretty easy to find, but might be more out of the center (a 10-minute walk in, for example).

GETTING AROUND

Figueres is very walkable and most visitors get around on foot. Travelers might want to take a taxi from the station: **Taxi Figueres** (tel. 97/250-5043, www.taxisfigueras.com) has a taxi rank on La Rambla de Figueres.

Sitges

Less than an hour (36km/22mi) south of Barcelona lies the beautiful coastal town of Sitges (pop. 30,000), whose whitewashed buildings and pristine beaches have long attracted day trippers from Barcelona, as well as those looking for a longer and more relaxing stay.

Sitges—known by some as the Spanish Riviera—really knows how to party, from its February carnival to the wildly popular Pride, held in mid-June. It has long been a famously gay-friendly destination and welcomes everyone with wide-open arms. The town has always attracted artists, such as Catalan painter Santiago Rusiñol in the late 19th century, but cemented its fun-loving and alternative reputation in the 1960s. Wander its old town and palm tree–lined promenade, relax on one of its 17 (!) beaches, and take in the "Americano" seafront villas, so called because many were built by wealthy Spaniards returning from Cuba and Puerto Rico in the 19th century who were known as *Americanos* (the most famous of these was Facundo Bacardi, founder of the famous rum brand).

SIGHTS
PASSEIG MARITIM

Running for more than 2.5 kilometers (1.5 miles) along Sitges' coast, the Passeig Maritim is a pedestrianized promenade where people walk, rollerblade, jog, and generally enjoy the cool sea breeze. The palm-tree-lined paved walkway runs past several beaches, including Platja de Sitges and Platja Terramar. Lined with *chiringuitos* (laid-back beach bars that tend to be very relaxed and full of beachgoers during the day and more of a sunset/drinks destination at night), it's the ideal place to promenade and enjoy a drink or meal along the seafront.

MUSEU CAU FERRAT

Carrer de Fonollar, 6; tel. 93/894-0364; www. museusdesitges.cat/en/museum/cau-ferrat/cau-

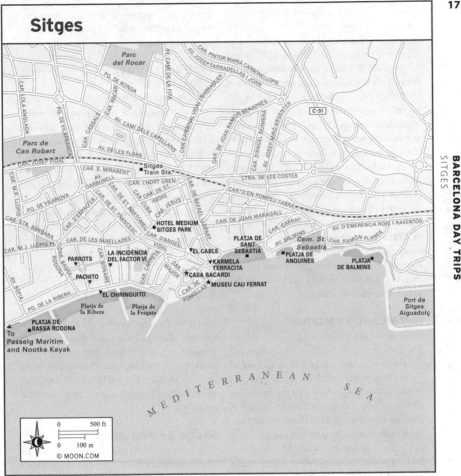

Sitges

ferrat-museum; Tues-Sun 10am-7pm; €10 (includes entry Maricel Museum)

The former home and studio of Catalan painter Santiago Rusiñol (1861-1931) became a museum in 1933. It features ancient art collected by Rusiñol, as well as an excellent array of work by Rusiñol himself, who was one of the pioneers of Catalan Modernism. Other paintings include works by Ramon Casas and Pablo Picasso. Rusiñol's modern style—his main subjects are nature and solitary women such as "La morfinòmana" ("the Morphine addict")—was an inspiration for Picasso.

The museum also has an interesting and unusual collection of ironwork—a craft showcased in the work of many Modernista architects, most notably that of Antoni Gaudí.

Admission includes entry into the next-door **Maricel Museum** (Calle Fonollar; tel. 93/894-0364; www.museusdesitges.cat/en/museum/maricel/maricel-museum; Tues-Sun 10am-7pm; €10), which houses centuries of Catalan sculpture and art.

CASA BACARDI
Plaça de l'Ajuntament, 11; tel. 93/894-8151; www.bacardi.com/casa-bacardi-sitges; Museum and

Bacardi shop, Wed-Sat midday-2pm, 4pm-8:30pm, Sun midday-2pm, 4pm-7:30pm

Don Facundo Bacardi Masso was born in Sitges and emigrated to Cuba in 1830, where he founded the white rum brand, Bacardi. Back in his birthplace, Casa Bacardi opened in 2010 in Sitges' old covered market building, offering visitors guided tours (available in English, twice a day, €12, €10 for students and seniors) where they can learn the history of the brand and taste some of its famous mojito cocktails. The museum charts the history of the Bacardi company and the rum-making process. Mixology masterclasses teach visitors the secret of making a great cocktail. Tickets can be purchased online and should be booked in advance—tours can sell out, especially on weekends. The only way to explore Casa Bacardi is on a tour, but if you want to skip that, you can head straight to the stylish bar to sample some cocktails.

AMERICANO MANSIONS

Carrer Illa de Cuba

These homes were built by "Americanos," Catalans who had emigrated to Cuba and Puerto Rico, made their fortune, and returned to Sitges, injecting money into the town. The new bourgeoisie began a feverish period of erecting mansions inspired by the most fashionable architectural styles of the day, such as Catalan modernism. Over 50 Americano buildings are still standing in Sitges, many centered around Carrer Illa de Cuba (Island of Cuba street), close to the train station.

AgiSitges (www.agisitges.com) offers a two-hour Americanos walking tour, in English for private groups (time can be decided when booking) and a more general "Walk through Sitges' History" tour (from €10pp, starts at 11am in front of the Tourism Office at the train station; see website for upcoming tours).

★ BEACHES

There is a total of 17 sandy *platges* (Catalan for beaches; singular is *platja*) in and around Sitges, so you are really spoiled for choice.

From June-September there are various activities along the beaches, from water sports to aerobics classes.

Platja de Sitges
(Sitges Beach)

Platja de Sitges is the main city beach and, as such, also tends to be the busiest with everyone from young couples to families. The main stretch of sand is split into eight interlinked beaches (including **Platja de la Ribera, Platja de l'Estanyol,** and **Platja de la Barra**), all with facilities like toilets, beach bars, and sun lounger rental (around €10/day). Walk west of the center to avoid the busiest spots. The water here tends to be calm and good for swimming or just floating around on a *lilo*, and the golden sands draw both locals and tourists.

Platja de Bassa Rodona

Sitges' main gay beach has a central location within Platja de Sitges' eight beaches (opposite Passeig Marítim, 2) and plenty of rainbow flags to help guide the way. It can become packed during the summer, so arrive early to grab the best spot. There are parasols and sun loungers for rent (from €10/day), and those looking for a bit more activity can hire pedal boats.

Platja de Anquines

Just west of the Plajta de Sitges, a 10- to 15-minute walk from the city center, Platja de Anquines is a man-made beach originally built for the guests of the Hotel Terramar (the beach is right in front of the hotel). Today, the pretty cove is a public beach, ideal for families and those looking to get active. The fact that it is a cove means the waters are calm and ideal for family-friendly paddling, while its position just west of the center means it tends to be quieter than the more central beaches.

The beach is home to **Nootka Kayak** (Passeig Marítim, 80; tel. 93/810-0256; www.nootka-kayak.com), which rents out kayaks

1: whitewashed buildings in Sitges; 2: Tarragona's Roman Amphitheater.

(from €15/hour) and paddle boards (from €18/hour) as well as offering kayak and paddleboard excursions, led by a guide, up the coast.

Platja de Balmins

At the very beginning of the seafront promenade and just east of the center (a 15-minute walk), Platja de Balmins is a popular naturist beach, so—if you fancy—you can leave the swimsuit at home. (Wearing swimsuits is also perfectly fine.) Divided into two different coves by a rocky outcrop (the nudists tend to stick to the more secluded side), the beach has a beautiful backdrop of mountains and whitewashed villas.

Platja de Sant Sebastià

Behind Sitges' Port, a 15-minute walk from the center, this beach is one of the most popular with locals and tends to be quieter than the more central city beaches. Historically, it was the base for the boats of Sitges' fishermen. There's a beach bar and umbrella and sun lounger rental (from €10/day). A beachfront promenade lined with restaurants and cafés is a good spot for a lunchtime bite to eat.

BARS AND NIGHTLIFE

Sitges is famous for its nightlife, and all over the city you'll find bars offering drinks and tapas that are buzzing with punters; like many Spanish bars, they stay open into the early hours of the morning.

The town's famed gay scene is focused around Calle Primer de Maig (known by locals as Carrer de Pecat, or "Street of Sin") and Plaça de la Indústria, while a more diverse selection of bars can be found around Plaça del Cap de la Vila, Sitges' main square.

Being a seaside town, there are also a host of beach bars and restaurants. In fact, Sitges is the home of Spain's very first *chiringuito* (beach bar).

EL CHIRINGUITO

Passeig de la Ribera, 31; tel. 93/894-7596; daily 10am-1am

The cute blue and white façade of this beachside tapas bar hints at a long history—it was the very first *chiringuito* in Spain when it opened in 1913. The name took off and soon was being used for beach bars up and down the Spanish coast. The bar, with a cute seafront terrace, has pride of place along the promenade and is a fantastic slice of history. Skip the standard tapas and stick to drinks, enjoying a fantastic sunset view in this little slice of local history.

PACHITO

Carrer Primer de Maig, 3; tel. 93/894-7813; www.pachitositges.es; Fri-Sat 9pm-3am

Pachito, or "Little Pacha," is part of the Pacha nightclub chain famed for its Ibiza club, but was actually one of the first Pacha clubs to open, way back in 1969. It's just behind the Passeig Marítim in the town center and is popular with a diverse gay and straight crowd who like a boogie and a *copa* (spirit and mixer).

PARROTS

Plaça de la Indústria, 2; tel. 93/894-1350; daily 5pm-2:30am

It's hard to miss Parrots. One of Sitges' most legendary gay bars has pride of place on Plaça de la Indústria, with a rainbow awning and large terrace. It's where many locals and tourists start the night, indulge in some serious people-watching over a multi-colored cocktail, and then see where the evening takes them.

FOOD

EL CABLE

Carrer Barcelona, 1; tel. 93/894-8761; www.elcable. cat; Mon-Fri 7pm-11:30pm, Sat-Sun midday-3:30pm, 7pm-11:30pm

Run by the Andreu family since 1940, El Cable is a local favorite for hearty and tasty tapas dishes in a friendly and welcoming atmosphere. Try the *patatas bravas* (potatoes in a spicy sauce), crispy fried squid, and spicy chistorra sausage. It gets busy, so don't be shy about elbowing your way to the bar.

LA INCIDÈNCIA DEL FACTOR VI

Carrer Bonaire, 25; tel. 93/894-8262; www.factorvi. com; Tues-Sun 1pm-3pm, Tues-Thurs 7pm-1am, Fri-Sat 7pm-2:30am, Sun 7pm-1am

A haven for wine lovers close to the seafront, this stylish restaurant has a menu of fresh local classics that have been given a contemporary twist. In an indoor terrace setting, try dishes like crab ravioli with lobster and charcoal-grilled cod cheek with thyme, tomatoes, onions, and fennel. Its fixed-price lunch menu, with three courses and wine for €19.50, is a particularly good deal (served Mon-Fri only).

KARMELA TERRACITA

Carrer de la Carreta, 24; tel. 93/894-1927; www. karmelaterracita.com; Thurs-Tues 1pm-11pm; €10-€15

This lovely beachside restaurant with an outdoor terrace is wildly popular for its tasty local tapas dishes. Try the Xató, Sitges' most typical dish, a salad of endives, anchovies, and tuna with a sauce made from almonds, breadcrumbs, vinegar, garlic, olive oil, and salt. Fresh tapas dishes include grilled prawns, razor clams, and mussels alongside classics like meatballs, *patatas bravas*, and padron peppers.

ACCOMMODATIONS

HOTEL MIM SITGES PARK

Avenida Sofia, 12; tel. 93/811-3500; www. hotelmimsitges.com; €125

A two-minute walk from the beach, this sleek hotel channels urban cool with its rooftop Sky Bar and pool area and indoor spa, where guests can indulge in treatments including deep-tissue massages, detox facials, and manicures. Rooms are spacious, and some come with stunning sea views. A delicious hot and cold buffet breakfast is the ideal start to the day.

HOTEL MEDIUM SITGES PARK

Carrer Jesús, 16; tel. 93/894-0250; www. mediumhoteles.com/en/spain/sitges/centro/hotel-medium-sitges-park; €120

Set in a Modernista building, this hotel is just a short stroll to the beach. With a sizeable outdoor pool, bar, and sun lounger area, it's also a lovely place to relax. In the heart of the old town, it makes a great base from which to explore Sitges' famous nightlife. Rooms include singles, doubles, twins, and triples, and some have their own terrace.

FESTIVALS AND EVENTS

CARNIVAL

http://www.visitsitges.com/en/carnaval-sitges-2018

The seaside town swells by over a quarter of a million people during its week-long carnival, held every year in late February. Carnival is traditionally a last chance for a huge party before the privations of Lent, and few places put on as excellent a party as Sitges. From gigantic street parades to fabulous costumes and all-night parties, this fiesta attracts people from across the world. Each day has a packed schedule of events for young and old, from outdoor concerts to traditional dancing and children's parades. Top tip: book accommodations well in advance, because places fill up quickly.

PRIDE

Being a top LGBT destination, it's not surprising Sitges hosts a fantastic Pride celebration. The event usually lasts for a week in June and includes a parade along the seafront with floats, concerts, beach parties, and more. Pride 2019 is the tenth anniversary of the event, so expect some extra-special celebrations. Check dates and what's on at www. gaysitgespride.com

GETTING THERE

The easiest way to get to Sitges is by train.

Train

The regional Rodalies train (line R2) (www. rodalies.gencat.cat) passes through stations Passeig de Gràcia and Estacio Sants in Barcelona on the way to Sitges. The final destination of the train will be either Vilanova i la Geltru or St. Vincenç de Calders (look out for this name on the train/boards).

Buy tickets (€7.20 return, €4.10 one way) from ticket desks or the ticket machines located inside the stations (they are not available to buy online). Trains run approximately every 20 minutes (around 70 departures per day) and the journey takes between 30-40 minutes. The first train of the day from Barcelona Sants is at 5:45am and the last train back from Sitges is at 10:50pm. From the train station in Sitges, it's a 10-minute walk into town.

Bus

MonBus (www.monbus.cat) runs buses that leave from Plaça Espanya and Ronda Universitat in Barcelona (55 minutes from Ronda Universitat and 45 minutes from Plaça Espanya). The bus runs about twice an hour and one-way tickets are €4.10. The first bus departs at 6:10am and the last bus home from Sitges is at 10pm. Get off the bus at Avenida Sofia, 43, and it's a 10-minute walk into the center of Sitges.

There is also a night bus that runs between Pg. de Vilafranca in Sitges and Plaça Catalunya and Plaça Espanya in Barcelona, which takes around 35 minutes. There are at least three departures during the night from Sitges back to Barcelona. The frequency and times depend on the day; check the website, www.monbus.cat/es/horaris-nocturn, for bus timetables.

Car

From Barcelona, take the C-32 south, which takes just under an hour. It is difficult to find parking in the center of Sitges but there is a free municipal car park on Carrer de Sant Honorat.

GETTING AROUND

Once in Sitges, the town is small enough for most visitors to get to most places on foot. Buses (operated by Transports Ciutat Comtal) can come in handy when visiting beaches further from the center. There are only three bus lines in Sitges. The most useful for visitors is the L2, which goes from the center to Platja de Anquines. A one-way ticket is €1.50.

Tarragona

Perched on a hill overlooking the Mediterranean, Tarragona (pop. 130,000), 100 kilometers (62 miles) south of Barcelona, has a long and interesting history. It was first settled by the Iberians and Carthinogens before becoming an important Roman military base, which was called Tarraco. Today, travelers come for its history—the city is home to a slew of well-preserved Roman remains, including a spectacular seaside amphitheater—and stay for its beaches and quality cuisine. The city's old town, with its narrow lanes and hidden plazas, is a joy to explore.

SIGHTS
Museu d'Història de Tarragona
(Tarragona History Museum)

Carrer dels Cavallers, 14; tel. 97/724-2220; tarragona.cat/patrimoni/museu-historia
This museum includes the Roman amphitheatre, circus, and several other Roman ruins that together make up a UNESCO World Heritage Site. Visitors can pay per sight (€3.30 per venue) or buy a pass (the €7.40 pass allows entry into the four Roman venues, and the €11.05 pass allows entry into all Tarragona History Museum venues across the city). You can buy the pass online or at any of the participating venues. All sights below are part of the Tarragona History Museum.

★ ROMAN AMPHITHEATRE
Parc de l'Amfiteatre romà; tel. 97/724-2579; winter, Tues-Fri 9am-7:30pm, Sat 9am-7pm, Sun 9am-3pm,

Tarragona

Mon 9am-3pm, Tues-Sat 9am-9pm, Sun 9am-3pm; €3.30

Built in the 2nd century BC, with a privileged position looking out over the sea, Tarragona's Roman amphitheater is a well-preserved slice of history. The stands, which could hold an audience of up to 14,000 people, were carved straight out of the underlying rock. It would have been typically used for gladiator fights and public executions; during the persecution of Christians in 259, Tarraco's bishop, Fructuosus, and his deacons were burned alive. Eventually the medieval Santa Maria del Miracle church was built over the

amphitheater, whose ruins were excavated in the mid-20th century. Today, visitors can walk into the middle of the arena and climb the surrounding seating area.

ROMAN CIRCUS AND PRAETORIUM

Rambla Vella; tel. 97/723-0171; Apr 12-Sept 30, Tues-Sat 9am-9pm, Sun 9am-3pm; Oct 1-Apr 11, Tues-Sat 9am-7pm, Sun 9am-3pm; €3.30

Once the scene of dramatic Roman chariot races watched by a crowd of as many as 30,000 spectators, Tarragona's Circus—an ancient racetrack—was built in the first century AD. Today, the Circus is half-excavated, and much remains buried under surrounding 10th-century buildings; visitors can see the eastern side with its stands and decorative façade. The sight is also worth visiting to see the Praetorium, a tower that once connected the lower city to the forum through the circus. It was used during the Spanish Civil War as a prison. Today, visitors can climb the tower for panoramic views over the seafront.

ROMAN WALLS

Avinguda de Catalunya, 1; winter, Tues-Fri 9am-7:30pm, Sat 9am-7pm, Sun 9am-3pm; summer Mon 9am-3pm, Tues-Sat 9am-9pm, Sun 9am-3pm; €3.30

One of the first projects the Romans undertook was to build a stone wall surrounding their military base, Tarraco, an important form of defense. The walls were six meters (20 feet) high and eventually went as far as the port, essentially marking the borders of the town. Of the original 3,500-meter (11,500-foot) wall, around 1,100 meters (3600 feet) remain today, bordering the city's old town. The Passeig Arqueològic (Archeological Walk), starting on Avinguda de Catalunya, takes you around the perimeter of the walls.

COLONY FORUM

Carrer de Lleida; tel. 97/725-0795; summer, Mon 9am-3pm, Tues-Sat 9am-9pm, Sun, 9am-3pm, winter, Tues-Fri 9am-7:30pm, Sat 9am-7pm, Sun 9am-3pm, €3.30

The social hub of Roman Tarraco, the Colony Forum, built around 30 BC, is a square plot with stone columns that would have been surrounded by shops, temples, and other public buildings. Walk over the footbridge and look down to see the streets of Tarraco, with Roman-era homes and shops.

Catedral de Tarragona

Pla de la Seu; tel. 97/722-6935; www. catedraldetarragona.com; Nov 2-Mar 18, Mon-Fri 10am-5pm, Sat 10am-7pm; Mar 20-Jun10, Mon-Sat 10am-7pm; Jun 12-Sept 9, Mon-Sat 10am-8pm, Sun 3pm-8pm; Sept 11-Oct 31, Mon-Sat 10am-7pm; €5

Sitting grandly at the top of a stone staircase,

the Cathedral of Tarragona was built in the 12th century on the site of an earlier basilica, which, before that, was an Arab Mosque and, before that, a Roman temple. Its style nods to both Romanesque and Gothic architecture; the main façade is a mixture of the two (of its three doors, one is Gothic and two are Romanesque).

Access is through the cloisters, around the corner from the front of the building, except for during mass (weekdays 9:30am, Sat 9:30am and midday, and Sun 9:30am, 11am, and 12:30pm). Dating from the 11th-12th centuries, the eastern gallery of the cloister features a 10th-century Arabic inscription that comes from the former mosque. The capitals (tops of the stone columns) in the cloisters are decorated with religious scenes, including—rather bizarrely—one that depicts a cat's funeral being conducted by rats.

Entry to the museum also includes the **Museu Diocesà** (Mar-June, Mon-Sat 10am-7pm; June-Sept, Mon-Sat 10am-8pm, Sun 3pm-8pm; Sept-Oct, Mon-Sat 10am-7pm; Nov-Mar, Mon-Fri 10am-5pm, Sat 10am-7pm), just off the Cloisters. The museum, which comprises two rooms and the chapterhouse, holds 14th-century religious sculptures, Gothic paintings, and intricate tapestries.

Museu Nacional Arqueològic de Tarragona
(National Archeological Museum of Tarragona)

Plaça del Rei, 5; tel. 97/723-6209; www.mnat.cat; Tues-Sat 9:30am-8:30pm, Sun 10am-2pm, €4.50

The National Archaeological Museum of Tarragona (MNAT) contains a wealth of mainly Roman artefacts and is a fascinating place to explore and learn more about Roman Tarraco. The museum takes visitors through the eight-century history of Tarraco in a roughly chronological order, with highlights including amazingly well-preserved mosaics. Learn about the town's Roman society, economy, and architecture through sculpture, jewelery, bronzes, and pottery. The museum's main location on the Plaça del Rei was being renovated at the time of writing, with a project completion date at the end of 2020. A temporary MNAT collection is on display at Tinglado, 4, on the Costa Wharf, in the Port of Tarragona.

BEACHES
Platja del Miracle
Tarragona's long, central city beach is popular with families and is bordered by the Passeig Marítim Rafael Casanova promenade. It is the easiest to access from the city center (a 10-minute walk), and it is watched over by lifeguards. Its golden sands are a lovely place to relax, and the waters off the beach are calm and perfect for a dip.

FOOD
As an historic port, Tarragona has a long seafaring and fishing tradition, so is an excellent place to sample some fresh-off-the-boat seafood. Head to **El Serrallo**, the fishermen's district, packed with homely restaurants offering fresh fish and seafood, for a substantial lunch. A local oily fish, Peix Blau de Tarragona, has a Protected Designation of Origin (D.O.), such is its quality.

Other local specialities include *Cassola de romesco*, a casserole with a base of romesco sauce, *arròs negre* (black rice cooked in squid ink), and *arrossejat* (seafood and rice).

★ CENTRAL MARKET OF TARRAGONA
Plaça de Corsini; tel. 97/789-7888; Mon-Sat 8:30am-9pm
Tarragona's main central market was built in 1915, with thin, cast-iron columns and a grand, high vaulted ceiling. It features Modernista touches such as the green, white, and red ceramics on its roof. The market recently underwent a €50-million renovation, reopening in 2017. It's a good place to pick up some local produce, from charcuterie and hams to cheese, olives, and cakes.

AQ
Carrer de les Coques, 7; tel. 97/721-5954; www. aq-restaurant.com; daily 1:30pm-3:30pm, 8:30pm-11pm, closed on Sun and Mon from late June-early Sept; mains €15-€20
The AQ refers to Ana and Quintín, the owners of this stylish restaurant, whose sleek interiors include stone walls and seating around the bar looking onto the open kitchen. Dishes fuse Catalan flavors with international inspiration—take the oysters, served natural (without additions), Mexican style, or Japanese style. Thai vegetable chop suey, cuttlefish with pil pil sauce and black garlic, and Vietnamese Goi Con lobster spring rolls are just some of the dishes on offer.

TXANTXANGORRI
Plaça de la Font, 16; tel. 97/723-0062; daily midday-1am; €10-€15
Just one of the many pleasant bars and restaurants lining the lovely Plaça de la Font, this Basque pintxo bar is an ideal place for a leisurely lunch or dinner on the terrace (a great place to people-watch). Order pintxos at the bar or dishes from the menu, which includes tapas, salads, and rice and meat dishes (try the seafood rice dishes at lunchtime, a local favorite). Its busy outdoor terrace is where locals come for a relaxing evening drink.

★ CAL JOAN
Carrer d'Espinach, 4; tel. 97/721-9223; Tues-Sun 1pm-3:45pm, Fri-Sat 8:30pm-10:45pm; €15 weekday menu
In Tarragona's fishing neighborhood of El Serrallo, this great local restaurant is the place to go for seafood paella, plates stacked high with prawns and mussels caught just hours earlier, and delicious fish dishes and seafood platters. It's a traditional place with white tablecloths, exposed brick walls, and wooden beams in the ceiling, and it's a favorite with locals, especially for lunch. Its €15 *menu del día* (Mon-Fri) includes two substantial courses, with dishes such as mussels, seafood paella, and fideuà, as well as dessert and a drink.

ACCOMMODATIONS

AC HOTEL TARRAGONA

Avenida Roma, 8; tel. 97/724-7105; www.marriott.
com/hotels/travel/reuta-ac-hotel-tarragona; €85
Just opposite the leafy Parc de la Ciutat, a 10-minute stroll to Tarragona's Roman monuments, this four-star hotel is well positioned to explore the city. Its 115 rooms are simple and stylish, with wooden floors, light-colored furnishings, and amenities like TVs, air conditioning, and 24-hour room service. The fitness center with Turkish bath is the ideal place to decompress at the end of the day.

HOTEL PLAÇA DE LA FONT

Plaça de la Font, 26; tel. 97/724-6134; www.
hotelpdelafont.com; €60
In the heart of Tarragona's old town on the pretty Plaça de la Font, this hotel is in an excellent location for exploring the city's historic sights and visiting the beach, just 500 meters (1600 feet) away. Rooms, available in doubles or triples (some with views over the square), are on the basic side, but reasonable and comfortable, with air conditioning, hairdryers, and TVs. The hotel's terrace, on the square, offers a *menu del día* and is a good place for a nightcap.

GETTING THERE

The best way to travel between Barcelona and Tarragona is by train, for its speed and comfort.

Train

The high-speed AVE trains run from Barcelona Sants and take 35 minutes (from €13 each way, cheaper when booked in advance). The first train leaves at 6:05am, and the last train back from Tarragona is at around 11pm; there are over 20 trains a day. The AVE

station in Tarragona (Camp de Tarragona) is a 15-minute taxi from the center (around €10).

Slower trains leave from Estació França, Passeig de Gràcia, and Sants, and arrive at Tarragona Train Station, close to the seafront, taking just over an hour. The first trains from Passeig de Gràcia leave at 5:56am and the last train back from Tarragona is at roughly 10:15pm. Trains depart approximately every 30 minutes.

Book tickets for both trains online (www.renfe.com) or at ticket booths and machines in the stations.

Bus

Spanish bus company **ALSA** (www.alsa.com) runs around seven buses a day from Barcelona's Estación Nord to Tarragona (one way €8.90, duration one and a half hours). The first bus is at 9am and the last bus from Tarragona is at 9:10pm. The bus drops passengers at the bus station on Carrer de Pere Martell, a 10-minute walk into the center.

Car

From Barcelona, take the C-32 toll road south along the coast (fastest route; around one hour, 20 minutes). There is free parking at the Platja del Miracle city beach and paid parking around the city (including at the Central Market and Plaça de la Font).

GETTING AROUND

Once in Tarragona, it is easy to get between the main sights on foot. Taxis are recommended when arriving from Camp de Tarragona train station. **Radio Taxi Tarragona** (tel. 97/722-1414 or 97/723-6064) is one taxi option. There is also a bus from the station (from 6:20am roughly every 20 minutes, journey time 18 minutes, ticket €1.50 one-way).

Penedès Wine Region

Whether you're a wine buff already or someone who is eager to learn the basics, a trip to the rolling hills of Catalonia's Penedès wine region makes an excellent day out. Speed past vineyard after vineyard on the train, then enjoy a leisurely day exploring some local wineries, vineyards, and cellars and, of course, sampling their produce. While other kinds of wines are produced here, Penedès is undoubtedly most famous for its production of Cava, a Spanish sparkling wine; around 95 percent of all Cava is made in the region.

From Barcelona, it is easy to visit the two main towns of the region, **Sant Sadurní d'Anoia** and **Vilafranca del Penedès**, within the same day trip, by either train or car; Vilafranca is just 10 minutes further by train, so stop at Sant Sadurní first, visit a vineyard, then hop on the train and spend the afternoon in Vilafranca before returning to Barcelona in the evening. If planning to stay overnight in Penedès, opt for Vilafranca, which is livelier than Sant Sadurní, with a wider range of restaurant options. Many people also make the day trip from Sitges.

Spring and fall are great times to visit the region; September/October is harvest time and coincides with Cava Week, a celebration of bubbly held annually in Sant Sadurni d'Anoia. Reservations are recommended for visits and wine tastings, to ensure there are tours and tastings available on your chosen day. Most of the bigger Cava companies offer tours and tastings in English; if looking at smaller wineries, a glance on their website or a quick email should let you know if they offer tours or tastings in English.

SANT SADURNÍ D'ANOIA

Sant Sadurní d'Anoia (pop. 12,500), the so-called "capital of Cava," is the premier destination for travelers wanting to learn more about the Spanish sparkling wine. Cava production dates back to the 1860s, when Spanish winemakers began using the Champagne method to make their own sparkling wines.

The town itself is a serene spot among the rolling hills of vineyards, with a pint-sized center that is easy to stroll. With museums dedicated to cava and a decent range of food options, visitors can easily while away some time in town between vineyard visits.

Wineries and Tasting Rooms
★ FREIXENET

Plaça Joan Sala, 2; tel. 93/891-7000; www.freixenet. es; Mon-Sat 9am-6pm, Sun 9am-3pm

Right outside the train station, Freixenet is one of Spain's most famous and biggest Cava brands and one of the easiest to visit straight off the train. The sparkling wine is produced right here on Freixenet's sprawling estate, and visitors can learn all about it on a 90-minute guided tour. The tour takes in the cellars (so extensive that they are explored on a fun train ride, which chugs past thousands of bottles of cava back up to ground level), where you will learn all about the production process. The visit ends in a tasting of two glasses of Cava (adults €15, children aged nine to 17 €10; available every day and in English; book online in advance).

CODORNÍU

Avenida Jaume de Codorníu; tel. 93/891-3342; www. visitascodorniu.com/visit/codorniu-visit; Mon-Fri 9am-5pm, Sat-Sun 9am-2:30pm

One of the oldest family companies in Spain has been making wine for over 450 years and was the first winery to produce Cava, in 1872. Its impressive winery building was designed in 1895 by acclaimed Modernista architect Josep Puig i Cadafalch. The style is unmistakably Modernista, with its exposed brickwork and curved windows. The winery is not within walking distance of the station, so if you arrive by train, take a taxi. (The 5-minute journey should be around €5.)

Wine and Cava Tours

You can explore the region on your own by either train or car, but there are several companies that offer vineyard tours from Barcelona, including:

- **Barcelona Discovery** (www.barcelona-discovery.com): This company, which promotes eco-friendly travel, offers several wine tour options in English around Barcelona, including a tour of the Gramona biodynamic winery (www.gramona.com) close to Sant Sadurní d'Anoia (€120 per person), and a picnic among the vineyards in the village of Alella, which includes a visit to a winery and a tasting of organic wines and typical Catalan food (€95 per person).

- **Catalunya Bus Turistic** (www.catalunyabusturistic.com): The region-wide version of the popular city tour bus offers a day trip to Penedès to visit three different wineries: Freixenet, Torres, and Jean Leon (€74 per person). Tours, conducted in English, leave from Barcelona's Plaça de Catalunya at 8am (Mondays, Wednesdays, Fridays, and Sundays) and last until 4:15pm. The trip includes a tasting at Jean Leon, a guided visit and tasting of four wines and four cheeses at Torres, and a guided visit and tasting with appetizers at Freixenet. Tickets can be booked online.

Guided tours take visitors around the winery, where they will learn the history of the buildings and the Cava-making method and enjoy a tasting of two Cavas. The caves are especially atmospheric, with their low ceilings and stone walls lined with thousands of bottles of cava. Bookings must be made in advance via the website. There is a wine bar where visitors can sample some cava if not taking part in a tour. (English tours: Nov-Feb, Mon-Fri at 11:45am, Tues and Thurs 1:30pm; Mar-Oct, Mon-Fri 11:45am and 3:30pm, Sat 2:30pm.)

There are several other tours available, some pairing cava with food and others exploring the vineyards by bike. Check the Codorníu website for details.

SOLÀ RAVENTÓS

Carrer de la Indústria, 38-40; tel. 93/891-0837; www. solaraventos.com; Mon-Fri 9am-1pm, 3pm-7pm, Sat-Sun 10am-2pm

This small family-run winery, a 10-minute walk from the train station, offers tours, in English, led by its friendly owner and his son, during which visitors can learn all about the production process of a smaller winery, as well as enjoy a tasting. A more personal tour experience than at the bigger Cava brands, visitors are shown the atmospheric stone cellars, where the winemaker explains the cava-making process. He is happy to answer any questions, and the visit feels more like being shown around by a friend than the slicker operations at the bigger producers.

Tastings are available Mon-Fri 9am-1pm and 3pm-7pm, Sat-Sun 10am-2pm. Book the visit (€5) in advance, via the winery's website.

Food
CAL BLAY VINTICINC

Carrer de Josep Rovira, 27; tel. 93/891-0032; Mon 1pm-4pm, Wed-Sun 1pm-4pm, Fri-Sat 9pm-11pm; from €16

Set inside a former Modernista winery, Cal Blay showcases local ingredients in classic Catalan dishes like roast Penedès duck and monkfish in Cava sauce. Its fixed-price lunch options and cava theme (there are photos of vineyards and historic scenes on the walls, and over a hundred different cavas on the wine list) make it a great lunch option between vineyard visits. It offers a set, five-course lunch menu for €35 (including bread, water, coffee, and half a bottle of Cava or wine), and a daily lunchtime menu (three courses) for €16.

CAL TICUS

Carrer Raval, 19; tel. 93/818-4160; www.
ticusrestaurant.cat; Tues-Sun 1pm-4pm, Fri-Sat
9pm-11pm; €15

This popular family-run restaurant does Catalan and local classics, using seasonal ingredients and a modern twist. The menu features dishes like mussels with cava, coriander, and ginger, and lamb with seasonal vegetables and a Merlot sauce. With a four-course lunch menu for just €15 (including drink), it's also a reasonable option in the center of town.

Accommodations
HOSTAL SANT SADURNÍ

Calle de San Antoni, 99; tel. 93/891-4335; www.hss.
com.es; €80

This small, ten-room hotel is located right in the center of Sant Sadurní d'Anoia, within easy walking distance to many restaurants, shops, and wineries. Rooms are simple but spotless, with TVs, air conditioning, and ensuite bathrooms. No breakfast is offered, and the reception isn't manned 24 hours a day, so let the hotel know what time you're planning to arrive.

Getting There
TRAIN

Take the suburban Rodalies train (R4 towards Sant Vicenç de Calders) from Barcelona Sants or Plaça de Catalunya to Sant Sadurní d'Anoia. The journey takes around 45 minutes. The first train is at 5:28am and the last train back is at 10:32pm. Trains leave every half hour and cost €4.20 one-way.

Freixetren tickets are available at ticket machines in all Rodalies stations, including Barcelona Sants and Plaça de Catalunya stations; return journey (on the Rodalies train, same as above) and entry into the Freixenet winery costs €11. Be aware that you will still need to book your tour time via the Freixenet website.

CAR

From Barcelona, take the AP-7 west to Sant Sadurní d'Anoia. The journey is 50 kilometers (31 miles) and takes around 50 minutes. There is free parking outside the Freixenet winery and a free car park on Carrer de la Indústria.

Getting Around

Once in town, the best way to get around is walking. If you're planning on visiting wineries located further out, a taxi is the best bet. For a local taxi, call 93/891-0428.

VILAFRANCA DEL PENEDÈS

Vilafranca del Penedès (pop. 40,000), the capital of the Penedès region, makes more red and white than sparkling wines, and is home to an interesting wine museum, as well as one of Spain's most famous wineries. The town itself, founded in the mid-12th century, is picturesque, with an historic medieval town center (home to the gothic church of Santa Maria) and a royal palace dating back to the 13th century, which is now home to the town's wine museum.

Sights
VINSEUM

Plaça de Jaume I, 1; tel. 93/890-0582; www.vinseum.
cat; May 2-Sept 30, Tues-Sat 10am-7pm, Sun
10am-2pm; rest of the year, Tues-Sat 10am-2pm,
4pm-7pm, Sun 10am-2pm; €7

This museum, housed in the 13th-century Palau Reial, charts the history and culture of winemaking in Penedès, from what happens during the harvest and how the wine is made to the very beginnings of winemaking in the region. Collections include the result of local archaeological excavations, from the Paleolithic to the Middle Ages, as well as a fascinating Wine Collection of objects from centuries past that were used in the winemaking process (information is available in English).

The museum's wide-ranging collection features over 17,000 items, and a wine tasting at the end is included in the ticket price.

Vineyard and Winery

TORRES

Finca el Maset, 08796 Pacs del Penedès;
93/817-7330; www.torres.es; English tours: Mon-Fri
11am,1pm, 3:30pm, Sat 11:30am, 1pm, 3:30pm, Sun
11:30am

The Torres family has been making wines since 1870, steadily growing into one of Spain's most emblematic wine brands and the country's largest winery. Its Mas La Plana vineyard makes the award-winning cabernet of the same name. Tours take visitors through the beautiful vineyards (in autumn, the golden, burnt orange colors look like a postcard), rows upon rows of vines that stretch as far as the eye can see. Afterwards, visitors are taken deep down into the cellars where the wine is aged. Hearing and appreciating the history of the brand, as well as the production process, makes the tasting at the end of the tour all the better.

The Torres winery is located 3 kilometers (2 miles) outside of Vilafranca, so visitors arriving by train will need to take a taxi from the center of town. (The 10-minute journey is around €7.)

A one hour, 45-minute tour (€12) includes a visit to the vineyards, cellars, and a tasting of two wines. (Tour times in English: Nov 6-Mar 23, Mon-Fri 11am, 1pm, and 3:30pm, Sat 11.30am, 1pm, and 3:30pm, Sun 11:30am; March 24-Nov 4, Mon-Fri 11am, 1pm, and 3:30pm, Sat 3:30pm.)

Food

EL PURGATORI

Plaça del Campanar, 6; tel. 93/892-1263; Mon-Thurs
7pm-12:30am, Fri-Sat 7pm-1:30am; €12

This great local haunt has a terrace right next to the town's Basílica de Santa Maria and is a real favorite with Spaniards, which gives it a pleasantly un-touristy feel. It specializes in cheeses, including local varieties, and also has a good range of tapas, like fried octopus and truffled eggs. The extensive wine list features dozens of local options and plenty of cava. Grab an outdoor table and enjoy a relaxed evening in the old town.

Accommodations

MASTINELL CAVA AND HOTEL

Ctra. Vilafranca a Sant Martí, km 0.5, Vilafranca
del Penedès; tel. 93/115-6132; www.hotelmastinell.
com; €200

This five-star hotel is the perfect dose of luxury among the vineyards surrounding Vilafranca del Penedès and is ideal for those wanting the ultimate wine tourism break. With its own cellar and winery, and treatments including wine and cava baths (grapes have health benefits!), it's a luxurious hotel for an incredible, pampered stay. Its design, a series of interlinking circles that resemble cava bottles in a rack, has an industrial edge, yet it is low enough to blend into the surrounding hills. Its 13 rooms are cozy and come with a welcome bottle of cava and fantastic views over the vineyards, as well as additions like rainforest showers, Nespresso machines, and slippers and robes. A swimming pool and restaurant mean you might never want to leave the hotel, but you should—it's just a 15-minute walk into Vilafranca.

Getting There

Train

FROM BARCELONA

Take the suburban Rodalies train (R4 towards Sant Vicenç de Calders) from Barcelona Sants or Plaça de Catalunya to Vilafranca del Penedès. The journey takes around 55 minutes. The first train is at 5:28am and the last train back is at 10:24pm. Trains leave every half hour and cost €4.20 each way.

FROM SANT SADURNÍ D'ANOIA

Take the R4 towards Sant Vicenç de Calders from Sant Sadurní d'Anoia station one stop to Vilafranca del Penedès. First train is at 6:12am and the last train from Vilafranca is at 10:24pm. Journey time is around 10 minutes and trains leave around every 30 minutes.

FROM SITGES

Take the Radalies train R2S south towards Sant Vicenç de Calders, then change onto the R4 north towards Manresa and get off at

Vilafranca del Penedès (journey time around one hour). First train from Sitges is at 6:38am and trains leave every hour. Last train home from Vilafranca is at 8:40pm.

Car

From Barcelona, take the AP-7 from Barcelona to Vilafranca del Penedès; the journey time is one hour. From Sant Sadurní d'Anoia, it's a 20-minute drive along the AP-7 to Vilafranca del Penedès. The drive from Sitges to Vilafranca is around 25 minutes along the C-32 and C-15 heading northwest. There is a central car park on Plaza Penedès (€2.60/hour), and bigger wineries will offer free parking.

Madrid

From its beginnings as a Moorish walled town,

through its expansion during Spain's Golden Age, the siege that gripped the city during the Spanish Civil War and the nearly 40 years of dictatorship that followed, Madrid has had a tumultuous and fascinating history. Today, it is the nucleus of Spanish business and politics, yet Madrid retains a small-town feel thanks to its friendly, laid-back locals, who raise the act of enjoying life's simple pleasures to an art form. It manages to mix the old and new with ease: this is a city where you can have breakfast in a 160-year-old bakery, have tapas in an old covered market, then dine in an edgy three-Michelin-starred restaurant by night.

Art runs through the veins of the city. The famed "Golden

Highlights

Look for ★ to find recommended sights, activities, dining, and lodging.

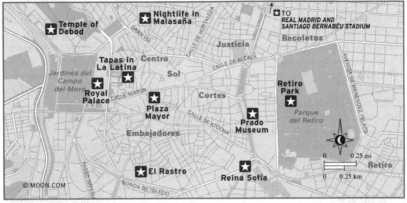

★ **Plaza Mayor:** Madrid's main square has seen it all during its 400-year history, from bull-fights and bloody deaths (during the Spanish Inquisition) to markets, football matches, and open-air concerts. Today, it's a great place for people watching (page 208).

★ **Royal Palace:** The largest royal palace in Europe has a checkered history and is a fascinating insight into the city's evolution (page 209).

★ **Temple of Debod:** Every evening, crowds gather at this Egyptian temple to watch the beautiful sunset (page 211).

★ **El Rastro:** Madrid's biggest street market (Sundays and public holidays only) is an excellent place to explore. Get there early to watch the stall holders setting up (page 218).

★ **The Prado Museum:** One of the world's most famous art galleries, the Prado houses a treasure trove of works by Spanish and European masters. Don't miss Spain's royal court painter Diego Velázquez—his "Las Meninas" shook up European art and is one of the museum's most famous paintings (page 223).

★ **Reina Sofía:** Spain's national museum of 20th-century art brings together some of the most famous contemporary artists from around the world. If you are to see just one piece of art while in Madrid, make it "Guernica," Pablo Picasso's haunting depiction of the bombing of a Basque town during the Spanish Civil War (page 228).

★ **Retiro Park:** Madrid's most famous green space is a beloved weekend favorite where locals go to picnic, play sports, or simply stroll (page 233).

★ **Tapas in La Latina:** La Latina is home to some of the best tapas in the city, centered on Calle de Cava Baja. Hope you've got an appetite (page 247)!

★ **Nightlife in Malasaña:** Ernest Hemingway famously said no one goes to bed in Madrid until they have killed the night, and nowhere is this more so than in the indie-cool neighborhood of Malasaña, whose tapas bars, lively restaurants, and late-night drinking dens throb with people of all ages (page 256).

★ **Real Madrid and Santiago Bernabéu stadium:** This temple to football and home of Real Madrid is a must-visit for any soccer fan. Take a tour or see a match; the sound of the crowd cheering for one of the world's greatest teams is a sound you'll never forget (page 284).

Triangle" of art galleries showcases the very best of Spanish and international art, and Madrid is also home to dozens of more off-the-beaten-track galleries, museums, and cultural spaces.

And not for nothing are Madrid locals known as *Gatos* (Cats), for the city truly comes alive after sunset. One of the joys of visiting is slotting yourself into the city's schedule—dining late, enjoying a cocktail after midnight, and taking in some flamenco, live music, or hitting a club in the early hours of the morning.

Madrid is proud of its diversity. It's an open, unstuffy, and unpretentious city. It is said that everyone in Madrid comes from somewhere else, and locals are friendly, warm, and always up for a chat. The city and its residents are welcoming, whoever you are.

HISTORY

Madrid was little more than a sleepy backwater until Habsburg King Philip II decided to make it the capital of Spain in 1561.

The first written account of the city refers to it as Mayrit, a hilltop fortress built on the site of today's Royal Palace by the Moors in 854, on the borders of Al Andalus and the kingdoms of Castile and León. In 1085, Christian King Alfonso VI of León attacked the settlement (with the aim of returning Christianity to the area). When a nimble soldier scampered up the city walls, the king proclaimed he was just like a *gato* (cat). Gato became a nickname for Madrileños, and to this day it is used to refer to the city's inhabitants, especially those with four Madrileño grandparents.

After the Royal Court moved to Madrid, the city experienced a Golden Age of arts and literature, with leading figures including Miguel de Cervantes (author of *Don Quixote*), playwright Lope de Vega, and court painter Diego Velázquez.

In 1700, Charles II, who had severe disabilities caused by years of inbreeding, died and left no heir. The stage was set for a new royal Spanish dynasty: the Bourbons, who rule to this day. In 1701, the French Philip V took to the throne, Spain's first Bourbon king. He brought with him a strong French influence, from music, clothing, and gastronomy to the ideals of the enlightenment.

Charles III, who became king in 1759 on his arrival from Naples, was nicknamed "the best king-mayor of Madrid" for the many projects he undertook to improve the city, from building schools and hospitals to introducing the Spanish lottery and Christmas cribs from Naples.

On May 2, 1808, Madrileños rose up against French occupiers and the new king, Joseph Bonaparte (brother of Napoleon), but were soon repressed. The uprising is depicted in two of Goya's most famous paintings, both in the Prado Museum, "The Second of May 1808" and "The Third of May 1808." The 19th century was a turbulent time politically, but during this period there was also a great effort to modernize the city. Madrid's first train line opened in 1851 and street paving and sewage were improved.

After the outbreak of the Spanish Civil War in 1936, General Francisco Franco aimed to quickly take Madrid, but its inhabitants had other ideas. When the Republican government fled to Valencia, local defenders and International Brigades volunteers held off Franco's Nationalist troops, who reached as far as the Casa de Campo during the Siege of Madrid. But on March 28, 1939, a depleted Madrid, its inhabitants on the verge of famine, surrendered, ushering in the rule of Franco, which lasted from 1939 until his death in 1975.

Spain's return to democracy in 1978 saw a period of hedonism and celebration that became known as the Movida Madrileña, a hotbed of music, partying, and creativity whose

Hemingway's Madrid

From his first visit in 1923, Ernest Hemingway loved Madrid, which he called "the most Spanish of all cities." He was fascinated by bullfighting, and covered the Spanish Civil War as a foreign correspondent for the North American Newspaper Alliance (his experiences inspired the novel *For Whom the Bell Tolls*).

Over his decades exploring Madrid, Hemingway carved out favorite niches to which he would return time and again:

- **The Westin Palace:** Hemingway often stayed at what was then the Palace Hotel. He would enjoy a martini at the bar and the hotel's proximity to the leafy Retiro Park, where he would often stroll.

- **El Corte Inglés Callao:** The Corte Inglés department store now stands on the spot formerly occupied by Hotel Florida, where Hemingway watched the Siege of Madrid in the nearby Casa de Campo from the ninth floor (now the department store's gourmet food hall). You can get the same view from the Gourmet Experience's ninth-floor terrace.

- **Cervecería Alemana:** This 1904 beer hall was a favorite of Hemingway's. Today, a photo of the writer hangs above his window seat.

- **The Matadero:** A young Hemingway was a regular fixture at the city's former slaughter-house, where he would watch *novilleros*—trainee/apprentice bullfighters—practice killing. Though today the complex is more culture than killing, the original buildings have been preserved to hold exhibitions, markets, and a cinema.

- **La Venencia:** This wood-clad sherry bar, where the fortified Spanish wine is served from huge barrels and the bar staff write your order in chalk on the bar, hasn't changed much since the days of the Civil War, when Republicans would meet to hear the latest news. Some rules have remained too: no tipping (a Socialist principle) and no photos (you could be a Fascist spy, after all).

- **Las Ventas Bullring:** Hemingway was a bullfighting aficionado and wrote a book about the Spanish tradition, *Death in the Afternoon* (1932). Hemingway visited Madrid's Las Ventas bullring many times and it is still in use today.

- **Sobrino de Botín:** The oldest restaurant in the world was a favorite hangout of Hemingway's. He would write there in the mornings before meeting friends for a hearty lunch of roast suckling pig. He loved it so much it is mentioned in *Death in the Afternoon* and *The Sun Also Rises*.

- The **Hemingway Walking Tour**, run by the Wellington Society, is a great option if you want to explore the writer's relationship with the city in more depth.

MADRID

famous poster boy is film director Pedro Almodóvar. Post Movida has seen urban renewal and regeneration, coupled with a crippling economic crisis that affected the entire country. In recent years, Madrid has been on the upswing, with ambitious building projects, international celebrations (World Pride), and a steady increase in tourist numbers.

Planning and Orientation

PLANNING YOUR TIME

Two or three nights provides an ideal introduction to the city, allowing visitors to get a taste of its history, culture, and culinary scene. Of course, the longer the stay, the better you will get to know the city. If you have a week, you can see the major sights and slow down, enjoying life's little pleasures the way Madrileños do.

Neighborhoods known for their nightlife (especially Malasaña) rise slowly. If you arrive at 9am, expect closed shops and eerily empty streets; most people will still be sleeping off the night before. Sol and Centro is always busy, whereas some other neighborhoods might experience an early-afternoon lull as shops close for lunch. Madrid is a late-night city; it's a perfectly normal sight to see small children running out and about with their families at midnight, especially in warmer months.

Daily Reminders

The Prado is open daily. It's free to visit during the last two hours it's open.

MONDAY

- Thyssen-Bornemisza offers free admission midday-4pm.
- Admission to the Fundación Mapfre (Mapfre Foundation) is free.
- Many other sights are closed, including Real Monasterio de las Descalzas Reales, Conde Duque Centro Cultural, ABC Museum, Museo de Historia (Museum of the History of Madrid), Museo del Romanticismo (Romanticism Museum), Lope de Vega House Museum, National Museum of Decorative Arts, National Archeological Museum, Museo Sorolla (Sorolla Museum), Chapel of San Antonio de la Florida, Museo de Traje (Garment Museum), and Museo Cerralbo (Cerralbo Museum).

TUESDAY

- Reina Sofía is closed.
- Thyssen-Bornemisza hours are reduced.

SATURDAY

- Museo del Romanticismo is free after 2pm.
- Most league football matches take place on weekends (Sat-Sun).

SUNDAY

- Museo del Romanticismo is free.

Advance Bookings and Reservations

Tickets for most of Madrid's major museums can be bought online ahead of time for a small extra booking fee, by choosing the date of your visit and your desired ticket. One advantage is not having to stand in the ticket line.

It is advisable to book football matches in advance. Most league matches will go on sale about two weeks before the match date. (Only high-price VIP tickets are generally available further in advance.) You can book football tickets on the teams' official websites.

Sightseeing Passes
PASEO DEL ARTE CARD

This card (€29.60) can be used to visit the collections of Madrid's three major art galleries: the Prado Museum, the Reina Sofía, and the Thyssen-Bornemisza Museum; it gets you a 20-percent discount on the entry price of the three museums. It can be purchased at any of the museums' ticket offices or on the museums' websites, and is valid for one year from the date of purchase or the date selected online. The ticket must be redeemed at the ticket office of the museum where you made your online purchase.

What's New?

PRADO BICENTENARY

The Prado will celebrate its bicentenary in 2019 with a program of events and exhibitions. The official celebrations will kick off on November 19, 2018, and include the exhibition "Prado 200," which will explore the construction and evolution of the museum in the 19th and 20th centuries. The exhibition "Circa 1819" will focus on artworks created in the years around the founding of the museum in 1819, and will show in the Jerónimos building.

BARS, RESTAURANTS, AND SHOPS

- **Café Comercial:** Locals were so saddened when one of Madrid's oldest cafés (established in 1887) suddenly closed its doors in 2015 that many left love letters on its boarded-up doors. Happily, new owners re-opened the café in 2017 and retained many of its original features.

- **Sala Equís:** This former XXX cinema has been transformed into one of the city's coolest bars and cultural spaces.

- **Santa Ana Street Market:** This street, strung with colorful bunting, features a host of spaces housing vintage clothing and furniture stores, as well as bakeries and bars. It's a hip addition to El Rastro market.

RIVER REJUVINATION

Madrid's trickle of a river, the Manzanares, used to be an area with nothing much going for it, but since 2011, when it was transformed into **Madrid Río**—a riverside walkway with parks, cafés, play areas, and skateparks—it has become one of local Madrileños' favorite destinations.

SUSTAINABILITY MEASURES

Madrid's city council has called for a three-pronged approach to sustainable tourism: environmental, social, and economic. Efforts include encouraging visitors not to waste water (Madrid sits high on the Spanish plain and gets very little rainfall), pushing for more electric buses, and welcoming electric car rental companies like Car2Go and emov (which can be rented just by tapping on an app).

THE CITY SPREADS OUT

These days, Madrid's outer barrios are attracting more and more visitors. The **Matadero** cultural center is a must-visit attraction in the Arganzuela neighborhood, while the fascinating **Museo Sorolla** and **Anden 0** ghost metro station make Chamberí well worth a visit. Parks like **Quinta de Molinos** and **Parque el Capricho**, to the north of Madrid, are some of the city's natural treasures.

EIGHT MUSEUMS PASS OR FOUR MUSEUMS PASS

This pass allows you to visit either four (€8) or eight (€16) of Madrid's under-the-radar museums as many times as you like over a 15-day period. The covered museums included are the Museum of Romanticism, National Museum of Anthropology, National Museum of Decorative Arts, Garment Museum, Ethnological Heritage Research Center (CIPE), Cerralbo Museum, Museum of the Americas, National Archaeological Museum, and the Sorolla Museum. The pass can be bought from any of the participating museums.

ORIENTATION

Madrid's main neighborhoods, or *barrios*, are located either north or south of the city's most famous road, the **Gran Vía**. Sol and Center, La Latina, Lavapiés, Barrio de Las Letras, and Paseo del Prado and Atocha are to the south,

Greater Madrid

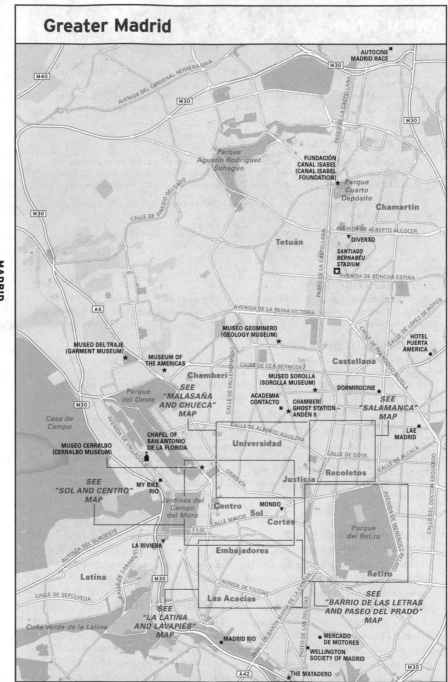

AUTOCINE
MADRID RACE

M30

M40

AVENIDA DEL CARDENAL HERRERA ORIA

M30

PASEO DE LA CASTELLANA

M30

Parque
Agustín Rodríguez
Sahagún

FUNDACIÓN
CANAL ISABEL
(CANAL ISABEL
FOUNDATION)

Parque
Cuarto
Depósito

Chamartín

CALLE DE SINESIO DELGADO

M30

AVENIDA DE ALBERTO ALCOCER

Tetuán

DIVERXO

SANTIAGO
BERNABÉU
STADIUM

AVENIDA DE CONCHA ESPINA

A6

AVENIDA DE LA REINA VICTORIA

PASEO DE LA CASTELLANA

CALLE DE LÓPEZ DE HOYOS

MUSEO GEOMINERO
(GEOLOGY MUSEUM)

MUSEO DEL TRAJE
(GARMENT MUSEUM)

CALLE DE FRANCISCO SILVELA

HOTEL
PUERTA
AMERICA

MUSEUM OF
THE AMERICAS

Chamberí

CALLE DE CEA BERMÚDEZ

Castellana

CALLE DE VALLEHERMOSO

MUSEO SOROLLA
(SOROLLA MUSEUM)

Parque
del Oeste

SEE
"MALASAÑA
AND CHUECA"
MAP

ACADEMIA
CONTACTO

CHAMBERÍ
GHOST STATION –
ANDÉN 0

DORMIRDCINE

SEE
"SALAMANCA"
MAP

Casa de
Campo

M30

AVENIDA DE VALLADOLID

CHAPEL OF
SAN ANTONIO
DE LA FLORIDA

Universidad

CALLE DE ALBERTO AGUILERA

LAE
MADRID

MUSEO CERRALBO
(CERRALBO MUSEUM)

CALLE DE GOYA

CALLE DE ALCALÁ

SEE
"SOL AND CENTRO"
MAP

MY BIKE
RÍO

GRAN VÍA

Justicia

Recoletos

AVENIDA DEL DOCTOR ESQUERDO

Jardines del
Campo
del Moro

Centro

MONDO

AVENIDA DE MENENDEZ PELAYO

CALLE MAYOR

Sol

Cortes

AUTOVÍA DEL SUROESTE

LA RIVIERA

Embajadores

Parque
del Retiro

CALLE DE CARAMUEL

Latina

M30

Retiro

CALLE DE SEPÚLVEDA

RONDA DE TOLEDO

SEE
"BARRIO DE LAS LETRAS
AND PASEO DEL PRADO"
MAP

Cuña Verde de la Latina

SEE
"LA LATINA
AND LAVAPIÉS"
MAP

Las Acacias

RONDA DE SANTA MARÍA DE LA CABEZA

MADRID RÍO

MERCADO
DE MOTORES

PASEO DE LAS DELICIAS

WELLINGTON
SOCIETY OF MADRID

M30

A42

THE MATADERO

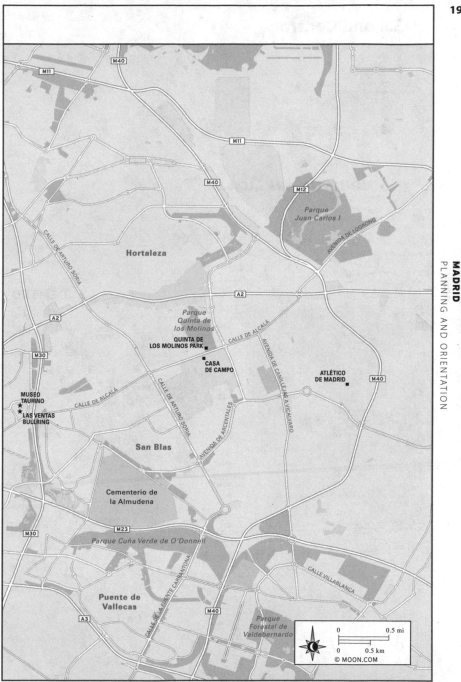

M40

M11

M11

M40

M12

Parque
Juan Carlos I

AVENIDA DE LOGRONO

CALLE DE ARTURO SORIA

Hortaleza

A2

A2

Parque
Quinta de
los Molinos

QUINTA DE
LOS MOLINOS PARK

CALLE DE ALCALÁ

AVENIDA DE CANILLEJAS A VICÁLVARO

M30

CASA
DE CAMPO

ATLÉTICO
DE MADRID

M40

MUSEO
TAURINO

CALLE DE ALCALÁ

CALLE DE ARTURO SORIA

AVENIDA DE ARCENTALES

LAS VENTAS
BULLRING

San Blas

Cementerio de
la Almudena

M30

M23

Parque Cuña Verde de O'Donnell

CALLE VILLABLANCA

CALLE DE LA PUENTE CARMAIZONA

Puente de
Vallecas

A3

M40

Parque
Forestal de
Valdebernardo

0   0.5 mi

0   0.5 km

© MOON.COM

Sol and Centro

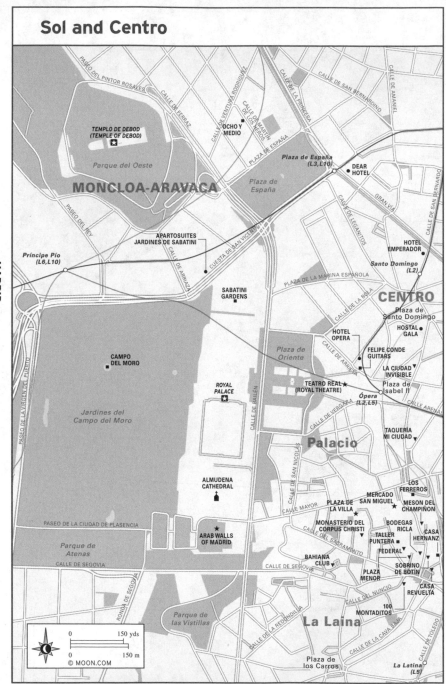

PASEO DEL PINTOR ROSALES

CALLE DE FERRAZ

CALLE DE VENTURA RODRÍGUEZ

CALLE DE SAN MARTÍN DE LOS HEROS

CALLE DE LA PRINCESA

CALLE DE SAN BERNARDINO

CALLE DE AMANIEL

**TEMPLO DE DEBOD
(TEMPLE OF DEBOD)**

OCHO Y
MEDIO

Parque del Oeste

PLAZA DE ESPAÑA

**Plaza de España
(L3, L10)**

**DEAR
HOTEL**

MONCLOA-ARAVACA

*Plaza de
España*

GRAN VÍA

CALLE DE SAN BERNARDO

PASEO DEL REY

**APARTOSUITES
JARDINES DE SABATINI**

CUESTA DE SAN VICENTE

CALLE DE LEGANITOS

**HOTEL
EMPERADOR**

**Príncipe Pío
(L6, L10)**

CALLE DE ARRIAZA

**Santo Domingo
(L2)**

PLAZA DE LA MARINA ESPAÑOLA

CENTRO

**SABATINI
GARDENS**

CALLE DE LA BOLA

Plaza de
Santo Domingo

**HOSTAL
GALA**

PASEO DE LA VIRGEN DEL PUERTO

**CAMPO
DEL MORO**

*Plaza de
Oriente*

**HOTEL
OPERA**

CALLE DE ARRIETA

**FELIPE CONDE
GUITARS**

**LA CIUDAD
INVISIBLE**

*Jardines del
Campo del Moro*

**ROYAL
PALACE**

CALLE DE BAILÉN

**TEATRO REAL
(ROYAL THEATRE)**

*Ópera
(L2, L5)*

**Plaza de
Isabel II**

CALLE ARENAL

CALLE DE VERGARA

**TAQUERÍA
MI CIUDAD**

CALLE DE SAN NICOLÁS

Palacio

**ALMUDENA
CATHEDRAL**

**LOS
FERREROS**

**MERCADO
SAN MIGUEL**

**MESON DEL
CHAMPIÑON**

CALLE MAYOR

**PLAZA DE
LA VILLA**

PASEO DE LA CIUDAD DE PLASENCIA

**ARAB WALLS
OF MADRID**

**MONASTERIO DEL
CORPUS CHRISTI**

**BODEGAS
RICLA**

**CASA
HERNANZ**

CALLE DEL SACRAMENTO

**TALLER
PUNTERA**

FEDERAL

*Parque de
Atenas*

CALLE DE SEGOVIA

**BAHIANA
CLUB**

**SOBRINO
DE BOTÍN**

**PLAZA
MENOR**

CALLE DE SEGOVIA

CALLE DEL NUNCIO

**CASA
REVUELTA**

RONDA DE SEGOVIA

**100
MONTADITOS**

CALLE DE LA REDONDILLA

La Laína

CALLE DE LA CAVA BAJA

CALLE DE TOLEDO

*Parque de
las Vistillas*

0   150 yds

0   150 m

© MOON.COM

Plaza de
los Carros

*La Latina
(L5)*

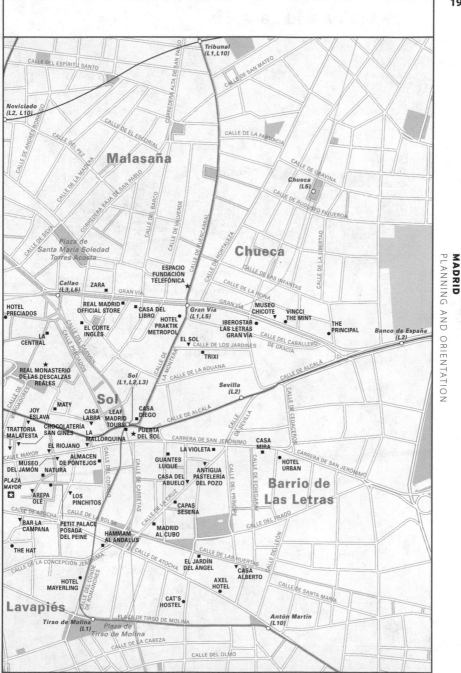

Tribunal
(L1, L10)

CALLE DEL ESPÍRITU SANTO

CALLE DE SAN MATEO

Noviciado
(L2, L10)

CALLE DE ANDRÉS BORREGO

CORREDERA ALTA DE SAN PABLO

CALLE DE EL ESPORIAL

CALLE DEL PEZ

CALLE DE LA FARMACIA

CALLE DE SILVA

CALLE DE LA MADERA

Malasaña

CALLE DE GRAVINA

Chueca
(L5)

CALLE DE AUGUSTO FIGUEROA

CORREDERA BAJA DE SAN PABLO

CALLE DEL BARCO

CALLE DE VALVERDE

CALLE DE FUENCARRAL

CALLE DE HORTALEZA

Plaza de
Santa María Soledad
Torres Acosta

Chueca

CALLE DE LA LIBERTAD

ESPACIO
FUNDACIÓN
TELEFÓNICA

CALLE DE LAS INFANTAS

Callao
(L3, L5)

ZARA

GRAN VÍA

CALLE DE LA REINA

GRAN VÍA

MUSEO
CHICOTE

HOTEL
PRECIADOS

REAL MADRID
OFFICIAL STORE

CASA DEL
LIBRO

Gran Vía
(L1, L5)

VINCCI
THE MINT

EL CORTE
INGLÉS

HOTEL
PRAKTIK
METROPOL

IBEROSTAR
LAS LETRAS
GRAN VÍA

THE
PRINCIPAL

Banco de España
(L2)

LA
CENTRAL

CALLE DE PRECIADOS

EL SOL

CALLE DE LOS JARDINES

CALLE DEL CABALLERO
DE GRACIA

CALLE DEL CARMEN

CALLE DE LA MONTERA

TRIXI

REAL MONASTERIO
DE LAS DESCALZAS
REALES

Sol
(L1, L2, L3)

CALLE DE LA ADUANA

CALLE DE ALCALÁ

Sevilla
(L2)

CALLE DE BORDADORES

Sol

MATY

JOY
ESLAVA

CASA
LABRA

LEAF
MADRID
TOURS

CASA
DIEGO

CALLE DE ALCALÁ

CALLE DE SEVILLA

CALLE DE CEDACEROS

TRATTORIA
MALATESTA

CHOCOLATERÍA
SAN GINÉS

LA
MALLORQUINA

PUERTA
DEL SOL

CARRERA DE SAN JERÓNIMO

CASA
MIRA

EL RIOJANO

LA VIOLETA

CARRERA DE SAN JERÓNIMO

CALLE MAYOR

ALMACEN
DE PONTEJOS

GUANTES
LUQUE

HOTEL
URBAN

MUSEO
DEL JAMÓN

NATURA

CALLE DEL CORREO

CALLE DE CARRETAS

CASA DEL
ABUELO

ANTIGUA
PASTELERÍA
DEL POZO

CALLE DEL PRÍNCIPE

CALLE DE ECHEGARAY

PLAZA
MAYOR

**Barrio de
Las Letras**

AREPA
OLE

LOS
PINCHITOS

CALLE DE LA CRUZ

CAPAS
SESEÑA

CALLE DE ATOCHA

CALLE DE LA BOLSA

CALLE DEL PRADO

BAR LA
CAMPANA

PETIT PALACE
POSADA
DEL PEINE

HAMMAM
AL ANDALUS

MADRID
AL CUBO

CALLE DEL LEÓN

THE HAT

CALLE DE LAS HUERTAS

CALLE DE LA CONCEPCIÓN JERÓNIMA

CALLE DE ATOCHA

EL JARDÍN
DEL ÁNGEL

CASA
ALBERTO

HOTEL
MAYERLING

CALLE DEL CONDE
DE ROMANONES

AXEL
HOTEL

CALLE DE SANTA MARÍA

Lavapiés

CAT'S
HOSTEL

Antón Martín
(L10)

Tirso de Molina
(L1)

Plaza de
Tirso de Molina

PLAZA DE TIRSO DE MOLINA

CALLE DE LA CABEZA

CALLE DEL OLMO

La Latina and Lavapiés

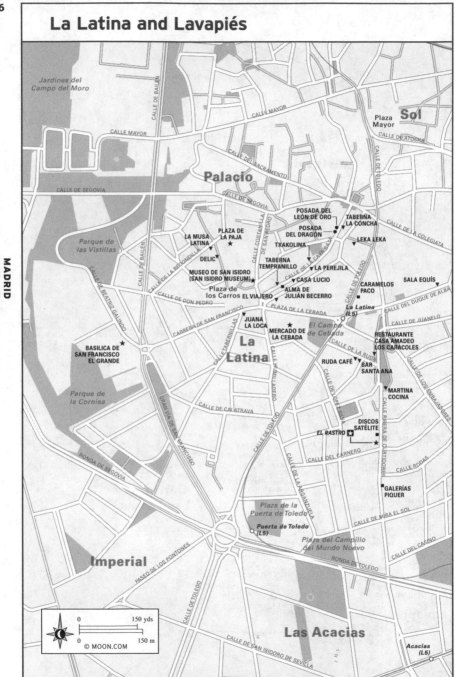

Jardines del
Campo del Moro

CALLE DE BAILÉN

CALLE MAYOR

CALLE MAYOR

Plaza
Mayor

Sol

CALLE DE ATOCHA

CALLE DEL SACRAMENTO

CALLE DE SEGOVIA

Palacio

CALLE DE TOLEDO

CALLE DE SEGOVIA

POSADA DEL
LEÓN DE ORO

TABERNA
LA CONCHA

CALLE DE LA COLEGIATA

Parque de
las Vistillas

LA MUSA
LATINA

PLAZA DE
LA PAJA

POSADA
DEL DRAGÓN

LEKA LEKA

CALLE COSTANILLA DE SAN PEDRO

CALLE DE BAILÉN

DELIC

TXAKOLINA

CALLE DE LA REDONDILLA

TABERNA
TEMPRANILLO

CALLE DE LA CAVA BAJA

MUSEO DE SAN ISIDRO
(SAN ISIDRO MUSEUM)

LA PEREJILA

CALLE DE BEATRIZ GALINDO

Plaza de
los Carros

CALLE DE DON PEDRO

EL VIAJERO

CASA LUCIO

ALMA DE
JULIÁN BECERRO

CARAMELOS
PACO

SALA EQUÍS

CALLE DE TOLEDO

CALLE DEL DUQUE DE ALBA

PLAZA DE LA CEBADA

La Latina
(L5)

CALLE DEL DUQUE DE ALBA

CARRERA DE SAN FRANCISCO

JUANA
LA LOCA

CALLE DE JUANELO

BASÍLICA DE
SAN FRANCISCO
EL GRANDE

MERCADO DE
LA CEBADA

El Campo
de Cebada

RESTAURANTE
CASA AMADEO
LOS CARACOLES

La
Latina

CALLE DE LA RUDA

CALLE TABERNILLAS

CALLE HUMILLADERO

RUDA CAFÉ

BAR
SANTA ANA

Parque de
la Cornisa

CALLE DE LOS EMBAJADORES

CALLE DE VALEMBRILLA

MARTINA
COCINA

CALLE DE CALATRAVA

GRAN VÍA DE SAN FRANCISCO

CALLE DE TOLEDO

DISCOS
SATÉLITE

RONDA DE SEGOVIA

EL RASTRO

CALLE RIBERA DE CURTIDORES

CALLE DEL CARNERO

CALLE RODAS

CALLE DE LA ARGANZUELA

GALERÍAS
PIQUER

Plaza de la
Puerta de Toledo

CALLE DE MIRA EL SOL

Imperial

PASEO DE LOS PONTONES

Puerta de Toledo
(L5)

Plaza del Campillo
del Mundo Nuevo

CALLE DEL CASINO

RONDA DE TOLEDO

CALLE DE TOLEDO

0   150 yds

0   150 m

© MOON.COM

CALLE DE SAN ISIDRO DE SEVILLA

Las Acacias

Acacias
(L5)

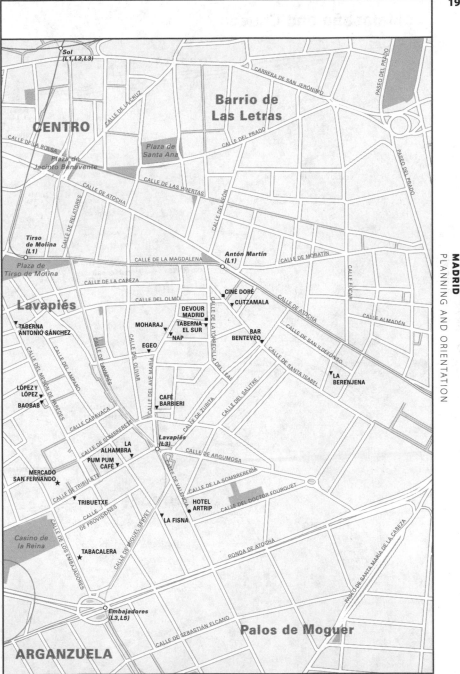

Malasaña and Chueca

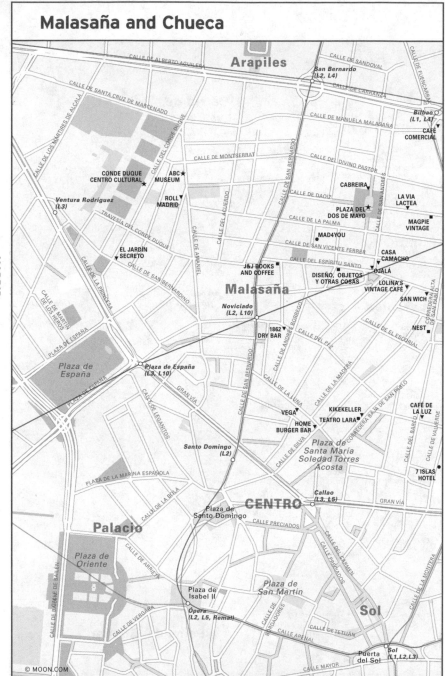

Arapiles

CALLE DE ALBERTO AGUILERA

CALLE DE SANDOVAL

San Bernardo
(L2, L4)

CALLE DE FUENCARRAL

CALLE DE SANTA CRUZ DE MARCENADO

CALLE DE CARRANZA

CALLE DE MANUELA MALASAÑA

Bilbao
(L1, L4)

CAFÉ
COMERCIAL

CALLE DE LOS MARTIRES DE ALCALA

CALLE DE MONTSERRAT

CALLE DEL DIVINO PASTOR

CALLE DEL CONDE DUQUE

CONDE DUQUE
CENTRO CULTURAL ★

ABC ★
MUSEUM

CABREIRA

LA VIA
LACTEA

Ventura Rodríguez
(L3)

ROLL ▼
MADRID

CALLE DE DAOIZ

PLAZA DEL
DOS DE MAYO ★

MAGPIE
VINTAGE

TRAVESÍA DEL CONDE DUQUE

CALLE DE LA PALMA

CALLE DE SAN ANDRÉS

CALLE DEL ACUERDO

MAD4YOU

EL JARDÍN
▼ SECRETO

CALLE DE SAN VICENTE FERRER

CASA
CAMACHO

CALLE DE AMANIEL

CALLE DEL ESPIRITU SANTO

J&J BOOKS ■
AND COFFEE

OJALÁ

DISEÑO, OBJETOS
Y OTRAS COSAS

LOLINA'S ▼
VINTAGE CAFÉ

CALLE DE SAN BERNARDINO

Malasaña

SAN WICH

CALLE DE LA PRINCESA

Noviciado
(L2, L10)

CALLE DE ANDRÉS BORREGO

NEST

CALLE DE EL ESCORIAL

CALLE DE MARTIN
DE LOS HEROS

1862 ▼
DRY BAR

CALLE DEL PEZ

CALLE DE ESPAÑA

PLAZA DE ESPAÑA

Plaza de España
(L3, L10)

CALLE DE LA MADERA

Plaza de
España

Plaza de España

CALLE DE SAN BERNARDO

CALLE DE LA LUNA

CORREDERA BAJA DE SAN PABLO

CAFÉ DE
LA LUZ ▼

GRAN VÍA

VEGA ▼

KIKEKELLER ■

CALLE DE LEGANITOS

HOME ▼
BURGER BAR

TEATRO LARA ■

CALLE DEL BARCO

CALLE DE VALVERDE

Santo Domingo
(L2)

CALLE DE SILVA

Plaza de
Santa María
Soledad Torres
Acosta

7 ISLAS
HOTEL

PLAZA DE LA MARINA ESPAÑOLA

Callao
(L3, L5)

GRAN VÍA

CENTRO

CALLE DE LA BOLA

Plaza de
Santo Domingo

CALLE PRECIADOS

Palacio

CALLE DE ARRIETA

CALLE DEL CARMEN

CALLE PRECIADOS

CALLE DE BAILEN

Plaza de
Oriente

Plaza de
San Martín

CALLE DE LA MONTERA

Plaza de
Isabel II

Plaza de
San Martín

CALLE DE VERGARA

Ópera
(L2, L5, Ramal)

CALLE ARENAL

CALLE DE TETUÁN

Sol

CALLE DE BORDADORES

Puerta
del Sol

Sol
(L1,L2,L3)

CALLE MAYOR

© MOON.COM

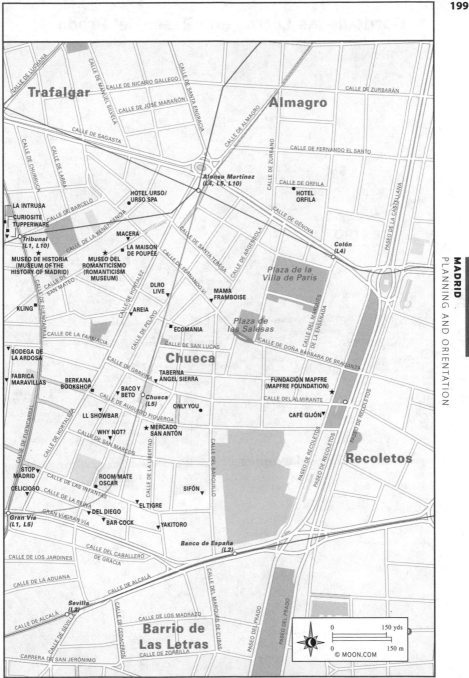

Trafalgar

Almagro

CALLE DE ZURBARÁN

CALLE DE LUCHANA

CALLE DE MANUEL SILVELA

CALLE DE NICASIO GALLEGO

CALLE DE SANTA ENGRACIA

CALLE DE ALMAGRO

CALLE DE JOSÉ MARAÑÓN

CALLE DE SAGASTA

CALLE DE FERNANDO EL SANTO

CALLE DE CHURRUCA

CALLE DE LARRA

CALLE DE ZURBANO

PASEO DE LA CASTELLANA

Alonso Martínez
(L4, L5, L10)

CALLE DE ORFILA

HOTEL
ORFILA

HOTEL URSO/
URSO SPA

CALLE DE GÉNOVA

LA INTRUSA

CURIOSITE
TUPPERWARE

CALLE DE BARCELO

CALLE DE LA BENEFICENCIA

MACERA

CALLE DE SANTA TERESA

CALLE DE ARGENSOLA

Colón
(L4)

Tribunal
(L1, L10)

LA MAISON
DE POUPÉE

MUSEO DE HISTORIA
(MUSEUM OF THE
HISTORY OF MADRID)

MUSEO DEL
ROMANTICISMO
(ROMANTICISM
MUSEUM)

CALLE DE FERNANDO VI

Plaza de la
Villa de París

CALLE DE SAN MATEO

DLRO
LIVE

MAMA
FRAMBOISE

KLING

AREIA

CALLE DE PELAYO

ECOMANIA

Plaza de
las Salesas

CALLE DE FUENCARRAL

CALLE DE LA FARMACIA

CALLE DE SAN LUCAS

CALLE DE DOÑA BÁRBARA DE BRAGANZA

CALLE DEL MARQUÉS DE LA ENSENADA

BODEGA DE
LA ARDOSA

Chueca

CALLE DE GRAVINA

TABERNA
ÁNGEL SIERRA

FABRICA
MARAVILLAS

BERKANA
BOOKSHOP

BACO Y
BETO

FUNDACIÓN MAPFRE
(MAPFRE FOUNDATION)

Chueca
(L5)

ONLY YOU

CALLE DEL ALMIRANTE

CALLE DE AUGUSTO FIGUEROA

CAFÉ GIJÓN

LL SHOWBAR

WHY NOT?

MERCADO
SAN ANTÓN

CALLE DE SAN MARCOS

CALLE DE LA LIBERTAD

CALLE DEL BARQUILLO

PASEO DE RECOLETOS

Recoletos

STOP
MADRID

ROOM MATE
OSCAR

CALLE DE LAS INFANTAS

SIFÓN

CELICIOSO

CALLE DE LA REINA

DEL DIEGO

EL TIGRE

Gran Vía
(L1, L5)

GRAN VIAGRAN VÍA

BAR COCK

YAKITORO

Banco de España
(L2)

CALLE DEL CABALLERO

DE GRACIA

CALLE DE LOS JARDINES

CALLE DE LA ADUANA

CALLE DE ALCALÁ

CALLE DEL MARQUÉS DE CUBAS

PASEO DEL PRADO

PASEO DEL PRADO

Sevilla
(L2)

CALLE DE ALCALÁ

CALLE DE SEVILLA

CALLE DE CEDACEROS

CALLE DE LOS MADRAZO

**Barrio de
Las Letras**

CARRERA DE SAN JERÓNIMO

CALLE DE ZORRILLA

| 0 | 150 yds |
| 0 | 150 m |

© MOON.COM

Barrio de las Letras and Paseo del Prado

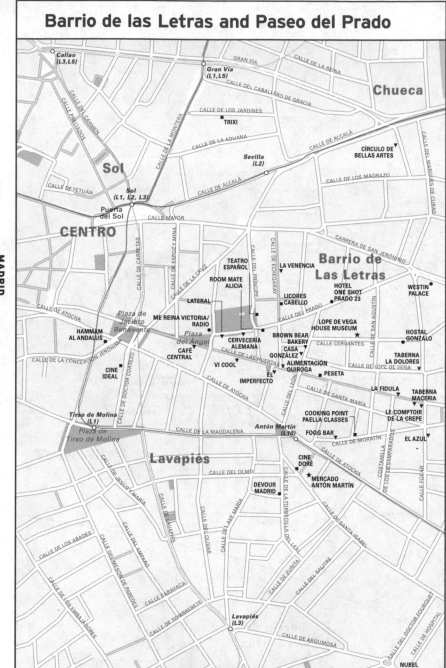

Retiro
(L2)

CALLE DE ALCALÁ

PUERTA DE
ALCALÁ

Banco de España
(L2)

PALACIO DE CIBELES
(CYBELE PALACE)

CALLE DE ALFONSO XII

NATIONAL MUSEUM
OF DECORATIVE ARTS

CALLE JUAN DE MENA

CALLE DE ALFONSO XI

HOTEL PALACIO
DEL RETIRO

MUSEO NACIONAL
THYSSEN-BORNEMISZA
(THYSSEN-BORNEMISZA
MUSEUM)

CALLE RUIZ DE ALARCÓN

PASEO DEL PRADO

PARQUE
DEL RETIRO

CALLE DE FELIPE IV

NH COLLECTION
PASEO DEL PRADO

CALLE ACADEMIA

RENT &
ROLL

Parque
del
Retiro

Paseo del Prado

CALLE CASADO DEL ALISAL

CALLE MORETO

THE PRADO MUSEUM
(MUSEO DEL PRADO)

PASEO DEL PRADO

CALLE DE LA ALAMEDA

CAIXAFORUM

CALLE ALMADÉN

CALLE DEL CENICERO

CALLE DE ALFONSO XII

PASEO DE FERNÁN NÚÑEZ

KAPITAL

CUESTA DE
MOYANO

CUESTA DE MOYANO

Atocha
(L1)

CALLE DE SANTA ISABEL

PASEO DE LA INFANTA ISABEL

CALLE DOCTOR VELASCO

0   150 yds
0   150 m
© MOON.COM

MUSEO NACIONAL CENTRO
DE ARTE REINA SOFÍA
(REINA SOFÍA MUSEUM)

To
Atocha Train Station

NATIONAL MUSEUM
OF ANTHROPOLOGY

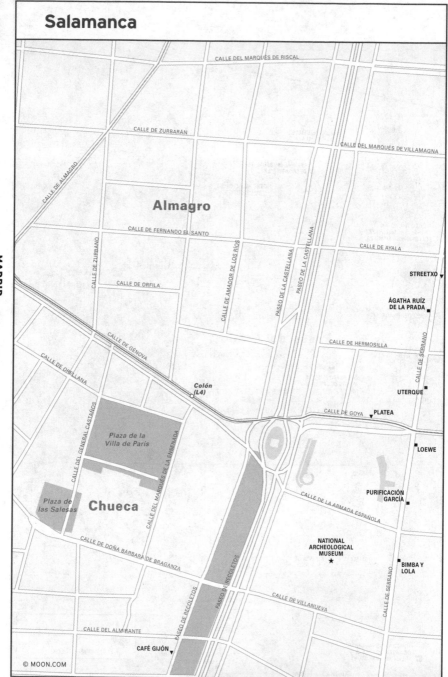

Salamanca

CALLE DEL MARQUÉS DE RISCAL

CALLE DE ZURBARÁN

CALLE DEL MARQUÉS DE VILLAMAGNA

CALLE DE ALMAGRO

Almagro

CALLE DE FERNANDO EL SANTO

CALLE DE AYALA

CALLE DE ZURBANO

CALLE DE AMADOR DE LOS RIOS

PASEO DE LA CASTELLANA

PASEO DE LA CASTELLANA

STREETXO ▾

CALLE DE ORFILA

ÁGATHA RUÍZ
DE LA PRADA ■

CALLE DE HERMOSILLA

CALLE DE SERRANO

CALLE DE GÉNOVA

CALLE DE ORELLANA

Colón
(L4)

UTERQUE ■

CALLE DE GOYA ▾ PLATEA

CALLE DEL GENERAL CASTAÑOS

Plaza de la
Villa de París

CALLE DEL MARQUÉS DE LA ENSENADA

■ LOEWE

PURIFICACIÓN
GARCÍA ■

CALLE DE LA ARMADA ESPAÑOLA

Plaza de
las Salesas

Chueca

CALLE DE DOÑA BÁRBARA DE BRAGANZA

NATIONAL
ARCHEOLOGICAL
MUSEUM
★

■ BIMBA Y
LOLA

PASEO DE RECOLETOS

PASEO DE RECOLETOS

CALLE DE SERRANO

CALLE DE VILLANUEVA

CALLE DEL ALMIRANTE

CAFÉ GIJÓN ▾

© MOON.COM

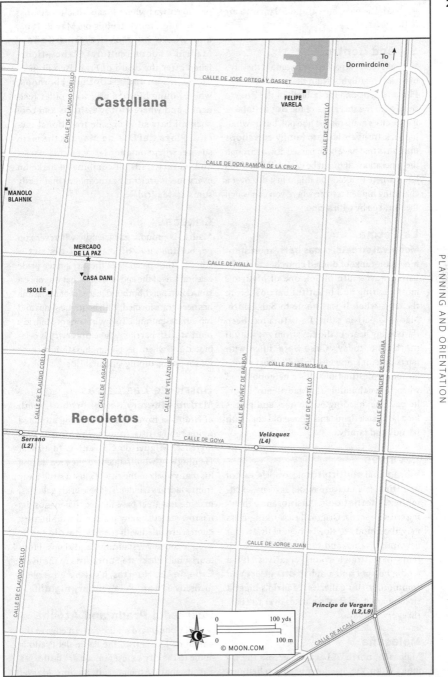

while Malasaña, Chueca, and Salamanca are to the north.

Sol and Centro

Madrid's center is packed with some of the city's historical highlights, from the grandeur of the **Plaza Mayor** and the hubbub of the **Puerta del Sol** to the sheer size of the **Royal Palace**. It's the city's main tourist hotspot, but its winding backstreets are home to **family-run shops and bars** that have been passed down through the generations. It might be crowded, but if you know where to look, you might just discover a charming hidden terrace where you can watch the world go by with a vino.

La Latina

Medieval streets, tapas bars, and a stunning panorama of domed churches make La Latina, just south of Sol, one of Madrid's most exciting and beautiful barrios. From the days when it was home to San Isidro, Madrid's patron saint, La Latina has been the beating heart of the city; from **medieval markets** to today's **Cava Baja**, lined with tapas bars, it's one of Madrid's most popular foodie destinations. It's a neighborhood where you can indulge in Madrileños' favorite pastime: heading out to bars and plazas for a laid-back drink and a good old chat with friends and family.

Lavapiés

Vibrant and **multicultural** Lavapiés, east of La Latina, is a mixture of old taverns, exciting new **international cuisine**, and a thriving creative scene. Originally a working-class neighborhood, it slowly began to attract new immigrants, and in recent years cheap rents have drawn young creatives. It's a foodie hotspot and a hub of **street art** and community-run galleries. Madrid's biggest street market, **El Rastro**, takes over the barrio every Sunday.

Malasaña

Malasaña, north of Lavapiés across the famous Gran Vía, has long been a rebellious barrio; it was where locals rose up against occupying French troops on May 2, 1808, and where **La Movida Madrileña**—Madrid's countercultural scene—flourished after the death of Francisco Franco. Today, it's an **indie-cool** neighborhood, where young hipsters mix with older residents, and where **vintage shops** and cool cocktail bars sit alongside traditional taverns. **Plaza del Dos de Mayo** is the main square, where outdoor terraces, play parks, and market stalls all combine to make an everyone-is-welcome atmosphere that really sums up Madrid.

Chueca

Madrid is proudly gay-friendly wherever you go, but the city's official **LGBT district** is Chueca, the epicenter of the city's huge pride celebrations at the end of June. What was once a run-down neighborhood just east of Malasaña has been transformed, with boutique shops and hip new restaurants. Today, it is one of Madrid's most **stylish** barrios, where **diversity** is celebrated and where people gay and straight come for shopping, dining, and nightlife.

Barrio de Las Letras

Madrid's literary neighborhood, south of Gran Vía from Chueca, has long attracted writers and artists, from Spain's most famous novelist, Miguel de Cervantes, to Ernest Hemingway, who frequented the area during his many visits to the city. It's just a stroll away from Madrid's Golden Triangle of art galleries, making it a great base for art aficionados. Its narrow streets, many peppered with literary quotes, are filled with **traditional old tapas bars**, cool new restaurants, and shops. From tourist hub **Plaza de Santa Ana** to the lively **Calle de Las Huertas**, it's also a great place to discover Madrid's **legendary nightlife**.

Paseo del Prado and Atocha

A major boulevard on the eastern edge of the Barrio de Las Letras, the Paseo del Prado is home to the city's most famous **art galleries** and its main Atocha train station. Marvel

Madrid Itinerary Ideas

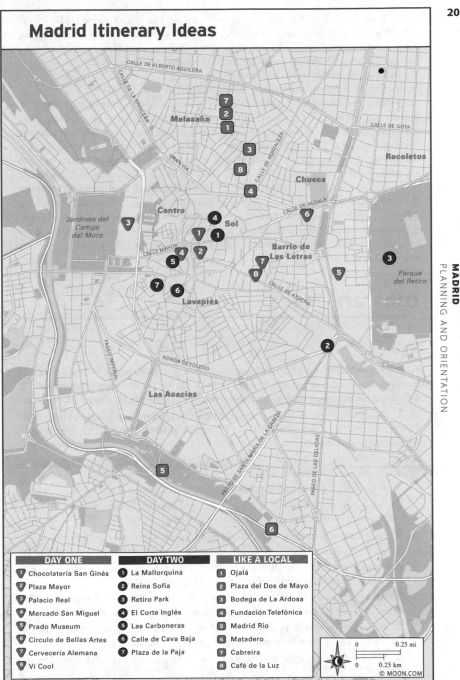

CALLE DE ALBERTO AGUILERA

CALLE DE LA PRINCESA

CALLE DE GOYA

Malasaña

GRAN VIA

CALLE DE HORTALEZA

Recoletos

Chueca

CALLE DE ALCALÁ

Centro

Jardines del
Campo
del Moro

Sol

CALLE MAYOR

Barrio de
Las Letras

Parque
del Retiro

CALLE DE ATOCHA

Lavapiés

PASEO IMPERIAL

RONDA DE TOLEDO

Las Acacias

PASEO DE SANTA MARÍA DE LA CABEZA

PASEO DE LAS DELICIAS

DAY ONE	DAY TWO	LIKE A LOCAL
1 Chocolatería San Ginés	1 La Mallorquina	1 Ojalá
2 Plaza Mayor	2 Reina Sofía	2 Plaza del Dos de Mayo
3 Palacio Real	3 Retiro Park	3 Bodega de La Ardosa
4 Mercado San Miguel	4 El Corte Inglés	4 Fundación Telefónica
5 Prado Museum	5 Las Carboneras	5 Madrid Río
6 Círculo de Bellas Artes	6 Calle de Cava Baja	6 Matadero
7 Cervecería Alemana	7 Plaza de la Paja	7 Cabreira
8 Vi Cool		8 Café de la Luz

0   0.25 mi

0   0.25 km

© MOON.COM

at the **Prado**'s Golden Age masters; see **Guernica**, Picasso's powerful depiction of the horrors of war in the **Reina Sofía**; and walk through almost a millennium of art history in the **Thyssen-Bornemisza**. Newer openings like the **Caixa Forum**, with its stunning vertical garden, are excellent examples of Madrid's modern architecture. The grandeur of the museums extends to the barrio's other big attraction, **Retiro Park**, one of Europe's most impressive city parks and a true highlight of any trip to Madrid.

Salamanca

Salamanca, with its **luxury hotels, high-end restaurants,** and **designer shops,** is **Madrid's most exclusive neighborhood** and worth seeing even if you're just window shopping. The neighborhood's wide boulevards are home to some lovely hidden gems, from buzzing local markets to some great under-the-radar museums.

Beyond the Center

Where once tourists stuck to central Madrid, today, sights and scenes are expanding like never before, making exploring beyond the center a vital part of any visit. North of the center, Madrid's business district is home to modern architecture and the enduring temple of Spanish football, **Real Madrid's Santiago Bernabéu**. Along the River Manzanares, the **Matadero** is a former slaughterhouse converted into a thriving cultural space, and the **Casa de Campo**, Madrid's biggest park, is fun for all the family.

Itinerary Ideas

DAY 1

Take in **Plaza Mayor, Palacio Real,** and the **Prado Museum,** which houses a wealth of European masterpieces, taking time for a **vermouth** and a bite at a **local market** in between. In the evening, enjoy drinks at some of Hemingway's old haunts in the literary quarter of **Las Letras.**

1 Start your first day in Madrid with a classic local experience: dunking some fresh churros into a cup of thick hot chocolate at **Chocolatería San Ginés,** which is conveniently open 24 hours a day.

2 Stroll around the heart of the city, taking in the 400-year-old **Plaza Mayor** and its winding side streets (pop into the Convent of Corpus Cristi for biscuits handmade by nuns—possibly the most unusual cookie-buying experience you'll ever have).

3 A five-minute walk away, visit the largest Royal Palace in Europe, the **Palacio Real**. Next door, stroll around the tranquil Sabatini Gardens.

4 Back towards Sol, stop at **Mercado San Miguel** for a vermouth and a bite to eat.

5 It's a 20-minute walk to the **Prado Museum**, where you can see masterpieces by Velázquez, Goya, and El Greco. (The middle of the day is when the museum tends to be at its quietest.) Plan to spend up to three hours taking everything in.

6 After your Prado visit, soak up the panoramic views from the nearby **Círculo de Bellas Artes** (a 10-minute stroll away), which has one of the best rooftop bars in Madrid.

7 Weave into the literary neighborhood of Las Letras to check out some old Hemingway haunts, like **Cervecería Alemana** on the pretty Plaza Santa Ana.

8 For dinner, sample a laid-back take on tapas by Michelin-starred chef Sergei Arola at **Vi Cool.**

DAY 2

See Picasso's "Guernica" in the **Reina Sofía,** then spend some time relaxing with locals in Retiro Park. Take in the grand architecture of **Gran Vía** and hit some top tapas bars on **Calle de Cava Baja,** Madrid's famed tapas street.

1 Have a sweet breakfast of a *napolitana de crema* from **La Mallorquina,** going strong since 1894.

2 Walk downhill through Lavapiés towards the **Reina Sofía** and marvel at Picasso's famous anti-war mural, *Guernica.* Spend about three hours exploring the museum.

3 Spend a lazy hour or two in **Retiro Park,** Madrid's loveliest green space. Grab a bite to eat at a lakeside kiosk, rent a rowing boat, or simply enjoy the peace with a picnic under the trees.

4 Walk up the cinematic Gran Vía, taking in the early-20th-century architecture of Madrid's most famous streets, including its iconic Schweppes sign. Stop for a drink on the ninth-floor terrace of **El Corte Inglés** department store and enjoy the panoramic views from its terrace.

5 At night, catch a stunning flamenco performance at **Las Carboneras** (even better if you can take a flamenco tour before the show).

6 Explore the tapas bars of **Calle de Cava Baja,** just a two-minute walk away.

7 End your evening with a drink on the beautiful **Plaza de la Paja,** just around the corner from Calle de Cava Baja.

MADRID LIKE A LOCAL

Explore the indie-cool neighborhood of **Malasaña** in the morning, then take in the current exhibition at **Fundación Telefónica,** a hidden gem that even locals miss. Cycle along **Madrid Río,** the city's rejuvenated riverside park, then end your day back in Malasaña for a dose of Madrid's legendary **nightlife.**

1 Enjoy a laid-back brunch at hip local favorite **Ojalá** in the barrio of Malasaña.

2 Wander around the neighborhood, taking in the street art and browsing the vintage stores. See **Plaza del Dos de Mayo,** which holds a monument to Madrileños who rose up against French troops in 1808.

3 Have a vermouth in **Bodega de La Ardosa,** one of the neighborhood's traditional old taverns, famed for its *tortilla de patatas.*

4 Pop into the **Fundación Telefónica,** inside what was Europe's first skyscraper. There are always interesting free exhibitions of 21st-century art, technology, and design.

5 Hop on the metro at Gran Vía and get off at Puerta de Toledo, then head downhill towards the river. Walk or rent bikes to cycle along **Madrid Río**—the riverside park non-locals seldom visit.

6 Walk or cycle along the river to the **Matadero,** Madrid's former slaughterhouse that is now an exciting cultural center with regular exhibitions, markets, a cinema, and a café.

7 For dinner, take the metro to Malasaña and enjoy some quality tapas at **Cabreira,** just off Plaza del Dos del Mayo.

8 End the night with cocktails in Malasaña at **Café de la Luz.**

Sights

SOL AND CENTRO

TOP EXPERIENCE

★ Plaza Mayor

Metro: Sol

Madrid's grand central square has been the scene of many different events throughout its over 400-year history, from markets and bullfights to public trials and executions during the Spanish Inquisition. When it was built (on the site of the former Plaza de Arrabal) in 1617 by architect Juan Gómez de Mora, the square brought a much-needed open space to the densely packed, narrow streets of the city center. Today, Plaza Mayor is a place to see life in all its forms, from early-morning delivery men and menu-touting waiters to locals rushing to work and tourists snapping photographs.

The cobbled square is surrounded on four sides with a covered arcade, featuring 237 wrought-iron balconies and 118 arches, that houses shops and restaurants. A statue of Philip III on horseback, sculpted by Giambologna in 1616, dominates the center of the square.

One of the square's most famous buildings is the **Casa de Panadería** (Bakery House), on the northern side. It was built in 1619; today, only the original cellar and ground floor remain. In the early 1990s, Spanish artist Carlos Franco was chosen to redecorate the façade of the building with frescoes depicting mythological figures interwoven with scenes from the city's history. It was originally the main bakery in Madrid and therefore set the price of bread across the city; today it's the headquarters of Madrid's tourist board.

The square has had several facelifts over the years; a tram ran through it until the 1960s, when the square was dotted with trees. Today, there is a weekly **stamp and coin market**

(Sunday mornings), as well as regular events such as concerts. The square gets a festive feel in December, when the balconies are strung with fairy lights and a Christmas market sets up stalls, selling a mixture of Christmas novelty items and hand-crafted nativity scenes (*belenes*).

The touristy restaurants surrounding the square are generally not the best quality or the best deal. If you want to sit at one of the terraces surrounding the square, do so just for a drink (a great opportunity for people watching). If you're hungry, do as the locals do: grab a *bocadillo de calamares* (a beloved local delicacy that is sold in the side streets surrounding the square), take a seat on a bench, and watch the world go by.

Puerta del Sol

Metro: Sol

Originally, this crescent-shaped "square" was the site of one of the gates in the 15th-century city wall, and its easterly location meant the rising sun would illuminate it. (Hence the square's name: the *Puerta del Sol*, or "Gate of the Sun.") Today, the square is often used more as a thoroughfare or meeting place, but there are several sights worth keeping an eye out for.

To the northeast of the Puerta del Sol is the stone-and-bronze statue of *El Oso y el Madroño* ("The Bear and the Strawberry Tree"), a symbol of Madrid that appeared on the city's coat of arms as early as the 13th century, when bears roamed the countryside around what was then a small town. (This enduring symbol of Madrid also features on the logo of the local football club, Atlético de Madrid.) This statue was made by Spanish sculptor Antonio Navarro Santafé in 1967.

In the center of the square is a statue of Charles III, who was nicknamed "the best mayor-king of Madrid" for the many public works he undertook to improve the city during his reign, from opening hospitals and schools to opening Retiro Park to the public.

The grand building to the south of the square has worn several hats over the years, from the old city post office to the headquarters of the Ministry of the Interior and State Security during the regime of Francisco Franco (1939-1975). Today it is the seat of Madrid's regional government. Just in front of this building is a plaque laid into the pavement reading "KM 0"—kilometer 0 marks the central point of all the roads in Spain.

Its central location and wide-open spaces mean the Puerta del Sol is often the scene of protests and demonstrations. In 2011, it became the center of anti-austerity protests by the so-called *indignados* (indignant ones), a group inspired to protest the harsh consequences of Spain's economic crisis.

Mercado San Miguel

Plaza de San Miguel; tel. 91/542-4936; www. mercadodesanmiguel.es; Sun-Wed 10am-midnight, Thurs-Sat 10am-2am; Metro: Sol

Just off Plaza Mayor is San Miguel Market, a wrought-iron-covered food market that was built in 1916 and renovated in 2009 into a temple of stalls selling food and drink from around Spain. It is undoubtedly touristy, but well worth a visit for its huge range of produce. From olives and *jamón Ibérico* (Iberian cured ham) to tapas, oysters, and a huge range of wines, cider, and cocktails, you could spend hours eating and drinking your way through the market. It can get very busy, so head there for a pre-lunch vermouth or else embrace the crowds and get ready to swoop when you spot a free table.

★ Royal Palace

Calle de Bailén; tel. 91/454-8700, www. patrimonionacional.es/real-sitio/palacios/6039; Mon-Sun, 10am-6pm (winter), 10am-8pm (summer); €10, €14 with kitchen tour; Metro: Opera

Madrid's Royal Palace dominates the Plaza de Oriente, a tree-lined square with manicured gardens and rows of statues of Spanish kings from the Middle Ages. While it is the official residence of Spain's royal family, King Felipe and Queen Letizia choose to live in the modest, 300-room Zarzuela Palace, on the outskirts of the city, using the Royal Palace for state occasions only.

The palace was built on the site of a 9th-century Moorish fortress, which burned down on Christmas Eve 1734. Many works of art were lost in the flames. "Las Meninas," the masterpiece by court painter Diego de Velázquez that today hangs in the Museo del Prado, was only saved by being thrown out of a window.

King Philip V ordered a new palace built on the same site. Construction took place between 1738 and 1755, and the result was a French-inspired building that has echoes of Versailles, with one difference: size. Madrid's Royal Palace is gigantic; it has over 3,000 rooms, making it the largest palace by floor area in Europe to this day. The last monarch to live in the palace was Alfonso XIII, who fled Spain during the Spanish Civil War.

Today, visitors can tour the palace and get a good taste of the lavish lifestyles of Spanish monarchs through the ages. Highlights include the royal chemist, the royal armory that houses armor and weapons used by the Spanish Royal Family since the 13th century, and the painting gallery, home to works such as "Salome with the Head of John the Baptist," by Caravaggio. Opened to the public in October 2017, the Royal Kitchen is a detailed example of the historic kitchens of European royal palaces. A visit to the Royal Kitchen is €5; a combined palace and kitchen ticket is €14.

Unlike many royal palaces in Europe, you can almost touch the exterior; there are no fences to keep away the tourists, which only enhances the size and grandeur of the building.

The changing of the guard is held every Wednesday and Saturday from 11am-2pm (10am-midday in July, Aug, and Sept) at the Puerta del Príncipe on Calle Bailén. The more elaborate Solemn Changing of the Guard is held on the first Wednesday of each month

at midday. It lasts approximately 50 minutes and takes place in the Plaza de la Armería; free entry is available via the Puerta de Santiago gate on Calle Bailén (get there early for a good spot).

Admission is free every Monday through Friday 4pm-6pm.

Almudena Cathedral

Calle de Bailén, 10; tel. 91/542-2200; www. catedraldelaalmudena.es; Sept-June, Mon-Sun 9am-8:30pm; July-August 10am-9pm; cathedral museum Mon-Sat 10am-2:30pm; the cathedral cannot be visited during religious services; admission is free but a donation is encouraged; Metro: Opera

Many people are surprised to learn that one of the newest examples of architecture in central Madrid is the city's cathedral—the Almudena. Although plans for the building were drawn up in 1879, war, lack of funds, and disagreements about the design held up construction, and it was not consecrated (by Pope John Paul) until 1993.

The building has gone through several designs and phases. First, it was to be like the great French 18th-century Gothic cathedrals of Reims and Chartres. When it was feared that a Gothic design would clash with the cathedral's surroundings, Spanish architects Fernando Chueca Goitia and Carlos Sidro changed the original design to give the cathedral a baroque exterior in keeping with the Royal Palace next door.

The cavernous interior is worth a look for the modern stained-glass windows, but has little else to recommend a long visit (though it is a cool rest stop in the sweltering summer months). It is worth a visit for a climb up the cathedral's dome, accessed through the chapterhouse and vestry. At more than 70 meters (230 feet) high, it gives visitors great views over the next-door Royal Palace and across La Latina to the dome of the Basilica of San Francisco el Grande. The **Cathedral Museum** (Mon-Sat 10am-2:30pm; €6),

---

1: Plaza Mayor; 2: Puerta del Sol; 3: Royal Palace; 4: Arab Walls.

located inside the cathedral, houses artwork and artefacts relating to the history of the Church in Madrid, as well as the city's two patron saints, Santa María la Real de la Almudena and San Isidro Labrador.

Arab Walls of Madrid

Emir Mohamed I Park, Cuesta Ramón, 1; Metro: Sol

Madrid's Arab Walls were built soon after the establishment of the settlement of Mayrit in 852 by Muhammed I of Córdoba. (Fun fact: Madrid is the only European capital city whose origins and name are Arab.) The walls, which ran for around 980 meters (3,220 feet) and enclosed an area of four hectares (9.9 acres), were part of a fortress defending the Muslim citadel of Mayrit, which was located on the site of today's Royal Palace.

The Arab Walls remain one of the very oldest remnants of the city. While much of the original walls have been destroyed, the best-preserved example is in the small Emir Mohamed I Park, next to the Almudena Cathedral. While you could be forgiven for walking straight past the wall today, it was an impressive construction at the time, according to historians. It is a worthwhile stop-off when visiting the cathedral and Royal Palace to get an idea of Madrid's incredibly diverse history.

★ Templo de Debod
(Temple of Debod)

Calle Ferraz, 1; tel. 91/366-7415; Tues-Fri: 10am-2pm, 6pm-8pm, Sat and Sun: 9:30am-8pm; free; Metro: Plaza de España

One of Madrid's more unexpected sights, this ancient Egyptain temple with two stone arches is located in the Parque del Oeste, near the Royal Palace. It was dismantled and sent brick-by-brick by the Egyptian government as a thank-you gift for Spain's help in saving temples that were threatened by flooding caused by the construction of the Aswan High Dam in 1960. It opened to the public in 1972 and today is one of the few examples of ancient Egyptian architecture outside Egypt, and the only one in Spain.

The temple was originally built as a

Madrid's Modern Architecture

Compared to many cities, Madrid is very traditional in its architecture. (You'll find no other-worldly creative flourishes of the likes of Antoni Gaudí here.) But the city does have some impressive modern architecture, if you know where to look.

What Madrid has been doing particularly well is renovation—taking old buildings and transforming them into boundary-pushing modern architecture while at the same time preserving crucial period details. Key examples of this are the renovation of the Mahou beer brewery into the ABC Museum and an old electricity power station into the Caixa Forum.

Below are some other great examples of architecture in Madrid:

- **Kio Towers** (Plaza de Castilla; Metro: Plaza de Castilla): The world's first inclined skyscrapers, dubbed the Gate of Europe, opened in Madrid 1996. They were designed by American architects Philip Johnson and John Burgee. Each 26-story building is 115 meters (377 feet) tall with an inclination of 15 degrees, making them look like they are leaning into each other.

- **Caixa Forum** (Paseo del Prado, 36, Metro: Atocha): One of Madrid's most spectacular examples of modern architecture is the Caixa Forum cultural center on the grand Paseo del Prado. Swiss architects Herzog & Meuron transformed an old electricity power station by adding a rust-covered top half and making the whole building appear to float. The pièce de résistance is the hanging garden, a vertical wall of greenery designed by French botanist Patrick Blanc.

- **Madrid-Barajas Airport Terminal 4**: You might spot one of Madrid's most impressive recent architectural additions before you've even left the airport. Terminal 4 was designed by Antonio Lamela and Richard Rogers, and the wave-like design, which includes lots of natural light from skylights, won the 2006 Stirling Prize.

- **Hotel Puerta America** (Avenida de América, 41, Metro: Cartagena): There are few projects where you can see the work of so many esteemed architects in one place. This luxury hotel is the brainchild of 19 different architects, including Jean Nouvel, Norman Foster, and Zaha Hadid, who each got their own floor in which to create their unique vision.

- **Cuatro Torres Business Area**: Madrid's four skyscrapers dominate the skyline to the north of the city, close to the Kio Towers and house offices, a hotel, and restaurants. The buildings include the Cepsa Tower (Paseo de la Castellana, 259 A), designed by Norman Foster, and the Torre de Cristal, "Glass Tower" (Paseo de la Castellana, 259 C), designed by César Pelli. This area is close to the Fundación Canal Isabel, so is worth checking out if visiting the gallery.

- **ABC Museum**: Aranguren & Gallegos Architects transformed what was the first Mahou brewery in Madrid into the ABC Museum of illustration and graphic art. The modern steel outer shell, and glass and concrete renovations inside, give the building a modern make-over while respecting the original architecture.

one-room shrine 15 kilometers (9.5 miles) from Aswan in the 2nd century BC. It was extended during the Ptolemaic dynasty into a small temple dedicated to Isis of Philae and was completed by Roman emperors Augustus and Tiberius.

The sight is a popular place to watch the sun set; settle on a spot on the grass in front of the temple or around its edges and watch as it is bathed in golden light—the views across Madrid and the Casa de Campo behind are lovely, too. Visits inside are available, but are restricted to 30 people at once for a maximum of 30 minutes, which can make lines long, especially on weekends.

Teatro Real
(Royal Theatre)

Plaza de Isabel II; tel. 90/224-4848; www.teatro-real. com; Metro: Opera

The cool gray neoclassical façade of the Teatro Real (Royal Theatre)—Madrid's main opera

1: Teatro Real; 2: Plaza de la Villa.

house—dominates the Plaza de Isabel II. It opened its doors in 1850 with the opera *La Favorita* by Geatano Donizetti, and held the Spanish premiere of Giuseppe Verdi's *La Forza del Destino* ("The Force of Destiny").

The Teatro Real housed the Madrid Royal Conservatory from 1867-1925, when the building was closed due to damage from the construction of Madrid's metro. Restoration was long and arduous, hampered by the Spanish Civil War. The building eventually reopened in 1966 as a concert hall, and reopened again as an opera house in 1997. Since then, it has quickly become one of the leading opera houses in Spain. As well as opera, the Teatro Real holds regular concerts, dance performances, and workshops.

Several tours are available, including a general guided tour (Mon-Sun, every half hour from 10:30am-1pm; €8), artistic tour (Mon-Sun 9:30am; duration 1 hour 15 minutes; €12), and technical tours (Mon-Sun 10am; duration 1 hour 15 minutes; €16) and a night tour, during which visitors can go behind the scenes after a performance. The tours allow visitors to explore the theater's stage, rehearsal rooms, dressing rooms, and royal box; it also recounts the history of the building and discusses its architecture and how a modern opera house works. During the artistic tour, visitors learn about the process of staging an opera, from the costume department to the rehearsal rooms, while the technical tour looks at the nuts and bolts of staging an opera, from moving stages to building the sets.

All tours are in Spanish but can be conducted in English on request. (Email visitasguiadas@teatro-real.com.)

Espacio Fundación Telefónica

Calle Fuencarral, 3; tel. 91/580-8700; www.espacio. fundaciontelefonica.com; Tues-Sun 10am-8pm; free admission; Metro: Gran Vía
The Telefonica Building, Europe's first skyscraper, dominates Gran Vía. It was completed as the headquarters of Spain's national telecommunications company in 1929. Architect Ignacio de Cárdenas was inspired by the Manhattan skyscrapers of the day, but added his own Madrid Baroque touches to the exterior. During the Spanish Civil War, it was the home of the Office of Foreign Press, and correspondents including Martha Gellhorn and Ernest Hemingway regularly ran the gauntlet of sniper fire down Gran Vía (nicknamed sniper alley) to file their reports.

Today, as well as housing the flagship store of Telefónica, Spain's national telecommunications company, it is home to the Espacio Fundación Telefonica, a four-floor space with regular exhibitions of 21st-century art, technology, and design, as well as talks and concerts. It's a true hidden gem, and even many locals have never visited. Its exhibitions are eclectic and diverse; recent shows have focused on the works of the architect Norman Foster, the photography of the Magnum photo agency, and ahead-of-their time dancers, from Isadora Duncan to Josephine Baker.

It's worth popping inside to see the building itself—the area where the Espacio Fundación Telefónica is located has had a modern makeover, featuring exposed iron and a steel spiral staircase.

Real Monasterio de las Descalzas Reales

Plazade las Descalzas; tel. 91/454-8800; Tues-Sat 10am-2pm, 4pm-6:30pm, Sun 10am-3pm; www. patrimonionacional.es/real-sitio/palacios/6095, €6 admission; Metro: Opera
This former 16th-century palace was converted into a convent in 1559 when the widowed sister of Philip II decided she wanted to become a nun. The convent attracted lots of women from the nobility of the time, many of whom brought their belongings with them, which made for a rich collection of artwork, tapestries, and sculptures. The building houses a cloistered community of nuns to this day and was seen by very few people until the 1980s, when part of the building was opened as a museum.

1: Plaza de la Paja; 2: Basilica de San Francisco el Grande.

Madrid Street Art

Two Madrid neighborhoods have particularly attracted graffiti artists—the indie-cool Malasaña and the multicultural Lavapiés. Some of the most vibrant examples of Madrid street art are listed below. (You can also take a street art walking tour with **Cool Tours Spain**.) Keep an eye out for stickers plastered to the walls, especially in Malasaña, where everyone from Marilyn Monroe to corrupt local politicians have had their time in the graffiti limelight.

For one weekend in April, artists descend on Malasaña to paint its shop fronts, walls, windows, and bollards, in a festival known as **Pinta Malasaña** (www.pintamalasana.com). A jury selects 100 artists to take part in the street art festival.

TUPPERWARE

Frenchman Louis Lambert (aka 3TTMan) is known for his large-scale, colorful murals. He designed the exterior of this Malasaña bar, in a burst of color and cartoonish characters that bring the spirit of La Movida to life.

MERCADO DE LA CEBADA

The vivid exterior of this local La Latina market is a great example of a street art aesthetic being used to decorate a permanent building. Its multi-colored roof and bright, colorful signage make the market really stand out among the neighborhood's historic buildings.

PACO DE LUCÍA METRO STATION

Spanish graffiti artist Okuda's pieces pop up around the city, and his style of multicolored geometric patterns is easy to recognize. A great example is his mural of flamenco legend Paco de Lucía in the metro station of the same name. Find another Okuda piece decorating the pizza oven in the Lavapiés Italian restaurant **NAP**.

MALASAÑA

Parisian graffiti artist Christian Guemy, also known as C215, has left intricately designed portraits on the walls of Malasaña, giving a face to the people of the streets—the homeless, children, and even smokers out for a quick cigarette break.

The convent can only be visited as part of a guided tour, which lasts around 50 minutes. Tickets can be booked online in advance. The tour takes visitors up a grand wooden stairway lined in frescoes to the upper floor of the convent and past several of its 33 chapels, including the resting place of Juana, the founder of the convent. The nuns' former bedrooms are home to several intricate tapestries based on drawings by Reubens and woven in the 17th century in Brussels.

The convent's unusual name ("Convent of the Barefoot Nuns") comes from the Discalced (Barefoot) Carmelites, a cloistered Catholic order founded in the 16th century.

Plaza de la Villa

Metro: Sol

Plaza de la Villa, the former medieval heart of the city, was Madrid's main square before the nearby Plaza Mayor was built. It is both a beautiful open space and an example of three periods of architecture.

The **Lujanes' House and Tower**, on the western side of the square, dates to the 15th century and was built as the Lujanes family mansion. While Muslim rulers were long gone by the time the tower was built, Islamic architectural influence is reflected in the shape of the arches towards the top of the tower, in what is known as the Mudéjar style. The tower

mural by Okuda at Paco de Lucía metro station

TABACALERA

This former tobacco factory in Lavapiés is now a community-run cultural space, and its walls are peppered with street art, including a multicolored bear in the unmistakable style of Okuda (see above) on the walls of the Tabacalera looking onto Calle Miguel Sirvet.

MERCADO ANTÓN MARTÍN

If you're visiting Mercado Antón Martín in Lavapiés, cast your eye upwards to take in the woman who looks out over the market—**Isabellita**. She was named by locals, who thoroughly embraced the work by Irish street artist Fin DAC.

is older than the main building; it was built at the beginning of the 15th century, and the building itself was constructed toward the end of that century.

At the north end of the square is the **Cisneros' House**, a palace built in the 16th century by architect Benito Jiménez de Cisneros, a nephew of Cardinal Cisneros (the founder of Madrid's Complutense University), after whom the building was named. Casa Cisneros was constructed in the Plateresque style, a Spanish architectural style that blended Gothic, Mudéjar, and Renaissance elements.

The eastern side of the square is dominated by the **Casa de la Villa**, built in the Baroque style in the 17th century. It was the seat of Madrid's city council from 1693 until 2007. Its triangular roofs are in the style of the Habsburgs, Spain's Austrian rulers.

Although all three buildings have been restored over the years, they provide an interesting direct comparison of more than 300 years of architectural style.

The statue in the center of the square, added in 1980, is of **Álvaro de Bazán**, a Spanish admiral who fought in the Battle of Lepanto.

LA LATINA
Plaza de la Paja
Metro: La Latina

One of Madrid's loveliest squares, Plaza de la Paja was the center of the city's commercial life, with its regular market, before the construction of the Plaza Mayor. It was surrounded by grand mansions, and today is home to cool restaurants and bars whose terraces spill out onto the lively plaza.

To the south of the square, a wrought-iron gate leads into a hidden garden that once belonged to one of the grand mansions: the **Príncipe de Angolona gardens** (Plaza de la Paja, 6; Oct-Feb, daily 10am-6pm; Mar-Sept, daily 10am-10pm; free). The original garden dates back to 1750 and was remodeled by artist and garden designer Javier de Winthuysen in 1920. A sit on one of the benches dotted around the garden is a relaxing stop-off among all the sightseeing.

Museo de San Isidro
(San Isidro Museum)
Plaza de San Andrés, 2; tel. 91/366-7415; Tues-Sun 9:30am-8pm, June 15-Sept 15 Tues-Sun 10am-7pm; free; Metro: La Latina

In the heart of La Latina, this small but excellent (and free) museum charts the history of Madrid, from the days when elephants and rhinos roamed the countryside, through Roman occupation and Moorish rule to the Middle Ages and beyond. Artefacts, maps, paintings, and some interesting interactive displays (in English and Spanish) bring the city's history to life. Rarely busy, it is a pleasant place for a leisurely history lesson.

The museum is named after Madrid's patron saint, San Isidro Labrador. On a courtyard inside the museum, visitors can see the **Pozo del Milagro** (the Well of the Miracle), whose waters, it is said, San Isidro rose to save his son from drowning.

Basílica de San Francisco el Grande
(Royal Basilica of Saint Francis the Great)
Calle San Buenaventura, 1; tel. 91/365-3800; general admission €5, reduced admission for seniors and students €3; Metro: La Latina

This church, with its huge, frescoed dome—said to be the biggest in Spain and the third or fourth largest in the world—dominates La Latina. It was built between 1761 and 1768 on the site of a medieval Franciscan monastery that was, according to legend, founded by St. Francis of Assisi in 1217. At 33 meters (108 feet) in diameter, the dome certainly dominates the church, which was once the national pantheon, where famous artists and politicians were entombed. The church is home to paintings from the 17th to the 19th centuries, including works by Zurbarán and Goya.

Mercado de la Cebada
Plaza de la Cebada; www.mercadodelacebada.com; Mon-Fri 9am-2pm, 5pm-8:30pm, Sat 9am-6pm; Metro: La Latina

This huge local market, noticeable for its multicolored, wave-like roof, mainly sells fresh fruit, vegetables, meat, and fish, but on a Saturday afternoon, the fish stalls will cook up anything you buy in an informal seafood party.

LAVAPIÉS
Originally a working-class neighborhood, Lavapiés is filled with *corralas*—typical apartment buildings whose balconies looked out over a central courtyard (see an example at Calle del Sombrerete, 13, best viewed from Calle Mesón de Paredes).

★ El Rastro
Plaza de Cascorro and Calle Ribera de Curtidores; Sun. and public holidays 9am-3pm; Metro: La Latina

Madrileños aren't used to waking early on the weekend but make an exception for El Rastro, Madrid's biggest street market, held every Sunday and public holiday. Spain's most famous flea market has stalls selling both new and second-hand products, and shops along the route also open their doors. The market seems to sell everything, from old flamenco records and leather products

La Movida Madrileña

La Movida, which translates as "the scene," was a shrugging off of the shackles of dictatorship for Spaniards after the death of General Franco and Spain's return to democracy in 1978. All at once, Madrileños embraced all the freedoms that they had for so long been denied—sex, drugs, and rock 'n' roll were the order of the day; it was legal to smoke marijuana in the street, and bar closing times were loose, to say the least.

The Movida was also associated with a new wave of creativity in film, music, and fashion. One of the most famous people identified with the Movida Madrileña was Oscar-winning film director **Pedro Almodóvar**, born in La Mancha, who came to Madrid in the late sixties to make films. His first full-length film, *Pepi, Luci, Bom y otras chicas del montón* ("Pepi, Luci, Bom and Other Girls on the Heap"), was released in 1980. His movies are melodramas of heightened emotion, dazzling color palettes, and his famous *chicas Almodóvar* (Almodóvar girls), who include Carmen Maura and Penelope Cruz.

Another successful name to emerge from La Movida was fashion designer **Ágatha Ruíz de la Prada**, whose color-popping designs (which bring to mind the shades of Almodóvar's films) can be found in her flagship store on Calle Serrano, Madrid's Golden Mile of designer stores.

Perhaps more than specific names, what has most endured from the time of the Movida is Madrileños' love of *salir de copas*—going out for a drink—as well as their open and welcoming attitude.

MADRID
SIGHTS

to antiques, old furniture, and even pets, and browsing, chatting, and haggling will give you an authentic taste of Madrid life. Aim to arrive for opening time if you want to sniff out the best bargains and avoid the crowds, which tend to be at their busiest at around 11am.

While the main drag of stalls is Ribera de Curtidores, it is in the smaller side streets to the right-hand side where you might find some real treasures—from products to little bars where you can enjoy a beer or a vermouth. A good way to end your shopping spree is to stop off at a bar along the route for a caña or vermouth. Popular options include **Bar Santa Ana** (Calle de la Ruda, 9), **Restaurante Casa Amadeo los Caracoles** (Plaza de Cascorro, 18), and the nearby **Taberna Antonio Sánchez** (Calle del Mesón de Paredes, 13).

The Santa Ana street market, on **Calle de Santa Ana**, a new addition to the Rastro in 2018, sees cool furniture shops and vintage-clothes shops bring their wares out onto the street and features a lively atmosphere, including live music.

Mercado San Fernando

Calle de Embajadores, 41; www. mercadodesanfernando.es, Metro: Lavapiés; Mon 9am-3pm, 5pm-9pm, Tues-Thurs 9am-9pm, Fri-Sat 9am-11pm, Sun 11am-5pm

This buzzing neighborhood market opened in 1944, replacing a nearby open-air market. It is a working local market with a mixture of fresh food stalls (fruit and veg, fish, meat) and prepared food stalls with cuisine from around the world, from Mexican tacos, to pizzas and sushi. There are bars dotted around and a craft beer shop in the middle of the market. While it is usually open during the day only, it stays open until 11pm on Friday evenings—go then for a buzzing local vibe.

Tabacalera

Calle de Embajadores, 53; www.latabacalera.net; Tues-Sun 6pm-10pm; free; Metro: Embajadores

Tobacco factory turned alternative cultural hub, the Tabacalera has been a community-run arts and culture space since 2009, showcasing modern art, photography, music, and much more. The key is that the local community runs the space, so events reflect the neighborhood's diversity, from make-your-own-longboard workshops to wrestling and poetry recitals. It's also a great spot to take in some of Madrid's best street art. Check online for upcoming events or just drop in to see the latest exhibitions. Be aware that its website is not always up to date.

MALASAÑA
Plaza del Dos de Mayo
Metro: Bilbao/Tribunal
Malasaña's main square gets its name from the uprising of May 2, 1808, of Madrileños against Napoleon's invading troops. The monument in the center of the square commemorates two of the heroes of the uprising, Luis Daoiz and Pedro Velarde, captains who were stationed in the barracks that was once on the square.

Today, the square is popular with everyone, from young people to families (there are three play parks for kids) and older locals who walk their dogs or stop for a beer in the outdoor cafés. It's a great place for a local taste of Madrid, to people-watch and to enjoy a laidback drink. On weekends, stall holders set up a small market selling records, jewelery, and other local products.

Conde Duque Centro Cultural
Calle Conde Duque, 9; tel. 91/318-4450; www.condeduquemadrid.es; Tues-Sat 10am-2pm, 5:30pm-9pm, Sun 10:30am-2pm; Metro: Ventura Rodríguez
Now a vital cultural hub, the building that houses the Conde Duque Culturla Center was originally commissioned by Philip V and built in 1717 to house the elite Royal Guard Corps, whose job it was to protect the king. Architect Pedro de Ribera designed a building that could house 600 guards and 400 horses. Its 25,000-square-meter (269,000-square-foot) floor space and 228-meter-tall (748-foot) façade made it, for many years, the largest building in the capital.

Over the years it housed the military, a prison, and an observatory before in 1983 being handed over to the city council to use as a new cultural space. It was renovated

and cleaned up in 2011, and today lends its name to the hip Conde Duque area west of Malasaña.

The huge, rectangular space includes a large central square and two smaller patios. Inside are the City Archive, several libraries, a theater, and an exhibition space. It's a great place to check out the latest free exhibition or see an open-air film or concert during the summer.

ABC Museum
Calle de Amaniel, 29; tel. 91/758-8379; www.museo.abc.es; Tues-Sat 11am-8pm, Sun 10am-2pm; free; Metro: Noviciado
The off-the-beaten-track ABC Museum, in what was Madrid's first Mahou brewery, is dedicated to drawing, illustration, and graphic art. It is free to enter and holds regular events and temporary exhibits alongside its permanent collection, which spans the 20th century and features the work of more than 1,500 artists. It is a fascinating spot, as much to see how the original brewery has been transformed into a spacious, light-filled space, as for its interesting exhibits.

Museo de Historia de Madrid
(Museum of the History of Madrid)
Calle de Fuencarral, 78; tel. 91/701-1863; Tues-Sun 10am-8pm; free; Metro: Tribunal
Located on the shopping street Fuencarral, the Museum of the History of Madrid is a lavish Baroque building in a shade of pink that means it can't go unnoticed. The museum charts the lives of Madrileños and the development of their city from 1561—the year it became the Spanish capital—to the present day. The museum houses over 60,000 items related to the city's history, from paintings and maps to sculptures, furniture, and weapons. Don't miss the scale model of Madrid, made in 1830 by León Gil de Palacio, to get a sense of just how small the city was back then. Goya's

---

1: outdoor terrace on Plaza del Dos de Mayo; 2: Conde Duque Centro Cultural; 3: Fundación Mapfre; 4: Prado Museum.

painting "Allegory of the City of Madrid" is another must-see.

CHUECA
Museo del Romanticismo
(Romanticism Museum)

Calle de San Mateo, 13; tel. 91/448-0163; www.mecd. gob.es; Tues-Sat 9:30am-6:30pm, Sun 10am-3pm; €3; Metro: Alonso Martínez

Set in an 18th-century palace on an unassuming street in Chueca, the Romanticism Museum houses an interesting collection of paintings, furniture, clothing, and decorative art that gives visitors an insight into Romanticism, a cultural movement taken up by artists, intellectuals, and politicians during the first half of the 19th century. Pieces include works by Goya, Esquivel, and Madrazo, a porcelain doll collection, 15 pianos, and the pistol with which Spanish writer Mariano José de Larra committed his infamous suicide.

In the center of the museum is a tranquil courtyard café, a great spot for a leisurely summer breakfast or afternoon drink. You can buy tickets online and pick them up at the museum's ticket office. Free entry is available on Saturdays from 2pm and on Sundays.

Fundación Mapfre
(Mapfre Foundation)

Paseo de Recoletos, 23; tel. 91/602-5221; www. undacionmapfre.org; Mon 2pm-8pm, Tues-Sat 10am-8pm, Sun 11am-7pm; €3; Metro: Colón

The charitable and cultural arm of Spanish insurer MAPFRE, the Mapfre Foundation holds regular exhibitions of painting, sculpture, and photography in the grand surroundings of its museum, in a late-19th century building on the Paseo de Recoletos.

After recent renovations, it now has an exhibition space of 1,000 square meters (10,764 square feet). Although a favorite with locals, the gallery rarely features on tourist itineraries, but it should; prices are low and the museum attracts big-name exhibitions. The permanent exhibition space, the Espacio Miró, is dedicated to the work of the Catalan painter.

There's also a small exhibition hall just up the road at Calle Bárbara de Braganza, 13, so make sure you check beforehand where the exhibition you want to see is being held. You can buy tickets online or at the ticket booth at the museum. Admission is free on Mondays.

Mercado San Antón

Calle de Augusto Figueroa, 24B; tel. 91/330-0730, www.mercadosananton.com; daily 10am-midnight; Metro: Chueca

This 100-plus-year-old local market in Chueca was renovated in 2011 and reopened as a thriving gastronomic space. The ground floor has fresh food stalls, the first floor is home to stalls serving everything from regional Spanish cuisine to international flavors, and the top floor is a restaurant and roof terrace, a great place to chill on a summer's day.

BARRIO DE LAS LETRAS
Lope de Vega House Museum

Calle de Cervantes, 11; tel. 91/429-9216; www. casamuseolopedevega.org; Tues-Sun 10am-6pm; free; Metro: Antón Martín

This home in the heart of what is now Madrid's literary quarter is where Golden Age playwright Lope de Vega lived for the last 25 years of his life, until he died aged 72 in 1635. Now the Lope de Vega House Museum, the restored home is full of period furniture and artwork. Visitors can see the writer's study, as well as his dining room, bedroom, and kitchen. Don't miss the pretty courtyard, filled with orange trees.

Free 45-minute tours are available in English, Spanish, and French. Tours start every 30 minutes and must be booked in advance by telephone or email (casamuseolopedevega@madrid.org).

Mercado Antón Martín

Calle de Santa Isabel, 5; tel. 913690620; www. mercadoantonmartin.com; Mon-Sat 9am-11:30pm; Metro: Antón Martín

Straddling the neighborhoods of Las Letras and Lavapiés, Antón Martín is a thriving local market that manages to expertly mix traditional stalls selling fruit and vegetables, fish, and meat with a deli run by two Italian brothers, a vegan stall, and a cereal café.

PASEO DEL PRADO AND ATOCHA

Madrid's three most famous art galleries are handily located in the same area, at three points that form what has become known as the city's **"Golden Triangle"** of art. The Prado, Reina Sofía, and Thyssen-Bornemisza museums are all located along the Paseo del Prado, a wide, tree-lined boulevard.

TOP EXPERIENCE

★ The Prado Museum
(Museo del Prado)

Paseo del Prado; tel. 91/330-2800; www. museodelprado.es; Mon-Sat 10am-8pm, Sun 10am-7pm; €15; Metro: Banco de España

One of the world's most renowned art galleries, the Prado Museum holds three floors of treasures spanning the 12th to the early 20th centuries based on the former Spanish Royal Collection. It is the place to see works of some of Spain's greatest painters as well as masterpieces from further afield.

The grand, neoclassical building was constructed in 1785 as a Natural History Museum on the orders of Charles III. It did not become an art museum until November 1819, when it opened as the Royal Museum of Painting and Sculpture.

The three-floor museum is filled with light, and while it is seldom empty, it's spacious enough that it rarely feels too packed. Its wide, main gallery, a long corridor with curved ceilings, is lined with paintings and sculpture. It takes around three hours to see all the highlights, but a visit during the museum's free hours (the last two hours of the day) is sufficient for a whistle-stop tour of some of its major works.

The Prado will celebrate its bicentenary in 2019 with a program of events and exhibitions. An extension of the Prado, a renovation of the **Hall of Realms** (once part of the Buen Retiro Palace) by architect Normal Foster, is due to open in 2019.

TICKETS AND PRACTICAL INFORMATION

The museum's ticket office is at the Puerta de Goya on Calle Felipe IV, and the entrance is around the back at the Puerta de los Jerónimos. Avoid the lines by buying tickets online in advance.

You can pick up a floor plan and **audio guide** (€4 for the permanent collection, €3.50 for temporary exhibits, €6 for both) at the ground floor information point. Children's audio guides—aimed at 5-12-year-olds—are also available (free when rented by an accompanying adult). Audio guides are an excellent way to gain a better understanding of the history and context behind key works.

There is a café with free Wi-Fi and a bookshop stocking art books and souvenirs.

VISITING THE PRADO

The museum is laid out according to national schools. The **Spanish Painting Collection** (ground, first, and second floors) includes

Prado Fast Facts

The Prado holds 12th- to early-20th-century European art, with an emphasis on pieces from some of Spain's most famous painters.

· **Number of floors:** 3

· **Recommended visit:** 3 hours

· **Least crowded time:** 1:30pm-3:30pm (when everyone else is eating lunch)

· **Free hours:** Last two hours of each day

· **Most famous piece:** "Las Meninas" (Floor 1, Room 12)

· **Worth seeking out:** "The Cardinal" (1510-11) by Raphael, a masterpiece in Renaissance painting (Ground floor, Room 49)

pieces by Velázquez and Goya, and if you are on a tight schedule you may want to dedicate your time to these master artists. The **Italian Painting Collection** (first floor) includes Rennaissance works from Raphael to Caravaggio, and the largest collection of Venetian art outside Venice, with works by Titian, Tintoretto, Vernoses, and the Bassano. The **Early Netherlandish and Flemish Painting Collection** (ground floor) has more than 1,000 paintings, including Van der Weyden's "Virgin and Child," Bosch's "Garden of Earthly Delights," and nearly 90 works by Rubens.

The Prado also has smaller collections of French and German painters, as well as over 900 sculptures, from ancient to modern. There are also regular temporary exhibits in the Jerónimos Building, an extension off the ground floor completed in the late 2000s.

Some of the museum's highlights include:

Ground Floor:

- **"The Garden of Earthly Delights," Hieronymous Bosch (circa 1500), Room 56A:** Starting on the ground floor, this wonderfully detailed triptych depicts, from left to right, the passage from the Garden of Eden to Hell. One of the world's most famous masterpieces, its style was completely different to the Netherlandish painters of the time. On the left, God shows Adam his new creation, Eve; in the middle, on earth, humanity succumbs to carnal pleasures shown by naked women and red fruit; and on the right is the consequence—hell—with a burning city in the background.

- **"Second of May, 1808," Francisco de Goya (1814), Room 64-65:** Continue on the ground floor into room 64-65, where Goya's brutal painting depicts the uprising in Madrid on May 2, 1808 of local Madrileños against Napoleon's forces during the Peninsula War. Its companion piece, **The Third of May, 1808**, in the same room, shows the execution of locals by firing squad.

- **"Black Paintings," Francisco de Goya (1820-23), Room 67:** An entire room is dedicated to Goya's "Black Paintings," a melancholic and disturbing collection of scenes that the artist painted directly onto the walls of his house.

First Floor:

- **"The Family of Charles IV," Francisco de Goya (1800), Room 32:** What at first appears to be a regular portrait of the Spanish royal family hides secrets added by the artist, Goya. The King's brother, Infante Antonio Pascual, sports a scared look on his just-visible face. His fear might be explained by the fact that next to him in the painting is his wife, Infanta María Amalia, who had died two years before. Goya also depicts himself, in the background left-hand side of the painting, harking back to Velázquez's "Las Meninas."

- **"The Emperor Charles V at Muhlberg," Titian (1548), Room 24:** The Prado holds one of the world's most extensive collections of works by Titian, and this portrait, commemorating Charles V's victory over Protestant forces at Muhlberg, showcases the painter's masterly touch.

- **"David and Goliath," Caravaggio (circa 1599), Room 6:** Note the expert use of chiaroscuro, as seen in the contrast between David's muscular arm and back bathed in light, unlike his head, which remains in darkness.

- **"The Adoration of the Shepherds," El Greco (1614), Room 10:** Greek-born El Greco was adopted by Spain and this is considered his final painting, depicting the visit of the shepherds to the newborn baby Jesus. Note the light emanating from the baby Jesus, illuminating those gathered around him.

- **"Bearded Woman," Jose de Ribera (1631), Room 8:** Spanish painter Ribera's depiction of a bearded woman bestows a dignity onto the subject of the

Pacing Yourself at the Prado

Locals, who have the luxury of close proximity to the Prado, tend to dip into the museum to see one or two of their favorite paintings. While this strategy might not be so easy if you're intent on packing in as much as possible, you could take inspiration by pinpointing a few key painters or periods you want to see beforehand—for example Goya's "Black Paintings," or the major court paintings of Velázquez, or, better still, by planning a couple of visits (there is a "Two Visits" ticket option for €22 that counts for two separate visits to the museum in the space of a year). The Prado's website is also a good resource to consult before your visit. It has suggestions of key paintings to see during one-, two-, or three-hour visits, so you can create your own bespoke tour.

If you are on a tight schedule, one strategy would be to dedicate your time to the big Spanish masters: Velázquez and Goya.

Velázquez
Velázquez is the center of the Prado's collection, both figuratively and physically; his paintings, around 50 of the 120 he is thought to have painted, have been shown in the museum since 1899, set around his masterpiece **Las Meninas** (Floor 1, Room 12).

Don't miss Velázquez's other works, however (spread out across rooms 12, 14-16, and 18). His depiction of the mythical subject Mars in the painting "Mars" (room 15A) is arresting for its humanizing of the subject—here the god of war is shown as a dejected and mustachioed soldier, wearing nothing but his helmet and underwear, his shield at his feet. Art critics have suggested the painting could be a metaphor for Spain itself: a once-great world power that was beginning a period of decline.

Francisco de Goya
The single most represented artist in the Prado, Francisco de Goya, was still alive when the museum opened in 1819. The sheer breadth of his work and style is clear in the collection (Floor 0, rooms 64-67 and 75, and floor 1, rooms 32 and 34-38), from the seductive nude and clothed portraits of the **Maja Desnuda** and the **Maja Vestida** (room 36) to his famous depictions of the uprising of locals against French troops and their ultimate execution in **The Second of May, 1808** and **The Third of May, 1808** (rooms 64-65). An entire room is dedicated to Goya's infamous **Pinturas Negras** (Black Paintings—room 67), a nightmarish gaggle with themes of evil, terror, and death that the artist painted onto the walls of his home.

painting—Magdalena Ventura, who was married with three sons when she suddenly grew a full beard, aged 37.

- **"Las Meninas," Diego de Velázquez (1656), Room 12:** "Las Meninas" is the Prado's star attraction and has astounded and split critics for centuries. The life-size canvas depicts the Infanta Margarita Teresa, with two *meninas* (ladies-in-waiting) along with many members of the Spanish court frozen in mid-action as if in a snapshot. Rich with hidden meaning, "Las Meninas" is one of the most analyzed paintings in art history. The museum's most famous painting always has a crowd of admirers around it,

but is big enough that you can always get a decent view.

Other highlights of the Spanish collection include "Knight with a Hand on His Chest" (room 10A) by El Greco, an enigmatic portrait of a Spanish nobleman from 1580.

Museo Nacional Thyssen-Bornemisza
(Thyssen-Bornemisza Museum)

Paseo del Prado, 8; tel. 91/791-1370; www. museothyssen.org; Tues-Sun 10am-7pm, Mon midday-4pm; admission €12, reduced €8 for students with a valid student card and over 65s; Metro: Banco de España

The Thyssen-Bornemisza Museum bridges

the gap between the Prado and the Reina Sofia, with international artworks from the 13th to the 20th centuries. It is the Thyssen's extraordinary breadth of art that makes it so fascinating; it gives the visitor a rare tour of the history of almost a millennium of art, all within the walls of just one museum.

Set in the grand surroundings of the Villahermosa Palace, the museum is light, with terracotta-colored walls surrounding the artwork. It showcases one of the largest private collections in the world, started by German-Hungarian entrepreneur Baron Heinrich Thyssen in the 1920s and continued by his son, Baron Hans Heinrich and his wife, Miss Spain 1961, Carmen Cervera.

TICKETS AND PRACTICAL INFORMATION

The museum has a particularly good **audio guide** (€5), loaded with several different options, from the classic main audio guide, a two-and-a-half-hour tour that covers 50 works of art, to a handy 30-minute version that only covers masterworks. A 40-minute family tour brings paintings to life in an accessible way for younger visitors. A recent addition to the audio-guide selection is a set of themed 45-minute tours, which cover the likes of jewelry, fashion, food, and wine culture. **Multimedia guides** (€6), on a tablet with interactive information covering 39 artworks, are another interesting way to explore the museum. All guides are available at the audio-guide desk in the entrance hall.

A three-hour visit would be sufficient to explore the highlights at a leisurely pace, while an hour would give you a quick run-through of some of the main draws (the museum's floor-plan leaflet features a selection of key works and their room numbers). While it can be busy on weekends, the Thyssen tends to be quieter than either the Prado or the Reina Sofía.

A good museum shop sells the usual postcards, prints, and magnets, alongside products designed to tie in with temporary exhibits.

The museum has shorter opening hours on Mondays, but it is free all day—ticket booths are closed and visitors can just walk straight into the museum.

VISITING THE THYSSEN

The Thyssen is split into three floors, arranged in roughly chronological order, with the oldest works on the second floor and newest works on the ground floor. Start your visit by taking the elevator up to floor 2, where you will see some of the museum's oldest pieces.

Floor 2:

You'll find "The Virgin and Child Enthroned with Saints Dominic and Martin and Two Angels" (1290), the museum's oldest painting, in Room 1. It was created by the Master of the Magdalen and retains its original frame, which dates to the second half of the 13th century.

Walk along to Room 5, where you will see Hans Holbein the Younger's famous "Portrait of Henry XIII of England" (c.1537). The Tudor king appreciated Holbein's skill of painting lifelike portraits so much, he commissioned him to paint his possible future wives after Jane Seymour so he would have a good idea of what his fourth wife might look like before he met her.

An extension on the second floor houses Carmen Cervera's collection, dominated by 19th-century landscapes, as well as temporary exhibitions.

Floor 1:

Level 1 is home to Dutch painting of the 17th century as well as key works of Romanticism, Impressionism, and 19th-century American paintings. Don't miss room 32, which holds landscapes by Claude Monet ("The Thaw at Vétheuil"), Vincent van Gogh ("Les Vessenots" in Auvers), and Pierre Auguste Renoir ("Woman with a Parasol in a Garden"). In the last of these, Renoir uses a wholly impressionist style to depict a woman and man in the middle of a green countryside scene. Although many have assumed it was

1: Museo Nacional Thyssen-Bornemisza; 2: Reina Sofía; 3: Caixa Forum; 4: Palacio de Cibeles.

painted in an actual countryside, Renoir in fact painted it in the garden of his studio in Montmartre.

Ground Floor:

The ground floor is a treasure trove of 20th-century highlights, including "Hotel Room" (1931) by Edward Hopper (room 40), "Dream Caused by the Flight of a Bee around a Pomegranate a Second before Waking" (1944) by Salvador Dalí (room 45), "Harlequin with a Mirror" (1923) by Pablo Picasso (room 45), and "Woman in Bath" (1963) by Roy Lichtenstein (Room 48).

This last piece, now a classic of the Pop Art genre, sits at the end of a long corridor in Room 48, which means visitors are greeted with the arresting canvas as they walk along the gallery. It was made using the Benday dot technique, a process that had been used to print comic strips since 1879. Lichtenstein and his Pop Art contemporaries used comic book and advertising imagery to explore the connections between art and popular culture.

★ Museo Nacional Centro de Arte Reina Sofía
(Reina Sofía Museum)

Calle de Santa Isabel, 52; tel. 91/774-1000; www. museoreinasofia.es; Wed-Sat 10am-9pm, Sun 10am-7pm, Mon 10am-9pm; admission €10; Under 18s, students aged 25 and under, over 65s and disabled people can enter for free with ID; Metro: Atocha

Spain's national museum of 20th-century art, the Reina Sofía is home to a vast collection of Spanish and international art from the late 19th century to the present day.

The museum, inaugurated in 1992, is set in what was once Madrid's first general hospital; walking down its long gallery balconies, you can picture the doors that today open onto galleries, leading to the different hospital wards. The current building is Francisco Sabatini's rebuild from the early 1800s. The museum was named after (then-) Queen Sofía, and in 2005, an 8,000-square-meter (86,000-square-foot) extension, designed by French architect Jean Nouvel, opened; it

Reina Sofía Fast Facts

The Reina Sofía holds 20th-century Spanish art.

- **Number of floors:** 5
- **Recommended visit:** 3 hours
- **Least crowded time:** 1pm-3pm (Spanish lunch time)
- **Free hours:** Mon-Sat 7pm-9pm, Sun 1:30pm-7pm
- **Most famous piece:** Picasso's "Guernica" (second floor)
- **Worth seeking out:** The surrealist film "Un Chien Andalou" (1929) by Luis Buñuel is played on a loop in room 205.

houses an auditorium, a library, and new galleries for temporary exhibits.

The building is a light-filled space that is set around a central courtyard garden, an ideal place to get away from the crowded galleries and contemplate. Sculptures in the garden include "Carmen," a huge standing mobile by Alexander Calder, and "Pajaro Lunar" (Moonbird) by Joan Miró.

Two other spaces in Madrid's Retiro Park are also part of the Reina Sofía—the **Palacio de Cristal** (Crystal Palace) and the **Palacio de Velázquez** (Velázquez Palace).

TICKETS AND PRACTICAL INFORMATION

Enter the museum through the Sabatini Building or the Nouvel Building (this second entrance is usually less busy). **Audio guides** (€4.50) are available on the ground floor. These only pertain to the second floor of the museum and cover several of its most famous paintings. (The commentary is somewhat dry, but useful if you want to gain a better understanding of key works.) You can download a map from the website or pick one up from the information point on the ground floor.

A three-hour visit is enough to take in the

Picasso's Guernica

"A work of art must make a man react . . . It must agitate him and shake him up."—Pablo Picasso.

Pablo Picasso's depiction of the bombing of the Basque town of Guernica during the Spanish Civil War has come to be regarded as one of the world's most powerful portrayals of warfare, and a stinging indictment of the war that ripped the country apart between 1936 and 1939.

The huge black, white, and gray mural shows the agony, violence, and horrific results of the bombing of Guernica on April 26, 1937 by German and Italian allies of Nationalist leader General Francisco Franco. (Preliminary drawings of the mural line the walls as you make your way towards the finished piece.)

Picasso, who was exiled in Paris, completed the oil painting in June 1937. It was exhibited in the Spanish Pavillion of the Paris International Exposition in 1937 and then toured the world, bringing attention to the Spanish conflict.

Franco expressed interest in having the painting return to Spain in the late 1960s, but Picasso stipulated in his will that it should never return until Spain was a republic; it was finally returned to Spain by New York's Museum of Modern Art in 1981. A tapestry copy of "Guernica" hangs in the United Nations in New York.

As you're viewing the painting, note the following elements:

- **Women and children:** Because many of the town's men were away fighting, Guernica was full of mainly women and children on the day of the bombing. Women are the main characters in the painting, representing the innocent victims of war.

- **The chicken:** The bombardment happened on market day and animals ran away in fear.

- **The horse:** For some, this animal represents Spaniards; for others, fascism.

- **The bull** is said to represent Spain.

MADRID SIGHTS

key works at a not-too-rushed pace. The best time to visit is between 1pm and 3pm (Spanish lunchtime). Visit in the early morning and chances are you'll be sharing the space with school trips.

The gift shop is a great place to pick up some souvenirs (postcards, fridge magnets, and tote bags are favorites), while La Central bookshop, in the Nouvel building, has a good assortment of art books and some interesting souvenirs such as Salvador Dalí bags and polka dot notebooks.

The museum also offers free hours in the afternoons (Mon-Sat 7pm-9pm, Sun 1:30pm-7pm).

VISITING THE REINA SOFIA

The Sabatini building has five floors (0, 1, 2, 3, and 4)—the ground floor and third floor show temporary exhibitions, while the permanent exhibitions are spread over the first, second, and fourth floors.

The permanent exhibition includes works by Dalí, Miró, and Juan Gris, and is divided into three collections. The museum is big and can be difficult to navigate. Many visitors start on the second floor (Collection 1) at the nucleus of the Reina Sofía—Pablo Picasso's "Guernica."

Floor 2: Collection 1 (1900-1945)

Located on the second floor, Collection 1 traces the very beginnings of Spanish modern art, with the Cubism of Pablo Picasso and Juan Gris sitting alongside the more Surrealist works of Salvador Dalí (Room 205) and Joan Miró. This is where many of the museum's masterpieces are located, and the only floor that the audio guide covers. The works of Salvador Dalí can be found in room 205. Picasso's "Guernica" is in Room 206, on the second floor. The huge mural depicts the bombing of the Basque town during the Spanish Civil War. It dominates an entire wall of the room (it is forbidden to take photos of this particular painting), while the walls opposite hold 28 photographs taken by Dora Marr—Picasso's then-lover—depicting the making of "Guernica." The photos are interesting in that they reveal which elements changed over time (the fallen soldier became smaller and more disjointed) and which stayed the same (the woman cradling the dead child was present from the beginning). There are information sheets available in the room giving the history and background of the painting. The surrounding rooms, which hold art created during the Spanish Civil War, put "Guernica" in more context. They feature Civil War posters and a particularly moving set of photographs of Spanish child refugees taken by American photographer Walter Rosenblum.

Floor 4: Collection 2 (1945-1968)

Collection 2 explores the post-war period of tense geopolitical wrangling and includes works by Louise Bourgeois, Mark Rothko, Marcel Duchamp, and Claes Oldenburg.

Museum Extension: Collection 3 (1962-1982)

Collection 3, located in the museum's extension, explores political, social, and cultural changes including the 1968 uprisings, the rise of feminism, and economic crisis. Closer to home, the collection explores La Movida Madrileña, which spawned a flurry of creativity, from fanzines to photography. This section tends to have more sculptural and audiovisual works.

Caixa Forum

Paseo del Prado, 36; tel. 91/330-7330; www. caixaforum.es/madrid/home; daily 10am-8pm; €4; Metro: Atocha

Between the Prado and the Reina Sofía sits one of Madrid's lesser-known cultural institutions, the Caixa Forum. But once seen, this incredible building, which opened in 2008, is not forgotten. French botanist Patrick Blanc designed the huge vertical garden—home to 15,000 plants belonging to 250 different species—that dominates the entrace. The main building, a great example of industrial architecture, appears to levitate. Run by the social and cultural arm of Spanish bank CaixaBank, it holds regular exhibitions, talks, and

Puerta de Alcalá

workshops and houses a top floor café and a great bookshop.

Museo Nacional de Artes Decorativas
(National Museum of Decorative Arts)

Calle de Montalbán, 12; tel. 91/532-6499; www.mecd. gob.es/mnartesdecorativas/portada.html; Tues-Sat 9:30am-3pm, Thurs 5pm-8pm, Sun 10am-3pm; €3; Metro: Banco de España

Inspired by London's Victoria and Albert Museum, this four-floor museum, set in a grand building close to El Parque de Buen Retiro, focuses on the industrial arts, both from across Spain and around the world. The collection provides a fascinating glimpse of everyday items from the 14th century to the present day. There is an impressive oriental art collection, started by King Charles III, including ceramics and porcelain, glassware, furniture, and textiles, while the 18th-century tiled Valencian kitchen is a real highlight.

Museo Nacional de Antropología
(National Museum of Anthropology)

Calle de Alfonso XII, 68; tel. 91/530-6418; www.mecd. gob.es/mnantropologia; Tues-Sat 9:30am-8pm, Sun 10am-3pm; €3; under 18s and over 65s free; Metro: Atocha

This three-floor museum, located near Retiro Park and the Atocha train station, takes visitors on a tour through world cultures in its permanent exhibition, which features a range of artefacts, artwork, and clothing from indigenous cultures from the Philippines, East Asia, Africa, and the Americas. Key items in the collection include piña fabrics (traditional Philippine clothing made from pineapple-leaf fibers), Gelede masks from Nigeria, and Amazon feather adornments. A must-see, despite it not pertaining to world cultures at all, is the "Giant of Extremadura"—a 2.35-meter-tall (7 feet 8 inches) skeleton of one of the tallest Spaniards ever, Agustín Luengo Capilla.

Entry is free on Saturdays from 2pm and all day on Sundays.

Palacio de Cibeles
(Cybele Palace)

Plaza de Cibeles, 1; tel. 91/480-0008; www. centrocentro.org; exhibitions Tues-Sun 10am-8pm; viewing platform Tues-Sun 10:30am-1:30pm and 4pm-7pm; admission for viewing platform €2 adults, 50 cents for under 12s; Metro: Banco de España

Built between 1904 and 1917, the grand Cybele Palace, designed by Antonio Palacios, was originally the headquarters of the Spanish Post Office and Telegraph Company, surely making it one of the most ornate post offices in the world. Today, it is home to Madrid's City Hall and the CentroCentro cultural center; it has comfy sofas and free Wi-Fi on the ground floor and temporary exhibitions on the upper floors. Its observation platform (€2) is a great spot for views across the city to the Sierra de Guadarrama mountains beyond.

In front of the building is a huge roundabout crowned by a fountain of the Roman goddess Cybele. Made in 1782, the main figure of Cybele was sculpted by Francisco Gutiérrez. The lions, which represent the mythological characters Hippomenes and Atalanta, were sculpted by French artist Roberto Michel. Until 1862, the fountain's two standpipes provided water for water carriers, who distributed it to houses around the city. Today, the fountain is an important monument for Real Madrid fans, who congregate around it—and are known to splash around in it—after a victory.

Puerta de Alcalá

Plaza de la Independencia, 1; Metro: Retiro

The grandiose, granite Puerta de Alcalá (Alcalá Gate) was the first modern triumphal arch in Europe, older than both the Arc de Triomphe and the Brandenburg Gate. It was commissioned by Charles III in 1774 as a monumental gate in the city walls on the road

Retiro Park Walking Tour

As Madrid's green lung, Retiro Park is a popular destination for both locals and tourists, who come to walk, play sports, or have picnics on its many grassy and shady areas. To explore the park thoroughly, a walk around its key highlights will take you across its length and breadth. Walking it in one go could take an hour, but taking it at a leisurely pace, with stops to sit and soak up the atmosphere or for a drink at a little kiosk by the lake, could easily take up a whole morning or afternoon.

Retiro Park

- Enter the park from its northern end at the Retiro metro station (Line 2).

- Walk toward the estanque, or lake, Retiro's best-known spot, with its grand backdrop of a statue of King Alfonso XII. Rent a boat on the lake or snap some photos, then enjoy a caña (little beer) at one of the surrounding terraces.

- Walk toward the end of the lake, past the Alcachofa Fountain and toward the Palacio de Velázquez (Velázquez Palace), a late 19th-century neoclassic building that today houses temporary exhibits tied to the Reina Sofía Museum.

- Continue on toward one of the park's most beautiful buildings: the Palacio de Cristal, a glass and cast-iron pavilion inspired by London's Crystal Palace. It was built in 1887 to house flora and fauna from the Philippines, and today it holds temporary exhibitions organized by the Reina Sofía.

- Keep walking to the Cecilio Rodríguez gardens, towards the southwest corner of the park. Rodríguez was the director of Madrid's parks and gardens, and he designed this landscaped garden himself. He also created La Roselada, Retiro's beautiful rose garden with more than 4,000 varieties of the flower, located at the southern end of the garden.

- In stark contrast to the beauty of the rose garden is one of Retiro's most unusual monuments. El Ángel Caído (the Fallen Angel), just east of the rose garden, is said to be the only permanent public statue depicting the devil in the world.

- Walking northwest, you come to the Bosque del Recuerdo (Forest of Remembrance), 191 trees planted for the 191 victims of the 2004 terror attacks on Madrid's commuter trains.

- Keep walking northward through the greenery to Madrid's oldest tree, on Plaza Parterre, just inside the Puerta de Felipe IV: a Mexican conifer (ahuehuete) planted in 1633.

- Loop back around the lake, passing the Casa de Vacas theater and the Casita del Pescador, a little house with paintings on the façade that looks like it has stepped right out of a fairytale. It was built when Retiro was renovated in the 19th century after being badly damaged during the Peninsular War.

that led to the town of Alcalá de Henares—hence the name. The monument was designed by Francesco Sabatini, who was responsible for the Sabatini gardens next to Madrid's Royal Palace. Today it is one of Madrid's most famous landmarks and is lit up beautifully at night.

TOP EXPERIENCE

★ El Parque de Buen Retiro
(Retiro Park)

Plaza de la Independencia, 7; tel. 91/400-8740; Oct-Mar, 6am-10pm; Apr-Sept, 6am-midnight; Metro: Retiro

Madrid's most famous green space, Retiro Park is where Madrileños young and old come to relax, play sports, sunbathe, and enjoy a family day out. Originally laid out by Philip IV in the 17th century, the park was used exclusively by royalty until it was opened to the public in 1868. It's a great place to while away a weekend afternoon; you can rent a boat on the lake or enjoy a drink at one of the surrounding terraces.

On weekends, street performers surround the lake, which has a grand backdrop of a monument to Alfonso XII flanked by marble lions. The park has several playgrounds for children, and its green, shady patches are popular for weekend picnics.

ROWING IN RETIRO PARK

Renting a rowboat on Retiro's picturesque lake is an iconic Madrid experience, and fun for all the family. Boats can be rented from the wooden kiosk at the northern end of the lake for €6 per boat (for 45 mins) from Monday to Friday, and €8 on weekends and public holidays. Regular rental hours are Mon-Sun, from 10am to 5:30pm or 8:30pm (depending on the time of year). There is no shade on the lake, so make sure to take a hat/sunglasses/sunscreen in summer.

For those who don't fancy the effort of rowing, there is a solar-powered boat that chugs its way around the lake (Tues-Sun 10am-2pm, 4pm-sunset, €2). It is boarded at the same point where rowboats are rented (at the northern end of the lake).

SALAMANCA
Museo Arqueológico Nacional
(National Archeological Museum)

Calle de Serrano, 13; tel. 91/577-7912; www.man. es,general; Tues-Sat 9:30am-8pm, Sun 9:30am-3pm; admission €3; Metro: Serrano

Spain's National Archaeological Museum

MADRID
SIGHTS

Santiago Bernabéu Stadium

shares its grand building with Spain's National Library. Inside is a treasure trove of Iberian ancient history, from Roman mosaics and Moorish artefacts to intricately sculpted busts such as the "Lady de Elche," which dates to the 4th century BC. A copy of the prehistoric cave paintings of Altamira, in northern Spain, gives visitors a glimpse of one of the country's finest historic treasures—the real caves are usually closed to the public in an effort to protect the ancient artwork. Admission is free on Saturdays after 2pm and on Sunday mornings (9:30-12:30).

Mercado de la Paz

Calle de Ayala, 28; Mon-Fri 9am-8pm, Sat 9am-2:30pm; Metro: Serrano

This local food market has been going strong since 1882. This is the place to pick up fresh food for a picnic, or join the devoted locals at Casa Dani, which does a great tortilla and offers one of the best-value *menus del día* (a fixed-price lunchtime menu) in the city.

BEYOND THE CENTER
★ Santiago Bernabéu Stadium

Avenida de Concha Espina, 1; tel. 913984300; www. realmadrid.com; Metro: Santiago Bernabéu

The home of one of the world's most famous football teams, the Santiago Bernabéu has been the stage for the stars of Real Madrid since 1947, and the 80,000-seat stadium is a place of pilgrimage for many die-hard football fans.

The stadium, which was named after the former owner of the club, has held the Champions League final four times and was the host of the 1982 World Cup final.

A behind-the-scenes **stadium tour** (€25 adults, €18 children; Mon-Sat 10am-7pm, Sun 10:30am-6:30pm) is a 90-minute look around the stadium's highlights, from the dressing rooms, players' tunnel, and VIP pitch-side box to the impressive silver-filled trophy room. The self-guided tour allows visitors access to many different areas of the stadium, with ample photo opportunities (including the chance to have your photo taken with cardboard cutouts of your favorite players) and some incredible panoramic views over one of Europe's biggest football stadiums.

The Best Club Ever room includes an audiovisual display on the history of Real Madrid, as well as the team's many trophies. There is an optional interactive audio guide in English (€5).

The stadium has a reasonably priced café (Real Café) and three more exclusive restaurants: the Asador de la Esquina, Puerta 57, and Zen Market. All four have views out onto the pitch.

The Matadero

Paseo de la Chopera, 14; tel. 91/517-7309; www. mataderomadrid.org; 9am-10pm daily; free; Metro: Legazpi

The Matadero was built in 1911 as Madrid's slaughterhouse (*matadero*) and livestock market in the Arganzuela district bordering the River Manzanares. It is said Ernest Hemingway liked to come here in the early morning to watch apprentice bullfighters practice killing.

The site is constructed around several different pavilions. While they were designed as functional spaces by architect Luis Bellido, the pavilions also incorporate Neo-Mudéjar (Moorish revival architecture) flourishes such as patterned tiles, giving the whole space the air of something altogether fancier than a slaughterhouse.

After it closed in 1996, it was converted into a huge cultural center, housing spaces for exhibitions of art and design, theater, concerts, and **La Cineteca** (films €3.50), Spain's only cinema dedicated to documentaries. If you have time to catch a movie, the cinema's Azcona screening room is an incredible space; its woven walls are made from old irrigation hoses and steel tubing, all illuminated by LED tubes. (Tickets are available on the Matadero's website.)

The Matadero holds regular weekend

1: Matadero; 2: Chamberí Ghost Station – Andén 0.

Bullfighting: Culture and Controversy

a matador's 'suit of lights'

Bullfighting has long been associated with Spain, and is elegant, artistic, brutal, savage, and a tradition to be cherished or a cruelty to be banned . . . depending on who you talk to.

While some form of fighting bulls has been around since Roman times, the current style, with a matador with a cape and sword who kills a bull in the ring, first started in the 18th century in Andalusia, in southern Spain. The tradition really took off; bullrings were built in many towns and cities, and it went international, gaining fans in Mexico and other parts of South America. Matadors, with their elaborate *trajes de luces* (suits of light—so named for their reflective sequins and golden threads), became the megastars of the day.

Bullfighting quickly became entwined with Spain's image of itself and soon came to symbolize the entire country. Today in souvenir shops, bulls adorn everything from tea towels to key rings. But since the 1970s bullfighting has been in decline. Only around one in ten Spaniards ever attends bullfights, and a 2016 poll found that 19 percent of Spaniards support bullfighting while 58 percent oppose it.

Animal-rights activists have vocally campaigned against the tradition (Spain's animal-rights party, Pacma, is a key campaigner to ban bullfighting), and several towns have declared themselves "anti-bullfighting towns." The practice has been banned in the Canary Islands since 1991, and both Catalonia and the Balearic Islands have also tried to ban it. (Bullfighting is dangerous for humans as well as bulls: bullfighter Victor Barrio died in 2016 during a live televised bullfight in Teruel, the first matador to be gored to death since 1985.)

If you are thinking of attending a bullfight while in Spain, bear in mind that many Spaniards are strongly opposed to the cruelty of killing bulls "for sport." There are regular demonstrations in Madrid against bullfighting.

The debate rages over whether Spain will ever ban bullfighting. The reality is that the tradition might just peter out when it fails to attract younger fans, which has been the prevailing trend.

markets, including farmers' markets and design markets showcasing clothes, jewelery, and accessories designed by local artists. (Check the Matadero website for market times.) This is also a great stop-off point if you're walking along the city's riverside park, Madrid Rio.

Fundación Canal Isabel
(Canal Isabel Foundation)
Calle Mateo Inurria, 2; tel. 91/545-1501; www.
fundacioncanal.com; Mon-Sun 11am-8pm except Wed
11am-3pm; free admission; Metro: Plaza de Castilla

This intimate gallery lies in the shadow of the world's first leaning skyscrapers, the KIO towers, in Madrid's business district. Run by the cultural foundation of Madrid's water supplier, Canal Isabel II, it holds a varied program of temporary exhibitions, with recent shows including a retrospective of American photographer Vivian Maier, a look at the work of French painter Toulouse-Lautrec, and an exhibition charting the history of Barbara Millicent Roberts, aka Barbie. Its slightly out-of-the-center location means it's rarely packed and an under-the-radar local gem.

Chamberí Ghost Station–Andén 0
Plaza de Chamberí; tel. 90/244-4403; www.
*metromadrid.es/es/viaja_en_metro/Anden_0_y_*
museos_suburbanos/anden_0/; Thurs 10am-1pm, Fri
11am-7pm, Sat-Sun 11am-3pm; admission free; Metro:
Iglesia

Chamberi was one of the eight original stations on Madrid's first metro line, opened in 1919. In the 1960s, the introduction of new, longer trains meant station platforms had to be lengthened. There wasn't enough room to extend Chamberí's platform, so it was closed in 1966. The station could still be glimpsed when traveling in the metro between the stations of Iglesia and Bilbao, a hazy, blink-and-you-miss-it vision that intrigued commuters for decades. It was transformed into a museum, **Platform 0**, and reopened in 2008, recreating what the station would have looked like in the 1920s, complete with contemporary

advertisements, the old ticket booth, and turnstiles.

Plaza de Toros de Las Ventas (Las Ventas Bullring)
Calle de Alcalá, 237; tel. 687739032, www.
lasventastour.com; Oct-May, daily 10am-5:30pm;
June-Sept, daily 10am-6:30pm; Metro: Las Ventas

One of the world's grandest bullrings, Madrid's Plaza de Toros de Las Ventas was built in 1931 and has welcomed some of the world's most famous matadors to the ring and famous bullfighting aficionados (including Ernest Hemingway) to the stands. Designed in a neo-Mudéjar (Moorish) style, the 23,798-seat venue has an exterior punctuated with hand-painted tiles. Seat prices differ depending on how close you are to the ring, and whether you are in the sun (cheaper) or the shade (more expensive). Seating is divided into ten *tenidos*, or groups of 27 rows of seats. While the tradition has seen a wane in popularity, due in part to criticism from animal-rights activists, there are still plenty of local fans, especially during the fiesta dedicated to Madrid's patron saint San Isidro in May, when bullfights take place every day. During the general March-October season, bullfights take place every Sunday. The bullring is also the site of the **Museo Taurino**, which covers the history of bullfighting. Tours of both the bullring and museum are available. The bullring is also used as a concert venue and has hosted the likes of Coldplay and Radiohead.

Museo Taurino
Calle de Alcalá, 237; tel. 91/356-2200; www.
lasventastour.com/en/; Mon-Sun 10am-5:30pm;
Metro: Ventas

Museo Taurino, located within Las Ventas bullring, covers the history of bullfighting. Exhibits include matadors' *traje de luces* (suit of lights), as well as sections dedicated to famous bullfighters like Manolete, photographs, paintings, and other paraphernalia.

Tours, which go around both the bullring and museum, are available, with an audioguide or as a private tour (from €12.90, reservations required). The self-guided tour with audioguide takes visitors around different "stops" inside the bullring, recounting the history of the building, as well as what happens during a bullfight and the different traditions and customs associated with it. The tour ends at the small Museo Taurino. It's a good alternative if you want to learn more about bullfighting but do not want to see an actual bullfight.

Museo Sorolla
(Sorolla Museum)
Paseo del General Martínez Campos, 37; tel. 91/310-1584; www.mecd.gob.es/msorolla; Tues-Sat 9:30am-8pm, Sun 10am-3pm; admission €3; Metro: Iglesia

The Sorolla Museum showcases the life and work of Spanish artist Joaquín Sorolla (1863-1923), dubbed "the painter of light" and known for his landscapes, portraits, and socially charged paintings. The gallery, set in what was the artist's home, is an intimate space a world away from the crowds of the Prado. The building is still laid out as a home, so you can see Sorolla's light-filled studio and walk through the beautiful gardens, designed by the artist himself. Admission is free on Saturdays after 2pm and all day on Sundays.

Chapel of San Antonio de la Florida
Glorieta San Antonio de la Florida, 5; tel. 91/542-0722; www.sanantoniodelaflorida.es; Tues-Sun 9:30am-8pm; free admission; Metro: Príncipe Pío

This neoclassical chapel, next to the River Manzanares, is best known for its ceiling and dome frescoes by Francisco de Goya, which depict the miracles of St. Anthony of Padua. The present chapel was built by Felipe Fontana from 1792 to 1798 and commissioned by King Charles (Carlos) IV, along with the frescoes by Goya and his assistant, Asensio Juliá. In 1919, Goya's remains were transferred to the chapel from Bordeaux, where he had died in 1828. They were later moved to the chapel next door, specially built for services so that the original could be preserved as a monument to Goya.

On the feast of St. Anthony, June 13, unmarried women have traditionally come to the chapel to pray for a husband and to stick their hand into a fountain full of pins. According to the tradition, if one of the pins sticks to your palm, you'll soon find a husband.

Museo del Traje
(Garment Museum)
Av. Juan de Herrera, 2; tel. 91/550-4700; www.mecd.gob.es/mtraje/inicio.html; Tues-Sat 9:30am-7pm, Sun 10am-3pm; €3; Metro: Moncloa

The wonderful—and slightly off the beaten track—Garment Museum is dedicated to Spanish fashion and clothing in all its forms, from regional costumes from around Spain and historical outfits to garments by famous modern fashion designers from Spain and abroad, such as Cristóbal Balenciaga, Hubert de Givenchy, and Paco Rabanne. The museum is set in the former Spanish Museum of Contemporary Art, a modernist gray building designed by Spanish architect Jaime López de Asiain, for which he won Spain's National Architecture Award in 1969.

Museo Cerralbo
(Cerralbo Museum)
Calle Ventura Rodríguez, 17; tel. 91/547-3646; www.mecd.gob.es/mcerralbo/home.html; Tues-Wed 9:30am-3pm, Thurs 9:30am-3pm, 5pm-8pm, Fri-Sat 9:30am-3pm, Sun 10am-3pm; €3; Metro: Plaza de España

Opened in 1944 and housed in the former home of its founder, the Museo Cerralbo showcases art and historical objects collected by the 17th Marquis of Cerralbo, who died in 1922. The lavish 19th-century building is sumptuously decorated with baroque furniture, huge chandeliers, and paintings by the likes of El Greco, Jacopo Tintoretto, and Zurbarán. Don't miss the magnificent mirrored ballroom. Admission is free Thursday evenings and Sundays.

Madrid Specialties

Churros

One of the joys of Madrid is that you can sample regional specialities from all over the country, but there are certain local dishes that you definitely shouldn't miss.

- **Cocido Madrileño:** This hearty winter stew, eaten at lunchtime, is made with pork, vegetables, and chickpeas. The components are usually eaten separately: soup, chickpeas, and vegetables, then meat.

- **Callos a la Madrileña:** Madrid-style tripe might not sound like the most appetizing dish, but it is a local speciality. Made with slow-cooked beef or lamb tripe, chorizo, garlic, tomatoes, sweet paprika, and other spices, the tripe is served in a tasty stew-like sauce, which has a smoky taste thanks to the paprika.

- **Tortilla de patatas:** Spanish omelette, made with eggs, potato, and onion (there's often a debate about whether it is better with or without onion), is a tapa that you're likely to find in any bar, from firmly no-frills joints to more high-end establishments. Ask for a pintxo (*pincho*), or slice, which usually comes with a piece of crusty bread.

- **Bocadillo de Calamares:** Forget eating at one of the overpriced restaurants on Plaza Mayor. Instead, do as the locals do and get a *bocadillo de calamares*, a crusty baguette stuffed with deep-fried, battered squid rings. The side streets around the square are packed with bars selling bocadilos de calamares, which have become the typical snack associated with the area.

- **Churros and Chocolate:** A popular food whether for breakfast or a late-night snack, *churros* are served simply, with perhaps a scattering of sugar and with thick hot chocolate. **Chocolatería San Ginés** is the most famous place in Madrid to eat churros and chocolate.

Museum of the Americas

Avenida de los Reyes Católicos, 6; tel. 91/549-2641; www.museodeamerica.mcu.es; Tues, Wed, Fri, Sat 9:30am-3pm, Thurs 9:30am-7pm, Sun 10am-3pm; €3; free admission for under 18s, over 65s and students with a valid student card; Metro: Moncloa

Artefacts from Spain's American colonies furnish this fascinating museum, which gives visitors an insight into both the indigenous people of the Americas and their Spanish colonizers. The two-floor museum is split into five sections, charting the discovery of the Americas, as well as society, religion, language, and the "reality of America," which explains how the continent has developed over the centuries. The more than 25,000 objects in the collection include Mayan funeral urns and vases, Inca figurines and headdresses, and shields and clothing from around the continent. Admission is free on Thursdays from 2pm and every Sunday.

Museo Geominero
(Geology Museum)

Calle de Ríos Rosas, 23; tel. 91/349-5759; www.igme.es/museo/; Mon-Sun 9am-2pm; free; Metro: Ríos Rosas

Madrid's Geology Museum, full of dark wood cabinets, seems transported from a different age of exploration and discovery, displaying minerals and fossils from Spain and its former colonies. It is located in the headquarters of the Geological and Mining Institute of Spain, and even if you have little interest in rocks, the building and its 250 showcases are well worth a look.

Food

Madrileños love their food, for it is more than just sustenance. It's a chance to socialize and enjoy life, whether that's over a long lunch or packed into a crowded tapas bar.

Typical Madrid cuisine is hearty fare, including rich meat stews like *cocido Madrileño*, but one of the perks of visiting the Spanish capital is that its restaurants showcase cuisine from every single region of Spain. This is the best place to try Galician octopus or Andalusian fried fish outside of those regions. However, while many visitors anticipate paella, the famous dish is actually from Valencia and not a very common sight in the capital. There are a few good places to try the dish, so do your homework beforehand to avoid the low-quality tourist traps.

Surprisingly for a city that lies more than 300 kilometers (186 miles) from the sea, Madrid is home to some of Spain's best seafood. Traditionally, the best catch would be sent straight to Madrid, which is home to **Mercamadrid**, the world's second-largest fish market (after Tokyo's Toyosu market). Fish and seafood that travelers are likely to encounter on menus include *bacalao* (salt cod), *merluza* (hake), *gambas* (prawns, often served *al ajillo*—with garlic), *sardinas* (sardines), *calamari* (squid), *pulpo a la gallega* (Galician-style octopus, served with paprika), *boquerones* (anchovies), and *bonito* (tuna).

The city is also home to some fine tapas bars, where *raciónes* (larger plates for sharing) are a popular offering.

SOL AND CENTRO
Spanish
SOBRINO DE BOTÍN

Calle Cuchilleros, 17; tel. 91/366-4217; www.botin.es; Mon-Sun 1pm-4pm, 8pm-midnight; Metro: Sol

The Guinness World Records certificate in the window proves it: Sobrino de Botín is officially the world's oldest restaurant. Opened in 1725 by Frenchman Jean Botín, the restaurant was taken over by his nephew after his death—hence the name, which means "Nephew of Botín." It was a favorite of Ernest Hemingway, who mentioned the restaurant in *The Sun Also Rises* and *Death in the Afternoon*; he would scribble away there before meeting friends for lunch—no doubt ordering the speciality of roast suckling pig or roast lamb, which are still slowly cooked in the wood-fired oven that dates to 1725. Despite renovations and expansions over the years—the restaurant is now set over four floors—Botín has retained the feel of a traditional old tavern; it is cozy, warm, and convivial. While hardly a local hangout (it's much more of a tourist favorite), it is still worth a visit to enjoy dining in a little piece of living history.

Tapas
CASA ALBERTO
Calle de las Huertas, 18; tel. 91/429-9356; www. casaalberto.es; Tues-Sat midday-1:30am, Sun midday-4pm; €9; Metro: Sol
This classic old tavern in the center of Madrid opened in 1821. Sit in the front bar area and have tapas and drinks (try a vermouth, with soda water—*con sifón*—if you want to dilute it a little), or eat local classics like Madrid-style tripe and oxtail stew in the restaurant at the back. It's undeniably touristy, but one of Madrid's most historical bars.

CASA REVUELTA
Calle Latoneros, 3; tel. 91/366-3332; Tues-Sat 10:30am-4pm, 7pm-11pm, Sun 10:30am-4pm; €3; Metro: Sol
Wildly popular no-frills bar Casa Revuelta specializes in deep-fried battered cod, the bones carefully picked out by the waiters beforehand. Despite its central location, just steps from the Plaza Mayor, it's always packed with locals. Order *tajadas de bacalao* (deep-fried cod pieces) and wash down with a *caña* (little beer).

CASA DEL ABUELO
Calle de la Victoria, 12; tel. 91/000-0133; www. lacasadelabuelo.es/; Sun-Thurs midday-midnight, Fri-Sat midday-1am; €8.90; Metro: Sol
Casa del Abuelo ("Grandad's House") has been cooking up succulent garlic prawns since 1906 and is now something of a Madrid institution. Choose between

gambas a la plancha (grilled prawns) or *gambas al ajillo* (prawns fried with garlic, which arrive sizzling in a ceramic dish), washed down with a small glass of *chato*, the house sweet red wine. Its central location, just off Sol, only does prawns, whereas its other three locations do a range of traditional tapas.

MESON DEL CHAMPIÑON
Calle Cava de San Miguel, 17; tel. 91/559-6790; www. mesondelchampinon.com; Tues-Sat midday-2am, Sun-Mon midday-1:30am; €6.20; Metro: Sol
Meson del Champiñon ("House of the Mushroom") is set in a row of beautiful curved buildings that were converted from storerooms for the Plaza Mayor into restaurants and bars in the 1960s. It specializes in mushrooms, cooked on an open plancha and served sizzling hot, topped with garlic, parsley, and bacon. The key to eating the mushroom is to skewer it with two cocktail sticks then push it, whole, into your mouth to savor all the lovely juices.

★ CASA LABRA
Calle Tetuán, 12; tel. 91/531-0081; www.casalabra.es; Mon-Sun 11am-3:30pm, 6pm-11pm; Metro: Sol
The hugely popular Casa Labra has been frying up delicious pieces of battered cod (*tajadas de bacalao*—€1.45) since 1860. Try those with their other speciality, cod croquettes (€1), washed down with an ice-cold beer. Weekends can see a line out the door, so try to be strategic—off-peak hours will mean there is no line and more chance of snagging a ledge or table.

MUSEO DEL JAMÓN
Calle Mayor, 7; tel. 91/531-2367; www. museodeljamon.com; Mon-Thurs 7am-12:30am, Fri-Sat 7am-1am, Sun 10am-12:30am; Metro: Sol
Not a museum, but a bar specializing in—you guessed it—jamón, Museo del Jamón is always packed with locals enjoying a beer and a bite to eat. There's a restaurant, but do as locals do and prop up the bar, surrounded by hanging ham legs; it's a great place for a

MADRID
FOOD

cheap snack. Try some *jamón ibérico* (€13 per *ración*), or a *bocadillo de jamón* (ham baguette—€1.30). There is a counter, too, where you can buy vacuum-packed meats.

BAR LA CAMPANA

Calle Botoneras, 6; tel. 91/364-2984; Sun-Thurs 9am-11pm, Fri-Sat 9am-midnight; €2.90; Metro: Sol

Bar La Campana is the place to get a calamari sandwich, the most popular snack around Plaza Mayor. Squid rings coated in batter and deep fried are stuffed into a crusty baguette bun. The little bar has seating inside, but patrons usually spill out and sit on the plaza's benches and surrounding streets while they eat. Expect lines on weekends. Vegetarians can opt for a *bocadillo de tortilla* (tortilla baguette), another popular local snack.

Cafés

LOS PINCHITOS

Calle de Esparteros, 9; tel. 91/531-7556; Mon-Wed 8:30am-11pm, Thurs-Sun 8:30am-midnight; Metro: Sol

A traditional Spanish *cafeteria* (café) that's a firm favorite with fur-coat-wearing *abuelas*, Los Pinchitos is a great place for a cheap breakfast just off the Puerta del Sol. Churros dipped in hot chocolate or a tostada with tomato are the most popular orders. Amiable waiters take orders from the middle of a rectangular bar that dominates the middle of the space. Order at the bar, then eat there or at one of the tables.

LA CIUDAD INVISIBLE

Costanilla de los Ángeles, 7; tel. 91/542-2540; www. laciudad-invisible.com; Mon-Thurs 1pm-midnight, Fri 1pm-2am, Sat midday-2am, Sun midday-11pm; Metro: Opera

Cool café and travel bookshop La Ciudad Invisible might resemble a modern cyber café during the day—it's a popular spot with remote workers on their laptops—but it's a good place to grab a coffee and enjoy the laid-back vibe. Browse some of its many travel guides (in Spanish and English) to plan your next adventure. Staff are friendly, and the menu includes cakes, snacks, and tapas dishes.

International

FEDERAL

Plaza del Conde de Barajas, 3; tel. 91/852-6848; www.federalcafe.es; Mon-Thurs 9am-11pm, Fri-Sat 9am-midnight, Sun 9am-8pm; €4-€8; Metro: Sol

Started by an Australian couple, hip Federal is a popular brunch spot for its wide-ranging, if on the expensive side, menu of everything from pancakes to a morning bacon burger—and there are plenty of vegetarian options, too. The restaurant is on a pretty square and has a big outdoor terrace. You can find a second location at Plaza de las Comendadoras, 9, in Malasaña.

TAQUERÍA MI CIUDAD

Calle de las Hileras, 5; tel. 91/559-8711; www. taqueriamiciudad.com; Mon-Sun 1:30pm-5pm, Mon-Thurs 8pm-2am, Fri-Sun 8pm-2:30am; €1.50; Metro: Opera

The decor may be basic, but Taquería Mi Ciudad offers one of the most refreshingly spicy slices of Mexico in Madrid. Tacos, quesadillas, guacamole, and refried beans are the order of the day, accompanied by four increasingly spicy sauces and a Mexican beer or margarita. There's a stand-up little hole-in-the wall branch around the corner (Calle de las Fuentes, 11) if you just want a quick snack.

TRATTORIA MALATESTA

Calle Coloreros, 5; tel. 91/365-9097; www. trattoriamalatesta.com/; Mon-Sun 1:30pm-4pm, 8:30pm-11pm; €13; Metro: Sol

Quality Italian cuisine in the center of Madrid is the preserve of Trattoria Malatesta, a cozy restaurant with a terrace and an exposed-brick dining area downstairs that's ideal for a date. It specializes in Neapolitan-style pizzas cooked in its wood-fired oven and homemade pastas. Leave room for a dessert—the tiramisu is heavenly.

Holy Biscuits!

One of the most curious shopping experiences in Madrid has to be buying the biscuits baked by the cloistered nuns of the **Monasterio del Corpus Christi** (Plaza del Conde de Miranda, 3; Metro: Sol), founded in the 17th century. Ring the buzzer, ask for "dulces" in Spanish, and you'll be let into the convent. Walk around to a spinning tray split by a curtain. A nun on the other side (it's a closed order so she can't be seen) will ask what you'd like, and you can choose from a list fixed to the wall (half a kilogram/one pound is around €10). Biscuits come in little boxes, so are probably best eaten while in Madrid rather than taken on a flight home.

BAHIANA CLUB

Calle Conde, 4; tel. 91/541-6563; www.bahianaclub.
es; Mon-Thurs 7pm-2am, Fri 7pm-2:30am, Sat
12:30pm-2:30am, Sun 12:30pm-12:30am; €10-15;
Metro: La Latina/Sol

The laid-back Bahiana Club has a lovely outdoor terrace and is just a few minutes from the Plaza Mayor, yet it feels like it could be in a quaint Spanish village, set, as it is, on a cobbled back street. Opened by a group of Uruguayan and Brazilian friends, the restaurant's menu is a mixture of Spanish and international influences, with everything from croquettes to pizzas and Uruguayan steak.

AREPA OLÉ

Calle Postas, 26; tel. 91/364-0992; www.arepaole.
com; Mon-Sun 10am-midnight; €4.60; Metro: Sol

Just off Plaza Mayor, local chain Arepa Olé serves up Venezuelan *arepas* (corn pockets stuffed with a variety of different fillings) as well as other popular snacks like *tequeños* and yuca fries. It's a great fast-food option, whether you want to sit in (there's an outdoor terrace, too) or take away.

Bakeries and Sweets
LA MALLORQUINA

Calle Mayor, 2; tel. 91/521-1201; www.
pastelerialamallorquina.es; Mon-Sun 8:30am-9:15pm;
€1.30; Metro: Sol

One of Madrid's most famous bakeries, La Mallorquina is right on the Puerta del Sol and has been selling mouth-watering baked goods since 1894. Don't be put off by the crowds—just elbow your way in and order

their speciality, a *napolitana de chocolate*, a chocolate-filled pastry. If you ask for it to take away (*para llevar*), the white-coated staff will wrap it in their signature bright pink paper and tie it with string. On weekends you'll see lots of locals walking around with these perfectly pink packages.

EL RIOJANO

Calle Mayor, 10; tel. 91/366-4482; www.
confiteriaelriojano.com; Mon-Sun 10am-2pm,
5pm-9pm; €2.50; Metro: Sol

El Riojano, a wonderful little bakery with tantalizing displays of pastries, sweets, and local specialities like *torrijas* (a French-toast-style bread) and *buñuelos* (similar to profiteroles), was founded in 1855 by the pâtissier to the queen. There is a café at the back of the shop; it's a great place for breakfast or an afternoon pastry and coffee.

CHOCOLATERÍA SAN GINÉS

Pasadizo de San Gines, 5; tel. 91/365-6546; https://
chocolateriasangines.com; open 24 hours; Metro:
Opera

Chocolatería San Ginés in central Madrid has been making churros and chocolate since 1894. The long, donut-like fried snacks are incredibly popular with both locals and tourists, especially dunked into the thick, pudding-like hot chocolate. San Ginés is open 24 hours a day, and is a great pit stop at the end of a night out. Place your order at the bar, then hand your receipt to one of the white-coated waiters and take a seat. There can be lines, but they tend to move quickly.

MADRID
FOOD

Walking Tour of Madrid de los Austrias

Madrid de los Austrias is one of the oldest parts of the city, built during the Habsburg dynasty. The name comes from the Austrian heritage of the Hapsburgs—"Madrid de los Austrias" is "Madrid of the Austrians." Plan at least an hour to take this tour—and two or three if you want to explore the sights or stop for a drink or snack.

- Start on **Plaza Mayor**—keep an eye out for scenes from the square's history engraved onto the benches surrounding its street lights, as well as the **Casa de la Panadería** (Bakery House) on the north side of the square. Originally Madrid's main bakery, it is today the main tourist information office.

- Exit onto Calle de Toledo, noting the picturesque view from the archway looking down the street towards the dome of the church of Nuesta Señora Buen Consejo. Walk past **Casa Hernanz**, a store where *espadrilles* have been crafted since 1840.

- After Casa Hernanz, take a right and walk up Calle Cuchilleros—named after the knife-makers who used to work there. On the right side of the street is the world's oldest restaurant, **Sobrino de Botín**—proof of its claim to fame, a Guinness World Records Certificate, is framed proudly in the window. The restaurant appears in Ernest Hemingway's *The Sun Also Rises:* "We lunched upstairs at Botin's. It is one of the best restaurants in the world. We had roast young suckling pig and drank rioja alta." Hemingway, too, would often lunch on the house specialty, roast suckling pig, with friends.

- Turn left onto **Plaza de Conde de Barajas,** a tranquil square in a hectic city center that holds a Sunday art market, where local painters show and sell their work.

- Turn right and walk towards Plaza de Conde de Miranda and the **Convent of Corpus Cristi**—the cloistered nuns here make and sell their own biscuits. Look out for the "venta de dulces" sign below the door buzzer, which you should press if you want to buy some nun biscuits.

- Walk down the little alleyway by the convent and you will emerge onto **Plaza de la Villa**, a beautiful square that was the setting of Madrid's city hall, the Casa de la Villa, until the late 2000s. Take note of the different architectural styles of the three buildings on the square: to the left (standing with your back to Calle Mayor), the **Lujanes' House and Tower** was built in the 15th century—its tower features Mudéjar details. **Cisneros' House,** to the north end of the square, was built in the 16th century and features Gothic, Renaissance, and Mudéjar elements. To the right, the **Casa de la Villa,** built in the 17th century, shows a foreign influence—the triangular roofs are of the typical Austrian style of the country's Habsburg rulers.

- Walk down Calle Mayor until you come to the crossroads. To the right is the **Almudena Cathedral**, a surprisingly modern addition to Madrid's architectural scene. Despite fitting in

MADRID
FOOD

ANTIGUA PASTELERÍA DEL POZO

Calle Pozo, 8; tel. 91/522-3894; www. antiguapasteleriadelpozo.com; Tues-Sat 9:30am-2pm, 5pm-8pm, Sun 9:30am-2pm; Metro: Sol

Antigua Pastelería del Pozo, founded in 1830, is the oldest pastry shop in Madrid, and a testament to the city's traditional forms of baking. Stepping through the door is like traveling back in time; the old, wooden counters and the beautiful old till are still used today. Try its *empanadas*—pastries filled with meat or tuna—or its simple yet delicious croissant, glazed in orange.

Sobrino de Botín

well with the Royal Palace next door, the cathedral was only consecrated by Pope John Paul II in 1993. Straight on, to the left of the cathedral, is the Arab Wall, one of the oldest remnants of the city, constructed in the 9th century to surround the castle built by Muhammad I of Córdoba on the site of today's Royal Palace.

- Turn left and walk over the Segovia Viaduct. On the other side, turn left and walk up until you reach the Costanilla de San Andrés. Turn left and you emerge onto the beautiful **Plaza de la Paja**, one of Madrid's oldest market squares. Before the Plaza Mayor was built, this square was the bustling heart of the city, holding a market from the 13th century. Noble families lived in grand houses around the square; today you can visit a little-known garden of one such house, **The Garden of the Prince of Anglona**. Enjoy a drink on one of the square's lovely terraces.

- To learn more about the history of Madrid, cross the Plaza de los Carros to the **San Isidro Museum,** a fantastic free museum (usually very quiet) that recounts the history of the city using interactive displays. Named after the patron saint of Madrid, the museum also contains the Well of Miracles, where San Isidro is said to have made the waters rise to save his young son, who had fallen down the well.

- If your stomach is beginning to rumble, head to **Calle Cava Baja**, one of Madrid's most famous tapas streets. Here, stand up, pack in, and order a caña or wine to wash down some delicious tapas.

Budget
100 MONTADITOS

Plaza Puerta Cerrada, 6; tel. 90/219-7494; www. spain.100montaditos.com; Mon-Sun 9am-midnight; €1-€1.20; Metro: Sol

Spanish chain 100 Montaditos does 100 different varieties of *montadito* (or mini baguette). It has regular offers (on Sundays and Wednesdays, everything on the menu is €1) and attracts a mixed crowd, from students to little old ladies after a bargain. There are 30 locations across Madrid, including one near Plaza Mayor at Plaza Puerta Cerrada, 6.

Madrid Food Markets

Madrid's markets sell fresh produce, stuff like jamón, cheese, and olives that make ideal picnic food; they're also home to restaurant/bar stalls where you can grab a seat at a little counter and enjoy some fresh food right then and there. For diving into the food culture, the lively atmosphere, rich aromas, and delicious tastes simply cannot be beat.

Some locals still buy their fruit and vegetables and other fresh produce from the neighborhood market. Stall holders include families who have been serving Madrileños for decades and really know their stuff, making it a much more personal experience than going to a supermarket.

Mercado San Miguel is the only market on the list that does not sell fresh produce; it is solely made up of food and drink stalls selling dishes to eat there on site. Other markets, like Mercado de la Cebada, are mainly made up of fresh produce stalls, and still others are a mixture of both fresh produce and little restaurant stalls selling food and drink that you can eat at a counter.

Mercado San Miguel

- **Mercado San Miguel:** This beautifully restored wrought-iron-covered market just off the Plaza Mayor is one of the historic center's biggest tourist draws, so don't expect chill local vibes. It's worth a look, though, for its fresh tapas, tasty vermouth (Madrileños' favorite aperitif), and sweet treats (page 209).

- **Mercado San Antón:** This local market in Chueca is over 100 years old. It also holds a restaurant and roof terrace (page 222).

- **Mercado Antón Martín:** Straddling the neighborhoods of Las Letras and Lavapiés, Antón Martín contains the usual stalls, plus an Italian deli, a vegan stall, and a bakery (page 222).

- **Mercado San Fernando:** This buzzing neighborhood market in Lavapiés has a craft beer shop in its midst. Go before 11pm (closing time) on a Friday evening for a buzzing local vibe (page 219).

- **Mercado de la Cebada:** This huge local market in La Latina is noticeable for its multicolored roof. On Saturday afternoons, the fish stalls will cook up anything you buy in an informal seafood party (page 218).

- **Mercado de la Paz:** A local food market in the upmarket barrio of Salamanca. Join the locals for a great tortilla at Casa Dani (page 234).

LA LATINA

La Latina is renowned as Madrid's "tapas area," thanks in big part to one street in particular: **Calle de Cava Baja**. This street is lined with tapas bars, including some of the city's most famous, visited by everyone from the Prime Minister to people on their very first trip to Madrid. Some tapas bars are standing room only—order at the bar and pack in, balancing your drink and food on the bar or little ledges around the edge. Others have seats, and still others have restaurant areas, usually at the back.

Spanish
CASA LUCIO
Calle Cava Baja, 35; tel. 91/365-3252; www.casalucio. es; Mon-Sun 1pm-4pm, 8:30pm-midnight; €20; Metro: La Latina

Madrid institution Casa Lucio has welcomed everyone from politicians and royalty to actors and local regulars. This is the place to try Madrid classics like *cocido Madrileño*, a meat and chickpea stew, and *huevos rotos* ("broken eggs"), fried eggs with ham on a bed of potatoes. The decor is that of a 19th-century tavern, and the owner, Lucio Blázquez, presides over his beloved restaurant with wit and warmth (he began working there when he was 12, then bought the restaurant; voila, Casa Lucio was born). Reservations are highly recommended.

★ LA MUSA LATINA
Costanilla de San Andrés, 12; tel. 91/354-0255; www. grupolamusa.com/restaurante-lamusalatina; Sat-Tues 10am-1am, Wed 10am-1:30am, Thurs-Fri 10am-2am; €6/tapa; Metro: La Latina

Part of a cool young chain of restaurants in Madrid, La Musa Latina offers a modern take on tapas, with a menu of creative Spanish and international fusion dishes including *ropa vieja* (spicy pulled beef) tacos, avocado and tomato served in a "mash it yourself" pestle and mortar, roasted seabass, and hoisin-glazed short ribs. Its outside terrace is lovely, but inside the design juices are really flowing: check out the vertical garden and, downstairs, the retro video games and ping pong table. It attracts a trendy local crowd and a mixture of ages. Also great for breakfast.

★ Tapas
TXAKOLINA
Calle de Cava Baja, 26; tel. 91/366-4877; Mon-Thurs 7pm-11pm, Fri 7pm-midnight, Sat noon-1am, Sun 11am-11pm; Metro: La Latina

Txakolina specializes in Basque *pintxos*: little gourmet bites that usually come balanced atop a slice of crusty baguette. The huge *pintxos*, which range in price from €2.50-€5, are lined up on the counter, so simply point at what strikes your fancy and the barman will make you up a plate. Order a *Txakoli*, a Basque white wine, which the barman will pour into a glass from a great height to add some fizz.

★ JUANA LA LOCA
Plaza Puerta de Moros, 4; tel. 91/364-0525; www. juanalalocamadrid.com; Mon-Thurs 1pm-5pm, 7pm-midnight, Fri 1pm-5pm, 7pm-1am, Sat 1pm-7pm, 8pm-1am, Sun 1pm-7pm, 8pm-midnight; €9.50; Metro: La Latina

Juana la Loca specializes in modern pintxos. Its pintxos and sharing dishes blend traditional Spanish flavors with creative twists. According to many locals, it has the best *tortilla de patatas* in Madrid, a hefty, unctuous slice made with caramelized onions. Stand at the bar with a beer and a pintxo, or take a seat for a more leisurely meal.

★ TABERNA TEMPRANILLO
Calle Cava Baja, 38; tel. 91/364-1532; Mon 1pm-4pm, Mon-Sun 1pm-4pm, 8pm-midnight; €12; Metro: La Latina

The floor-to-ceiling wine rack dominates rustic wine bar Taberna Tempranillo on Cava Baja. It proudly sells only Spanish wines, and offers a wide selection by the glass. It has a relaxed atmosphere and a menu of traditional dishes including jamón, chorizo, cheeses, and *raciónes*, bigger tapas portions ideal for sharing.

TABERNA LA CONCHA
Calle Cava Baja, 7; tel. 61/691-0671; www. laconchataberna.com; Mon-Thurs 1pm-1am, Fri-Sun 1pm-2am; €8; Metro: La Latina

One of Cava Baja's best tapas bars, Taberna la Concha does a delicious vermouth cocktail called a Manuela and a great range of tapas, including plenty of vegetarian and gluten-free options. Don't bother with a table downstairs; this is a place to cram into the bar area with the locals and enjoy the atmosphere.

LA PEREJILA

Calle Cava Baja, 25; tel. 91/364-2855; Tues-Sun 1pm-4pm, Tues-Sat 8:15pm-1am; €10; Metro: La Latina

Walking into La Perejila is like stepping into the backstage dressing room of a vintage theater actress; there's a piano, various trinkets, a chandelier, and walls covered in old photographs, fans, and other paraphernalia. This bar does delicious *raciónes* and *rebanadas* (toasts with different toppings—€5).

Cafés
RUDA CAFÉ

Calle de la Ruda, 11; tel. 91/832-1930; www.rudacafe. com; Mon-Fri 8am-8pm, Sat-Sun 9am-8pm; Metro: La Latina

Just down from La Latina metro on the border the neighborhood shares with Lavapiés, this small café with exposed brick walls specializes in proper coffee, a caffeine kick that makes a great start to the day. There's also a selection of delicious homemade cakes and herbal teas on offer.

MARTINA COCINA

Plaza de Cascorro, 11; tel. 91/083-4380; Tues-Wed 9am-midnight, Thurs-Fri 9am-1am, Sat 10am-1am, Sun 10am-11pm; Metro: La Latina

A cozy café between La Latina and Lavapiés, Martina Cocina, with its big communal wooden table and a selection of little round tables at the back, is a popular work spot for people on laptops. Décor is distressed-cool, with exposed bulbs hanging from the ceiling. It has a range of quiches, empanadas, and more traditional breakfast staples like tomato bread, as well as an extensive menu of coffees and teas. The café is a great option for breakfast, but equally good for a quick lunch or an evening drink.

International
LEKA LEKA

Calle San Bruno, 3; tel. 91/000-5073; www.lekaleka. com; Mon-Sun 1pm-3am; €12; Metro: La Latina

This laid-back restaurant/bar on a little cobbled street just behind Cava Baja is a popular local hangout, with regular live music. Its food takes inspiration from South America and includes Venezuelan *arepas* (stuffed corn pockets) and other tasty bites. There's a cute terrace outside and a good-value *menu del día* weekday lunch (€12).

LAVAPIÉS

Until the 1980s, Lavapiés was a neighborhood mainly made up of working-class Spaniards. Thanks to its reasonable rents, it started to attract newly arrived immigrants from around the world, with large contingents from Ecuador, Morocco, Colombia, China, Senegal, and Bangladesh. Today, it is home to around 90 nationalities, leading Spanish newspaper *El País* to write "Lavapiés is almost the United Nations." The neighborhood is a tantalizing mix of traditional taverns and restaurants serving cuisine from around the world, from Indian food at Moharaj to Senegalese at Baobab.

Spanish
TABERNA EL SUR

Calle de la Torrecilla del Leal, 12; tel. 91/527-8340; Mon-Sun midday-midnight; €8; Metro: Antón Martín

Popular restaurant Taberna El Sur does a good range of Spanish and Latin American dishes, many available in half or full portions; the walls are lined with Pedro Almodóvar film posters. Try the *ropa vieja* (Cuban shredded beef) or the melt-in-the-mouth mushroom croquettes. Prices are reasonable, and the atmosphere is lively and welcoming.

Tapas
TABERNA ANTONIO SÁNCHEZ

Calle del Mesón de Paredes; tel. 91/539-7826; www. tabernaantoniosanchez.com; Mon-Sat midday-4pm, 8pm-midnight, Sun midday-4:30pm; €7-€14; Metro: Tirso de Molina

Opened by bullfighter Antonio Sánchez in 1830, Taberna Antonio Sánchez is a traditional old bar with a bullfighting theme; its walls are covered in photographs of old bullfighters, and its menu features Madrid classics like *cocido Madrileño* and *torrijas*, a Spanish riff on French toast popular at Easter.

LA BERENJENA

Calle del Marqués de Toca, 7; tel. 91/467-5297; Tues-Wed 8pm-1am, Thurs 2pm-5pm, 8pm-2am, Fri-Sat 1:30pm-2:30am, Sun 1:30pm-midnight; €10; Metro: Antón Martín

Tapas bar La Berenjena is a special find—it elevates traditional tapas with international and modern twists. It's a small space, so don't worry about elbowing your way in and balancing your plate on the bar or on the wooden ledges around the side. Dishes include fish and chips, caprese salad, and Galician-style octopus.

BAR SANTA ANA

Calle de la Ruda, 9; tel. 67/913-7988; Tues-Wed 2pm-midnight, Thurs 7pm-9pm, Fri 7pm-2am, Sat 11:30am-2am, Sun 11am-9pm; Metro: La Latina

This popular neighborhood bar makes a great pit stop while you are shopping at the surrounding El Rastro flea market on Sundays. Pack into the busy bar area, decorated with a mixture of Cuban-influenced trinkets, and order a beer. The small bar menu features some Cuban and Spanish dishes.

RESTAURANTE CASA AMADEO LOS CARACOLES

Plaza de Cascorro, 18; tel. 91/365-9439; www.loscaracolesdeamadeo.com; daily 11am-11pm; Metro: La Latina

This Rastro institution has been serving up Madrid-style snails, based on a treasured family recipe, since it opened in 1942. Try a portion from the huge vat served up by amiable owner Amadeo, who has been working the bar for 75 years (he will be 90 in 2019). Other classic tapas include chorizo, pork shoulder, and pig's ear.

TRIBUETXE

Calle del Tribulete, 23; tel. 91/139-7304; Tues-Sun 1pm-midnight; €3-8 per pintxo; Metro: Lavapiés

Delicious Basque-style pintxos are the speciality of Tribuetxe, a local favorite in Lavapiés that does a mixture of Basque and Andalusian-inspired tapas and a good range of wines by the glass. It can get very busy, so you'll most likely need to stand at the bar or around the edges while balancing your food, but pack in with the locals and prepare for your tastebuds to be thoroughly tickled.

Cafés

PUM PUM CAFÉ

Calle del Tribulete, 6; tel. 91/199-9854; www.pumpumcafe.com; Mon-Fri 9am-8pm, Sat-Sun 10am-8pm; Metro: Lavapiés

This cool café, with exposed brick walls and planters hanging from the ceiling, is a laid-back spot for breakfast or brunch. It can get busy on weekends, when the brunch crowd have been known to line up outside—such is the popularity of Pum Pum's food offerings. There are plenty of vegan and vegetarian offerings, as well as delicious homemade cakes and tasty coffee. Later in the day, the café does toasts, burgers, and salads.

International

MOHARAJ

Calle del Ave María, 18; tel. 91/527-1787; www.moharaj.com; Mon-Sun 1pm-5pm, 8pm-midnight; €10; Metro: Lavapiés

You don't go to Indian restaurant Moharaj for the décor; in fact, if you can sit on the outdoor terrace, all the better. It does do great value curries, though. Ask for dishes *mas picante* if you like spice—they tend to tone down the heat for the Spanish palate. Moharaj has all the classics, including tandoori chicken, jalfrezi, and rogan josh.

BAOBAB

Calle de Cabestreros, 1; tel. 63/211-5681; Wed-Mon 2pm-5pm, 8pm-11pm; €7; Metro: Lavapiés

Baobab does traditional Senegalese dishes like *thieboudienne*, a rice dish made with fish and tomato, and *mafe*, a meat stew with a peanut sauce. It's an authentic place that's a favorite of the local Senegalese community, and a great place to discover the country's most famous dishes.

CUTZAMALA

Calle de Santa Isabel, 5; tel. 63/892-1528; Mon-Fri 1pm-10pm, Sat midday-4pm; €7; Metro: Antón Martín

Cutzamala is a Mexican stall in Mercado de Antón Martín that, despite its diminutive size, does big flavors across dishes including pork and chicken tacos, guacamole, and quesadillas. Drinks include Mexican beers and margaritas. Customers eat at tall wooden tables and stools just next to the stall.

LA ALHAMBRA

Calle del Tribulete, 4; tel. 91/530-1823; Mon-Sun 10am-midnight; Metro: Lavapiés

La Alhambra is a Moroccan restaurant that is famous for its tagines. Don't be put off by the no-frills vibe—the rich Moroccan stews, served with couscous, really hit the spot. Cash only; be aware that no alcohol is served.

NAP

Calle del Ave María, 19; tel. 91/125-0742; Mon-Sun 1:30pm-4pm, 8pm-midnight; €9.50; Metro: Lavapiés

NAP, with its graffiti-decorated pizza oven, does an impressive take on a Neapolitan-style pizza.

LÓPEZ Y LÓPEZ

Calle de Cabestreros, 2; tel. 91/029-9926; Wed-Sun 1:30pm-5:30pm, 8pm-12:30am, Mon-Tues 8pm-12:30am; €12.50; Metro: Lavapiés

López y López is a cool local haunt that does artisanal pizzas with toppings like Catalan butifarra spicy sausage, anchovies in vinegar, and courgette and garlic. It attracts a hip young local crowd.

EGEO

Calle de San Carlos, 17; tel. 91/826-4644; www.egeolavapies.com; Mon-Tues 6:30pm-midnight, Wed 1:15pm-midnight, Thurs-Sat 1:15pm-1am, Sun 1:15pm-midnight; suvlaki €4; Metro: Antón Martín

Souvlakis, Greek pitas stuffed with chicken, pork, or pumpkin "meatballs" (the veggie option), are the speciality of Egeo, a laid-back restaurant that prides itself on using 100-percent Greek products. Order at the bar and take a seat at a wooden table in this relaxed local favorite.

MALASAÑA
Spanish
★ CABREIRA

Calle Ruis, 2; tel. 91/445-1895; www.cabreira.es/es/; Thurs-Mon 1pm-5pm, 8pm-1am, Wed 8pm-1am; €11; Metro: Tribunal

Café Comercial

Cabreira mixes traditional decor with a menu full of delicious *raciónes*. Its speciality is seafood; try the Galician octopus seasoned with paprika or the succulent garlic prawns. There are plenty of vegetarian dishes, too, from the classic *tortilla de patatas* to honey-coated aubergine and padrón peppers. Its lovely outdoor terrace, just off Plaza del Dos de Mayo, is a great place for dinner during warmer months.

OJALÁ

Calle de San Andrés, 1; tel. 91/523-2747; www. grupolamusa.com/en/ojala-restaurant; Sat-Tues 10am-1am, Wed 10am-1:30am, Thurs-Fri 10am-2am; €7; Metro: Tribunal

Whether you fancy a lazy brunch or a late-night meal, Ojalá has you covered. This local favorite features a hanging garden, wooden interiors, and a downstairs sand-covered "beach" designed by architect Andrés Jacque. Food includes modern tapas dishes, wraps, and burgers as well as international-inspired main courses like Mac 'n Cheese and Fish and Chips.

Tapas
BODEGA DE LA ARDOSA

Calle de Colón, 13; tel. 91/521-4979; www.laardosa. es; Mon-Thurs 8am-2am, Fri 8am-2:30am, Sat 11am-2:30am, Sun 11am-2am; tapas €3.25; raciónes €12; Metro: Tribunal

One of Madrid's most historic taverns, Bodega de La Ardosa has been going strong since 1892 and its popularity shows no sign of waning. Don't mind the crowds; head in, order a beer and a slice of tortilla (€2.95—said to be one of the city's best), and find a spot at one of the high barrel tables. It does a range of traditional tapas and is a good spot for a quick bite.

Cafés
CAFÉ COMERCIAL

Glorieta de Bilbao, 7; tel. 91/088-2525; www. cafecomercialmadrid.com; Mon-Fri 8:30am-2am, Sat-Sun 9am-2am; breakfast €3.80; Metro: Bilbao

Founded in 1887, Café Comercial was one of Madrid's most famous 19th-century cafés, known for its *tertulias*—literary and artistic gatherings. It closed without warning in 2015, much to the dismay of the locals, who made a shrine of little notes on its closed doors. It reopened in 2016 with new owners and a slicker design, but thankfully it has managed to retain the period features of the former, including its mirrored walls, marble columns, and revolving doors. It's a great place for a leisurely breakfast—try the chocolate and churros.

STOP Madrid

MADRID FOOD

International
ROLL MADRID

Calle de Amaniel, 23; tel. 91/805-7930; www.
rollmadrid.com; Sun-Thurs 11am-1am, Fri-Sat
11am-2:30am; €9; Metro: Noviciado

This contemporary "neo-American" restaurant and bar, set in a beautiful high-ceilinged building, is popular for everything from lazy brunches to late-night drinks. It has a good range of craft beers and is great for a more substantial breakfast or brunch (eggs, pancakes, and French toast are all delicious). Reservations can be made online.

HOME BURGER BAR

Calle de Silva, 25; tel. 91/115-1279; www.
homeburgerbar.com/; Mon-Thurs 1:30pm-4pm,
8:30pm-midnight, Fri-Sat 1:30pm-5pm,
8:30pm-midnight, Sun 1:30pm-5pm, 8:30pm-11pm;
€11; Metro: Callao

American-style diner Home Burger Bar is the place to come if you're craving a whopping great burger. Meat is 100 percent ecological and you can make any burger vegetarian, or opt for the falafel burger or vegetarian club. Try the Hickory Burger (Hickory BBQ sauce, cheddar, bacon, and onion) or the Tandoori Club sandwich. There is also a children's menu.

VEGA

Calle de la Luna, 9; tel. 91/070-4969; Mon-Sun
1pm-midnight; €7.90; Metro: Santo Domingo

Modern vegan restaurant Vega is a great option for a bargain menu del día—three hearty, nutritious courses including things like curries, rice dishes, and soups, for under €8. The atmosphere is cool, and dishes are fresh and creative with an international flavor. At night, options include Thai curry and vegan tapas.

SAN WICH

Calle de Espíritu Santo, 3; tel. 91/53145142; www.
sanwichmadrid.com; Mon-Thurs 1:30pm-4pm,
8pm-midnight, Fri-Sun 1:30pm-4:30pm,
8pm-midnight, €15, Metro: Tribunal

For a taste of Chile in Madrid, San Wich, a little sandwich shop, does Chilean hamburgers and other local favorites like empanadas, completo hot dogs (a hot dog topped with chopped tomatoes and avocado), and alfahores (a sweet snack of two cookies with a dulce de leche filling). There's a decent range of Chilean beers and wines, as well as the country's signature cocktail, the Pisco Sour. Staff are friendly and the food is delicious.

CHUECA
Spanish
BACO Y BETO

Calle de Pelayo, 24; tel. 91/522-8441; www.
baco-beto.com; Mon-Fri 8pm-1am, Sat 2pm-4:30pm,
8pm-1am; €10; Metro: Chueca

Off the tourist trail, local Chueca favorite Baco y Beto is a friendly, family-run place with a homey atmosphere. There's a front bar area where you can stand with a drink and a tapa, or a back area with tables for a sit-down meal. Its tapas and raciónes use the best local ingredients, and it has a good range of wines by the glass. Popular dishes include grilled octopus, pork marinated in bitter orange, garlic mushrooms, and plantains with guacamole.

Tapas
EL TIGRE

Calle de las Infantas, 30; tel. 91/532-00-72;
Sun-Thurs noon-1:15am, Fri-Sat noon-4am; €2.50;
Metro: Gran Vía

Unsurprisingly popular with students but usually filled with people of all ages, El Tigre is famous for its heaped plates of free tapas. Order a beer or cider (€2.50) and you'll be given a plate piled high with everything from tortilla de patatas and croquettes to little sandwiches filled with jamón. The packed crowds only add to the atmosphere at this great bargain-eating option.

★ STOP MADRID

Calle de Hortaleza, 11; tel. 91/521-8887; www.
stopmadrid.es/en/; Mon-Sun 12:30pm-2am; tapa €6;
Metro: Gran Vía

Ignoring its not-very-catchy name, STOP Madrid is one of the city's oldest taverns and a great pit stop if you're exploring Gran Vía. Opened in 1929, the bar does traditional tapas, including canapés, cold cuts, and cheeses, and a good range of wines by the glass. Alternately, try a vermouth, a fortified wine that's a favorite aperitif of Madrileños. Grab a low wooden stool and soak up the atmosphere alongside locals enjoying a leisurely glass of wine, or drop in for a quick drink while shopping on Gran Vía. Some bars in Madrid transport you back in time, and this is one of them.

International
★ YAKITORO

Calle Reina, 41; tel. 91/737-1441; www.yakitoro.com/ en/; Mon-Sun 1pm-midnight; around €5 per plate; Metro: Banco de España

The brainchild of Spanish celebrity chef Alberto Chicote, Spanish-Japanese hybrid Yakitoro specializes in yakitoros: skewers packed with different ingredients (options include eggplant tempura with red miso and paprika, crisp duck confit with spinach and orange, and grilled and caramalized beef bone marrow). The dining room is spacious, with big windows and leafy greens dotted around a central cooking station where chefs cook the skewers over charcoal, sending an incredible aroma around the room. It's a popular place, so reservations are highly recommended.

Cafés
CELICIOSO

Calle de Hortaleza, 3; tel. 91/531-8887; www. celicioso.com/; Mon-Sun 10:30am-9:30pm; €2.80; Metro: Gran Vía

Bakery and coffee shop Celicioso specializes in cupcakes, cookies, and other baked goods. All of its products are 100-percent gluten-free, and there is also a range of sugar-free options and other healthy choices like juices, protein bowls, salads, and sandwiches. It's a magnet for the trendy and health-conscious, but generally has a very mixed crowd. There are three other locations in Madrid: Calle Barquillo, 19; Plaza del Callao, 2 (Corte Inglés Gourmet Experience); and Camino de la Zarzuela, 23.

Bakeries
MAMA FRAMBOISE

Calle de Fernando VI, 23; tel. 91/391-4364; www. mamaframboise.com; Mon-Fri 9am-9pm, Sat-Sun 10am-9pm; €3.50; Metro: Chueca

Popular local bakery Mama Framboise does beautiful pastries, as well as savory snacks like sandwiches, quiche, and toasts. Its wooden tables and mismatched seating give a cool, vintage vibe, and its offerings are a real treat—raspberry croissants, macarons, and chocolates of different colors (with names like "the Audrey Hepburn" and "the Sophia Loren") are just some of the tantalizing items on offer.

BARRIO DE LAS LETRAS

Barrio de Las Letras is also known as "Huertas" for the **Calle de Las Huertas**, the area's most famous street. The narrow street, which drops steeply down through the barrio, is home to some excellent restaurants and bars and is one of the capital's favorite nighttime destinations.

Spanish
★ TABERNA MACERIA

Calle de las Huertas, 66; 91/429-5818; www. tabernamaceira.com; Mon-Thurs 1:15pm-4:15pm, 8pm-12:15am, Fri-Sat 1:30pm-4:45pm, 8:30pm-1am, Sun 1:30pm-4:45pm, 8pm-midnight; €9; Metro: Antón Martín

Taberna Maceria is a laid-back tavern with wooden tables and little stools that specializes in the cuisine of Galicia, in northwest Spain. Try pulpo a la gallega (Galician-style octopus, cooked with paprika) and pimientos de padrón (juicy, fried green peppers). Wash down the tasty food with a crisp, white Galician Albariño wine, served the traditional way in small ceramic bowls.

VI COOL

Calle de las Huertas, 12; tel. 91/429-4913; Mon-Sun 1pm-4pm, 8pm-midnight; www.vi-cool.com, €18; Metro: Antón Martín

Michelin-starred Catalan chef Sergi Arola's casual dining offering includes his take on traditional tapas. The menu is split into cold and hot *raciónes* (sharing dishes larger than tapas size), including Iberian ham with tomato, ceviche, meatballs with a Manchego cheese fondue, and Vi Cool's take on Madrid's classic calamari sandwich. The long, thin restaurant, with tables against a banquette and huge murals of classic Spanish ingredients on the walls, is a great place to taste food inspired by a Michelin-starred chef without the hefty pricetag.

Tapas

★ CASA GONZÁLEZ

Calle del León, 12; tel. 91/429-5618; www. casagonzalez.es; Mon-Thurs 9:30am-midnight, Fri-Sat 9:30am-1am, Sun 11am-6pm; €5-15; Metro: Antón Martín

Casa González, a cozy little deli/wine bar in the literary quarter of Las Letras, was founded in 1939 as a neighborhood store by Vicente González and was a popular hangout—and secret meeting place—of Republicans during the Spanish Civil War. González's descendants converted the shop into a restaurant specializing in quality Spanish produce. Grab the window seat overlooking a pretty street and sample some top-quality Spanish meats, cheeses, and tapas, as well as over 40 Spanish wines by the glass (the majority under €3). The moustachioed owner, Paco, is a friendly and welcoming presence.

EL AZUL

Calle Fúcar, 1; tel. 91/429-0773; www.elazuldefucar. com; Mon-Thurs 1pm-midnight, Fri-Sat 10am-12:30am, Sun 10am-midnight; €8.90; Metro: Antón Martín

From breakfast and brunch to its excellent value *menu del día*, El Azul offers a menu packed with delicious vegetarian fare (some meat options are available, too). Decor is Scandi-minimalist, with wooden floors and benches, and the atmosphere is laid-back and local.

ALIMENTACIÓN QUIROGA

Calle de las Huertas, 19; tel. 91/029-2863; www. alimentacionquiroga.com; Mon-Sun 9am-midnight; €6; Metro: Antón Martín

This charming deli-meets-wine-bar is a great place to sample some fabulous Spanish wines, meats, and cheeses. The place, dominated by a central wooden wine display, is surrounded by shelves of incredible gourmet ingredients from Spain and further afield. There are tables dotted around, including some high tables and stools at the back, from where you can order wine by the glass, delicious cheese and meat boards, and toasts with toppings like mushrooms, garlic and parmesan, and smoked salmon and brie.

LATERAL

Plaza Santa Ana, 12; tel. 91/420-1582; www. lateral.com; Sun-Wed midday-midnight, Thurs-Sat midday-2am; €6; Metro: Sol

Popular local tapas chain Lateral has a vast choice of good-value tapas to satisfy everyone, from the most meat-loving carnivore to strict vegetarians. Its location on Plaza Santa Ana, with both indoor and outdoor seating on a pretty terrace, is a good choice as many of the other restaurants around the popular square are overpriced.

International Bakeries

BROWN BEAR BAKERY

Calle del León, 10; tel. 91/369-0587; www. brownbearbakery.es/; Mon-Sun 8:30am-9pm; breakfasts from €2.80; Metro: Antón Martín

The cute, American-influenced Brown Bear Bakery in the Las Letras barrio is the place to come for gooey brownies, tasty loaves, and the satisfyingly large "New York Brunch" (options include pancakes, French toast, and bagels), available weekends only. There are also plenty of Spanish favorites, like *napolitanas* (a kind of chocolate croissant).

PASEO DEL PRADO AND ATOCHA

Cafés

NUBEL

Calle Argumosa 43, Reina Sofía Museum; tel. 91/530-1761; www.nubel.es; Mon, Wed, and Sun 9am-1am, Thurs 9am-2am, Fri-Sat 9am-2:30am; Metro: Atocha

This cool café/restaurant is located in the space-age Nouvel extension of the Reina Sofía Museum, and it makes a good stop-off either before or after you explore the artworks within. It is popular for brunch (€18 weekends) and is open all day, from breakfast and lunch to coffee and cake and dinner. Staff are friendly and the surroundings are stylish, with curved sofas and cool armchairs; the whole area is set under what looks like a giant red spaceship.

SALAMANCA

Spanish

CASA DANI

Calle de Ayala, 28; tel. 91/575-5925; www.casadani.es; Mon-Sat 6:30am-8:30pm; menu del día €.9.50; Metro: Serrano

If you spot a crowd in the Mercado de la Paz, chances are it's for Casa Dani, a no-frills restaurant where locals enjoy one of the best *menus del día* (fixed-price lunch menus) around. For more of a snack, order a slice of Dani's famous *tortilla de patatas*; you won't regret it. It's gooey, caramelized, and absolutely delicious. Expect to elbow your way to the bar on weekends, when it's packed.

International

STREETXO

Calle de Serrano, 52; tel. 91/531-9884; www.streetxo.com; Sun-Thurs 1:30pm-4pm, 8:30-11pm, Fri-Sat 1:30pm-4:30pm, 8:30pm-11pm; €8-€20; Metro: Serrano

If you want to try three-Michelin-star cuisine but can't afford the price tag, visit this casual dining option by Madrid's only three-Michelin-starred chef, David Muñoz. It is located in the Gourmet Experience (the top-floor gourmet food hall of the Corte Inglés department store). The bar, inspired by Asian food stalls, is extremely popular, so expect a wait. It's a frenetic, exciting place, where chefs, who cook behind the bar, serve diners themselves. The menu is dominated by spicy, far-Eastern flavors, and dishes change on a regular basis. While not Michelin prices, it is still an expensive tapas option, but worth it for the experience alone.

Cafés

CAFÉ GIJÓN

Paseo de Recoletos, 21; tel. 91/521-5425; www.cafegijon.com; Mon-Sun 7:30am-1:30am; Metro: Banco de España

One of Madrid's grand old cafés, Café Gijón was the scene of many a *tertulería* (literary discussion) during the late 19th and early 20th centuries. It became the meeting place for a group of intellectuals, writers, and artists known as the "Generation of 36." Today, little has changed of its décor—including red and white checkerboard floor, red velvet banquettes, and dark wood furniture—making it popular with tourists for its vintage ambiance. It can be a little too touristy at times, so avoid for meals; but it's worth a visit for a coffee while in the area.

BEYOND THE CENTER

Fine Dining

DIVERXO

Calle de Padre Damián, 23; 91/570-0766; www.diverxo.com/en; Tues-Sat 2pm-1am; €250; Metro: Cuzco

Madrid's only three-Michelin-starred restaurant, DiverXO is the brainchild of edgy chef David Muñoz, who earned his third Michelin star in 2014 at the age of just 34. There are two options: the WOW tasting menu (€195) or the XEF tasting menu (€250). The whole experience puts a big dose of fun into fine dining, from the décor (which includes flying pigs) and the wacky plating to the friendly staff and creative dishes, which pair unusual flavors into one harmonious whole. The dishes—including guinea fowl dumpling, monkfish macerated in maple syrup, and cotton candy ice-cream—are named "canvas 1," "canvas 2," and so on, and are artworks in their own right, explosive in both color and taste. To reserve, buy a ticket (€100) via the restaurant's website (the €100 will be deducted from your bill). Reservations up to six months in advance are recommended.

Bars and Nightlife

Madrid is famed for its nightlife, and its residents are confirmed night owls—you might be too if you had so many excellent entertainment options on your doorstep.

Spaniards like a drink, but socially, often with food, which means scenes of public drunkenness are rare. You'll notice that beer options include a *caña*, a handy small size that, in summer, means your drink won't get warm. In most places, a caña is around €2.50, while a glass of wine is around €3-€4.

Many bars open early as cafés and have an all-day existence, catering to the breakfast crowd and daytime before the after-work and nighttime crowd piles in for beers, wine, and cocktails. Bars here are multi-generational places; there is no age limit to having a good time. Most places in the capital aren't image-conscious or stuffy, and hardly any have a dress code.

NIGHTLIFE DISTRICTS

TOP EXPERIENCE

★ Malasaña

The center of the Madrid Movida (or "scene") in the late '70s and '80s, Malasaña has always been Madrid's alternative barrio with a taste for late nights and rock 'n' roll. It has transformed into Madrid's hip heartland in recent years, with a host of cool bars and indie music clubs that sit alongside some of the neighborhood's classic old bars, a few of which have been going for well over a century. In summer, the action spills out onto the streets, especially around the Plaza del Dos de Mayo, the terrace-lined square at the center of Malasaña.

Chueca

Since the '80s, the neighborhood of Chueca

cocktails in Malasaña

has transformed from a down-at-heel barrio to one of the city's most stylish, thanks in large part to the gay community, who have made Chueca Madrid's famous LGBT neighborhood. Home to classic cocktail bars, fun drag shows, and clubs, as well as the old bars that just keep on going, Chueca is a diverse and welcoming place for a party.

Calle de las Huertas

This steep street in Barrio de las Letras is packed with a great mixture of classic old places like Casa Alberto and cool, newer openings. The nearby Plaza de Santa Ana is home to the Teatro Español, a great location to see Spanish theater, and the ME Reina Victoria Hotel, home to Radio, one of the most exclusive rooftop bars in the city.

Lavapiés

This traditional working-class and immigrant neighborhood has become one of the city's coolest for its buzzing bars and interesting cultural offerings. It retains its wonderful old taverns and old-man bars alongside a raft of exciting new openings, making it a popular nightlife area with locals.

BARS

Sol and Center

PLAZA MENOR

Calle Gómez de Mora, 3; tel. 66/581-3821; Metro: Sol
Plaza Menor, a hidden gem close to the Plaza Mayor, is a series of cave-like rooms, popular with locals for a late-night cocktail or gin and tonic with a slice of cake (the carrot cake is amazing). Staff are friendly, and it's a surprisingly tourist-free spot right in the center.

BODEGAS RICLA

Calle Cuchilleros, 6; tel. 91/365-2069; Mon, Wed, Thurs 11:30am-3:30pm, 7pm-midnight, Fri 11:30am-3:30pm, 7pm-1am, Sat 12:30pm-4pm, 7pm-1am, Sun 12:30pm-5pm; Metro: Sol
This charming little bar, with bright green wooden doors and a beautiful tiled bar, is run by a mother and son and does good, cheap wine as well as some classic tapas like

boquerones (anchovies in vinegar) and cabrales cheese. It's also a great, authentic place to try one of Madrid's favorite aperitifs: *vermút de grifo*, or vermouth on tap.

La Latina

DELIC

Costanilla de San Andrés, 14; tel. 91/364-5450; www.delic.es; Tues-Thurs 11am-2am, Fri-Sat 11am-2:30am, Sun 11am-2am; Metro: La Latina
Grab an outdoor terrace seat at Delic on the beautiful Plaza de la Paja or head inside this cute bar with a vintage touch for great cocktails, snacks, and incredible desserts (the banana and dulce de leche cake is to die for).

EL VIAJERO

Plaza de la Cebada, 11; tel. 620638159; www.elviajeromadrid.com; Tues-Fri 5pm-2pm, Sat midday-2:30am, Sun midday-midnight; Metro: La Latina
Three-story bar and restaurant El Viajero in La Latina has the neighborhood's loveliest roof terrace, an intimate space with dreamy views over the barrio's domed churches. It's a great spot for a cocktail on a summer evening.

Lavapiés

CAFÉ BARBIERI

Calle del Ave María, 45; tel. 91/527-3658; www.cafebarbieri.es/; Mon-Thurs 8am-1am, Fri 8am-2am, Sat 9am-2am, Sun 9am-1am; Metro: Lavapiés
Café Barbieri has an air of crumbling elegance, and judging by the red velvet seats, marble-topped tables, and mirrored walls, little has changed since it opened in 1902. It's good for a laid-back breakfast, an afternoon coffee, or a late-night drink; musicians regularly take to the small stage at the back.

BAR BENTEVEO

Calle de Santa Isabel, 15; tel. 91/139-8503; Tues-Thurs 9am-1am, Fri 9am-2am, Sat 10am-2am, Sun 10am-1am; Metro: Antón Martín
The owners of Bar Benteveo have taken a functional, but not exactly pretty, neighborhood bar and transformed it by . . . not really doing much at all. There are a few stylish little seats here and there, but the main

red-topped bar and simple wooden tables are unchanged, giving the place a lovely mixture of the old and the new. The trendy young clientele come for everything from breakfast to beers after a film at the Cine Doré, just up the road.

SALA EQUÍS

Calle del Duque de Alba, 4; tel. 91/429-6686; www.salaequis.es; Sun-Thurs noon-1am, Fri-Sat noon-2.30am, Metro: Tirso de Molina

A bar whose previous life was as Madrid's last erotic cinema might not sound like the best idea for a night out, but Sala Equís, which opened at the end of 2017, is one of the hottest new openings in Madrid. Set in a grand old building, one screening room is now a high-ceilinged bar, the staggered levels used as seating. There's a smaller upstairs bar, and one cinema screen is still running—but these days it shows classics and indie films, many in English.

Malasaña
CAFÉ DE LA LUZ

Calle de la Puebla, 8; tel. 91/523-1199; Mon-Thurs 10am-2am, Fri-Sat 10am-2:30am, Sun 10am-1am; Metro: Gran Vía

The charming Café de la Luz is a vintage-style café just off Gran Vía with cozy sofas and a warm and welcoming atmosphere. It's open from breakfast time but is at its best after dark, when you can sink back into a soft armchair and enjoy a cocktail or two.

LOLINA'S VINTAGE CAFÉ

Calle del Espíritu Santo, 9; tel. 91/523-5859; www.lolinacafe.com; Sun-Thurs 9:30am-midnight, Fri-Sat 10am-2:30am; Metro: Tribunal

Lolina's Vintage Café is decorated like an eccentric aunt's apartment; furniture from the '60s and '70s includes fringed lamps, golden mirrors, and old radios. Like many Madrid bars, it opens early for breakfast (a bargain at €2.50) and closes late, catering to the cocktail crowd. Try one of its signature mojitos.

KIKEKELLER

Calle Corredera Baja de San Pablo, 17; tel. 91/522-8767; www.kikekeller.com; Thurs-Sat 7:30pm-3am; Metro: Callao

Interiors and furniture shop by day, cool underground bar by night, Kikekeller is a super-cool hangout that might also give you a dose of design inspiration. It's only open on Thursdays, Fridays, and Saturdays, but is a stylish and pleasingly secret bar ideal for a cocktail or gin and tonic.

Lolina's Vintage Café

FABRICA MARAVILLAS

Calle de Valverde, 29; tel. 91/521-8753; www.
fmaravillas.com; Mon-Wed 6pm-midnight, Thurs
6pm-1am, Fri 6pm-2am, 12:30pm-2am, Sun
12:30pm-midnight; Metro: Gran Vía

Despite Spaniards' affection for beer, Fabrica Maravillas is so far the only craft beer bar in Madrid with its own on-site microbrewery (just behind the bar). It's a must-visit for craft beer fans; staff are friendly and knowledgeable, and there are always several new brews to sample. The Malasaña, a light lager inspired by the surrounding neighborhood, is a refreshing light option, while there are also stouts, pale ales, and a cider.

EL JARDÍN SECRETO

Calle Conde Duque, 2; tel. 91/541-8023; www.
eljardinsecretomadrid.com; Mon-Thurs 6pm-1am,
Fri-Sat 6:30pm-2:30am, Sun 5:30pm-2:30am; Metro:
Plaza de España

El Jardín Secreto is a little bar decorated in lush tapestries and candles like something out of the Arabian Nights. It's a cool and cozy spot for a late-night cocktail and its dessert menu will be a sure-fire hit with chocoholics.

TUPPERWARE

Calle Corredera Alta de San Pablo, 26; Tues-Sat
7:30pm-3:30am, Sun 7:30pm-midnight; Metro:
Tribunal

Kitch Malasaña bar Tupperware has a 1960s vibe and eclectic music. The crowd is mixed but tends to center around thirtysomethings out for a fun but laid-back vibe. It can get pretty packed on weekends, but there's a downstairs dance floor if you want to pull a few shapes. Its exterior mural is by French street artist 3TTMan, known for his huge, colorful murals.

LA VIA LACTEA

Calle Velarde, 18; tel. 91/446-7581; Sun-Thurs
7pm-3am, Fri-Sat 7pm-3:30am; Metro: Tribunal

A popular bar during the Madrid Movida, La Via Lactea ("the Milky Way") opened in 1979 and quickly became one of the key hangouts of the Madrid "scene" of the 1980s. Its

soundtrack is pure rock 'n' roll, and it's a great place for a beer and a game of pool.

CASA CAMACHO

Calle de San Andrés, 4; tel. 91/531-3598; Mon-Fri
midday-2am, Sat midday-2:30am; Metro: Tribunal

One of Malasaña's beloved old bars, Casa Camacho has barely changed since it opened in the 1920s. It's a standing-room-only place, with wooden barrels sitting behind the bar. It can get packed at night, so head there in the early evening for a vermouth, or try the house speciality, a "yayo"—a mixture of vermouth, gin, and soda water.

Chueca

AREIA

Calle de Hortaleza, 92; tel. 91/310-0307; www.
areiachillout.com; Mon-Wed 4pm-3am, Thurs-Fri
4pm-3:30am, Sat 1pm-3:30am, Sun 1pm-3am; Metro:
Chueca

The decor at Areia—beach hut meets eastern palace—means it's a great place to chill, whether for a laid-back weekend lunch, afternoon coffee, or late-night cocktail and dance to the nightly DJ. Its comfy sofas and cushions—not to mention its indoor sandy beach—make it a cool place to lounge.

SIFÓN

Plaza del Rey, 4; tel. 91/532-6159; www.sifonmadrid.
com; Tues-Thurs 10am-midnight, Fri 10am-1am, Sat
midday-1am, Sun midday-6pm; Metro: Chueca

This cool bar (with vintage touches like wooden floors, old columns, and distressed stools) does delicious vermouth, either inside or on its outdoor terrace. A menu of tapas and *latas* (a selection of tinned fish) make an excellent accompaniment.

Barrio de Las Letras

CERVECERÍA ALEMANA

Plaza Santa Ana, 6; tel. 91/429-7033; www.
cerveceriaalemana.com; Sun-Mon 11am-12:30am,
Wed-Thurs 11am-12:30am, Fri-Sat 11am-2am; Metro:
Sol

Cervecería Alemana is one of the most emblematic bars in Madrid and was a favorite of

Ernest Hemingway (a photo of the American writer hangs above his favorite window seat). There is a good beer menu and a range of traditional tapas dishes.

LA VENENCIA

Calle Echegaray, 7; tel. 91/429-7313; Mon-Thurs 12:30pm-3:30pm, 7pm-1am, Fri 12:30pm-4pm, 7pm-1:30am, Sat 7pm-1:30am, Sun 12:30pm-4pm, 7pm-1am; Metro: Sol

Legendary Madrid sherry bar La Venencia was a popular Republican watering hole—and Hemingway hangout—during the Spanish Civil War. It upholds its socialist principles to this day, with a ban on tipping (which is contrary to socialism) and photos (in case you're a fascist spy). Order a *manzanilla*, a pale fino sherry, and prop up the bar with the regular mixture of curious tourists and old hands who have been visitng the bar for decades.

TABERNA LA DOLORES

Plaza Jesús, 4; tel. 91/429-2243; Mon-Thurs 11am-12:30am, Fri-Sat 11am-1:30am, Sun 11am-midnight; Metro: Antón Martín

You can't miss the colorful tiles outside this traditional old bar, going strong since 1908. Inside, the walls are lined with beer steins, and the best pre-lunch drink is a vermouth, said to be the ideal aperitif for its ability to whet your appetite for food.

EL IMPERFECTO

Plaza de Matute, 2; tel. 91/366-7211; Mon-Thurs 3pm-2am, Fri-Sun 2pm-2:30am; Metro: Antón Martín

Two things hit you on walking into this little bar in Las Letras: the walls covered in pop culture memorabila and the intense aroma of fresh mint, all ready for its delicious mojitos. There's a small terrace in front, but head inside to be smacked in the face (in the best possible way) by its quirky décor. There's a laid-back atmosphere in the bar, which is just as good for a smoothie or milkshake as for a late-night cocktail.

FOGG BAR

Calle de Moratín, 5; tel. 91/821-3804; www.foggbar. es; Mon-Thurs 7pm-midnight, Fri-Sat 7pm-1am; Metro: Antón Martín

This wood-clad bar in Las Letras has two specialties: craft beer and cheese. It's a great place to sample some Spanish craft beers; the bar works with a range of small breweries around the country. Cheese boards (from around €8) are artistically presented and a great accompaniment. It gets busy, so head there early—before 8pm—if you want to grab a seat.

RADIO

Plaza Sta. Ana, 14; tel. 91/701-6000; www.melia.com/ en/hotels/spain/madrid/me-madrid-reina-victoria/ the-roof; Mon-Thurs 7pm-2am, Fri 5pm-3am, Sat 1pm-3am, Sun 1pm-3am; Metro: Sol

The place to see and be seen in Madrid, Radio—the rooftop bar of the ME Reina Victoria hotel, on Plaza Santa Ana—is a glamorous spot, with panoramic views over the city's rooftops. The crowd is stylish and it's a popular place to watch the sun set—so you might end up standing rather than getting a table.

Paseo del Prado and Atocha

CÍRCULO DE BELLAS ARTES

Calle de Alcalá 42; tel. 91/360-5400; www. circulobellasartes.com/azotea; Mon-Thurs 9am-2am, Fri 9am-3am, Sat 11am-3am, Sun 11am-2am; Metro: Banco de España

One of the best rooftop bars in Madrid, Círculo de Bellas Artes will take your breath away with its panoramic views across the city. It costs €4 to go up to the rooftop, but it's well worth it for the iconic views across the Gran Vía and beyond. There are cool bed areas where you can lie down with a *tinto de verano*, a popular Sangria alternative, or high tables and stools. The atmosphere is laid-back during the day (literally), and more dressed-up by night.

Salamanca
PLATEA
Calle de Goya, 5-7; tel. 91/577-0025; www.
plateamadrid.com; Sun-Wed midday-12:30am,
Thurs-Sat midday-2:30am; Metro: Serrano

Converted 1950s cinema Platea is a feast for the senses, with food stalls, a restaurant, and a cocktail bar now inhabiting the lovingly preserved surroundings. Grab a table in the central area in front of the stage, then walk around and choose some tasty tapas options from the surrounding stalls, which include cheese, jamón, sushi, Basque pintxos, and lots of other tapas options. The stage plays host to entertainers, from DJs to acrobats.

WINE BARS
Lavapiés
LA FISNA
Calle del Amparo, 91; tel. 91/539-5615; www.lafisna.
com; Mon-Thurs 10:30am-2pm, 7pm-midnight, Fri
10:30am-midnight, Sat 1pm-4:30pm, 8pm-midnight;
Metro: Lavapiés

Wine connoisseurs will love intimate little wine bar La Fisna in the heart of Lavapiés. Its high tables are a lovely place to sit and enjoy some quality Spanish wines, all at decent prices and the vast majority available by the glass.

Barrio de Las Letras
ALIMENTACIÓN QUIROGA
Calle de las Huertas, 19; tel. 91/029-2863; www.
alimentacionquiroga.com; Mon-Sun 9am-midnight;
€12; Metro: Antón Martín

Charming deli-meets-wine bar Alimentación Quiroga has been serving excellent-quality Spanish meats and cheeses, and wine by the glass, since 1958. It started life as a shop where patrons could taste the produce before buying; now there are high tables at the back where locals enjoy wine, toasts, and platters of meat and cheese. It's the ideal place for an evening aperitif.

COCKTAIL BARS
Madrid is home to several classic old cocktail bars, where waiters are smart, the decor is vintage, and the clientele has included everyone from star bullfighters and acclaimed writers to the most famous Hollywood actors of the '50s and '60s. Many of the most famous cocktail bars are located in Chueca, just north of Gran Vía—which makes it easy to try out a few different places in one night. These cocktail bars have changed little in decades, and they tend not to subscribe to new fads; expect a list of traditional cocktails and a stylish, refined atmosphere.

Sol and Center
MUSEO CHICOTE
Gran Vía, 12; tel. 91/532-6737; www.
grupomercadodelareina.com/en/museo-chicote-en/;
Mon-Thurs 7pm-3am, Fri 7pm-3:30am, Sat 7pm-3am,
Sun 7pm-midnight; Metro: Gran Vía

Museo Chicote opened in 1931 and quickly became the center of Madrid's glamorous nightlife, over the years welcoming the biggest names in cinema and the arts, from Ava Gardner and Grace Kelly to Frank Sinatra. Sink into a cozy 1930s leather booth, backlit in pink, and enjoy an expertly mixed cocktail. Check out the wall of fame of past notable visitors in the entrance.

Malasaña
1862 DRY BAR
Calle del Pez, 27; tel. 60/953-1151; Mon-Wed
3:30pm-2am, Thurs-Fri 3:30pm-2:30am, Sat-Sun
12:30pm-2am; Metro: Noviciado

Opened in 2016, 1862 Dry Bar is one of the most popular and chic cocktail bars to open recently in Malasaña for its old-school philosophy of serving classic cocktails without messing too much with them (as can be the fashion nowadays). People tend to pack the main upstairs stand-up bar area, or head downstairs to sink into a sofa and enjoy one of the wide range of cocktails on offer.

Chueca
DEL DIEGO
Calle Reina, 12; tel. 91/523-3106; www.deldiego.com;
Mon-Thurs 7pm-3am, Fri-Sat 7pm-3:30am; cocktails
€9-€10; Metro: Banco de España

Renowned barman Fernando del Diego left his post at the nearby Museo Chicote in 1992 to open his own bar, Del Diego, an old-fashioned joint with low, wooden tables and low-hanging light shades. It's a family affair (Fernando runs the bar with his two sons), and the atmosphere is friendly, warm, and welcoming, with professional service and exemplary cocktails. Try a Del Diego, the bar's own creation of vodka, apricot brandy, and lime.

BAR COCK

Calle Reina, 16; tel. 91/532-2826; www.barcock.com; Sun-Thurs 7pm-3am, Fri-Sat 7pm-3:30am; cocktails €11; Metro: Banco de España

Suggestive name aside, Bar Cock is one of the capital's most famous cocktail bars. The high-ceilinged, wood-clad room, with its comfortable sofas and beautiful mirrored bar, has been the favorite hangout of everyone from Hemingway to Pedro Almodóvar and George Clooney.

MACERA

Calle San Mateo, 21; tel. 91/011-5810; www.maceradrinks.com; Tues-Wed 1pm-2am, Thurs 1pm-2:30am, Fri-Sat 1pm-3:30am, Sun 4pm-2am; Metro: Tribunal

Craft cocktail bar Macera makes all of its own spirits, bestowing them with incredible flavors for a truly bespoke cocktail experience. The interior is industrial-chic, and hand-labeled spirit bottles provide a cool backdrop to the bar.

LGBTQ+
Chueca
TABERNA ÁNGEL SIERRA

Calle de Gravina, 11; tel. 91/531-0126; www.tabernadeangelsierra.es; Sun-Thurs midday-2am, Fri-Sat midday-2:30am; Metro: Chueca

This old tavern was here long before Chueca cemented itself as Madrid's LGBTQ neighborhood, but today draws a diverse crowd befitting its surroundings—it even gained the official stamp of approval from Spanish film director Pedro Almodóvar, who filmed a scene of his 1995 film, The Flower of My Secret, in the bar. It's an ideal place to try a vermouth, accompanied by a snack like jamón, cheese, or empanadas.

LL SHOWBAR

Calle Pelayo, 11; tel. 91/523-3121; www.llshowbar.com; Sun-Thurs 8pm-3am, Fri-Sat 8pm-3:30am; Metro: Chueca

This bar, decked out with glitter balls and fairy lights, has been hosting drag shows for over two decades. Today, acts like Nacha La Macha and Supremme Deluxe sing, dance, and entertain the crowds (in Spanish). Shows start at around 11:30pm and are free—check who is due to perform on the bar's website.

WHY NOT?

Calle de San Bartolomé, 7; tel. 91/521-8034; daily 10am-3am

This cocktail bar is an icon of Madrid's LGBT community and is pretty much always packed (it's tiny). Its low, vaulted ceiling and baroque décor, complete with chandelier and black and white photographs of great actresses, lend it a stylish touch. It's a popular place to start a night out, with a lively atmosphere and a diverse crowd.

LIVE MUSIC
Sol and Center
EL SOL

Calle Jardines, 3; tel. 91/532-6490; www.salaelsol.com; €12 with drink; Metro: Sol

Since 1979, intimate club El Sol, in the center of Madrid, has been hosting Spanish and international bands. It was a key location of the Madrid Movida and attracted the biggest writers, actors, and directors of the day. Today, El Sol has a packed schedule of live music and DJs—check its website for upcoming shows. Concerts are usually at 10pm and DJ sets at 1am.

Barrio de Las Letras
LA FIDULA

Calle de las Huertas, 57; www.lafidula.es; Sun-Thurs 7pm-3am, Fri-Sat 7pm-3:30am; Metro: Antón Martín

Chueca: Madrid's LGBTQ+ Neighborhood

rainbow flags in Chueca

Spain's record on LGBT rights is progressive. In 2005, it was just the third country in the world to legalize gay marriage, in measures that also allowed same-sex couples to adopt.

The city's main LGBT quarter, bedecked with rainbow flags and gay-owned businesses, is Chueca, just north of the Gran Vía. The neighborhood is the epicenter of the city's huge Pride celebrations in late June and early July.

You don't have to be LGBT to enjoy Chueca; this inclusive, diverse neighborhood is for everyone.

It is also vital to point out that Madrid as a whole is an incredibly welcoming and LGBT-friendly city. LGBT visitors should feel just as safe and comfortable in any central neighborhood as they would in Chueca, so there is no need to feel like you need to stick to this area.

- **Visit Chueca** (www.visitchueca.com/en) is a great resource with lots of information about events, tours, and great new places to visit.

Neighborhood highlights include:

- **Berkana Bookshop** (Calle de Hortaleza, 62): This beloved bookstore was one of the main reference points for young LGBT Spaniards before the age of the internet.

- **Taberna Ángel Sierra:** This century-old bar is a popular hangout at the start of the night for everyone in the diverse barrio, from drag queens to little old ladies. Pack in with the locals and order a *vermút de grifo* (vermouth on tap).

- **LL Showbar:** One of the best drag clubs in the capital, there are great drag shows every night of the week.

- **Why not?:** This buzzing cocktail bar, with a low, vaulted ceiling and chandelier, packs in people at night for its lively atmosphere.

- **San Antón Market:** Renovated local market with two floors of food stalls and a rooftop restaurant and terrace.

- **Baco y Beto:** Excellent local tapas bar with mouth-wateringly good croquettes and a range of international spins on classic Spanish flavors.

Flamenco in Madrid

Flamenco dresses

One of the most enduring symbols of Spain, flamenco actually has a multiethnic provenance, with gypsy, Sephardic Jewish, and Muslim influences combining in this traditional form of dance, music, and singing. It has a strong folk tradition and grew with people who worked in the fields and the mines, much like the blues in the United States. In 2010, UNESCO named flamenco one of the Masterpieces of the Oral and Intangible Heritage of Humanity.

While it is mainly associated with Andalusia, in southern Spain, Madrid is one of the best places to see a flamenco show; many of the top dancers live in the capital and dance in some of its most famous *tablaos* (flamenco shows). Madrid's small flamenco scene is nestled among the narrow streets of Barrio de Las Letras, the literary quarter. Here you can find some of the city's most famous shows, as well as flamenco shops selling flamenco clothing, guitars, and accessories.

Some of the best *tablaos* in Madrid include:

· **Las Carboneras** (Plaza del Conde de Miranda, 1; tel. 91/542-8677; www.tablaolascarboneras. com; €36; Metro: Sol): This tablao was founded by three flamenco dancers; just near Plaza Mayor, it features twice-nightly shows (ticket options include show and drink or show and dinner) and an intimate atmosphere. Performers, including some of Spain's top flamenco dancers, rotate on a weekly basis, so there is always something new to see. Tickets can be booked online.

· **Villa Rosa** (Plaza de Santa Ana, 15; tel. 91/521-3689; www.tablaoflamencovillarosa.com; €35; Metro: Sol): Founded in 1911, this is one of the capital's oldest flamenco tablaos and is immediately recognizable by its wonderful tiled façade. Inside, the tiles continue, with Andalusian scenes on the walls. There are two flamenco shows a night and you can opt for dinner-and-show or drink-and-show tickets, which can be booked online.

· **Las Tablas** (Plaza de España, 9; tel. 91/542-0520; www.lastablasmadrid.com; €29; Metro: Plaza de España): Near Plaza de España, this is one of the capital's newer tablaos but has quickly built an excellent reputation. There are shows at 8pm and 10pm every night, and tickets can be booked online. Like the other tablaos, guests can choose whether to watch the show with dinner or with just a drink.

Since 1978, this intimate bar has been one of the best places to see live music around Huertas. The focus is on Spanish singer-songwriters, and entry is free—visitors can decide what to pay the singer after the performance. There are also regular open-mic nights; see the website for upcoming shows.

CAFÉ CENTRAL

Plaza del Ángel, 10; tel. 91/369-4143, www. cafecentralmadrid.com; Sun-Thurs 11:30am-2:30am, Fri-Sat 11:30am-3:30am; concerts around €18; Metro: Sol

Café Central has been bringing homegrown and international jazz music to Madrid since 1982, and has been named one of the best places to listen to jazz by American magazine *Down Beat*. Many acts play a short residency over a week or so; shows start at 9pm and tickets go on sale at 6pm. It's an intimate space, with a bar and dinner menu (optional) including tapas, fish, and meat dishes.

Beyond the Center
LA RIVIERA

Paseo Bajo de la Virgen del Puerto; tel. 91/365-2415; www.salariviera.com; concerts from €15; Metro: Puerta del Angel

Down the steep Calle de Segovia from La Latina is La Riviera, a popular club whose music output is eclectic, from indie concerts to electronic DJ sets. It attracts a mixed crowd depending on the event, but is always popular with a hip, twentysomething crowd. Check upcoming concerts and buy tickets on its website.

CLUBS

Clubs in Madrid are a very late-night affair—most do not open until at least midnight and don't start to fill up until around 2am. Spaniards are confirmed night owls, and clubbing until 5am-6am is perfectly common. Most clubs offer free or discounted entry for those who turn up before a certain time (usually around 1am), while those who turn up at the busiest time will pay the premium.

Clubs are generally laid-back when it comes to dress code, but it's wise to avoid flip-flops and shorts in all circumstances and go for a smart-casual look.

Chueca
DLRO LIVE

Calle Pelayo, 59; tel. 91/319-5302; Thurs midnight-5:30am, Fri-Sat midnight-6am; from €10 cover; Metro: Alonso Martínez

Gay club DLRO Live, in the heart of Chueca, is a weekend favorite with gay and gay-friendly alike. It is spread over two floors; a more chill upper floor and a downstairs dance haven. As well as nightly DJs, the club has regular live music and performers.

Paseo del Prado and Atocha
KAPITAL

Calle de Atocha, 125; tel. 91/420-2906; www. grupo-kapital.com/kapital/; Wed-Thurs midnight-5:30am, Fri-Sat midnight-6am; around €20 cover; Metro: Atocha

Kapital, Madrid's most famous megaclub, is set over seven stories and caters to a mixed crowd of locals, VIPs, and tourists. Music, too, is eclectic, from house and dance to R&B, pop, and karaoke. It hosts regular fiesta nights with top DJs. Dress code is smart.

Beyond the Center
MONDO

Calle de Alcalá, 20; tel. 69/239-7477, www. mondodisko.es; Thurs-Sat midnight-6am, from €15 cover; Metro: Sevilla

One of the city's best underground nightclubs, Mondo brings some of the world's top electronic acts to Madrid. It is the place to dance until dawn to the best DJs going—just make sure to book your tickets in advance. Ticket prices differ depending on both the DJ/act playing and the time you arrive at the club.

JOY ESLAVA

CalleArenal, 11; tel. 91/366-3733; https://
joy-eslava.com; Mon-Thurs midnight-5am, Fri-Sat
midnight-6am, Sun midnight-5:30am; Metro: Opera

Joy Eslava, set in a 19th-century theater just off the Puerta del Sol, is both a club and music venue. The club is a mixed bag, but you can guarantee a large tourist presence and the fact that it will be open 365 days a year. It's worth checking upcoming gigs, as it's an intimate concert venue that attracts some great bands.

Performing Arts

From one of Spain's finest opera houses, the Royal Theatre, to intense flamenco shows and indie cinemas, Madrid's performing arts scene has something to suit every taste.

THEATER
TEATRO ESPAÑOL

Calle del Príncipe, 25; tel. 91/389-6335; www.
teatroespanol.es/; prices depend on the show, from
€5; Metro: Sol

Teatro Español, on Plaza de Santa Ana, opened in 1895 on the site of a Medieval open-air theater. The faces of famed playwrights are engraved onto the façade, among them Federico Garcia Lorca, who was murdered during the Spanish Civil War. The 763-seat space plays host to regular performances of both classic works and more modern plays in Spanish, which sometimes have English subtitles.

TEATRO LARA

Calle Corredera Baja de San Pablo, 15; tel.
91/523-9027; www.teatrolara.com; prices depend on
the show, from €7; Metro: Santo Domingo

Hidden behind an unassuming façade, the beautiful Teatro Lara dates back to 1880. The main theater, which holds 480 people, is plush, with decorative gold balconies looking out onto a sea of red velvet seats in the stalls. Today it hosts plays and concerts by Spanish and international artists. Check the upcoming program and buy tickets on the theater's website.

CINEMAS

Madrileños love going to the cinema. To see films in English, not dubbed into Spanish, look on the cinema's website (or at the box office) for the original version subtitled in Spanish ("VOSE"). Tickets at major cinema chains are around €10, but afternoon showings tend to be slightly cheaper.

CINE DORÉ

Calle de Santa Isabel, 3; tel. 91/369-3225; www.mecd.
gob.es/cultura/areas/cine/mc/fe/cine-dore.html; box
office: 4:15pm-15 mins before the last film; €2.50 or
€2 for students; Metro: Antón Martín

One of Madrid's oldest cinemas, the Cine Doré is a must-visit for cinephiles, who will fall in love with its art-deco façade, foyer café, and packed schedule of old and modern classics. The cinema, which dates back to the 1910s, survived bombing during the Civil War and today is home to the Filmoteca Española, charged with preserving old film stock. Each month it runs a different film program, showcasing a particular theme or the work of a particular actor or director. Previous seasons have included the films of Pedro Almodóvar and Gus Van Sant. It shows English-language films in English with Spanish subtitles.

CINE IDEAL

Calle del Dr Cortezo, 6; tel. 91/369-0669; www.
yelmocines.es/cartelera/madrid/yelmo-cines-ideal;
Metro: Tirso de Molina

Originally opened in 1916, Cine Ideal shows all the latest releases on its nine screens. Most films are shown in the original language with Spanish subtitles, so you can avoid the dubbing that is so prevalent in many Spanish

1: Teatro Español; 2: Cine Doré.

cinemas. Buy tickets and choose your seats online or at the box office.

AUTOCINE MADRID RACE

Calle de la Isla de Java, 2; tel. 67/574-4984; www. autocinesmadrid.es; Metro: Begoña

Autocine Madrid RACE became the largest drive-in cinema in Europe when it opened in early 2017, with space for 350 cars. In summer, there are 150 deck chairs for those who didn't drive. It screens a variety of films, from old classics to new blockbusters (at the time of writing, all films were dubbed into Spanish, but there are plans to offer original-version options with Spanish subtitles in the near future). There's also a diner where you can have drive-in staples like burgers and hot dogs (€5-€15) delivered right to your car. Most showings are after 10pm, so the crowd is more adults than families.

Festivals and Events

Easter/Holy Week

Various locations

Holy week begins in earnest on **Jueves Santo** (Holy Thursday), and continues over the long Easter weekend. Brotherhoods belonging to different churches around the city parade huge statues of Christ and the Virgin Mary. Penitents dress in hooded robes, while women wear the traditional lace *mantilla*, or religious veil. The parades, with their heady incense, shrieking trumpets, and crashing percussion, are a feast for the senses. Central parades go down Calle Mayor and across the Plaza Mayor—times are published on local tourism websites, such as www.esmadrid.com, in the run-up to Easter. Make sure to eat some *torrijas*, a Spanish version of French toast that is popular at Easter, which are sold at Easter in most local bakeries and in markets such as Mercado San Miguel.

Festival of San Isidro
MAY 11-MAY 15

Various locations including Plaza Mayor, Plaza del Oriente, and San Isidro Park; www.sanisidro.madrid.es

Madrid celebrates its patron saint, San Isidro Labrador, with music, dancing, and religious services. During the festivities, attendees don traditional dress and dance *chotis*. Many festivities are centered around San Isidro Park (Paseo de la Ermita del Santo, 74; Metro: Marqués de Vadillo), just south of the river, where families take picnics. Free events such as concerts take place in the Plaza Mayor, where a temperory stage is usually set up, as well as many other locations around the city, including the Debod Temple, Retiro Park, and Las Vistillas park. The *Gigantes y Cabezudos* (Giants and Bigheads) parade takes place in the center, around Plaza de la Villa (but locations change, see official website), during which huge papier-mâché models in traditional dress are paraded through the streets. Bullfights take place every day for 20 days, attracting some of the most famous matadors to Las Ventas Bullring.

Veranos de la Villa
(Summer in the City)
JUNE-SEPTEMBER

Various locations; www.veranosdelavilla.com/en/

Madrid City Council plans an interesting schedule of both free and ticketed events from June through September under the banner Summer in the City, from street performances and dancing to theater, cinema, and children's activities. Check the website for program details. It mainly attracts locals, but is well worth seeking out some of the public performaces if you happen to be visiting the city over the summer.

Mulafest
LATE JUNE
Av. Partenón, 5; tel. 90/222-1515; www.mulafest.com; day tickets €15, weekend tickets €36 when purchased on the Mulafest website

This urban trends festival, which takes place in the huge surroundings of Madrid's IFEMA conference center (around 30 minutes north of the city center on public transport), near the metro station Feria de Madrid (line eight—the light pink line) at the end of June, includes performances by some of the world's best DJs and electronic artists, as well as a tattoo convention, skate park, and urban beach. It's popular with young Madrileños in their late teens and twenties, as well as locals of all ages interested in alternative culture.

Madcool
JULY
IFEMA conference center, Av. Partenón, 5; tel. 90/222-1515; www.madcoolfestival.es; three-day ticket from €150, day tickets from €76

This rock and alternative music festival has attracted the likes of The Who, Neil Young, and Foo Fighters. With a new location in the cavernous grounds of the IFEMA conference center, 30 minutes north of Madrid, the festival is expected to attract around 80,000 people each day. The three-day festival takes place in July.

Madrid Pride
LATE JUNE/EARLY JULY
Various locations; www.madridorgullo.com

Madrid is a great LGBT+ destination, and there is no better time to feel the inclusive, fun-loving atmosphere than during the city's pride celebrations, one of the biggest in the world, welcoming around 2 million people every year. Festivities include a drag queen stiletto race, concerts by international artists (with stages around the city including at the Puerta del Sol and the Puerta de Alcalá), and a huge Pride march down the Paseo del Prado. Accommodation gets booked up well ahead of time, so it might be more expensive to visit during this week. Make sure to book in advance.

Verbenas
AUGUST
Various locations

There are three different *verbenas* (open air festivals) that take place in central Madrid in August. **San Cayetano** (Aug 2-8) in the Embajadores area, **San Lorenzo** (Aug 9-11) in Lavapiés, and the biggest, **La Paloma** (Aug 12-15) in La Latina, are fiestas dedicated to three of Madrid's patron saints. The city's old streets are decked with colorful bunting, and restaurants set up open-air bars on the street. Locals wear traditional dress and dance the traditional *chotis* in the street. The fiestas are also a chance for locals to let their hair down and party well into the night.

Madrid International Jazz Festival
NOVEMBER
Various locations including Conde Duque Cultural Center and Fernán Gómez Centro Cultural de la Villa; www.festivaldejazzmadrid.com

Performers from around the world descend on Madrid for the city's International Jazz Festival, Jazz Madrid. Performances take place at venues around the city, including the Conde Duque Cultural Center in Malasaña (Calle Conde Duque, 11) and the Fernán Gómez Centro Cultural de la Villa, in Salamanca (Plaza de Colón, 4). Along with live jazz, the festival includes films, discussions, and lectures related to the genre. Find information about performances and venues on the festival's website.

Plaza Mayor Christmas Market
DECEMBER 1-31
Plaza Mayor, Mon-Thurs 9am-9pm, Fri-Sun 9am-10pm

Madrid goes festive in the run-up to Christmas with its main Christmas market on Plaza Mayor. It sells mainly figures for nativity scenes and other decorations, as well as silly hats and wigs for people to wear on December 28, the *Día de los Santos Inocentes*—Spain's version of April Fool's Day. The city puts on a special Christmas bus, **Naviluz**, an open-topped bus that takes you around the city's Christmas lights. The bus runs from the very end of November to the first week of January. Tickets can be purchased online (www.esmadrid.com/en/whats-on/christmas-bus). The buses run around every five minues from Plaza de Colón, and the Christmassy journey takes around 40-50 minutes. Tickets cost €3 and under-sevens go free. (Wrap up and stay warm!)

While Plaza Mayor is Madrid's main Christmas market, there are also smaller seasonal markets around the city, including at **Plaza Isabel II**, in front of the Teatro Real (selling mainly Christmas sweets like *turrón*), **Plaza de Callao**, and **Plaza España** (a market selling artisanal produce from around Spain).

New Year's Eve
Puerta del Sol

Every New Year's Eve, Madrileños pack the Puerta del Sol to count down to midnight from the big clock on the Casa de Correos building, to the south of the square. As per tradition, people eat 12 grapes—one for every

stroke of midnight, which is said to bring good luck for the year ahead. The festivities from the square are broadcast across Spain on national television.

Three Kings Day Parade
JANUARY 5
Central Madrid, from Nuevos Ministerios and ending at Plaza de Cibeles

In Spain, the Epiphany is more important than Christmas Day; it is a public holiday, and traditionally it is the Three Kings who bring children presents, not Santa Claus, making January 5 a night of feverish excitement for Spanish children. Madrid hosts a huge Three Kings parade, which starts at around 6:30pm at Nuevos Ministeros and makes its way down the Paseo de la Castellana, finally ending at Plaza de Cibeles in front of the City Hall. The floats carry wonderful characters including the Three Kings themselves, who throw out sweets for eager little hands to catch.

Most Spaniards spend January 6 with family, eating the traditional *Roscón de Reyes*, or Kings' Cake, a round glazed cake with a hole in the middle that you'll notice in many bakery shop windows in the run-up to January 6.

Shopping

Unlike other European capitals, Madrid has managed to resist the total takeover by big chains. They're there, but so are the old, family-run shops that have been expertly making one quality product for generations. From traditional Spanish capes, fans, and flamenco attire to shops specializing in leather goods, shoes, or even potato chips, there is a good range of these little shops to explore.

Bear in mind that smaller shops in Madrid (i.e., non-chains) usually open from around 9am-2pm, then close over lunch and open again from around 4pm-8pm.

SHOPPING DISTRICTS
Gran Vía and Fuencarral

Gran Vía, Madrid's most famous street, was built in the early 1900s, its grand buildings displaying a range of architectural styles. Today, it is one of the city's main shopping streets and is home to major Spanish fashion stores like Zara and Mango, as well as a range of shoe shops, sports boutiques, and bookstores.

Fuencarral, a pedestrianized street that leads from Gran Vía metro station up into Malasaña, is one of Madrid's most popular shopping streets and is home to both local and international brands. From global names like Muji and New Balance to cool Spanish labels like Kling, and a number of good shoe and makeup shops, there is plenty of choice for those wanting to hit the shops.

Malasaña

Malasaña is the place to go for vintage stores and offbeat finds, as well as cool young designers and boutiques. **Calle Valarde**, just off Plaza del Dos de Mayo, is particularly lined with vintage stores, while many of the other streets just off the square are dotted with little boutiques, bookstores, and one-off shops where you might pick up a unique souvenir.

Salamanca

High-end fashion mavens should head straight to Salamanca, Madrid's most luxe neighborhood. Running north from the Puerta de Alcalá, **Calle de Serrano** is known as the city's "Golden Mile" of designer stores, featuring everything from Spanish names like Ágatha Ruíz de la Prada, Balenciaga, and Manolo Blahnik to the likes of Chanel, Dior, and Louis Vuitton. You will also find large branches of Spanish high-street favorites like Zara and Mango.

SOL AND CENTRO
Clothing and Accessories
CAPAS SESEÑA

Calle de la Cruz, 23; tel. 91/531-6840; www.sesena.com/en/; Mon-Fri 10am-8pm, Sat 10:30am-8pm; Metro: Sol

Perhaps the ultimate souvenir—if you have the money to spare—is a Spanish cape (from €470) from Capas Seseña. The Seseña family has been hand-crafting capes since the shop opened in 1901, and today it is said to be the only shop in the world that is entirely dedicated to capes. It is said Picasso asked to be buried in one, and they have graced the shoulders of everyone from Luis Buñuel to Bruce Springsteen.

TALLER PUNTERA

Plaza Conde de Barajas, 4; tel. 91/364-2926; www.puntera.com; Mon-Sat 10am-2:30pm, 4pm-8:30pm, Metro: Sol

Taller Puntera is more than just a leather shop; it is a workshop open to the public, where visitors can see the leather being crafted and peruse the shelves packed with beautiful leather goods, from colorful satchels to bags, belts, and wallets. Prices range from around €20 for a small card wallet to upwards of €200 for bags. The spacious shop also holds regular leather-working classes, if you want to go a step further than buying.

MATY

Calle Maestro Victoria, 2; tel. 91/531-3291; www.maty.es; Mon-Fri 10am-1:45pm, 4:30pm-8pm, Sat 10am-2pm, 4:30pm-8pm; Metro: Sol

Delve into the gigantic dress-up box that is Maty for flamenco dresses, skirts, and accessories, including castanets, flowers for your hair, fans, earrings, and more. The Aladdin's cave of dressing up doesn't stop at flamenco; there are outfits fit for any costume party.

NATURA

Calle Postas, 16; tel. 91/169-7292; www.naturaselection.com; Mon-Sat 10am-10pm; Metro: Sol

Clothes for women (with a few options for men), homewares, and travel and lifestyle items can all be found at Spanish chain Natura, established in Barcelona in 1992. The brand has a strong focus on sustainability and gives some of its proceeds to environmental projects including forest protection and health care. Clothing has a relaxed vibe, with floaty trousers and pretty, patterned tops and dresses for between €20-€50, while the travel section—including things like passport holders and inflatable pillows—could come in handy for your trips.

CASA DIEGO

Puerta del Sol 12; tel. 91/522-6643; www.casadediego.info; Mon-Sat 9:30am-8pm; Metro: Sol

Casa Diego has been making beautiful

abanicos (Spanish fans), along with umbrellas, walking sticks, and traditional shawls, since 1858. The family-run business has even provided the Spanish royal family with all their accessory needs. The small shop on the Puerta del Sol consists of a glass-fronted counter holding fans, from behind which smart shop assistants produce an array of products for customers to peruse.

GUANTES LUQUE

Calle de Espoz y Mina, 3; tel. 91/522-3287; www. guantes-luque.negocio.site; Mon-Fri 10am-1:30pm, 5pm-8pm, Sat 10:30am-1:30pm; Metro: Sol

Hand-made gloves in supple leather are the speciality of Guantes Luque, just off the Puerta del Sol, but the family-run business, which was founded in 1912, makes almost any kind of glove imaginable, in a huge variety of materials, styles, and price ranges. They make a lovely souvenir from one of Madrid's most traditional old shops.

ZARA

Gran Vía, 34; tel. 91/521-1283; www.zara.com; Mon-Sun 10am-10pm; Metro: Gran Vía

The jewel in the crown of Spanish fashion behemoth Inditex, Zara is Spain's most famous fashion brand. Its Gran Vía store is spread over four floors and has clothes and accessories for women, men, and children. Prices tend to be cheaper in Spain than in Zara stores abroad.

REAL MADRID OFFICIAL STORE

Gran Vía, 31; tel. 91/755-4538; www.shop.realmadrid. com; Mon-Sat 10am-9pm, Sun 11am-8pm; Metro: Gran Vía

For every imaginable souvenir linked to Madrid's most famous football club, this spacious store has you covered. Football shirts, caps, scarves, mugs, keyrings, and more make great souvenirs or gifts for sports fans. There are several shops around the city, including at Calle del Carmen, 3 and Calle del Arenal, 6.

ALMACEN DE PONTEJOS

Calle del Correo, 4; tel. 91/521-5594; www. almacendepontejos.com; Mon-Fri 9:30am-2pm, 4:30pm-8:15pm, Sat 9:30am-2pm; Metro: Sol

Just south of the Puerta del Sol, around the little square of Plaza de Pontejos, is Madrid's traditional textile district, home to some haberdashery shops that have been open for well over a century. Almacen de Pontejos has been keeping locals stocked up with buttons, thread, zips, and fabric since it opened in 1913. It's one of Madrid's perfectly preserved old shops, where assistants disappear into the burrows of back rooms to find exactly the right item for customers. Keen crafters might pick up some gems.

Shoes
CASA HERNANZ

Calle de Toledo, 18; tel. 91/366-5450; www. alpargateriahernanz.com; Mon-Fri 9am-1:30pm, 4:30-8pm, Sat 10am-2pm; Metro: Sol

Casa Hernanz, just off Plaza Mayor, has been making *espadrilles* since 1840. The summer favorite for women, men, and children comes in hundreds of different designs and colors. Expect lines out the door in summer. Service is brusque, but you can nab a Spanish classic from €10 upwards.

Food and Wine
LA VIOLETA

Plaza de Canalejas, 6; tel. 91/522-5522; www. lavioletaonline.es; Mon-Sat 10am-8pm; Metro: Sol

La Violeta has been making violet-flavored sweets for decades, in homage to the flower of Madrid. The beautifully wrapped packages, which locals give as traditional presents for everything from birthdays to Holy Communions, make a lovely gift.

CASA MIRA

Carrera de S. Jerónimo, 30; tel. 91/429-8895; www.casamira.es/; Mon-Sat 10am-2pm, 5pm-9pm, Sat 10am-2pm, 5pm-9pm, Sun 10:30am-2:30pm, 5:30pm-9pm; Metro: Sol

When 21-year-old Luis Mira came to Madrid

Best Souvenirs

If you're eager to bypass the typical tourist merchandise and take home something a little more special from Madrid, consider one of the following items.

FOOD AND DRINK

Spanish classics, including **saffron**, a bottle of local **vermouth** or **wine**, and local **La Violeta candies** (available from **La Violeta,** Plaza de Canalejas, 6), all make lovely gifts.

For gourmet food, consider browsing markets like **Mercado Antón Martín**, as well as the ninth-floor **Gourmet Experience** of the Corte Inglés department store (Plaza del Callao). Smaller specialty shops like **Alma de Julián Becerro** (Calle Cava Baja, 41) and **Los Ferreros** (Calle Ciudad Rodrigo, 5) are also good options. Something particularly "in" at the moment in Madrid is tinned fish, or conserves. They come in tins with amazing designs and can be picked up in any supermarket, as well as more gourmet shops. Tuna, sardines, and the like are a great addition to a self-made Spanish hamper once you get home.

FANS

The first mention of fans in Spain was in the royal court of the 14th century, and over the years, the intricately decorated items became an essential accessory for high society ladies (there was even a "secret language of fans" during the 19th century, when ladies who were out with chaperones could send secret messages to their potential suitors by holding their fans in a certain way). Today, it's common to see Spanish women with fans—they are a handy way to cool yourself in summer. **Casa Diego** has been making the traditional Spanish accessory for over 150 years.

LEATHER

Spain is known for its leather goods. **Taller Puntera**, a leather workshop and store, has a great range of bespoke items, from coin purses to handbags, that have been made right there on site.

ESPADRILLES

The rope-soled shoe was originally a typical footwear of the working classes before being catapulted into fashion's consciousness when Lauren Bacall wore a pair in the film *Key Largo* (1948). This Spanish summer staple crops up in shops across the city, but one of the oldest makers of the rope-soled shoes is **Casa Hernanz**, just off Plaza Mayor.

FLAMENCO ACCESSORIES

Whether you want some castanets or decide to really do it up with a flamenco dress, **Maty** has you covered.

CAPES

Capas Seseña is allegedly the only place in the world that's dedicated to capes and capes alone. Picasso reportedly requested to be buried in one of their traditional Spanish designs.

FOOTBALL GEAR

Football fans should visit Real Madrid's official shop if they would like a football shirt to take home, or browse any number of souvenir shops for scarves, keyrings, and mugs sporting the slogans of Real Madrid or Atletico Madrid.

from Valencia and started selling his *turrón*, a nougat treat popular at Christmas, he probably did not expect that his business would be going strong more than 170 years later. Casa Mira, with its rotating window displays packed with tantalizing treats, still specializes in *turrón*, alongside other local sweets.

LOS FERREROS

CalleCiudad Rodrigo, 5; tel. 91/548-0223; Mon-Fri 10am-3pm, 6pm-10pm, Sat 10am-4pm; Metro: Sol

Los Ferreros, just off the Plaza Mayor, is in its fourth generation of ownership by the Ferrero family and has been selling local meats, cheeses, and other Madrid produce for over a century. The shop is small, and lined on three sides with glass-fronted fridges holding an array of meats and cheeses. Stock up on local wines, a bottle of vermouth, or some paprika and saffron to take home as mementos of Madrid, all while supporting a local family-run business.

Design and Décor
MADRID AL CUBO

Calle de la Cruz, 35; tel. 62/745-2053; Mon-Fri 10:30am-10pm, Sat 11am-10:30pm, Sun 11am-3pm; Metro: Sol

Skip the tourist shops around Puerta del Sol and try Madrid al Cubo if you're looking for a more creative souvenir. The little shop sells a range of Madrid-themed products, many designed by local artists. From artwork, coasters, and books to T-Shirts, *Lolea sangria* (look out for its fun, polka dot bottles), and unusual postcards, this is a one-stop shop for quirky mementos.

EL JARDÍN DEL ÁNGEL

Calle de las Huertas, 2; tel. 91/369-7932; www. jardindelangel.es; Mon-Sun 10am-9pm; Metro: Antón Martín

El Jardín del Ángel, a florist and homewares shop at the top of Huertas, is worth visiting just to see its wonderfully decorated front garden and showroom. The small garden, which used to be the cemetery of the adjoining church, is strewn with fairy lights and bird boxes. Inside, plants are on show alongside other products such as furniture and garden accessories. Smaller, suitcase-friendly souvenirs include ceramic garlic graters, candle holders, and little plant pots.

La Central

Lottery Lineup

Doña Manolita

If you're in Madrid in the run-up to Christmas and see an endless crowd of people lining up just off the Puerta del Sol, chances are they're waiting to buy a lottery ticket at **Doña Manolita** (Calle del Carmen, 22; tel. 91/522-7639; www.loteriamanolita.com; Mon-Fri 9am-8:30pm, Sat 9:30am-8:30pm, Sun 10am-8:30pm; Metro: Callao/Sol). This tiny shop, which consists of a glass-fronted counter with staff on one side and customers on the other, has become famous throughout Spain for its luck in getting the winning ticket in Spain's famous Christmas Lottery. People come from around Spain just to buy a ticket, with most buying a *décimo*, or a tenth of a ticket, for €25.

Books
LA CENTRAL
Calle del Postigo de San Martín; tel. 91/790-9922; www.lacentral.com; Mon-Thurs 10am-9:30pm, Fri-Sat 10am-10pm, Sun 11am-9pm; Metro: Callao

La Central, a large, spacious bookshop, with other outposts in Barcelona and the Reina Sofía museum, is a great place to browse. Its over 70,000 volumes include good English-language, children's, and recipe book selections. It's also a good place to pick up an unusual gift; each floor has a small gift area with items like tote bags, notebooks, and calendars. There is a café at the back of the store, where you can read in peace.

OCHO Y MEDIO
Calle de Martín de los Heros, 11; tel. 91/559-0628; Mon-Thurs 11am-12:30am, Fri 11am-1am, Sat midday-1am; Metro: Plaza de España

Just off Madrid's most cinematic street, Gran Vía, which at one time was home to dozens of cinemas, is the wonderful Ocho y Medio, which specializes in books—in Spanish and English—all about the silver screen. It also stocks films, film posters, and other paraphernalia and has a cute café, the ideal place for a post-movie analysis.

CASA DEL LIBRO
Gran Vía, 29; tel. 90/202-6402; www.casadellibro.com; Mon-Sat 9:30am-9:30pm, Sun 11m-9pm; Metro: Gran Vía

Founded in 1923, Casa del Libro (House of the Book) is one of Spain's most famous bookshop chains. The Gran Vía store is its largest and has a huge range of books. While most are in Spanish, there are well-stocked English, French, and German sections.

Music
FELIPE CONDE GUITARS
Calle de Arrieta, 4; tel. 91/541-8738; www. condehermanos.com; Mon-Fri 9am-2pm, 5pm-8pm, Sat 10am-1:30pm; Metro: Opera

Since 1915, the Conde family has been handcrafting guitars for everyone from flamenco legend Paco de Lucía to Bob Dylan and Leonard Cohen. Felipe Conde Guitars is an intimate store and workshop where you can see the beautifully made instruments in person. They're not cheap (from €2,355 to upwards of €10,000), but if you're in the market for a guitar, you can't beat the quality and craftsmanship that goes into these classic models.

Department Stores
EL CORTE INGLÉS
Plaza del Callao, 2; tel. 91/379-8000; www. elcorteingles.es; Mon-Sat 10am-10pm, Sun 11am-9pm; Metro: Callao

Spain's most famous and last remaining department store chain, El Corte Inglés (which translates as "The English Cut") has branches across the city. Its most central are located on Plaza del Callo (home to the Gourmet Experience food court on the ninth floor, with views over the iconic Schweppes sign on Gran Vía) and Calle de Preciados, 3, its original building, just off the Puerta del Sol. It sells everything from clothing and homeware to electrical products, books, and music. Both central branches have a supermarket in the basement, a good place to stock up on local produce.

LA LATINA
Food and Wine
ALMA DE JULIÁN BECERRO
Calle de Cava Baja, 41; tel. 91/366-1524; www. julianbecerro.com; daily 10am-10pm; Metro: La Latina

Among the tapas bars on Cava Baja, this gourmet food shop is an excellent place to pick up some of Spain's most famous food: *jamón Ibérico*, or acorn-fed Iberian cured ham. The Becerro family have been producing the finest Spanish ham since the 1930s, and in this shop, decked in hanging ham legs, you can pick up vacuum-packed meats that will travel easily.

CARAMELOS PACO
Calle de Toledo 53-55; tel. 91/354-0670; www. caramelospaco.com; Mon-Sat 10am-2pm, 5pm-9pm, Sun 11am-3pm; Metro: La Latina

It will be hard for lovers of candy to walk past the window display of this beloved neighborhood sweet shop, which has been drawing children to press their noses against the window in wide-eyed delight since it opened in the 1930s. It's a great place to stock up on Spanish candies, whether to take home or to enjoy as you wander the city. Sugar-free and gluten-free varieties are also available.

LAVAPIÉS
Markets
GALERÍAS PIQUER
Calle de la Ribera de Curtidores, 29; Mon-Fri 11am-2pm, 5pm-8pm, Sat-Sun 11am-2pm; Metro: La Latina

Just off the main drag of the Rastro flea market (Ribera de Curtidores) is this wonderful gallery of antique shops and bric-a-brac stalls that, on Sundays and public holidays, becomes an extension of the market itself. Most of the 70 shops, set over two levels, are relatively modern, but stock a selection of vintage gems, from furniture and lighting to old magazines, clothing, and jewelry.

Music
DISCOS SATÉLITE
Calle de la Ribera de Curtidores, 8; tel. 66/964-5590; Mon-Fri 5pm-9pm, Sat-Sun 10am-2pm; Metro: La Latina

The Rastro flea market might be most famous for its antiques, but it is also a great place to hunt for vinyl LPs. This record shop, along the market's main street of Ribera de Curtidores, stocks an eclectic range of genres. Whether you're looking for '60s rock or '80s Spanish pop, you're bound to come away with a great find. It is especially busy with record fans on Sundays when the market is on.

MALASAÑA
Clothing and Accessories
LA INTRUSA
Calle Corredera Alta de San Pablo, 33; tel. 91/445-7170; www.laintrusashowroom.com; Mon 4pm-9pm, Tues-Sat 11am-9pm; Metro: Tribunal

La Intrusa brings together women's clothes and jewelry as well as artwork by Spanish designers, and it is a great place to pick up a unique souvenir from Madrid. Clothing is quirky, with patterned T-shirts and cute and colorful dresses and skirts. Jewelery includes unusual necklaces, earrings, and bracelets by local designers at a reasonable price. There is another shop in Las Letras (Calle de León, 17).

MAGPIE VINTAGE
Calle Velarde, 3; tel. 91/448-3104; www.magpie.es/; Mon-Sat 11am-9pm, Sun 1am-8pm; Metro: Tribunal

Whether you fancy a pair of vintage sunglasses, a 1960s miniskirt, or some authentic '80s sportswear, look no further. Magpie Vintage is a hodge-podge of men's and women's clothes and accessories from throughout the 20th century. This vintage clothing shop is a great place if you love to root out a bargain.

KLING
Fuencarral, 71; tel. 91/521-5779; www.kling.es/; Mon-Sun 11am-9pm; Metro: Tribunal

Spanish brand Kling does bright, vintage-themed womenswear and accessories, inspired by everything from 1960s mods to 1990s grunge. The store is spread over two floors, a bright and spacious upstairs and a smaller basement where the fitting rooms are located. There is an outlet store at Calle del Duque de Alba, 10, a great place to nab a bargain.

Design and Décor
NEST
Plaza de San Ildefonso, 3; tel. 91/523-1061; www.nest-boutique.com; Mon-Fri 11am-2:30am, 4pm-8:30pm, Sat 11am-8:30pm, Sun-midday-7pm; Metro: Tribunal

Nest sells beautiful gifts, jewelery, and other quirky items—including maps of Madrid designed by local artists, wrapping paper with classic record covers, red lip-shaped jewelery holders, and vintage-style postcards—and it is one of the only places in the city that sells cards (Spaniards don't tend to send birthday or greeting cards). The shop is festooned with bunting, and its walls and tables are covered in lovely products, from fairy lights to diaries. There's a Baby Nest section at the back for children.

CURIOSITE
Calle Corredera Alta de San Pablo, 28; tel. 91/141-3305; www.curiosite.es; Mon-Sat 11am-9pm; Metro: Tribunal

Full of offbeat gift ideas (ham-leg cushion, anyone?), Curiosite will keep the kids amused and might just be where you pick up some of your most unusual souvenirs from Madrid. With items for tech enthusiasts, keen travelers, and lovers of all things weird and wonderful, it's a fun place to browse. Products range from the humorous—Gin and Titanic ice-tray molds in the shape of the ill-fated ship and the iceberg that sank it—to kid-friendly buys like inflatable globes and unicorns and giant coloring-in posters.

DISEÑO, OBJETOS Y OTRAS COSAS
Calle del Espíritu Santo, 27; tel. 91/070-1654; www.dooc.eu; Mon-Sat 11am-3pm, 5pm-9pm; Metro: Tribunal

Diseño, Objetos y Otras Cosas ("Design, Objects and Other Things"), in the heart of Malasaña, is a great place to find unusual and off-the-wall interior inspiration, from neon lamps to lipstick-themed mirrors. There are items for every room of the house that start at reasonable prices.

Books
J&J BOOKS AND COFFEE
Calle del Espíritu Santo, 47; tel. 91/521-8576; www. jandjbooksandcoffee.es; Mon-Thurs 4pm-11:30pm, Fri 4pm-1:30am, Sat midday-11:30pm, Sun midday-6pm; Metro: Noviciado
Second-hand bookshop J&J Books and Coffee is a bit of an expat meeting place; it holds regular quiz nights in its upstairs café/bar, while downstairs you can browse the shelves of second-hand English-language books for that Hemingway or travelogue that's next on your reading list.

CHUECA
Design and Décor
ECOMANIA
Calle de Belen, 4; tel. 91/319-0090; www.eco-mania. es; Mon-Sat 11am-9pm; Metro: Chueca
Ecomania, a little shop in Chueca, specializes in eco-friendly products, and stocks everything from upcycled jewelery and homewares to beauty products, stationery, and toys. Its products are a mixture of organic, sustainably-sourced, and fair trade, so you can feel good about making a positive impact while you shop.

LA MAISON DE POUPÉE
San Mateo 26; tel. 91/139-9714; Mon-Fri 11am-3pm, 5pm-9pm; Metro: Tribunal
This cool boutique is where fashion, art, and design converge in clothing, jewelery, homewear, and other finds, many made by local designers. The joy of exploring the store is that you are never quite sure what you are going to find: vintage dinner plates decorated with Wonder Woman, pretty floral summer dresses, statement earrings and necklaces, and

vintage reading glasses are just some of the products on offer.

Books
BERKANA BOOKSHOP
Calle de Hortaleza, 62; tel. 91/522-5599; www. libreriaberkana.com; Mon-Sat 10:30am-9pm, Sun midday-2pm, 5pm-9pm; Metro: Chueca
When this LGBT bookshop was faced with closure in 2016, a crowdfunding effort helped it to survive. It was one of the main reference points for young LGBT Spaniards before the age of the internet. It has a good selection of books with genres ranging from biography and poetry to guidebooks and comics, mainly in Spanish but with a few English editions.

BARRIO DE LAS LETRAS
Clothing and Accessories
PESETA
Calle de las Huertas, 37; tel. 91/052-5971; www. peseta.org; Mon-Sun 11am-9pm; Metro: Antón Martín
PeSeta started life selling its own in-house products, specializing in unique textiles, and has now branched out to working with a host of local designers on everything from men's and women's clothing and accessories to great gift ideas. Shirts, dresses, and tops come in PeSeta fabrics that feature bold patterns and colors. Although prices are slightly higher than your average souvenir, this is a great place to find a more bespoke memento from Madrid. There are other branches in Malasaña (Calle del Noviciado, 9, and Calle de San Vicente Ferrer, 8).

Food and Wine
LICORES CABELLO
Calle Echegaray, 19; tel. 91/429-6088; Mon-Sat 10am-3pm, 5:30pm-10pm; Metro: Sevilla
Licores Cabello is a speciality wine shop that has been in the same family for generations. There is barely room to move around the store, so packed it is with wine bottles that line its wooden shelves. The friendly and knowledgeable owners really know their vino, so it's

a great place to pick up a bottle, from Catalan cavas to rich red Riojas and Riberas.

PASEO DEL PRADO AND ATOCHA
Books
CUESTA DE MOYANO

Calle Claudio Moyano; www.cuestamoyano.es/index. asp; Mon-Sun 9:30am-1:30pm, 4:30pm-7pm; Metro: Atocha

Cuesta de Moyano, a row of wooden stalls on a pedestrianized, sloping street near Retiro Park, has been selling second-hand books since 1925. Most are in Spanish, but you might find editions in other languages. It's a good place for a browse if you're near the park.

SALAMANCA
Clothing and Accessories
ÁGATHA RUÍZ DE LA PRADA

Calle de Serrano, 27; tel. 91/319-0501; www. agatharuizdelaprada.com/en; Mon-Sat 10am-8:30pm; Metro: Serrano

A prominent member of the Madrid Movida, Ágatha Ruíz de la Prada makes clothes that stand out for their bright colors as much as for their bold patterns. Her clothing, for women and girls, ranges from eye-catching sweatshirts and T-shirts to vividly patterned special-occasion dresses. The one thing that unites all the clothing is their strong sense of fun. Her flagship store in Madrid has ranges for women, men, and children, as well as homewear and accessories.

BIMBA Y LOLA

Calle de Serrano, 22; tel 91/576-1103; www. bimbaylola.com; Mon-Sat 10am-8:30pm, Sun midday-8pm; Metro: Serrano

Homegrown label Bimba y Lola is one of the coolest recent names on the Spanish fashion scene. Founded by sisters Uxia and Maria Dominguez in 2005 and named after their dogs, the brand specializes in feminine and offbeat pieces with bold colors and designs. It has been championed by the likes of *Vogue*. Dresses are priced around €150. (Look out for regular sales to nab a bargain.)

UTERQUE

Calle de Serrano, 40; tel. 91/575-4585; www.uterque. com; Mon-Sat 10am-9:30pm, Sun midday-9pm; Metro: Serrano

Part of the wildly successful Inditex group, Uterque is the classy older sister of fellow fashion behemoth Zara, with slightly elevated prices to match. Unlike Zara, Uterque designs for women only, with a large selection across dresses, skirts, trousers, and shirts, as well as footwear and accessories. With dresses from around €100, a big dose of Spanish style won't break the bank.

PURIFICACIÓN GARCÍA

Calle de Serrano, 28; tel. 91/435-8013; www. purificaciongarcia.com; Mon-Sat 10am-10pm, Sun 11am-9pm; Metro: Serrano

Prolific Spanish designer Purificación García creates lines of women's, men's, and children's clothing as well as accessories, bags, and jewelry. There is a sense of whimsy to Garcia's clothing, which combines sharp tailoring with quirky patterns or motifs. Her Salamanca store is a long, clean space where the products take center stage.

FELIPE VARELA

Calle de José Ortega y Gasset, 30; tel.91/577-9220; www.felipevarela.com; Mon-Sat 10:30am-8pm; Metro: Serrano

Known to be one of the favorite designers of Spain's Queen Letizia, Felipe Varela set up his eponymous brand in Madrid in 1994, after working for fashion houses including Dior and Thierry Mugler. His Madrid store, with huge front windows and black interiors, is a stylish spot filled with elegant dresses, jackets, and other women's wear.

LOEWE

Calle de Serrano, 34; tel. 91/577-6056; www.loewe. com; Mon-Sat 9am-8pm; Metro: Serrano

Founded in Madrid in 1846 by leather craftsmen, today Loewe is one of the world's foremost luxury leather brands. It is famous for its handbags, but also does exquisite lines of menswear, womenswear, and other accessories. Products are high-end, with prices to match.

Shoes
MANOLO BLAHNIK

Calle de Serrano, 58; tel. 91/575-9648; www. manoloblahnik.com; Mon-Sat 10am-2pm, 4pm-8pm; Metro: Serrano

Despite starting his shoe business in London, Manolo Blahnik will always be revered in his native Spain (he was born in the Canary Islands). Visit his store in the swanky Salamanca neighborhood to peruse his collections for women and men.

Department Stores
ISOLÉE

Calle de Claudio Coello, 55; tel. 90/287-6136; www. isolee.com; Mon-Fri 11am-8:30pm, Sat 11am-9pm; Metro: Serrano

This 600-square-meter (6,500-square-foot) department store is filled with quality products, from women's, men's, and children's fashion to designer sneakers, gourmet food, and a well-stocked beauty department. It's good for a browse, whether you're looking to stock up on makeup, buy some provisions for a picnic, or want to pick up a new item of clothing from Madrid.

BEYOND THE CENTER
Markets
MERCADO DE MOTORES

Paseo de las Delicias, 61; tel. 67/231-9582; www. mercadodemotores.es; Metro: Delicias

Monthly weekend market Mercado de Motores (check website for upcoming dates) takes place in the atmospheric surroundings of Madrid's railway museum, the platforms packed with over 100 different stalls selling everything from food and vintage fashion to accessories and homewares made by local designers. There are food trucks outside and musicians playing, so you can really make a day of it.

Recreation and Activities

PARKS

Retiro is Madrid's most famous park, and rowing a boat on the lake there (page 233) is a quintessential Madrid experience. But the city has many additional green spaces that are well worth exploring if you want to get a more local feel for the city. The Casa de Campo is Madrid's largest green space, and holds the city's zoo, theme park, and a great public swimming pool that opens during the summer months. Madrid Rio, opened in 2011, is a wonderful riverside park, a popular weekend hangout for families and people young and old.

MADRID RIO

Puente de Segovia, Metro: Principe Pio

Madrid's River Manzanares is more trickle than torrent, but the area around it was given a serious makeover between 2006 and 2011. Today it is Madrid Rio, a lovely riverside park ideal for strolling, cycling, or just watching your children have the time of their lives in the 17 different play areas along the route. The park, which runs either side of the river, also features examples of modern architecture like the Arganzuela Bridge, a tubular bridge designed by French architect Dominique Perrault, close to the entrance off Calle de Toledo.

The easiest way to get down to the park from the city center is to walk downhill to the steep Calle de Segovia, which takes you straight to the river. Turning right will take you to the entrance of Casa de Campo; left will take you along the main section of Madrid Rio towards the Matadero cultural center.

CAMPO DEL MORO

Paseo Virgen del Puerto; Oct-Mar, daily 10am-6pm; Apr-Sept, daily 10am-8pm; Metro: Opera

These English-style gardens below the Royal

Palace were laid out in the 19th century and feature pristine lawns where the odd peacock wanders. It takes its name ("Moors' Field" in Spanish) from the camp established by the Muslim soldiers who laid siege to Madrid between 1100 and 1200.

What was once the private grounds of Spanish royalty is today a lovely area for a stroll that hides a spectacular view of the palace at the end of the Pradera lawn, which runs east to west through the park. On the Pradera is the Fuente de las Conchas (Fountain of the Shells), designed by Ventura Rodríguez in the 18th century.

Enter from the Paseo Virgen del Puerto.

SABATINI GARDENS

Calle de Bailén, 2; daily 8am-9pm; Metro: Opera
When visiting the Royal Palace, don't miss the gardens, just to the right of the main building, where the royal stables used to stand. Opened in 1978, the gardens take their name from architect Francesco Sabatini, who designed the original stables.

They are laid out in a neoclassical style, with box hedges, little mazes, and fountains. The northern end of the central rectangular lake is a popular spot for photographs of the palace—the huge building reflected in the waters is a memorable sight.

PARQUE DEL OESTE

Paseo de Moret, 2; Mon-Sun 9:30am-8:30pm; Metro: Plaza de España
Few parks can boast Spanish Civil War remnants, a rose garden with more than 600 varieties of the flower, and an authentic Egyptian temple—but Madrid's Parque del Oeste (Park of the West) has all three. Created in 1906, this 100-acre park, to the west of the city center, is a real local favorite with plenty of green spaces ideal for picnics.

The Egyptian temple, **Temple of Debod**, is one of the few Egyptian temples outside of Egypt, while bunkers dotted around the park hark back to its relatively recent past as one of the fronts in the Siege of Madrid during the Spanish Civil War (1936-39).

The rose garden, **Roselada Ramón Ortiz**, is named after Madrid's city gardener, who created it in 1955. The garden is best visited in May when it hosts an international rose competition.

The **Teleférico de Madrid** has an access point in the park, on Paseo del Pintor Rosales.

CASA DE CAMPO

If the Retiro is Madrid's manicured showpiece park, the Casa de Campo is its rugged, sprawling older sibling. Madrid's largest park is a vast royal hunting ground that stretches 17.6 square kilometers (6.8 square miles), encompassing everything from a swimming pool and lake to a theme park, zoo, and cable car. When Philip II decided to move the Royal Court to Madrid, he used the Casa de Campo as his own personal hunting ground. The Casa de Campo did not become a public park until 1931, when the government of the Second Republic gave it to the people of Madrid. During the Spanish Civil War (1936-1939), the front line of the Siege of Madrid ran through the park, which today is still dotted with the remnants of the three-year-long battle for the Spanish capital; several bunkers are still standing.

Today, the park is a favorite recreation spot for locals; the trails around the park are great for hiking, running, or cycling, and there are picnic benches scattered around. One central point is the lake, which is surrounded by cute wooden chalet-style restaurants with terraces looking out over the water. The park was once infamous for its prostitutes, who generally only come out at night and are decreasing in numbers since the park was closed to traffic.

There are several worthwhile attractions here:

The **Teleférico de Madrid**, Madrid Cable Car (Paseo del Pintor Rosales; tel 90/234-5002), connects the Parque del Oeste (near Arguelles metro station) to the interior of the Casa de Campo. There are decent views of the Royal Palace and Cathedral, but the majority of the ride takes you over the park. Tickets can

only be bought at the Teleférico (noon-8pm daily, €4.50 one-way).

Madrid Zoo Aquarium (Casa de Campo; tel. 91/154-7479; Mon-Fri 11am-5:30pm, Sat-Sun 10:30am-6pm; www.zoomadrid.com/; €23.30 adults; Metro: Casa de Campo) is one of the few zoos in the world to house giant pandas, including the first panda cub born in the zoo, Chulina ("Cutie" in Spanish). The zoo is home to some 6,000 animals of 500 species, and it offers the prospect of a fun day out with children.

Madrid Amusement Park (Casa de Campo; tel. 91/200-0795; Sat-Sun midday-10pm, longer hours in summer; €32.90 but discounts available online; Metro: Batán) is no Disney World, but it does what it says on the tin: it's an amusing day out for all the family, with rides ranging from the adrenaline-fuelled to the gentle.

Casa de Campo Municipal Swimming Pool (Paseo Puerta del Ángel, 7, via the metro, Lago; tel 91/463-0050; Mon-Sun 11am-9pm; €4.50 for adults, €3.60 for children, €1.35 for over-65s; Metro: Lago) is a popular complex with two outdoor pools and a children's pool. Expect lines in summer.

QUINTA DE LOS MOLINOS PARK

Calle de Alcalá, 502; Mon-Sun 6:30am-10pm; Metro: Torre Arias

One of the best places to see the white and pink almond tree blossom during the springtime, Quinta de los Molinos Park is well off the beaten track but definitely worth a visit if you're looking to head out of the center and want to witness one of nature's most beautiful displays. Located a 25-minute metro ride northeast of the center, the park features olive, pine, and eucalyptus trees, but is most famous for its almond trees, which blossom around February/March. The 25-hectare park has more formal, Romantic-style gardens to the north and a more rugged landscape of trees to the south. In summer, it hosts concerts as part of the Veranos de la Villa festival.

1: Madrid Río; 2: Casa de Campo.

CYCLING

For many years, Madrid was the opposite of a bike-friendly city, with hectic traffic, few bike lanes, and significant traffic pollution. Although no Copenhagen or Amsterdam, Madrid has been making changes to encourage more locals and visitors to hop on two wheels—and to educate drivers about sharing the roads with cyclists. Still, if you are not used to navigating busy roads, stick to the city's parks. **Retiro Park** and **Madrid Rio** are particularly suited to exploring on two wheels.

RENT & ROLL

Calle de Esperteros, 16; tel. 91/148-4967; www. rentandrollmadrid.com; Mar 29-Oct 24, Mon-Fri 10am-8pm, Sat-Sun 9am-9pm, Oct 25-Mar 28, Mon-Fri 10am-7pm, Sat-Sun 9am-8pm; bike rentals €5/hour, €15/day

Rent & Roll, located near Retiro, rents out bikes, roller blades, roller skates, and longboards, and offers organized bike tours.

MY BIKE RIO

Calle Aniceto Marinas, 26; tel. 91/139-4652; www. mibikerio.com; Mon-Fri 10:30am-2:30pm, 4pm-8pm, Sat-Sun 10am-8pm; bike rentals €10/two hours, €30/ day

My Bike Rio, near Principe Pio, rents out bikes, tandems, tricycles, and go-karts to use along Madrid Rio, the riverside park with designated bike paths and no risk of traffic. Pop into the nearby Casa de Campo, which has an entrance off Madrid Rio close to Principe Pio metro, if you're looking for a more rugged ride.

BICIMAD

www.bicimad.com

Madrid's city bike scheme, BiciMAD, has more than 2,000 electric bikes; a few are docked every 300 meters (1,000 feet) across the city. There are two ticket options: an annual pass, for which you sign up online, or an occasional card, which is the best option for tourists. Sign up via the screens at the docking stations (languages include English) and choose a one-, three-, or five-day pass—the card itself is free and you use it every time you want to get a bike out of a docking station. You will be charged at the end of your chosen time period for how many hours you used the bike (prices start at €2 per hour—bikes are meant to be used on short journeys, so after one hour the price jumps to €4 for the second and subsequent hours). A sum of €150 will be "blocked" on your credit card as a deposit, which will be unblocked once you have paid at the end of your one-, three-, or five-day period.

TOP EXPERIENCE

★ FOOTBALL MATCHES

Soccer, or *fútbol*, is Spain's favorite sport, and Madrid is home to two of the country's most famous teams. There are league matches most weekends, either on a Saturday or Sunday, and cup matches on weekdays during the season, which starts in August and ends in May.

If you want to see a match while in Madrid, your best bet is to check the teams' official websites in the weeks leading up to your trip. Tickets normally go on sale a week ahead of match day, usually on a Monday morning. You can also buy tickets via www.ticketmaster.es, which sells tickets at the official price.

You are welcome to take your own non-alcoholic drinks and food into Spanish football stadiums. (Alcohol is not sold in the stadiums.)

REAL MADRID

Santiago Bernabéu stadium, Avenida de Concha Espina, 1; www.realmadrid.com; tickets from €45; Metro: Santiago Bernabéu

Real Madrid play at the Santiago Bernabéu stadium, to the north of the city close to the business district. The stadium, with its 81,000 capacity, really sings on match day. The atmosphere is electric, and the crowds are good natured. Team chants and songs are common.

Alcoholic drinks are not sold inside the stadium—but the majority of fans fill the surrounding bars for a pre-match beer ahead of the game. This is when the excitement really starts to build. It's worth arriving to the area early for the experience.

Spectators will go through a security checkpoint on the way into the stadium. On-site food options include the reasonably priced Real Café and the more exclusive Asador de la Esquina, Puerta 57, and Zen Market. All four have views out onto the pitch. .

Unsurprisingly for one of the world's richest football clubs, tickets and merchandise can be expensive. The cheapest tickets, usually the very highest rows, can be bought from around €45 on the official Real Madrid website and usually go on sale around two weeks before a match.

ATLÉTICO DE MADRID

Av. de Luis Aragones, 4; atleticodemadrid.com; tickets from €40; Metro: Estadio Metropolitano;

Atlético de Madrid recently moved to the Wanda Metropolitano stadium, even further north. The surroundings might be bigger and shinier, but the local spirit of Madrid's lifelong Atlético supporters is as passionate as ever. Fans often enjoy typical snacks such as sunflower seeds (ubiquitous in Spain) while watching the match, discarding the shells on the floor.

SPAS

HAMMAM AL ANDALUS

Calle de Atocha, 14; tel. 90/233-3334; www.madrid. hammamalandalus.com/en/; daily 9:30am-11:30pm; from €35; Metro: Tirso de Molina

Behind a simple door close to Plaza Mayor lies an underground oasis of calm and serenity, the ideal place to de-stress after sightseeing. Modeled after traditional Andalusian Arab baths, the Hammam Al Andalus has three different temperature pools, a steam room, and a relaxation room. The aromas of essential oils evoke Moorish Spain and the sound of the flowing water is a calming soundtrack. A 90-minute session is €35, while massages are extra. Sessions run every two hours starting at 10am (the

Real Madrid and Atlético de Madrid: A City Rivalry

Madrid is the home of two great football teams: Real Madrid and Atlético Madrid. The former is the international megastar that was named "Team of the 20th Century" by FIFA; the latter is the more "local" team, whose loyal supporters are used to the agony of losing.

Atlético supporters were traditionally working-class Madrileños. The team's original stadium, the Vicente Calderón, was located in the working-class neighborhood of Arganzuela, whereas Real Madrid's Santiago Bernabéu is close to the city's northern business district. (Atlético moved to the Wanda Metropolitano, in northern Madrid, in 2017, to the dismay of many die-hard fans.)

Real Madrid, known as *Los Blancos* after the white strip on their uniforms, was founded on March 6, 1902. Atlético Madrid, known as *Los Rojiblancos*, for their red-and-white-striped shirts, was founded on April 26, 1903 by three Basque students living in Madrid. It is said that red and white shirts were the cheapest to make because they were the same color of the most popular mattresses at the time; the team used the excess material for their football shirts, leading to its other nickname, *Los Colchoneros* (the Mattresses).

Soccer scarves

The long-standing rivalry between Real Madrid and Atlético Madrid is known as El Derbi Madrileño, or the Madrid Derby. On match days, the city bristles with electric energy as the two home teams prepare to battle it out.

Neither team escapes the embarrassing association with Spanish dictator Francisco Franco; Atlético, which merged with the football team of the Spanish airforce in the 1940s, was perceived as the team of the regime, but Franco, ever the glory supporter, switched allegiances when Real Madrid started to enjoy European-wide success in the 1950s. One minister is alleged to have uttered: "Real Madrid are the best ambassadors we've ever had."

When it comes to statistics, Real Madrid are the real goliaths; of 161 league matches, they've won 86, Atlético has won 39, and 36 were draws.

least busy and most advisable time to go), and reservations are required. While children over five are allowed, it is more geared towards adults.

URSO SPA

Calle de Mejía Lequerica, 8; tel. 91/444-4458; www.hotelurso.com; Mon-Fri 11am-9pm, Sat-Sun 10am-9pm; Metro: Tribunal

Set inside the **Hotel Urso** in Chueca, the luxurious Urso Spa offers a range of treatments. The relaxing space includes three treatment rooms, a hydrotherapy pool, oriental steam hammam, and relaxation and fitness areas. Several different bespoke packages are available, including seasonal treatments and treatments especially tailored to men. Hourlong facials start at €145, while body massages start at around €120.

TOURS

There is a huge range of tours available in Madrid, whatever your interest, from tapas tours to walking tours covering Hemingway in Madrid, to tours that delve into the history and modern-day culture of flamenco. There are also a number of free walking tours on offer, many of which start on either the Plaza Mayor or Puerta del Sol. These can provide a good primer on Madrid's history.

Walking Tours

DEVOUR MADRID

Calle de la Torrecilla del Leal, 10; tel. 69/511-1832; www.madridfoodtour.com; Mon-Sun 8am-11pm; Metro: Antón Martín

Devour Madrid provides a range of food tours exploring different sides of Madrid's gastronomy, art, and history. Its four-hour **Tapas, Taverns, and History** tour (€99 per person) combines an enjoyable tapas bar crawl through central Madrid with an introduction to the city's history. The friendly and knowledgable guides are just as passionate about Spain's turbulent history as they are about the best Spanish wines, hams, and tapas. Devour Madrid's tours are a great introduction to Madrid and are particularly recommended for travelers who are visiting the city for the first time. Take the tour near the start of your stay for some great insider tips on how to get the most out of the rest of your trip.

FLAMENCO TOUR

theflamencoguide.com

Madrileña and keen flamenco dancer Yolanda Martín is passionate about flamenco and transmits her knowledge and enthusiasm through her private Flamenco Tour (€95 per person), a must for anyone intrigued by this most Spanish of art forms that, as you'll discover, has diverse and multicultural origins. The tour takes a fun route around Madrid's informal Flamenco quarter in the Barrio de Las Letras, with Yolanda giving you a fascinating history of the traditional music and dance in a local tavern, before visiting flamenco shops as well as a famous flamenco school. Put your newfound knowledge to the test at the end of the evening at a *tablao* (flamenco show), which is included in the price of the tour. The private tours, which are suitable for children, are an intimate experience—more like meeting a good friend than following around behind a stuffy tour guide.

WELLINGTON SOCIETY OF MADRID

Paseo de las Delicias, 75; tel. 60/914-3203; www.wellsoc.org

The eccentric Yorkshireman Stephen Drake-Jones offers several historical tours through the Wellington Society of Madrid. One of the most popular is the four-hour **Hemingway Walking Tour** (€110 per person), during which Drake-Jones weaves history and quirky anecdotes, along with a big dose of humor, to tell the tale of Ernest Hemingway's time in Madrid. The tour includes—aptly—stops for drinks and tapas at four of Don Ernesto's favorite watering holes.

COOL TOURS SPAIN

tel. 63/839-9784; www.cooltourspain.com

Cool Tours Spain explores Madrid's burgeoning **street art scene** (€15). The two-hour guided tour takes you around Lavapiés, one of the city's coolest and most multicultural barrios, visiting centers of urban art like the Tabacalera. The well-informed guides explain the history of street art in Madrid and the different techniques used by local artists.

LEAF MADRID TOURS

Plaza Puerta del Sol; tel.61/148-5028; www.leafmadrid.com

Started by a group of young Madrileños with a passion for showing off their city, Leaf Madrid offers free walking tours with fun, informative guides that will help you bone up on Madrid's history, culture, and traditions by recounting local tales and legends. Choose between two tours: the three-hour Madrid de los Austrias tour, which takes you around Madrid's oldest neighborhood, and the nearly three-hour Bourbon Madrid tour, which includes sights like the Spanish parliament and Retiro Park. Although the tours are "free," you are encouraged to pay your guide what you thought the tour was worth at the end. Places on both tours can be booked ahead of time on the website.

Bike Tours

TRIXI

Calle de los Jardines 12; tel. 91/523-1547; www.trixi.com

Trixi runs different tours around Madrid, including its daily Madrid tour (11am, €25 per person). This three-hour tour is a great introduction to the city; friendly, patient, and knowledgeable guides provide a history of the city, as well as useful tips for your stay. It takes in sights including the Royal Palace, Plaza Mayor, the literary neighborhood of Barrio de Las Letras, and Retiro Park, one of the best places to cycle in the city. A soft drink is included towards the end of the tour, when you'll have a rest at a café. Other available tours include one around Madrid's most famous parks (€30 per person), and private tours tailored to the individual rider.

Bus Tours

MADRID CITY TOURS

tel. 90/202-4758; www.madridcitytour.es; adults €21/ one day or €25/two consecutive days, children €9/ one day or €12/two consecutive days

These red tourist buses, which are equipped with audio guides in English and which stop near all the city's major sights, are a comfortable way to explore. You can buy a one- or two-day ticket and hop on and off the bus as many times as you like. Tickets are available from the main Tourist Information Center on Plaza Mayor and online. There are two routes to choose from: the **Historical Route** takes in sights including the Prado Museum, Cybele Palace, Gran Vía, Temple of Debod, and the Royal Palace, while **Modern Madrid** takes in the upmarket Salamanca neighborhood, the Santiago Bernabéu stadium, and Madrid's business district.

CLASSES

Cooking

A popular group activity in Madrid is taking part in a cooking class to learn how to make Spanish delicacies, including paella and tapas.

COOKING POINT PAELLA CLASSES

Calle de Moratín, 11; tel. 91/011-5154; www.cookingpoint. es; Mon-Sat 10am-2pm, Metro: Antón Martín

Cooking Point's paella classes (€70 adult, €35 children) start with a visit to the nearby Antón Martín market to buy fresh produce. Back in the kitchen, you'll learn how to prepare traditional sangria, a gazpacho starter, and then the star of the show: authentic paella. The chef will explain the history of Spain's most famous dish while you cook. The four-hour class includes three hours of shopping and cooking and a final hour to enjoy your freshly cooked creation. The school also offers a tapas-making class.

Language

A number of academies offer intensive language courses that will teach you the fundamentals of Spanish in under a week.

ACADEMIA CONTACTO

Calle Raimundo Lulio, 7; tel. 91/364-2454; www. academiacontacto.com; Metro: Iglesia

This school in the residential neighborhood of Chamberí, just north of the center, has a range of courses available, including its *Intensive 20*, a 20-hour course held Monday-Friday from 9:30am-1:30pm available across all levels (€145 per week). Classes are small—two to nine people—to give learners the most student-teacher time possible. The company also offers a classes-plus-internship course, which puts students into a Spanish company to really flex their language muscles—a good option if you're planning on using Spanish in your career.

LAE MADRID

Calle Montesa, 35; tel. 91/219-6991; www.laemadrid. com; Metro: Manuel Becerra

LAE Madrid has a wide range of courses, from a week-long intensive (20 hours, €195) that includes a coffee and current affairs breakfast, to evening and one-to-one classes. It even has a kids-and-family class designed especially for little ones. The school also organizes regular cultural activities, when you can put your Spanish to the test and learn more about Spanish traditions.

Accommodations

Madrid has accommodation to suit all budgets, from hostels to the finest five-star hotels. *Hostals* are a good budget choice; they're small, usually family-run guesthouses on one or two floors of a larger building (don't be put off by the name; the Spanish "hostal" means *guesthouse*, not hostel).

Madrid's center is relatively compact, so anywhere within the central barrios (Sol and Centro, Malasaña, Chueca, or La Latina) is a good base. The city center is compact and walkable, so basing yourself there means you are within easy reach of all the major sights and nightlife. Many hotels are located on or around the Gran Vía, Madrid's main shopping street. This is a good central location.

As of this writing, Madrid is encouraging home-rental websites like Airbnb to display more information online, so travelers can better tell which rental properties adhere to the city's regulations. Many buildings in the city center have, in a few short years, become almost exclusively tourist rentals, angering some residents who feel they are being priced out of their neighborhoods. Renting apartments via online booking platforms is not illegal, but it is worth keeping in mind the issues surrounding tourist rentals when choosing accommodation.

SOL AND CENTRO
Under €100
★ HOTEL PRAKTIK METROPOL

Calle de la Montera, 47; tel. 91/521-2935; www. praktikmetropol.com; doubles €74; Metro: Gran Vía

The boutique Hotel Praktik Metropol mixes vintage touches with Scandinavian-cool decor and wallet-friendly prices. Part of a small chain with hotels in Madrid and Barcelona, it is located in a grand building on Gran Vía, within easy walking distance of all the major sights. Its 68 rooms include singles, doubles, and suites with balconies. Don't miss chilling out on a sun lounger on the cool roof terrace, which has panoramic views over the city.

CAT'S HOSTEL

Calle Cañizares, 6; tel. 91/369-2807; www.catshostel. com; twins and doubles from €45, dorms from €10; Metro: Tirso de Molina

Cat's Hostel is a popular budget option set in a 17th-century former palace with a central courtyard and underground bar. Rooms are clean and beds comfortable; options include private singles and doubles and female-only and mixed dorms. Known as a party hostel, it's a good option for younger visitors wanting to meet fellow travelers; there are nightly activities like bar crawls, free tours, and tapas tastings. Make sure to check its website because it often offers discounts for early booking.

★ THE HAT

Calle Imperial, 9; tel. 91/772-8572; www. thehatmadrid.com; doubles €95, dorms €27; Metro: Sol

The Hat takes hostels to a new, boutique level and is one of Madrid's most popular budget accommodation options. The designer hostel is just off Plaza Mayor and has clean white interiors with hip creative touches, including its pièce de résistance: the stunning rooftop bar (where guests can enjoy a complementary beer on arrival). The hostel offers double and family rooms with ensuite bathrooms, as well as mixed and female-only dorms with air conditioning and shared bathrooms. It also offers free breakfast and a range of social activities.

★ HOSTAL GALA

Costanilla de Los Ángeles, 15; tel. 91/032-5119; www. hostalgala.com; €50; Metro: Santo Domingo

Guesthouse Hostal Gala is located just off the Gran Vía and within easy walking distance to all the major sights; its friendly staff are happy

Where to Stay . . .

If it's your first time . . .
. . . stay in **Sol/Centro**, within easy walking distance to all the main sights.
If you're here for the art . . .
. . . stay along the **Paseo del Prado and Atocha**, in the heart of Madrid's Golden Triangle of art.
If you're a foodie . . .
. . . book a room in **La Latina**, one of the city's oldest neighborhoods and the heart of its tapas scene.
If you want to party . . .
. . . head to **Malasaña**, Madrid's hippest barrio, or **Chueca**, the heart of the city's LGBT scene.
If you want to follow in literary footsteps . . .
. . . stay in **Barrio de las Letras**, Madrid's literary neighborhood, which was home to iconic Golden Age writers.
If you want to feel like a local . . .
. . . stay in **Lavapiés**, a formally down-at-heel barrio that is now the center of Madrid's international food scene and home to an increasing number of new bars and restaurants, as well as classic old taverns.
If you want to revel in luxury . . .
. . . **Salamanca** is Madrid's most exclusive barrio, home to its "Golden Mile" of designer stores and fine dining restaurants.

to give recommendations. It's a great budget option, with a range of family rooms for four, five, or six adults, but some rooms can be a bit noisy—inquire whether any interior rooms are available to avoid street noise. Breakfast is available for an extra €3.90.

€100-200

HOTEL OPERA

Cuesta Santo Domingo, 2; tel. 91/541-2800; www.hotelopera.com/en; €150-€200; Metro: Opera

Opera by name, opera by nature. Hotel Opera is located just next to Madrid's opera house, the grand Royal Theatre, and offers guests rousing weekend dinners serenaded by opera singers at its Café de la Ópera. The hotel's 79 rooms include doubles and family-sized options, as well as suites with a terrace and hot tub.

HOTEL MAYERLING

Calle del Conde de Romanones, 6; tel. 91/420-1580; www.mayerlinghotel.com; €120; Metro: Tirso de Molina

The stylish Hotel Mayerling, a converted textile warehouse, is located close to Plaza Mayor and the Puerta del Sol. Its 22 rooms include doubles and triples, all equipped with TVs and air conditioning. There is a morning breakfast buffet and a sun terrace, where you can relax after a long day of sightseeing.

PETIT PALACE POSADA DEL PEINE

Calle Postas, 17; tel. 91/523-8151; www.petitpalaceposadadelpeine.com; €150; Metro: Sol

Just off the Plaza Mayor, the Petit Palace Posada del Peine boasts over 400 years of history, making it one of the oldest hotels in the city. But the rooms are modern and high-tech, each coming with its own iPad (available from reception). Options include compact doubles and family rooms with four, five, and six beds, ideal for groups traveling together. There's a buffet breakfast and free bike rentals; it's a cool, eco-friendly way to explore the city.

DEAR HOTEL

Gran Vía, 80; tel. 91/412-3200; www.dearhotelmadrid.com; €170; Metro: Plaza de España

With a prime location on Gran Vía, the stylish

boutique Dear Hotel is a cool place to stay. Rooms feature Scandinavian-chic design, which means light wood, minimalist style, and cozy textiles. Options range from the deluxe doubles to suites and family rooms (two rooms with a shared entrance). Its 14th floor is home to the Nice to Meet You restaurant and lounge. Its roof has a stunning skypool, a plunge pool that juts out over the street, with incredible views over the city.

IBEROSTAR LAS LETRAS GRAN VÍA

Gran Vía, 11; tel. 90/081-1676; www.iberostar.com/ en/hotels/madrid/iberostar-las-letras-gran-via; €180; Metro: Gran Vía

Immerse yourself in the literary vibe of the nearby Barrio de Las Letras at the literature-themed Iberostar Las Letras Gran Vía. Rooms feature literary quotes on the walls, and guests can relax with a good book in the library. There is a large range of room options, including spacious doubles, family rooms, and a deluxe double complete with terrace and jacuzzi.

HOTEL PRECIADOS

Calle de Preciados, 37; tel. 91/454-4400; www. preciadoshotel.com; €143; Metro: Santo Domingo

Just steps from Gran Vía, the four-star Hotel Preciados is set in an elegant balconied building. Staff are friendly and rooms are spacious and comfortable, with all the mod cons including air conditioning and power showers, while some have balconies or terraces. There is a good buffet breakfast and a ground-floor restaurant and bar with an outdoor terrace.

APARTOSUITES JARDINES DE SABATINI

Cuesta San Vicente, 16; tel. 91/542-5900; www. jardinesdesabatini.com; €129; Metro: Plaza de España

The ApartoSuites Jardines de Sabatini, a short walk from the Royal Palace, sells itself as a hotel with the comfort and space of an apartment. Rooms, a mixture of doubles and four-guest suites, come with kitchenettes, ideal for families or for travelers who want the option to cook for themselves. Don't miss the rooftop bar, with stunning views over the Royal Palace, and—surprisingly—the in-house vintage car collection (a free guided tour is available for all guests).

HOTEL EMPERADOR

Gran Vía, 53; tel. 91/547-2800; www.emperadorhotel. com; €120; Metro: Santo Domingo

Located right on Madrid's Gran Vía, Hotel Emperador is a great location for exploring the city. The four-star hotel has a range of rooms, from well-priced doubles to suites with their own balcony. The real pièce de résistance is its sizable rooftop pool, which is free to guests. The sky bar is a great place to wind down at the end of the day and has spectacular views across Madrid.

€200-300

THE PRINCIPAL

Calle Marqués de Valdeiglesias, 1; tel. 91/521-8743; www.theprincipalmadridhotel.com; €270; Metro: Banco de España

The Principal is a luxurious five-star option right on Gran Vía, featuring a wonderful rooftop terrace with panoramic views across the city. Its 76 rooms and suites are elegantly decorated and light-filled. The Ático restaurant, on the sixth floor, has a menu created by Michelin-starred chef Ramón Freixa, while the wellness suite is the place for a sauna or massage treatment. Various deals are available on its website; advance reservations are recommended.

AXEL HOTEL

Calle de Atocha, 49; tel. 91/088-3380; www. axelhotels.com/en/axel-hotel-madrid/hotel.html; €200; Metro: Antón Martín/Sol

The quirky Axel Hotel is specifically focused on an LGBT clientele, but bills itself as "hetero-friendly," so all are welcome. Its 88 rooms have a kitsch design, with neon signs, bold prints, and stylish design touches. There's a gym,

Best Accommodations

Hotel Urban

★ **Hotel Urban:** An Art Deco slice of luxury with an artistic soul and its own museum, not to mention a wonderful rooftop with pool, bar, and views.

★ **Room Mate Alicia:** A great location with friendly staff in Madrid's literary quarter. Suites come with their own terrace and plunge pool.

★ **Hotel Praktik Metropol:** Stylish, boutique accommodation for a reasonable price in the heart of the city.

★ **Posada del León de Oro:** A former coaching inn turned boutique hostel; check out the ruins of the former city wall and enjoy some of the city's best tapas right on your doorstep.

★ **Hotel Urso:** Relax in style in the luxurious spa and top-notch rooms of this five-star hotel.

★ **Hostal Gala:** Central guesthouse, just off Gran Vía, with lots of family room options—ideal for groups traveling together.

★ **The Hat:** Boutique hostel with hip, young vibe and stylish rooftop bar. Organizes regular social activities for guests; a great option for travelers on a budget.

sauna, and massage room. Its downstairs restaurant serves modern tapas, while the Sky Bar is a great place to watch the sunset over a drink or have a dip in the rooftop pool.

VINCCI THE MINT

Gran Vía, 10; tel. 91/203-0650; www.vinccihoteles. com/eng/Hotels/Spain/Madrid/Vincci-The-Mint; €270; Metro: Banco de España

The four-star Vincci The Mint brings a fun and quirky design to a grand, classic Gran Vía building right in the heart of Madrid. Gone is the stuffy old reception desk, in favor of checking in at the bar (with complimentary drink, of course). Enjoy a drink on the rooftop bar, a cool, laid-back space with its own food truck. Rooms include doubles (top-floor tower rooms have a terrace) and suites.

Over €300
★ HOTEL URBAN

Carrera de S. Jerónimo, 34; tel. 91/787-7770; www.
hotelurban.com; €320; Metro: Sevilla

The five-star Hotel Urban blends art, cuisine, and top-quality service, resulting in one of Madrid's most luxurious boutique hotels. Just a few minutes from the Puerta del Sol and Madrid's major art galleries, the glass-fronted hotel has an Art Deco interior and its own gallery dedicated to the art of Papua New Guinea. Artworks can also be found in its 96 designer rooms and suites, which are comfortable and include modern amenities like Nespresso machines and designer toiletries. The hotel rooftop, with its bar, sauna, and pool, is the ideal place to relax at the end of a long day. Staff are friendly and only too happy to make recommendations or reservations for guests—if you even leave the hotel to dine. Michelin-starred restaurant Cebo does a modern spin on classic Mediterranean cuisine, while the icy-cool Glass Mar is a seafood spot with great cocktails. Breakfasts are fantastic, with both buffet and a la carte options to set you up for the day.

LA LATINA
€100-200
★ POSADA DEL LEÓN DE ORO

Calle Cava Baja, 12; tel. 91/119-1494; www.
posadadelleondeoro.com; €170; Metro: La Latina

The 17-room Posada del León de Oro is a former coaching inn, where travelers would stay on long journeys by horse before the invention of the railway. It has been stylishly renovated into a four-star hotel set around its traditional central courtyard, with a location right in the heart of La Latina on Cava Baja, the neighborhood's famous tapas street. Rooms are decorated in a bright and modern style, but they retain period touches like wooden beams. Options include doubles, family rooms, and a spacious attic room with a jacuzzi. The hotel's **Enotaberna restaurant** showcases tapas from around Spain.

POSADA DEL DRAGÓN

Cava Baja, 14; tel. 91/119-1424; www.
posadadeldragon.com; Metro: La Latina

This boutique hotel, right on Cava Baja, is set in a traditional *corrala* courtyard building on the ruins of Madrid's old Christian walls, some of which are visible running through the hotel. Its name comes from the mythical dragon that was said to guard this area of Madrid. Its 27 bright and comfortable rooms include exterior rooms looking out over the rooftops of La Latina; the smaller corrala rooms look onto the central "corrala" courtyard. There is a good tapas bar on the ground floor.

LAVAPIÉS
€100-200
HOTEL ARTRIP

Calle de Valencia, 11; tel. 91/539-3282; www.
artriphotel.com/en; €155; Metro: Lavapiés

One of the few hotels in Lavapiés, Hotel Artrip is a modern, bright hotel within easy walking distance of Madrid's main art galleries. It's a good option for those who'd prefer to be out of the main tourist center and in a more local barrio. Its 17 rooms include double, triple, and family rooms, as well as two penthouses at the top of the building. Breakfast is included.

MALASAÑA
Under €100
MAD4YOU

Costanilla de San Vicente; tel. 91/521-7549; www.
mad4youhostel.com/en; double €90, dorm beds
€18-28; Metro: Tribunal

Set in the hip neighborhood of Malasaña, boutique hostel Mad4You is a great option for younger travelers on a budget. Rooms include singles and doubles as well as four-, six-, and eight-bed mixed and female-only dorms. A decent breakfast is included, and the interior patio is a cool place to hang out and meet fellow travelers.

€100-200
7 ISLAS HOTEL
Calle de Valverde, 14; tel. 91/523-4688; www.7islashotel.com; €130; Metro: Gran Vía

Inspired by the Canary Islands, the boutique 7 Islas Hotel, just off Gran Vía, brings a beachside vibe to central Madrid with its light wood floorboards and stylish nautical touches. Its 79 rooms include doubles and three penthouse rooms with their own terraces. Booking on its website gets you perks like a free minibar. The family-run hotel also doubles as an art gallery, hosting regular exhibitions on the ground floor near its 7 Craft Bar restaurant and bar.

Over €300
★ HOTEL URSO
Calle de Mejía Lequerica, 8; tel. 91/444-4458; www.hotelurso.com/en; €333; Metro: Tribunal

Old world glamour mixes with hip, modern design at Urso Hotel, set in a restored palace in the cool Malasaña neighborhood. The hotel offers elegant rooms, air conditioning, a gym, and a luxurious spa where you can enjoy some "me time" after a day pounding the cobblestones. The helpful concierge, who speaks good English, is knowledgeable about Madrid's top sights and best local hangouts.

CHUECA
€100-€200
ROOM MATE OSCAR
Plaza de Pedro Zerolo, 12; tel. 91/701-1173; www.room-matehotels.com/en/Oscar; Metro: Gran Vía

Part of the stylish and budget-friendly Spanish chain of Room Mate hotels, Room Mate Oscar is located in the heart of Chueca. Its futuristic lobby leads onto corridors that look like they could have come straight off a spaceship; happily, rooms are bright, with bursts of color on the walls. Options range from standard doubles to suites with their own terraces. At the top of the hotel is one of Madrid's coolest hidden hangouts, a small rooftop pool and bar surrounded by comfy sun loungers. Entry to the pool and terrace is free for hotel guests.

€200-300
ONLY YOU
Calle del Barquillo, 21; tel. 91/005-2746; www.onlyyouhotels.com; €250; Metro: Chueca

Set in an historic 19th-century mansion, Only You has already become a benchmark for its award-winning design by Lázaro Rosa-Violán. Its 125 rooms each have lovely individual touches. Options range from doubles to the incredible Moments Suite (with a 40-meter/131-foot terrace space). Breakfast is served all day long, a great idea in a city where late nights—and late mornings—are the norm. The hotel's YOUnique restaurant melds Mediterranean flavors with a modern touch.

Over €300
HOTEL ORFILA
Calle de Orfila, 6; tel. 91/702-7770; www.hotelorfila.com; €400; Metro: Alonso Martínez

The 32-room Hotel Orfila is a family-owned haven in the heart of buzzing Madrid. A great spot to recharge your batteries before you head back out into the heady energy of the city, the hotel is set in a 19th-century mansion with a lovely garden terrace. Rooms are spacious and the decor is sumptuous; think drapes, vases, and intricately detailed wallpaper. The **Garden de Orfila** restaurant serves seasonal specialties and a Sunday brunch designed by two-Michelin-starred chef, Mario Sandoval.

BARRIO DE LAS LETRAS
Under €100
HOSTAL GONZALO
Calle de Cervantes, 34; tel. 91/429-2714; www.hostalgonzalo.com; €50; Metro: Antón Martín

Comfortable little guesthouse Hostal Gonzalo is close to Madrid's major art galleries and smack-bang in the middle of its literary quarter, which is full of great restaurants and bars.

Rooms are simply decorated but clean, bright, and comfortable—and at €50-70 for a double, they are a great budget option in the center of the city.

€100-200
★ ROOM MATE ALICIA

Calle del Prado, 2; tel. 91/389-6095; www. room-matehotels.com/en/alicia; €180; Metro: Antón Martín

It would be hard to find a better location than Room Mate Alicia, a designer boutique hotel nestled in a corner of Plaza Santa Ana. The Room Mate chain was founded by three Madrid friends and now has hotels around the world. Front desk staff are friendly and happy to give recommendations. Many rooms have big windows looking out onto the square, while each upper-floor suite includes a spacious terrace with a plunge pool—ideal for cooling off during the summer—as well as nice touches like yoga mats and weights for those who don't want to miss a workout. There is a good buffet breakfast of hot and cold items served until the pleasantly late time of midday.

HOTEL ONE SHOT PRADO 23

Calle del Prado, 23; tel. 91/420-4001; www. hoteloneshotprado23.com/; €130; Metro: Sol

In the heart of Madrid's literary quarter, Hotel One Shot Prado 23 is a design boutique hotel with an artistic theme throughout, including a special focus on photography. It's a short walk from the Prado and Reina Sofía museums. Economy doubles are a great money-saver, while other options include doubles, family rooms, and a terrace room complete with spacious outdoor terrace.

€200-300
ME REINA VICTORIA

Plaza Sta. Ana, 14; tel. 91/276-4747; www.melia.com/ es/hoteles/espana/madrid/me-madrid-reina-victoria; €225; Metro: Sol

The huge white building that dominates Plaza de Santa Ana was once the favorite hangout of Madrid's star matadors. Today, it's a luxury designer hotel with bags of style and all the mod cons. Rooms range from doubles to suites overlooking the square. The **Ana la Santa** restaurant does modern Mediterranean cuisine while **Radio**, the hotel's glamorous rooftop bar, is the

Room Mate Alicia

Rooftop Pools

Room Mate Oscar's rooftop pool

Madrid has several rooftop pools that are a great option if you want somewhere relaxing and glamorous to cool off during the sweltering summer days.

ROOM MATE OSCAR

Plaza de Pedro Zerolo, 12; tel. 91/701-1173; www.room-matehotels.com/en/oscar; Metro: Gran Vía
The rooftop pool at Room Mate Oscar, a boutique hotel in Chueca, might be pint-sized, but it is a luscious and cooling dip on a hot summer's day. Entry includes towels and a complementary glass of cava, and the stunning views over Madrid's rooftops are priceless. Full-day (10am-7pm) entry is €35 per person Mon-Thurs and €60 per person from Fri-Sun and on public holidays. Morning (10am-2pm) or afternoon (3pm-7pm) entry is available for €35 from Fri-Sun and on public holidays. Entry to the pool and terrace is free for hotel guests.

HOTEL EMPERADOR

Gran Vía, 53; tel. 91/547-2800; www.emperadorhotel.com; May-Sept, 10am-9pm; full day Mon-Fri €40, half day Mon-Fri €30, Sat-Sun and public holidays €50; Metro: Santo Domingo
Hotel Emperador hosts a good-sized pool right on Gran Vía with exquisite views over the city, a solarium with sunbeds, sunshades, and a cocktail bar. Tickets include a complementary drink. Hotel guests can use the pool free of charge.

place to see and be seen. It's a pet-friendly hotel for those who want to bring their pooch.

PASEO DEL PRADO AND ATOCHA

€200-300

WESTIN PALACE

Plaza de las Cortes, 7; tel. 91/360-8000; www. westinpalacemadrid.com/en; €234; Metro: Banco de España/Sol
Formerly the Palace Hotel, one of Hemingway's favorite lodgings, the huge Westin Palace provides a real dose of old-world glamour. Its 467 rooms, from the deluxe room to the royal suite, are elegantly decorated with soft carpets, marble bathrooms, and comfortable beds. The hotel's restaurants and bars include **La Rotunda**, which sits under a magnificent stained-glass dome and hosts a Sunday Opera and Brunch, and the **1912 Museo Bar**, where Hemingway and Salvador Dalí liked to down

a few cocktails. Other amenities include a gym and sauna.

HOTEL PALACIO DEL RETIRO, AUTOGRAPH COLLECTION

Calle de Alfonso XII, 14; tel. 91/523-7460; www.marriott.com/hotels/travel/madre-hotel-palacio-del-retiro-autograph-collection; €250; Metro: Retiro

This 50-room, five-star hotel is set in a palatial home built overlooking Retiro Park at the beginning of the 20th century. Rooms are stylish, with period features including original wooden floors and ceiling moldings. They are all equipped with plasma TVs, iPod docking stations, and luxury toiletries, while many look out onto the park. Other facilities include a small fitness room, buffet breakfast, and The Suite bar.

NH COLLECTION PASEO DEL PRADO

Plaza Cánovas del Castillo, 4; tel. 91/330-2400; www.nh-collection.com/hotel/nh-collection-madrid-paseo-del-prado; €200; Metro: Banco de España

Set in a Baroque-style palace designed in 1904 by Antonio Palacios, who also built the nearby Palacio de Cibeles (now home to Madrid's City Hall), this stylish hotel is ideally situated on the Paseo del Prado, close to Madrid's "Golden Triangle" of art galleries. Superior premium rooms, as well as junior and standard suites, feature artisanal touches like locally produced carpets and artwork from the Canary Islands. A Guest Relations team is on hand to help guests with advice or bookings.

SALAMANCA
€100-200
DORMIRDCINE

Calle del Príncipe de Vergara, 87; tel. 91/411-0809; www.dormirdcine.com/en; €90; Metro: Diego de León

Film fans will love Dormirdcine, a design hotel with a cinematic theme located in Madrid's upmarket Salamanca neighborhood. Its 85 rooms—singles, doubles, and three suites—are all individually designed and feature street-art-style wall murals by international artists based on different films. Breakfast is served each morning in the hotel's café and guests can relax in its cinema bar in the evening.

BEYOND THE CENTER
€100-200
HOTEL PUERTA AMERICA

Avenida América, 41; tel. 91/744-5400; www.hoteles-silken.com/hoteles/puerta-america-madrid/; €125; Metro: Avenida de América

Hotel Puerta America was designed by 19 different architecture and design studios from 13 different countries, resulting in an innovative and unique space. Rarely have so many of the world's top architects united to create one vision. The multicolored façade was the work of Jean Nouvel, who also built the extension to the city's Reina Sofía Museum, while the futuristic interiors were designed by the likes of Zaha Hadid and Norman Foster, who each got their own floor to play with. While the hotel is located to the north of the city, it provides a free shuttle into the center.

Information and Services

TOURIST INFORMATION CENTERS

Madrid's main Tourist Information Center (9:30am-9:30pm daily) is located on the city's historic Plaza Mayor (number 27), and offers face-to-face assistance, a self-service information point, and ticket sales.

Other tourist information points can be found close to key sights around the city, including the Tourist Information Point Paseo del Prado, close to the Prado Museum (Plaza de Neptuno), the Atocha Tourist Information Point, near Atocha Train Station (Ronde de Atocha), Plaza de Callao Tourist Information point, on Gran Vía (Plaza de Callao), and two Tourist Information Points in Adolfo Suárez

Madrid-Barajas airport (Terminal 2, lounges 5 and 6 and Terminal 4, lounges 10 and 11).

HEALTH AND SAFETY

Madrid's inland location and high altitude (it is the highest capital city in Europe) mean summers are dry and very hot (temperatures can regularly top 40 degrees Celsius/104 Fahrenheit in July and August). A summer visit could mean slowing down considerably, keeping out of the scorching sun and tailoring your activities to the heat—for example, incorporating pool trips and indoor, air-conditioned activities into your plans.

Emergency Numbers

In an emergency, dial **112**. There is also a **tourist helpline and emergency number** (90/210-2112), in English, French, German, and Italian.

Hospitals

Hospital General Gregorio Marañón (Calle del Dr. Esquerdo, 46; tel. 91/586-8000), one of the city's main hospitals, is in quite a central location. **Anglo-American Medical Unit** (Unidad Médica, Calle Conde de Aranda, 1; tel. 91/435-1823) is a private clinic where all the doctors speak Spanish and English. The clinic has a wide range of specialties, with consultations ranging from €125-€150.

Pharmacies

Farmacia Mayor (Calle Mayor, 13; tel. 91/213-6178) is open 24 hours a day, while other central pharmacies include

Farmacia Cuchilleros (Calle Cuchilleros, 12; tel. 91/366-5238), **Farmacia Gran Vía 26** (Gran Vía, 26; tel. 91/521-3148), and **Farmacia Velázquez** (Calle de Velázquez, 70; tel. 91/435-1347) in the Salamanca neighborhood.

Farmacia de la Reina Madre (Calle Mayor, 59; tel. 91/548-0014), founded in 1576, is the oldest pharmacy in Madrid, and has been at its current location since 1913. It's worth peeping in to see the traditional pharmacy; it is said to have an original prescription belonging to Spanish writer Miguel de Cervantes.

COMMUNICATIONS

Wi-Fi

Madrid has dozens of free Wi-Fi hotspots, including on the city buses and at newspaper kiosks. You just need to register online at www.gowex.com and then look out for "GOWEX Wi-Fi" or "Madrid Wi-Fi." Wi-Fi is also available in over 100 public buildings, from libraries to cultural centers, and a number of museums. These days, many bars and restaurants have free Wi-Fi; look for a sign, or ask a member of staff.

Newspapers

Spain's biggest daily newspaper is **El País**, on the center-left; **El Mundo**, on the center-right, is another popular read. *El País* has an online English edition.

Newspaper kiosks are dotted around the city and many sell foreign newspapers, including *The New York Times*, *Le Monde*, *The Times*, and *The Guardian*.

Getting There

AIR

Madrid has one international airport, the **Adolfo Suárez Madrid–Barajas Airport** (MAD, www.aeropuertomadrid-barajas.com/eng/), located 12 kilometers (7.5 miles) northeast of the city center. It has four terminals, and scheduled flights to and from dozens of North American and European cities.

Airport Transportation

METRO

There are two metro stations in the airport on Line 8 (pink), one at Terminal 1-2-3 and one at Terminal 4 (there is a metro station in between the two stops, called Barajas; this is the town of Barajas, not the airport). The metro runs from 6:05am to 1:30am. Take Line 8 from the airport to Nuevos Ministerios, then take Line 10 (royal blue) further into the center (it goes to both Tribunal in Malasaña and Plaza de España on Gran Vía). Change onto Line 1 (light blue) at Tribunal if you are heading to Sol.

The price of a metro ticket, including airport supplement, is €4.50-€5, depending on how many stations you will travel. It takes around 15-20 minutes total to reach Nuevos Ministerios station from the airport, then another 15 minutes to get to Sol, Gran Vía, or Malasaña.

RENFE CERCANÍAS

If you're heading to central Madrid, one of the quickest and cheapest ways is to take the RENFE Cercanías commuter train. There is a cercanías station in Terminal 4, next to the metro, and trains leave every 30 minutes (between 6am and 11:15pm). (If you arrive at Terminal 1, 2, or 3, take the free shuttle bus to Terminal 4 to board the train).

Take the C-1 two stops to Chamartín, then change onto C-3 or C-4 and get off at Sol. From the airport to Sol takes around 25 minutes. A single ticket is €2.60.

BUS

A special airport express bus (line 203) stops at Atocha train station and outside Cibeles Palace. The bus runs 24 hours a day, 365 days a year. It stops at Atocha during the day, but it changes its stop to Cibeles during the night. The journey takes around 30 minutes in good traffic and tickets are €5, cash only. The buses run every 15 minutes during the day and every 35 minutes at night. They are particularly useful if you are staying around Paseo del Prado, Atocha, or towards the western end of Gran Vía. (The fact it runs 24 hours a day also makes it a good option for travelers who have to get to the airport between 1:30am-6am, when the metro is closed.) Buses depart from just outside Terminal 1, 2, 3, and 4.

TAXI

Taxis are a fixed price of €30 to anywhere in the center and are a good, easy option, especially if you have a lot of luggage. Taxis, which are white with a red diagonal stripe, are easy to find by following the signs to the taxi ranks just outside each terminal. It takes approximately 30-40 minutes to get from the airport to the city center, depending on traffic.

TRAIN

Spain's national rail network is operated by **RENFE** (www.renfe.com), and Madrid is well-connected to cities across the country.

Puerta de Atocha is Madrid's main railway station, and the point from which many long-distance trains embark. The station is connected to the Metro (Line 1) and has a range of shops and cafés, as well as a memorial to the 191 people killed in the 2004 terror attacks that targeted commuter trains in the city.

Chamartín Station, to the north of the

1: Puerta de Atocha railway station; 2: Madrid Metro

city, is a common starting point for trains heading north. For travelers arriving at Chamartín, the best way to go to the city center is to take a direct *cercanía* (local train) that goes direct to Sol (the station on the Puerta del Sol) in under 10 minutes. Tickets cost €1.70 and can be purchased from ticket machines in the station. Trains leave every 10-15 minutes.

You can purchase train tickets at machines and ticket desks inside train stations, as well as online.

BUS

Madrid's main station for long-distance buses is the **Estación Sur de Autobuses**, on Line 6 of the Madrid Metro (station: Méndez Álvaro), sometimes referred to as **Méndez** **Álvaro bus station**. Located to the southeast of the city, it's a 15-minute metro ride to Sol (the station on Puerta del Sol in the center of the city). There are also many other more local bus companies that operate out of the Estación Sur.

CAR

From Barcelona, take the **AP-2/E-90** towards Zaragoza, then follow the signposts to Madrid. The drive takes about six hours. Be prepared to pay around €25 in tolls along the way, via cash or chip-and-pin credit card. If you are driving into the city, you'll arrive via one of Madrid's two ring roads, the **M-30** and the **M-40** or the **Paseo de la Castellana**, which runs from north to south.

Getting Around

Madrid is a very walkable city and its center is best explored on foot. The metro—clean, safe and easier to use than the bus—is the best option for destinations that are slightly more out of the way or for when your feet start to ache.

PUBLIC TRANSIT

The **Tarjeta Multi** (Public Transport Card, €2.50), a swipeable plastic card, is now required to ride the metro. The card is available at machines in all metro stations and is valid for up to 10 years. Once the pass expires, you can continue to top up the Public Transport Card with single tickets. A 10-trip ticket, valid for Metro zone A and all buses, costs €12.20 and can be loaded onto a Tarjeta Multi.

Travelers may be interested in the **Tourist Travel Pass** (www.esmadrid.com), which can be used on all kind of public transport across Madrid, allowing for unlimited trips within your chosen timeframe. For most tourists, the **Zone A pass,** covering Zone A of the metro as well as the €3 airport supplement, will be sufficient. For Zone A, passes are €8.40 (1 day), €14.20 (2 days), €18.40 (3 days), €26.80 (5 days), or €35.40 (7 days). Children under 11 get a 50-percent discount; those under age 4 travel for free. The **Zone T pass**, covering the entire metro and bus network as well as some commuter trains, is also available and useful if you plan on making daytrips to El Escorial. The 1, 2, 3, 5, or 7-day Tourist Travel Passes come pre-loaded onto a Tarjeta Multi Card.

Metro

Metro Madrid (www.metromadrid.es) operates the city's metro. A **single metro ticket** costs €1.50-€2. Riders must possess a Tarjeta Multi Card (€2.50, available at all metro stations) to ride the metro.

Madrid's metro is modern, reasonably priced, and fast. It is the world's seventh longest metro and services the city and the surrounding areas. The most central station is Sol, on the Puerta del Sol, connected to Lines 1, 2, and 3. There are 12 color-coded metro lines, as well as three light rail lines that serve the far south and far north of the city. Metro maps are available from metro stations. The metro is open from 6am to 1:30am.

Bus

Although you will usually get everywhere you need to go much easier on the metro, buses are especially useful during the night, when the metro does not run. Madrid's bus network is operated by the **Empresa Municipal de Transportes** (EMT, www.emtmadrid.es) and travels throughout the city from 6:30am–11:30pm. There are also more than 25 late-night bus routes, called *búhos* (Spanish for "owls"), all departing from Plaza de Cibeles; fares are the same, but the frequency is lower. Buses have free Wi-Fi and air-conditioning, but can be slower than the metro, especially during rush hour. Some 791 buses run on compressed natural gas and 20 are run on electric motors.

Buy single **tickets** (€1.50) on board the bus. (Note that buses do not accept notes larger than a ten-euro note.) If you have a Tarjeta Multi, just press it against the card reader when you board the bus.

You can plot your bus route, in English, on the EMT website.

TAXI

Official Madrid taxis are white with a diagonal red stripe; you can pick up a taxi at ranks or hail one on the street. A green light on the roof means the taxi is available, and there is usually a "libre" (free/available) sign placed on the passenger side of the windscreen. Passengers can pay in cash or by card. There is a supplement of €3 for rides from Madrid's IFEMA conference center, the Atocha and Chamartín train stations, and the Estación del Sur and Avenida de América bus stations.

You can also order cars through apps including Uber and Cabify, which are becoming increasingly popular in Madrid, but which have faced a backlash from taxi drivers.

If you wish to take a private taxi, you might try Radio Taxi Madrid Airport (911760081), but bear in mind that private taxi companies will turn on the meter as soon as they pick you up.

Often the best bet is taking an official Madrid taxi by hailing one or using the My Taxi app.

CAR

Madrid's excellent public transport system means renting a car while visiting is usually unnecessary. Parking in Madrid, where congestion is a big issue, can be difficult. While some street parking is available (pay at streetside parking meters), opting for a spot in a carpark can be easier; central ones include beneath the Plaza Mayor and beneath the Mercado de Cebada in La Latina.

Car parking is around €30–€40 a day, depending on where you park. Some hotels do have parking, usually in garages under the hotel building, which in some cases is free and in others is to be paid for as an extra—check this when booking.

Major car rental companies, including **Avis** (Gran Vía, 60; tel. 90/210-3739; www.avis.com) and **Europcar** (Calle San Leonardo, 8; tel. 91/541-8892; www.europcar.com), have branches at Adolfo Suárez Madrid-Barajas Airport and Atocha train station as well as at city-center locations.

BICYCLE

Madrid has a city bike scheme, **BiciMAD**, which has more than 2,000 bikes docked in 165 stations around the city. However, cycling in Madrid is really only recommended for experienced cyclists.

Madrid Day Trips

Located in the geographic center of Spain, Madrid is a great base from which to explore the country. What's more, some of Spain's most stunning cities are within easy reach of the capital, from Segovia and its perfectly preserved Roman aqueduct, to the cultural gem of Toledo, where historically Christians, Jews, and Muslims lived in peace, leaving the city a rich mixture of architectural styles.

For those who want to escape the big city and explore some nature, the Sierra de Guadarrama mountains are an hour outside the city and a great place for hiking or winter sports like skiing and snowboarding. You can also delve into Spanish history at the renaissance monastery/palace of El Escorial and the macabre (and controversial) monument that holds General Francisco Franco's remains.

Highlights

Look for ★ to find recommended sights, activities, dining, and lodging.

★ **Segovia's Roman Aqueduct:** Constructed in the 1st century AD, Segovia's Roman aqueduct remains one of the best-preserved in the world (page 304).

★ **Alcázar (Castle) of Segovia:** This fairy-tale castle features fantastic spires and turrets against a mountainous backdrop (page 306).

★ **Toledo Cathedral:** This 13th-century place of worship is Toledo's crowning glory, and one of Spain's finest Gothic cathedrals (page 312).

★ **Valle de la Fuenfría:** Walk the ancient Roman road that winds through the sierra and take in the mountains, pine forests, and Roman relics along the way (page 319).

PLANNING YOUR TIME

Toledo is the most popular day trip from Madrid and is well-worth a visit, as long as you are prepared to share the city with thousands of other tourists eager to explore its treasures. **Segovia** is extremely popular, too, with its fairytale castle and Roman aqueduct that dominate the skyline. In both cases, planning an overnight stay can provide you with a better feel for the place; you can enjoy the nightlife with the locals once the day trippers and tour buses have headed home.

Most locals head to the **Sierra de Guadarrama** and its mountain villages for a day trip, and decent transport links mean you can easily get to the mountains—whether you're planning on hiking, skiing, or just exploring a quaint mountain village—in a day without having to stay overnight.

El Escorial and the **Valley of the Fallen** are ideal for a combined day trip, while some tourists manage to visit in a morning or afternoon. El Escorial is accessible via public transit, while the Valley of the Fallen is not—you'll either have to drive to reach it or join a day tour from Madrid.

Segovia

Segovia (population 52,000), 90 kilometers (56 miles) northwest of Madrid, is famous for the grandeur of its architecture, its traditional Castilian cuisine, and its long, fascinating history. There is something magical about a city that was supposedly founded by Hercules himself, and whose urban landscape is framed by a soaring Roman aqueduct, a fairytale castle, and the picturesque peaks of the Sierra de Guadarrama beyond.

Segovia was founded as a Celtic settlement, but control of the city soon passed to the Romans, whose engineering prowess would give the city one of its most enduring and famous sights—the enormous aqueduct that dominates the city center. In the Middle Ages, Segovia's position on trading routes transformed the city into a center of the wool and textile trade. At the same time, a thriving Jewish community developed in the city. Segovia was long a favorite of royalty; Isabel the Catholic, one of Spain's most powerful monarchs, was crowned Queen of Castile in the Plaza Mayor.

Today, the city is a medley of architectural styles and a veritable guide to architecture through the ages, from medieval walls and a Gothic Cathedral to the fairytale Alcázar fortress. Visitors should explore its narrow streets and consider staying the night; the city's nightlife is mainly left to locals once the tourists have boarded their tour buses back to Madrid.

SIGHTS
★ Roman Aqueduct

What was a relatively short aqueduct channeling water 15 kilometers (9 miles) from the nearby mountains to the small Roman town of Segovia is today one of the most well-preserved and impressive examples of Roman engineering in the world. Locals are used to having this Goliath of engineering slap-bang in the middle of their city, but for those visiting for the first time, its grandeur and dominance is staggering.

It is a testament to the Romans' engineering prowess that the aqueduct was still in use right up to the 20th century. At 813 meters (2,667 feet) in length and 28.5 meters (94 feet) high at its highest point, the aqueduct is best viewed from the Plaza Azoguejo; you can climb the stairs to the left of the square to get a higher view of the structure. Incredibly, the

Previous: Toledo; Toledo door details; Segovia aqueduct.

Madrid Day Trips

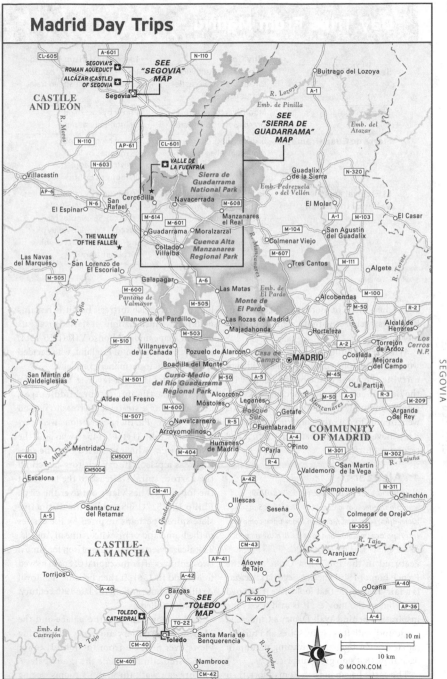

CL-605 A-601 N-110
SEGOVIA'S
ROMAN AQUEDUCT ⊠
ALCÁZAR (CASTLE) ⊠
OF SEGOVIA
SEE "SEGOVIA" MAP
Segovia
Buitrago del Lozoya

CASTILE AND LEÓN
R. Lozoya A-1
Emb. de Pinilla

N-110 AP-61 CL-601
SEE "SIERRA DE GUADARRAMA" MAP
Emb. del Atazar

N-603
⊠ VALLE DE LA FUENFRÍA
Sierra de Guadarrama National Park
Guadalix de la Sierra N-320
Emb. Pedrezuela o del Vellón

Villacastín
AP-6
N-6 San Rafael Cercedilla Navacerrada M-608 El Molar
El Espinar
M-614 M-601 A-1 M-103 El Casar
THE VALLEY OF THE FALLEN ★ Guadarrama Moralzarzal Manzanares el Real M-104 San Agustín del Guadalix
Collado Villalba **Cuenca Alta Manzanares Regional Park** Colmenar Viejo
Las Navas del Marqués San Lorenzo de El Escorial
M-607 Tres Cantos M-111 Algete
M-505 Galapagar A-6 Las Matas Emb. de El Pardo Alcobendas M-100
M-600 M-505 **Monte de El Pardo** M-50 R-2
Pantano de Valmayor
Villanueva del Pardillo Las Rozas de Madrid Hortaleza Alcalá de Henares
M-510 M-503 Majadahonda Los Cerros N.P.
Villanueva de la Cañada Pozuelo de Alarcón Casa de Campo ⊛ MADRID Coslada A-2 Torrejón de Ardoz
Boadilla del Monte Mejorada del Campo
San Martín de Valdeiglesias M-501 **Curso Medio del Río Guadarrama Regional Park** M-50 A-5 M-45 La Partija
Aldea del Fresno Alcorcón Leganés M-50 A-3 R-3 R-209
M-600 Móstoles Bosque Sur Getafe Arganda del Rey
M-507 Navalcarnero R-5 Fuenlabrada **COMMUNITY OF MADRID**
Arroyomolinos A-4
Méntrida Humanes de Madrid Parla Pinto M-301 M-302
N-403 CM5007 R-4
Escalona CM5004 A-42 Valdemoro San Martín de la Vega R. Tajuña
CM-41 Ciempozuelos M-311 Chinchón
Santa Cruz del Retamar Illescas Seseña Colmenar de Oreja
A-5 M-305
CASTILE-LA MANCHA
CM-43 R. Tajo
AP-41 Aranjuez R-4
Torrijos Añover de Tajo
A-42 Ocaña A-40
Bargas **SEE "TOLEDO" MAP** N-400 AP-36
Emb. de Castrejón TOLEDO CATHEDRAL ⊠ TO-22 A-4
R. Tajo ⊠ Toledo Santa María de Benquerencia R. Algodor
CM-40 Nambroca
CM-401 CM-42

0 — 10 mi
0 — 10 km
© MOON.COM

Day Trips From Madrid

	Why Go?	Travel Time from Madrid
Segovia	Roman aqueduct, Alcázar fortress, fairytale castle, Gothic cathedral	1 hour, 15 minutes by car; 30 minutes by high-speed train
Toledo	Moorish architecture, El Greco, Gothic cathedral	1 hour by car; 30 minutes by high-speed train
Sierra de Guadarrama	hiking, skiing, charming mountain villages	1 hour by car; 1 hour, 45 minutes by local train (*cercanías*); 60 to 90 minutes by bus
El Escorial and the Valley of the Fallen	Spanish Civil War history, grand monastery where Charles I is buried	40 minutes by car; 50 minutes by commuter train (to El Escorial); 55 minutes by bus to El Escorial. Valley of the Fallen is not accessible via public transit.

166 arches, made of more than 20,000 granite bricks, were set without a single drop of mortar.

When it was built, each of the tallest arches would have displayed a bronze lettered sign carrying the name of the builder along with the date of construction. Because no such signs remained, for many years historians were unable to date the construction. Today, it is believed it was built between the first and second century AD.

★ Alcázar

Plaza Reina Victoria Eugenia; tel. 92/146-0759; www.alcazardesegovia.com; Apr-Oct, Mon-Sun 10am-8pm; Nov-Mar, Mon-Sun 10am-6pm; complete entry (palace, museum and tower) €8, museum and palace €5.50, John II tower €2.50

Featured in the 1967 film *Camelot* as the French home of Sir Lancelot, Segovia's Alcázar is a fairytale castle that looks like it stepped right out of the movies. It is said it was the inspiration behind Walt Disney's Cinderella castle and, with its soaring spires and turrets, moat, drawbridge, and stunning mountain backdrop, that's no great surprise.

The castle began life as a Roman fort, then became a Moorish fortress, but little remains of its former incarnations. It started to take its current shape under Alfonso VIII (1155-1214) and his wife Eleanor of England, who decided to make it their permanent residence.

The fortress was a favorite home of the kings of Castile during the Middle Ages, and served as a strategic fortress to defend the kingdom. Further renovations were carried out by John II (1406-1454), who built the "New Tower," which was used over the centuries as a prison (today, visitors can climb the narrow, spiral staircase to the terrace at the top, which has views out over the city); Philip II (1527-1598) added the distinctive slate spires, perhaps inspired by the castles of the homeland of his wife, Anne of Austria. The alcázar served as a state prison for almost two centuries after the capital of Spain moved to Madrid in 1561. It then became the Royal Artillery School and, in the late 19th century, a military college.

Today, you can visit the palace and the Museum of Artillery and soak up amazing views over Segovia from the John II tower (a 152-step climb). Inside the grand palace, visitors can walk through its rooms, seeing

Segovia

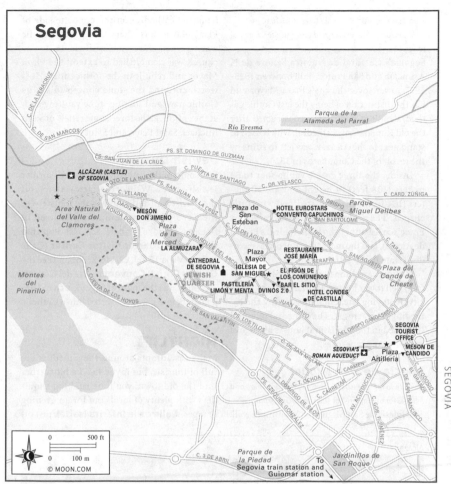

Río Eresma

Parque de la Alameda del Parral

C. DE LA VERACRUZ
C. DE SAN MARCOS
PS. ST. DOMINGO DE GUZMAN
PS. SAN JUAN DE LA CRUZ
C. PUERTA DE SANTIAGO
POZO DE LA NUEVE
C. DR. VELASCO
PS. OBISPO
C. CARD. ZÚÑIGA

★ **ALCÁZAR (CASTLE) OF SEGOVIA**

Area Natural del Valle del Clamores
C. VELARDE
C. DAOIZ
RONDA DON JUAN II
PS. SAN JUAN DE LA CRUZ
▼ **MESÓN DON JIMENO**
Plaza de la Merced
C. MARQUÉS DEL ARCO
Plaza de San Esteban
C. VALDELÁGUILA
★ **HOTEL EUROSTARS CONVENTO CAPUCHINOS**
C. SAN BARTOLOMÉ
C. SAN NICOLÁS
Parque Miguel Delibes
C. TARAY

Montes del Pinarillo
C. CUESTA DE LOS HOYOS
LA ALMUZARA ▼
CATHEDRAL DE SEGOVIA ✝
JEWISH QUARTER
PASTELERÍA LIMÓN Y MENTA
C. DE SAN CAMPOS
Plaza Mayor
IGLESIA DE SAN MIGUEL ★
RESTAURANTE JOSÉ MARÍA ★
C. SERAFÍN
EL FIGÓN DE LOS COMUNEROS ▼
▼ **BAR EL SITIO**
DVINOS 2.0 ▼
HOTEL CONDES DE CASTILLA ●
C. JUAN BRAVO
C. SAN AGUSTÍN
Plaza del Conde de Cheste

C. DE SAN VALENTÍN
PS. LOS TILOS
C. DE SAN MILLÁN
C. DEL OBISPO GANDÁSEGUI
SEGOVIA TOURIST OFFICE
MESÓN DE CÁNDIDO ▼
SEGOVIA'S ROMAN AQUEDUCT ★
Plaza Artillería ▼
C. DE SAN FRANCISCO
EL TEODOSIO
EL GRANDE
PS. ST. DOMINGO DE SILOS
C. T. OCHOA
C. DE ROMÁN
C. CARRETAS
C. EZEQUIEL GONZÁLEZ
AV. ACUEDUCTO
C. GOB. FERNÁNDEZ JIMÉNEZ

0 — 500 ft
0 — 100 m
© MOON.COM

Parque de la Piedad
To Segovia train station and Guiomar station
Jardinillos de San Roque
C. 3 DE ABRIL

where generations of kings and queens lived. The Throne Room holds the carved wooden thrones of the Catholic Monarchs, Isabella and Ferdinand (Isabel y Fernando), under their motto "Tanto monta, monta tanto" ("They amount to the same, the same they amount to"—a comment on the equality the pair shared as joint monarchs). The Sala de Piñas (Hall of Pineapples) is so-called because of the hundreds of pineapple shapes that adorn its ceiling.

Many of the rooms are lined with depictions of Spanish monarchs; in the Hall of the Fireplace, decorated with original 16th-century furniture, there are portraits of Felipe II and Felipe III, while the Hall of Kings holds 52 sculptures of medieval kings and queens.

The palace is also rich in intricately woven tapestries; note the depictions of Isabella and Ferdinand that surround the Royal Chamber.

There are regular tours in Spanish (€1), but English-language private tours must be booked in advance (€40). Alternately, audio guides in English can be rented (€3).

Cathedral de Segovia

Plaza Mayor; tel. 92/146-2205; Mon-Sun

9am-9:30pm; visit to the bell tower 10:30am, 12:30pm, and 4pm; church and tower ticket €7, bell tower €5

Segovia's Catedral de Nuestra Señora de la Asunción and San Frutos, built between 1525-1577, towers over the city's Plaza Mayor and has the distinction of being the last Gothic cathedral built in Spain. It was constructed after the old Romanesque cathedral, which used to stand next to the Alcázar, was left in ruins by the revolt of the Comuneros in 1520.

Inside, the three gothic vaults soar to 33 meters (108 feet) in height and are 50 meters (164 feet) wide, and are lined with little chapels. The golden altarpiece was carved by Francisco Sabatini (who built Madrid's Puerta de Alcalá), and the majestic stained-glass windows date to the 17th century.

Visitors can climb the 90-meter-high (295-foot) bell tower for spectacular views over the city; if staying late, don't miss seeing the cathedral lit up at night. The cathedral museum (included in the admission) houses a range of artworks and tapestries.

Iglesia de San Miguel

Calle de la Infanta Isabel, 1; tel. 616956104; Thurs and Sun 11:30am-2pm, Fri-Sat 11am-2pm, 5pm-7pm

The Iglesia de San Miguel, a two-minute walk from the cathedral on the opposite side of Plaza Mayor, was where Isabel the Catholic was crowned Queen of Castile in 1474. The church was demolished to extend the Plaza Mayor and rebuilt in the 16th century. It is worth entering the stone church to see its Gothic nave and soaring stone vaulting and, at the entrance, the three stone reliefs of Saint Michael, Saint Peter, and Saint Paul.

Jewish Quarter

Just south of the cathedral is the city's former Jewish quarter. Wander the narrow streets off the tourist trail and follow in the footsteps of the city's Jewish community, who lived in the area from as far back as 1215. Pop into the **Jewish Quarter Visitor Center** (Calle Judería Vieja 12; tel. 92/146-2396) and see the **Corpus Christi Convent** (Plaza del Corpus, 7), which was the main of Segovia's five synagogues before it was converted into a Catholic Church in 1410.

NIGHTLIFE

Many restaurants around the aqueduct are full of tourists, but if you head a bit further into the old town, you'll be rubbing shoulders with plenty of locals out for an evening of tapas. **Calle de la Infanta Isabel**, just off

Alcázar

the Plaza Mayor, is a good place to start; it's lined in tapas bars and restaurants, from the historic to the modern, that are all reasonably priced and packed with locals come evening.

DVINOS 2.0

Calle de la Infanta Isabel, 12; tel. 64/434-6252; Mon-Wed 12:30pm-4:45pm, 7:15pm-midnight; Thurs-Fri 12:30pm-4:45pm, 7:15pm-2am; Sat 1pm-2:30am; Sun 12:30pm-midnight; €1.80

Located on Segovia's famous "bar street" where locals come on an evening to eat, drink, and be merry, DVinos is a no-frills joint that packs them in for its offer of a tapa and a *caña* (little beer) for just €1.80. It's sufficiently off the tourist trail for you to feel like you're mingling with a local crowd. Tapas include Spanish favorites along with international flavors like hummus and mini nachos.

BAR EL SITIO

Calle de la Infanta Isabel, 9; tel. 92/146-0996; daily 9am-midnight; €5 tapas, €15-€20 restaurant

The wildly popular front-of-house tapas bar packs in the crowds for its chilled beers, wine, and free plates of tapas; this is the place to stop on a tapas crawl or for an early-evening bite. For a more substantial sit-down dinner, the upstairs restaurant, a cozy space with wooden beams and furniture that feels like a medieval dining room, specializes in traditional dishes like oxtail, calamari, Galician-style octopus, and steak.

EL FIGÓN DE LOS COMUNEROS

Travesía del Patín, 4; tel. 92/146-0309; www. figondeloscomuneros.com; daily 10am-midnight; €5 tapas, €15-€20 restaurant

Down a little side street just off the buzzing Calle de la Infanta Isabel, this dark-wood-clad restaurant and bar is dripping in medieval charm, and the front bar area is a place locals like to hang out over a *caña* or two. Its restaurant specializes in traditional local dishes (and is much less tourist-heavy than some of the more well-known local restaurants), from roast suckling pig to *cocido* (a meat, vegetable,

and chickpea stew from Madrid), which it serves every Thursday lunchtime.

FOOD

Wandering around Segovia, it's hard to miss the many references to the city's star dish: *cochinillo* (roast suckling pig). Restaurants display beaming plastic pigs (or, in some cases the real thing, somewhat less smiley) sitting in pots in their windows, while souvenirs, from magnets to tea towels, all feature the humble hog.

The pig is cooked simply (roasted in a wood-fired oven) and comes out crispy on the outside, and so soft on the inside you can slice it with nothing more than a plate (yes, a plate—chefs show off how tender the meat is by slicing it up with this blunt instrument, which is also what the locals do). Go for lunch service to give you time to walk off the heavy meal during the afternoon. Good places to try it are Restaurante José María, Meson Don Jimeno, and Meson de Candido. Everywhere gets busy, so reservations are a must.

Servings are usually one portion of the suckling pig, sometimes with potatoes, and diners can order starters, sides like salads, and desserts. Some restaurants offer a lunchtime fixed-price menu, which might include a starter and dessert as well as the roast suckling pig.

RESTAURANTE JOSÉ MARÍA

Calle Cronista Lecea, 11; tel. 92/146-1111; www. restaurantejosemaria.com; Mon-Thurs 10am-1am, Fri 10am-2am, Sat 10am-2am, Sun 10am-1am; €40

Near the Plaza Mayor, Restaurante José María is a renowned favorite where visitors can expect the full show—and prices to match. Waiters will cut your suckling pig with a plate beside your table, and owner José María will welcome you with open arms. The spacious dining room, with period wooden beams, is a permanent hubbub of diners, many of them tourists after a true taste of Segovia. There are plenty of traditional options besides roast suckling pig, too, including several vegetarian dishes. The front bar area does some great tapas dishes.

MESON DON JIMENO

Calle Daoiz, 15; tel. 92/146-6350; Wed-Mon 11am-5:30pm; €20-25

This local favorite is a less expensive option for *cochinillo* than some of the more tourist-heavy restaurants, and does a good range of other local dishes, from soups to salads. Close to the Alcázar, it's a good pit stop for lunch, and its checked tablecloths, wooden beams and yellow walls lend it a country kitchen ambiance.

MESON DE CANDIDO

Plaza Azoguejo, 5; tel. 92/142-5911; www. mesondecandido.es; Mon-Sun 1pm-4:30pm, 8pm-11pm; €24

Set in an atmospheric 18th-century building, Meson de Candido has great views over Segovia's aqueduct, especially from its second-floor dining room. It is renowned for its buttery-soft *cochinillo* and delicious roast lamb, both cooked in its wood-fired oven. Reservations are a must.

LA ALMUZARA

Calle Marqués del Arco, 3; tel. 92/146-0622; Wed-Sun midday-midnight; €11

For vegetarians, this cute family-run restaurant is a good antidote to the mostly carnivorous offerings in Segovia, with meatless dishes like couscous, crepes, tofu, and seitan as well as salads and a mixture of vegetarian and meaty pastas and pizzas. Their vegetarian lasagne is especially tasty. It has more of a local vibe than the many tourist spots in the city center.

PASTELERÍA LIMÓN Y MENTA

Calle Isabel la católica, 2; tel. 92/146-2257; www. pastelerialimonymenta.com; Mon-Fri 9am-8:30pm, Sat-Sun 9am-9pm; €2

This lovely bakery on the Plaza Mayor has been making a local speciality, *ponche segoviano*, a kind of layer cake covered in marzipan, for over 30 years. Buy it whole or by the slice, to take out or to enjoy in the bakery's café. Its cabinets are stacked with so many treats you might just want to try everything.

ACCOMMODATIONS

HOTEL EUROSTARS CONVENTO CAPUCHINOS

Plaza Capuchinos, 2; tel. 92/141-5250; www. eurostarshotels.co.uk/eurostars-convento-capuchinos.html; €210

Eurostars Convento Capuchinos, a beautifully converted convent dating back to 1637, mixes a modern aesthetic—including minimalist design and boutique furnishings—with the building's over-400-year history; original features such as wooden beams have been lovingly preserved. Its 62 rooms are bright and comfortable, and many have mountain views, while its spa (additional charge) and gourmet Villena restaurant are the ideal places to relax after a long day of sightseeing.

HOTEL CONDES DE CASTILLA

Calle José Canalejas, 5; tel. 92/146-3529; www. hotelcondesdecastilla.com; €85

Set in a restored 13th-century palace, this cozy hotel is just a couple of minutes' walk from the central Plaza Mayor and Segovia Cathedral, and within easy walking distance to the aqueduct and Alcázar. Rooms are comfortable, with dark wood floors, air conditioning, and flat-screen TVs, and the price—especially if booked well in advance, when discounts are available—is reasonable.

INFORMATION AND SERVICES

Segovia Tourist Office (Plaza Azoguejo, 1; tel. 92/146-6720; www.turismodesegovia.com; Mon-Sat 10am-6:30pm, Sun 10am-5pm) has maps, brochures, books, and information on tours and all of the city's sights.

GETTING THERE

The easiest and fastest way to get to Segovia is by the high-speed AVE train, just a 30-minute journey from central Madrid.

Train

Renfe (www.renfe.com) offers two options for those traveling by train from Madrid to Segovia. The high-speed AVE train leaves frequently (from around 6:30am and every 30-45 minutes throughout the day, last train back to Madrid at around 10:15pm) from Madrid's Chamartín station and gets to Segovia's Guiomar station in under 30 minutes (tickets between €10-€20). The station is around 6 kilometers (4 miles) outside the city center, but you can take a bus (the L11 or L12, fares are €1 one-way, journey time into Segovia around 20 minutes; buses leave approximately every 20 minutes from outside the AVE station) or a taxi (around €8 for a 15-minute journey) into the center if you don't relish the walk.

The less frequent regional train, which also leaves from Madrid's Chamartín station, takes around one hour and 45 minutes but is a cheaper option, with tickets usually around €7 each way. (First train around 11:15am, last train back to Madrid 8:45pm; two to three trains a day.) This train will take you to Segovia train station, 1.5 kilometers (1 mile) from the city center.

Tickets can be booked online ahead of time at www.renfe.com.

Bus

The cheapest way to get to Segovia is by bus.

Avanzabus (tel. 91/272-2832; www.avanzabus. com) runs regular buses from Madrid's Moncloa station to Segovia. The journey takes around 1 hour and 20 minutes, and you can buy one-way, return, or open-return tickets (from €4 one-way). The first bus leaves Madrid at around 6:30am and the last bus leaves Segovia at around 9:45pm; there are approximately 40 buses a day from Madrid to Segovia. The bus arrives at Segovia Estacio (Avenida del Obispo Quesada, 1), a 20-minute walk or five-minute taxi ride to the center.

Car

Take the A-6 motorway northwest from Madrid to the N-603 national highway north to Segovia. Travel time is 1 hour 15 mins.

There is a large car park close to the aqueduct (parking around €15/day) that is open 24 hours a day and offers day, 24-hour, and weekend parking passes that you can also book online (www.parkia.es/en/aparcamientos/parking-acueducto-segovia).

GETTING AROUND

Once you are in Segovia, the old city, where all the main sights, restaurants, and hotels are located, is easily walkable. You might want to get a taxi to the station if carrying luggage. Try **Radio Taxi Segovia** (tel. 92/144-5000, www.radiotaxisegovia.es).

Toledo

When Madrid was nothing more than a rugged backwater, Toledo (pop. 83,000) was one of Spain's most important cities, a shining example of architecture, culture, and religion.

Sitting high upon a rocky outcrop above the Tagus River, 74 kilometers (46 miles) south of the Spanish capital, Toledo has been a UNESCO World Heritage Site since 1986 and is one of the most popular day trip options from Madrid. It became the capital of the Visigoth kingdom of Hispania in the 6th century and, when the Moors established Al-Andalus in 711 AD, it became an important Muslim center, located as it was on the northern frontier of their new kingdom. This period is often viewed as a utopian time of peace, when Muslims, Christians, and Jews lived together in what has been termed by historians as "la convivencia." But these halcyon times could not last and, with the expulsion of the Jews in 1492, Toledo's experiment in multiculturalism was well and truly destroyed. Charles I set his court in Toledo, making the city the imperial capital until 1561, when Philip II moved the capital to Madrid.

The city was the center of Spanish religion, declared the "seat of the church in Spain" after Alfonso VI conquered the Moors in 1085. It remained the center of power in Spain until the 16th century, when the move of Spain's capital to Madrid marked the beginning of the end for Toledo's power.

Toledo has been a steel and sword-making city since around 500 BC, and its weapons were used by Hannibal during the Punic Wars. It is said the Romans were astonished by the quality and hardness of Toledo steel, and the Roman legions adopted Toledo weaponry. These days, swords are a common souvenir from the city.

Tourists flock to Toledo for its diverse history, visiting the Christian, Jewish, and Muslim sights that made the city renowned for its mixture of cultures. Its Gothic cathedral, Jewish Quarter, and miniature mosque, Cristo de la Luz, shed fascinating light on Toledo's history for the modern visitor, and the picturesque golden shades of the city's skyline are the ideal subject for snap-happy travelers.

The city's cuisine, too, is a big draw. Sweet-toothed visitors make a beeline for Toledo's marzipan shops (it is said to have been invented right here in the city). When lunchtime calls, it's time to try some local cuisine, from rich, hearty stews to tapas at the local market.

SIGHTS
★ Toledo Cathedral

Plaza del Ayuntamiento; tel. 92/522-2241; www.catedralprimada.es; Mon-Sat 10am-6:30pm, Sun and public holidays 2pm-6:30pm; €12.50

One of the world's most majestic Gothic cathedrals and considered by many to be the pinnacle of Spain's gothic churches for its size, detail, and artistic riches, Saint Mary's Cathedral was built by Ferdinand (Fernando) III in 1227 on top of an earlier mosque. Today, the gargantuan, mainly Gothic cathedral still has a few mudéjar (a Moorish-influenced style) touches, such as the chapter house, just off the cloister, with its mudéjar wooden ceiling.

The *coro* (choir stalls) feature intricately carved wood depicting scenes from the capture of Granada by Rodrigo Alemán, while the Transparente, a baroque altarpiece behind the sanctuary, is illuminated by the skylight above. The shafts of sunlight lend the piece a magical, spiritual quality.

The cathedral houses many art treasures

Toledo view

Toledo

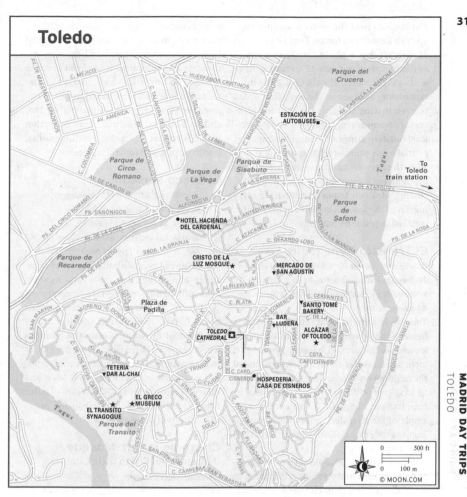

by Spanish, Italian, and Flemish painters. The sacristy, for many visitors, is the highlight of the cathedral, holding works by the likes of El Greco, Velázquez, and Zubarán.

Mammoth in its grandeur, the cathedral has five naves and 88 columns, as well as stained glass windows dating back to the 14th, 15th, and 16th centuries. The Mozarabic chapel in the southeast corner was expressly dedicated to services for Toledo's Mozarabic population (Christians who lived under Muslim rule at the time of Al-Andalus). Its central Virgin and Child mosaic was made in a Vatican workshop.

Services in the Mozarabic Rite are still given today.

Alcázar of Toledo

Calle de la Union; tel. 92/523-8800; www.museo.ejercito.es; Thurs-Tues 11am-5pm; €5, €2.50 (reduced)

At the highest point of the old city is the Alcázar, a grand stone fortification that dates back to Roman times and which was renovated under Charles I and Philip II in the 16th century. In 1521, Hernán Cortés was received in the Alcázar by Charles I after conquering the Aztecs. In the Siege of the Alcázar during the Spanish Civil War (1936-39), the

Nationalists held the fortress against huge Spanish Republican forces. Today it is the site of Toledo's **Army Museum**. The extensive museum, spread out over 13 themed halls as well as eight more halls that trace the military history of Spain in chronological order, is a fascinating hodgepodge of stuff: 17th-century Spanish army uniforms and magnificent jousting armor sit alongside weaponry, official army photographs, and decorations. The ethnography collection features pieces brought back from Spanish colonies, including Mexican armor and intricate carvings from the Spanish colonies in the Pacific. Admission is free on Sundays.

El Tránsito Synagogue

Calle Samuel Levi; tel. 92/522-3665; Nov 1-Feb 28, Tues-Sat 9:30am-6pm; Mar 1-Oct 31, Tues-Sat 9:30am-7:30pm, Sun and public holidays 10am-3pm; €8, admission free for students

Toledo's *judería* (the old Jewish quarter) is home to the Sinagoga del Tránsito, otherwise known as the Samuel ha-Levi Synagogue, after the treasurer to Pedro I who founded the building on special decree from the king in 1355 (the building of synagogues was by then banned in Spain). It's an excellent example of mudéjar decoration, the Moorish-inspired style that flourished after the Islamic rule of Spain.

Its stucco walls, a tangle of floral and geometric patterns and Arabic script, bring to mind the Alhambra in Granada. They surround the huge Wall of the Torah Ark, where the synagogue's Torah would have been kept. It's easy to imagine Toledo's Jewish community gathering for prayers here—the men downstairs, the women upstairs—and gazing over this ornate place of safekeeping for their holy book. The synagogue's Hebrew inscriptions, which run around the edge of the space, are one of the best examples of Medieval Jewish epigraphy in the world. Don't forget to look up: the building is topped with an exquisite mudéjar decorative wooden ceiling that dates to the 14th century.

After the expulsion of the Jews in 1492, the synagogue was used as a priory, church, and monastery. In 1877, it was declared a National Monument and, in the mid-20th century, was resorted and renovated. It has been home to the **Museo Sefardí**, which charts the history of Judaism and Jewish culture in Spain, since 1964 (free entry on Saturdays after 2pm and on Sundays). The museum's collection includes typical Sephardic wedding outfits, Jewish scrolls, and funeral statues.

El Greco Museum

Paseo Tránsito; tel. 92/599-0980; www.mecd. gob.es/mgreco/inicio.html; Mar 1-Oct 31, Tues-Sat 9:30am-7:30pm; Nov 1-Feb 28, Tues-Sat 9:30am-6pm; Sun and public holidays, 10am-3pm; €3

Located in Toledo's Jewish quarter, this museum—spread over two buildings—pays homage to one of the city's most famous sons, who, although he was born in Crete (hence "El Greco," the Greek), spent much of his life in Toledo. The museum, which recreates the home of El Greco, houses the painter's works, especially from the later period, as well as paintings by some of his contemporaries. Notable works include the "View and Plan of Toledo" (1608), "The Tears of Saint Peter" (1580-89), and the "Apostolate" series of paintings of Jesus' apostles.

Cristo de la Luz Mosque
(Mesquita del Cristo de la Luz)

Calle Carmelitas Descalzas, 10; tel. 92/526-5419; Mar 1-Oct 15, Mon-Sun 10am-6:45pm; Oct 16-Feb 28, Mon-Sun 10am-5:45pm; €2.80, free for under 11s

Glimpse one of the few remaining signs of Toledo's Moorish culture at the Mesquita del Cristo de la Luz (the Cristo de la Luz Mosque), the last remaining mosque in Toledo—which, at the peak of Moorish rule, was home to ten.

The small mosque, with a façade featuring horseshoe arches typical of the Moorish style, is fascinating in that its style is practically unchanged since it was built in 999 AD in the city's Medina, then home to wealthy Muslim families. The eight-by-eight-square-meter (86 square feet by 86 square feet) building is decorated with a series of arches that bring to mind

Marzipan

Marzipan is one of Toledo's most famous foods, and a must-try when visiting the city. The first written reference to this treat, made from ground almonds and sugar, was in Toledo in the 16th century.

It is said that marzipan was brought to Spain by the Moors. Its origins have also been attributed to the nuns of the Convent of San Clemente in Toledo, who, during a particularly bad famine when wheat was unavailable, mixed a paste of sugar and almonds to feed the local people.

Toledo marzipan is today protected by a D.O. (designation of origin), and is one of the world's most famous varieties. Santo Tomé Bakery (Calle Santo Tomé, 3 and Plaza Zocodover, 7, www.mazapan.com) has been making marzipan since 1856. Inside, long, glass-fronted display cases hold marzipan, laid out in individual pieces and in boxes, a good option for those who want to take some home. The shop also sells pastries and chocolates. You won't be able to miss the giant statue of Don Quixote, made entirely out of marzipan; it's the tallest marzipan structure in the world.

Locals typically eat marzipan as a snack, with a coffee or after lunch. The most popular form is small pieces of marzipan, the simplest (and many would say, best) version of the food.

Córdoba's great mosque, but on a miniature scale; the mosque's vaults and arches are said to have been inspired by the Great Mosque of Córdoba, which was built just a few years before. The mosque's layout, which would have made it easy for students to gather around a teacher, has led historians to surmise that it could have been used as a school, or *madrasa*.

FOOD
BAR LUDEÑA
Plaza Magdalena, 10; tel. 92/522-3384; Sun-Fri 10:30am-4:30pm, 8pm-11:30, Sat 10:30am-4:30pm, 8pm-midnight; €15

It's easy to fall into a tourist trap in Toledo, but no such fate awaits at Bar Ludeña, a neighborhood bar with no pretensions but delicious and hearty local food. It serves Toledo specialities like *carcamusa*, a pork and vegetable stew. Try its *menú del día*, a three-course set lunch, including wine, for less than €15. With eight starters and eight main courses, there are plenty of local classics to choose from.

MERCADO DE SAN AGUSTÍN
Cuesta Águila, 1-3; tel. 69/610-4308; Sun-Thurs 10am-1:30pm, Fri-Sat 10am-2pm

This four-story market, opened in 2014, brings together local cuisine and international flavors in a laid-back space ideal for trying lots of different bites. Its 24 stalls include wine bars, pintxos (Basque tapas), and seafood, as well as burgers, Japanese food, and Italian food. Its upstairs cocktail bar is a cool place to while away the evening, and its terrace is a popular warm weather spot.

TETERIA DAR AL-CHAI
Plaza Barrio Nuevo, 5; tel. 92/522-5625; Mon-Tues 9:30am-9:30pm, Wed 9:30am-1:30pm, Thurs 9:30am-9:30pm, Fri 9:30am-midnight, Sat 4pm-12:30am, Sun 4pm-10pm, €10

With its mudéjar-inspired decor and its sweet mint tea, Teteria Dar Al-Chai lets you experience some of the sights, smells, and tastes of Moorish Toledo. Located in the Jewish quarter close to the synagogue, it specializes in teas and desserts, with an extensive tea menu and a good range of crepes and waffles. There is an outdoor terrace in summer.

ACCOMMODATIONS
HOSPEDERIA CASA DE CISNEROS
Calle Cardenal Cisneros, 12; tel. 92/522-8828; www.hospederiacasadecisneros.com; €49

Located in the heart of Toledo's old town, this small, charming guesthouse is an excellent value. It is set in a converted 16th-century building close to the cathedral; its ten ensuite rooms are packed with historical touches such

TOLEDO

MADRID DAY TRIPS

as original wooden beams and exposed brick walls. There is a buffet breakfast and a must-visit roof terrace with impressive views over the cathedral. Staff are friendly and happy to give tips and recommendations.

HOTEL HACIENDA DEL CARDENAL

Paseo de Recaredo, 24; tel. 92/522-0862; www. haciendadelcardenal.com; €87

With an historic setting, including gardens surrounded by original 11th-century Arab walls, this hotel, set in a building from the 18th century, takes guests back in time. The beautiful outdoor area includes a small pool and terrace. Rooms are spacious—some with four poster beds—and come with all the necessary amenities, like air conditioning and flat-screen televisions. The hotel's restaurant, set in a romantic courtyard, is a great choice for a charming dinner of local classics.

GETTING THERE

The cheapest travel option to visit Toledo from Madrid is by bus, though it takes twice as long as the high-speed train, which for speed and ease is the best option.

Train

The high-speed AVE train, operated by RENFE (www.renfe.com), goes from Madrid's Puerta de Atocha train station to Toledo in just over 30 minutes (€10.30 each way). Trains start at between 8am-9am and the last train back is usually at around 9:30pm. (Around 15 trains run each way per day.)

Toledo's train station is a 20-minute walk from the old city. Alternately, you can hop in a taxi (around €6 for a journey of under 10 minutes) or take the bus (number 5 stops outside the station and takes you to Plaza Zocodover). Tickets are €1.40 one way, and buses run every 15 minutes from just after 7am to 11pm.

Bus

Spanish bus company **ALSA** (tel. 90/242-2242; www.alsa.es) runs regular buses from the Intercambiador de Plaza Elíptica (on Line 6 and Line 11 of the Madrid metro). You can buy tickets online at Alsa's website. Make sure to choose a "direct" ticket when purchasing for the quickest journey (around an hour). The first buses leave Madrid at around 6:30am and the last bus from Toledo is at around 10:30pm. Buses leave around every 30 minutes throughout the day until around 11pm and buses arrive at Toledo's Estación de Autobuses (Avenida Castilla la Mancha, 4); it is a 15-minute walk into the center or a five-minute taxi ride (around €5).

Car

From Madrid, go down the A-42 motorway south toward Toledo. The drive (75 kilometers/46 miles) takes around an hour. You can park for free at the bus and train stations and then walk into the center (the winding, small streets of the old town are best avoided in a car!).

GETTING AROUND

The best way to explore Toledo's old town is on foot. The narrow streets are not vehicle friendly, so wear comfy shoes.

Sierra de Guadarrama National Park

You can be out of Madrid's busy city center and out among the peaks and forests of the **Sierra de Guadarrama National Park** (www.parquenacionalsierraguadarrama.es) in less than an hour, whether you're looking for a leisurely mountain hike, a day skiing on the pistes, or an opportunity to explore one of the Sierra's charming small towns.

The Sierra de Guadarrama mountain range runs from southwest of Madrid to northeast of the city, over roughly 80 kilometers (50 miles). The highest peak is Peñalara at 2,428 meters (7,966 feet). It is an extremely popular getaway for Madrid families, and the Sierra's sights can get busy on weekends in high season. It is slightly more off the beaten track for international visitors, who tend to stick to the well-trodden day trips of Toledo and Segovia, but if you are looking to escape to nature close to Madrid, it is definitely worth a visit.

The sierra is covered in sweeping pine and oak forests, and at higher altitudes features glacial lakes and granite fields (rocky outcrops often concentrated around the mountains' peaks). No one peak tends to stand out above the others, giving the mountains an undulating feel, their wavy outline a backdrop to many of the little villages nestled at lower altitudes. The sierra is crisscrossed with trails for hikers of all abilities.

GETTING THERE

The best way to travel to the Sierra de Guadarrama and reach your exact destination is by car. There are also decent public transport links to the main towns in the Sierra, from where you can set off on hikes. From Madrid, take the **A-6** northwest, then the **M-601** north to reach Cercedilla, one of the region's gateways, in about an hour.

If you're taking public transit from Madrid, the region is accessible via bus and train. **Bus 691** goes from Madrid's Moncloa station to Navacerrada and Peñalara. The **C2 cercanía** local train goes from Madrid's Chamartín Station direct to Cercedilla in just over an hour. Stay on the train until Cotos for Peñalara, or switch to the C9 in Cercedilla to reach Puerto de Navacerrada ski resort in around 15 mins. Manzanares El Real is somewhat separate, and accessible via **bus 724** from Madrid.

CERCEDILLA

The small mountain town of Cercedilla (pop. 7,000) is a good starting point for hikers and those looking to head up to the sierra's ski resorts. (It's just a 15-minute train ride from Puerta de Navacerrada ski resort.) While the town is pleasant enough, with a few good café-restaurants to sate hungry stomachs and an alpine mountain village feel, it is more of a jumping-off point than a destination in itself. The nearby Valle de la Fuenfría is a valley of pine forest that is a popular weekend spot for walking; it's also the site of a former Roman road.

Hiking

There are several hikes that start in the town of Cercedilla, covering a range of abilities. Pick up a hiking map and information on hikes from and around Cercedilla from the **Valle de la Fuenfría Visitors Center** (Ctra. de las Dehesas, km 2, Cercedilla; tel. 91/852-2213; www.parquenacionalsierraguadarrama. es/en/visit/contact-vc/vc-fuenfria; Oct-May, daily 9am-4:30pm; June and Sept, weekdays 9am-4:30pm, weekends and public holidays 9am-8pm; July and Aug, daily 9am-8pm).

Note that this is a 2-kilometer (1.2-mile) walk from the train station, so bear that extra effort/distance in mind when planning your hike!

Trails are color-coded and correspond to colored dots on trees along the trails, making the routes easy to navigate.

Sierra de Guadarrama National Park

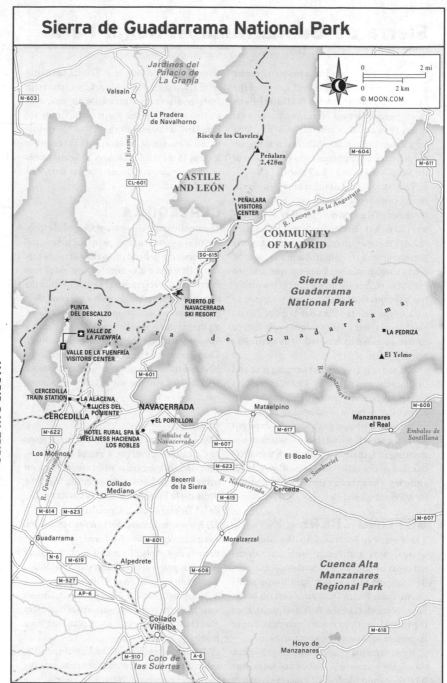

Jardines del
Palacio de
La Granja

Valsaín

La Pradera
de Navalhorno

Risco de los Claveles

N-603

R. Eresma

CASTILE
AND LEÓN

CL-601

Peñalara
2,428m

PEÑALARA
VISITORS
CENTER

R. Lozoya o de la Angostura

M-604

M-611

COMMUNITY
OF MADRID

SG-615

Sierra de
Guadarrama
National Park

PUNTA
DEL DESCALZO

PUERTO DE
NAVACERRADA
SKI RESORT

Sierra   de   Guadarrama

LA PEDRIZA

VALLE DE
LA FUENFRÍA

El Yelmo

R. Manzanares

VALLE DE LA FUENFRÍA
VISITORS CENTER

M-601

CERCEDILLA
TRAIN STATION

LA ALACENA

LUCES DEL
PONIENTE

CERCEDILLA

NAVACERRADA

EL PORTILLON

Mataelpino

Manzanares
el Real

M-608

M-622

HOTEL RURAL SPA &
WELLNESS HACIENDA
LOS ROBLES

Embalse de
Navacerrada

M-617

Embalse de
Santillana

Los Molinos

M-607

El Boalo

R. Guadarrama

M-623

R. Navacerrada

R. Samburiel

Collado
Mediano

Becerril
de la Sierra

Cerceda

M-615

M-614   M-623

M-607

Guadarrama

M-601

Moralzarzal

N-6   M-619

Alpedrete

M-608

Cuenca Alta
Manzanares
Regional Park

M-527

AP-6

Collado
Villalba

M-618

M-510   A-6   Coto de
las Suertes

Hoyo de
Manzanares

0   2 mi
0   2 km
© MOON.COM

Outdoor Recreation in the Sierra de Guadarrama

HIKING

Hiking in the Sierra de Guadarrama can be a fulfilling experience of getting back to nature and taking in the fresh air and scenic views far from the big, busy city. There are just a few things to bear in mind before setting off.

First, weekends are the busiest time, so the trails will be crowded, but you'll have the security of lots of other people around. Weekdays are much quieter and you'll likely have the trails to yourself.

Check the weather reports before you go; the weather in the mountains can differ considerably from the weather in Madrid. It tends to be colder at the higher altitudes, so make sure to take some layers.

For most of the trails, a pair of comfortable walking shoes or sneakers should suffice. It's also a good plan to bring a backpack with water and a few snacks. Some hikes are not suitable during winter (roughly November through February).

For all hikes, it is recommended you drop into the local tourist information center or visitors' center to pick up an up-to-date map. Staff will also have advice about weather conditions up in the mountains.

Hiking Madrid (www.hikingmadrid.com) runs Saturday and Sunday group hikes in the Sierra and also organizes private hikes for all fitness levels. The group hikes, run in English, are a great way to meet visitors and locals and explore the sierra as part of an organized trip.

SKIING

The Sierra de Guadarrama ski season usually lasts from December until March, depending on snowfall. Madrileños flock to the slopes on winter weekends, so go on a weekday, if possible, for more powder to yourself. The popular Navacerrada ski resort has the usual pricey café/restaurant.

One issue to consider when driving to the ski resorts is parking; set off early because spaces fill up fast and cars can be turned away once the car parks are full. If you're driving in winter, it's recommended to take chains on your car.

CAMINO DEL AGUA

This easy, family-friendly hike (5.7 kilometer/3.5 mile, round trip) starts at the Valle de la Fuenfría Visitors Center and follows the "Path of Water," through thick forest canopies, past ponds and viewpoints that peek through the trees to the blanket of pines and more peaks of the sierra beyond. It's a circular loop, and is well signposted along the way.

CAMINO PURICELLI

This straightforward 10-kilometer (6.2-mile) loop through the forests surrounding Cercedilla starts and ends at Cercedilla train station. Turn left off the train and head towards the tunnel under the train tracks. Don't go through the tunnel; instead, continue straight ahead until you come to the start of the trail (a dirt trail heading uphill);

it's marked by dark blue points on the tree trunks. The trail (easy/moderate) is part dirt, part old cobbled road that winds through the trees, which provide much-needed shade during the summer.

★ VALLE (VALLEY) DE LA FUENFRÍA: CALZADA BORBÓNICA

This hike (2.9km/1.8mi, one way) follows the best-preserved portion of the ancient Roman Road that linked Titulcia village, in the Community of Madrid, to Segovia, and is suitable for all the family. Walking along the cobbles of the sierra's ancient Roman road is a spine-tingling experience, and there are plenty of curiosities along the way, such as the Roman bridge, the **Puente del Descalzo**. The road, which dates back to the reign of

Emperor Vespasian, crosses the bridge and weaves through thick pine forests. The trail begins at the Valle de la Fuenfría Visitors Center or, if driving, the Majavilán car park, and ends at the Majavilán car park.

Food
LA ALCENA DE CERCEDILLA
Calle de San Andrés, 42; tel. 91/852-2186; www. laalacenadecercedilla.com; Fri-Sat 1:30pm-midnight, Sun 1:30pm-4pm; €€20

A 10-minute walk from Cercedilla train station, this traditional mountain restaurant, with its cozy, wood-lined dining room, is the place for a hearty weekend lunch. Its huge roasting oven cooks local meats, from roast suckling pig to steaks, to perfection. There are also tapas like croquettes and blood sausage, and several vegetarian options.

Accommodations
LUCES DEL PONIENTE
Lina de Avila, 4, Cercedilla; tel. 91/852-5587; www. lucesdelponiente.com; €90

This mountain hotel makes a good base, with comfortable rooms, a big terrace, and an indoor swimming pool where you can relax after a day on the pistes. Rooms include standard doubles and doubles with a terrace looking over the mountains.

Getting There
The C2 *cercanía* (local train) goes from Chamartín Station direct to Cercedilla in just over an hour. (First train at around 6:15am, last train back at around 10:30pm; trains run every 30 minutes to every hour, depending on the time of day. The fare is €5.50 each way.)

Drivers can take the A-6 motorway northwest out of Madrid to the M-601 in Collado Villalba. Take exit 39 from the A-6 and follow the M-601 north to Cercedilla. The journey (around 60km/37mi) takes approximately an hour from Madrid.

NAVACERRADA
The gateway to Madrid's closest ski resort, Navacerrada (pop. 3,000) is a mountain village with typical wood and stone houses and a smattering of restaurants and shops geared towards the hiking and ski trade. In summer, it's a pretty spot for a day out from Madrid, and is the starting point for several hikes out to the Siete Picos (Seven Peaks) area of the sierra.

Food
EL PORTILLON (NAVACERRADA)
Paseo de los Españoles, 5; tel. 91/856-0256; Tues-Sun 10:30am-midnight; €20

Set in a beautiful stone and wood chalet in the village of Navacerrada (10km/6.2mi below the ski resort), El Portillon is a cozy spot for a hearty lunch of quality local ingredients; the meat dishes are particularly good. Tapas and drinks are served in the bar area, while meals are served in the upstairs dining room. It's a lovely setting; if visiting in winter, the entire restaurant is decorated with twinkling fairy lights. Reservations are recommended.

Accommodations
HOTEL RURAL SPA & WELLNESS HACIENDA LOS ROBLES
Avenida de Madrid, 27; tel. 91/856-0200; www. haciendalosrobles.com; €90

Around 10 kilometers (6.2 miles) from the Navacerrada ski resort, this rural hotel is a great base whether you're heading to the mountains in winter or summer. Relax in its spa or enjoy its grounds in warmer weather by making use of the tennis courts, outdoor pool, and children's playground. Rooms include doubles and suites with a double bed and one or two sofa beds, ideal for families. The hotel restaurant serves traditional local dishes.

Getting There
Be aware that the Puerto de Navacerrada stop on the *cercanía* train is for the ski resort, 10 kilometers (6.2 miles) up the mountain from Navacerrada; there is no cercanía station in the village itself, so your best bet is to take the bus from Madrid.

Bus 691 goes from Madrid's Moncloa station to Navacerrada. The journey takes around one hour. Two buses an hour leave from 7am to 10am on weekdays, and four an hour leave from 8am-10am on weekends; after 10am buses run around every hour. The fare is €5.10 each way.

By car, take the A-6 motorway northwest out of Madrid, then take exit 39 for the M-601 towards Puerto de Navacerrada, which will take you to Navacerrada.

PUERTO DE NAVACERRADA SKI RESORT

Calle Dos Castillas, 3, tel. 90/288-2328; www. puertonavacerrada.com, open during the winter (Dec-Mar)

It comes as a surprise to many visitors to Madrid that there is a ski resort a day trip's distance away from the city. Puerto de Navacerrada is a family-friendly resort that is very popular with Madrileños on weekends during the winter. The area is also worth visiting in summer for its hiking trails and scenery.

Skiing
PUERTO DE NAVACERRADA

A popular destination for families, especially on weekends, Puerto de Navacerrada (prices: adult weekday day pass €27, weekend day pass €32; you can rent equipment at the ski station for around €15 for boots, skis, helmet, and ski poles) is a medium-sized resort with 19 pistes and five kilometers (3 miles) of cross-country ski trails as well as a snow park for snowboarders. The slopes are split into the higher, more difficult pistes for advanced/upper-intermediate skiers and the lower pistes for beginners and lower-intermediate skiers. The pistes are sheltered and picturesque, running down between pine forests. Visitors can take lessons at one of the ski schools, such as **Escuela de Esquí de Navacerrada** (www.eeenavacerrada.com). There is a cafeteria-style restaurant onsite for snacks or lunch.

Hiking
SIETE PICOS

During the Middle Ages, the Sierra de Guadarrama was known as the Sierra de Dragón ("Dragon Sierra") because of the shape of these seven peaks, which resemble the jagged back of the mythical creature. On this 8.5-kilometer (5.3-mile) round-trip trail, you will traverse rocky outcrops and pretty mountain meadows along the route, which has fantastic views down over the forested valleys below.

The circular trail, which is ideal for more experienced hikers, begins at the Puerto de Navacerrada ski resort (head towards the Cogorros military area and ascend by the cross-country skiing track). It is intermediate level, with high, steep sections, not suitable during the winter. When you reach the Collado Ventoso prairie, follow the trail to your right (the Schmid trail), marked with yellow circles, to get back to where you started at Puerto de Navacerrada.

Getting There

You can get the cercanía local train (C9) from Cercedilla up to the Puerta de Navacerrada ski resort. The ride takes about 15 minutes. (The fare can be bought in conjunction with the fare from Madrid-Cercedilla, the first leg of the train journey, €8.70 one way.) The train runs every two hours starting at 9:35am. The last train is at 5:35pm.

By car from Navacerrada, continue up the M-601, following the signs for Puerto de Navacerrada Estación de Esquí. Set off early if you're driving, because spaces fill up fast and cars can be turned away once the car parks are full.

PEÑALARA

Peñalara is the highest peak of the Sierra de Guadarrama, at 2,428 meters (7,966 feet). The area is characterized by its rocky, granite landscape dotted with glacial lakes. Trails run from the Peñalara Visitors Center around the area, giving visitors great views of the peak above.

Hiking

Located at Los Cotos pass, at the entrance to the Peñalara Massif, **Peñalara Visitors Center** (Ctra M-604, km 42, Puerto de los Cotos, Rascafría; tel. 91/852-0857; www.parquenacionalsierraguadarrama.es/en/visit/contact-vc/vc-penalara; Nov-Mar 8am-6pm, Apr-Oct 8am-9pm) is the place to pick up maps and information about surrounding trails.

ZABALA REFUGE HIKE

This 4.8-kilometer (3-mile) round-trip hike takes in some of the glaciated landscape surrounding Peñalara, the highest peak in the Sierra de Guadarrama. It's intermediate level, with some steep sections, and is not suitable in winter.

Start the hike from the Peñalara Visitors Center, then follow the route (marked by white symbols) up to La Gitana viewpoint (Mirador de la Gitana), which has views out over the pine forests below and has a sundial dedicated to Spanish poet Federico García Lorca.

Leave the viewpoint to your right and follow the forest track up the ascending trail. You will come to a crossroads leading to the Peñalara peak, or, to the right, the Zabala Refuge, a shelter open since 1927, from where you will have stunning views over a crystal-clear lagoon. From here, you can hike back the way you came to reach the Peñlara Visitors Center.

Getting There
FROM CERCEDILLA

From Cercedilla station, take the C9 commuter train (*cercanía*) uphill in the direction of Navacerrada and Cotos. The fare from Madrid, including the first leg on the C2 train between Madrid and Cercedilla, is €8.70 each way. The C9 leaves Cercedilla every two hours, starting at 9:35am. The last train from Cotos to Cercedilla is at 6:43pm. Get off at Cotos, which is a five-minute walk from the Peñalara Visitors Center.

It is a 20-kilometer (12.5-mile), 20-minute drive up to Peñalara Visitors Center from Cercedilla. Take the M-622 towards Navacerrada, then take the M-601 north towards Navacerrada Ski station. From there take the SG-615 north towards Puerto de Cotos, where there is a free car park near the Peñalara visitors center.

FROM MADRID

Bus 691 goes from Madrid's Moncloa bus station to Peñalara (stop: Valdesquí; €5.50 one way, journey time around 90 minutes). There are three or four buses an hour between 8am-10pm, and then one every hour thereafter.

MANZANARES EL REAL

At the foot of the Sierra de Guadarrama, the little town of Manzanares el Real (pop. 8,000) takes its name from the River Manzanares and is home to the 15th-century Castillo de los Mendoza; it's also the starting point of several hikes, including La Pedriza. Whether you like history, the outdoors, or a bit of both, it makes a great day out from Madrid. The town looks out over the Santillana reservoir, an important part of the water supply to Madrid, which sparkles in the sunlight, the surrounding peaks reflected in its clear, blue waters. Manzanares el Real's cafés and restaurants make a great post-hike lunch, or just a lovely place to wander during a morning or afternoon trip out of Madrid.

Sights
CASTILLO DE LOS MENDOZA

28410, Manzanares el Real; tel. 91/853-0008; Tues-Fri 10am-5:30pm, Sat-Sun 10am-6pm; €5
With its neat turrets and square stature, Manzanares's *castillo* looks like a classic storybook castle that a child might draw. One of the Madrid region's best-preserved fortifications, it was built in the 15th century. Inside there is a collection of 17th-century furniture and tapestries (based on sketches by Rubens), as well as suits of armor; visitors are free to walk outside the castle and see its exteriors without paying the entry fee.

Hiking

Nature trails snake off from the town and around the reservoir.

Manzanares El Real Tourist Office (Calle del Cura, 5; tel. 91/878-0196; www. manzanareselreal.org/en/; Tues-Fri 9:30am-2:30pm, Sat-Sun 9am-3pm) is a good port of call before setting off on a hike. You can pick up maps showing local trails.

La Pedriza Visitors Center (Camino de la Pedriza, Manzanares el Real; tel. 91/853-9978; www.parquenacionalsierraguadarrama.es/en/visit/contact-vc/vc-pedriza; Oct-May, daily 9am-4:30pm; June and Sept, weekdays 9am-4:30pm, weekends and public holidays 9am-8pm; July and Aug, 9am-8pm) has maps and guides for hiking trails around La Pedriza. The center is a 15-minute walk from the center of Manzanares El Real.

COLLADO DEL CHAPARRAL

At 4 kilometers (2.5 miles) each way, the Collado del Chaparral route starts at the lake viewing point (the "descansadero de Samburiel"), part of the **Camino de Santiago** (Way of Saint James), the route pilgrims walk to Santiago de Compostela in Galicia (the part of the camino for pilgrims walking from the south). After about 1.5 kilometers (1 mile), you will have views over La Pedriza. Continue along the path to Collado, 992 meters (3,255 feet) above sea level. Continue for a further 500 meters (1,640 feet) for views back down over Madrid to the south. (Re-trace your steps on the return route.)

LA PEDRIZA

Some two kilometers (1.2 miles) to the north outside the town of Manzanares el Real, this outcrop is a landscape of jutting, jagged rock formations. Compared to the pine forests of much of the sierra, the area is unusual for its stark, granite hills that give it an almost lunar atmosphere. With so many rocks, it is a popular destination for rock climbers, and there are also several different hiking routes for all ability levels.

There are red and white markers signaling routes along the River Manzanares that go past waterfalls, streams, and even the odd mountain goat. The route along the river (the length depends on how far you go) is a popular one and is an easy, family-friendly route.

A 6-kilometer (3.7-mile) round-trip hike starts in Manzanares and follows the Avenida de la Pedriza up toward the El Tranco parking area. Cross the bridge there and follow the path on the right bank of the river Manzanares for a kilometer (half a mile) up to an area called Casa Julián. From here you can re-trace your steps, or head back to the village immediately along the Avenida de la Pedriza.

Getting There

From Madrid, take bus 724 from Plaza de Castilla (Metro lines 1, 9, and 10) to Manzanares El Real. The journey takes around 45 minutes; buses leave at roughly 30-minute intervals throughout the day on weekdays (first bus at 7am, last bus back at around 9:30pm) and every 45 minutes to an hour at weekends (first bus 8am, last bus back at 10pm). Tickets are €4.20 each way.

By car, take the M-30 north out of Madrid and join the M-607 and take the exit onto the M-609. Follow the M-609 and M-608 to Manzanares El Real. There is a large, free car park in front of the castle.

El Escorial and the Valley of the Fallen

Those fascinated by history should consider a day trip that combines a visit to the monastery and palace of El Escorial and the Valley of the Fallen, Francisco Franco's colossal—and controversial—basilica and memorial to those who died during the Spanish Civil War. Both complexes are a testament to immense power—and reflect the rulers who commissioned them. Visiting both sights together is a fascinating, whistle-stop tour through half a century of some of Spain's most infamous historical moments.

EL ESCORIAL

The town of San Lorenzo de El Escorial (population 15,000), more commonly referred to as El Escorial, developed during and after the construction of the mammoth monastery-palace complex nearby. For its architecture alone, the great hulk of renaissance design, it is worth a visit—not to mention its vast palace, library, and monastery.

El Escorial is a pretty mountain town, with a center filled with little shops and tapas bars, ideal for a leisurely lunch after exploring the monastery. The historical center of the town is around **Plaza de la Cruz**, a quaint square surrounded with pale yellow buildings and a covered arcade lined with columns. Here, locals sit out at terraces for a morning coffee and enjoy the fresh air of the sierra.

Sights
EL ESCORIAL MONASTERY

Calle de Juan de Borbón y Battemberg, San Lorenzo de el Escorial; Oct-Mar, Tues-Sun 10am-6pm; Apr-Sept, Tues-Sun 10am-8pm; €10, €5 reduced admission

One of the most important buildings of the Spanish renaissance, this UNESCO World Heritage Site is 2 kilometers (1.2 miles) from the town of El Escorial, in the foothills of the Sierra de Guadarrama mountains.

El Escorial is one of the most popular day trips from Madrid for its sheer grandeur and size, as well as for the breadth of use; it was a palace, monastery, library, university, and pantheon, where most of Spain's monarchs are buried. Its gardens, themselves dotted with little houses and curiosities, are beautiful. Its setting, too, is majestic, surrounded as it is by the thickly forested foothills of the Sierra de Guadarrama.

The grand yet austere granite construction was commissioned in the 16th century by Philip II, who envisioned it as a palace and monastery, as well as a burial place for his father, Charles I, and mother, Isabella of Portugal. It was also intended to be an architectural embodiment of Spain's position as the most important country in the world. At the time it was built, Spain was amassing a vast empire in the Americas and its power was unparalleled.

The complex was built on farmland at the foot of the Guadarrama mountains. It was designed by architect Juan Bautista de Toledo, who had spent much of his career in Rome, where he had worked on St. Peter's Basilica. His ground plan was said to represent the grid on which Saint Lawrence, the monastery's namesake, was martyred (he was roasted alive on a gridiron). When Bautista died in 1567, his apprentice, Juan de Herrera, took over the project and saw it to its completion. Above the main entrance to the monastery is a sculpture of St. Lawrence, holding the symbolic gridiron, the instrument of his death.

The Courtyard of the Kings is the first thing visitors will see upon entering El Escorial. Its name comes from the Kings of Judah, whose statues decorate the outside of the Basilica. Inside, the Basilica has a great cupola, inspired by St. Peter's in Rome, and a grand chapel complete with red marble steps

Touring El Escorial and the Valley of the Fallen

The Valley of the Fallen is not served by public transport, but it's popular to visit the site on tours from Madrid that also cover El Escorial.

- **Bus Vision** (Carrerea de S. Jerónimo, 3; tel. 91/429-2767; www.busvision.net; adults €49, children from 7-15 €39, under 7s free) does a five-hour, half-day bus tour of El Escorial and the Valley of the Fallen with an English-speaking guide that includes admittance to both sites. Pick-up is at around 11am. Book online for discounts.

- **Madrid Day Tours** (tel. 91/789-6684; www.madriddaytours.com) offers a half-day (five-hour) private tour by car that encompasses both sites and includes hotel pick-up and drop-off in Madrid. Prices range from €85 per person for a group of four (the more people in a group, the lower the prices) that includes transport and entry to the sights, to €595 for the "First Class Tour," during which the group will be accompanied by a guide inside the sights.

and a 30-meter-high (90-foot) altarpiece that includes bronze sculptures and paintings.

Under the basilica, the Royal Pantheon contains the remains of the majority of Spanish kings and queens beginning with Charles I. Next door, the Salas Capitulares (Chapter Rooms) showcase the rich array of artwork collected by Spanish royalty over the years, with paintings by Spanish, Italian, and Flemish painters including El Greco, Titian, and Hieronymus Bosch.

Visitors can also see the House of the Kings, which includes the rooms of Philip II, the Art Gallery, the Architectural Museum, and the Library, whose vaulted ceilings are decorated with frescos by Pellegrino Tibaldi.

The royal grounds are vast and certainly worth making time to explore. The Garden of the Friars, off the monastery's north façade, is a perfectly manicured garden of square hedges and fountains; it was commissioned by Felipe II as a place to contemplate and relax.

Tickets can be purchased online. The walk from town is around 20 minutes through the monastery's gardens.

Food
LA CUEVA
Calle de San Antón, 4; tel. 91/890-1516; www. mesonlacueva.com; Tues-Sun 1:30pm-4pm, 9pm-midnight; €20
This restaurant, which was built in 1768, is

located in the atmospheric *cave* (basement) of a building just a block away from the monastery. Local meats, cheeses, soups, and classics like *callos a la Madrileña* (Madrid-style tripe), croquettes, and *tortilla española*, all feature on the menu; it specializes in steaks.

KU4TRO
Calle Floridablanca, 28, San Lorenzo de El Escorial; tel. 61/913-5831
Cool local tapas bar Ku4tro is close to the monastery palace of El Escorial and is a good place to stop for a drink and a bite to eat. Its menu features an array of interesting and creative tapas dishes, ideal for sharing. Try its unusual take on the classic *patatas bravas*; the sauce comes inside a hollowed-out potato instead of drizzled over the top.

AMETSTUDIO
Calle Pablo Picasso, 4, San Lorenzo de El Escorial; tel. 62/870-6683; www.ametstudio.com; Fri 9pm-11:30pm, Sat 2pm-3:30pm, 9pm-11:30pm, Sun 2pm-3:30pm; €50
If you're looking for a dining experience that will work all your senses, make time for a trip to AMETStudio, a fine dining restaurant close to the monastery of El Escorial. The restaurant offers one tasting menu, which—at €50 per person for a seven-course seasonal menu, including wine—is excellent value. The dishes, including smoked sardine with

squid mayonnaise, truffled egg, and pork cheeks with pumpkin, use local ingredients from the sierra and are plated as intricately as at any Michelin-starred restaurant. The atmosphere in the small dining room is relaxed and cozy, with exposed brick walls and a half-open kitchen where diners can peek into the creative nerve center of the restaurant. In winter, they light the big chimney, creating a magical atmosphere. There are only a handful of tables, so booking ahead is essential.

CAVA ALTA

*Calle Floridablanca, 17; tel. 91/890-1912; www.
cavalta.es; Tues-Sat 1pm-4pm, 9pm-11:45pm, Sun
1pm-4pm; €15*
This lovely local restaurant serves rustic local dishes with a creative twist. The front bar area is the place to come for tapas and a drink, while its dining room is a comfortable and welcoming spot for a more substantial lunch. Local meats and classics such as *huevos rotos* ("broken eggs") sit alongside a good range of vegetarian dishes.

Getting There
TRAIN
From Madrid's Atocha or Chamartín stations, take the *cercanías* (local train) C3 to El Escorial (around 50 minutes to one hour, €8.10 return). The first train leaves at around 6:50am and there are trains every hour throughout the day. The last train back from El Escorial is at around 10pm. From the train station it is a pleasant, 20-minute walk through the Jardín del Principe gardens to the monastery.

BUS
Bus company Herranz lines 661 and 664 go to El Escorial from the Intercambiador de Moncloa (metro lines 3 and 6). Buses leave every 15 minutes on weekdays and every 30 minutes at weekends, with the first bus departing at around 7am and the last bus from El Escorial at 10:30pm on weekdays, 10pm on weekends. The journey takes around 55 minutes. Tickets are €4.20 each way and are bought on the bus.

The bus drops passengers off at San Lorenzo de El Escorial bus station (Calle de Juan de Toledo, 3). From here, it is a short, 10-minute walk to the monastery.

CAR
From Madrid, take the A-6 motorway northwest out of the city and follow the M-600 towards El Escorial (there will be signs along the way). Driving time is around 40 minutes. There is free parking right outside the monastery and metered parking along Calle Floridablanca, a two-minute walk away.

THE VALLEY OF THE FALLEN

*Carretera de Guadarrama/El Escorial; tel.
91/890-5411; Tues-Sun 10am-7pm; €9, €4 reduced
admission*
This mammoth stone memorial and Roman Catholic basilica was the brainchild of Spanish dictator General Francisco Franco, who ruled Spain from 1939 until his death in 1975.

Originally conceived as a memorial to those who died during the Spanish Civil War (1936-39), it has long been one of Spain's most controversial monuments, a sight which many believe glorifies Franco's Nationalists and his subsequent dictatorship. It was built, in part, by political prisoners rounded up by Franco after the war, some of whom died during the construction process.

As many towns and cities across the country have removed symbols of Franco, many Spaniards wonder when the biggest symbol of all might be removed, repurposed, or closed. In 2018, the Spanish government voted to remove Franco's remains from the Valley of the Fallen in order to make the site a "civil cemetery," but with strong opposition from Franco's family, the fate of the dictator was unclear at the time of writing. Despite or perhaps because of its infamous history, it is a popular day trip from Madrid, which many combine with a visit to El Escorial, 15 kilometers (9 miles) to the south.

The structure was started in 1940 and was not inaugurated until 1959, in part because of the immense scale of the build. It comprises an expansive underground basilica and a granite cross that sits high above on the hillside; the cross, 152 meters (500 feet) tall, is the tallest memorial cross in the world and is visible on the hillside as you come in to land in Madrid.

Franco himself is buried in the underground basilica, the only person buried here who did not die during the civil war. His grave is often strewn with flowers; the basilica is a pilgrimage site for the small number of staunch Franco supporters who visit every November 20 (the anniversary of Franco's death) to pay homage to their former leader—a ritual that is itself another point of controversy.

There are 40,000 people, both Republican and Nationalist, who died during the Civil War and who are buried in the valley outside the basilica, though the site currently contains no information about the Civil War or Franco's dictatorship. The graves are completely unmarked. Relatives of those buried there have called for their loved ones' remains to be removed so they can be given a proper burial; others have suggested the site should be turned into a museum. Madrid's mayor, Manuela Carmena, has suggested changing the site's name to the Valley of Peace, but at the time of writing, no firm decisions had been taken on the future of the monument.

You can take a funicular up to the base of the cross (€1.50 one way) for stunning views across the sierra. There is also a snack bar and restaurant just to the left of the monument and plenty of picnic benches if you want to bring your own lunch.

Getting There

The site, nestled down a long, winding road through the pine forests, is almost impossible to reach by public transport. Your best bet is to hire a car or to visit through an organized day trip. From Madrid, take the A-6 motorway and then the M-600 highway, and follow the signs for the Valle de los Caídos. Driving time is around 35 minutes.

From El Escorial, follow the M-600 to the Valley of the Fallen (around 20 minutes). There is parking next to the site.

Valley of the Fallen

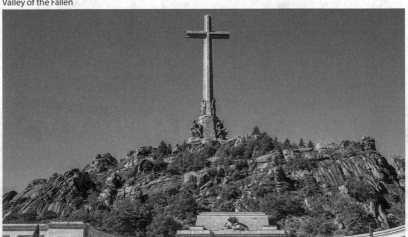

Background

History

Before the Roman conquest of Spain, the main group living along the Mediterranean coast was the Iberians. One group belonging to the Iberians were the Laietani, who inhabited the area around present-day Barcelona. They are commemorated in the name of one of the city's main streets, the Via Laietana.

THE ROMANS

Roman armies first invaded the Iberian Peninsula—what they called Hispania—in 218 BC. Initially, their biggest urban areas were centered

around the south of the country. It was not until 15 BC that the Romans founded a colony in present-day Barcelona, which they named Julia Augusta Faventia Paterna Barcino (or Barcino for short). It was a small town, a military camp that was eclipsed in size by is southerly neighbor, Tàrraco (modern-day Tarragona).

Spanish goods, such as wine and olive oil, were exported all over the Roman Empire; pottery especially designed for Spanish wine was even found in the ruins of Pompeii. Barcino was a center of production for the popular, incredibly pungent, Roman fish sauce *garum*. (Fish, fish parts, salt, and flavorings would be put into stone vats under the hot sun and left to ferment for several weeks.) Today, traces of Roman Barcelona can be seen at the Barcelona City History Museum (MUHBA), as well as in its remaining Roman walls and the huge columns of the Temple of Augustus.

The Romans occupied Segovia in 80 BC and built what is, today, one of the world's most impressive examples of Roman engineering, the city's 36-arch Roman aqueduct. Toledo was another important town for the Romans—it contained a Roman circus, city walls, and public baths. Today, visitors can see its Roman bridge, the Puente de Alcántara.

Jewish communities began to settle in many Roman cities, including Barcelona, beginning in the 2nd century; many of them were part of the Jewish diaspora who had fled west after the Roman destruction of the temple of Jerusalem in the first century AD. These Spanish Jews would create the Sephardic branch of Judaism.

THE MOORS

After the fall of the Roman Empire in the fifth century AD, the Visigoths, a Germanic group, held much of Spain and established their capital in Toledo, making the city an important center of learning. But by early 716,

the Muslims known as Moors had conquered most of the Iberian Peninsula, apart from the far northwest and other mountainous regions in the north. The new Islamic state was named Al-Andalus.

The Moors controlled much of Spain for nearly 700 years, until 1492. Barcelona had a relatively short Moorish period; by 801 it was back under Christian control. Madrid, a small town still many centuries away from being made the Spanish capital, was located at a strategic point close to Toledo on the border of Al-Andalus and the more northerly Christian kingdoms. Therefore, in the 9th century, Emir Muhammed I of Córdoba built a fortress high up over the River Manzanares, in what is now Madrid; its purpose was to protect Toledo from Christian invasion. It was built on the site of today's Royal Palace, and remnants of the city's original Arab walls still remain close by.

In contrast to Barcelona and Madrid, Toledo was one of the most important kingdoms of the Moors, who held it until 1085. It was a great center of learning, and over the centuries gained the reputation of being home to Muslims, Jews, and Christians who all lived in a state of relative peace known as *convivencia*. (Under the Moors, people had the option of converting to Islam but did not have to; Christians and Jews were allowed to retain their religions as long as they agreed to certain conditions, such as not attempting to convert others and agreeing to have no authority over Muslims.)

THE MIDDLE AGES

When Barcelona and other counties in the same region united with the Kingdom of Aragon in 1137, the Principality of Catalonia was born. It had its own constitutional system of courts and was the base for the Kingdom of Aragon's great mercantile and naval power.

By the Middle Ages (12th-13th centuries), Catalonia's commercial empire was rapidly expanding; its empire stretched as far as Sardinia, Naples, and Sicily, and it had consulates in 126 locations across the Mediterranean including Constantinople, Venice, and Beirut. The Catalan language spread through Catalonia's colonies, too.

Barcelona experienced huge growth and prosperity during this period. The city's mercantile class of traders and shipbuilders helped create the city, constructing palaces in the Ribera district and putting money towards churches like the Gothic Santa Maria del Mar. The city was renowned for its shipbuilding (its medieval shipyards now house the city's maritime museum). In the early 14th century, mariners from the Crown of Aragon—to which Catalonia belonged—were exploring the Atlantic coast of Africa as far as the Canary Islands.

The marriage of Isabel of Castile and Fernando of Aragón (often referred to as Isabella and Ferdinand in English) in 1469 would change Spain forever, and was the main catalyst in the creation of the Spain we know today. It wasn't until after their marriage that the various Christian kingdoms united to form the nation of Spain as it exists now.

When they married—she 18, he 17—the two largest Christian kingdoms in Spain merged. They would go on to conquer Granada and Navarra, widening their power and reach even further. A busy couple, they started the Spanish Inquisition, conquered Granada (the Moors' last stronghold) in 1492, and the same year expelled from Spain all Jews who refused to convert to Christianity (they would expel all Muslims in 1500). They also sponsored Christopher Columbus's first voyage (he was looking for a western route to Asia but ended up landing in the Americas).

The rise of the Catholic Monarchs, as they have been dubbed, and Spain's feverish exploration of the New World, marked a period of decline for Catalonia and Barcelona; its seafaring industry, so focused on eastward exploration, was affected by the push west to the Americas and the New World.

Isabella and Ferdinand were also concerned with spreading their influence around Europe; their daughter Catalina married England's King Henry VIII (she was known there as Catherine of Aragon). Their daughter Juana (often dubbed Juana La Loca or Juana the Mad) was deemed unfit to rule after the death of her husband, so when Ferdinand died in 1516, his grandson, the 17-year-old Charles (Carlos I) (1516-1556), took the throne. By 1519, Charles had been elected Holy Roman Emperor (Charles V) and, thanks to the combination of his maternal and paternal lineages, ruled Spain and its empire, the Low Countries, Austria, and parts of Italy, France, and Germany. Spain now had its first Habsburg king.

EMPIRE

By the 16th century, Christopher Columbus's early voyages had spawned dozens more; Spanish colonizers were intent on conquering as much of the New World as possible. Conquistadores Hernán Cortés and Francisco Pizarro conquered the Aztec (1521) and the Inca (1532-1572) empires during this period. The colonies, which by the end of the century included Florida, Mexico, and much of Central and South America, sent back a stream of silver, gold, and other treasures to Spain, enriching the Spanish crown.

Charles's son, Felipe II (1556-1598), established his capital in Madrid in 1561. Madrid was a blank slate that allowed Felipe to establish a court without claims or gripes from already established aristocrats, and without too much Church influence (the previous capital, Toledo, had been more or less controlled by the Church).

For everything Felipe II got right, something else seemed to go wrong. He won the naval battle of Lepanto against the Ottoman Turks, but severely misjudged the Spanish Armada against England and his former sister-in-law, Elizabeth I (1588). He presided over seemingly unbounded wealth that flowed in from the Americas, but he ended up with no money. His biggest legacy today is the vast monastery palace at El

Escorial, into which he poured money and where he died.

At the turn of the 17th century, Spain was experiencing its *Siglo de Oro* ("Golden Century"), during which artists like Diego de Velázquez immortalized the royal family in paintings such as "Las Meninas" and writer Miguel de Cervantes was penning the first great Western novel, *Don Quixote de La Mancha.*

But while its cultural life was thriving, its military and economic life was in decline. A series of inept kings presided over a bleak few centuries for Spain, during which it would lose many of its colonies and plummet into economic disaster.

BOURBONS

After many years of marrying cousins, aunts, and other family members to ensure power remained in the family, the last Habsburg king, Charles II died in 1700, childless, sickly, and—many said—deformed. His successor was a young French relative, Felipe V (1700-Jan 1724 and Sept 1724-1746), the grandson of Louis XIV.

Spain's first Bourbon king brought a French touch to the court; styles changed and the new influence was reflected in everything from architecture (Madrid's Royal Palace, built under the orders of Felipe V, was said to have been inspired by plans for the Louvre) to fashion, music, and dance.

The argument over who would succeed Charles II turned into an all-out war: the War of the Spanish Succession (1701-1714). Charles II was related to both the Austrian Habsburgs and the French Bourbon dynasties, and the war pitted the two sides and their supporters against each other for who would succeed Charles II and take the Spanish throne. Catalonia backed the Habsburg side— which would turn out to be the wrong bet. When Felipe V was confirmed king, in 1714, he punished the region by abolishing its independent rights and its government, the Generalitat. He also disbanded the University of Barcelona and banned the use of Catalan in

government. He demolished large parts of La Ribera district to build a citadel, which would guard the city and prevent future rebellions. The citadel, which stood on what today is the Parc de la Ciutadella, was loathed by locals in Barcelona as a symbol of the central Spanish government and how it had taken away many of their rights.

INDUSTRIAL REVOLUTION AND 19TH CENTURY

Towards the end of the 18th century, the effect of the French Revolution and the subsequent Napoleonic Wars spilled over into Spain.

By 1808, Spain was under occupation by the French, under Napoleon. Charles (Carlos) IV (1788-1808) was forced to abdicate in favor of Joseph Bonaparte, Napoleon's older brother. The people of Madrid rose up against the new king on May 2, 1808 (the uprising is depicted in Goya's famous painting, "The Second of May 1808," now on display in Madrid's Museo del Prado). Spaniards stood up to the French, with support from the British and Portuguese, led by the Duke of Wellington. A new liberal constitution was drawn up in 1812 and the French were out of Spain by 1813.

The 19th century was a politically shaky time for Spain, which was increasingly torn apart by rifts between liberal reformers, who wanted to modernize Spain and get away from the firm grip of the Church, and the conservative Catholic Church itself.

Under Ferdinand (Fernando) VII (1814-33), Spain lost many of its American colonies, which declared independence, adding to the political instability at home. His successor, daughter Isabel II (1843-68), who took the throne at the age 13, oversaw a period of economic progress thanks to building work, mining, and railways, but the country remained torn between a more liberal future and a more conservative, Church-dominated one. After various political wrangles, Spain's *Cortes* (its lower parliament and senate) declared the short-lived First Republic in 1873, made up of liberals, radicals, and democrats.

The Republic was plagued by in-fighting and attacks from all sides, and it would not last for long. By 1874, the army had put Isabel's son Alfonso XII (1874-1885) on the throne, to the relief of conservatives. In reality, most Spaniards supported the king because of the return to stability he brought after the tumultuous First Republic.

As the century neared its end, industry was booming, especially in Catalonia and the Basque Country. Inequality and poor working conditions spawned militant labor movements; as the factory owners and fat cats got richer, the workers saw none of the huge profits. Many subscribed to the ideas of anarchism, which arrived in Spain around this time.

When Catalans were called up to fight in Spanish Morocco in 1909 to sort out the confrontation between Rifian tribes and Spanish workers in the iron mines near Melilla (a confrontation that would eventually lead to the Rif War, 1920-1927), they protested with violence, attacking churches and other religious institutions in what would be called Barcelona's Tragic Week. Around the same time there was a rise in Catalan nationalism, with a renewed focus on Catalan language, culture, and the drive for an independent Catalan state.

The years between 1923 and 1936 were marked by a continued power struggle between the left and the right. When Alfonso XIII (1886-1931), who was known for meddling, was at the peak of unpopularity, General Primo de Rivera led an army in his support and established Spain's first military dictatorship in 1923, which would last until 1930. A new Republican government, spearheaded by liberal reformers, won elections in 1931 and issued a range of reforms such as votes for women, giving Catalonia back its own parliament and—to the horror of the Catholic Church—legalizing divorce. In 1933, right-wingers won national elections. This inspired liberal groups around the country, as well as Catalan Nationalist groups, to fight against the new government, and in

1934 Catalan President Lluis Companys declared independence for Catalonia. Political divisions deepened, and the country became increasingly violent. In February 1936, the left-wing, communist-led Popular Front narrowly defeated the right-wing National Front.

The scene was set for a showdown—but even the army generals who started it could barely have envisaged how an attempted coup would start one of Spain's most bloody and divisive conflicts.

SPANISH CIVIL WAR

A rebellion against Spain's Republican government by five military generals, including Francisco Franco—the youngest general in any of the European armed forces—began in Morocco at 5pm on Friday, July 17, 1936 with an uprising in Spain's Moroccan colonies. But while past attempts to overthrow the government had succeeded almost immediately, this one did not. It marked the beginning of the three-year Spanish Civil War, during which the rebels (known as the Nationalists) would fight those loyal to the Republican government (the Republicans) for control of Spain.

The Nationalists were characterized by right-wing political beliefs, their belief in a united Spain (and the elimination of regional autonomy, such as that of Catalonia), and a reverence for the role of the Church as a moral compass for Spain. The Republicans were a mixed bag of left-leaning groups including socialists, communists, and anarchists. They ranged considerably in how left-wing they were, which would lead to divisions within the Republican side as the war progressed.

The Nationalists powered through Spain, capturing many cities within days until they held huge swathes of the north and Andalusia. Airlifted into Seville, they moved northward towards Madrid.

The capital fought hard against the attackers, aided by foreigners who had come to Spain to fight with the Republicans for democracy (joining the International Brigades). The Republicans managed to hold off Franco's first assault in November and would hold out for a further two years, in what would be called the Siege of Madrid. While their side continued to hold the Spanish capital from Nationalist forces, the Republican government fled besieged Madrid for Valencia in late 1936.

From the beginning, the Republicans were beset by infighting; street fighting even broke out in Barcelona in 1937. Meanwhile, the Nationalists ploughed on, taking the northern coast and winning a series of decisive victories at Teruel (early 1938) and the Ebro Valley (July 1938). In early 1939, the Republican government and thousands of Republicans fled to France.

Madrid was still holding on by its fingertips when the Nationalists entered the city on March 28, 1939. Franco declared victory on April 1. Worn down and on the verge of starvation, the residents of Madrid had no other option but to surrender.

Historians have put the death toll of the Spanish Civil War as high as 500,000. It ripped communities apart, with next-door neighbors sometimes falling on opposite sides of the conflict. Each side meted out killings—the Nationalists murdered thousands of Republicans, and the Republicans murdered Nationalist sympathizers, including 7,000 priests, monks, and nuns. One of the war's most significant events, the 1937 bombing of the Basque town of Guernica by the German Condor Legion and several planes from the Italian air force, is emotionally depicted in Picasso's famous anti-war painting "Guernica," which today is on display in Madrid's Reina Sofía.

When the Second World War began, just five months after the end of the Spanish Civil War, Spain was far too depleted to join in.

LIFE UNDER FRANCO

Franco, who would rule for 36 years until his death in 1975, defined the Spanish state as one coherent unit and strongly opposed independence movements in Catalonia and the Basque Country.

Franco positioned himself as head of state and head of government, with the sole legal party being the fascist Falange. A key principle of Francoism was national unity; Franco severely limited the freedoms of Spain's autonomous regions, including more or less banning the use of regional languages. For example, it was forbidden to name children Catalan names.

Many Republican political figures fled Spain after the Civil War, and those who remained were persecuted by the Franco regime. Many people who fought with the Republicans or shared their political beliefs were arrested, subjected to unfair trials, and executed.

For regular citizens under Franco, especially during the early years of the dictatorship, life was grim and a sense of paranoia pervaded Madrid and Barcelona. Franco had a large network of secret police and censorship—of "liberal" theater, films, and books—was rife. Franco extolled traditional family and family roles, so many women stayed at home. The Catholic Church also played a strong part in the fabric of daily life.

Until the early 1950s, Spain was a pariah in the international community; it was barred from joining the United Nations in 1946 because of its historically close relationship with the Axis powers during the Spanish Civil War and the Second World War. In 1953, Franco signed the Pact of Madrid with Dwight D. Eisenhower, which would allow three US airbases to be located in Spain in exchange for American financial and military aid. This was strategically important for the United States in the middle of the Cold War, and signaled to Franco that the international community was thawing in its relations towards Spain.

By the late 1950s, Spain was part of international organizations, including the United Nations (which it joined in 1955), the IMF, and World Bank. Spain experienced an unprecedented period of growth during the 1960s as urbanization and tourism boomed. The period of growth (roughly 1959-1974) was dubbed *El Milagro Español*—"the Spanish Miracle."

The "miracle" was the result of reforms put

in place by technocrats, whom Franco allowed to make a raft of changes. Industry boomed in the Basque Country and Barcelona, and the automotive industry—led by Spanish company SEAT—was a key economic driver. In 1946 there were 72,000 private cars in Spain, which rose to over a million in 1966. The Franco government also promoted Spain as a tourist destination, which contributed to the country's economic growth.

Franco, nearing the end of his life, named Prince Juan Carlos de Borbón y Borbón as his successor in 1973, and named Admiral Carrero Blanco as Prime Minister. In December of that year, Carrero Blanco was assassinated by Basque terror group ETA. With Franco on his last legs, the future of Spain was looking increasingly uncertain.

RETURN TO DEMOCRACY

Franco died on November 20, 1975. His successor, King Juan Carlos, had been secretly plotting to return the country to democracy, and the first democratic elections for 41 years were held on June 15, 1978. The Union of the Democratic Center (UCD) of Adolfo Suárez won 165 of 350 seats, while the center-left PSOE (Partido Socialista Obrero Español, Spanish Socialist Workers' Party) and PSC (Socialist Party of Catalonia) won a total of 118 seats. Spain's new constitution was signed in 1978, and the government approved autonomy statutes for Catalonia and the Basque Country in 1979, giving the regions authority over education, police, culture, and more.

The days after Franco were not just dramatic on a political level, but on a social level, too. Spaniards who for decades had lived under an oppressive military dictatorship were now free, and they took to the streets in celebration across the country. This new countercultural scene—typified by indie music, drugs, and late-night partying, as well as an outpouring of cultural creativity, from fashion to film—was christened *La Movida Madrileña* ("the Madrid Scene") because it began in and centered around the Spanish capital. The most famous son of La Movida was the film director Pedro Almodóvar, whose films—which would go on to win Oscars—typified the technicolor optimism of those years.

The new days of democracy did not go without a couple of hitches. In February 1981, Lieutenant Colonel Antonio Tejero and 200 Civil Guard officers stormed the lower parliament building in Madrid in an attempted coup. They held hostages for 18 hours, during which King Juan Carlos made a televised address denouncing the coup and calling for democracy to be restored. Tejero soon surrendered.

In 1982, the PSOE won the elections, and during the next decade a range of liberal social changes were brought in; abortion (in certain circumstances) and divorce were legalized.

The 1992 Barcelona Olympics and Paralympics were a huge turning point—both for Barcelona and for Catalonia, which saw the games as theirs and not Spain's. Infrastructure was improved, beaches were created, green spaces flourished, and the city gained a confidence that propelled it to its current position as "the capital of the Mediterranean." Even today, over 26 years later, people still refer to the Olympics as a watershed moment for Barcelona.

CONTEMPORARY SPAIN

In a coordinated terrorist attack on March 11, 2004, bombs were detonated on several *cercanías*, commuter trains in Madrid. The bombings were the single deadliest terror attack on European soil to date, with 192 people killed and over 2,000 injured.

The Spanish government initially blamed Basque terror group ETA for the attack, which took place three days before Spain's general election. It soon transpired that it was, in fact, an al-Qaeda terrorist cell that carried out the attacks. By quickly and wrongly blaming ETA, the conservative government lost a lot of support, and the PSOE government of José Luis Rodríguez Zapatero was voted in.

One of Zapatero's most notable actions was

the legalization of same-sex marriage in 2005, making Spain only the third country in the world to do so. As part of the same legislation, same-sex couples were allowed to adopt. He also withdrew Spanish troops from Iraq.

Economic crisis hit the country in 2008. Zapatero's response to the crisis was criticized, and the PSOE lost the 2011 general election, which was won by the center-right Popular Party (*Partido Popular*, aka PP), led by Mariano Rajoy.

Seemingly out of the blue, in June 2014 King Juan Carlos announced he was to abdicate in favor of his son, Felipe. Juan Carlos, who had been so revered for his part in helping return to democracy after the death of Franco, had seen his popularity plummet in recent years after a series of scandals, including a corruption investigation.

Spain's political system, so long a back-and-forth between the PP and the PSOE, was shaken up in 2014 by new, left-wing *Podemos* (We Can), which had grown out of the *indignados* (indignant ones), an anti-austerity movement that opposed the government's handling of Spain's economic crisis.

Podemos and the center-right *Ciudadanos* (Citizens) won seats in parliament, but Podemos made perhaps its most important mark in the mayoral races of 2015. Podemos-supported candidates became mayors of Spain's three biggest cities. The new mayor of Madrid, Manuela Carmena, was a former communist judge and Barcelona's first female mayor, Ada Colau, had been a vocal part of the city's anti-eviction activists.

In recent years, Spain has come out the other side of its economic crisis, with tourism especially booming; Spain is now the second most visited country in the world, with 82 million visitors in 2017.

In 2018, after a crippling corruption scandal, Prime Minister Mariano Rajoy lost a vote of no confidence in parliament and was replaced by PSOE Prime Minister Pedro Sánchez.

Art and Architecture

ARCHITECTURAL STYLES

Barcelona and Madrid could not be more different when it comes to their architectural styles. Throughout history, Barcelona has had waves of building frenzy that have resulted in its famed mixture of styles, especially the medieval Gothic buildings of its Barri Gòtic and the Modernista buildings from the turn of the 20th century.

Madrid's buildings are, on the whole, newer; it did not become capital of Spain until the 16th century. The capital's buildings from that period on often reflect who was in charge—the austere design of the Habsburgs, then the French-influenced, more intricate and elaborate style of the Bourbons.

While we begin here with talking about Gothic architecture, both cities of course do have examples of earlier buildings.

Roman Barcelona peeks from around corners, from the city's Roman walls to its ancient Roman streets and homes buried beneath the Plaça del Rei, which can be seen in the Museum of the History of Barcelona. Segovia, a popular day trip from Madrid, is dominated by its aqueduct, an incredible example of Roman ingenuity and engineering. In Madrid, there are whisperings of the city's Moorish past; just next door to its Cathedral there's a section of the old Arab walls of Madrid.

Gothic

Barcelona is home to the highest concentration of 13th-15th century buildings in Spain, and walking around its Barri Gòtic (Gothic Quarter) is like stepping back in time.

Elsewhere in Spain, such as in Toledo, churches and cathedrals were influenced by

Historical Timeline

15BC: The Romans establish a colony, Barcino, on the location of present-day Barcelona.

12th-13th centuries: Barcelona experiences a golden age in trade, culture, and seafaring, signified by the construction of palaces and churches such as the Basilica de Santa Maria del Mar.

1469: Isabella (Isabel) of Castile weds Ferdinand (Fernando) of Aragón, setting the stage for the creation of modern Spain.

1561: Hapsburg King Philip II establishes his capital in the undeveloped town of Madrid.

1656: Spain's royal court painter, Diego Velázquez, shakes up the art world with "Las Meninas."

1714: Felipe V abolishes Catalonia's independent rights and government.

1735: Felipe V commissions Madrid's Royal Palace.

1808: Madrileños rise up, unsuccessfully, against Napoleon's invading troops.

1864: Construction starts on the Eixample ('Expansion'), a new neighborhood in Barcelona designed by Ildefons Cerdà.

1868: Madrid's Retiro Park opens to the public.

1883: Antoni Gaudí takes over construction of Barcelona's Sagrada Familia.

1888: First examples of Catalan Modernist architecture displayed at Barcelona's World's Fair.

1909: Called to fight in Spanish Morocco, Catalans protest violently.

1923: Ernest Hemingway visits Madrid for the first time, declaring it "the most Spanish of all cities."

1929: The International Exposition, Barcelona, renovates the area of Montjuïc, spawning famous buildings and sights including the Palau Nacional, Poble Espanyol, and the Font Màgica (Magic Fountain).

1936: Five military generals, including Franco, rebel against the Spanish government, kicking off the Spanish Civil War.

1937: Franco allies bomb the Basque town of Guernica. Picasso completes a brutal depiction of the bombing, titled "Guernica."

1939: Franco sacks Madrid and declares the end of the Spanish Civil War.

1939-1975: Franco rules Spain in a fiercely nationalistic military dictatorship. Catalan language and culture are effectively banned.

1972: Madrid receives a gift from Egypt: the ancient Temple of Debod.

1975: Franco dies, leaving democracy-seeking King Juan Carlos in power.

1978: Spain holds its first democratic election in 41 years. In response, a joyful counterculture movement known as *Movida Madrileña* is unleashed, with Madrid's Malasaña neighborhood at its epicenter.

1992: The Olympics are held in Barcelona, propelling the city to international status.

the French Gothic style—you'll see flying buttresses and towering buildings with a touch of Spanish design, like ornate altar pieces, thrown in. Barcelona, on the other hand, had its own unique take. Catalan Gothic was a more austere, plain, and unadorned version of English or French Gothic, typified by its lack of spires, its broad vaults unsupported by flying buttresses, its flat-roofed belltowers, and its lack of aisles. The style can be seen in the city's cathedral, built between 1298 and 1448, and the churches of Santa Maria del Mar and Santa Maria del Pi.

Barcelona's medieval building boom was, in part, thanks to its shipbuilding and trading prowess. Merchants were becoming wealthier and wanted fancy buildings to show for it. They built up much of today's La Ribera neighborhood—constructing the huge palaces along Carrer Montcada that, again, look austere and uninviting from outside, but open out into galleried courtyards and high-ceilinged rooms on the inside. Five of these palaces are now home to the Picasso Museum. The streets in this area are named after the professions of the men who worked there and helped build the area: Agullers (needle-makers), Corders (rope-spinners), Escudellers (shield-makers). Medieval building know-how is also on display at Barcelona's *Drassanes* or shipyards, now home to the city's Maritime Museum.

Segovia's cathedral—built between 1525 and 1577—was one of the last pure Gothic buildings in Spain.

Mudéjar

From the 12th century until as late as the 17th century, the style of Mudéjar architecture was used in buildings across Spain. The style was a Christian adaption and interpretation of Arab architecture under the Moors, using Moorish techniques and design to decorate buildings such as churches. Mudéjar style is characterized by its use of brickwork, Islamic script, geometric patterns, and intricate ceramic work; it can be seen in cities such as Toledo, Segovia, and Zaragoza.

Baroque

Beginning in the late 17th century, Baroque architecture peppered Madrid, the country's relatively new capital city, with memorable buildings, such as its Plaza Mayor and the Casa de la Villa, home of Madrid's City Hall, which were dubbed Castilian Baroque.

As with Catalan Gothic, Spain had its own spin on Baroque. Pioneered by the Churriguera brothers, who came from a Spanish family of sculptors and architects, Churrigueresque architecture was a style of Spanish Baroque focused on elaborate ornamentation, intricate detailing, and over-the-top decoration. An example in Madrid is the Museum of the History of Madrid, a powder-pink confection with an ornate stone entranceway.

French Influence

The rise of the Bourbons (from 1700) brought a distinct French and Italian influence to Madrid's architecture—it is said that the Royal Palace, constructed after the old one burned down on Christmas Eve 1734, was inspired by plans by Bernini for the Louvre in Paris.

The Prado Museum, designed by Juan de Villanueva (1739-1811) —who also redesigned the Plaza Mayor after it was damaged by a fire—shows an emerging neoclassic trend, one that would continue into the 19th century with the construction of the Palacio de las Cortes, home to Madrid's lower parliament.

Modernisme

Today, the architectural style most people associate with Barcelona is Catalan Modernisme (roughly 1888-1910), a unique version of Art Nouveau that took on its own personality in Catalonia.

While *Modernisme* refers to a style that branched through literature, painting, furniture design, and the visual arts, it was in architecture that it found its most famous and enduring examples. The Eixample (literally "expansion"), a grid-pattern of streets and city blocks north of the old town designed by

Ildefons Cerdà, was the ideal creative playground for a host of Modernista architects, many of whom were employed by rich businessmen and industrialists to build homes in the new neighborhood for them. Cerdà designed the Eixample as a much-needed expansion of Barcelona, whose population had outgrown its cramped, unhygienic old town. With its wide boulevards, grid pattern, and green space, it was designed as a more livable area for every citizen. In reality, it became a rich area populated mainly by Barcelona's up-and-coming bourgeoisie.

The first examples of Modernisme were on display at Barcelona's 1888 World's Fair, notably the *Castell dels Tres Dragons* restaurant by Lluís Domènech i Montaner (1850-1923), who would be an important voice in defining Modernime and would go on to design two of Barcelona's most exciting Modernista buildings: the Palau de la Música Catalana (1908) and the Hospital de la Santa Creu i Sant Pau (1901-1930). In 1878, Domènech i Montaner wrote *In Search of a National Architecture*, in which he laid out the main principles of a modern, national Catalonian architecture.

Other important Modernista architects were Josep Puig i Cadafalch (1867-1956), who designed Casa Amatller, and—of course—the movement's most famous son, Antoni Gaudí. The ambition of Gaudí outstripped his contemporaries; he was in fact so ambitious that his main work, the Sagrada Familia, remained unfinished—he knew he would never complete it in his lifetime.

Modernisme was strongly tied in with an idea of Catalan identity. It featured the same motifs again and again, often related to nature— look at Gaudí's buildings and you will see plants, flowers, and animals worked into their exteriors.

Modernisme took important local crafts and artisanal work—ceramics, iron forging, stained glass, fine woodwork, exposed brickwork—and elevated it. The style also featured new techniques; Gaudí pioneered the technique of *trencadís*, making mosaics out of broken tiles, something that can be seen today across Barcelona. A modern example is Joan Miró's homage to Gaudí in his sculpture "Woman and Bird," close to the former bullring (now the Las Arenas shopping center).

As the 20th century progressed, Modernisme fell out of fashion, and Barcelona's great Modernista buildings fell into disrepair; exteriors were neglected, and La Pedrera even housed a bingo hall. By the end of the 20th century, the city realized what a treasure it had and made more of an effort to take care of its buildings.

Contemporary Architecture

The Olympic Games transformed Barcelona and heralded a new era for the city's modern architecture. As Barcelona cleaned itself up, it commissioned new buildings, such as the Museu d'Art Contemporani de Barcelona (1995), designed by American architect Richard Meier, the gherkin-shaped Torre Agbar (2005) by Jean Nouvel, and several designs that were specially built for the games, including the Communications Tower (1992) by Santiago Calatrava, the Hotel Arts (1994), with its Frank Gehry-designed fish sculpture (1992) out front, and the next-door Torre Mapfre.

Madrid's business district includes four skyscrapers and the KIO Towers, two unusual tilting buildings that were the world's first inclined skyscrapers when they were completed in 1996. Older buildings have received shiny, new extensions, such as with the Reina Sofía Museum in Madrid, which in 2005 opened an 8,000-square-meter (86,000-square-foot) expansion designed by French architect Jean Nouvel.

Both cities have also taken old buildings and transformed them for new uses. Richard Rogers (who also designed the wavy-ceilinged terminal 4 of Madrid's airport) transformed Barcelona's Les Arenes bullring into a shopping center with viewing platform, while in Madrid both the Matadero slaughterhouse and the Conde Duque army barracks are now cultural centers. One of Madrid's most impressive transformations is that of an old electricity station into the Caixa Forum museum—architects Herzog & de Meuron encased the museum in oxidized cast-iron, giving it a rusty appearance that contrasts with the vertical garden designed by botanist Patrick Blanc.

Markets, too, have been given makeovers, from Madrid's glass and wrought-iron Mercado de San Miguel to the colorful arches of Barcelona's Mercado Santa Caterina, by Enric Miralles.

ART

Spain's artistic output, from the Golden Age to 20th-century surrealists, is world famous.

One of the most famous painters of the Spanish Golden Age (16th-17th centuries) was Diego Velázquez. He worked as a court painter under King Felipe IV and produced some of Spain's most well-known works, such as "Las Meninas" (1656), which depicts the young Infanta Margarita Teresa, her ladies in waiting, and other members of the court. By inserting himself into the painting and making the viewer the subject of the painting-within-the painting, Velázquez made an enigmatic portrait, which has become one of the most studied in Western art. Many of his works can be seen today in the Prado Museum in Madrid. Other Golden Age painters on display include El Greco, Zurbarán, and José de Ribera.

Straddling the old masters and a more modern style, Francisco de Goya (1746-1828) became a court painter in 1786, painting Spanish monarchs and aristocrats. His historical depictions, including "The Second of May 1808" and "The Third of May 1808," document Spain's changing status in the world. In later life and increasingly unwell, Goya's output became much more melancholy and macabre. His Black Paintings, applied straight onto the walls of his house, are dark depictions that include witches and Saturn devouring his own son.

Born in Malaga, southern Spain, Pablo Picasso (1881-1973) began as a classical painter when he moved to Barcelona with his family as a teenager. His talent was apparent from a young age and some of his earliest works can be seen in Barcelona's Museu Picasso. After living and working in Paris, Picasso pioneered the Cubist movement, an abstract style that would bring traditional painting well into the 20th century. Picasso's most famous work, his huge mural depicting the bombing of Guernica during the Spanish Civil War, hangs in the Reina Sofía Museum in Madrid.

Other key Spanish 20th-century artists include the surrealists Salvador Dalí (1904-1989) and Joan Miró (1893-1983).

The Landscape

GEOGRAPHY

Spain is the fourth largest country in Europe, after Russia, Ukraine, and France, with an area of 506,000 square kilometers (195,368 square miles). The country is a diverse one, with landscapes ranging from the lush green countryside and frequent rainfall of the northwestern region of Galicia, to the arid, desert landscapes of Almería in the southeast. Over half of the country is forest area (54.8 percent), and the coastline is more than 1,600 kilometers (994 miles) long.

At over 600 meters (1,969 feet) above sea level, Madrid is one of the highest capital cities in Europe. Spain's biggest city is located in the center of the country, over 300 kilometers (186 miles) from the nearest coast.

Barcelona, on the country's east coast, is bordered on one side by the Serra de Collerola mountain range and on the other by the Mediterranean Sea.

CLIMATE

In general, Spain has a Mediterranean climate of hot summers and mild winters.

Madrid, located on Spain's central plateau, or *Meseta*, is one of the highest capital cities in Europe and experiences very hot, dry summers and cold winters, with regular blue skies no matter what the season.

Barcelona, due to its location on the coast, is slightly cooler, with warm summers, mild winters, and higher rates of rainfall than Madrid.

The average winter temperatures in Madrid are around 7°C (45°F); January is the coldest month, with temperatures of around 5-6°C (41-42°F). Average summer temperatures in Madrid are around 32C (90F), but temperatures can rise to the high 30s C (upper 90s F) and top 40°C (104°F), especially in July and August, the city's hottest months.

In Barcelona, winter temperatures vary from around 10-16°C (50-60°F), and summer temperatures in July and August hover around 29°C (84°F).

ENVIRONMENTAL ISSUES

The biggest environmental issue affecting both Barcelona and Madrid is urban pollution, specifically air pollution caused in large part by traffic. This can have a serious effect on the health of the cities' inhabitants.

Madrid, after taking emergency measures (such as banning cars from the city center and reducing the speed limit on the highway into the city on days of particularly high pollution), is looking at longer-term solutions. One is a permanent ban on cars belonging to non-residents in the center of the city. Barcelona, too, has introduced measures such as banning old, more polluting cars from the streets. This is one reason why the best mode of transport for visitors is public transport.

Government and Economy

ORGANIZATION

Spain's modern political system took shape with the Constitution of 1978, when Spain returned to democracy after 36 years under the dictatorship of General Francisco Franco.

The country is a parliamentary monarchy—the king (King Felipe VI) is the head of state, and the prime minister (official title: President of the Government) is head of the government. Legislative power belongs to the *Cortes Generales*, split into the Congress of Deputies (350 seats) and the Senate (265 members).

Spain's semi-autonomous communities also hold power in regional parliaments. For example, Catalonia's regional parliament, the *Generalitat*, has its own president and oversees areas including education, culture, and Catalonia's own police force, the *Mossos d'Esquadra*.

POLITICAL PARTIES

For the past few decades, Spanish politics has been dominated by two political parties, the center-right Popular Party (*Partido Popular,* or PP) and the center-left Socialists (*Partido Socialista Obrero Español*, or PSOE).

The Partido Popular traces its beginnings to the People's Alliance, founded in 1976 by former Francoist minister Manuel Fraga. Between the late 1970s and late 1980s it joined with other conservative groups, and in 1989 renamed itself the People's Party (PP). The PP was in government from 1996-2004 under Prime Minister José María Aznar and from 2011-18 under Prime Minister Mariano Rajoy.

The PSOE was founded in 1879 and took part in coalition governments during the Second Republic from 1931-33 and from 1936-39 during the Spanish Civil War. Today a social democratic party, it originally had strong links with Marxism, which it abandoned

Spain's Tourism Backlash

Like other cities across the world, Barcelona and Madrid are grappling with the question of how to balance soaring tourist numbers with the rights of local residents; in 2016 Barcelona, a city of 1.6 million, had 32 million visitors.

In Barcelona and Madrid, locals are worried about the effect of tourism on rent prices (many feel they are being priced out of the city center). Other concerns range from antisocial tourist behavior to the way mass tourism is changing the character of city centers.

Barcelona City Council is making efforts to address the issue, closing down thousands of illegal apartment rentals and working with home rental sites like Airbnb (which accounts for 18 percent of all overnight bookings in Barcelona) to implement stricter rules; renters now have to register their homes with the council and display their registration number on their Airbnb listing.

Barcelona has also implemented a "tourist tax"; all hotel stays are taxed, depending on the number of stars the hotel has—from 75 cents per person per night in a 3-star hotel to €2.25 per person per night in a 5-star hotel. This tax also applies to apartment rentals.

Madrid City Council is also working on ways to promote sustainable tourism in terms of environmental, social, and economic impact.

Conscientious travelers will want to keep all of this in mind as they tour through the cities. Here are a few tips:

- Research local accommodations, and in Barcelona, make sure any apartment rentals are registered with the local council (you can check whether an address is licensed or not at this website: www.meet.barcelona.cat/habitatgesturistics/en).

- Consider staying in less touristy neighborhoods (i.e., avoid the Barri Gòtic in Barcelona). This will spread out tourism and give you a more authentic experience. Alternatively, stick to hotels and hostels.

- Respect local customs and avoid antisocial behavior, e.g., public drunkenness, or wandering around the city in swimwear off the beach (this is actually illegal, and you could face a fine).

- Consider visiting during the low season (January or February, or November) when lines will be shorter and there will be fewer tourists.

- Get off the beaten track and explore little-known sights and neighborhoods—this spreads out the tourist burden from just the center of the city to other neighborhoods, many of which would appreciate the extra tourists.

- Support local, independent businesses and avoid big chains—putting your money back into the local economy is important (a common gripe of locals in Barcelona is that cruise-ship passengers disembark and look around but spend no money because they are sleeping and eating on board the ship).

- Use public transport.

- Reduce plastic waste by carrying your own reusable water bottle.

- Learn a few phrases in Spanish—even hello, goodbye, and thank you show you're making an effort.

when Spain returned to democracy in the late 1970s.

The PSOE was in power from 1982-1996 under Prime Minister Felipe González and from 2004-2011 under Prime Minister José Luis Rodríguez Zapatero. The party's Pedro Sánchez became Spanish Prime Minister on June 2, 2018.

Many Spaniards felt dissatisfied with the two major political parties, which they criticized for being equally corrupt and ineffective. From around 2014, the two main parties were challenged by new political parties such as *Podemos* (We Can)—a left-wing party that grew out of the *indignados* (indignant ones) movement, which rose up in 2011 in reaction to the 2008 financial crisis and subsequent austerity measures—and *Ciudadanos* (Citizens), a center-right party that formed in Catalonia.

In the run-up to the 2015 general election, many Spaniards hoped that these new parties might shake up Spain's stagnant political system. In fact, the new parties split the votes in the 2015 general election. Despite gaining the most votes, the PP lost 64 seats and the PSOE had its worst election results since Spain's return to democracy. The election marked the moment Spain changed from a two party to a multi-party system. Neither of the main parties was able to form a government, so a new general election was held in 2016, after which the PP's Mariano Rajoy was able to form a government.

In June 2018, PP Prime Minister Mariano Rajoy, who had been Prime Minister since 2011, had a vote of no confidence brought against him in the Spanish parliament by PSOE leader Pedro Sánchez. Rajoy lost the vote, and days later Sánchez was sworn in as prime minister of a minority government.

Sánchez is governing thanks to a shaky alliance with Podemos and smaller regional parties; his PSOE—with just 85 seats—does not have a majority in Spain's lower parliament.

With elections predicted for 2020, Sánchez has been quick to make symbolic changes that do not rely on support of his minority government in parliament, such as nominating one of the most female-majority cabinets in the world (he gave 11 of 17 cabinet posts to women, including the ministries of finance, the economy, defense, and the interior).

ELECTIONS

General elections are normally held every four years; the Congress and the Senate usually serve terms that run for a max of four years, but the Prime Minister has the power to dissolve both at any time.

The Congress of Deputies is made up of 350 members of parliament directly elected for a four-year term. Each of Spain's 50 provinces is entitled to a minimum of two seats (the Spanish enclaves of Ceuta and Melilla are entitled to one). The rest of the seats are assigned to the provinces in proportion to their populations.

The elections to Spain's Senate usually take place at the same time as the elections for the Congress of Deputies. Of the Senate's 265 members, 208 are elected by a popular vote and 57 are appointed by Spain's regional legislatures.

ECONOMY

Spain is the world's 14th largest economy, with a GDP of $1.23 trillion ($38,000 per capita). It is the fifth largest economy in the Eurozone behind Germany, the United Kingdom, France, and Italy.

The 2008 economic crisis plunged Spain into recession and its government implemented tough austerity measures. At its peak, unemployment was more than 20 percent and youth employment was more than 50 percent, the second-highest in the EU after Greece. By 2015, Spain's GDP was growing at a rate not seen since before the recession hit, and since then it has been steadily improving. The Spanish economy has grown above 3 percent each year since 2015, above the EU average, and unemployment is down from its peak (at almost 26 percent) to 16 percent (in 2018).

Industry

Tourism, manufacturing, agriculture, and energy make up the main economic activities in Spain.

Cars and pharmaceuticals are Spain's main exports from manufacturing. Spain is Europe's second-largest car manufacturer (2.8 million a year, second to Germany) and the eighth-biggest in the world. Its biggest car companies include SEAT, while many

The Fight for Catalan Independence

Catalonia is an autonomous community within Spain, with its own regional parliament, the *Generalitat*, and control over areas such as police and education. Catalonia also has its own distinct culture, from the buildings of the great Modernista architects like Antoni Gaudí to social traditions like *castells* (human towers), which are a major part of local festivals throughout the region. It has its own flag, the red, yellow, and blue *estelada*, and its own national anthem, "Els Segadors" (The Reapers).

The independence movement began during the 1920s with the founding of the *Estat Català* (Catalan State) political party, which later formed the *Esquerra Republicana de Catalunya* (Republican Left of Catalonia, ERC). The modern independence movement really took shape in 2010 in response to a threat to autonomy by Spain's Constitutional Court, which ruled that parts of the 2006 Statute of Autonomy (such as calling Catalonia a "nation" within Spain) were unconstitutional. Mass protests and calls for independence ensued. Many Catalans feel that they are short-changed by the Spanish government, paying much more in taxes than the region gets back. (Another argument for independence is Catalonia's distinct language and culture.)

Since then, support for Catalan independence has been growing, and on October 1, 2017, the Generalitat held a referendum on the issue—one that was illegal according to the Spanish constitution, and strongly opposed by the Spanish government. Around 92 percent voted for independence out of a turnout of 43 percent—many people who opposed independence did not vote.

The Catalan parliament declared independence from Spain on October 27, 2017. The Spanish government immediately reacted by imposing direct rule over Catalonia and firing its president, Carles Puigdemont, and the Catalan government. Independence supporters, who had banged pots and pans every evening on their balconies in the run-up to the referendum to call for protest, filled the streets carrying the *estelada* and placards reading "independència." Young and old took to the streets, while protests for a united Spain were—conspicuously—much smaller (many people who did not support independence stayed at home and kept quiet).

After being charged with rebellion, sedition, and misuse of public funds, Puigdemont fled to Belgium with other members of parliament. Eight of those who remained—including Catalan Vice President Oriol Junqueras—were arrested and, as of writing, are still in Spanish prisons awaiting trial.

Catalonia is split into those who vocally and passionately call for independence, and those who want to remain part of Spain but shy away from protest. Displays of Catalan nationalism are tied in with cultural activities such as the building of castells and are never more apparent than on Catalonia's national day, *La Diada*, on September 11, when many independence supporters take to the streets waving Catalan flags.

global car brands have manufacturing bases in Spain.

When it comes to energy, Spain is particularly focused on renewables. It has the world's largest solar power industry and has invested particularly heavily in this area. Spain is also the world leader in renewable energy, and in 2014 became the first country whose main source of energy was wind power for an entire year.

Agriculture

Despite having the most land dedicated to agriculture in Europe after France, only around 17 percent of that land is for irrigation-based agriculture; the rest is used for pasture.

Some of Spain's most important agricultural exports are vegetables and citrus fruits—Spain is Western Europe's main producer of citrus fruits, and it grows the highest number of olives of any country in the world.

Spain is home to the largest area of vineyards in the world and is the number-one wine exporter (22.8 million hectoliters in 2017). But despite having the most vineyards, Spain's wine does not make the most money; the country sells its wine at a much cheaper price than its nearest competitors (€1.25/liter compared to France's €6/liter and Italy's €2.78/liter). Spain makes €2.8 billion compared to Italy's €6 billion and France's €9 billion, mainly due to the fact that the majority of Spanish wine is exported in bulk.

Pork, beef, milk, and poultry are Spain's main livestock products—Spain is the world's third-biggest pork exporter ($4.1 billion worth in 2017).

Tourism

Tourism has long been one of Spain's most important industries and in 2018, it became the country's biggest employer, overtaking the construction industry. It accounts for around 11 percent of annual GDP.

In 2017, Spain replaced the United States as the world's second most popular tourist destination—just after its northern neighbor, France. In 2017, Spain welcomed 82 million visitors, a 7-percent leap from 2016. Tourist spending also broke records in 2017, rising 12.4 percent from 2016.

When it comes to big tourist spenders, people from the United Kingdom spend the most, followed by Germans, the French, visitors from the Nordic countries, and Americans.

Spain is not just a huge destination for international tourism, but for internal tourism too. Most Spaniards holiday within Spain, contributing massively to the country's tourism industry.

The headquarters of the World Tourism Organization are located in Madrid.

People and Culture

DEMOGRAPHY

Spain has a population of 46 million people. Madrid is the biggest and most populous city, with three million inhabitants, followed by Barcelona (1.5 million) and Valencia (800,000). The Community of Madrid region is home to 6.4 million people, while the wider Barcelona region is home to 5.4 million.

Spain has one of the highest life expectancies in the world, with an average of 83.1 years old—85.7 for women and 80.3 for men. The country also has one of the lowest birth rates in Europe.

IMMIGRATION

Foreign-born residents now make up 9.5 percent of the Spanish population, down from a high of over 12 percent in 2011. Nationals from Romania and Morocco make up 31 percent of the total.

The most common countries of foreigners living in Spain are Romania, Morocco, the United Kingdom, Italy, China, and Ecuador.

Migrants can be grouped into economic migrants, those fleeing conflict (more recent arrivals from Syria and from boats across the Mediterranean), and older persons, usually northern Europeans, who retire to Spain.

RELIGION

Spain is a Roman Catholic country, and 70 percent of Spaniards describe themselves as such (a drop of 20 percent since 1978, when it was 90 percent). But while the majority of Spaniards are nominally Catholic, few attend Mass; 60 percent of those who declare themselves Catholic almost never attend religious services.

The traditions of Catholicism—especially when it comes to local saints' days, fiestas, and *Semana Santa* (Holy Week)—are often celebrated, but Spanish society, and Spaniards' outlook in general, is much more liberal than the conservative Catholic Church.

LANGUAGE

Spanish is the official language of the entire country of Spain, while individual autonomous communities also have co-official languages. Catalan is the co-official language in Catalonia.

In tourist sights, hotels, and popular nightlife areas, most people will probably speak English, but when you go off the beaten track or head to old, traditional bars, waiters (especially old ones) will probably not speak English. Learning a few basic phrases in Spanish is a good idea before you set off.

Essentials

Getting There

Most international travelers arrive in Spain by air. Some also arrive by train, especially as part of an inter-railing trip around Europe.

AIR

Madrid's **Adolfo Suárez Madrid–Barajas Airport** (MAD, www. aeropuertomadrid-barajas.com) is Spain's main international hub. It has four terminals and scheduled flights to and from dozens of North American and European cities.

Most flights to Barcelona arrive at **Barcelona Airport** (Aeroport

de Barcelona-El Prat; tel. 93/298-3838; www. aena.es). The airport has two terminals, the newer Terminal 1 and the older Terminal 2. Some budget airlines arrive at **Girona-Costa Brava**, 90 kilometers (56 miles) north of Barcelona, or **Reus airport**, about 100 kilometers (62 miles) to the south of Barcelona.

From the U.S. and Canada

Madrid's airport has direct routes from New York, Miami, Los Angeles, Boston, Philadelphia, Dallas, Chicago, and Atlanta, and receives flights from the U.S. on major airlines such as **American Airlines** (www.aa.com), **Delta** (www.delta.com), and **United** (www.united.com), along with budget airlines **Norwegian** (www.norwegian.com) and **Level Air** (www.flylevel.com). It receives flights from Canada on major airlines such as **Air Canada** (www.aircanada.com).

Barcelona's airport has direct routes from New York with American Airlines, Delta, United, and budget airline Norwegian.

Another option is to fly indirect via London, Amsterdam, or another European destination, which could end up cheaper. You can book the entire journey on the same airline, which could just involve a connecting flight in (for example) London Heathrow.

From the UK

There are direct flights to Madrid and Barcelona from several UK cities including London, Birmingham, Bristol, Manchester, Liverpool, and Edinburgh. Both airports receive flights from the UK on major airlines such as **British Airways** and **Iberia** and on budget airlines **Ryanair, easyJet**, and **Norwegian**.

From Australia and New Zealand

There are indirect flights to Madrid and Barcelona from Sydney, Melbourne, and Brisbane in Australia on a number of different airlines including **Quantas, Emirates**, and **Singapore Airlines**. (All flights will make one stop en route, as is the norm with flights from Australia.)

From New Zealand, airlines including **Etihad** and **Air New Zealand** fly to both cities with an average of two connections en route.

For the cheapest flights, many passengers fly to London and then on to Spain on a budget airline such as **easyJet** or **Ryanair**.

From South Africa

There are direct flights between Johannesburg and Madrid on Sundays, Tuesdays, and Thursdays with Iberia.

From other cities in South Africa, or to travel to Barcelona, flights fly indirect via other cities such as London or Frankfurt.

TRAIN

If you are traveling by train as part of a longer European vacation, consider purchasing a rail pass from **Eurail** (www.eurail.com) or **Rail Europe** (www.raileurope.com). You can choose how many countries you want to include in the train pass. Interrailing—traveling through several different European countries by train—is a popular summer travel experience, especially among students.

FROM FRANCE AND PORTUGAL

There are several routes to Spain from both neighboring France and Portugal (which can be connected to arrive from other, more-further-afield countries). The **AVE** high-speed train (www.renfe.com/viajeros/larga_distancia/productos/AVEFrancia) has direct routes between Marseille and Barcelona (4 hours 30 minutes) and Marseille and Madrid (7 hours 45 minutes). The same train has direct routes between Paris and Barcelona (6 hours 20 minutes), Lyon and Barcelona (5 hours), and Toulouse and Barcelona (3 hours and 15 minutes).

There is a nine hour night train between Lisbon and Madrid (opt for the bunk, as sitting in a seat for nine hours is not a comfortable experience), but with flights between the two cities lasting just 1 hour 20 minutes, this is the preferable option when it comes to time and cost.

BUS

In Spain, buses are the cheapest form of transport, but expect long journeys.

Eurolines (www.eurolines.com) is the main bus company for international journeys, connecting Spain to cities across Europe and Morocco. You can book tickets on its website. Eurolines operates routes to Madrid from Germany, Belgium, the Czech Republic, France, the Netherlands, Italy, Morocco, and Switzerland, and to Barcelona from all of the above plus the United Kingdom.

Flixbus (www.flixbus.co.uk) operates a route from London to Barcelona. The average journey time from London to Barcelona is between 24 and 30 hours.

Other major bus companies include **ALSA** (www.alsa.es) and **AVANZA** (www.avanzabus.com), which mainly offer routes between cities within Spain.

CAR
Driving from the UK

From the UK, you can take the Eurotunnel under the English Channel and then drive down through France. The drive from London to Barcelona is 1,500 kilometers (932 miles) and will likely take 15 hours, or two days. There will be around €130 worth of tolls along the way in France and Spain.

Ferry from the UK to Santander

- **Brittany Ferries** (www.brittany-ferries.co.uk) operates ferry services from Portsmouth and Plymouth in the UK to Santander, which is around six hours' drive from Barcelona or about five hours from Madrid:

- **From Portsmouth to Santander:** Three sailings a week on Tuesdays, Fridays, and Saturdays, 24-hour journey, from £470 (€530) one way for a car and two passengers.

- **From Plymouth to Santander:** Weekly sailing on Fridays or Sundays, 20-hour journey time, from £410 one way for a car and two passengers.

- **From Cork, Ireland to Santander:** Two sailings a week on a Wednesday and Friday, 26 hours and 32 hours long, from €150 one way for two passengers and a car.

When you arrive in Santander, it's a 420-kilometer (261-mile) drive to Madrid. Drive south along the A-1 (journey time around five hours and toll price is approximately €40). From Santander to Barcelona, a 700-kilometer (435-mile) trip, take the AP-68. Toll cost is approximately €125.

Ferry from the UK to Bilbao

Brittany Ferries also runs a route from Portsmouth to Bilbao. The 24- or 32-hour journey costs from €440 one way for a car and two passengers, and the ferry departs twice a week on Sundays and Wednesdays.

Bilbao is about a five-hour drive from either Barcelona or Madrid. To get to Madrid from Bilbao, drive 400 kilometers (250 miles) south via the A-67 towards Burgos, and then the A-1 towards Madrid. Toll prices vary but expect around €40. Driving time is approximately four to five hours.

To get to Barcelona from Bilbao, drive 600 kilometers (373 miles) southeast (driving time approximately six hours). Follow the AP-68 and AP-7 to Barcelona. Toll cost is around €115.

Getting Around

CITY TRANSPORTATION

Public Transportation

Public transportation in both Madrid and Barcelona is excellent and affordable, with single rides costing between €1.50 and €2.20, and is the recommended way to get around each city. Both cities have *metros* (underground subways) and bus routes that run until around 1am and connect the main neighborhoods and sights. In Madrid and Barcelona, night buses run when the metro is closed (usually between around 1am-6am). In both cities, you can buy single-ride passes, or save money by purchasing multi-ride transit cards.

Bicycle

Both cities have city bikeshares; however, cycling on Madrid's roads is really only recommended for experienced cyclists; those wanting to experience the city by bike would do better to cycle in one of its parks, such as Retiro Park or Madrid Río. The same goes in Barcelona, where it's better to stick to the bike lanes and the safety of places like the seafront promenade and—for more experienced bikers—routes through the Collserola mountains.

Note that the same drunk driving rules that apply to motor vehicle drivers also apply to cyclists in Spain.

Car

The very good public transport systems in both cities mean that renting a car is unnecessary, unless you are planning lots of trips out of the city. Companies such as **Car2Go** (www.car2go.com) and **Emov** (www.emov. es) let drivers sign up online, then search for nearby cars and rent them by the minute or the day using an app.

A recent trend in car and scooter rental is eco-friendly companies, such as scooter company **eCooltra** (www.ecooltra.com), which has a fleet of more than 3,000 electric scooters

across five European cities including Madrid and Barcelona. Rent the scooters via an app for an easy way to get around (be aware of the traffic in both cities, however).

TRAVELING BETWEEN BARCELONA AND MADRID

While flying is the quickest way to travel between Madrid and Barcelona, given the amount of time you have to spend waiting around in the airport, the most comfortable and easiest way to travel is by train. Atocha train station is in central Madrid, and the high-speed RENFE train will get you to Barcelona in under three hours.

Air

The fastest way to travel to Madrid from Barcelona is to fly; the short flight takes around 1 hour 20 minutes.

Iberia's *Puente Aereo* (air shuttle) between the two cities operates from Madrid's Terminal 4 with dozens of flights a day, but prices can be quite high. Check flights in advance to get the best deals: **Iberia Express** (www.iberiaexpress.com), Iberia's budget airline, flies between the two cities, as does Spanish low-coast airline **Vueling** (www. vueling.com); you can pick up return flights for under €100 when you book in advance.

Train

Spain's national rail network is operated by **RENFE** (www.renfe.com). The high-speed Tren de Alta Velocidad Española (**AVE**) train can zip between Barcelona Sants train station and Madrid's Atocha train station in between 2 hours 30 minutes and 3 hours, but prices are steep—around €100 each way is the norm. If you don't mind a long journey, slower trains can take anything between 6 and 9 hours to trundle across the country, but prices are cheaper, as little as €30 each way. Most trains

Side Trip to Zaragoza

Traveling from Barcelona to Madrid is quick via airplane or train. If you're in no hurry and want to explore more of Spain, then a stop-off midway turns what is usually an uninteresting journey into a cross-country amble. And the best place to stop is Zaragoza.

With a pretty setting on the Ebro river, Zaragoza is the capital of the autonomous community of Aragón. It was a thriving Roman city named after Emperor Cesar Augustus, and today, visitors can view remnants of its Roman walls, which can be seen on Plaza de César Augusto.

Most trains and buses stop in the city, 315 kilometers (196 miles) west of Barcelona. Buses will stop for just a short break, so your best bet would be getting off in Zaragoza and staying overnight, then catching a bus the next day to Barcelona. Buses drop off at Mercado Central, and from the train station, it's a 20-minute bus ride to the city center (line 34).

The city's compact old town is laid out to the south of the River Ebro and is easily walkable. The Mercado Central bus stop is in the middle of the old town and the Aljafería, a 20-minute stroll from the Basílica de Nuestra Señora de Pilar.

SIGHTS

Zaragoza's cathedral, **Cathedral-Basílica de Nuestra Señora del Pilar** (Plaza del Pilar; www.basilicadelpilar.es, Mon-Sat 6:45am-8:30pm, Sun 6:45am-9:30pm) is said to be the first church dedicated to Mary in history. It was built between 1681 and 1872 on the site of various Christian shrines to where the Virgin Mary is said to have appeared to Saint James around 40 AD. See it from across the river at sunset for a sparkling reflection to remember.

Unusually, Zaragoza has two cathedrals. Its second, **La Seo** (Plaza de la Seo, 4), was built between the 12th-17th centuries on the site of what had been first a Roman forum and then a mosque. Today, it is part of a UNESCO World Heritage Site, the **Mudéjar Architecture of Aragon**.

The **Aljafería** (Calle de los Diputados; tel. 97/628-9683; Apr 1-Oct 31, Mon-Sun 10am-2pm, 4:30pm-8pm; Nov 1-Mar 31, Mon-Sat 10am-2pm, 4pm-6:30pm, Sun 10am-2pm; entry €5) is an incredible fortified Moorish palace built in the 11th century. Today, it holds the *Cortes* (regional courts) of Aragón and is open to the public; look for distinctly Islamic architectural features such as horseshoe arches and geometrical designs.

FOOD

The best view of the city's Roman walls is from the Plaza de César Augusto and the **Mercado Central** (Av. De César Augusto; tel. 97/628-1998) a large, iron-covered market with a stone entrance that is a good place to pick up provisions. Alternately, head to the multitude of tapas bars surrounding the **Plaza del Pilar** and **Plaza de Santa Marta**.

between the two cities stop at both Zaragoza, around the mid-way point, and Tarragona, close to Barcelona.

A new budget high-speed train operated by RENFE is planned to run between Madrid and Barcelona starting in early 2019. The new train, named EVA, will arrive at a new station in El Prat de Llobregat, close to Barcelona-El Prat airport. The station is also connected to metro line 9.

Some foreign travelers, especially Americans and Australians, have had problems with their cards being accepted on Renfe's website; make sure you register before attempting to purchase tickets, so that if you have trouble receiving your PDF tickets, you can log into your account and see them there. If the Renfe website doesn't accept your credit card, you can use other sites such as www.loco2.com, which links directly to Renfe's ticketing system and which sells tickets (which you can either print at home or print off from in-station machines) at the same price as the Renfe website.

Driving in Spain

The legal driving age in Spain is 18 years old; all foreign drivers must also be this age to drive in Spain, regardless of the legal age in their home country. Most car rental companies require a minimum age of 21 to rent out vehicles. Drivers and cyclists must not drive/cycle if their blood-alcohol level exceeds 0.5 milligrams per milliliter.

Most Spaniards drive manual cars, but you can request automatic cars at all car rental companies.

Spaniards drive on the right-hand side of the road. Some motorways are tolled (look for the word *"peaje"* or toll); you take a ticket upon entering the section of motorway and then pay at booths with cash or credit card when you leave that section. Toll motorways tend to be the fastest route between major cities, so are a good option if you are looking for the quickest journey and don't mind paying the toll.

The price of fuel in Spain is €1.35/liter.

Bus

The bus is the cheapest mode of transport between Madrid and Barcelona, but also takes the longest. Spanish bus company **ALSA** (www.alsa.com) operates 18 daily buses (including overnight options) between the two cities, with ticket prices starting at €17. Expect an average journey time of between 7 hours and 8 hours 30 minutes.

Car

Madrid is 504 kilometers (313 miles) from Barcelona, and the drive between the two cities takes around six hours on the **AP-2/E-90 highway**, which is easy to navigate. There are tolls along the highway (around €25), so have some cash on hand; they also accept cards, but usually only the chip and pin variety. Zaragoza makes a good halfway stop between Madrid and Barcelona.

Taxi

Barcelona's taxis are black, with yellow panels on the side doors. Madrid's taxis are white, with a red stripe on the side. A green light indicates that the taxi is available. In both Madrid and Barcelona, passengers can hail taxis, wait at taxi ranks dotted around the city, or use the MyTaxi mobile app. You can pay in cash or by card.

Visas and Officialdom

PASSPORTS AND VISAS

Travelers from the **United States**, **Canada**, **Australia**, and **New Zealand** do not need a visa to enter Spain for a period of under 90 days. Travelers need a passport valid for at least three months after the end of your trip.

For those entering Spain from the **E.U.**, you will need a valid passport or ID card.

Travelers from **South Africa** require a Schengen visa to enter Spain, which is valid for up to 90 days travel around the 26 Schengen countries in Europe. To apply for the visa, contact your local Spanish embassy or consulate.

EMBASSIES AND CONSULATES

Most countries have a main embassy in Madrid and a consulate in Barcelona. Get in touch in case of a lost passport or if you get into any other kind of trouble.

In Madrid

The United States Embassy (Calle

de Serrano, 75; tel. 91/587-2200; https://es.usembassy.gov) is located in the Salamanca neighborhood.

The **Canadian Embassy** (Torre Espacio, Paseo de la Castellana, 259D; tel. 91/382-8400), **British Embassy** (Torre Espacio, Paseo de la Castellana 259D; tel. 91/714-6300; www.gov.uk/world/organisations/british-embassy-madrid), and **Australian Embassy** (Torre Espacio, Paseo de la Castellana 259D; tel. 91/353-6600; http://spain.embassy.gov.au) are located in the Torre Espacio skyscraper, in Madrid's business district to the north of the city center.

The **South African Embassy** (Calle de Claudio Coello, 91; tel. 91/436-3780; www.dirco.gov.za/madrid) and the **New Zealand Embassy** (Calle del Pinar, 7; tel. 91/523-0226) are located in the Salamanca neighborhood.

In Barcelona

The **United States Consulate** (Passeig de la Reina Elisenda de Montcada, 23; tel. 93/280-2227; www.es.usembassy.gov/embassy-consulates/barcelona; Mon-Fri 9am-1pm) is located in the Sarrià neighborhood.

The **Canadian Consulate** (Plaça de Catalunya, 9; tel. 93/270-3614; www.canadainternational.gc.ca/spain-espagne/offices-bureaux/consul_barcelona.aspx?lang=eng; Mon-Thurs 9am-1pm,

2pm-5:30pm; Fri and August 9am-2:30pm) is on Plaça de Cataunya, at the top of the Ramblas.

The **United Kingdom Consulate** (Avinguda Diagonal, 477; tel. 93/366-6200; gov.uk/world/organisations/british-consulate-general-barcelona/office/british-consulate-general-barcelona; Mon-Fri 8.30am-1.30pm) is in the Eixample neighborhood.

The **South African consulate** (Parc Empresarial Mas Blau II Alta Ribagorza, 6-8, Prat de Llobregat; tel. 93/506-9100) is in Prat de Llobregat, just south of the center.

The **Australian consulate** (Avinguda Diagonal 433; tel. 93/362-3792; www.spain.embassy.gov.au, Mon-Fri 10:30am-12:30pm) is located in Eixample.

New Zealand has an embassy in Madrid, but no consulate in Barcelona.

CUSTOMS

Those bringing more than €6,000 into the country need to declare the amount upon arrival. Travelers are permitted to carry 200 cigarettes, 50 cigars, one liter of spirits, and two liters of wine.

No animal food products can be taken in or out of Spain with the exception of powdered baby milk, which must be in its original sealed container. Vacuum-packed hard cheese or jamón should be OK, but it's a good idea to check your country's regulations before traveling.

Festivals and Events

SPRING

Easter / Holy Week (both cities): Brotherhoods process through the streets and events take place across both cities to celebrate Semana Santa or Holy Week.

San Isidro (Madrid, May 11-May 15): Madrileños don traditional dress and dance in the streets during this festival, which celebrates Madrid's patron saint, San Isidro.

Día de Sant Jordi (Barcelona, April 23): Barcelona's patron saint is celebrated by giving loved ones books and roses.

Primavera Sound (Barcelona, late May/early June): One of Barcelona's most famous music festivals draws performers from all over the world. Previous acts include Arcade Fire, Public Enemy, and The Cure.

SUMMER

Sónar (Barcelona, mid-June): One of the world's most famous electronic music festivals welcomes DJs and performers to Barcelona at the beginning of summer.

Sant Joan (Barcelona, June 23/24): During the so-called "night of fire," Barcelona celebrates the beginning of summer with bonfires on the beach and fireworks.

Pride (both cities, June and July): Both cities get decked out in rainbow flags to celebrate Pride. Madrid's is one of the biggest celebrations in the world.

Summer Verbenas (Madrid, August): Madrid celebrates three patron saints during its three big summer fiestas, with dancing, food stalls on the streets, music, and traditional dress.

Festa Major de Gràcia (Barcelona, mid-August): This local festival in the Gràcia neighborhood sees locals festoon the streets, and revel in parades and parties, for 10 days.

FALL

Festa de la Mercè (Barcelona, around Sept 24): Barcelona's annual city festival, dedicated to Our Lady of Mercy, is a lively celebration of all things Catalan, from local cuisine to soaring human towers (*castells*).

Madrid International Jazz Festival (Madrid, November): Throughout November, Madrid transforms into a jazz paradise, with performances by world-class artists across the city.

WINTER

Christmas Markets (both cities): in the run-up to Christmas, Madrid and Barcelona are decorated with beautiful lights and welcome Christmas markets to their streets and squares, selling everything from *turrón* to Christmas figurines.

Three Kings Parade / Epiphany (Madrid and Barcelona, January): In Spain, it's the Three Kings who traditionally bring children their presents, so the big parades that take place the night before the Epiphany draw huge crowds; eager children line the route to catch candies thrown down by the kings.

Carnival (Barcelona, Feb/March): Barcelona locals let their hair down before the somber 40 days and nights of Lent.

Food

One of the best things about visiting Spain is the food, and exploring its many different tapas bars, restaurants, and markets is a highlight of many a trip. Spanish cuisine is based on a Mediterranean diet rich in olive oil, fish, vegetables, and the country's unofficial national food: *jamón* (cured ham). The Spanish palate is quite mild, and spicy food is not common.

Both cities have excellent seafood, and with Barcelona right on the Mediterranean coast, fresh fish is abundant. When it comes to high-end dining, Barcelona and Madrid are also really starting to make a name for themselves, with more Michelin-starred restaurants than ever. Both cities also have thriving international food scenes, with Middle Eastern, Indian, and South American restaurants particularly abundant. (If you like it hot, in some Indian restaurants it's worth asking how spicy dishes are, and even requesting it "mas picante"—spicier.) Recent trends include burger restaurants, brunch spots (breakfast is traditionally not a big meal in Spain and usually consists of a *tostada*—toast—or a pastry, but lately the concept of brunch has really taken off), healthy food places (including plenty of vegetarian options), and cafés that take the quality of their coffee very seriously.

Spanish waiters rarely rush diners or drinkers off their table; once you have it, it's yours for as long as you want it.

When choosing where to eat, avoid places with people outside actively trying to get

The *Menu del Día*

The *menu del día* is a fixed-price lunchtime menu that was actually conceived by Spanish dictator Francisco Franco to ensure workers could get a decent, reasonably priced lunch at any restaurant. It is without doubt one of Spain's best—and best-value—culinary inventions. It usually consists of a starter, main course, and dessert or coffee as well as a drink (beer or glass of wine included) for between €10–€15, and it is usually available on weekdays only.

The *menu del día* is served everywhere from traditional, no-frills restaurants to fine dining options, where the price will probably exceed €15 but still be good value. Menus tend to change daily, and there are usually three or four options per course. The menu is usually advertised on a chalkboard outside the restaurant or on a separate sheet of paper inside. It is a great way to try eating Spanish-style; in Spain, the biggest meal of the day is usually lunch, and Spaniards tend to eat between 1:30pm and 3:30pm.

Be aware that in Spanish, the word *menu* refers to this fixed-price lunch menu. The Spanish word for "menu" is "carta."

Traditional *menus del día* feature mainly meat and fish options, but these days many other varieties of restaurant (serving, for example, vegetarian and international cuisine) also offer a *menu del día*.

tourists in, and be cautious of places that have menus with photos or menus in several different languages—they're usually tourist traps.

SPANISH EATERIES

Many establishments in both Barcelona and Madrid wear several hats; they might be great breakfast places, do a delicious lunch, and then get packed as a heaving bar come evening.

Tapas Bars

Tapas bars are a huge part of life in Spain; *tapear* (aka to "to do tapas") is its own verb, and many families make a ritual out of "doing tapas," especially on weekends. Spain's tapas tradition is an excellent starting point to explore the cuisine of Barcelona and Madrid, allowing visitors to sample lots of little dishes and see what strikes their fancy.

At first, authentic tapas bars can be an assault on the senses. The good ones are usually packed, with everyone clambering towards the bar, eating standing up, and throwing their discarded napkins on the floor (some say the more napkins on the floor, the better the tapas bar). If it's your first time trying out tapas bars (especially in Madrid, where this kind of bar tends to be more common than in

Barcelona), head out a little early (8pm) so you avoid hitting peak time (from 9pm), which should give you more space. Some tapas bars do not have menus at all, or they may have their menus written on the wall. In bars with no menus at all, ask the bartender what is on offer, have a look around to see what other patrons are eating, or just go for the most common tapa of all, a *pintxo* of *tortilla* (a slice of tortilla de patatas, a Spanish omelet made with eggs, potatoes, and often onions).

Drinks may come with a free tapa, although this is less common in Barcelona than elsewhere in Spain. Be careful of over-ordering; you can always order more, and Spaniards tend to order smaller bits, especially as part of a bigger tapas crawl. Some tapas bars have tables; most informal bars need no reservation, so you can just grab a table. Many tapas bars also have their front bar area, where people stand with a drink and a tapa (more as a snack than a whole meal), and a restaurant area in the back for those who want a more expansive, sit-down meal, where you order from a server rather than at the bar.

Bodegas, more common in Barcelona, serve wine out of huge barrels and also offer a range of tapas dishes. **Pinchos / Pintxos** (a Basque tapa usually served on top of a piece of crusty bread) will be available in Basque tapas bars (look out for *Euskal*, which means Basque), which are common in both Barcelona and Madrid.

Some vocabulary will help you on your tapas experience. A **tapa** (singular of tapas) is a small, one-person serving (approximately €2.50). A **ración** is a larger, plate-sized serving that is usually shared among two, three, or four (depending on how many dishes you're ordering). Typical tapas dishes include **albóndigas** (meatballs), **croquetas** (croquettes filled with different ingredients such as ham, but always including béchamel sauce), **bacalao** (cod, especially popular served battered), and **gambas al ajillo** (garlic prawns).

Restaurants

There is a big overlap in Spain between tapas bars and restaurants. Many tapas bars have a restaurant area in the back, many restaurants are tapas restaurants (i.e., they serve raciónes but with table service, and you order from a waiter), and the most famous tapas establishments can be stand-up bars or formal sit-down restaurants. In tapas restaurants, diners are expected to keep their cutlery between courses.

There are a good range of Michelin-starred restaurants in both Madrid and Barcelona, and the majority offer a tasting menu, which can often be paired with a wine menu.

A **taberna** is usually a family-run restaurant, and **marisquerías** are seafood restaurants.

Markets and Street Food

The modern incarnation of street food that includes food trucks has been slow to take hold in Spain, mainly due to the dominance of the tapas bar. Some common street-food trucks sell churros and ice-cream.

Markets, however, are a great place to try lots of different types of Spanish produce, and they are especially good for stocking up on supplies if you are self-catering or are preparing a picnic. Markets in Barcelona and Madrid take all forms, from renovated spaces that contain gourmet food stalls to neighborhood markets that mainly sell raw ingredients like meat, fish, and vegetables. Typical market food includes *jamón ibérico*, olives, and cheeses, as well as raw meat and fish, and fruit and vegetables. Both cities are home to covered markets that contain restaurant food stalls selling hot food to eat then and there, the most famous being La Boqueria in Barcelona.

Bakeries

Panaderías are bakeries that sell mainly bread, while **pastelerías** sell mainly cakes, pastries, and other sweet goods. Pastelerías are a good place to buy breakfast; some are purely takeaway, while others have indoor seating areas or a bar where patrons stand and eat a pastry along with a morning *café con leche* (coffee with milk), *café solo* (espresso), or *cortado* (espresso with a dash of milk).

TYPICAL SPANISH DISHES

Spain is split into 17 regions and each one has its own specialties. Happily, Madrid and Barcelona, as well as having their own local specialties, are great places to sample food from around the rest of Spain; being such big cities, they have attracted people from around the country who have brought their food with them.

The unofficial national food of Spain has got to be **jamón ibérico de bellota,** ham made from acorn-fed pigs that is sliced wafer thin and served as a ración. **Tortilla de patatas**—a Spanish egg, potato, and onion omelet—is available almost everywhere; ask for a "pincho de tortilla" or a slice of tortilla.

Be picky with **paella**: Spain's most famous dish is actually a regional dish that comes from Valencia, so it is not a local dish, especially in Madrid. It's worth researching where to find a good paella restaurant, because many tourist restaurants offer frozen paellas heated up in the kitchen; these are usually the ones advertising them with pictures outside.

Vegetarian Tapas

In traditional tapas bars, there are always at least one or two dishes that are suitable for those who do not eat meat or fish. Look for the following:

- **Tortilla de patatas**—potato and onion omelet

- **Pimientos de padrón**—green peppers

- **Patatas Bravas**—potatoes topped with a spicy sauce

- **Pisto Manchego**—a Spanish ratatouille

- **Queso**—cheese (there will usually be a ración of different kinds of Spanish cheese on any tapas menu)

- **Gazpacho**—cold tomato soup from Andalusia, popular in summer

- **Huevos rotos**—Literally "broken eggs," Spanish scrambled eggs is a popular sharing dish and sometimes comes with additions like asparagus. This also often comes with meat, so make sure to specify you do not want any meat ("sin carne").

- **Berenjenas con miel**—fried eggplant drizzled in honey

IN BARCELONA SPECIFICALLY:

- **Escalivada**—grilled eggplant, red peppers, and sometimes other vegetables served on toasted bread

- **Calçots**—green onion-like vegetable, eaten during "calçot season" at the end of winter

DIETARY RESTRICTIONS
Vegetarian Options

Spain, with its love of *jamón*, is not the most vegetarian-friendly country, but attitudes are changing and more and more vegetarian restaurants are popping up in both Barcelona and Madrid. Vegetarians, take note: *tortilla de patatas* will be your best friend while traveling in Spain.

In some more traditional places, the very concept of vegetarianism seems difficult to grasp—as evidenced by the waiter who, when told the diner is vegetarian, asks, "But you eat ham, don't you?"

"Soy vegetariano / a" (I'm vegetarian) should get you through most situations, but some Spaniards take that to mean you are pescatarian and still eat fish. (Some dishes that are advertised as vegetarian may actually contain fish such as *atún* (tuna)—this often happens with salads or sandwiches.) To make absolutely clear you eat neither, you can say "No como carne ni pescado" (I eat neither meat nor fish).

In Madrid, where it is common for bars to offer a free tapa with a drink, if the waiter brings something that contains meat or fish, feel free to say you are vegetarian, and ask if he or she has anything else ("tiene algo sin carne y pescado"—literally "Do you have anything without meat or fish?"). Often, the waiter will bring some olives or potato chips instead.

Gluten-Free Options

Spain is also wising up on gluten-free options, with some restaurants even advertising their non-gluten options on their menu and most supermarkets offering a selection of gluten-free produce. There are also plenty of traditional dishes that do not contain gluten, such as *tortilla de patatas*, *patatas bravas*, and *boquerones en vinagre* (anchovies in vinegar). Key phrases for persons with celiac disease include *libre de gluten* ("gluten-free") and *Soy celiaco/a* ("I'm celiac").

MEALTIMES

Spaniards typically eat a light breakfast—perhaps a quick *tostada* (toast topped with butter, jam, tomato, or ham) and *café con leche* (coffee with milk)—followed by a hearty lunch and then a lighter, late dinner. One thing you will immediately notice in Spain is that meal times are later than almost everywhere else. Lunch is usually eaten between 1:30pm-3:30pm, and dinner any time after 9pm. Arriving at a restaurant at 7pm, you will usually be met with a closed sign. Restaurants tend to open for dinner from around 8:30pm. The best plan is to adapt, or you risk missing out on great local restaurants and tapas bars; many of the places that open earlier cater only to tourists and are best avoided.

Thanks to Spain's late eating times, finding late-night eats is usually easy—it's not uncommon for places to still be serving food after midnight. Otherwise, there are plenty of casual places such as pizza bars and kebab shops where you can pick up a late-night meal.

Be aware that some tapas bars and restaurants close for the month of August. Travelers will always be able to find something that is open, but many of the smaller bars close during this month.

DRINKS

The minimum age to drink and purchase alcohol in Spain is 18. Alcohol is a strong part of tapas culture and for many Spaniards is consumed alongside food. Spaniards young and old enjoy a laid-back *caña* on a sunny terrace while watching the world go by.

While Spaniards love to drink—the concept of day drinking is perfectly normal here, and many *menus del día* include a glass of beer or wine with the meal—they do so in moderation. Seldom will you see a Spaniard fall-down drunk on the street, as is the case in some other countries. One key is that Spaniards rarely drink without also eating; the whole concept of *tapas* means that as you drink,

you are constantly eating, too. Key drinks in any bar, from the most low-key neighborhood joint to the hottest new opening, are beer and wine.

Beer

Beer has long been the favorite drink of Spaniards, and men and women both enjoy the cool sensation of an ice-cold **caña**, the smallest size of beer a place offers; it's also the most common order of beer in Spain—ordering a pint will usually mark you out as a foreigner. The exact size of a *caña* differs from bar to bar but is usually never more than half a pint. In Madrid, the local beer you are most likely to find on tap is **Mahou**, and in Barcelona, **Estrella Damm**.

Wine

Spanish wine is starting to get the attention it deserves, but the fact it has gone under the radar compared to French wine means prices are still low, and you can enjoy an excellent bottle for a very reasonable price (from as little as a few euros in a supermarket to €10 in a restaurant). Spain has the most vineyards of any country in the world and is the world's third-largest wine producer, with Rioja and Ribera del Duero varieties being particularly popular. Catalonia, where Barcelona is located, is the country's main producer of **Cava**, Spanish sparkling wine.

Most regular bars will offer either a house red and white, or small choice of a couple of different varieties. The most common tend to be Rioja and Ribera for reds (*vino tinto*) and Rueda and Albariño for whites (*vino blanco*). Rosé is available in places with a longer wine list but tends to be less popular.

Non-Alcoholic Drinks

Mineral water (*agua mineral*) is available everywhere; Spain is in the top five in Europe and top ten in the world when it comes to mineral water consumption. Solán de Cabras is the main mineral water in Madrid and Font Vella is the main brand in Barcelona. Madrid is renowned for its excellent tap water, and although most locals in Barcelona steer clear of their local tap water because of its bad taste, it is safe to drink. Many travelers will be advised, however, to buy bottled water in Barcelona, and restaurants in the city will usually not provide tap water.

RESERVATIONS

Reservations are worth making for popular restaurants. Some have online booking forms; for others, just call a day or two before (for high-end, Michelin-starred places, you'll need to call far in advance). However, it's not necessary to make reservations at casual tapas bars.

TIPPING

Tipping is not habitual or expected in Spain. Most Spaniards will leave nothing or a small coin after a sit-down drink (you do not tip bartenders in Spain), or they will leave some spare change after a meal, but in general there is very little tipping culture. After a bigger meal, a tip of 5-10 percent is more common.

Accommodations

As of writing, Madrid and Barcelona are encouraging home-rental websites like Airbnb to display more information online, so travelers can better tell which rental properties adhere to the city's regulations. Many buildings in the city center have, in a few short years, become almost exclusively tourist rentals, which has angered some residents who feel they are being priced out of their own neighborhoods. Renting apartments via online booking platforms is not illegal, but it is worth keeping the issues surrounding tourist rentals in mind when choosing accommodation.

HOTELS

Both cities have a good range of hotels, and different price points (graded on a star system, from one to five stars). Hotels can be booked online and will have multilingual staff. Checking in requires a passport, and check-in time is usually at around 3pm (early arrivals can usually leave luggage at the hotel while they head out to explore).

Hotels have en-suite bathrooms, and the majority provide toiletries like shampoo and soap. Many also offer a buffet-style breakfast, but this is not always included in the room price (check when booking).

Travelers will be charged a city tax on top of their hotel bill in Barcelona, the amount depending on the number of stars the hotel has (65 cents per person per night for 3-star hotels, €1.10 per person per night at 4-star hotels, and €2.25 per person per night at 5-star hotels).

PENSIONES

For those on more of a budget, opting for a *pensión* could save you on accommodation. These are small hotels that are usually around the two-star mark, are family-run, and are located on one floor of a larger building. Most rooms will include an en-suite bathroom. In Spanish, the word "hostal" usually refers to a *pensión*.

HOSTELS

Hostels (note the difference in spelling from "hostal," or *pensión*) are plentiful and increasingly stylish, aiming to attract a cool, young market. Design hostels are becoming more common in both cities and allow travelers on a budget to still sleep in style. Hostels usually have both mixed and female-only dorms (with shared bathrooms), and many also have private rooms (some with their own en-suite)—often a cheaper option than a hotel, but with just as much privacy. Dorm beds range from around €15 upwards and can include breakfast.

APARTMENT RENTALS

Renting an apartment can give you a more local feel than staying in a hotel, allowing you to experience local life during your stay, including cooking in the kitchen; this option usually costs less than a hotel. Websites like Airbnb have hundreds of options in both cities, but the site has been experiencing an increasing amount of backlash related to the phenomena of mass tourism.

If using apartment rental websites to book in Barcelona, make sure the apartment is registered on the city's database—registration numbers should be included in listings under the subheading "License or registration number" in the description of the apartment.

Conduct and Customs

GREETINGS

In both general Spanish and Catalan culture, people greet each other with a kiss on each cheek; this applies to men and women, and to women with other women, but rarely to men with men. In a more formal setting a handshake is a usual form of greeting.

Many Catalans are fiercely proud of their Catalan identity, so they do not take kindly to being referred to as Spanish. Similarly, there are some Catalans who, when asked a question in Spanish, might answer in Catalan, but this is generally quite rare, especially if it's a tourist asking the question. (Some Catalans might also prefer to answer in English than Spanish.)

THE SIESTA

Siesta—from the Latin sexta hora, or the sixth hour of the day from daybreak—is a post-lunch nap that was traditionally taken by Spaniards working in the fields to avoid the hottest part of the day.

Today, few Spaniards have a siesta (around 60 percent never partake of the nap), while for many, a quick post-lunch snooze is relegated to the weekends if they ever do enjoy one. One reason is that with the rise of urbanization, Spaniards no longer worked close to where they lived, so they could no longer have a siesta. Although the stereotype endures, most Spaniards today would laugh at the idea that they have a daily siesta.

The word "siesta" is also often confused with shop opening times. Shops tend to close for two or three hours in the middle of the day, but this is closing time for lunch rather than a siesta.

SMOKING

Since 2011, smoking has been banned in all bars and restaurants, as well as near playgrounds, schools, and hospitals, so smokers have to step outside to light up. Cigarettes can be bought from specialist tabacarías—tobacco shops.

DRUGS

Marijuana is illegal in Spain for commercial purposes but is legal for personal use, as long as it is in the privacy of your own home. Taking drugs, including cannabis, in the street, public places, or buildings is illegal and carries fines ranging from €300-€30,000. Other drugs such as cocaine and heroin are illegal.

DRESS

There is no "one way" of dressing in Spain, and most outfits will not raise an eyebrow. In general, however, both Madrileños and Barceloneses are smart but casual dressers. In Barcelona, swimwear and flip flops are the preserve of the beach, and don't consider wandering the city in a bikini or shirtless because it is illegal and you could be fined.

In churches, too, it is best to cover up. Sleeveless tops, shorts, and miniskirts are banned in Barcelona's cathedral, and although the rule is not always enforced, it is better to cover up.

Health and Safety

EMERGENCY NUMBERS

The main emergency telephone number in Spain is **112**, used to contact the police, fire brigade, and ambulance service. The operator will speak English.

CRIME AND THEFT

Barcelona and Madrid are, on the whole, very safe cities to travel around, but like all major tourist destinations, visitors should pay particular attention to their belongings and be aware of pickpockets and street scams. Barcelona has built up quite a reputation for its pickpockets, who tend to hang out in its metro system and on Las Ramblas, the city's main boulevard and tourist hub.

In both cities, keep your valuables safe, carry a securely fastened bag facing towards your body (avoid backpacks or carry them on your front), and try to avoid looking like a lost visitor. Pickpockets will target people who look like an obvious tourist: camera around the neck, looking at a big map out on the street. If you must consult a map, do so when you are sitting in a café or step into a side street where you are not so obvious.

It is best to have a cynical attitude towards being stopped on the street; this is how some pickpockets strike, working in teams or pairs, one distracting the victim while the other steals their wallet/purse. A polite "no gracias" and walking away should suffice.

Remember that most visitors are not victims of pickpocketing, so do not let the fear of it take over—just be prepared and be aware for a safe and enjoyable trip.

TERRORISM AND SECURITY

Unfortunately, Spain has not been immune to the recent spate of terror attacks that have struck European countries, including the UK, France, Belgium, and Germany. On August 17, 2017, a van drove down Las Ramblas in Barcelona, killing 14 people and injuring more than 100.

Being aware of the "run, hide, tell" guidelines is a good way for tourists to prepare for a (very unlikely) similar incident.

MEDICAL SERVICES

Spain's health care system is excellent, and your hotel or local embassy or consulate can put you in touch with an English-speaking doctor if needed. Travelers from the UK should carry their European Health Insurance Card (EHIC), which replaced the E111 card. Travelers from North America, as well as other countries, such as South Africa, Australia, and New Zealand, are advised to take out travel insurance, as non-EU citizens have to pay for anything other than emergency treatment.

PHARMACIES

Pharmacies are found on almost every street in both cities (look out for the green cross) and can offer advice, often in English, and medicines, many of which are only available on prescription in the UK and North America.

DRINKING WATER

Madrid's tap water (*agua del grifo*) is considered among the best in Spain, coming as it does straight from the surrounding Sierra. In Barcelona, on the other hand, the tap water is safe to drink but does not taste good, which means relying on bottled water. Some restaurants in Barcelona are even starting to offer filtered tap water—for a price.

Practical Details

WHAT TO PACK

What to pack depends on the length of trip and time of year, but there are some key pieces that will make your trip easier.

- **Luggage**: a wheelie suitcase is easy to pull along, while a bag with a zip and (ideally) another closure on top is ideal for taking around during the day. Backpacks are popular but can be targets for pickpockets, so consider a cross-body bag for when you're out during the day. A money belt is useful for storing essentials.

- **Clothing**: Pack layers for during the autumn and spring, when temperatures are likely to fluctuate. Summers are hot, with temperatures well over 30C (86F), so cool cotton clothing is ideal. Sunglasses should be brought no matter the time of year, especially in Madrid, which has more annual sunny days than Barcelona. Beachwear is fine for the playa, but in churches, shoulders and knees should be covered.

- **Toiletries and Prescriptions**: Don't forget sunscreen and any prescriptions you may need (including photocopies of the prescription label).

- **Travel adapters** (Spain's voltage is 220 volts, and plugs have two prongs) are essential for charging phones and other electrical gadgets. Pick up a couple of US-to-European adaptors before arriving at the airport, where they usually charge a premium. Once in Spain, adaptors are available at El Corte Inglés and at electronics shops (there are also lots of "corner shops" and hardware shops that sell everything). Otherwise, most decent hotels have them available to lend to visitors.

MONEY

Currency

The euro has been Spain's currency since 2002. Banknotes come in €5, €10, €20, €50, €100, €200, and €500 denominations. Coins come in 1, 2, 5, 10, 20, and 50 cents, and €1 and €2. The euro is used in 19 of the European Union's 28 member states.

Cash, Credit Cards, and ATMs

ATM machines are easily located in both cities and accept foreign debit and credit cards. (Before your trip, it's worth asking your bank what fees they charge for overseas withdrawals.) Spanish banks also include a small fee for clients of other banks to use their ATMs, and ATMs have instructions in several languages, usually including English.

Cards are regularly used in Spain and few places are cash-only. Most card systems now use chip and pin or contactless payment (for transactions under €20, no pin is needed).

Before your trip, inform your bank or credit card company of where you will be traveling; many will block cards used abroad after unexpected activity.

Sales Tax

In Spain, sales tax of 21 percent is added to purchases in shops but is usually included in the quoted price. (The tax is 10 percent in hotels and restaurants and is also normally included in the price.) Residents outside the EU are entitled to a refund on all 21 percent on any purchases that exceed €90, are on one receipt, and are taken out of the EU within three months.

BUSINESS HOURS

Smaller shops tend to open during the morning and take a break of a few hours in the middle of the day, then reopen for the late afternoon and evening. Typical hours might be 10am-2pm then 5pm-9pm. Bigger stores will stay open all day, but if you are thinking of visiting a particular shop, it's worth checking its opening hours beforehand.

BUILDING FLOORS

In Spain, as in much of Europe, the floors of buildings are numbered 0–Ground floor, 1–first floor, 2–second floor, and so on. So, what would be the second floor in the United States is the first floor in Spain.

PUBLIC HOLIDAYS

All national holidays are observed in both Madrid and Barcelona. Travelers can expect public buildings and places like banks to be closed, but most sights and restaurants will remain open.

National Public Holidays

* Año Nuevo/New Year's Day—January 1

* Reyes (Epiphany/Three Kings' Day)—January 6

* Viernes Santo (Good Friday)—March/April

* Día del Trabajo (Labor Day)—May 1

* Asunción de la Virgen (The Assumption)—August 15

* Día de la Hispanidad (Spain's National Day)—October 12

* Día de Todos los Santos (All Saints Day)—November 1

* Día de la Constitución (Day of the Constitution)—December 6

* Immaculada Concepción (The Immaculate Conception)—December 8

* Navidad (Christmas)—December 25

Madrid Public Holidays

* Jueves Santo (Holy Thursday)—March/April

* Día de la Comunidad de Madrid (Madrid Day)—May 2

* Fiesta de San Isidro (Feast of San Isidro, Madrid's patron saint)—May 15

* La Almudena (Celebrating Madrid's other patron saint)—November 9

Exchange Rates

* €1—$1.17USD

* €1—£0.88 GBP (British Pound)

* €1—.6 AUD (Australian Dollar)

* €1—1.5 CAD (Canadian Dollar)

* €1—17 ZAR (South African Rand)

* €1—1.8 NZD (New Zealand Dollar)

Barcelona Public Holidays

* Dilluns de Pasqua Florida (Easter Monday)—March/April

* Dilluns de Pasqua Granda (Pentecost)—May/June

* Dia de Sant Joan (Feast of Saint John the Baptist)—June 24

* Diada (Catalonia's National Day)—September 11

* Festes de la Mercè (city-wide fiesta)—September 24

* El Dia de Sant Esteve (Boxing Day/ St Stephen's Day)—December 26

COMMUNICATIONS
Phones and Cell Phones

To call Spain from outside the country, include your international access code, followed by Spain's country code (34) and the full number. To make an international call, dial the international access code (00), country code, area code, and number.

The EU abolished roaming charges between its different member countries in 2017, which means EU residents should not be charged more for using their phone in Spain as they would in their home country. However, different providers have different rules on how much data is included when abroad, so it is always worth checking before you leave.

Travelers from countries outside the EU tend to bring their smartphones and use available WiFi (both cities offer WiFi spots at points across the city).

Check with your local mobile providers to see what options they offer for customers traveling abroad; many have packages—at an extra cost—that allow customers to use international roaming or foreign networks.

Wi-Fi

Both cities have free WiFi hotspots. These days, many bars and cafes offer WiFi as well.

Tourist Information

SIGHTSEEING PASSES

Both cities offer sightseeing passes that can save you time and money.

Madrid

- **Paseo del Arte Card:** A good option if you're planning on visiting the city's major art galleries, this card gives holders 20 percent off entry into the Prado, Reina Sofía, and Thyssen-Bornemisza.

- **Eight Museums Pass or Four Museums Pass:** Handy if you're keen on exploring some of Madrid's smaller museums, this card allows entry into certain museums, including the Museum of Romanticism and National Museum of Anthropology, as many times as you like over a 15-day period.

Barcelona

- **Barcelona Card:** A comprehensive card that includes transport and discounts into 25 museums and attractions.

- **Art Ticket:** A good option if you're keen on sticking to Barcelona's best art museums, this card allows entry into six of them and is valid for six months.

- **ArqueoTicket:** Only really necessary if you want to visit all the participating museums, including the Archeological Museum and the Egyptian Museum.

- **Ruta del Modernisme:** Worth the purchase for architecture fans and those wanting to focus on Barcelona's Modernista buildings. It comprises a book and discount codes for the city's major Modernista sights.

MAPS

Maps are available from Tourist Information Centers, and most hotels and hostels also offer maps to their guests.

Traveler Advice

ACCESS FOR TRAVELERS WITH DISABILITIES

Neither Madrid nor Barcelona is perfect when it comes to access for disabled travelers—but both cities are making increased efforts to become more accessible. While most sidewalks have ramps, not all metro stations have elevators.

Madrid

Madrid City Council has produced an **Accessible Travel Guide** (www.esmadrid. com/sites/default/files/documentos/

Advice for Travelers of Color

Sienna Brown, founder of **Las Morenas de España** (Brown Women of Spain, www. lasmorenasdeespana.com), who is originally from New York and now resides in Javea, Spain, offers her perspective on travel in the country.

What has been your experience as a black woman living in Spain?
I've had an extremely positive experience living as a black woman in Spain over the past four years. I think that in the U.S., race is a topic that everyone avoids when trying to be politically correct. I spent a month in New York this past summer; after being in Spain for so long, I felt a lot more racial tension than I ever had in the past.

When I'm in Spain, I feel safe and welcomed, but I'm aware that it also has to do with my nationality. When you're a person of color from the U.S. or UK, you are automatically given higher societal standards and acceptance than what you would be given if you were from Africa. It's sad but the truth.

What stood out to me the most in my first year was how openly Spanish people were willing and eager to talk about race. It's something I wasn't used to coming from the states. Many Spaniards are very blunt, so they'll address someone as Black in the same way that they'll call their friend "fat" to their face but it's because they don't necessarily view it as something negative, just as what it is.

What inspired you to start Las Morenas de España?
I started Las Morenas de España four years ago because the narrative of what it's like to be black in Spain was extremely negative, and the majority of the stories were told by people who didn't know the cultural or historical context of Spain as a whole.

I wanted to redefine the narrative of what it means to be a woman of color, not just living, but thriving in the country. I found it was necessary to shed a light on people who were doing it so that others who were interested would feel inspired and empowered to do the same.

accessible_resources_2_edicion.pdf), with information for disabled travelers on disabled-friendly sights, routes, transport, restaurants, and accommodation.

Around 50 percent of Madrid's metro stops have wheelchair access—metro maps show which stations have elevators. Central stations with elevator access include Sol (Lines 1, 2, and 3), Callao (Line 3), and Iglesia (Line 1).

Madrid's museums are well prepared for disabled visitors, and free entry is offered at several sites. The Museo del Prado has audio and sign guides and wheelchairs can be hired at the locker area. (Access is wheelchair-friendly throughout the museum, except for some areas of the Villanueva building—something the museum is currently working on.) The Reina Sofía offers free entry to disabled visitors, as well as anyone accompanying them to provide necessary support. Elevators are marked in Braille, and the building is completely wheelchair accessible. Touch tours and descriptive visits are available for visually impaired visitors, as brochures in Braille. Wheelchairs can be checked out at the Information Points in the Sabatini and Nouvel buildings.

The Thyssen-Bornemisza offers free entry to disabled visitors, rents out wheelchairs, and has good access, interactive sign-language guides (see audio descriptions at https://www.museothyssen.org/en/visit/accessibility/services-resources/sign-language-guide-audio-descriptions).

Barcelona

Barcelona's metro does not have elevators at all stops. Central stations and stations close to big sights that do have disabled access include

Over the years, we've definitely accomplished that and more. There is still a long way to go but we're on the right path!

How diverse is Spain?

Compared to many other countries, Spain is not that diverse at all. That being said, the demographics are changing, but with mass immigration just starting in the early '90s the concept of "diversity" is still quite young in the country.

In the bigger cities like Madrid and Barcelona, you'll find much more diversity. In the Madrid neighborhood of Lavapiés alone there are now more than 80 nationalities represented. In smaller towns, it's quite rare that you'll see a diverse population, but when that happens, it's a great way to ignite conversations and be a pillar to shape the conversation and defy stereotypes that many get from mainstream media.

Are there any issues people of color may need to be aware of when traveling in Spain?

Compared to the U.S., absolutely not. I feel 1,000-percent safer with my health and well-being in Spain than I do in my home country. One piece of advice would be to always remember that the historical context of the U.S. and Spain are not the same.

Some people come in thinking that every stare, comment, or interaction is based on race and oftentimes, that's not the case.

One of the biggest things that people mention is that "Spanish people stare at me a lot" and while that might be true . . . many times, it's not with mal-intent but out of curiosity. It could be that they haven't seen someone like you before and while staring isn't the politest thing, I'd rather someone stare at me for five extra seconds on the street and reply with a smile, than fear if something is going to happen to me or I'll be attacked for the color of my skin.

You can find us at www.lasmorenasdeespana.com. Otherwise, feel free to email us with any questions (team@lasmorenasdeespana.com).

Catalunya (Line 3), Barceloneta (Line 4), and Sagrada Familia (Line 5). Buses are more accessible, with access ramps and special areas for wheelchairs.

Access to Park Güell is up a very steep street, so unless wheelchair users are accompanied by someone with muscles of steel, a taxi to the entrance could be a good bet. The Picasso Museum is completely accessible, and visitors can rent wheelchairs if needed. It also offers special visits exclusively for visually or auditory impaired visitors on the third Thursday of every month (www.bcn.cat/museupicasso/en/education/accessible-visits.html).

There are wheelchair access paths at the beach, and most of the city is flat.

Barcelona Turisme's website, Barcelona Access, can help disabled travelers with a range of tips, from transport to sights; visit www.barcelona-access.com/?idioma=3.

TRAVELING WITH CHILDREN

Spaniards love children, and Spanish society is very family-focused; a common sight on weekends is multiple generations of the same family all coming together for a big family lunch. Children are welcome everywhere, and it's perfectly common to see little ones running around the local plaza at all hours of the evening.

Museums, amusement parks, and public transport, to name but a few places, all offer discounts to children.

On the Madrid Metro, children under the age of 11 get a 50-percent discount on tourist travel cards (available covering from one day to 7 days).

Under 18s get free access to the Museo del Prado, Reina Sofía Museum, and the Thyssen-Bornemisza Museum.

Children under 14 get a 40-percent discount on RENFE ticket prices, and children under four who will share a seat with their parent go free. Visit www.renfe.com/EN/viajeros/tarifas/ninos.html.

FEMALE AND SOLO TRAVELERS

Spain is generally a very safe country for female and solo travelers. Women traveling alone should take the normal precautions of any trip—avoid deserted or dodgy areas at night, keep your wits about you, and don't leave drinks unattended. If you do need assistance, Spain's emergency number is 112. If you're looking to meet fellow travelers, hostels are a great accommodation idea. They often organize social events—such as tapas nights or bar crawls—for guests, which is a great, ready-made way of socializing if you're traveling alone.

SENIOR TRAVELERS

Spaniards revere their elders and Spain has one of the highest life expectancies in the world. Older Spaniards tend to be just as sociable as their younger family members, which means that in most restaurants, bars, and terraces, you're likely to see people of all different ages having a good time.

Over 65s are entitled to discounts at museums, theaters, and other entertainment events; a passport or valid ID is usually necessary to prove your age. Over 65s get into the Prado Museum for half-price (€7.50), into the Reina Sofía for free, and into the Thyssen-Bornemisza for a reduced price (€8).

LGBT TRAVELERS

Spain was just the third country in the world to legalize gay marriage, in 2005, at the same time giving adoption rights to same-sex couples. Spaniards, in general, have a live-and-let-live attitude, and the sight of same-sex couples hand in hand is perfectly common in both Barcelona and Madrid.

Both cities host huge Pride events every year; Madrid's is one of the biggest in the world. Madrid has its own "LGBT+" neighborhood,

Chueca, where many LGBT shops, bars, and other businesses are located. But establishments are very welcoming across the city in general, and same-sex couples should have no issues.

Barcelona's equivalent neighborhood is the Gaixample (a mixture of gay and Eixample), a rectangle bordered by Carrer Balmes, the Gran Via, Carrer Urgell, and Carrer Aragó.

Sitges, 35 kilometers (22 miles) south of Barcelona, is renowned as a LGBT destination; it's famed for its February carnival and summer Pride celebrations.

For more info, Madrid's Tourism Board provides dedicated advice for LGBT travelers at www.esmadrid.com/en/madrid-lgbt. Barcelona Tourism's guide to the Gaixample can be found at www.barcelonaturisme.com/wv3/en/page/393/gaixample.html.

TRAVELERS OF COLOR

Spain's big cities are less diverse than the likes of London, Paris, and New York, partly because mass migration only really took off in the 1990s and partly because, for many years, the main immigrants to Spain came from Latin America, so they already spoke the language. Today, Madrid and Barcelona are increasingly diverse, and travelers of color should feel confident visiting both.

Some travelers of color do find that some Spaniards can be quite naïve/culturally insensitive when it comes to race; examples include staring and asking bluntly about things such as hairstyles. In the vast majority of cases, these questions are posed out of curiosity with no malice intended. Also be aware that rudeness is not always a sign of racism; some waiters are just grumpy and are usually like that with everyone.

Something to be aware of is that, in some local festivals, the practice of using blackface—white people making their skin darker with makeup—has been a tradition for decades. (One example is during the Three Kings parades, when Balthazar is often played by a "blacked-up" white man). Attitudes to this are slowly changing, but many Spaniards see nothing wrong with the practice.

Resources

Glossary

SPANISH
abierto: open
aseos: toilet
avenida: avenue
barrio: neighborhood or quarter
banco: bank
caña: smallest size of beer
calle: street
cerrado: closed
iglesia: church
estación: station
mercado: market
museo: museum
plaza: square
playa: beach
salida: exit
tapear: to 'do tapas' / go out for tapas

CATALAN
avinguda: avenue

barri: neighborhood or quarter
bodega: cellar or wine bar
carrer: street
cava: Catalan sparkling wine
entrada: entrance
església: church
estació: station
festa: festival
generalitat: Catalan regional government
mercat: market
Moderisme: Catalan architectural style / Catalan Art Nouveau
museu: museum
obert: open
plaça: square
platja: beach
serveis: toilet
sortida: exit
seu: cathedral
tancat: closed

Spanish and Catalan Phrasebook

PRONUNCIATION

Spanish
It's worth noting that the "c" sound, when the letter comes before e or i, is pronounced differently in Spain than in South America. In Spain it is "lisped"—for example, the word gracias is pronounced grath-ee-ass.

VOWELS
a like ah, as in "hah": agua AGwa (water), pan PAN (bread), and casa CA-SA (house)
e like eh, as in "help": mesa MEH-sa (table) and tela TEH-la (cloth)
i like ee, as in "need": diez dee-ES (ten), comida ko-MEE-dah (meal), and fin FEEN (end)
o like oh, as in "go": peso PAY-soh (weight), ocho OH-choh (eight), and poco POH-koh (a bit)

u like oo, as in "cool": uno OO-noh (one), cu-arto KOOAHR-toh (room), when it follows a "q" the u is silent

CONSONANTS

b, d, f, k, l, m, n, p, q, s, t, w, x, y, z, and **ch** pronounced almost as in English; **h** occurs, but is silent—not pronounced at all (e.g., *hola* is pronounced oh-la and *hielo* (ice) is pronounced ee-el-oh)

c like k as in "keep": cuarto KOOAR-toh (room), caliente KAL-ien-tay (hot); c is lisped before e and i for example gracias.

g like g as in "gift" when it precedes "a," "o," "u," or a consonant: gato GAH-toh (cat), hago AH-goh (I do, make); before e or i, pronounce g like h as in "hat": giro HEE-roh (money order), gente HEN-tay (people)

j like h, as in "has": Jueves HWE-ves (Thursday), mejor meh-HOR (better)

ll like y, as in "yes": me llamo me YA-mo (I'm called), ellos AY-yohs (they, them)

ñ like ny, as in "canyon": año AH-nyo (year), señor SEH-nyor (Mr., sir)

r is lightly trilled, with tongue at the roof of your mouth: pero PEH-rrrro (but), tres Trrres (three), cuatro KOOAH-trrrro (four)

rr like a Spanish r, but with much more emphasis and trill. Let your tongue flap. Practice with burro (donkey), carretera (highway), and ferrocarril (railroad)

v like b as in "baby": vino BEE-no—the v can often be pronounced as a b or a v interchangeably, so listen out for words like vino and vale BALLAY (ok)

Note: The single small but common exception to all of the above is the pronunciation of Spanish **y** when it's being used as the Spanish word for "and," as in "Penelope y Javier." In such case, pronounce it like the English ee, as in "keep": Penelope "ee" Javier (Penelope and Javier).

Catalan

The 'lisp' sound common in other parts of Spain does not exist in Catalan, so the city is never pronounced Barthelona but Barcelona.

VOWELS

a like a as in "pan": Ciutat SEE-OO-TAT (city) and pa PA (bread)

e like eh as in "pencil": te tEH (tea) and cafè caFEH (coffee)

i like ee as in "police": país pie-EES (country)

o like oh as in "on": hora OR-AH (time/hour)

u like oo "pool": música MOO-zic-ah (music)

CONSONANTS

Letters not pronounced the same as English are:

c is soft followed by e or i, otherwise it is hard: cervesa SIR-VESA (beer)

ç like s as in "say": plaça pla-SAH (square), Barça BAR-SAH (nickname for FC Barcelona)

g like j as in "jacket" when followed by e or i: general (JE-NE-RAL) or hard when followed by other letters: Gaudí (GAU-DEE)

h always silent: hola OH-LA (hello), hotel OH-tel (hotel)

j soft like the French "je": jardi SHAR-DEE (garden)

l.l like l as in "lamp" (although there is more nuance in Catalan, this is the easiest way for non-Catalan speakers to pronounce it): Paral.lel PARA-LEL (metro stop in Barcelona)

r rolled at the start of a word and after l, m, n and s: Rambla RRRRambla, not rolled when in other parts of word, e.g., Miró and Girona

s like z as in "zero" when between vowels: casa CA-ZAH (house) and música MOO-ZI-CAH (music)

x like sh as in "shop" when at the beginning of a word: xocolata SHOCK-O-LA-TAH (chocolate). In other positions, pronunciation is similar to English, e.g., èxit

ESSENTIAL PHRASES

Phrases below are in Spanish first, and Catalan second:

Hello Hola / Hola

Good-bye Adios / Adéu

Nice to meet you Encantado/a (m/f) / Encantat

Please Por favor / Si us plau
Thank you Gracias / Gràcies
You're welcome De nada / De res
Excuse me Perdón / Perdoni
I don't speak Spanish/Catalan No hablo
español / No parlo Català
Do you speak English? ¿Habla inglés? /
Parla anglès?
Yes Si / sí
No No / no

TRANSPORTATION

bus autobús / autobús
train tren / tren
Where is...? ¿Dónde está...? / On és...?
How far is it...? ¿Qué tan lejos esta? / A
quina distància està?
What time does the bus leave? ¿A qué
hora sale el autobús? / A quina hora surt el
autobus?
Where can I buy a ticket? ¿Dónde puedo
comprar un billete? / On puc comprar un
bitllet?

ACCOMMODATIONS

hotel hotel / hotel
apartment piso / apartament
room habitación / habitació
key llave / clau
shower ducha / dutxa
soap jabón / sabó

FOOD

I would like... Quisiera... / Voldria...
The check please? La cuenta, por favor / El
compte, si us plau
I'm a vegetarian. Soy vegetariano/a / Sóc
vegetarià / vegetarian
Cheers! Salud! / Salut!
beer cerveza / cervesa
bread pan / pa
breakfast desayuno / esmorzar
cash efectivo / en efectiu (as in "pay in cash")
coffee café / cafè
dinner cena / sopar
glass vaso / got
ice hielo / glaç
lunch comida / dinar

restaurant restaurante / restaurant
water agua / aigua
wine vino / vi

SHOPPING

money dinero / diners
shop tienda / botiga
How much does this cost? ¿Cuánto
cuesta? / Quant costa?
I'm just looking Sólo estoy mirando /
només estic mirant

HEALTH

I need to see a doctor. Necesito ver un
médico / Necessito veure un metge
I need to go to the hospital. Necesito ir al
hospital / Necessito anar a l'hospital
I am diabetic. Soy diabético/a / Sóc
diabètic
I am pregnant. Estoy embarazada / Estic
embarassada
I am allergic to . . . Soy alérgico a... / Sóc
al.lèrgic a...
pain dolor / dolor
fever fiebre / febre
headache dolor de cabeza / mal de cap
stomachache doloar de estómago / mal
d'estomac
toothache dolor de muelas / dolor de dents
nausea náusea / nàusees
vomiting vómito / vòmits
medicine medicina / medicaments

NUMBERS

0 cero / zero
1 un/uno/una / un/a (m/f)
2 dos / dos/dues (m/f)
3 tres / tres
4 cuatro / quatre
5 cinco / cinc
6 seis / sis
7 siete / set
8 ocho / vuit
9 nueve / nou
10 diez / deu
11 once / onze
12 doce / dotze
13 trece / tretze

14 catorce / catorze
15 quince / quinze
16 dieciséis / setze
17 diecisiete / disset
18 dieciocho / divuit
19 diecinueve / dinou
20 veinte / vint
100 cien (to) / cent
1,000 mil / mil
1,000,000 millón / milió

TIME

What time is it? ¿Qué hora es? / Quina hora es?
It's two o'clock. Son las dos / Són les dues
morning mañana / matí
afternoon tarde / tarda
evening noche / vespre
night noche / nit
yesterday ayer / ahir
today hoy / avui
tomorrow mañana / demà
now ahora / ara
later más tarde / mès tard
earlier antes / abans

day día / dia
week semana / setmana
month mes / mes

DAYS AND MONTHS

Monday lunes / dilluns
Tuesday martes / dimarts
Wednesday miércoles / dimecres
Thursday jueves / dijous
Friday viernes / divendres
Saturday sábado / dissabte
Sunday domingo / diumenge
January enero / gener
February febrero / febrer
March marzo / març
April abril / abril
May mayo / maig
June junio / juny
July julio / juliol
August agosto / agost
September septiembre / setembre
October octubre / octobre
November noviembre / novembre
December diciembre / desembre

Suggested Reading

CULTURE

Hooper, John. *The New Spaniards*. A sociological look at Spanish identity, covering topics as diverse as politics, the Church and monarchy, bullfighting, art, and regional nationalism. An accessible and fascinating insight into what has historically made Spaniards Spaniards.

Tremlett, Giles. *Ghosts of Spain*. In this excellent delve into modern Spain, British journalist Tremlett explores how Civil War wounds are still not healed. A great general overview of contemporary Spain.

Webster Jason. *Duende*. A memoir about a man who moves to Spain, falls in love with flamenco, and embarks on a journey to learn flamenco guitar and discover the elusive *duende*—a special state of emotion that flamenco inspires.

TRAVELOGUES

Orwell, George. *Homage to Catalonia*. Orwell's classic account of his time fighting on the Republican side during the early days of the Spanish Civil War.

Tóibín Colm. *Homage to Barcelona*. Irish author Tóibín is head over heels in love with Barcelona, and here recounts the city's history through some of its most famous personalities, from artists to musicians, weaving in stories of when he first lived in Barcelona as a student.

HISTORY

Gellhorn, Martha. *The Face of War.* This collection of the great war correspondent's journalism includes articles written during the Spanish Civil War that really shine a light on the everyday struggles of Spaniards living through the horrors of war.

Hughes, Robert. *Barcelona.* A fantastic history that covers 2,000 years of Barcelona. It is especially good on its architecture and art.

Phillips, Jr, William D and Carla Rahn Phillips. *A Concise History of Spain.* From the Romans to the modern day, this whistle-stop tour of Spanish history is a great way to bone up quickly on the country's dramatic past.

Thomas, Hugh. *The Spanish Civil War.* The definitive account of the Spanish Civil War, Thomas's engrossing history is an essential companion for anyone wanting the full overview of the conflict.

ART AND ARCHITECTURE

O'Brian, Patrick. *Picasso: A Biography.* The most comprehensive biography of the great artist.

Van Hensbergen, Gijs. *Gaudí: The Biography.* Discover the man behind Barcelona's great architecture in this interesting biography, which examines how Gaudí's life and beliefs inspired his buildings.

FICTION

Cervantes, Miguel. *Don Quixote de La Mancha.* The pinnacle of the Spanish literary canon, Cervantes's masterpiece is often lauded as the first great novel in Western literature.

Dueñas, Maria. *The Seamstress.* This epic novel opens with its protagonist, Sira Quiroga, shopping in Madrid's textile district, then branches out as she travels to Spanish Morocco just before the breakout of the Spanish Civil War. An epic of romance and intrigue that was a bestseller around the world.

Hemingway, Ernest. *The Sun Also Rises.* Although most of the action is set around the fiesta of San Fermín, in Pamplona, the final scene of Hemingway's 1926 novel takes place in Madrid's legendary restaurant Botín—the oldest restaurant in the world.

Hemingway, Ernest. *For Whom the Bell Tolls.* The story of an American soldier fighting in Spain with the International Brigades is based on Hemingway's experience reporting in Spain during the Spanish Civil War and is often lauded as one of the best novels on the subject.

Ruiz Zafón, Carlos. *The Shadow of the Wind.* This worldwide bestseller is set in Barcelona just after the Spanish Civil War, following Daniel Sempere and his journey into the Cemetery of Forgotten Books and the mystery that lies within.

Suggested Films

Mujeres al borde de un ataque de nervios / Women on the Verge of a Nervous Breakdown (1988). D: Pedro Almodóvar. Almodóvar's earliest international hit is a riot of melodrama, color, and comedy, featuring an early performance by Antonio Banderas and an excellent star turn by Carmen Maura.

Land and Freedom (1995). D: Ken Loach. Liverpudlian David Carr travels to Spain to join the International Brigades and discovers the ideological conflicts that beset the Republicans during the Spanish Civil War. Loach's critically acclaimed film is a brutally realistic portrayal of the conflict.

Abre los Ojos / Open Your Eyes (1997). D: Alejandro Amenábar. Remade with Tom Cruise as *Vanilla Sky*, the Spanish original includes a memorable scene when the main character, César, walks down a completely empty Gran Vía in Madrid (which was reshot on Times Square in the U.S. remake). A mysterious tale that will leave you guessing until the end.

Todo Sobre mi Madre / All About My Mother (1999). D: Pedro Almodóvar. This Oscar-winning film is, unusually for Almodóvar, mainly set in Barcelona and deals with a mother's emotional journey in search of the father of her son.

Volver (2006). D: Pedro Almodóvar. In the pinnacle of Almodóvar's collaborations with actress Penelope Cruz, the actress plays a mother forced to take matters into her own hands after the death of her husband, all while dealing with the ghost of her own mother.

The Bourne Ultimatum (2007). D: Paul Greengrass. Jason Bourne's globetrotting takes him to Madrid in his third outing. He is seen striding across the platform at Atocha train station and in several scenes in streets around the city.

Biutiful (2010). D: Alejandro González Iñárritu. The gritty suburbs of Barcelona take center stage in Iñárritu's Oscar-nominated film. Javier Bardem stars as Uxbal, an underground businessman giving work to illegal immigrants who make designer goods for African street vendors. When he finds out he is dying, his world is turned upside down.

Internet Resources

TRAVEL AND TOURIST TIPS

www.spain.info is Spain's official tourism portal covering locations and sights across the country.

Barcelona
VISIT BARCELONA
www.barcelonaturisme.com
Barcelona's tourism board has information about the city's major sights as well as how to book tours.

Day Trips from Barcelona
GIRONA TOURISM
www.girona.cat/turisme/eng/activitats.php

VISIT SITGES
www.visitsitges.com

VISIT FIGUERES
www.en.visitfigueres.cat

MONTSERRAT TOURISM
www.montserratvisita.com

Madrid
VISIT MADRID
www.esmadrid.com
Madrid's tourist board has information about what's going on in the city, as well as handy guides and maps.

Day Trips from Madrid
VISIT SEGOVIA
www.visitsegovia.turismodesegovia.com

TARRAGONA TOURISM
www.tarragonaturisme.cat

TOLEDO TOURISM
www.turismo.toledo.es

TRANSPORTATION
Spain
RENFE
www.renfe.com
Spain's national rail operator.

ALSA
www.alsa.com
Long-distance bus company with routes between most major Spanish cities.

Barcelona
TRANSPORTS METROPOLITANS DE BARCELONA
www.tmb.cat
Barcelona's metro website.

Madrid
BICIMAD
www.bicimad.com
Madrid's public bicycle scheme. You can sign up online or with a card at the machines at cycle racks, which can be found around the city.

MADRID METRO
www.metromadrid.es
Madrid's metro, where you can check timetables, ticket prices, and journey times.

APPS
MY TAXI
Use to order local taxis in both Madrid and Barcelona

DUOLINGO
Handy for practicing your Spanish before you set off

WORDREFERENCE
Useful for translating words while on the go

Index

List of Maps

Photo Credits

Acknowledgments

A huge thank you to the dedicated team at Avalon Travel, especially Nikki Ioakimedes, who from the beginning has been a great source of encouragement and feedback. Thanks also to Darren Alessi for overseeing the photographs and Grace Fujimoto for managing production.

Thank you to my parents, Fiona and James, for sparking my love of travel and writing, as well as for being my informal proofreaders and number one fans! And Lucy and Rory for being my earliest travel buddies, whether we were singing in the back of the car or braving a body board for the first time.

Thanks to Fiona Govan for being a great mentor and friend. I've always appreciated your advice on writing and journalism.

Thank you to all the shopkeepers, bar and restaurant workers, tour guides, and little old ladies who have taught me so much about Spain and, in the case of the little old ladies, how to rock a fur coat. I hope Madrid and Barcelona's traditional businesses, which give the cities their unique feel, continue long into the future—and we can all help by making sure to pay them a visit when traveling.

Finally, thank you to Sara, without whom this book would not have been possible. Thank you for your unwavering support, your fantastic photographs, and for always being the very best travel companion. Long may our adventures continue.

Trips to Remember

MOON
TRIP OF A LIFETIME
ANGKOR WAT
TOM VATER

MOON
TRIP OF A LIFETIME
GALÁPAGOS ISLANDS

MOON
ICELAND
JENNA GOTTLIEB

MOON
TRIP OF A LIFETIME
MACHU PICCHU

MOON
MOROCCO

MOON
NEW ZEALAND
JAMIE CHRISTIAN DESPLACES

MOON
NORWAY

MOON
TRIP OF A LIFETIME
PATAGONIA
WAYNE BERNHARDSON

MOON
PRAGUE, VIENNA & BUDAPEST

MOON
ROME, FLORENCE & VENICE
ALEXEI J COHEN

MOON
VIETNAM
DANA FILEK-GIBSON

Epic Adventure

MOON
Drive & Hike
APPALACHIAN TRAIL
THE BEST TRAIL TOWNS, DAY HIKES, AND ROAD TRIPS IN BETWEEN
TIMOTHY MALCOLM

MOON
CAMINO DE SANTIAGO
SACRED SITES, HISTORIC VILLAGES, LOCAL FOOD & WINE
BEEBE BAHRAMI

MOON
USA NATIONAL PARKS
THE COMPLETE GUIDE TO ALL
59 PARKS
BECKY LOMAX

MAP SYMBOLS

═══	Expressway	○	City/Town	✈	Airport	⚲	Golf Course
───	Primary Road	◉	State Capital	✖	Airfield	🅿	Parking Area
⋯⋯	Secondary Road	⊛	National Capital	▲	Mountain	⛏	Archaeological Site
- - -	Unpaved Road	★	Point of Interest	✦	Unique Natural Feature	⛪	Church
──	Feature Trail	●	Accommodation			⛽	Gas Station
- - - -	Other Trail	▼	Restaurant/Bar	⤳	Waterfall	◯	Glacier
⋯⋯⋯	Ferry	■	Other Location	⚐	Park		Mangrove
═══	Pedestrian Walkway	▲	Campground	⊓	Trailhead		Reef
▭▭▭	Stairs			⛷	Skiing Area		Swamp

CONVERSION TABLES

°C = (°F − 32) / 1.8
°F = (°C x 1.8) + 32
1 inch = 2.54 centimeters (cm)
1 foot = 0.304 meters (m)
1 yard = 0.914 meters
1 mile = 1.6093 kilometers (km)
1 km = 0.6214 miles
1 fathom = 1.8288 m
1 chain = 20.1168 m
1 furlong = 201.168 m
1 acre = 0.4047 hectares
1 sq km = 100 hectares
1 sq mile = 2.59 square km
1 ounce = 28.35 grams
1 pound = 0.4536 kilograms
1 short ton = 0.90718 metric ton
1 short ton = 2,000 pounds
1 long ton = 1.016 metric tons
1 long ton = 2,240 pounds
1 metric ton = 1,000 kilograms
1 quart = 0.94635 liters
1 US gallon = 3.7854 liters
1 Imperial gallon = 4.5459 liters
1 nautical mile = 1.852 km

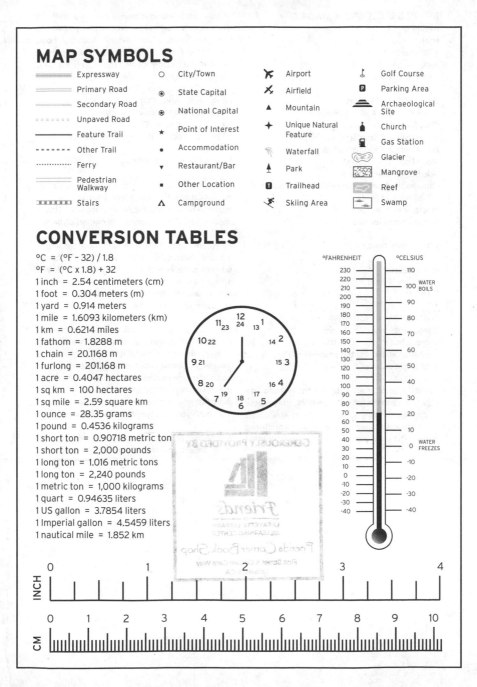

MOON BARCELONA & MADRID

Avalon Travel
Hachette Book Group
1700 Fourth Street
Berkeley, CA 94710, USA
www.moon.com

Editor: Nikki Ioakimedes
Series Manager: Kathryn Ettinger
Copy Editor: Chris Dumas
Production and Graphics Coordinator: Darren Alessi
Cover Design: Faceout Studios, Charles Brock
Moon Logo: Tim McGrath
Map Editor: Albert Angulo
Cartographers: Brian Shotwell, Andrew Dolan, Karin Dahl, Albert Angulo
Proofreader: Elina Carmona
Indexer: Sam Arnold-Boyd

ISBN-13: 978-1-64049-223-3

Printing History
1st Edition — April 2019
5 4 3 2 1

Front cover photo: Plaza Mayor at dusk, Madrid © Stefano Politi Markovina / Alamy Stock Photo
Back cover photo: Cibeles Museo, downtown Madrid © Beatrice Preve | Dreamstime.com

Printed in Canada by Friesens